with Microsoft®

PowerPoint® 2010 Introductory

Shelley Gaskin, Alicia Vargas, Donna Madsen, and Toni Marucco

Prentice Hall
Boston Columbus Indianapolis New York San Francisco Upper Saddle River
Amsterdam Cape Town Dubai London Madrid Milan Munich Paris Montreal Toronto
Delhi Mexico City Sao Paulo Sydney Hong Kong Seoul Singapore Taipei Tokyo

Associate VP/Executive Acquisitions Editor, Print: Stephanie Wall
Editorial Project Manager: Laura Burgess
Editor in Chief: Michael Payne
Product Development Manager: Eileen Bien Calabro
Development Editor: Linda Harrison
Editorial Assistant: Nicole Sam
Director of Marketing: Kate Valentine
Marketing Manager: Tori Olson Alves
Marketing Coordinator: Susan Osterlitz
Marketing Assistant: Darshika Vyas
Senior Managing Editor: Cynthia Zonneveld
Associate Managing Editor: Camille Trentacoste
Production Project Manager: Mike Lackey
Operations Director: Alexis Heydt
Operations Specialist: Natacha Moore
Senior Art Director: Jonathan Boylan
Cover Photo: © Ben Durrant
Text and Cover Designer: Blair Brown
Manager, Cover Visual Research & Permissions: Karen Sanatar
Manager, Rights and Permissions: Zina Arabia
AVP/Director of Online Programs, Media: Richard Keaveny
AVP/Director of Product Development, Media: Lisa Strite
Media Project Manager, Editorial: Alana Coles
Media Project Manager, Production: John Cassar
Full-Service Project Management: PreMediaGlobal
Composition: PreMediaGlobal
Printer/Binder: QuadGraphics-Taunton
Cover Printer: Lehigh-Phoenix Color
Text Font: Bookman Light

Credits and acknowledgments borrowed from other sources and reproduced, with permission, in this textbook appear on appropriate page within text. Photos appearing in PowerPoint chapters 1 and 3 supplied by Alicia Vargas and used with permission.

4 5 6 7 8 9 10 V064 16 15 14 13

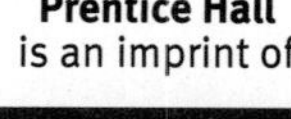

www.pearsonhighered.com

ISBN 10: 0-13-509800-9
ISBN 13: 978-0-13-509800-4

Brief Contents

Contents

PowerPoint

Chapter 1 Getting Started with PowerPoint 49

Chapter 2 Formatting PowerPoint Presentations 107

GO! System Contributors

We thank the following people for their hard work and support in making the *GO!* System all that it is!

Instructor Resource Authors

Adickes, Erich	Parkland College
Baray, Carrie	Ivy Tech Community College
Behrens, Sharon	Mid-State Technical College
Bornstein, Abigail	City College of San Francisco
Bowman, Valeria	National College
Callahan, Michael	Lone Star College
Clausen, Jane	Western Iowa Tech Community College
Cleary, Kevin	University at Buffalo
Colucci, William	Montclair State University
Coyle, Diane	Montgomery County Community College
Crossley, Connie	Cincinnati State Technical and Community College
Damanti, Lori	
Edington, Barbara	St. Francis College
Emrich, Stefanie	Metropolitan Community College of Omaha, Nebraska
Faix, Dennis	Harrisburg Area Community College
Federico, Hilda	Jacksonville University
Hadden, Karen	Western Iowa Tech Community College
Hammerle, Patricia	Indiana University/Purdue University at Indianapolis
Hearn, Barbara	Community College of Philadelphia
Hicks, Janette	Binghamton University/State University of New York
Hines, James	Tidewater Community College
Hollingsworth, Mary Carole	Georgia Perimeter College
Holly, Terri	Indian River State College
Holland, Susan	Southeast Community College-Nebraska
Jacob, Sherry	Kentucky Community and Technical College
Landenberger, Toni	Southeast Community College-Nebraska
Leinbach, Andrea	Harrisburg Area Community College
Lutz, Mary	Southwestern Illinois College
McMahon, Richard	University of Houston—Downtown
Miller, Abigail	Gateway Community and Technical College
Miller, Sandra	Wenatchee Valley College
Monson, Shari	Black Hawk College
Neal, Ruth	Navarro College
Niebur, Katherine	Dakota County Technical College
Nowakowski, Anthony	Buffalo State
Pierce, Tonya	Ivy Tech Community College
Piziak, Dee	University of Wisconsin-Milwaukee
Pogue, Linda	NorthWest Arkansas Community College
Reynolds, Mark	Lone Star College
Roselli, Diane	Harrisburg Area Community College
Shing, Chen-Chi	Radford University
St. John, Steve	Tulsa Community College
Sterr, Jody	Blackhawk Technical College
Thompson, Joyce	Lehigh Carbon Community College
Tucker, William	Austin Community College
Volker, Bonita	Tidewater Community College
Walters, Kari	Louisiana State University

Technical Editors

Matthew Bisi
Mary Corcoran
Lori Damanti
Barbara Edington
Sarah Evans
Adam Layne
Elizabeth Lockley
Joyce Nielsen
Janet Pickard
Sean Portnoy
Jan Snyder
Sam Stamport
Mara Zebest

Student Reviewers

Albinda, Sarah Evangeline	Phoenix College
Allen, John	Asheville-Buncombe Tech Community College
Alexander, Steven	St. Johns River Community College
Alexander, Melissa	Tulsa Community College
Bolz, Stephanie	Northern Michigan University
Berner, Ashley	Central Washington University
Boomer, Michelle	Northern Michigan University
Busse, Brennan	Northern Michigan University
Butkey, Maura	Central Washington University
Cates, Concita	Phoenix College
Charles, Marvin	Harrisburg Area Community College
Christensen, Kaylie	Northern Michigan University
Clark, Glen D. III	Harrisburg Area Community College
Cobble, Jan N.	Greenville Technical College
Connally, Brianna	Central Washington University
Davis, Brandon	Northern Michigan University
Davis, Christen	Central Washington University
De Jesus Garcia, Maria	Phoenix College
Den Boer, Lance	Central Washington University
Dix, Jessica	Central Washington University
Downs, Elizabeth	Central Washington University
Elser, Julie	Harrisburg Area Community College
Erickson, Mike	Ball State University
Frye, Alicia	Phoenix College
Gadomski, Amanda	Northern Michigan University
Gassert, Jennifer	Harrisburg Area Community College
Gross, Mary Jo	Kirkwood Community College
Gyselinck, Craig	Central Washington University
Harrison, Margo	Central Washington University
Hatt, Patrick	Harrisburg Area Community College
Heacox, Kate	Central Washington University
Hedgman, Shaina	Tidewater College
Hill, Cheretta	Northwestern State University
Hochstedler, Bethany	Harrisburg Area Community College Lancaster
Homer, Jean	Greenville Technical College
Innis, Tim	Tulsa Community College
Jarboe, Aaron	Central Washington University
Key, Penny	Greenville Technical College
Klein, Colleen	Northern Michigan University
Lloyd, Kasey	Ivy Tech Bloomington
Moeller, Jeffrey	Northern Michigan University
Mullen, Sharita	Tidewater Community College

Nelson, Cody	Texas Tech University
Nicholson, Regina	Athens Tech College
Niehaus, Kristina	Northern Michigan University
Nisa, Zaibun	Santa Rosa Community College
Nunez, Nohelia	Santa Rosa Community College
Oak, Samantha	Central Washington University
Oberly, Sara	Harrisburg Area Community College Lancaster
Oertii, Monica	Central Washington University
Palenshus, Juliet	Central Washington University
Pohl, Amanda	Northern Michigan University
Presnell, Randy	Central Washington University
Reed, Kailee	Texas Tech University
Ritner, April	Northern Michigan University
Roberts, Corey	Tulsa Community College
Rodgers, Spencer	Texas Tech University
Rodriguez, Flavia	Northwestern State University
Rogers, A.	Tidewater Community College
Rossi, Jessica Ann	Central Washington University
Rothbauer, Taylor	Trident Technical College
Rozelle, Lauren	Texas Tech University
Schmadeke, Kimberly	Kirkwood Community College
Shafapay, Natasha	Central Washington University
Shanahan, Megan	Northern Michigan University
Sullivan, Alexandra Nicole	Greenville Technical College
Teska, Erika	Hawaii Pacific University
Torrenti, Natalie	Harrisburg Area Community College
Traub, Amy	Northern Michigan University
Underwood, Katie	Central Washington University
Walters, Kim	Central Washington University
Warren, Jennifer L.	Greenville Technical College
Wilson, Kelsie	Central Washington University
Wilson, Amanda	Green River Community College
Wylie, Jimmy	Texas Tech University

Series Reviewers

Abraham, Reni	Houston Community College
Addison, Paul	Ivy Tech Community College
Agatston, Ann	Agatston Consulting Technical College
Akuna, Valeria, Ph.D.	Estrella Mountain Community College
Alexander, Melody	Ball Sate University
Alejandro, Manuel	Southwest Texas Junior College
Alger, David	Tidewater Community College Chesapeake Campus
Allen, Jackie	Rowan-Cabarrus Community College
Ali, Farha	Lander University
Amici, Penny	Harrisburg Area Community College
Anderson, Patty A.	Lake City Community College
Andrews, Wilma	Virginia Commonwealth College, Nebraska University
Anik, Mazhar	Tiffin University
Armstrong, Gary	Shippensburg University
Arnold, Linda L.	Harrisburg Area Community College
Ashby, Tom	Oklahoma City Community College
Atkins, Bonnie	Delaware Technical Community College
Aukland, Cherie	Thomas Nelson Community College
Bachand, LaDonna	Santa Rosa Community College
Bagui, Sikha	University of West Florida
Beecroft, Anita	Kwantlen University College
Bell, Paula	Lock Haven College
Belton, Linda	Springfield Tech. Community College
Bennett, Judith	Sam Houston State University
Bhatia, Sai	Riverside Community College
Bishop, Frances	DeVry Institute—Alpharetta (ATL)
Blaszkiewicz, Holly	Ivy Tech Community College/Region 1
Boito, Nancy	HACC Central Pennsylvania's Community College
Borger-Boglin, Grietje L.	San Antonio College/Northeast Lakeview College
Branigan, Dave	DeVry University
Bray, Patricia	Allegany College of Maryland
Britt, Brenda K.	Fayetteville Technical Community College
Brotherton, Cathy	Riverside Community College
Brown, Judy	Western Illinois University
Buehler, Lesley	Ohlone College
Buell, C	Central Oregon Community College
Burns, Christine	Central New Mexico Community College
Byars, Pat	Brookhaven College
Byrd, Julie	Ivy Tech Community College
Byrd, Lynn	Delta State University, Cleveland, Mississippi
Cacace, Richard N.	Pensacola Junior College
Cadenhead, Charles	Brookhaven College
Calhoun, Ric	Gordon College
Cameron, Eric	Passaic Community College
Canine, Jill	Ivy Tech Community College of Indiana
Cannamore, Madie	Kennedy King
Cannon, Kim	Greenville Technical College
Carreon, Cleda	Indiana University—Purdue University, Indianapolis
Carriker, Sandra	North Shore Community College
Casey, Patricia	Trident Technical College
Cates, Wally	Central New Mexico Community College
Chaffin, Catherine	Shawnee State University
Chauvin, Marg	Palm Beach Community College, Boca Raton
Challa, Chandrashekar	Virginia State University
Chamlou, Afsaneh	NOVA Alexandria
Chapman, Pam	Wabaunsee Community College
Christensen, Dan	Iowa Western Community College
Clay, Betty	Southeastern Oklahoma State University
Collins, Linda D.	Mesa Community College
Cone, Bill	Northern Arizona University
Conroy-Link, Janet	Holy Family College
Conway, Ronald	Bowling Green State University
Cornforth, Carol G.	WVNCC
Cosgrove, Janet	Northwestern CT Community
Courtney, Kevin	Hillsborough Community College
Coverdale, John	Riverside Community College
Cox, Rollie	Madison Area Technical College
Crawford, Hiram	Olive Harvey College
Crawford, Sonia	Central New Mexico Community College

Crawford, Thomasina	Miami-Dade College, Kendall Campus
Credico, Grace	Lethbridge Community College
Crenshaw, Richard	Miami Dade Community College, North
Crespo, Beverly	Mt. San Antonio College
Crooks, Steven	Texas Tech University
Crossley, Connie	Cincinnati State Technical Community College
Curik, Mary	Central New Mexico Community College
De Arazoza, Ralph	Miami Dade Community College
Danno, John	DeVry University/Keller Graduate School
Davis, Phillip	Del Mar College
Davis, Richard	Trinity Valley Community College
Davis, Sandra	Baker College of Allen Park
Dees, Stephanie D.	Wharton County Junior College
DeHerrera, Laurie	Pikes Peak Community College
Delk, Dr. K. Kay	Seminole Community College
Denton, Bree	Texas Tech University
Dix, Jeanette	Ivy Tech Community College
Dooly, Veronica P.	Asheville-Buncombe Technical Community College
Doroshow, Mike	Eastfield College
Douglas, Gretchen	SUNYCortland
Dove, Carol	Community College of Allegheny
Dozier, Susan	Tidewater Community College, Virginia Beach Campus
Driskel, Loretta	Niagara Community College
Duckwiler, Carol	Wabaunsee Community College
Duhon, David	Baker College
Duncan, Mimi	University of Missouri-St. Louis
Duthie, Judy	Green River Community College
Duvall, Annette	Central New Mexico Community College
Ecklund, Paula	Duke University
Eilers, Albert	Cincinnati State Technical and Community College
Eng, Bernice	Brookdale Community College
Epperson, Arlin	Columbia College
Evans, Billie	Vance-Granville Community College
Evans, Jean	Brevard Community College
Feuerbach, Lisa	Ivy Tech East Chicago
Finley, Jean	ABTCC
Fisher, Fred	Florida State University
Foster, Nancy	Baker College
Foster-Shriver, Penny L.	Anne Arundel Community College
Foster-Turpen, Linda	CNM
Foszcz, Russ	McHenry County College
Fry, Susan	Boise State University
Fustos, Janos	Metro State
Gallup, Jeanette	Blinn College
Gelb, Janet	Grossmont College
Gentry, Barb	Parkland College
Gerace, Karin	St. Angela Merici School
Gerace, Tom	Tulane University
Ghajar, Homa	Oklahoma State University
Gifford, Steve	Northwest Iowa Community College
Glazer, Ellen	Broward Community College
Gordon, Robert	Hofstra University
Gramlich, Steven	Pasco-Hernando Community College
Graviett, Nancy M.	St. Charles Community College, St. Peters, Missouri
Greene, Rich	Community College of Allegheny County
Gregoryk, Kerry	Virginia Commonwealth State
Griggs, Debra	Bellevue Community College
Grimm, Carol	Palm Beach Community College
Guthrie, Rose	Fox Valley Technical College
Hahn, Norm	Thomas Nelson Community College
Haley-Hunter, Deb	Bluefield State College
Hall, Linnea	Northwest Mississippi Community College
Hammerschlag, Dr. Bill	Brookhaven College
Hansen, Michelle	Davenport University
Hayden, Nancy	Indiana University—Purdue University, Indianapolis
Hayes, Theresa	Broward Community College
Headrick, Betsy	Chattanooga State
Helfand, Terri	Chaffey College
Helms, Liz	Columbus State Community College
Hernandez, Leticia	TCI College of Technology
Hibbert, Marilyn	Salt Lake Community College
Hinds, Cheryl	Norfolk State University
Hines, James	Tidewater Community College
Hoffman, Joan	Milwaukee Area Technical College
Hogan, Pat	Cape Fear Community College
Holland, Susan	Southeast Community College
Holliday, Mardi	Community College of Philadelphia
Hollingsworth, Mary Carole	Georgia Perimeter College
Hopson, Bonnie	Athens Technical College
Horvath, Carrie	Albertus Magnus College
Horwitz, Steve	Community College of Philadelphia
Hotta, Barbara	Leeward Community College
Howard, Bunny	St. Johns River Community
Howard, Chris	DeVry University
Huckabay, Jamie	Austin Community College
Hudgins, Susan	East Central University
Hulett, Michelle J.	Missouri State University
Humphrey, John	Asheville Buncombe Technical Community College
Hunt, Darla A.	Morehead State University, Morehead, Kentucky
Hunt, Laura	Tulsa Community College
Ivey, Joan M.	Lanier Technical College
Jacob, Sherry	Jefferson Community College
Jacobs, Duane	Salt Lake Community College
Jauken, Barb	Southeastern Community
Jerry, Gina	Santa Monica College
Johnson, Deborah S.	Edison State College
Johnson, Kathy	Wright College
Johnson, Mary	Kingwood College
Johnson, Mary	Mt. San Antonio College
Jones, Stacey	Benedict College
Jones, Warren	University of Alabama, Birmingham
Jordan, Cheryl	San Juan College
Kapoor, Bhushan	California State University, Fullerton
Kasai, Susumu	Salt Lake Community College
Kates, Hazel	Miami Dade Community College, Kendall
Keen, Debby	University of Kentucky
Keeter, Sandy	Seminole Community College

Kern-Blystone, Dorothy Jean	Bowling Green State
Kerwin, Annette	College of DuPage
Keskin, Ilknur	The University of South Dakota
Kinney, Mark B.	Baker College
Kirk, Colleen	Mercy College
Kisling, Eric	East Carolina University
Kleckner, Michelle	Elon University
Kliston, Linda	Broward Community College, North Campus
Knuth, Toni	Baker College of Auburn Hills
Kochis, Dennis	Suffolk County Community College
Kominek, Kurt	Northeast State Technical Community College
Kramer, Ed	Northern Virginia Community College
Kretz, Daniel	Fox Valley Technical College
Laird, Jeff	Northeast State Community College
Lamoureaux, Jackie	Central New Mexico Community College
Lange, David	Grand Valley State
LaPointe, Deb	Central New Mexico Community College
Larsen, Jacqueline Anne	A-B Tech
Larson, Donna	Louisville Technical Institute
Laspina, Kathy	Vance-Granville Community College
Le Grand, Dr. Kate	Broward Community College
Lenhart, Sheryl	Terra Community College
Leonard, Yvonne	Coastal Carolina Community College
Letavec, Chris	University of Cincinnati
Lewis, Daphne L, Ed.D.	Wayland Baptist University
Lewis, Julie	Baker College-Allen Park
Liefert, Jane	Everett Community College
Lindaman, Linda	Black Hawk Community College
Lindberg, Martha	Minnesota State University
Lightner, Renee	Broward Community College
Lindberg, Martha	Minnesota State University
Linge, Richard	Arizona Western College
Logan, Mary G.	Delgado Community College
Loizeaux, Barbara	Westchester Community College
Lombardi, John	South University
Lopez, Don	Clovis-State Center Community College District
Lopez, Lisa	Spartanburg Community College
Lord, Alexandria	Asheville Buncombe Tech
Lovering, LeAnne	Augusta Technical College
Lowe, Rita	Harold Washington College
Low, Willy Hui	Joliet Junior College
Lucas, Vickie	Broward Community College
Luna, Debbie	El Paso Community College
Luoma, Jean	Davenport University
Luse, Steven P.	Horry Georgetown Technical College
Lynam, Linda	Central Missouri State University
Lyon, Lynne	Durham College
Lyon, Pat Rajski	Tomball College
Macarty, Matthew	University of New Hampshire
MacKinnon, Ruth	Georgia Southern University
Macon, Lisa	Valencia Community College, West Campus
Machuca, Wayne	College of the Sequoias
Mack, Sherri	Butler County Community College
Madison, Dana	Clarion University
Maguire, Trish	Eastern New Mexico University
Malkan, Rajiv	Montgomery College
Manning, David	Northern Kentucky University
Marcus, Jacquie	Niagara Community College
Marghitu, Daniela	Auburn University
Marks, Suzanne	Bellevue Community College
Marquez, Juanita	El Centro College
Marquez, Juan	Mesa Community College
Martin, Carol	Harrisburg Area Community College
Martin, Paul C.	Harrisburg Area Community College
Martyn, Margie	Baldwin-Wallace College
Marucco, Toni	Lincoln Land Community College
Mason, Lynn	Lubbock Christian University
Matutis, Audrone	Houston Community College
Matkin, Marie	University of Lethbridge
Maurel, Trina	Odessa College
May, Karen	Blinn College
McCain, Evelynn	Boise State University
McCannon, Melinda	Gordon College
McCarthy, Marguerite	Northwestern Business College
McCaskill, Matt L.	Brevard Community College
McClellan, Carolyn	Tidewater Community College
McClure, Darlean	College of Sequoias
McCrory, Sue A.	Missouri State University
McCue, Stacy	Harrisburg Area Community College
McEntire-Orbach, Teresa	Middlesex County College
McKinley, Lee	Georgia Perimeter College
McLeod, Todd	Fresno City College
McManus, Illyana	Grossmont College
McPherson, Dori	Schoolcraft College
Meck, Kari	HACC
Meiklejohn, Nancy	Pikes Peak Community College
Menking, Rick	Hardin-Simmons University
Meredith, Mary	University of Louisiana at Lafayette
Mermelstein, Lisa	Baruch College
Metos, Linda	Salt Lake Community College
Meurer, Daniel	University of Cincinnati
Meyer, Colleen	Cincinnati State Technical and Community College
Meyer, Marian	Central New Mexico Community College
Miller, Cindy	Ivy Tech Community College, Lafayette, Indiana
Mills, Robert E.	Tidewater Community College, Portsmouth Campus
Mitchell, Susan	Davenport University
Mohle, Dennis	Fresno Community College
Molki, Saeed	South Texas College
Monk, Ellen	University of Delaware
Moore, Rodney	Holland College
Morris, Mike	Southeastern Oklahoma State University
Morris, Nancy	Hudson Valley Community College
Moseler, Dan	Harrisburg Area Community College
Nabors, Brent	Reedley College, Clovis Center
Nadas, Erika	Wright College
Nadelman, Cindi	New England College
Nademlynsky, Lisa	Johnson & Wales University
Nagengast, Joseph	Florida Career College
Nason, Scott	Rowan Cabarrus Community College

Ncube, Cathy	University of West Florida
Newsome, Eloise	Northern Virginia Community College Woodbridge
Nicholls, Doreen	Mohawk Valley Community College
Nicholson, John R.	Johnson County Community College
Nielson, Phil	Salt Lake Community College
Nunan, Karen L.	Northeast State Technical Community College
O'Neal, Lois Ann	Rogers State University
Odegard, Teri	Edmonds Community College
Ogle, Gregory	North Community College
Orr, Dr. Claudia	Northern Michigan University South
Orsburn, Glen	Fox Valley Technical College
Otieno, Derek	DeVry University
Otton, Diana Hill	Chesapeake College
Oxendale, Lucia	West Virginia Institute of Technology
Paiano, Frank	Southwestern College
Pannell, Dr. Elizabeth	Collin College
Patrick, Tanya	Clackamas Community College
Paul, Anindya	Daytona State College
Peairs, Deb	Clark State Community College
Perez, Kimberly	Tidewater Community College
Porter, Joyce	Weber State University
Prince, Lisa	Missouri State University-Springfield Campus
Proietti, Kathleen	Northern Essex Community College
Puopolo, Mike	Bunker Hill Community College
Pusins, Delores	HCCC
Putnam, Darlene	Thomas Nelson Community College
Raghuraman, Ram	Joliet Junior College
Rani, Chigurupati	BMCC/CUNY
Reasoner, Ted Allen	Indiana University—Purdue
Reeves, Karen	High Point University
Remillard, Debbie	New Hampshire Technical Institute
Rhue, Shelly	DeVry University
Richards, Karen	Maplewoods Community College
Richardson, Mary	Albany Technical College
Rodgers, Gwen	Southern Nazarene University
Rodie, Karla	Pikes Peak Community College
Roselli, Diane Maie	Harrisburg Area Community College
Ross, Dianne	University of Louisiana in Lafayette
Rousseau, Mary	Broward Community College, South
Rovetto, Ann	Horry-Georgetown Technical College
Rusin, Iwona	Baker College
Sahabi, Ahmad	Baker College of Clinton Township
Samson, Dolly	Hawaii Pacific University
Sams, Todd	University of Cincinnati
Sandoval, Everett	Reedley College
Santiago, Diana	Central New Mexico Community College
Sardone, Nancy	Seton Hall University
Scafide, Jean	Mississippi Gulf Coast Community College
Scheeren, Judy	Westmoreland County Community College
Scheiwe, Adolph	Joliet Junior College
Schneider, Sol	Sam Houston State University
Schweitzer, John	Central New Mexico Community College
Scroggins, Michael	Southwest Missouri State University
Sedlacek, Brenda	Tidewater Community College
Sell, Kelly	Anne Arundel Community College
Sever, Suzanne	Northwest Arkansas Community College
Sewell, John	Florida Career College
Sheridan, Rick	California State University-Chico
Silvers, Pamela	Asheville Buncombe Tech
Sindt, Robert G.	Johnson County Community College
Singer, Noah	Tulsa Community College
Singer, Steven A.	University of Hawai'i, Kapi'olani Community College
Sinha, Atin	Albany State University
Skolnick, Martin	Florida Atlantic University
Smith, Kristi	Allegany College of Maryland
Smith, Patrick	Marshall Community and Technical College
Smith, Stella A.	Georgia Gwinnett College
Smith, T. Michael	Austin Community College
Smith, Tammy	Tompkins Cortland Community Collge
Smolenski, Bob	Delaware County Community College
Smolenski, Robert	Delaware Community College
Southwell, Donald	Delta College
Spangler, Candice	Columbus State
Spangler, Candice	Columbus State Community College
Stark, Diane	Phoenix College
Stedham, Vicki	St. Petersburg College, Clearwater
Stefanelli, Greg	Carroll Community College
Steiner, Ester	New Mexico State University
Stenlund, Neal	Northern Virginia Community College, Alexandria
St. John, Steve	Tulsa Community College
Sterling, Janet	Houston Community College
Stoughton, Catherine	Laramie County Community College
Sullivan, Angela	Joliet Junior College
Sullivan, Denise	Westchester Community College
Sullivan, Joseph	Joliet Junior College
Swart, John	Louisiana Tech University
Szurek, Joseph	University of Pittsburgh at Greensburg
Taff, Ann	Tulsa Community College
Taggart, James	Atlantic Cape Community College
Tarver, Mary Beth	Northwestern State University
Taylor, Michael	Seattle Central Community College
Terrell, Robert L.	Carson-Newman College
Terry, Dariel	Northern Virginia Community College
Thangiah, Sam	Slippery Rock University
Thayer, Paul	Austin Community College
Thompson, Joyce	Lehigh Carbon Community College
Thompson-Sellers, Ingrid	Georgia Perimeter College
Tomasi, Erik	Baruch College
Toreson, Karen	Shoreline Community College
Townsend, Cynthia	Baker College
Trifiletti, John J.	Florida Community College at Jacksonville
Trivedi, Charulata	Quinsigamond Community College, Woodbridge
Tucker, William	Austin Community College
Turgeon, Cheryl	Asnuntuck Community College
Turpen, Linda	Central New Mexico Community College
Upshaw, Susan	Del Mar College
Unruh, Angela	Central Washington University
Vanderhoof, Dr. Glenna	Missouri State University-Springfield Campus

Vargas, Tony	El Paso Community College
Vicars, Mitzi	Hampton University
Villarreal, Kathleen	Fresno
Vitrano, Mary Ellen	Palm Beach Community College
Vlaich-Lee, Michelle	Greenville Technical College
Volker, Bonita	Tidewater Community College
Waddell, Karen	Butler Community College
Wahila, Lori (Mindy)	Tompkins Cortland Community College
Wallace, Melissa	Lanier Technical College
Walters, Gary B.	Central New Mexico Community College
Waswick, Kim	Southeast Community College, Nebraska
Wavle, Sharon M.	Tompkins Cortland Community College
Webb, Nancy	City College of San Francisco
Webb, Rebecca	Northwest Arkansas Community College
Weber, Sandy	Gateway Technical College
Weissman, Jonathan	Finger Lakes Community College
Wells, Barbara E.	Central Carolina Technical College
Wells, Lorna	Salt Lake Community College
Welsh, Jean	Lansing Community College Nebraska
White, Bruce	Quinnipiac University
Willer, Ann	Solano Community College
Williams, Mark	Lane Community College
Williams, Ronald D.	Central Piedmont Community College
Wilms, Dr. G. Jan	Union University
Wilson, Kit	Red River College
Wilson, MaryLou	Piedmont Technical College
Wilson, Roger	Fairmont State University
Wimberly, Leanne	International Academy of Design and Technology
Winters, Floyd	Manatee Community College
Worthington, Paula	Northern Virginia Community College
Wright, Darrell	Shelton State Community College
Wright, Julie	Baker College
Yauney, Annette	Herkimer County Community College
Yip, Thomas	Passaic Community College
Zavala, Ben	Webster Tech
Zaboski, Maureen	University of Scranton
Zlotow, Mary Ann	College of DuPage
Zudeck, Steve	Broward Community College, North
Zullo, Matthew D.	Wake Technical Community College

About the Authors

Shelley Gaskin, Series Editor, is a professor in the Business and Computer Technology Division at Pasadena City College in Pasadena, California. She holds a bachelor's degree in Business Administration from Robert Morris College (Pennsylvania), a master's degree in Business from Northern Illinois University, and a doctorate in Adult and Community Education from Ball State University. Before joining Pasadena City College, she spent 12 years in the computer industry where she was a systems analyst, sales representative, and Director of Customer Education with Unisys Corporation. She also worked for Ernst & Young on the development of large systems applications for their clients. She has written and developed training materials for custom systems applications in both the public and private sector, and has written and edited numerous computer application textbooks.

This book is dedicated to my students, who inspire me every day.

Alicia Vargas is a faculty member in Business Information Technology at Pasadena City College. She holds a master's and a bachelor's degree in business education from California State University, Los Angeles, and has authored several textbooks and training manuals on Microsoft Word, Microsoft Excel, and Microsoft PowerPoint.

This book is dedicated with all my love to my husband Vic, who makes everything possible; and to my children Victor, Phil, and Emmy, who are an unending source of inspiration and who make everything worthwhile.

Donna Madsen is a retired professor from Kirkwood Community College in Cedar Rapids, Iowa. She has B.A. and M.A. degrees in Business Education from the University of Northern Iowa and advanced studies in Instructional Design at the University of Iowa. In addition to teaching classes at Kirkwood, she managed a business computer learning center and coordinated a microcomputer specialist program. She served as an Education Instruction Specialist for IBM, was named Kirkwood Innovator of the Year sponsored by the League for Innovation, and received a Tribute to Women of Achievement from Waypoint. She enjoys traveling, reading, and quilting.

I dedicate this book to Ruth Rasmussen, my sister and best friend, and to all my family—David, Mary, Sophie, Bill, and Jim; Scott, Colleen, Dan, Sean, Jack, and especially my great-niece Maggie Rasmussen for her great ideas. I also dedicate this book to Kay Forest, my writing partner at Kirkwood Community College, who says that we "think on the same wave length."

Toni Marucco recently retired from Lincoln Land Community College in Springfield, Illinois, where she was a professor of business and technologies. She holds a bachelor's degree in merchandising, a master's degree in education, and a Ph.D. in educational administration and higher education. Earlier in her career she served as an Education Industry Specialist with IBM for 10 years. She has also served as a contributing author on several textbooks. She continues to teach several online classes and serves as a faculty advocate for Pearson Education. Currently she serves as interim director for the Illinois Office of Educational Services.

This book is dedicated to my husband, John, to my mother, Dorothy, and to my children, Kori, Gia, and Charlie, who supported the pursuit of my dream.

Teach the Course You Want in Less Time

A Microsoft® Office textbook designed for student success!

- **Project-Based** – Students learn by creating projects that they will use in the real world.
- **Microsoft Procedural Syntax** – Steps are written to put students in the right place at the right time.
- **Teachable Moment** – Expository text is woven into the steps—at the moment students need to know it—not chunked together in a block of text that will go unread.
- **Sequential Pagination** – Students have actual page numbers instead of confusing letters and abbreviations.

Student Outcomes and Learning Objectives – Objectives are clustered around projects that result in student outcomes.

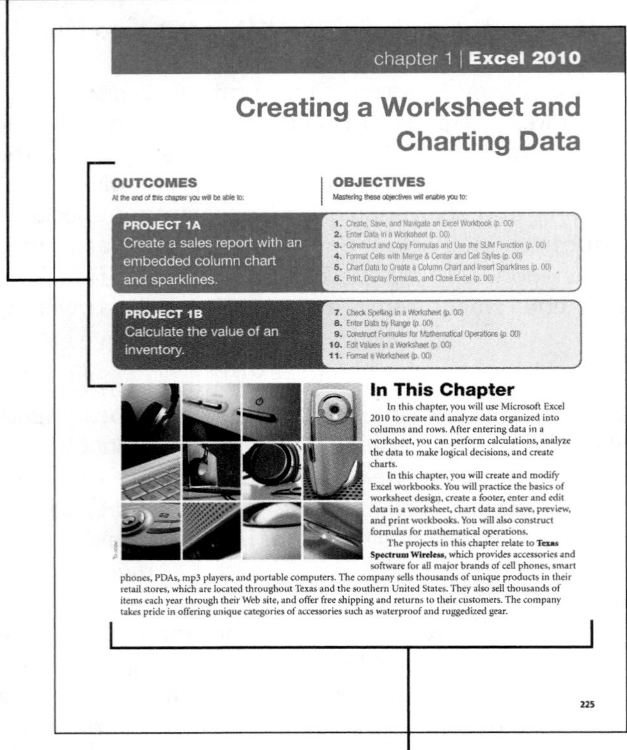
chapter 1 | **Excel 2010**

Creating a Worksheet and Charting Data

OUTCOMES
At the end of this chapter you will be able to:

OBJECTIVES
Mastering these objectives will enable you to:

PROJECT 1A
Create a sales report with an embedded column chart and sparklines.

1. Create, Save, and Navigate an Excel Workbook (p. 00)
2. Enter Data in a Worksheet (p. 00)
3. Construct and Copy Formulas and Use the SUM Function (p. 00)
4. Format Cells with Merge & Center and Cell Styles (p. 00)
5. Chart Data to Create a Column Chart and Insert Sparklines (p. 00)
6. Print, Display Formulas, and Close Excel (p. 00)

PROJECT 1B
Calculate the value of an inventory.

7. Check Spelling in a Worksheet (p. 00)
8. Enter Data by Range (p. 00)
9. Construct Formulas for Mathematical Operations (p. 00)
10. Edit Values in a Worksheet (p. 00)
11. Format a Worksheet (p. 00)

In This Chapter

In this chapter, you will use Microsoft Excel 2010 to create and analyze data organized into columns and rows. After entering data in a worksheet, you can perform calculations, analyze the data to make logical decisions, and create charts.

In this chapter, you will create and modify Excel workbooks. You will practice the basics of worksheet design, create a footer, enter and edit data in a worksheet, chart data and save, preview, and print workbooks. You will also construct formulas for mathematical operations.

The projects in this chapter relate to **Texas Spectrum Wireless**, which provides accessories and software for all major brands of cell phones, smart phones, PDAs, mp3 players, and portable computers. The company sells thousands of unique products in their retail stores, which are located throughout Texas and the southern United States. They also sell thousands of items each year through their Web site, and offer free shipping and returns to their customers. The company takes pride in offering unique categories of accessories such as waterproof and ruggedized gear.

225

Scenario – Each chapter opens with a story that sets the stage for the projects the student will create.

Project Activities – A project summary stated clearly and quickly.

Project Files – Clearly shows students which files are needed for the project and the names they will use to save their documents.

Project 1A Sales Report with Embedded Column Chart and Sparklines

myitlab
Project 1A Training

Project Activities

In Activities 1.01 through 1.16, you will create an Excel worksheet for Roslyn Thomas, the President of Texas Spectrum Wireless. The worksheet displays the first quarter sales of wireless accessories for the current year, and includes a chart to visually represent the data. Your completed worksheet will look similar to Figure 1.1.

Project Files

For Project 1A, you will need the following file:
New blank Excel workbook

You will save your workbook as:
Lastname_Firstname_1A_Quarterly_Sales

Project Results

Texas Spectrum Wireless
First Quarter Accessory Sales
1st Quarter Sales

Figure 1.1
Project 1A Quarterly Sales

226 Excel | Chapter 1: Creating a Worksheet and Charting Data

Project Results – Shows students how their final outcome will appear.

Key Feature

Microsoft Procedural Syntax – Steps are written to put the student in the right place at the right time.

Color Coding – Color variations between the two projects in each chapter make it easy to identify which project students are working on.

Objective 1 | Create, Save, and Navigate an Excel Workbook

On startup, Excel displays a new blank ***workbook***—the Excel document that stores your data—which contains one or more pages called a ***worksheet***. A worksheet—or ***spreadsheet***—is stored in a workbook, and is formatted as a pattern of uniformly spaced horizontal rows and vertical columns. The intersection of a column and a row forms a box referred to as a ***cell***.

Activity 1.01 | Starting Excel and Naming and Saving a Workbook

1 **Start** Excel. In the lower right corner of the window, if necessary, click the Normal button, and then to the right, locate the zoom—magnification—level.

Your zoom level should be 100%, although some figures in this textbook may be shown at a higher zoom level.

Another Way: Use the keyboard shortcut F12 to display the Save As dialog box.

2 In the upper left corner of your screen, click the **File tab** to display **Backstage** view, click **Save As**, and then in the **Save As** dialog box, navigate to the location where you will store your workbooks for this chapter.

3 In your storage location, create a new folder named **Excel Chapter 1** Open the new folder to display its folder window, and then in the **File name** box, notice that *Book1* displays as the default file name.

4 In the **File name** box, click *Book1* to select it, and then using your own name, type **Lastname_Firstname_1A_Quarterly_Sales** being sure to include the underscore (Shift + -) instead of spaces between words. Compare your screen with Figure 1.2.

Figure 1.2

Path to your new Excel Chapter 1 folder in address bar

File name with your name and underscores between words

Save button

Project 1A: Sales Report with Embedded Column Chart and Sparklines | Excel 227

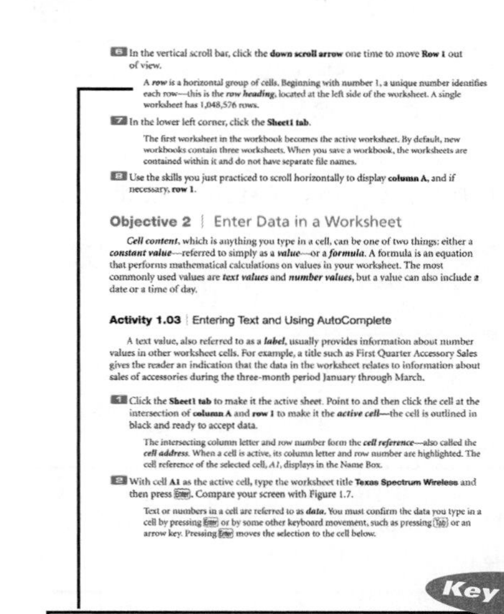

6 In the vertical scroll bar, click the **down scroll arrow** one time to move **Row 1** out of view.

A ***row*** is a horizontal group of cells. Beginning with number 1, a unique number identifies each row—this is the ***row heading***, located at the left side of the worksheet. A single worksheet has 1,048,576 rows.

7 In the lower left corner, click the **Sheet1 tab**.

The first worksheet in the workbook becomes the active worksheet. By default, new workbooks contain three worksheets. When you save a workbook, the worksheets are contained within it and do not have separate file names.

8 Use the skills you just practiced to scroll horizontally to display **column A**, and if necessary, **row 1**.

Objective 2 | Enter Data in a Worksheet

Cell content, which is anything you type in a cell, can be one of two things: either a ***constant value***—referred to simply as a ***value***—or a ***formula***. A formula is an equation that performs mathematical calculations on values in your worksheet. The most commonly used values are ***text values*** and ***number values***, but a value can also include a date or a time of day.

Activity 1.03 | Entering Text and Using AutoComplete

A text value, also referred to as a ***label***, usually provides information about number values in other worksheet cells. For example, a title such as First Quarter Accessory Sales gives the reader an indication that the data in the worksheet relates to information about sales of accessories during the three-month period January through March.

1 Click the **Sheet1 tab** to make it the active sheet. Point to and then click the cell at the intersection of **column A** and **row 1** to make it the ***active cell***—the cell is outlined in black and ready to accept data.

The intersecting column letter and row number form the ***cell reference***—also called the ***cell address***. When a cell is active, its column letter and row number are highlighted. The cell reference of the selected cell, *A1*, displays in the Name Box.

2 With cell **A1** as the active cell, type the worksheet title **Texas Spectrum Wireless** and then press Enter. Compare your screen with Figure 1.7.

Text or numbers in a cell are referred to as ***data***. You must confirm the data you type in a cell by pressing Enter or by some other keyboard movement, such as pressing Tab or an arrow key. Pressing Enter moves the selection to the cell below.

230 Excel

Key Feature

Sequential Pagination – Students are given actual page numbers to navigate through the textbook instead of confusing letters and abbreviations.

Key Feature

Teachable Moment – Expository text is woven into the steps—at the moment students need to know it—not chunked together in a block of text that will go unread.

End-of-Chapter

Content-Based Assessments – Assessments with defined solutions.

Objective List - Every project includes a listing of covered objectives from Projects A and B.

Content-Based Assessments — Summary — Key Terms

Content-Based Assessments — Skills Review | Project 1C GPS Sales

Content-Based Assessments — Mastering Excel | Project 1E Hard Drives

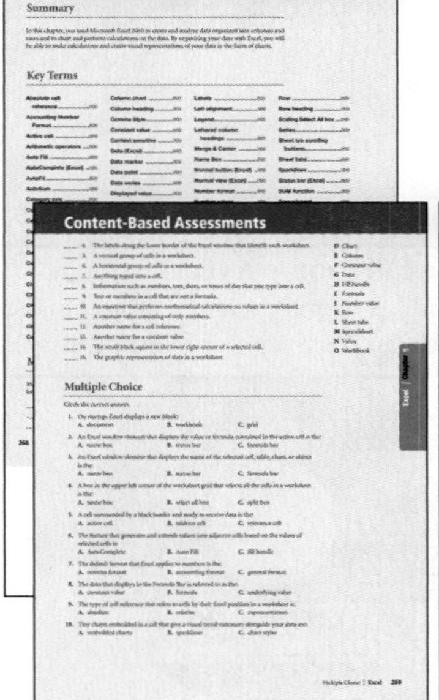

Content-Based Assessments — Multiple Choice

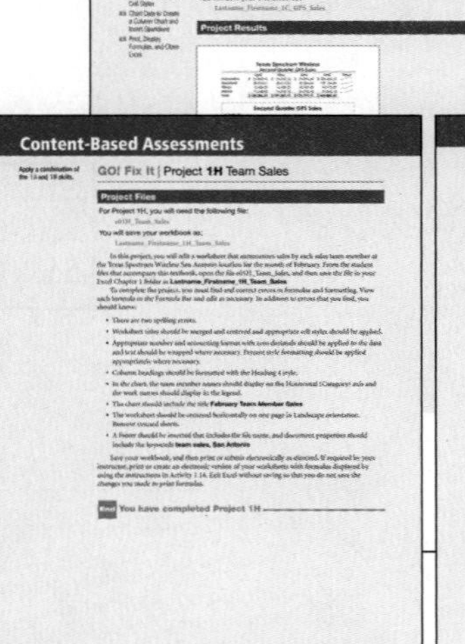

Content-Based Assessments — GO! Fix It | Project 1H Team Sales

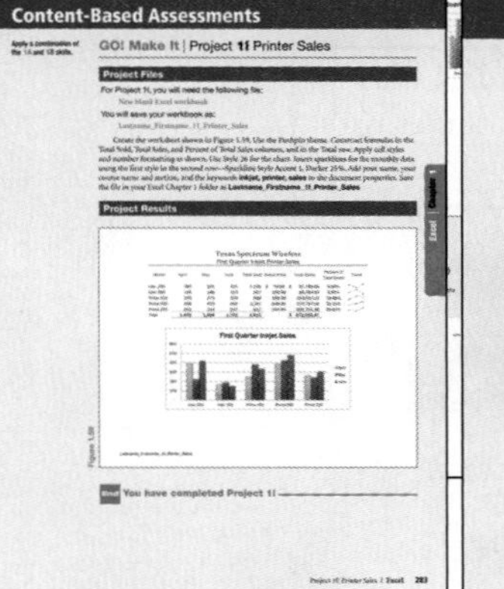

Content-Based Assessments — GO! Make It | Project 1I Printer Sales

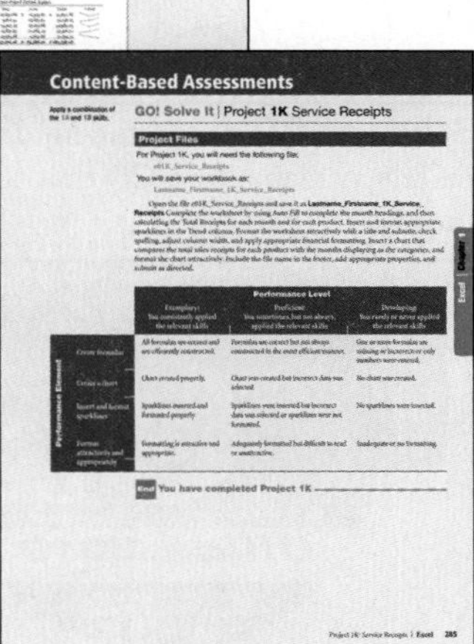

Content-Based Assessments — GO! Solve It | Project 1K Service Receipts

End-of-Chapter

Outcomes-Based Assessments – Assessments with open-ended solutions.

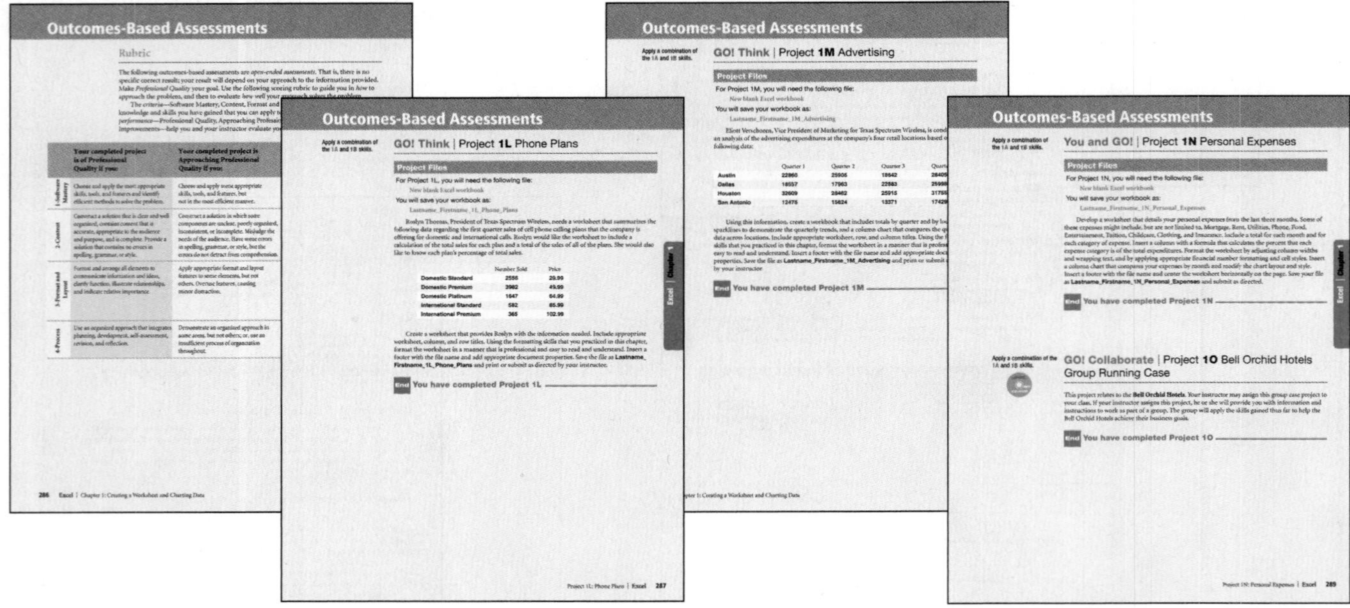

Task-Specific Rubric – A matrix specific to the **GO! Solve It** projects that states the criteria and standards for grading these defined-solution projects.

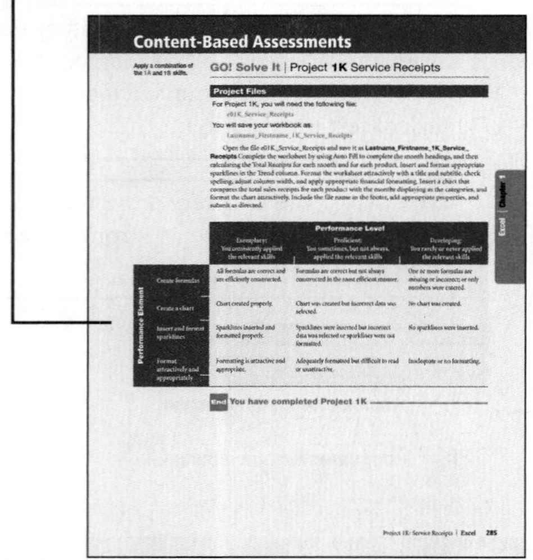

Outcomes Rubric – A matrix specific to the **GO! Think** projects that states the criteria and standards for grading these open-ended assessments.

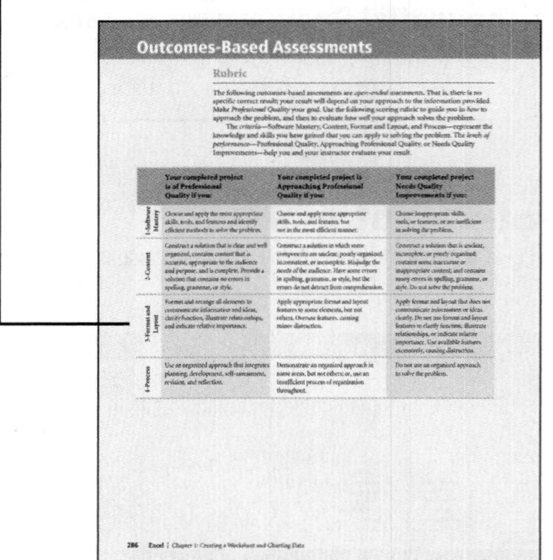

Student CD – All student data files readily available on a CD that comes with the book.

Student Videos – A visual and audio walk-through of every A and B project in the book (see sample images on following page).

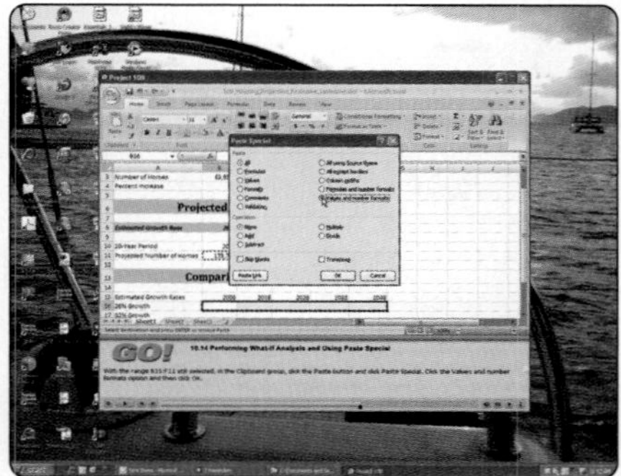

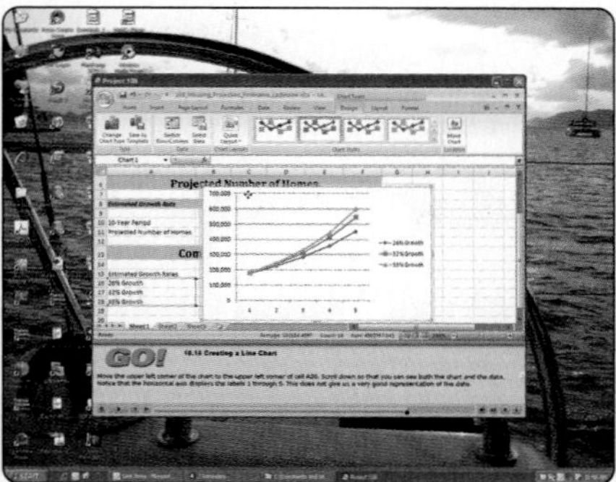

Student Videos! – Each chapter comes with two videos that include audio, demonstrating the objectives and activities taught in the chapter.

All Instructor materials available on the IRCD

Instructor Materials

Annotated Instructor Edition - An instructor tool includes a full copy of the student textbook annotated with teaching tips, discussion topics, and other useful pieces for teaching each chapter.

Assignment Sheets – Lists all the assignments for the chapter. Just add in the course information, due dates, and points. Providing these to students ensures they will know what is due and when.

Scripted Lectures – Classroom lectures prepared for you.

Annotated Solution Files – Coupled with the assignment tags, these create a grading and scoring system that makes grading so much easier for you.

PowerPoint Lectures – PowerPoint presentations for each chapter.

Scoring Rubrics – Can be used either by students to check their work or by you as a quick check-off for the items that need to be corrected.

Syllabus Templates - For 8-week, 12-week, and 16-week courses.

Test Bank – Includes a variety of test questions for each chapter.

Companion Website – Online content such as the Online Study Guide, Glossary, and Student Data Files are all at **www.pearsonhighered.com/go**.

Using the Common Features of Microsoft Office 2010

OUTCOMES

At the end of this chapter you will be able to:

OBJECTIVES

Mastering these objectives will enable you to:

PROJECT 1A

Create, save, and print a Microsoft Office 2010 file.

1. Use Windows Explorer to Locate Files and Folders (p. 3)
2. Locate and Start a Microsoft Office 2010 Program (p. 6)
3. Enter and Edit Text in an Office 2010 Program (p. 9)
4. Perform Commands from a Dialog Box (p. 11)
5. Create a Folder, Save a File, and Close a Program (p. 13)
6. Add Document Properties and Print a File (p. 18)

PROJECT 1B

Use the Ribbon and dialog boxes to perform common commands in a Microsoft Office 2010 file.

7. Open an Existing File and Save It with a New Name (p. 22)
8. Explore Options for an Application (p. 25)
9. Perform Commands from the Ribbon (p. 26)
10. Apply Formatting in Office Programs (p. 32)
11. Use the Microsoft Office 2010 Help System (p. 43)
12. Compress Files (p. 44)

olly/Shutterstock

In This Chapter

In this chapter, you will use Windows Explorer to navigate the Windows folder structure, create a folder, and save files in Microsoft Office 2010 programs. You will also practice using the features of Microsoft Office 2010 that are common across the major programs that comprise the Microsoft Office 2010 suite. These common features include creating, saving, and printing files.

Common features also include the new Paste Preview and Microsoft Office Backstage view. You will apply formatting, perform commands, and compress files. You will see that creating professional-quality documents is easy and quick in Microsoft Office 2010, and that finding your way around is fast and efficient.

The projects in this chapter relate to **Oceana Palm Grill**, which is a chain of 25 casual, full-service restaurants based in Austin, Texas. The Oceana Palm Grill owners plan an aggressive expansion program. To expand by 15 additional restaurants in North Carolina and Florida by 2018, the company must attract new investors, develop new menus, and recruit new employees, all while adhering to the company's quality guidelines and maintaining its reputation for excellent service. To succeed, the company plans to build on its past success and maintain its quality elements.

Project 1A PowerPoint File

Project Activities

In Activities 1.01 through 1.06, you will create a PowerPoint file, save it in a folder that you create by using Windows Explorer, and then print the file or submit it electronically as directed by your instructor. Your completed PowerPoint slide will look similar to Figure 1.1.

Project Files

For Project 1A, you will need the following file:

New blank PowerPoint presentation

You will save your file as:

Lastname_Firstname_1A_Menu_Plan

Project Results

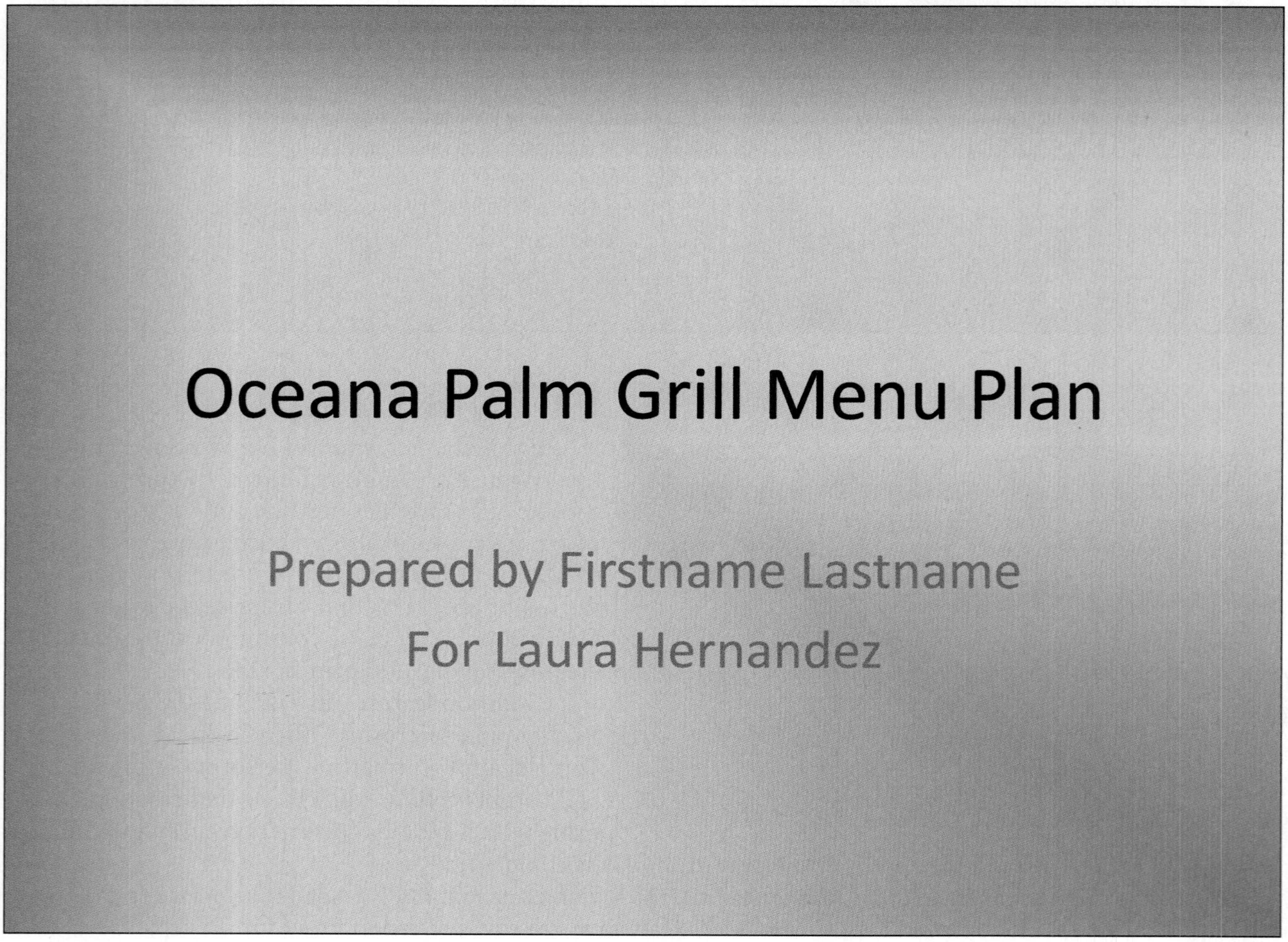

Oceana Palm Grill Menu Plan

Prepared by Firstname Lastname
For Laura Hernandez

Figure 1.1
Project 1A Menu Plan

Objective 1 | Use Windows Explorer to Locate Files and Folders

A ***file*** is a collection of information stored on a computer under a single name, for example, a Word document or a PowerPoint presentation. Every file is stored in a ***folder***—a container in which you store files—or a ***subfolder***, which is a folder within a folder. Your Windows operating system stores and organizes your files and folders, which is a primary task of an operating system.

You ***navigate***—explore within the organizing structure of Windows—to create, save, and find your files and folders by using the ***Windows Explorer*** program. Windows Explorer displays the files and folders on your computer, and is at work anytime you are viewing the contents of files and folders in a ***window***. A window is a rectangular area on a computer screen in which programs and content appear; a window can be moved, resized, minimized, or closed.

Activity 1.01 | Using Windows Explorer to Locate Files and Folders

1 Turn on your computer and display the Windows ***desktop***—the opening screen in Windows that simulates your work area.

> **Note | Comparing Your Screen with the Figures in This Textbook**
> Your screen will match the figures shown in this textbook if you set your screen resolution to 1024 × 768. At other resolutions, your screen will closely resemble, but not match, the figures shown. To view your screen's resolution, on the Windows 7 desktop, right-click in a blank area, and then click Screen resolution. In Windows Vista, right-click a blank area, click Personalize, and then click Display Settings. In Windows XP, right-click the desktop, click Properties, and then click the Settings tab.

2 In your CD/DVD tray, insert the **Student CD** that accompanies this textbook. Wait a few moments for an **AutoPlay** window to display. Compare your screen with Figure 1.2.

AutoPlay is a Windows feature that lets you choose which program to use to start different kinds of media, such as music CDs, or CDs and DVDs containing photos; it displays when you plug in or insert media or storage devices.

> **Note | If You Do Not Have the Student CD**
> If you do not have the Student CD, consult the inside back flap of this textbook for instructions on how to download the files from the Pearson Web site.

Figure 1.2

3 In the upper right corner of the **AutoPlay** window, move your mouse over—***point*** to—the **Close** button, and then ***click***—press the left button on your mouse pointing device one time.

4 On the left side of the **Windows taskbar**, click the **Start** button to display the **Start menu**. Compare your screen with Figure 1.3.

The ***Windows taskbar*** is the area along the lower edge of the desktop that contains the ***Start button*** and an area to display buttons for open programs. The Start button displays the ***Start menu***, which provides a list of choices and is the main gateway to your computer's programs, folders, and settings.

Figure 1.3

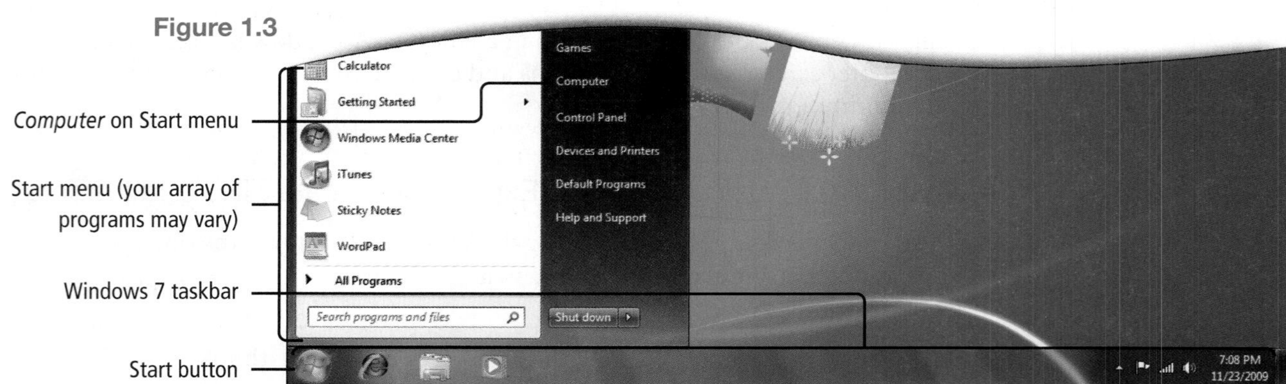

5 On the right side of the **Start menu**, click **Computer** to see the disk drives and other hardware connected to your computer. Compare your screen with Figure 1.4, and then take a moment to study the table in Figure 1.5.

The ***folder window*** for *Computer* displays. A folder window displays the contents of the current folder, ***library***, or device, and contains helpful parts so that you can navigate within Windows.

In Windows 7, a library is a collection of items, such as files and folders, assembled from *various locations*; the locations might be on your computer, an external hard drive, removable media, or someone else's computer.

The difference between a folder and a library is that a library can include files stored in *different locations*—any disk drive, folder, or other place that you can store files and folders.

Figure 1.4

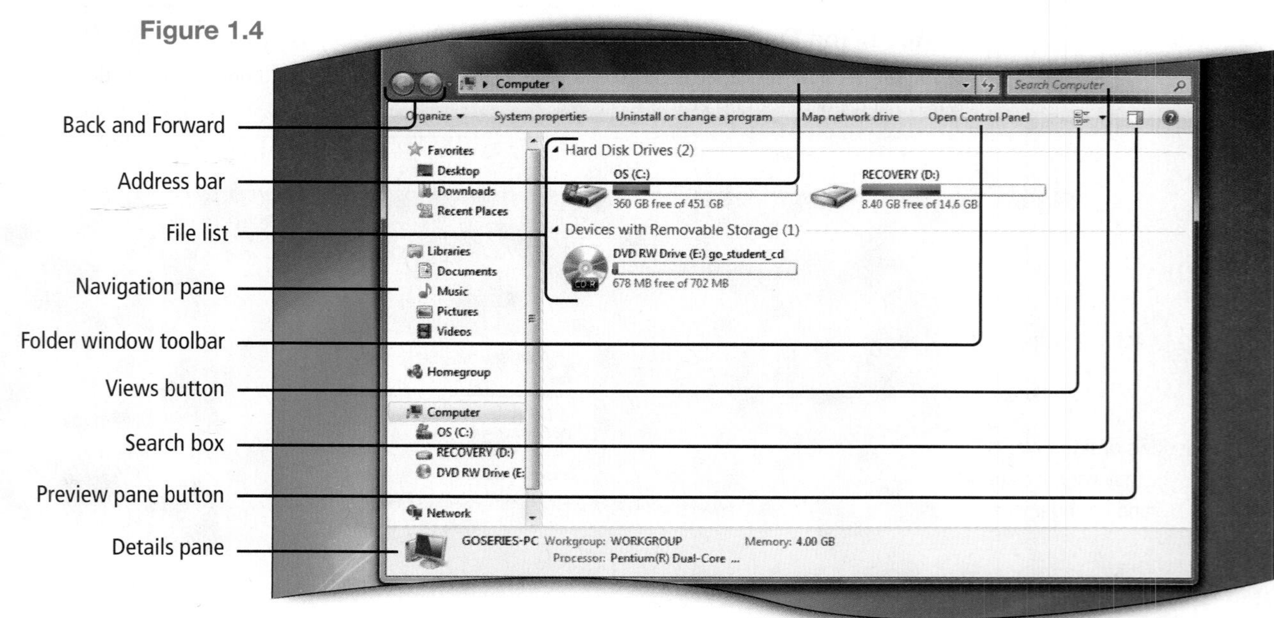

Window Part	Use to:
Address bar	Navigate to a different folder or library, or go back to a previous one.
Back and Forward buttons	Navigate to other folders or libraries you have already opened without closing the current window. These buttons work in conjunction with the address bar; that is, after you use the address bar to change folders, you can use the Back button to return to the previous folder.
Details pane	Display the most common file properties—information about a file, such as the author, the date you last changed the file, and any descriptive ***tags***, which are custom file properties that you create to help find and organize your files.
File list	Display the contents of the current folder or library. In Computer, the file list displays the disk drives.
Folder window for *Computer*	Display the contents of the current folder, library, or device. The Folder window contains helpful features so that you can navigate within Windows.
Folder window toolbar	Perform common tasks, such as changing the view of your files and folders or burning files to a CD. The buttons available change to display only relevant tasks.
Navigation pane	Navigate to, open, and display favorites, libraries, folders, saved searches, and an expandable list of drives.
Preview pane button	Display (if you have chosen to open this pane) the contents of most files without opening them in a program. To open the preview pane, click the Preview pane button on the toolbar to turn it on and off.
Search box	Look for an item in the current folder or library by typing a word or phrase in the search box.
Views button	Choose how to view the contents of the current location.

Figure 1.5

6 On the toolbar of the **Computer** folder window, click the **Views button arrow** —the small arrow to the right of the Views button—to display a list of views that you can apply to the file list. If necessary, on the list, click **Tiles**.

The Views button is a ***split button***; clicking the main part of the button performs a ***command*** and clicking the arrow opens a menu or list. A command is an instruction to a computer program that causes an action to be carried out.

When you open a folder or a library, you can change how the files display in the file list. For example, you might prefer to see large or small ***icons***—pictures that represent a program, a file, a folder, or some other object—or an arrangement that lets you see various types of information about each file. Each time you click the Views button, the window changes, cycling through several views—additional view options are available by clicking the Views button arrow.

Another Way

Point to the CD/DVD drive, right-click, and then click Open.

7 In the **file list**, under **Devices with Removable Storage**, point to your **CD/DVD Drive**, and then ***double-click***—click the left mouse button two times in rapid succession—to display the list of folders on the CD. Compare your screen with Figure 1.6.

When double-clicking, keep your hand steady between clicks; this is more important than the speed of the two clicks.

Figure 1.6

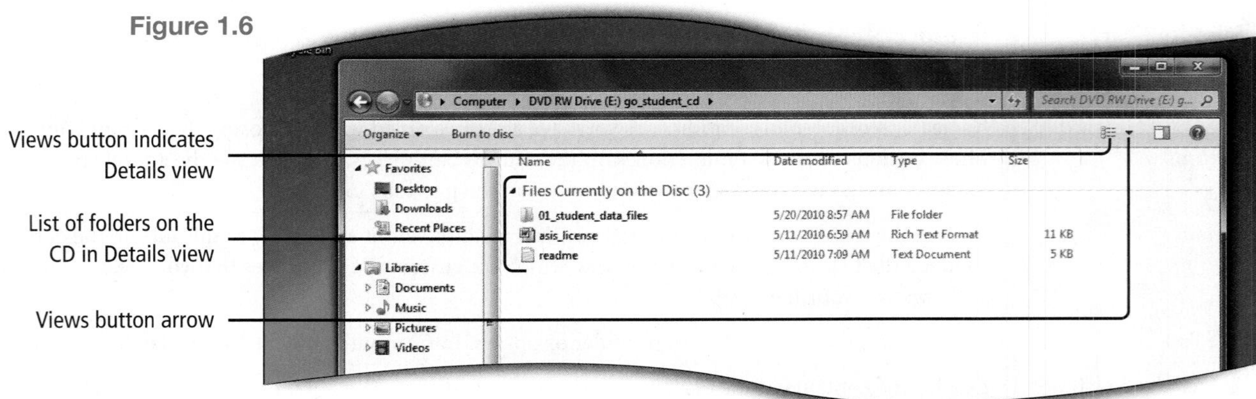

8 In the **file list**, point to the folder **01_student_data_files** and double-click to display the list of subfolders in the folder. Double-click to open the folder **01_common_features**. Compare your screen with Figure 1.7.

The Student Resource CD includes files that you will use to complete the projects in this textbook. If you prefer, you can also copy the **01_student_data_files** folder to a location on your computer's hard drive or to a removable device such as a ***USB flash drive***, which is a small storage device that plugs into a computer USB port. Your instructor might direct you to other locations where these files are located; for example, on your learning management system.

Figure 1.7

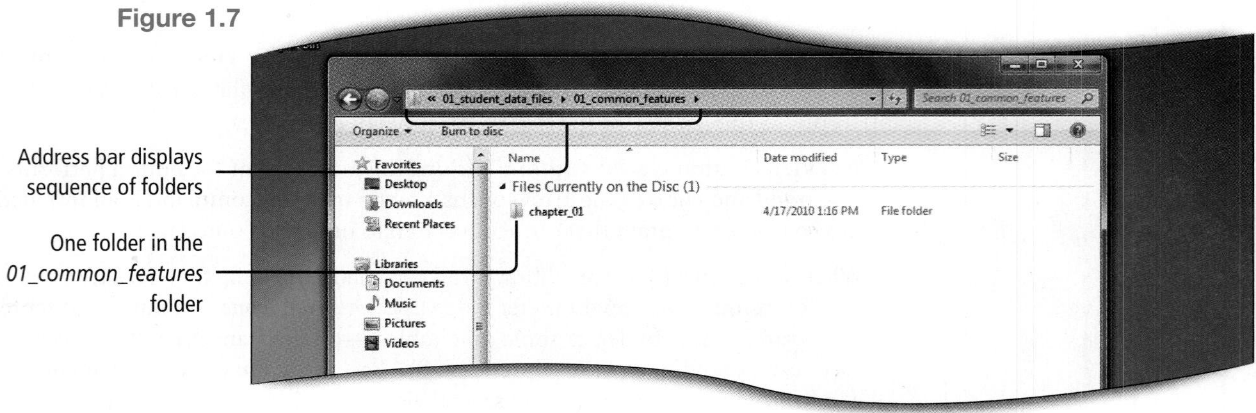

9 In the upper right corner of the **Computer** window, click the **Close** button to redisplay your desktop.

Objective 2 | Locate and Start a Microsoft Office 2010 Program

Microsoft Office 2010 includes programs, servers, and services for individuals, small organizations, and large enterprises. A ***program***, also referred to as an ***application***, is a set of instructions used by a computer to perform a task, such as word processing or accounting.

Activity 1.02 | Locating and Starting a Microsoft Office 2010 Program

1 On the **Windows taskbar**, click the **Start** button to display the **Start** menu.

2 From the displayed **Start** menu, locate the group of **Microsoft Office 2010** programs on your computer—the Office program icons from which you can start the program may be located on your Start menu, in a Microsoft Office folder on the **All Programs** list, on your desktop, or any combination of these locations; the location will vary depending on how your computer is configured.

All Programs is an area of the Start menu that displays all the available programs on your computer system.

3 Examine Figure 1.8, and notice the programs that are included in the Microsoft Office Professional Plus 2010 group of programs. (Your group of programs may vary.)

Microsoft Word is a word processing program, with which you create and share documents by using its writing tools.

Microsoft Excel is a spreadsheet program, with which you calculate and analyze numbers and create charts.

Microsoft Access is a database program, with which you can collect, track, and report data.

Microsoft PowerPoint is a presentation program, with which you can communicate information with high-impact graphics and video.

Additional popular Office programs include ***Microsoft Outlook*** to manage e-mail and organizational activities, ***Microsoft Publisher*** to create desktop publishing documents such as brochures, and ***Microsoft OneNote*** to manage notes that you make at meetings or in classes and to share notes with others on the Web.

The Professional Plus version of Office 2010 also includes ***Microsoft SharePoint Workspace*** to share information with others in a team environment and ***Microsoft InfoPath Designer and Filler*** to create forms and gather data.

Figure 1.8

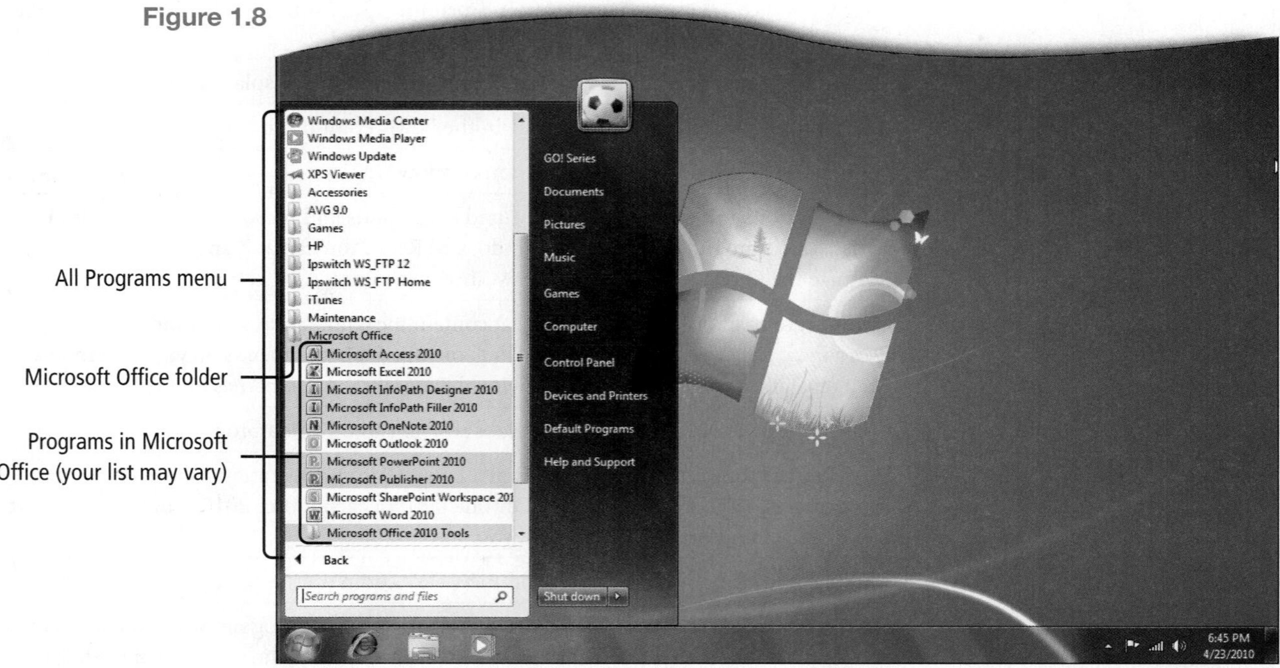

4 Click to open the program **Microsoft PowerPoint 2010**. Compare your screen with Figure 1.9, and then take a moment to study the description of these screen elements in the table in Figure 1.10.

Figure 1.9

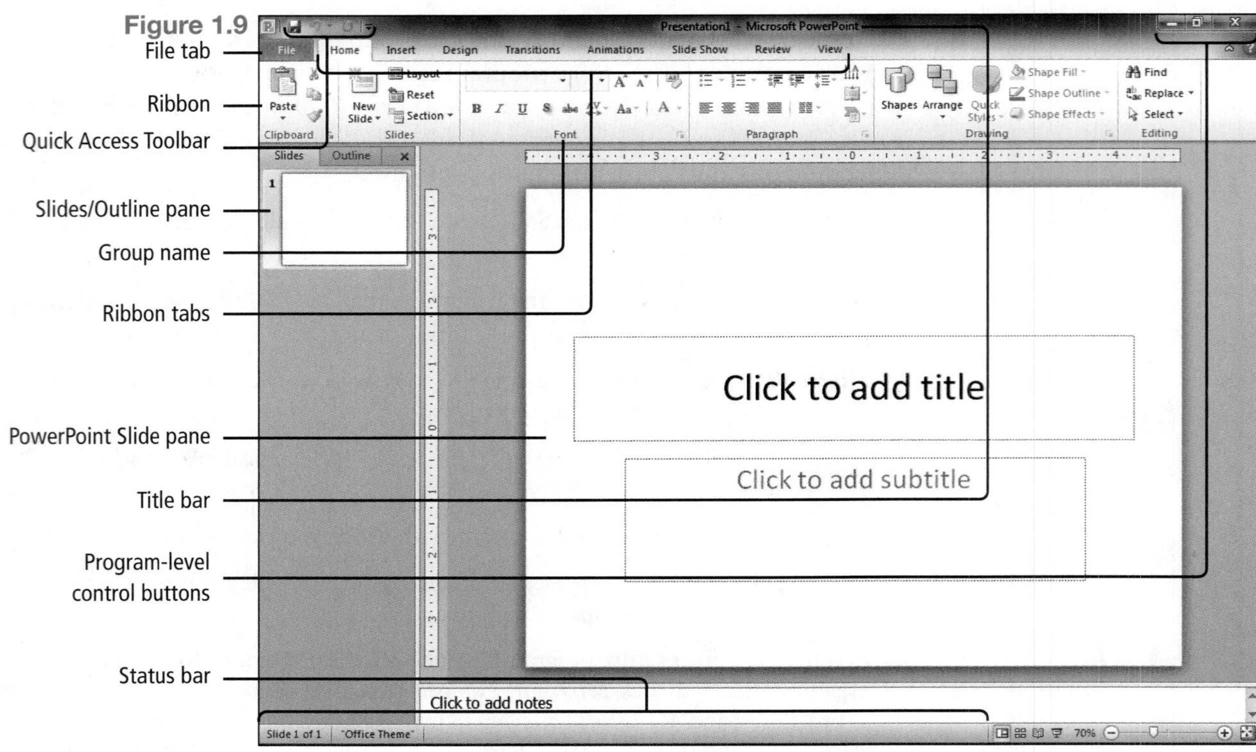

Screen Element	Description
File tab	Displays Microsoft Office Backstage view, which is a centralized space for all of your file management tasks such as opening, saving, printing, publishing, or sharing a file—all the things you can do *with* a file.
Group names	Indicate the name of the groups of related commands on the displayed tab.
PowerPoint Slide pane	Displays a large image of the active slide in the PowerPoint program.
Program-level control buttons	Minimizes, restores, or closes the program window.
Quick Access Toolbar	Displays buttons to perform frequently used commands and resources with a single click. The default commands include Save, Undo, and Redo. You can add and delete buttons to customize the Quick Access Toolbar for your convenience.
Ribbon	Displays a group of task-oriented tabs that contain the commands, styles, and resources you need to work in an Office 2010 program. The look of your Ribbon depends on your screen resolution. A high resolution will display more individual items and button names on the Ribbon.
Ribbon tabs	Display the names of the task-oriented tabs relevant to the open program.
Slides/Outline pane	Displays either thumbnails of the slides in a PowerPoint presentation (Slides tab) or the outline of the presentation's content (Outline tab). In each Office 2010 program, different panes display in different ways to assist you.
Status bar	Displays file information on the left and View and Zoom on the right.
Title bar	Displays the name of the file and the name of the program. The program window control buttons—Minimize, Maximize/Restore Down, and Close—are grouped on the right side of the title bar.

Figure 1.10

Objective 3 | Enter and Edit Text in an Office 2010 Program

All of the programs in Office 2010 require some typed text. Your keyboard is still the primary method of entering information into your computer. Techniques to ***edit***—make changes to—text are similar among all of the Office 2010 programs.

Activity 1.03 | Entering and Editing Text in an Office 2010 Program

1. In the middle of the PowerPoint Slide pane, point to the text *Click to add title* to display the [I] pointer, and then click one time.

   The ***insertion point***—a blinking vertical line that indicates where text or graphics will be inserted—displays.

   In Office 2010 programs, the mouse ***pointer***—any symbol that displays on your screen in response to moving your mouse device—displays in different shapes depending on the task you are performing and the area of the screen to which you are pointing.

2. Type **Oceana Grille Info** and notice how the insertion point moves to the right as you type. Point slightly to the right of the letter *e* in *Grille* and click to place the insertion point there. Compare your screen with Figure 1.11.

Figure 1.11

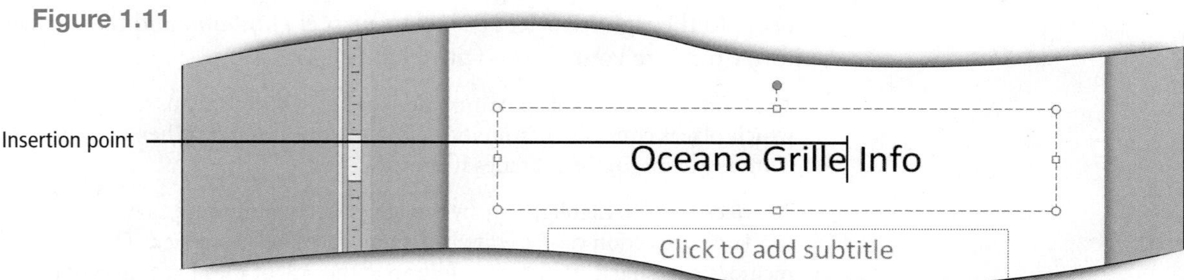

3. On your keyboard, locate and press the [Backspace] key to delete the letter *e*.

   Pressing [Backspace] removes a character to the left of the insertion point.

4. Point slightly to the left of the *I* in *Info* and click one time to place the insertion point there. Type **Menu** and then press [Spacebar] one time. Compare your screen with Figure 1.12.

   By ***default***, when you type text in an Office program, existing text moves to the right to make space for new typing. Default refers to the current selection or setting that is automatically used by a program unless you specify otherwise.

Figure 1.12

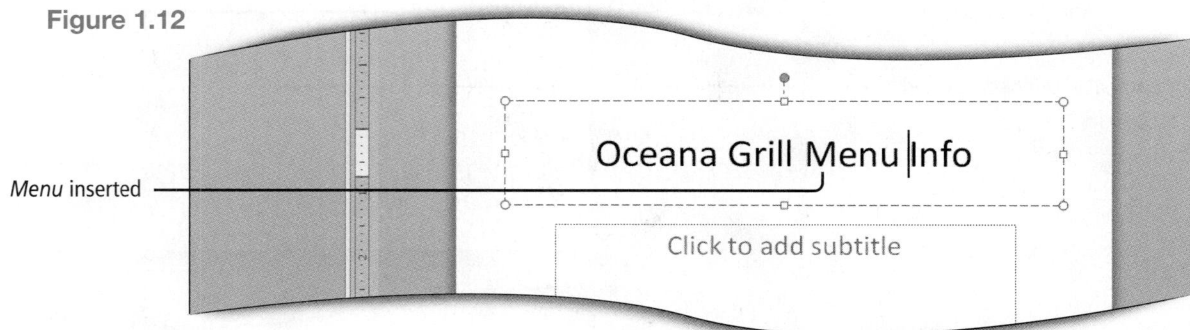

5 Press [Del] four times to delete *Info* and then type **Plan**

Pressing [Del] removes—deletes—a character to the right of the insertion point.

6 With your insertion point blinking after the word *Plan*, on your keyboard, hold down the [Ctrl] key. While holding down [Ctrl], press [←] three times to move the insertion point to the beginning of the word *Grill*.

This is a ***keyboard shortcut***—a key or combination of keys that performs a task that would otherwise require a mouse. This keyboard shortcut moves the insertion point to the beginning of the previous word.

A keyboard shortcut is commonly indicated as [Ctrl] + [←] (or some other combination of keys) to indicate that you hold down the first key while pressing the second key. A keyboard shortcut can also include three keys, in which case you hold down the first two and then press the third. For example, [Ctrl] + [Shift] + [←] selects one word to the left.

7 With the insertion point blinking at the beginning of the word *Grill*, type **Palm** and press [Spacebar].

8 Click anywhere in the text *Click to add subtitle*. With the insertion point blinking, type the following and include the spelling error: **Prepered by Annabel Dunham**

9 With your mouse, point slightly to the left of the *A* in *Annabel*, hold down the left mouse button, and then ***drag***—hold down the left mouse button while moving your mouse—to the right to select the text *Annabel Dunham*, and then release the mouse button. Compare your screen with Figure 1.13.

The ***Mini toolbar*** displays commands that are commonly used with the selected object, which places common commands close to your pointer. When you move the pointer away from the Mini toolbar, it fades from view.

To ***select*** refers to highlighting, by dragging with your mouse, areas of text or data or graphics so that the selection can be edited, formatted, copied, or moved. The action of dragging includes releasing the left mouse button at the end of the area you want to select. The Office programs recognize a selected area as one unit, to which you can make changes. Selecting text may require some practice. If you are not satisfied with your result, click anywhere outside of the selection, and then begin again.

Figure 1.13

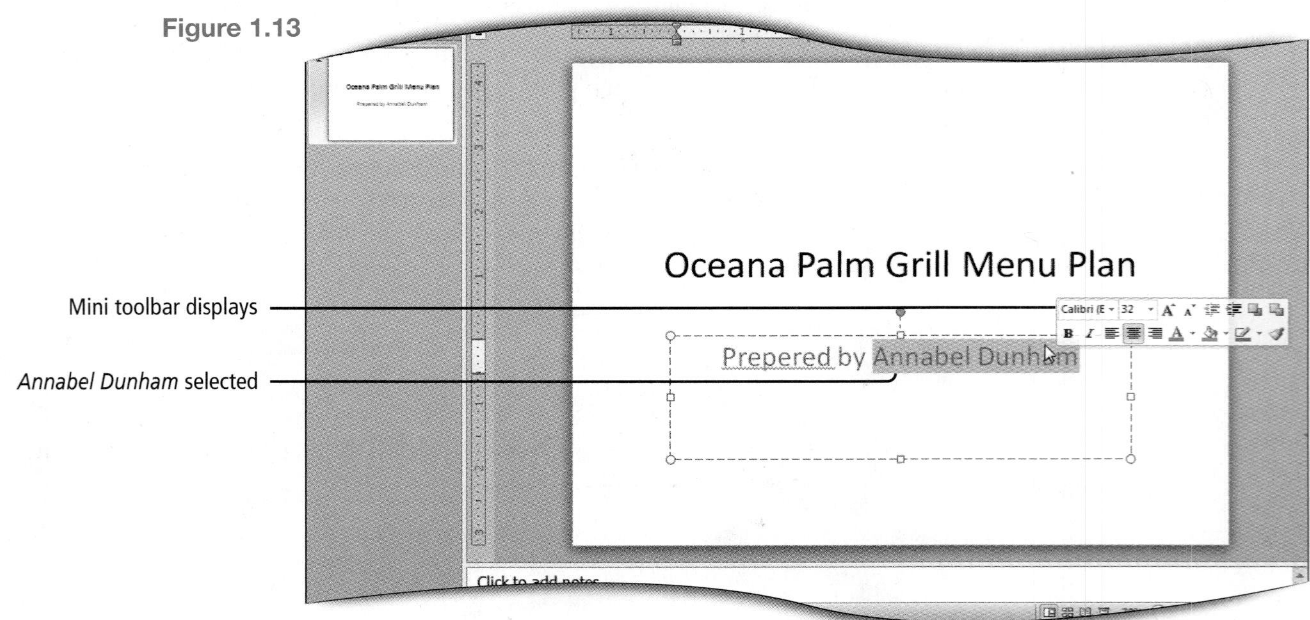

10 With the text *Annabel Dunham* selected, type your own firstname and lastname.

In any Windows-based program, such as the Microsoft Office 2010 programs, selected text is deleted and then replaced when you begin to type new text. You will save time by developing good techniques to select and then edit or replace selected text, which is easier than pressing the Del key numerous times to delete text that you do not want.

11 Notice that the misspelled word *Prepered* displays with a wavy red underline; additionally, all or part of your name might display with a wavy red underline.

Office 2010 has a dictionary of words against which all entered text is checked. In Word and PowerPoint, words that are *not* in the dictionary display a wavy red line, indicating a possible misspelled word or a proper name or an unusual word—none of which are in the Office 2010 dictionary.

In Excel and Access, you can initiate a check of the spelling, but wavy red underlines do not display.

12 Point to *Prepered* and then ***right-click***—click your right mouse button one time.

The Mini toolbar and a ***shortcut menu*** display. A shortcut menu displays commands and options relevant to the selected text or object—known as ***context-sensitive commands*** because they relate to the item you right-clicked.

Here, the shortcut menu displays commands related to the misspelled word. You can click the suggested correct spelling *Prepared*, click Ignore All to ignore the misspelling, add the word to the Office dictionary, or click Spelling to display a ***dialog box***. A dialog box is a small window that contains options for completing a task. Whenever you see a command followed by an ***ellipsis*** (...), which is a set of three dots indicating incompleteness, clicking the command will always display a dialog box.

13 On the displayed shortcut menu, click **Prepared** to correct the misspelled word. If necessary, point to any parts of your name that display a wavy red underline, right-click, and then on the shortcut menu, click Ignore All so that Office will no longer mark your name with a wavy underline in this file.

More Knowledge | Adding to the Office Dictionary

The main dictionary contains the most common words, but does not include all proper names, technical terms, or acronyms. You can add words, acronyms, and proper names to the Office dictionary by clicking Add to Dictionary when they are flagged, and you might want to do so for your own name and other proper names and terms that you type often.

Objective 4 | Perform Commands from a Dialog Box

In a dialog box, you make decisions about an individual object or topic. A dialog box also offers a way to adjust a number of settings at one time.

Activity 1.04 | Performing Commands from a Dialog Box

1 Point anywhere in the blank area above the title *Oceana Palm Grill Menu Plan* to display the pointer.

2 Right-click to display a shortcut menu. Notice the command *Format Background* followed by an ellipsis (...). Compare your screen with Figure 1.14.

Recall that a command followed by an ellipsis indicates that a dialog box will display if you click the command.

Figure 1.14

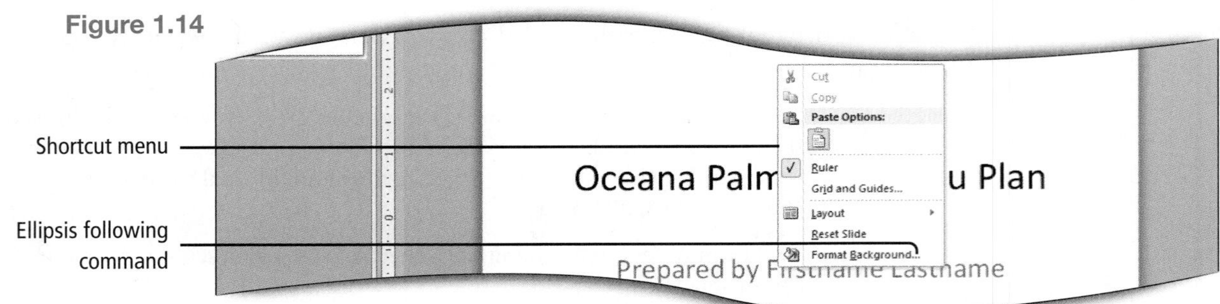

3 Click **Format Background** to display the **Format Background** dialog box, and then compare your screen with Figure 1.15.

Figure 1.15

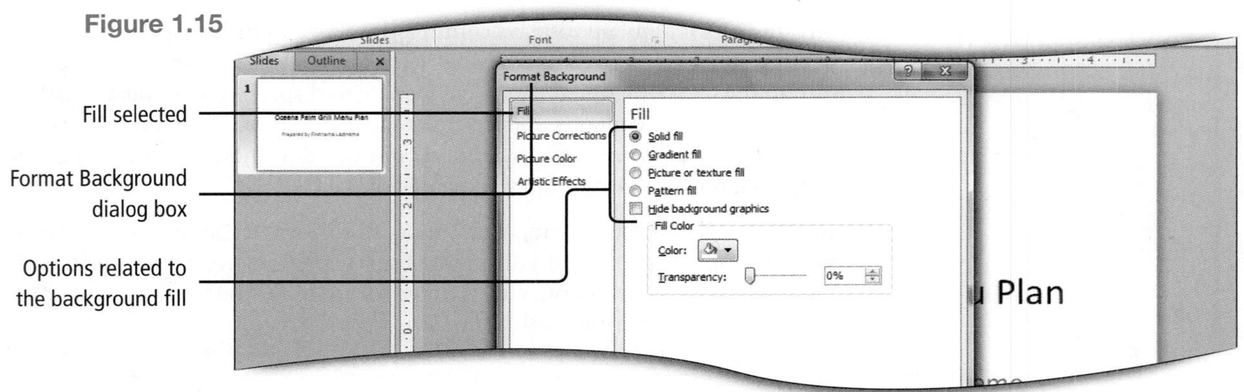

4 On the left, if necessary, click **Fill** to display the **Fill** options.

Fill is the inside color of an object. Here, the dialog box displays the option group names on the left; some dialog boxes provide a set of tabs across the top from which you can display different sets of options.

5 On the right, under **Fill**, click the **Gradient fill** option button.

The dialog box displays additional settings related to the gradient fill option. An ***option button*** is a round button that enables you to make one choice among two or more options. In a gradient fill, one color fades into another.

6 Click the **Preset colors arrow**—the arrow in the box to the right of the text *Preset colors*—and then in the gallery, in the second row, point to the fifth fill color to display the ScreenTip *Fog*.

A ***gallery*** is an Office feature that displays a list of potential results. A ***ScreenTip*** displays useful information about mouse actions, such as pointing to screen elements or dragging.

7 Click **Fog**, and then notice that the fill color is applied to your slide. Click the **Type arrow**, and then click **Rectangular** to change the pattern of the fill color. Compare your screen with Figure 1.16.

Figure 1.16

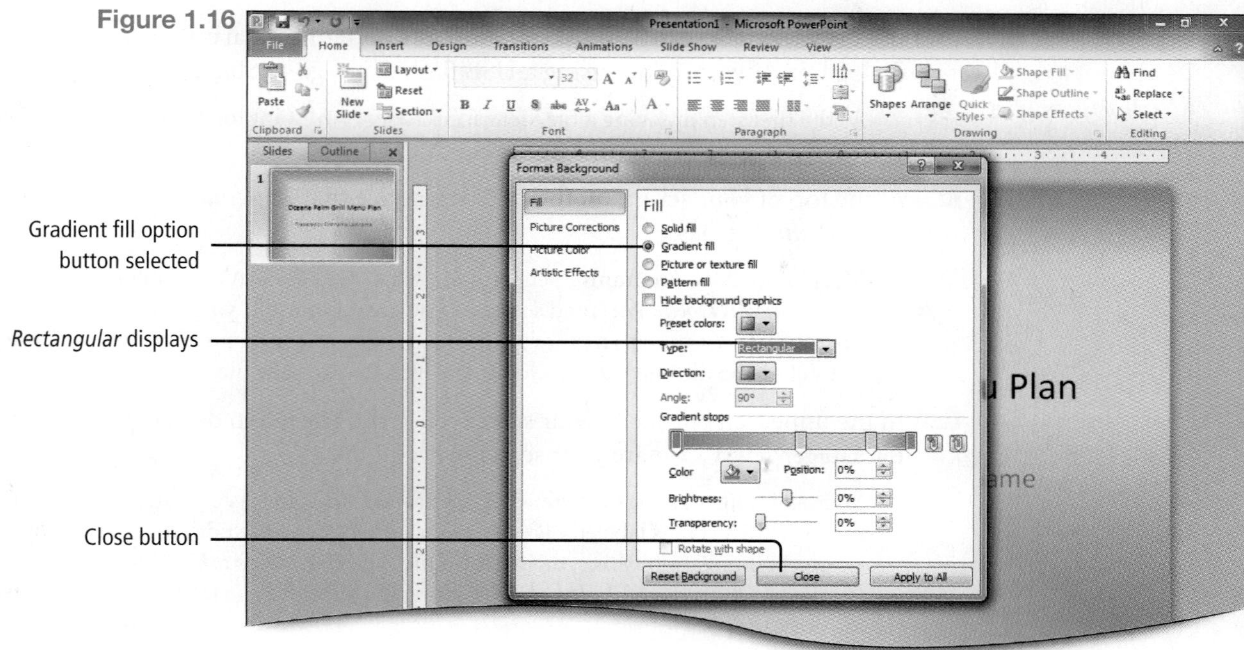

8 At the bottom of the dialog box, click **Close**.

As you progress in your study of Microsoft Office, you will practice using many dialog boxes and applying dramatic effects such as this to your Word documents, Excel spreadsheets, Access databases, and PowerPoint slides.

Objective 5 | Create a Folder, Save a File, and Close a Program

A ***location*** is any disk drive, folder, or other place in which you can store files and folders. Where you store your files depends on how and where you use your data. For example, for your classes, you might decide to store primarily on a removable USB flash drive so that you can carry your files to different locations and access your files on different computers.

If you do most of your work on a single computer, for example your home desktop system or your laptop computer that you take with you to school or work, store your files in one of the Libraries—Documents, Music, Pictures, or Videos—provided by your Windows operating system.

Although the Windows operating system helps you to create and maintain a logical folder structure, take the time to name your files and folders in a consistent manner.

Activity 1.05 | Creating a Folder, Saving a File, and Closing a Program

A PowerPoint presentation is an example of a file. Office 2010 programs use a common dialog box provided by the Windows operating system to assist you in saving files. In this activity, you will create a folder on a USB flash drive in which to store files. If you prefer to store on your hard drive, you can use similar steps to store files in your My Documents folder in your Documents library.

1 Insert a USB flash drive into your computer, and if necessary, **Close** [X] the **AutoPlay** dialog box. If you are not using a USB flash drive, go to Step 2.

As the first step in saving a file, determine where you want to save the file, and if necessary, insert a storage device.

2 At the top of your screen, in the title bar, notice that *Presentation1 – Microsoft PowerPoint* displays.

Most Office 2010 programs open with a new unsaved file with a default name—*Presentation1*, *Document1*, and so on. As you create your file, your work is temporarily stored in the computer's memory until you initiate a Save command, at which time you must choose a file name and location in which to save your file.

3 In the upper left corner of your screen, click the **File tab** to display **Microsoft Office Backstage** view. Compare your screen with Figure 1.17.

Microsoft Office ***Backstage view*** is a centralized space for tasks related to *file* management; that is why the tab is labeled *File*. File management tasks include, for example, opening, saving, printing, publishing, or sharing a file. The ***Backstage tabs***—*Info*, *Recent*, *New*, *Print*, *Save & Send*, and *Help*—display along the left side. The tabs group file-related tasks together.

Above the Backstage tabs, ***Quick Commands***—*Save*, *Save As*, *Open*, and *Close*—display for quick access to these commands. When you click any of these commands, Backstage view closes and either a dialog box displays or the active file closes.

Here, the ***Info tab*** displays information—*info*—about the current file. In the center panel, various file management tasks are available in groups. For example, if you click the Protect Presentation button, a list of options that you can set for this file that relate to who can open or edit the presentation displays.

On the Info tab, in the right panel, you can also examine the ***document properties***. Document properties, also known as ***metadata***, are details about a file that describe or identify it, such as the title, author name, subject, and keywords that identify the document's topic or contents. On the Info page, a thumbnail image of the current file displays in the upper right corner, which you can click to close Backstage view and return to the document.

More Knowledge | Deciding Where to Store Your Files

Where should you store your files? In the libraries created by Windows 7 (Documents, Pictures, and so on)? On a removable device like a flash drive or external hard drive? In Windows 7, it is easy to find your files, especially if you use the libraries. Regardless of where you save a file, Windows 7 will make it easy to find the file again, even if you are not certain where it might be.

In Windows 7, storing all of your files within a library makes sense. If you perform most of your work on your desktop system or your laptop that travels with you, you can store your files in the libraries created by Windows 7 for your user account—Documents, Pictures, Music, and so on. Within these libraries, you can create folders and subfolders to organize your data. These libraries are a good choice for storing your files because:

- From the Windows Explorer button on the taskbar, your libraries are always just one click away.
- The libraries are designed for their contents; for example, the Pictures folder displays small images of your digital photos.
- You can add new locations to a library; for example, an external hard drive, or a network drive. Locations added to a library behave just like they are on your hard drive.
- Other users of your computer cannot access your libraries.
- The libraries are the default location for opening and saving files within an application, so you will find that you can open and save files with fewer navigation clicks.

Figure 1.17

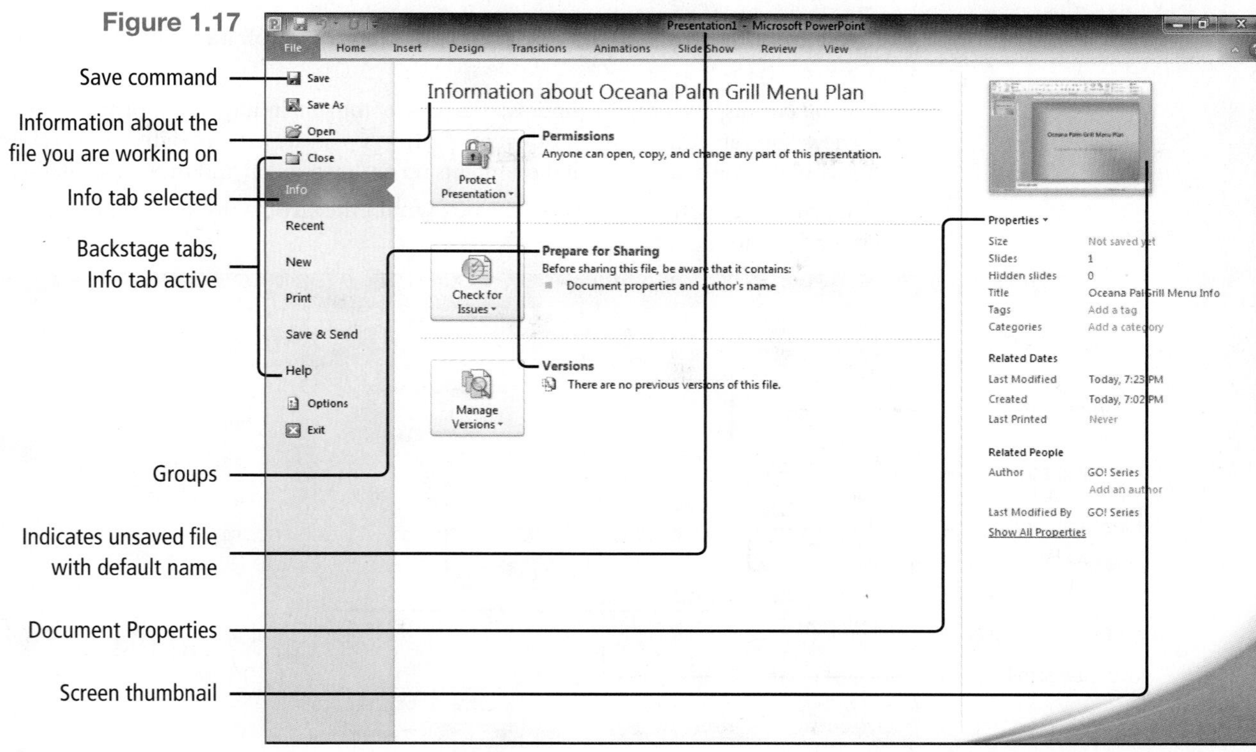

4 Above the **Backstage tabs**, click **Save** to display the **Save As** dialog box.

Backstage view closes and the Save As dialog box, which includes a folder window and an area at the bottom to name the file and set the file type, displays.

When you are saving something for the first time, for example a new PowerPoint presentation, the Save and Save As commands are identical. That is, the Save As dialog box will display if you click Save or if you click Save As.

> **Note** | Saving Your File
>
> After you have named a file and saved it in your desired location, the Save command saves any changes you make to the file without displaying any dialog box. The Save As command will display the Save As dialog box and let you name and save a new file based on the current one—in a location that you choose. After you name and save the new document, the original document closes, and the new document—based on the original one—displays.

5 In the **Save As** dialog box, on the left, locate the **navigation pane**; compare your screen with Figure 1.18.

By default, the Save command opens the Documents library unless your default file location has been changed.

Figure 1.18

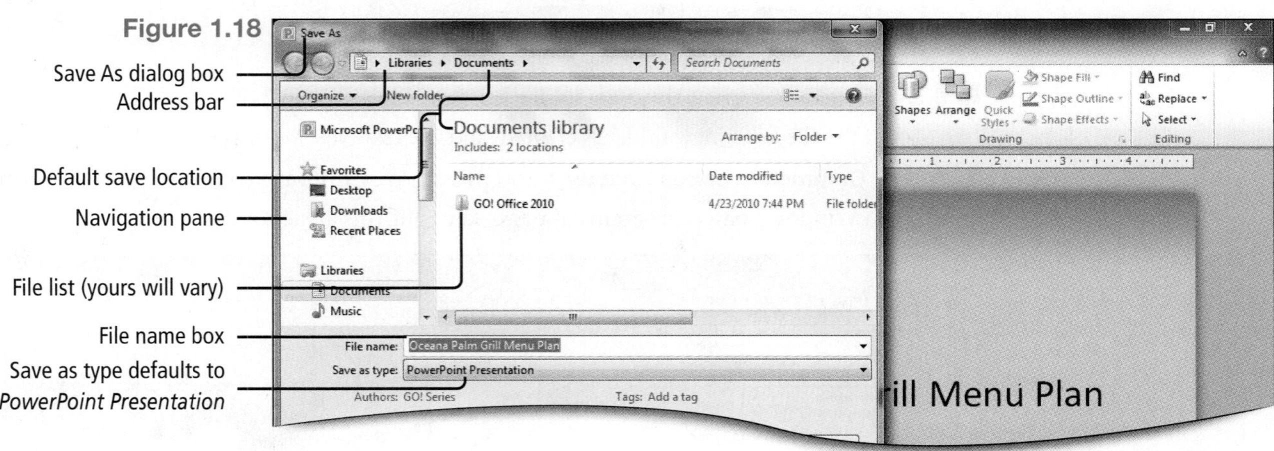

6 On the right side of the **navigation pane**, point to the **scroll bar**. Compare your screen with Figure 1.19.

A ***scroll bar*** displays when a window, or a pane within a window, has information that is not in view. You can click the up or down scroll arrows—or the left and right scroll arrows in a horizontal scroll bar—to scroll the contents up or down or left and right in small increments.

You can also drag the ***scroll box***—the box within the scroll bar—to scroll the window in either direction.

Figure 1.19

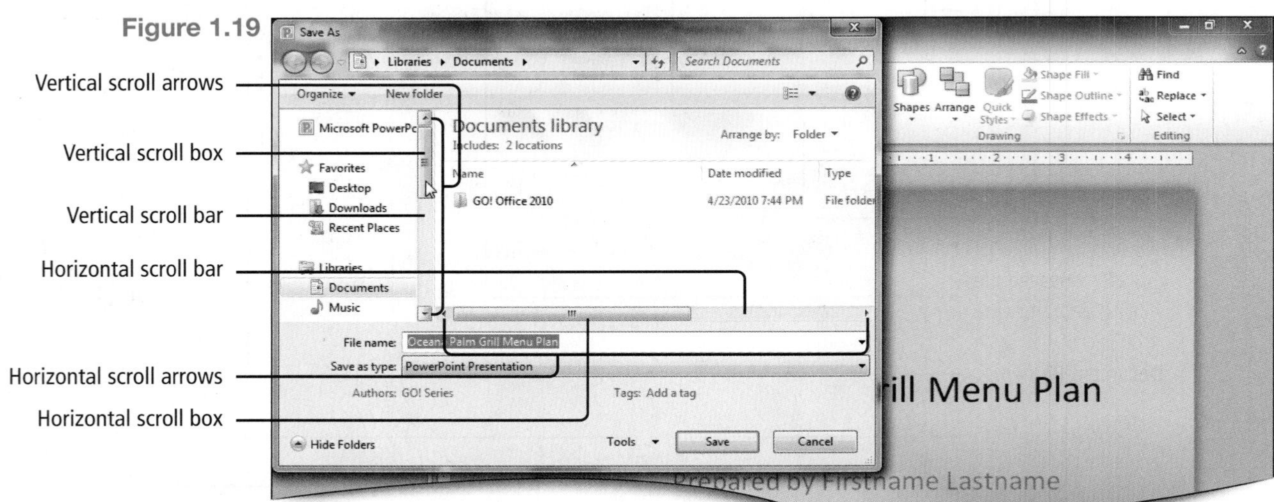

7 Click the **down scroll arrow** as necessary so that you can view the lower portion of the **navigation pane**, and then click the icon for your USB flash drive. Compare your screen with Figure 1.20. (If you prefer to store on your computer's hard drive instead of a USB flash drive, in the navigation pane, click Documents.)

Figure 1.20

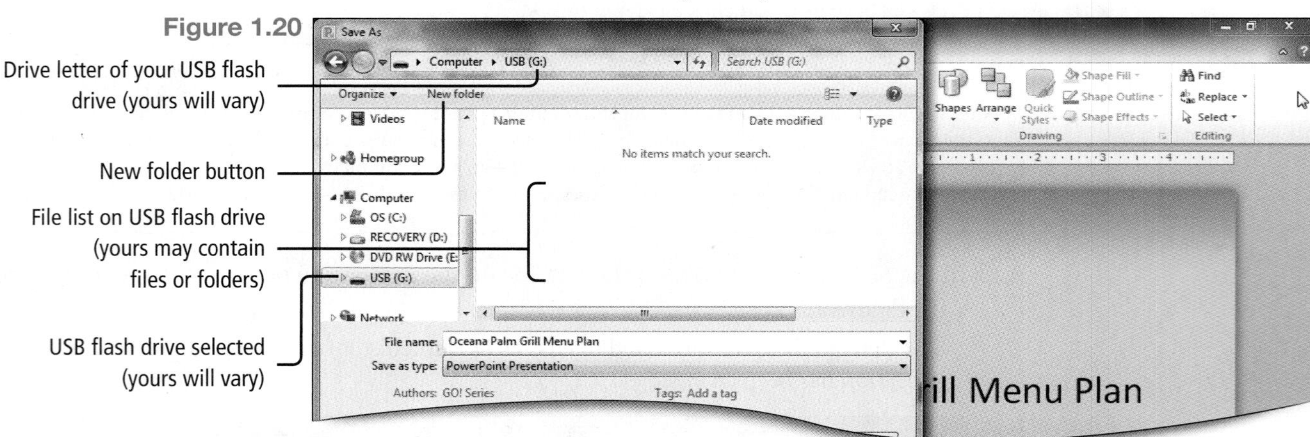

8 On the toolbar, click the **New folder** button.

In the file list, a new folder is created, and the text *New folder* is selected.

9 Type **Common Features Chapter 1** and press Enter. Compare your screen with Figure 1.21.

In Windows-based programs, the Enter key confirms an action.

Figure 1.21

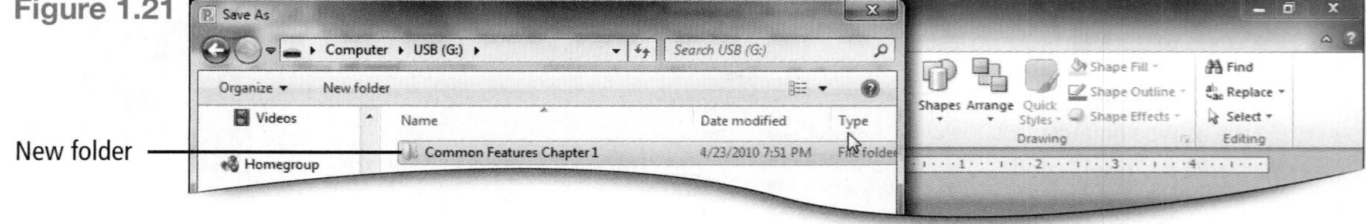

10 In the **file list**, double-click the name of your new folder to open it and display its name in the **address bar**.

11 In the lower portion of the dialog box, click in the **File name** box to select the existing text. Notice that Office inserts the text at the beginning of the presentation as a suggested file name.

12 On your keyboard, locate the [-] key. Notice that the Shift of this key produces the underscore character. With the text still selected, type **Lastname_Firstname_1A_Menu_Plan** Compare your screen with Figure 1.22.

You can use spaces in file names, however some individuals prefer not to use spaces. Some programs, especially when transferring files over the Internet, may not work well with spaces in file names. In general, however, unless you encounter a problem, it is OK to use spaces. In this textbook, underscores are used instead of spaces in file names.

Figure 1.22

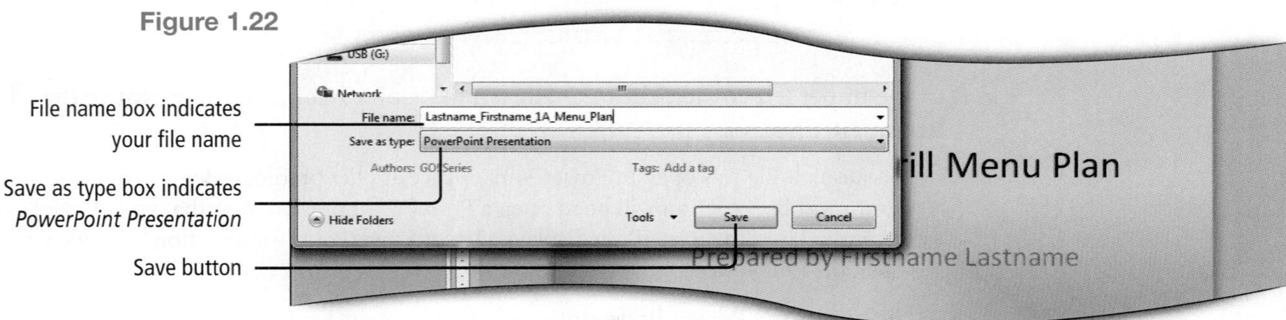

13 In the lower right corner, click **Save**; or press [Enter]. See Figure 1.23.

Your new file name displays in the title bar, indicating that the file has been saved to a location that you have specified.

Figure 1.23

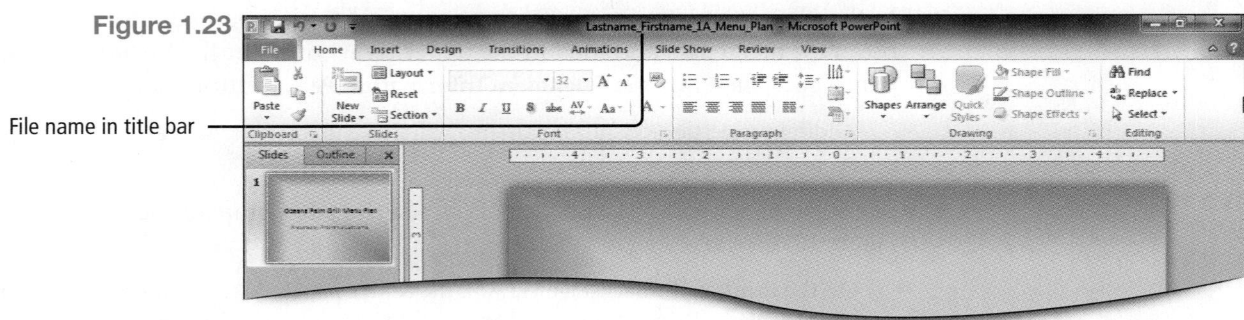

14 In the text that begins *Prepared by*, click to position the insertion point at the end of your name, and then press [Enter] to move to a new line. Type **For Laura Hernandez**

15 Click the **File tab** to display **Backstage** view. At the top of the center panel, notice that the path where your file is stored displays. Above the Backstage tabs, click **Close** to close the file. In the message box, click **Save** to save the changes you made and close the file. Leave PowerPoint open.

PowerPoint displays a message asking if you want to save the changes you have made. Because you have made additional changes to the file since your last Save operation, an Office program will always prompt you to save so that you do not lose any new data.

Objective 6 | Add Document Properties and Print a File

The process of printing a file is similar in all of the Office applications. There are differences in the types of options you can select. For example, in PowerPoint, you have the option of printing the full slide, with each slide printing on a full sheet of paper, or of printing handouts with small pictures of slides on a page.

Activity 1.06 | Adding Document Properties and Printing a File

> **Alert! | Are You Printing or Submitting Your Files Electronically?**
>
> If you are submitting your files electronically only, or have no printer attached, you can still complete this activity. Complete Steps 1-9, and then submit your file electronically as directed by your instructor.

1. In the upper left corner, click the **File tab** to display **Backstage** view. Notice that the **Recent tab** displays.

   Because no file was open in PowerPoint, Office applies predictive logic to determine that your most likely action will be to open a PowerPoint presentation that you worked on recently. Thus, the Recent tab displays a list of PowerPoint presentations that were recently open on your system.

2. At the top of the **Recent Presentations** list, click your **Lastname_Firstname_1A_Menu_Plan** file to open it.

3. Click the **File tab** to redisplay **Backstage** view. On the right, under the screen thumbnail, click **Properties**, and then click **Show Document Panel**. In the **Author** box, delete the existing text, and then type your firstname and lastname. Notice that in PowerPoint, some variation of the slide title is automatically inserted in the Title box. In the **Subject** box, type your Course name and section number. In the **Keywords** box, type **menu plan** and then in the upper right corner of the **Document Properties** panel, click the **Close the Document Information Panel** button [×].

   Adding properties to your documents will make them easier to search for in systems such as Microsoft SharePoint.

> **Another Way**
>
> Press Ctrl + P or Ctrl + F2 to display the Print tab in Backstage view.

4. Redisplay **Backstage** view, and then click the **Print tab**. Compare your screen with Figure 1.24.

   On the Print tab in Backstage view, in the center panel, three groups of printing-related tasks display—Print, Printer, and Settings. In the right panel, the ***Print Preview*** displays, which is a view of a document as it will appear on the paper when you print it.

   At the bottom of the Print Preview area, on the left, the number of pages and arrows with which you can move among the pages in Print Preview display. On the right, ***Zoom*** settings enable you to shrink or enlarge the Print Preview. Zoom is the action of increasing or decreasing the viewing area of the screen.

Figure 1.24

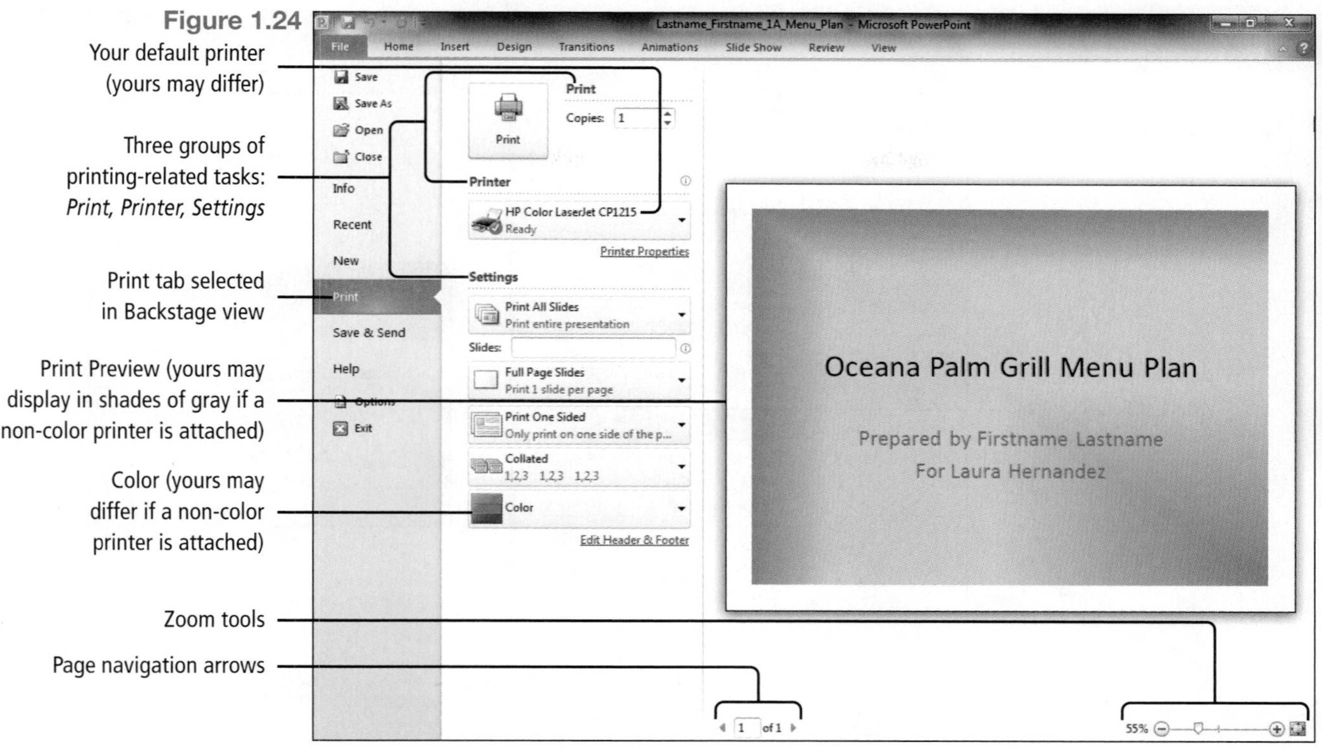

5 Locate the **Settings group**, and notice that the default setting is to **Print All Slides** and to print **Full Page Slides**—each slide on a full sheet of paper.

6 Point to **Full Page Slides**, notice that the button glows orange, and then click the button to display a gallery of print arrangements. Compare your screen with Figure 1.25.

Figure 1.25

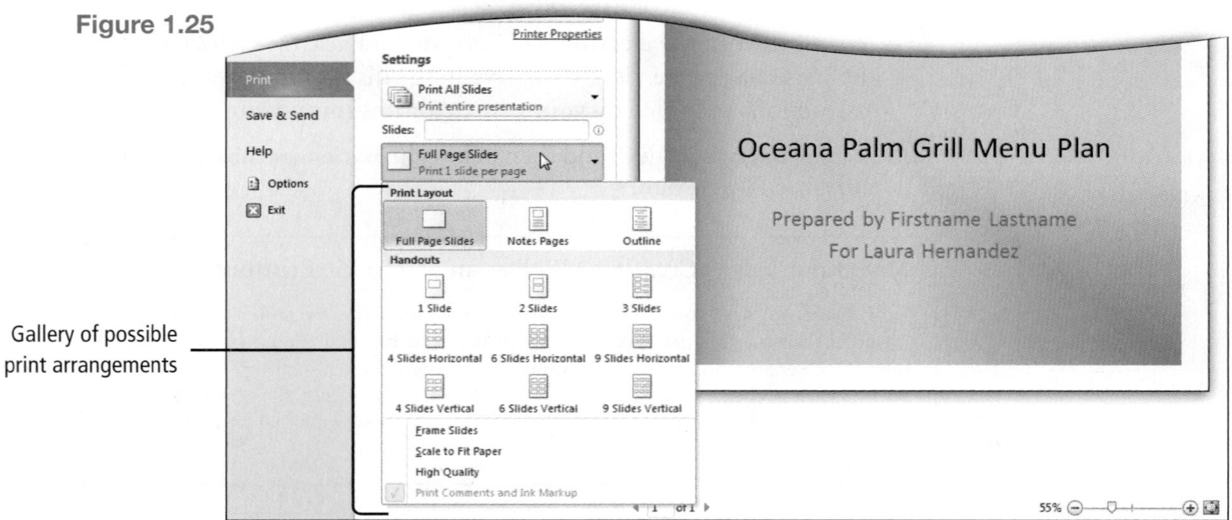

7 In the displayed gallery, under **Handouts**, click **1 Slide**, and then compare your screen with Figure 1.26.

The Print Preview changes to show how your slide will print on the paper in this arrangement.

Figure 1.26

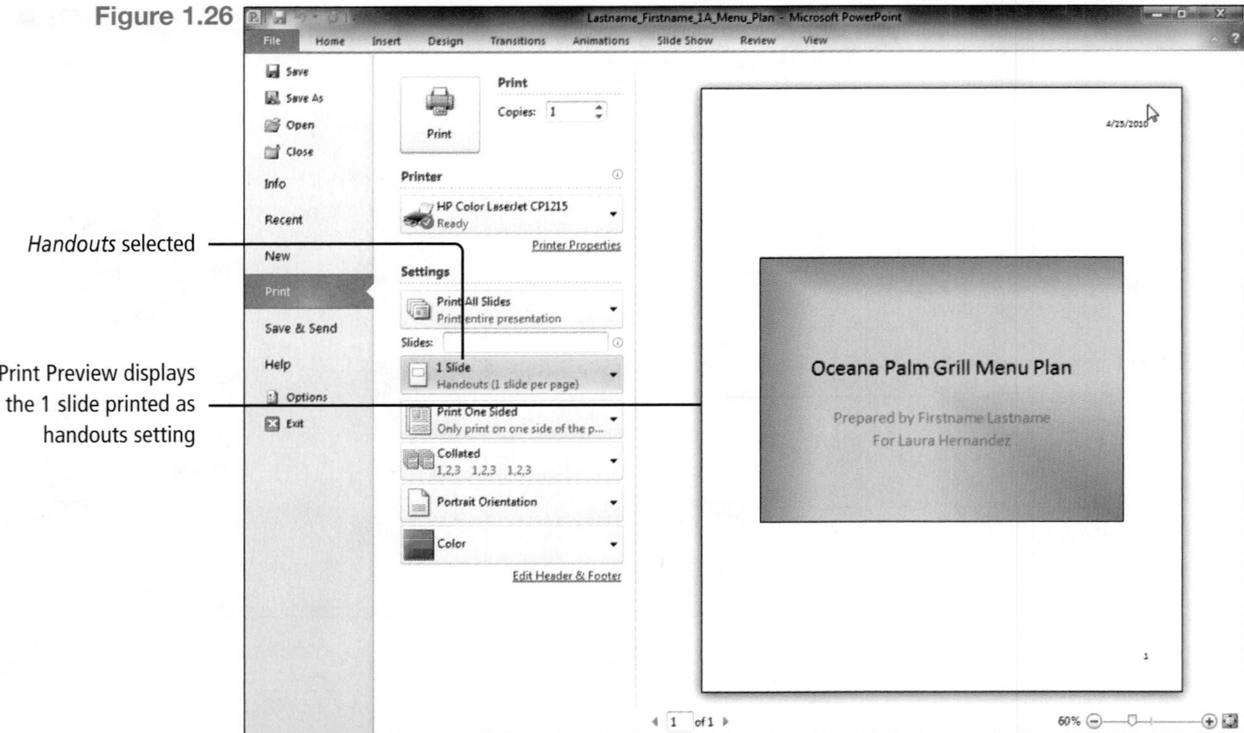

8 To submit your file electronically, skip this step and move to Step 9. To print your slide, be sure your system is connected to a printer, and then in the **Print group**, click the **Print** button. On the Quick Access Toolbar, click **Save**, and then move to Step 10.

The handout will print on your default printer—on a black and white printer, the colors will print in shades of gray. Backstage view closes and your file redisplays in the PowerPoint window.

9 To submit your file electronically, above the **Backstage tabs**, click **Close** to close the file and close **Backstage** view, click **Save** in the displayed message, and then follow the instructions provided by your instructor to submit your file electronically.

Another Way

In the upper right corner of your PowerPoint window, click the red Close button.

10 Display **Backstage** view, and then below the **Backstage tabs**, click **Exit** to close your file and close PowerPoint.

More Knowledge | Creating a PDF as an Electronic Printout

From Backstage view, you can save an Office file as a ***PDF file***. ***Portable Document Format*** (PDF) creates an image of your file that preserves the look of your file, but that cannot be easily changed. This is a popular format for sending documents electronically, because the document will display on most computers. From Backstage view, click Save & Send, and then in the File Types group, click Create PDF/XPS Document. Then in the third panel, click the Create PDF/XPS button, navigate to your chapter folder, and then in the lower right corner, click Publish.

End You have completed Project 1A

Project 1B Word File

Project Activities

In Activities 1.07 through 1.16, you will open, edit, save, and then compress a Word file. Your completed document will look similar to Figure 1.27.

Project Files

For Project 1B, you will need the following file:

cf01B_Cheese_Promotion

You will save your Word document as:

Lastname_Firstname_1B_Cheese_Promotion

Project Results

Memo

TO: Laura Mabry Hernandez, General Manager

FROM: Donna Jackson, Executive Chef

DATE: December 17, 2014

SUBJECT: Cheese Specials on Tuesdays

To increase restaurant traffic between 4:00 p.m. and 6:00 p.m., I am proposing a trial cheese event in one of the restaurants, probably Orlando. I would like to try a weekly event on Tuesday evenings where the focus is on a good selection of cheese.

I envision two possibilities: a selection of cheese plates or a cheese bar—or both. The cheeses would have to be matched with compatible fruit and bread or crackers. They could be used as appetizers, or for desserts, as is common in Europe. The cheese plates should be varied and diverse, using a mixture of hard and soft, sharp and mild, unusual and familiar.

I am excited about this new promotion. If done properly, I think it could increase restaurant traffic in the hours when individuals want to relax with a small snack instead of a heavy dinner.

The promotion will require that our employees become familiar with the types and characteristics of both foreign and domestic cheeses. Let's meet to discuss the details and the training requirements, and to create a flyer that begins something like this:

Oceana Palm Grill Tuesday Cheese Tastings

Lastname_Firstname_1B_Cheese_Promotion

Figure 1.27
Project 1B Cheese Promotion

Objective 7 | Open an Existing File and Save It with a New Name

In any Office program, use the Open command to display the ***Open dialog box***, from which you can navigate to and then open an existing file that was created in that same program.

The Open dialog box, along with the Save and Save As dialog boxes, are referred to as ***common dialog boxes***. These dialog boxes, which are provided by the Windows programming interface, display in all of the Office programs in the same manner. Thus, the Open, Save, and Save As dialog boxes will all look and perform the same in each Office program.

Activity 1.07 | Opening an Existing File and Saving it with a New Name

In this activity, you will display the Open dialog box, open an existing Word document, and then save it in your storage location with a new name.

1. Determine the location of the student data files that accompany this textbook, and be sure you can access these files.

   For example:

   If you are accessing the files from the Student CD that came with this textbook, insert the CD now.

   If you copied the files from the Student CD or from the Pearson Web site to a USB flash drive that you are using for this course, insert the flash drive in your computer now.

   If you copied the files to the hard drive of your computer, for example in your Documents library, be sure you can locate the files on the hard drive.

2. Determine the location of your **Common Features Chapter 1** folder you created in Activity 1.05, in which you will store your work from this chapter, and then be sure you can access that folder.

   For example:

   If you created your chapter folder on a USB flash drive, insert the flash drive in your computer now. This can be the same flash drive where you have stored the student data files; just be sure to use the chapter folder you created.

   If you created your chapter folder in the Documents library on your computer, be sure you can locate the folder. Otherwise, create a new folder at the computer at which you are working, or on a USB flash drive.

3. Using the technique you practiced in Activity 1.02, locate and then start the **Microsoft Word 2010** program on your system.

Another Way

In the Word (or other program) window, press Ctrl + F12 to display the Open dialog box.

4. On the Ribbon, click the **File tab** to display **Backstage** view, and then click **Open** to display the **Open** dialog box.

5. In the **navigation pane** on the left, use the scroll bar to scroll as necessary, and then click the location of your student data files to display the location's contents in the **file list**. Compare your screen with Figure 1.28.

   For example:

   If you are accessing the files from the Student CD that came with your book, under Computer, click the CD/DVD.

   If you are accessing the files from a USB flash drive, under Computer, click the flash drive name.

   If you are accessing the files from the Documents library of your computer, under Libraries, click Documents.

Figure 1.28

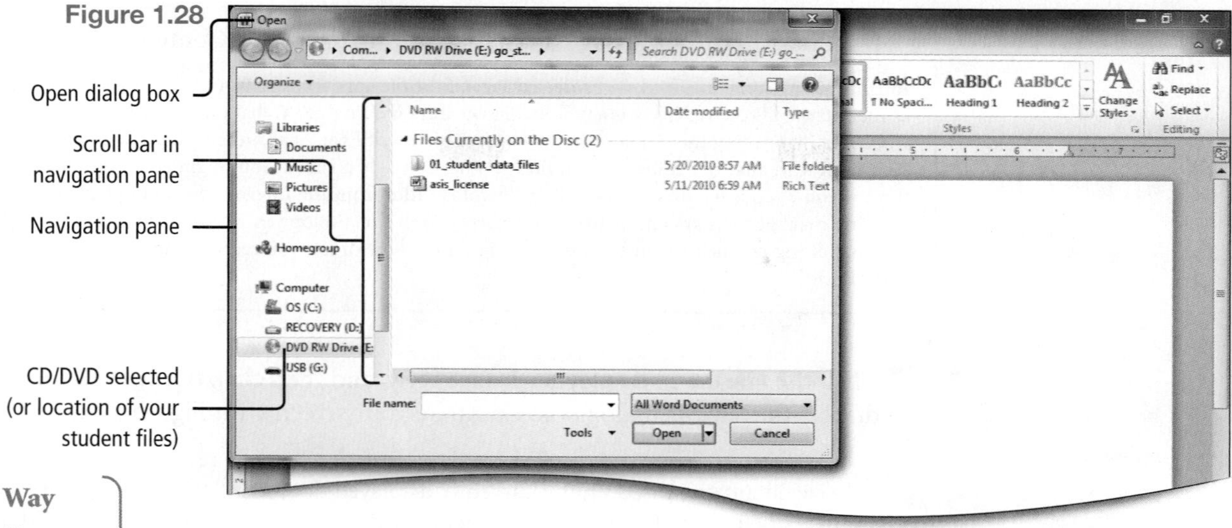

Another Way

Point to a folder name, right-click, and then from the shortcut menu, click Open.

6 Point to the folder **01_student_data_files** and double-click to open the folder. Point to the subfolder **01_common_features**, double-click, and then compare your screen with Figure 1.29.

Figure 1.29

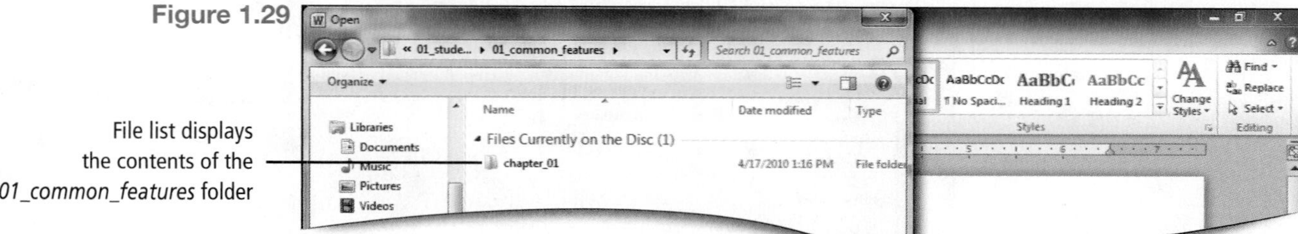

Another Way

Click one time to select the file, and then press Enter or click the Open button in the lower right corner of the dialog box.

7 In the **file list**, point to the **chapter_01** subfolder and double-click to open it. In the **file list**, point to Word file **cf01B_Cheese_Promotion** and then double-click to open and display the file in the Word window. On the Ribbon, on the **Home tab**, in the **Paragraph group**, if necessary, click the **Show/Hide** button ¶ so that it is active—glowing orange. Compare your screen with Figure 1.30.

On the title bar at the top of the screen, the file name displays. If you opened the document from the Student CD, (*Read-Only*) will display. If you opened the document from another source to which the files were copied, (*Read-Only*) might not display. ***Read-Only*** is a property assigned to a file that prevents the file from being modified or deleted; it indicates that you cannot save any changes to the displayed document unless you first save it with a new name.

Figure 1.30

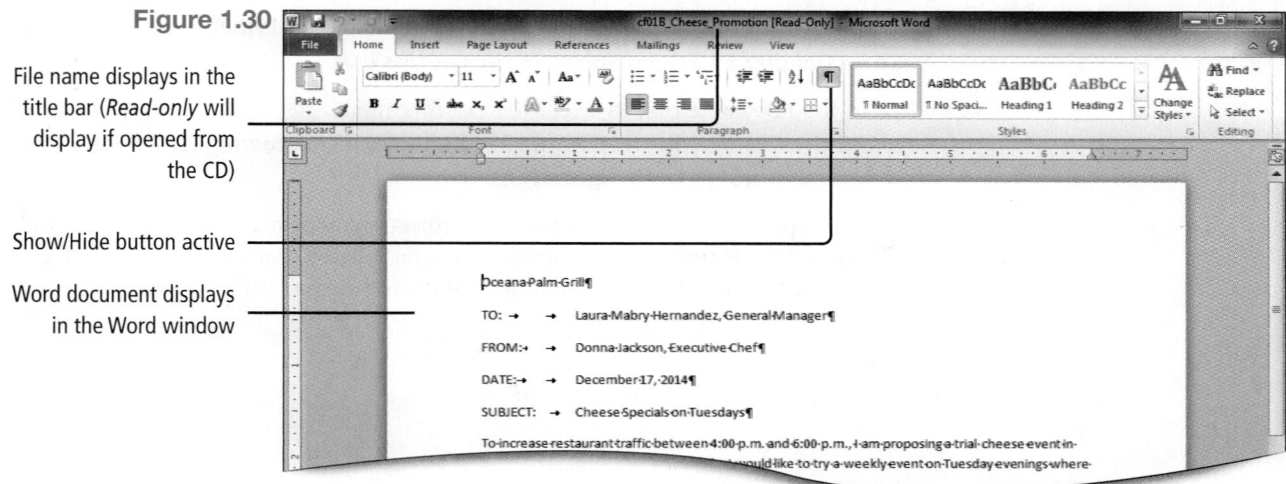

> **Alert! | Do You See a Message to Enable Editing or Enable Content?**
>
> In Office 2010, some files open in ***Protected View*** if the file appears to be from a potentially risky location, such as the Internet. Protected View is a new security feature in Office 2010 that protects your computer from malicious files by opening them in a restricted environment until you enable them. ***Trusted Documents*** is another security feature that remembers which files you have already enabled. You might encounter these security features if you open a file from an e-mail or download files from the Internet; for example, from your college's learning management system or from the Pearson Web site. So long as you trust the source of the file, click Enable Editing or Enable Content—depending on the type of file you receive—and then go ahead and work with the file.

> **Another Way**
>
> Press F12 to display the Save As dialog box.

8 Click the **File tab** to display **Backstage** view, and then click the **Save As** command to display the **Save As** dialog box. Compare your screen with Figure 1.31.

The Save As command displays the Save As dialog box where you can name and save a *new* document based on the currently displayed document. After you name and save the new document, the original document closes, and the new document—based on the original one—displays.

Figure 1.31

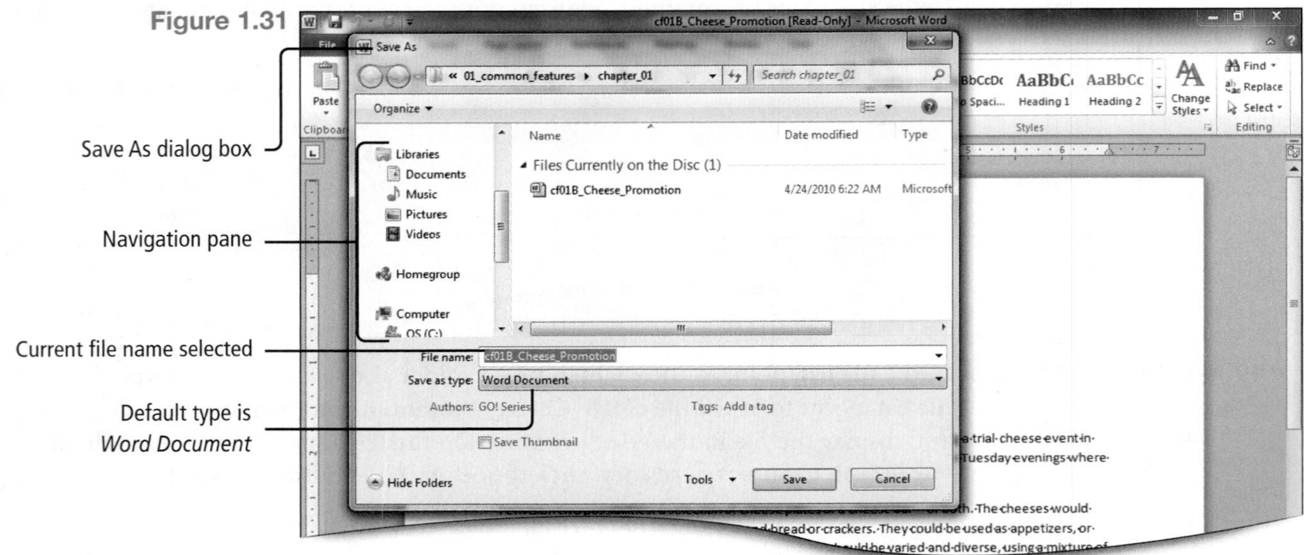

9 In the **navigation pane**, click the location in which you are storing your projects for this chapter—the location where you created your **Common Features Chapter 1** folder; for example, your USB flash drive or the Documents library.

10 In the **file list**, double-click the necessary folders and subfolders until your **Common Features Chapter 1** folder displays in the **address bar**.

11 Click in the **File name** box to select the existing file name, or drag to select the existing text, and then using your own name, type **Lastname_Firstname_1B_Cheese_Promotion** Compare your screen with Figure 1.32.

As you type, the file name from your 1A project might display briefly. Because your 1A project file is stored in this location and you began the new file name with the same text, Office predicts that you might want the same or similar file name. As you type new characters, the suggestion is removed.

Figure 1.32

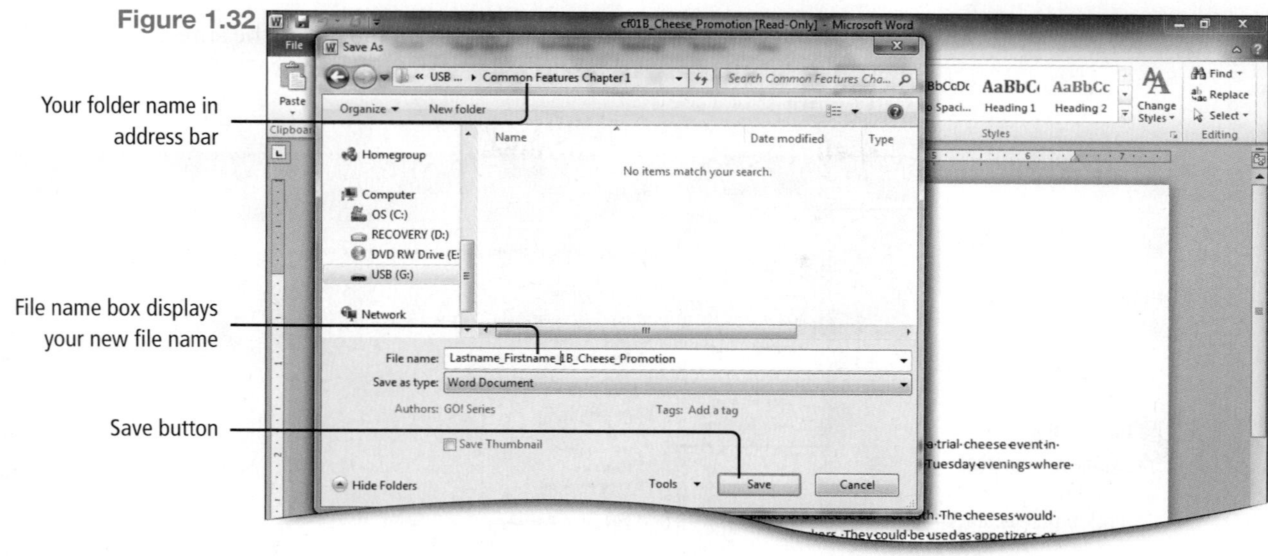

12 In the lower right corner of the **Save As** dialog box, click **Save**; or press Enter. Compare your screen with Figure 1.33.

The original document closes, and your new document, based on the original, displays with the name in the title bar.

Figure 1.33

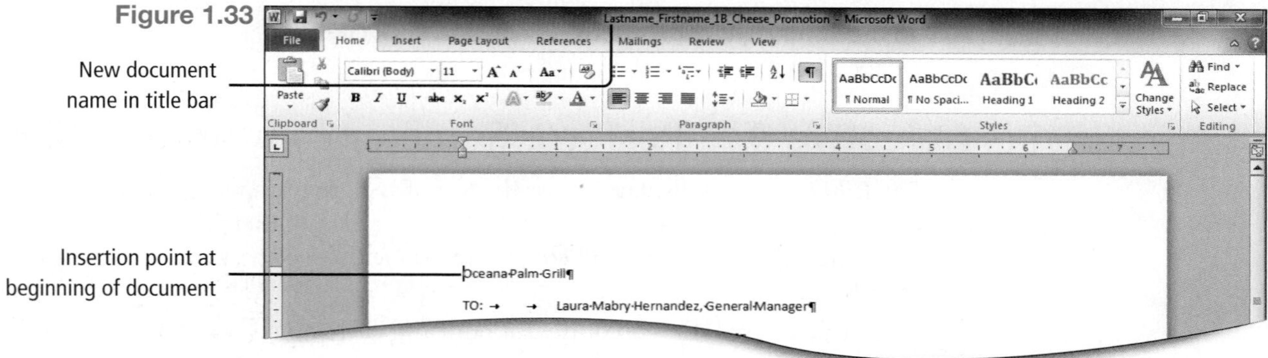

Objective 8 | Explore Options for an Application

Within each Office application, you can open an ***Options dialog box*** where you can select program settings and other options and preferences. For example, you can set preferences for viewing and editing files.

Activity 1.08 | Viewing Application Options

1 Click the **File tab** to display **Backstage** view. Under the **Help tab**, click **Options**.

2 In the displayed **Word Options** dialog box, on the left, click **Display**, and then on the right, locate the information under **Always show these formatting marks on the screen**.

When you press Enter, Spacebar, or Tab on your keyboard, characters display to represent these keystrokes. These screen characters do not print, and are referred to as ***formatting marks*** or ***nonprinting characters***.

3 Under **Always show these formatting marks on the screen**, be sure the last check box, **Show all formatting marks**, is selected—select it if necessary. Compare your screen with Figure 1.34.

Figure 1.34

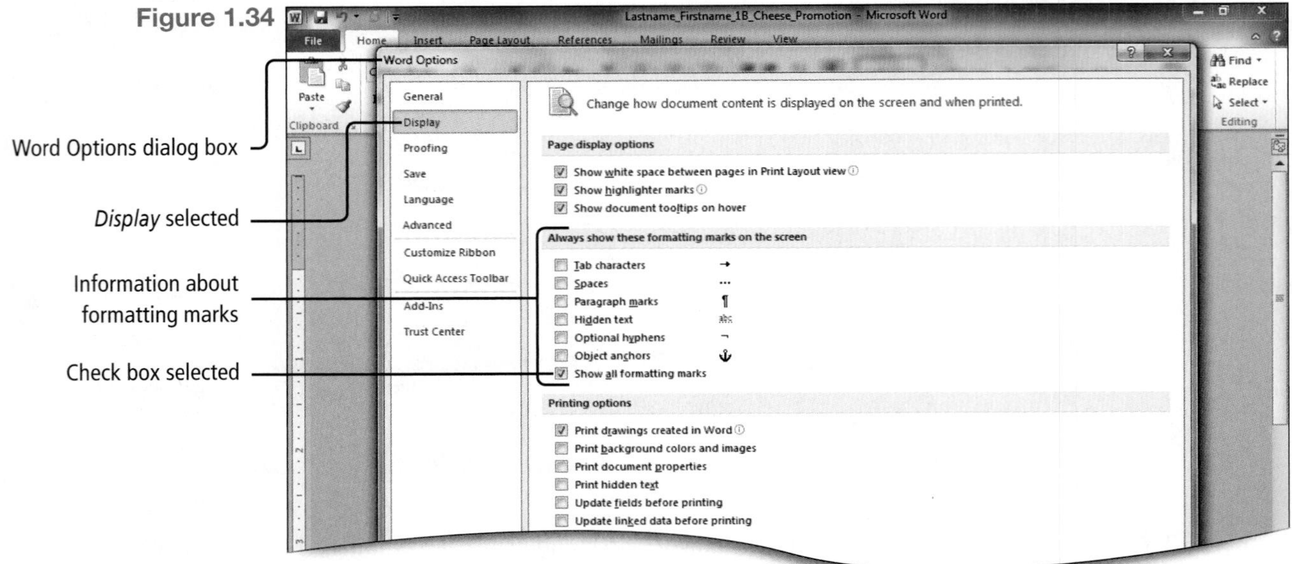

4 In the lower right corner of the dialog box, click **OK**.

Objective 9 | Perform Commands from the Ribbon

The ***Ribbon***, which displays across the top of the program window, groups commands and features in a manner that you would most logically use them. Each Office program's Ribbon is slightly different, but all contain the same three elements: ***tabs***, ***groups***, and ***commands***.

Tabs display across the top of the Ribbon, and each tab relates to a type of activity; for example, laying out a page. Groups are sets of related commands for specific tasks. Commands—instructions to computer programs—are arranged in groups, and might display as a button, a menu, or a box in which you type information.

You can also minimize the Ribbon so only the tab names display. In the minimized Ribbon view, when you click a tab the Ribbon expands to show the groups and commands, and then when you click a command, the Ribbon returns to its minimized view. Most Office users, however, prefer to leave the complete Ribbon in view at all times.

Activity 1.09 | Performing Commands from the Ribbon

1 Take a moment to examine the document on your screen.

This document is a memo from the Executive Chef to the General Manager regarding a new restaurant promotion.

2 On the Ribbon, click the **View tab**. In the **Show group**, if necessary, click to place a check mark in the **Ruler** check box, and then compare your screen with Figure 1.35.

When working in Word, display the rulers so that you can see how margin settings affect your document and how text aligns. Additionally, if you set a tab stop or an indent, its location is visible on the ruler.

Figure 1.35

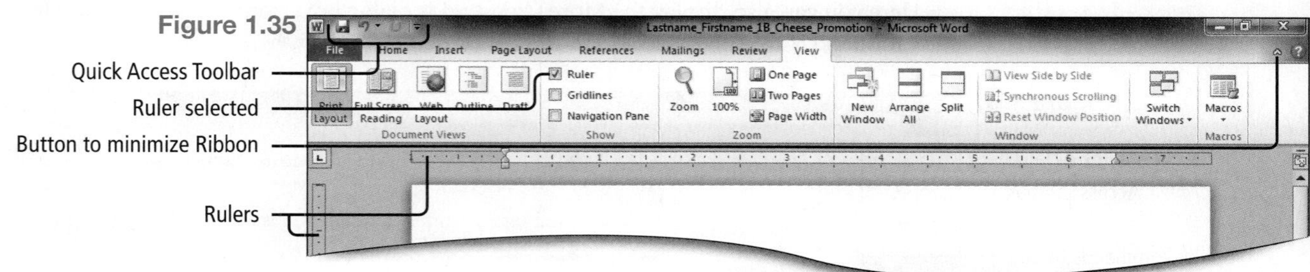

3 On the Ribbon, click the **Home tab**. In the **Paragraph group**, if necessary, click the **Show/Hide** button ¶ so that it glows orange and formatting marks display in your document. Point to the button to display information about the button, and then compare your screen with Figure 1.36.

When the Show/Hide button is active—glowing orange—formatting marks display. Because formatting marks guide your eye in a document—like a map and road signs guide you along a highway—these marks will display throughout this instruction. Many expert Word users keep these marks displayed while creating documents.

Figure 1.36

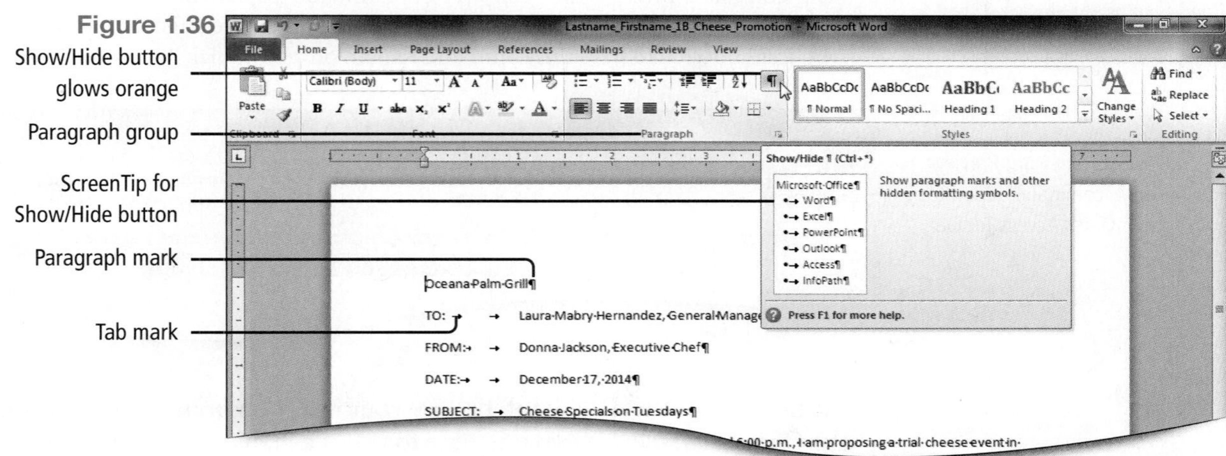

4 In the upper left corner of your screen, above the Ribbon, locate the **Quick Access Toolbar**.

The ***Quick Access Toolbar*** contains commands that you use frequently. By default, only the commands Save, Undo, and Redo display, but you can add and delete commands to suit your needs. Possibly the computer at which you are working already has additional commands added to the Quick Access Toolbar.

5 At the end of the Quick Access Toolbar, click the **Customize Quick Access Toolbar** button ▾.

6 Compare your screen with Figure 1.37.

A list of commands that Office users commonly add to their Quick Access Toolbar displays, including *Open*, *E-mail*, and *Print Preview and Print*. Commands already on the Quick Access Toolbar display a check mark. Commands that you add to the Quick Access Toolbar are always just one click away.

Here you can also display the More Commands dialog box, from which you can select any command from any tab to add to the Quick Access Toolbar.

Figure 1.37

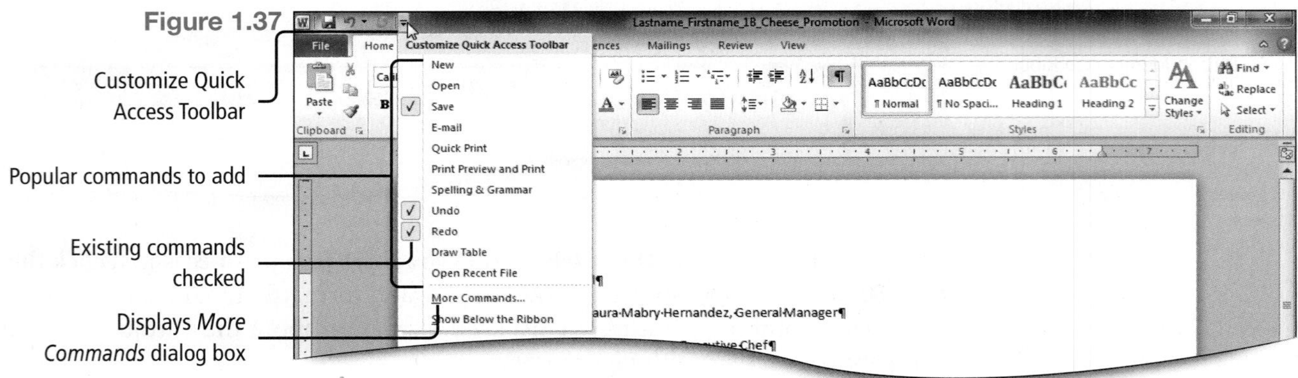

> **Another Way**
>
> Right-click any command on the Ribbon, and then on the shortcut menu, click Add to Quick Access Toolbar.

7 On the displayed list, click **Print Preview and Print**, and then notice that the icon is added to the **Quick Access Toolbar**. Compare your screen with Figure 1.38.

The icon that represents the Print Preview command displays on the Quick Access Toolbar. Because this is a command that you will use frequently while building Office documents, you might decide to have this command remain on your Quick Access Toolbar.

Figure 1.38

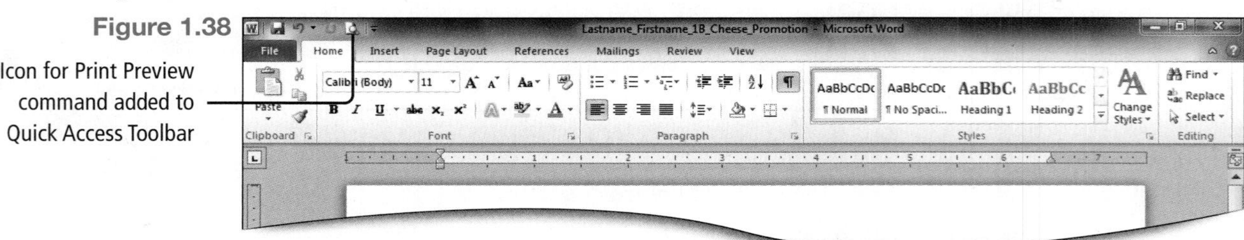

8 In the first line of the document, be sure your insertion point is blinking to the left of the O in *Oceana*. Press Enter one time to insert a blank paragraph, and then click to the left of the new paragraph mark (¶) in the new line.

The ***paragraph symbol*** is a formatting mark that displays each time you press Enter.

9 On the Ribbon, click the **Insert tab**. In the **Illustrations group**, point to the **Clip Art** button to display its ScreenTip.

Many buttons on the Ribbon have this type of ***enhanced ScreenTip***, which displays more descriptive text than a normal ScreenTip.

10 Click the **Clip Art** button.

The Clip Art ***task pane*** displays. A task pane is a window within a Microsoft Office application that enables you to enter options for completing a command.

11 In the **Clip Art** task pane, click in the **Search for** box, delete any existing text, and then type **cheese grapes** Under **Results should be:**, click the arrow at the right, if necessary click to *clear* the check mark for **All media types** so that no check boxes are selected, and then click the check box for **Illustrations**. Compare your screen with Figure 1.39.

Figure 1.39

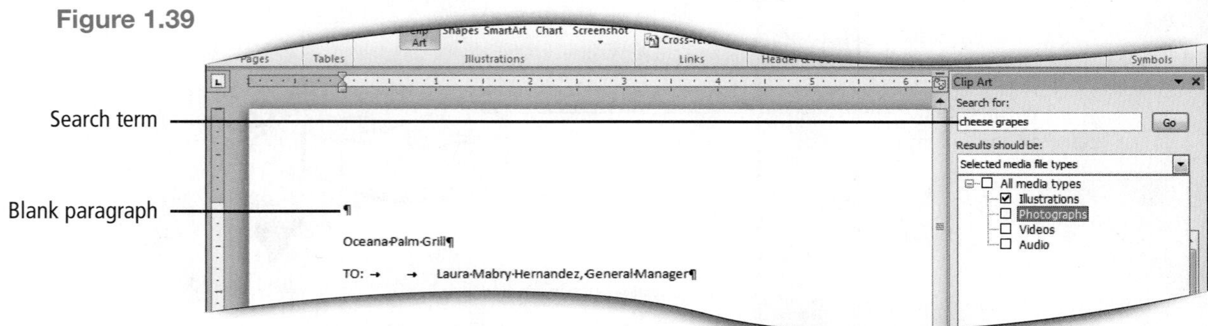

12 Click the **Results should be arrow** again to close the list, and then if necessary, click to place a check mark in the **Include Office.com content** check box.

By selecting this check box, the search for clip art images will include those from Microsoft's online collections of clip art at www.office.com.

13 At the top of the **Clip Art** task pane, click **Go**. Wait a moment for clips to display, and then locate the clip indicated in Figure 1.40.

Figure 1.40

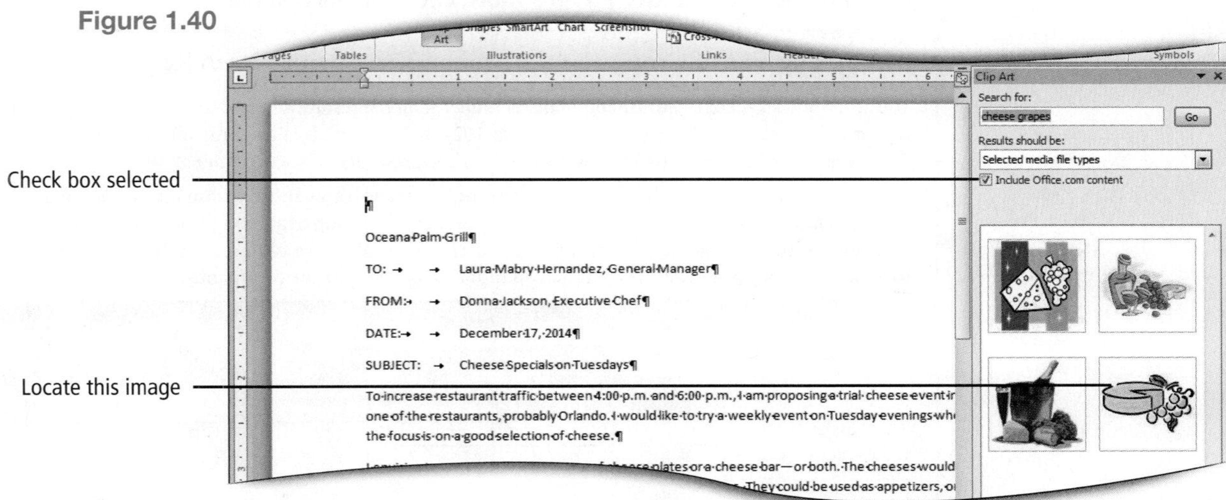

14 Click the image indicated in Figure 1.40 one time to insert it at the insertion point, and then in the upper right corner of the **Clip Art** task pane, click the **Close** [X] button.

> **Alert! | If You Cannot Locate the Image**
>
> If the image shown in Figure 1.40 is unavailable, select a different cheese image that is appropriate.

15 With the image selected—surrounded by a border—on the Ribbon, click the **Home tab**, and then in the **Paragraph group**, click the **Center** button [≡]. Click anywhere outside of the bordered picture to ***deselect***—cancel the selection. Compare your screen with Figure 1.41.

Figure 1.41

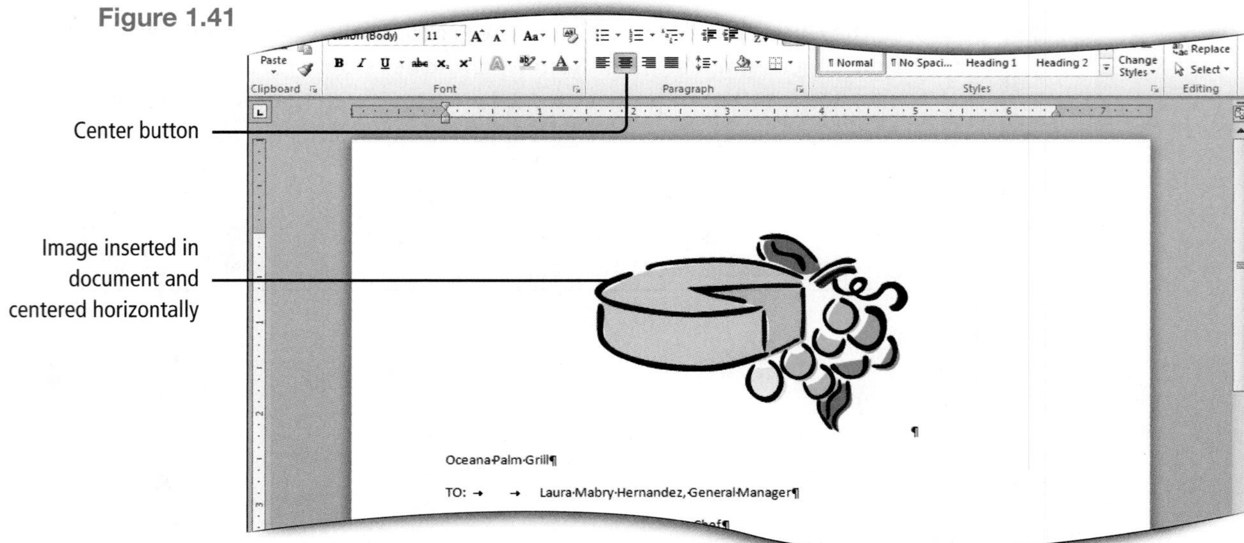

16 Point to the inserted clip art image, and then watch the last tab of the Ribbon as you click the image one time to select it.

The *Picture Tools* display and an additional tab—the *Format* tab—is added to the Ribbon. The Ribbon adapts to your work and will display additional tabs—referred to as ***contextual tabs***—when you need them.

17 On the Ribbon, under **Picture Tools**, click the **Format tab**.

Alert! | The Size of Groups on the Ribbon Varies with Screen Resolution

Your monitor's screen resolution might be set higher than the resolution used to capture the figures in this book. In Figure 1.42 below, the resolution is set to 1024 × 768, which is used for all of the figures in this book. Compare that with Figure 1.43 below, where the screen resolution is set to 1280 × 1024.

At a higher resolution, the Ribbon expands some groups to show more commands than are available with a single click, such as those in the Picture Styles group. Or, the group expands to add descriptive text to some buttons, such as those in the Arrange group. Regardless of your screen resolution, all Office commands are available to you. In higher resolutions, you will have a more robust view of the commands.

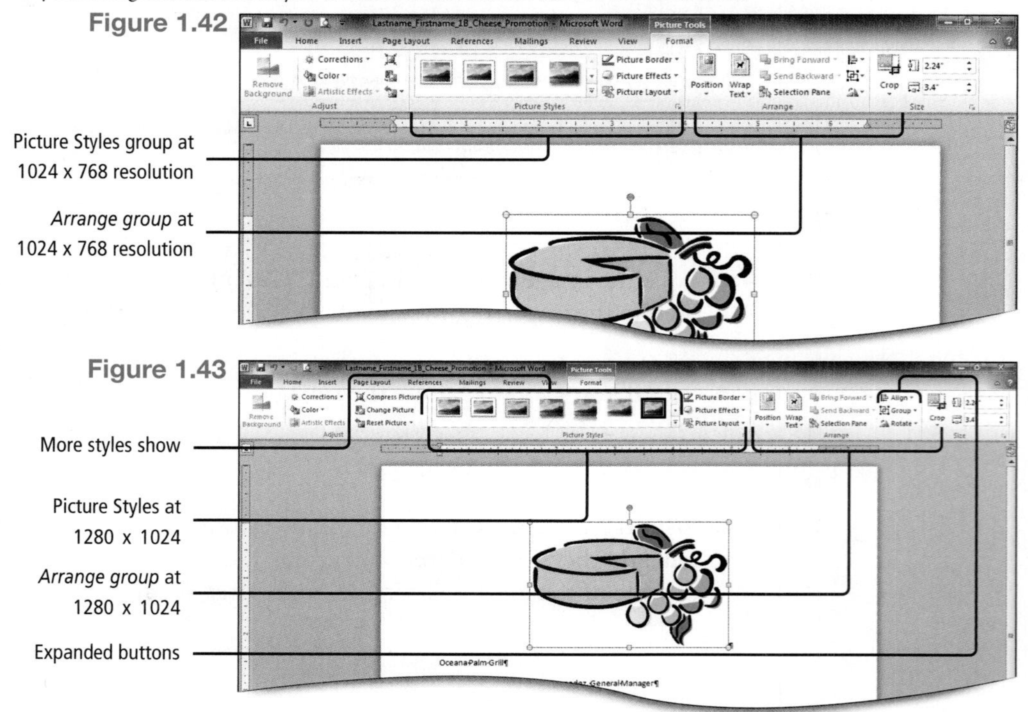

18 In the **Picture Styles group**, point to the first style to display the ScreenTip *Simple Frame, White*, and notice that the image displays with a white frame.

19 Watch the image as you point to the second picture style, and then to the third, and then to the fourth.

This is ***Live Preview***, a technology that shows the result of applying an editing or formatting change as you point to possible results—*before* you actually apply it.

20 In the **Picture Styles group**, click the fourth style—**Drop Shadow Rectangle**—and then click anywhere outside of the image to deselect it. Notice that the Picture Tools no longer display on the Ribbon. Compare your screen with Figure 1.44.

Contextual tabs display only when you need them.

Figure 1.44

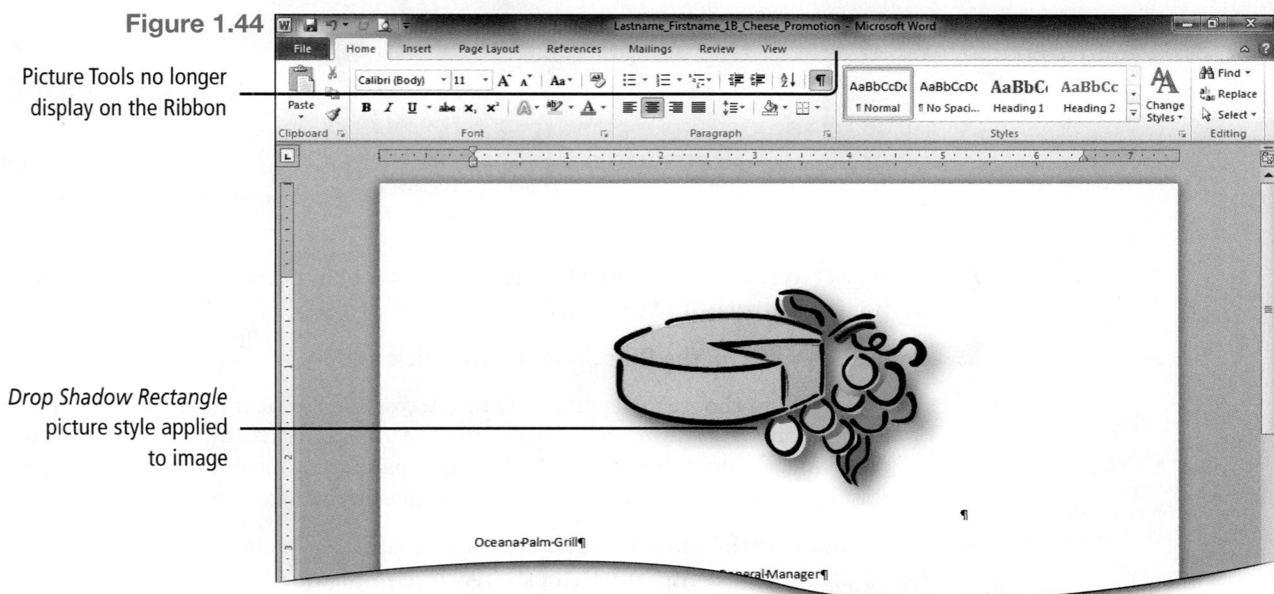

21 In the upper left corner of your screen, on the Quick Access Toolbar, click the **Save** button to save the changes you have made.

Activity 1.10 | Minimizing and Using the Keyboard to Control the Ribbon

Instead of a mouse, some individuals prefer to navigate the Ribbon by using keys on the keyboard. You can activate keyboard control of the Ribbon by pressing the Alt key. You can also minimize the Ribbon to maximize your available screen space.

1 On your keyboard, press the Alt key, and then on the Ribbon, notice that small labels display. Press N to activate the commands on the **Insert tab**, and then compare your screen with Figure 1.45.

Each label represents a ***KeyTip***—an indication of the key that you can press to activate the command. For example, on the Insert tab, you can press F to activate the Clip Art task pane.

Figure 1.45

KeyTips indicate that keyboard control of the Ribbon is active

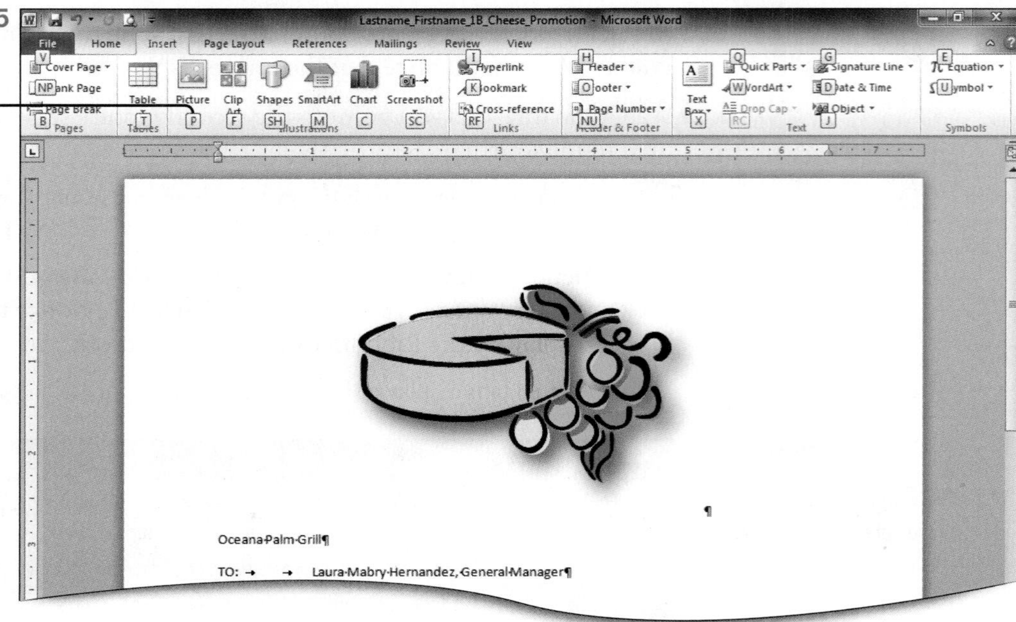

2 Press Esc to redisplay the KeyTips for the tabs. Then, press Alt again to turn off keyboard control of the Ribbon.

3 Point to any tab on the Ribbon and right-click to display a shortcut menu.

Here you can choose to display the Quick Access Toolbar below the Ribbon or minimize the Ribbon to maximize screen space. You can also customize the Ribbon by adding, removing, renaming, or reordering tabs, groups, and commands on the Ribbon, although this is not recommended until you become an expert Office user.

> **Another Way**
> Double-click the active tab; or, click the Minimize the Ribbon button at the right end of the Ribbon.

4 Click **Minimize the Ribbon**. Notice that only the Ribbon tabs display. Click the **Home tab** to display the commands. Click anywhere in the document, and notice that the Ribbon reverts to its minimized view.

> **Another Way**
> Double-click any tab to redisplay the full Ribbon.

5 Right-click any Ribbon tab, and then click **Minimize the Ribbon** again to turn the minimize feature off.

Most expert Office users prefer to have the full Ribbon display at all times.

6 Point to any tab on the Ribbon, and then on your mouse device, roll the mouse wheel. Notice that different tabs become active as your roll the mouse wheel.

You can make a tab active by using this technique, instead of clicking the tab.

Objective 10 | Apply Formatting in Office Programs

Formatting is the process of establishing the overall appearance of text, graphics, and pages in an Office file—for example, in a Word document.

Activity 1.11 | Formatting and Viewing Pages

In this activity, you will practice common formatting techniques used in Office applications.

1 On the Ribbon, click the **Insert tab**, and then in the **Header & Footer group**, click the **Footer** button.

> **Another Way**
>
> On the Design tab, in the Insert group, click Quick Parts, click Field, and then under Field names, click FileName.

2 At the top of the displayed gallery, under **Built-In**, click **Blank**. At the bottom of your document, with *Type text* highlighted in blue, using your own name type the file name of this document **Lastname_Firstname_1B_Cheese_Promotion** and then compare your screen with Figure 1.46.

Header & Footer Tools are added to the Ribbon. A ***footer*** is a reserved area for text or graphics that displays at the bottom of each page in a document. Likewise, a ***header*** is a reserved area for text or graphics that displays at the top of each page in a document. When the footer (or header) area is active, the document area is inactive (dimmed).

Figure 1.46

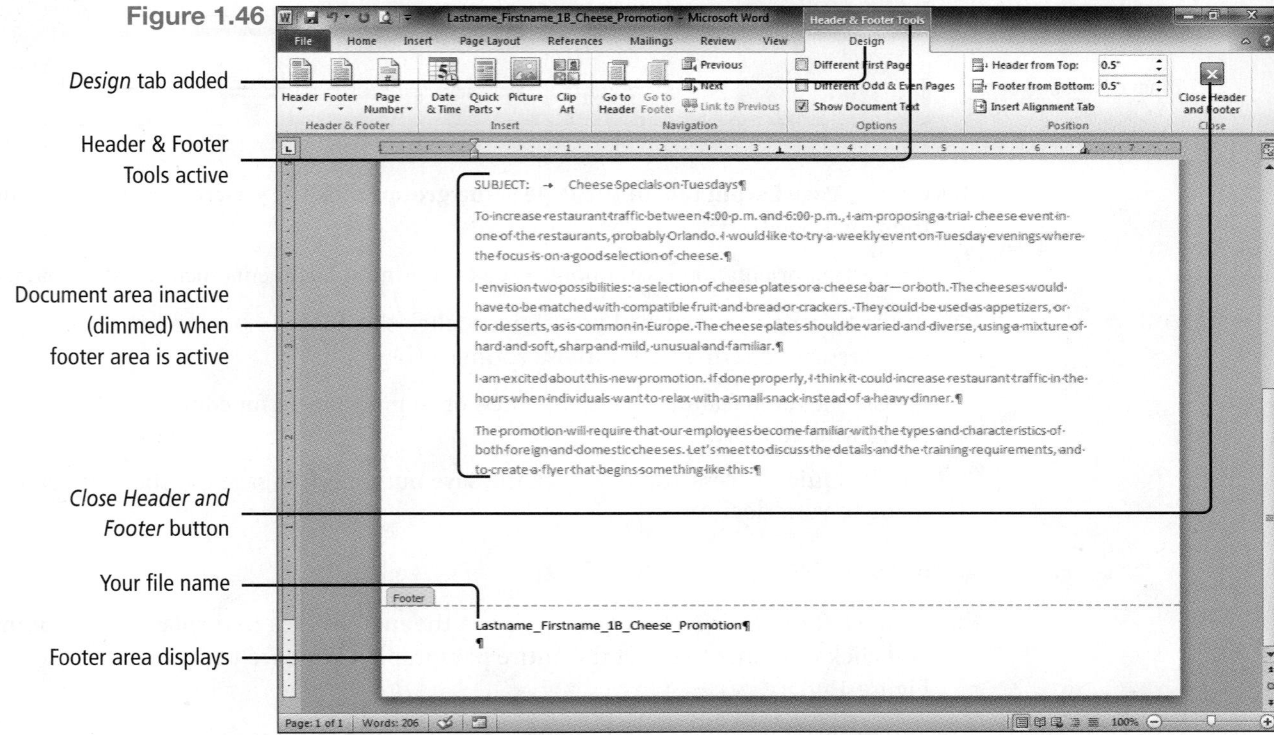

3 On the Ribbon, on the **Design tab**, in the **Close group**, click the **Close Header and Footer** button.

4 On the Ribbon, click the **Page Layout tab**. In the **Page Setup group**, click the **Orientation** button, and notice that two orientations display—*Portrait* and *Landscape*. Click **Landscape**.

In ***portrait orientation***, the paper is taller than it is wide. In ***landscape orientation***, the paper is wider than it is tall.

5 In the lower right corner of the screen, locate the **Zoom control** buttons [zoom control].

To ***zoom*** means to increase or decrease the viewing area. You can zoom in to look closely at a section of a document, and then zoom out to see an entire page on the screen. You can also zoom to view multiple pages on the screen.

6 Drag the **Zoom slider** [zoom slider] to the left until you have zoomed to approximately *60%*. Compare your screen with Figure 1.47.

Figure 1.47

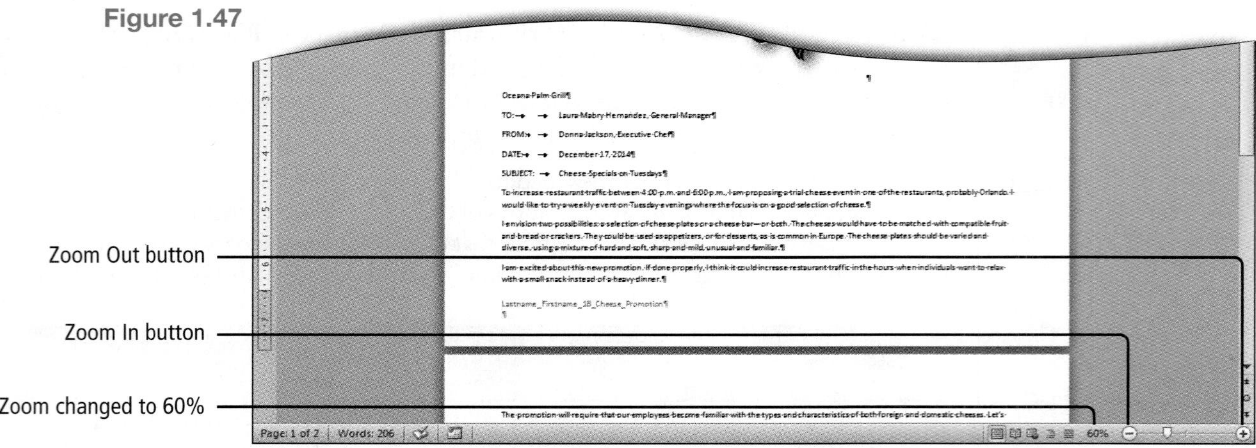

7 On the **Page Layout tab**, in the **Page Setup group**, click the **Orientation** button, and then click **Portrait.**

Portrait orientation is commonly used for business documents such as letters and memos.

8 In the lower right corner of your screen, click the **Zoom In** button as many times as necessary to return to the **100%** zoom setting.

Use the zoom feature to adjust the view of your document for editing and for your viewing comfort.

9 On the Quick Access Toolbar, click the **Save** button to save the changes you have made to your document.

Activity 1.12 | Formatting Text

1 To the left of *Oceana Palm Grill*, point in the margin area to display the pointer and click one time to select the entire paragraph. Compare your screen with Figure 1.48.

Use this technique to select complete paragraphs from the margin area. Additionally, with this technique you can drag downward to select multiple-line paragraphs—which is faster and more efficient than dragging through text.

Figure 1.48

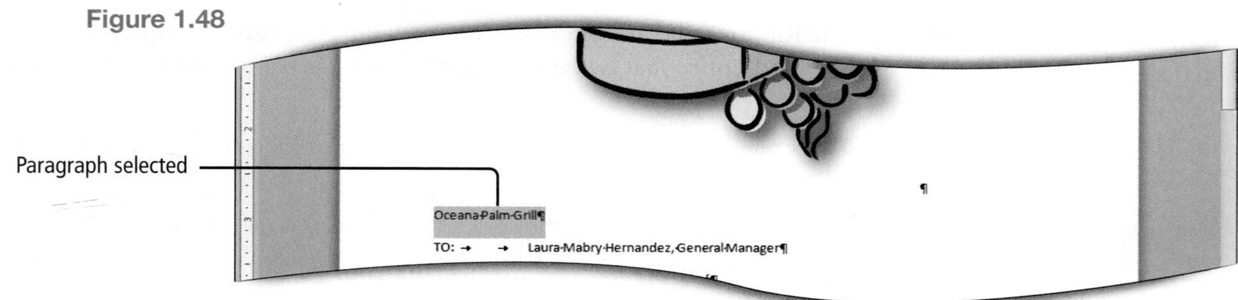

2 On the Ribbon, click the **Home tab**, and then in the **Paragraph group**, click the **Center** button to center the paragraph.

Alignment refers to the placement of paragraph text relative to the left and right margins. ***Center alignment*** refers to text that is centered horizontally between the left and right margins. You can also align text at the left margin, which is the default alignment for text in Word, or at the right margin.

3 On the **Home tab**, in the **Font group**, click the **Font button arrow** [Calibri (Body)]. At the top of the list, point to **Cambria**, and as you do so, notice that the selected text previews in the Cambria font.

A ***font*** is a set of characters with the same design and shape. The default font in a Word document is Calibri, which is a ***sans serif*** font—a font design with no lines or extensions on the ends of characters.

The Cambria font is a ***serif*** font—a font design that includes small line extensions on the ends of the letters to guide the eye in reading from left to right.

The list of fonts displays as a gallery showing potential results. For example, in the Font gallery, you can see the actual design and format of each font as it would look if applied to text.

4 Point to several other fonts and observe the effect on the selected text. Then, at the top of the **Font** gallery, under **Theme Fonts**, click **Cambria**.

A ***theme*** is a predesigned set of colors, fonts, lines, and fill effects that look good together and that can be applied to your entire document or to specific items.

A theme combines two sets of fonts—one for text and one for headings. In the default Office theme, Cambria is the suggested font for headings.

5 With the paragraph *Oceana Palm Grill* still selected, on the **Home tab**, in the **Font group**, click the **Font Size button arrow** [11], point to **36**, and then notice how Live Preview displays the text in the font size to which you are pointing. Compare your screen with Figure 1.49.

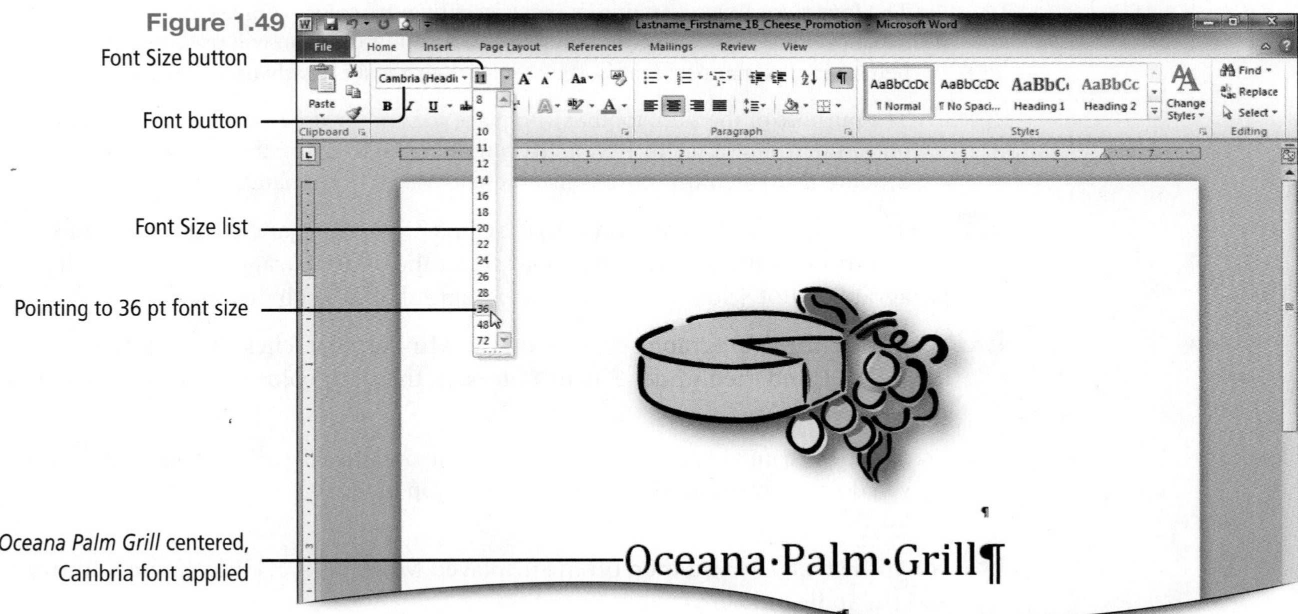

Figure 1.49

6 On the displayed list of font sizes, click **20**.

Fonts are measured in ***points***, with one point equal to 1/72 of an inch. A higher point size indicates a larger font size. Headings and titles are often formatted by using a larger font size. The word *point* is abbreviated as ***pt***.

7 With *Oceana Palm Grill* still selected, on the **Home tab**, in the **Font group**, click the **Font Color button arrow** [A]. Under **Theme Colors**, in the seventh column, click the last color—**Olive Green, Accent 3, Darker 50%**. Click anywhere to deselect the text.

8 To the left of *TO:*, point in the left margin area to display the [pointer] pointer, hold down the left mouse button, and then drag down to select the four memo headings. Compare your screen with Figure 1.50.

Use this technique to select complete paragraphs from the margin area—dragging downward to select multiple-line paragraphs—which is faster and more efficient than dragging through text.

Figure 1.50

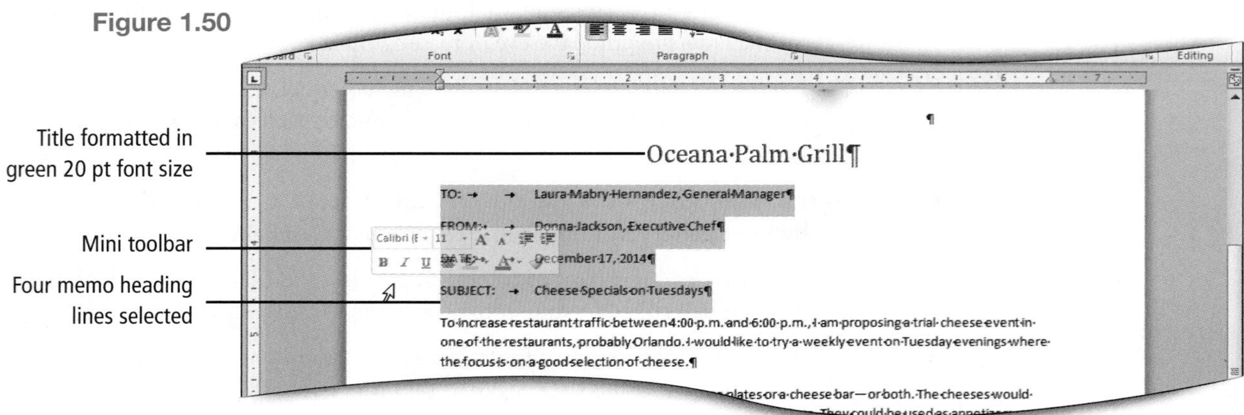

9 With the four paragraphs selected, on the Mini toolbar, click the **Font Color** button [A], which now displays a dark green bar instead of a red bar.

The font color button retains its most recently used color—Olive Green, Accent 3, Darker 50%. As you progress in your study of Microsoft Office, you will use other buttons that behave in this manner; that is, they retain their most recently used format.

The purpose of the Mini toolbar is to place commonly used commands close to text or objects that you select. By selecting a command on the Mini toolbar, you reduce the distance that you must move your mouse to access a command.

10 Click anywhere in the paragraph that begins *To increase*, and then ***triple-click***—click the left mouse button three times—to select the entire paragraph. If the entire paragraph is not selected, click in the paragraph and begin again.

11 With the entire paragraph selected, on the Mini toolbar, click the **Font Color button arrow** [A], and then under **Theme Colors**, in the sixth column, click the first color—**Red, Accent 2**.

It is convenient to have commonly used commands display on the Mini toolbar so that you do not have to move your mouse to the top of the screen to access the command from the Ribbon.

12 Select the text *TO:* and then on the displayed Mini toolbar, click the **Bold** button [B] and the **Italic** button [I].

Font styles include bold, italic, and underline. Font styles emphasize text and are a visual cue to draw the reader's eye to important text.

13 On the displayed Mini toolbar, click the **Italic** button [I] again to turn off the Italic formatting. Notice that the Italic button no longer glows orange.

A button that behaves in this manner is referred to as a ***toggle button***, which means it can be turned on by clicking it once, and then turned off by clicking it again.

14 With *TO:* still selected, on the Mini toolbar, click the **Format Painter** button. Then, move your mouse under the word *Laura*, and notice the mouse pointer. Compare your screen with Figure 1.51.

You can use the ***Format Painter*** to copy the formatting of specific text or of a paragraph and then apply it in other locations in your document.

The pointer takes the shape of a paintbrush, and contains the formatting information from the paragraph where the insertion point is positioned. Information about the Format Painter and how to turn it off displays in the status bar.

Figure 1.51

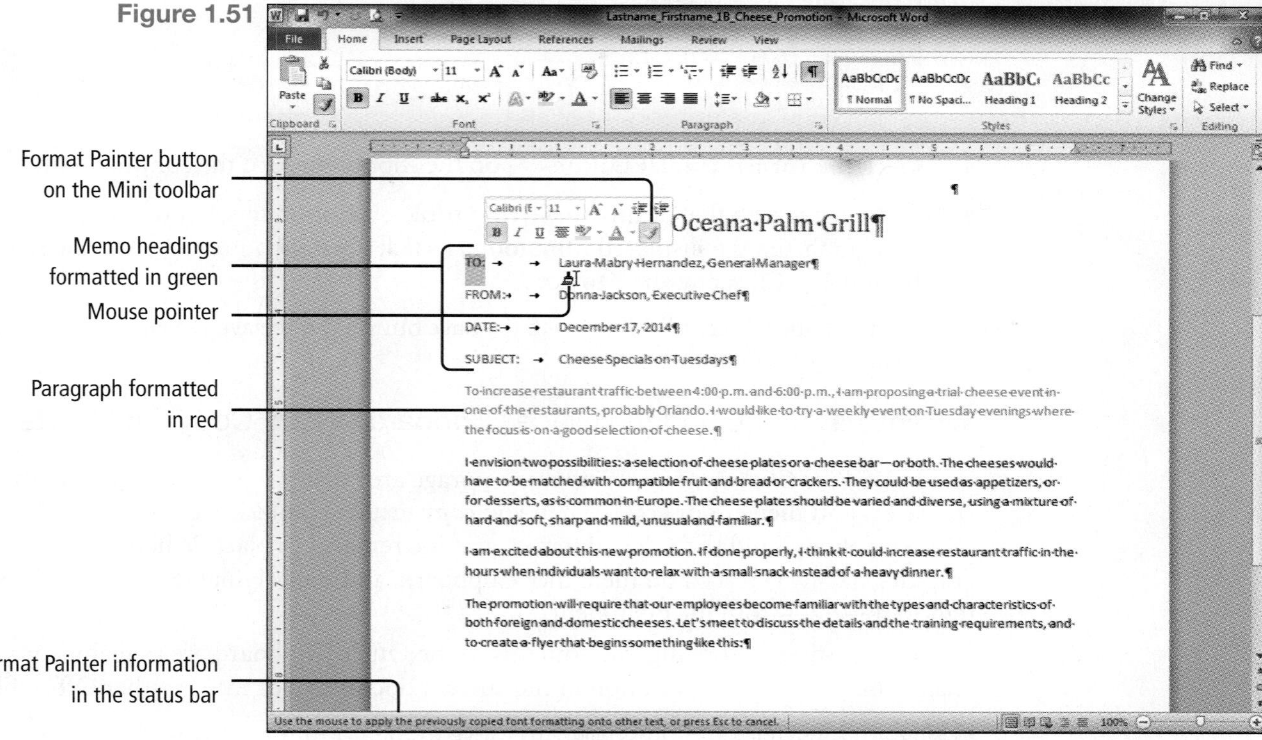

15 With the pointer, drag to select the text *FROM:* and notice that the Bold formatting is applied. Then, point to the selected text *FROM:* and on the Mini toolbar, *double-click* the **Format Painter** button.

16 Select the text *DATE:* to copy the Bold formatting, and notice that the pointer retains the shape.

When you *double-click* the Format Painter button, the Format Painter feature remains active until you either click the Format Painter button again, or press Esc to cancel it—as indicated on the status bar.

17 With Format Painter still active, select the text *SUBJECT:*, and then on the Ribbon, on the **Home tab**, in the **Clipboard group**, notice that the **Format Painter** button is glowing orange, indicating that it is active. Compare your screen with Figure 1.52.

Figure 1.52

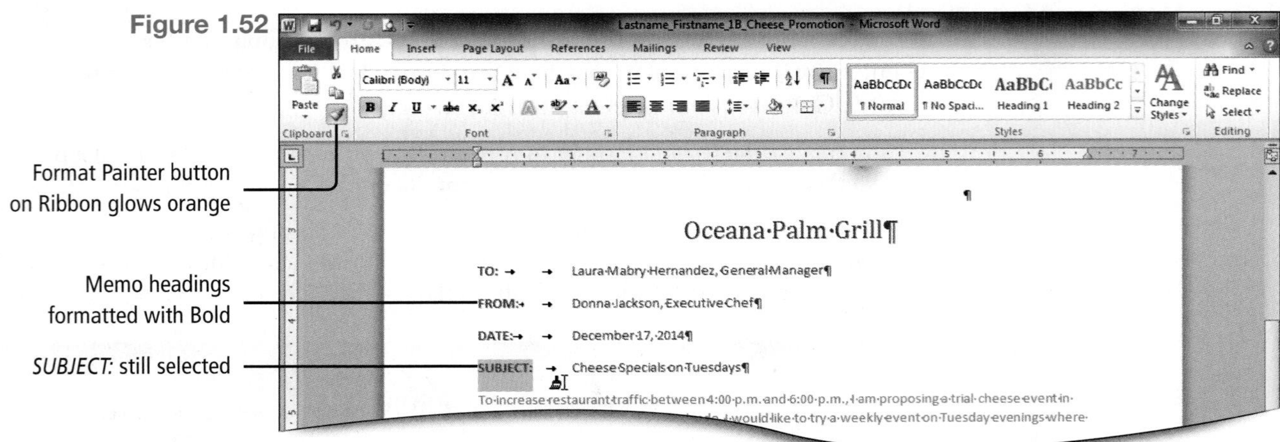

18 Click the **Format Painter** button on the Ribbon to turn the command off.

19 In the paragraph that begins *To increase*, triple-click again to select the entire paragraph. On the displayed Mini toolbar, click the **Bold** button [B] and the **Italic** button [I]. Click anywhere to deselect.

20 On the Quick Access Toolbar, click the **Save** button to save the changes you have made to your document.

Activity 1.13 | Using the Office Clipboard to Cut, Copy, and Paste

The ***Office Clipboard*** is a temporary storage area that holds text or graphics that you select and then cut or copy. When you ***copy*** text or graphics, a copy is placed on the Office Clipboard and the original text or graphic remains in place. When you ***cut*** text or graphics, a copy is placed on the Office Clipboard, and the original text or graphic is removed—cut—from the document.

After cutting or copying, the contents of the Office Clipboard are available for you to ***paste***—insert—in a new location in the current document, or into another Office file.

1 Hold down Ctrl and press Home to move to the beginning of your document, and then take a moment to study the table in Figure 1.53, which describes similar keyboard shortcuts with which you can navigate quickly in a document.

To Move	Press
To the beginning of a document	Ctrl + Home
To the end of a document	Ctrl + End
To the beginning of a line	Home
To the end of a line	End
To the beginning of the previous word	Ctrl + ←
To the beginning of the next word	Ctrl + →
To the beginning of the current word (if insertion point is in the middle of a word)	Ctrl + ←
To the beginning of a paragraph	Ctrl + ↑
To the beginning of the next paragraph	Ctrl + ↓
To the beginning of the current paragraph (if insertion point is in the middle of a paragraph)	Ctrl + ↑
Up one screen	PgUp
Down one screen	PageDown

Figure 1.53

> **Another Way**
>
> Right-click the selection, and then click Copy on the shortcut menu; or, use the keyboard shortcut Ctrl + C.

2 To the left of *Oceana Palm Grill*, point in the left margin area to display the [pointer] pointer, and then click one time to select the entire paragraph. On the **Home tab**, in the **Clipboard group**, click the **Copy** button [Copy].

Because anything that you select and then copy—or cut—is placed on the Office Clipboard, the Copy command and the Cut command display in the Clipboard group of commands on the Ribbon.

There is no visible indication that your copied selection has been placed on the Office Clipboard.

3 On the **Home tab**, in the **Clipboard group**, to the right of the group name *Clipboard*, click the **Dialog Box Launcher** button [Dialog Box Launcher], and then compare your screen with Figure 1.54.

The Clipboard task pane displays with your copied text. In any Ribbon group, the ***Dialog Box Launcher*** displays either a dialog box or a task pane related to the group of commands.

It is not necessary to display the Office Clipboard in this manner, although sometimes it is useful to do so. The Office Clipboard can hold 24 items.

Figure 1.54

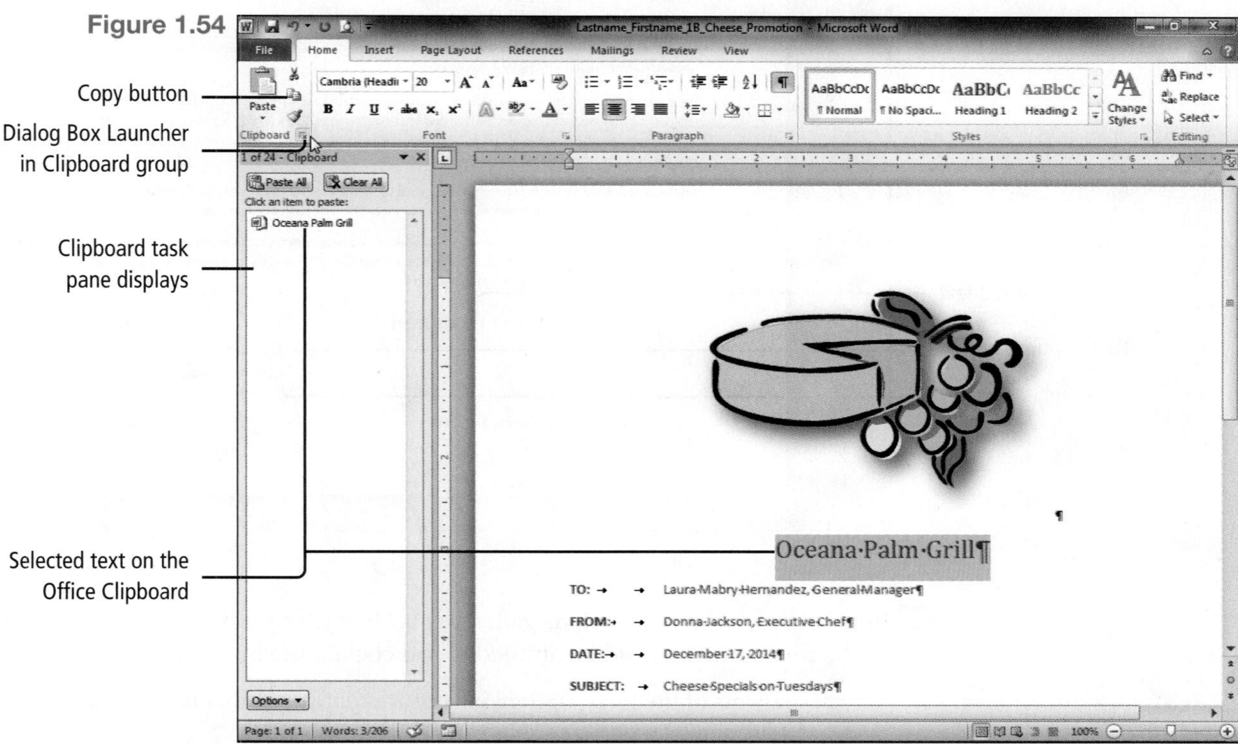

4 In the upper right corner of the **Clipboard** task pane, click the **Close** button [Close].

> **Another Way**
>
> Right-click, on the shortcut menu under Paste Options, click the desired option button.

5 Press Ctrl + End to move to the end of your document. Press Enter one time to create a new blank paragraph. On the **Home tab**, in the **Clipboard group**, point to the **Paste** button, and then click the *upper* portion of this split button.

The Paste command pastes the most recently copied item on the Office Clipboard at the insertion point location. If you click the lower portion of the Paste button, a gallery of Paste Options displays.

6 Click the **Paste Options** button that displays below the pasted text as shown in Figure 1.55.

Here you can view and apply various formatting options for pasting your copied or cut text. Typically you will click Paste on the Ribbon and paste the item in its original format. If you want some other format for the pasted item, you can do so from the ***Paste Options gallery***.

The Paste Options gallery provides a Live Preview of the various options for changing the format of the pasted item with a single click. The Paste Options gallery is available in three places: on the Ribbon by clicking the lower portion of the Paste button—the Paste button arrow; from the Paste Options button that displays below the pasted item following the paste operation; or, on the shortcut menu if you right-click the pasted item.

Figure 1.55

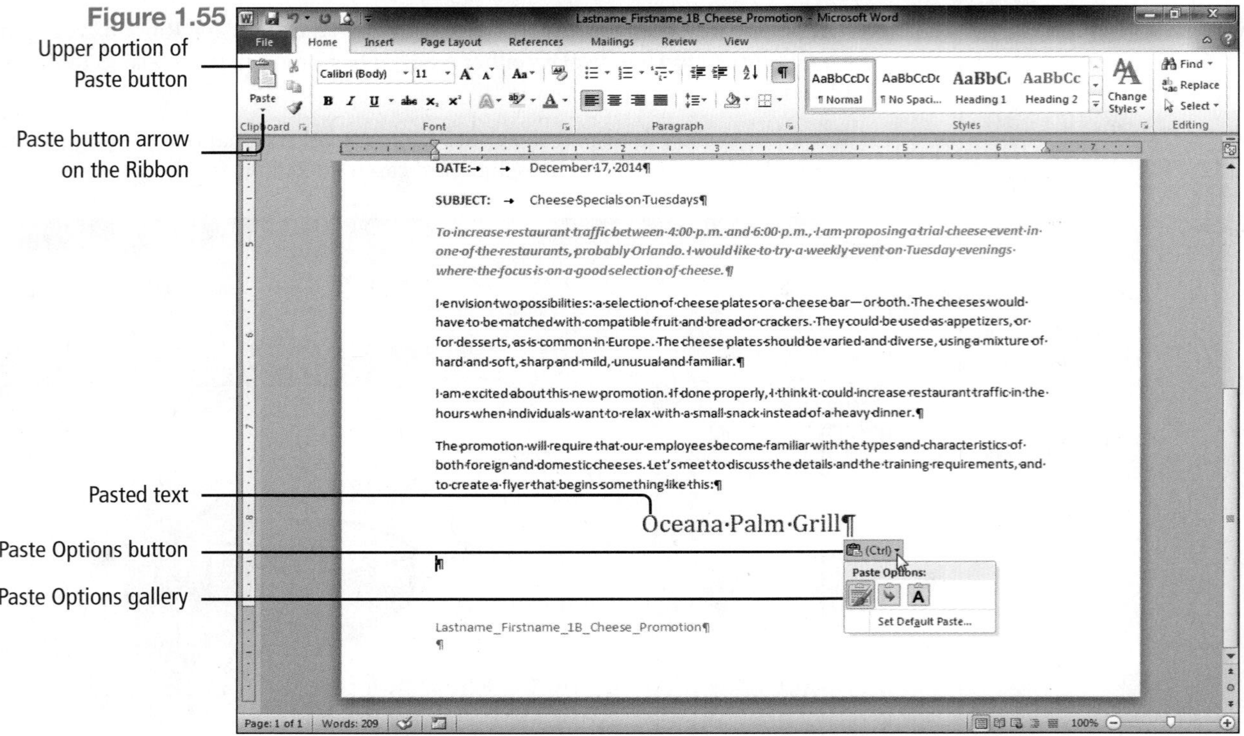

7 In the displayed **Paste Options** gallery, *point* to each option to see the Live Preview of the format that would be applied if you clicked the button.

The contents of the Paste Options gallery are contextual; that is, they change based on what you copied and where you are pasting.

8 Press Esc to close the gallery; the button will remain displayed until you take some other screen action.

Another Way

On the Home tab, in the Clipboard group, click the Cut button; or, use the keyboard shortcut Ctrl + X.

9 Press Ctrl + Home to move to the top of the document, and then click the **cheese image** one time to select it. While pointing to the selected image, right-click, and then on the shortcut menu, click **Cut**.

Recall that the Cut command cuts—removes—the selection from the document and places it on the Office Clipboard.

10 Press Del one time to remove the blank paragraph from the top of the document, and then press Ctrl + End to move to the end of the document.

11 With the insertion point blinking in the blank paragraph at the end of the document, right-click, and notice that the **Paste Options** gallery displays on the shortcut menu. Compare your screen with Figure 1.56.

Figure 1.56

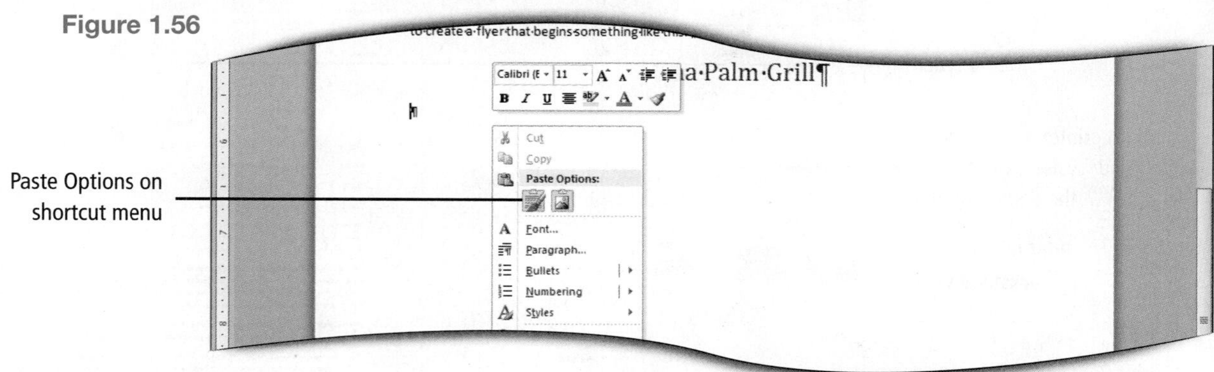

12 On the shortcut menu, under **Paste Options**, click the first button—**Keep Source Formatting**.

13 Click the picture to select it. On the **Home tab**, in the **Paragraph group**, click the **Center** button.

14 Above the cheese picture, click to position the insertion point at the end of the word *Grill*, press Spacebar one time, and then type **Tuesday Cheese Tastings** Compare your screen with Figure 1.57.

Figure 1.57

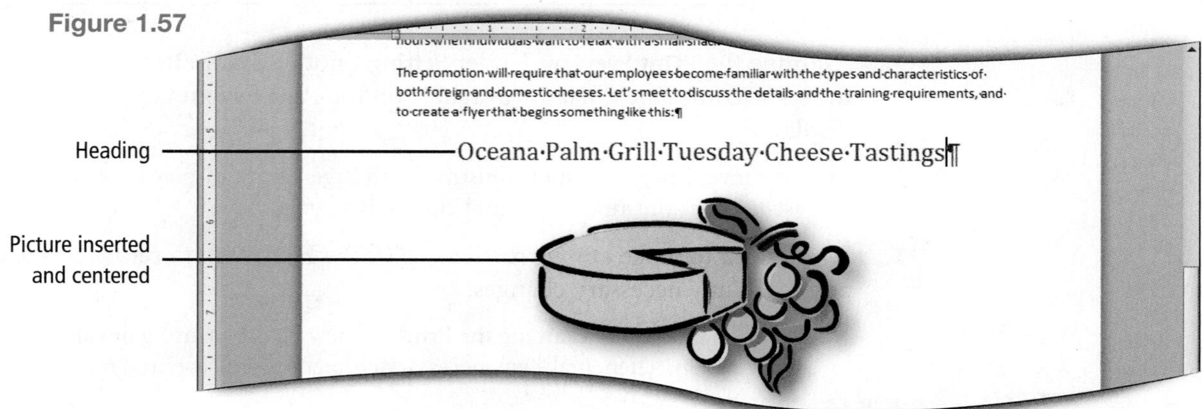

Activity 1.14 | Viewing Print Preview and Printing a Word Document

1 Press Ctrl + Home to move to the top of your document. Select the text *Oceana Palm Grill*, and then replace the selected text by typing **Memo**

2 Display **Backstage** view, on the right, click **Properties**, and then click **Show Document Panel**. Replace the existing author name with your first and last name. In the **Subject** box, type your course name and section number, and then in the **Keywords** box, type **cheese promotion** and then **Close** the **Document Information Panel**.

Another Way

Press Ctrl + F2 to display Print Preview.

3 On the Quick Access Toolbar, click **Save** to save the changes you have made to your document.

4 On the Quick Access Toolbar, click the **Print Preview** button that you added. Compare your screen with Figure 1.58.

Figure 1.58

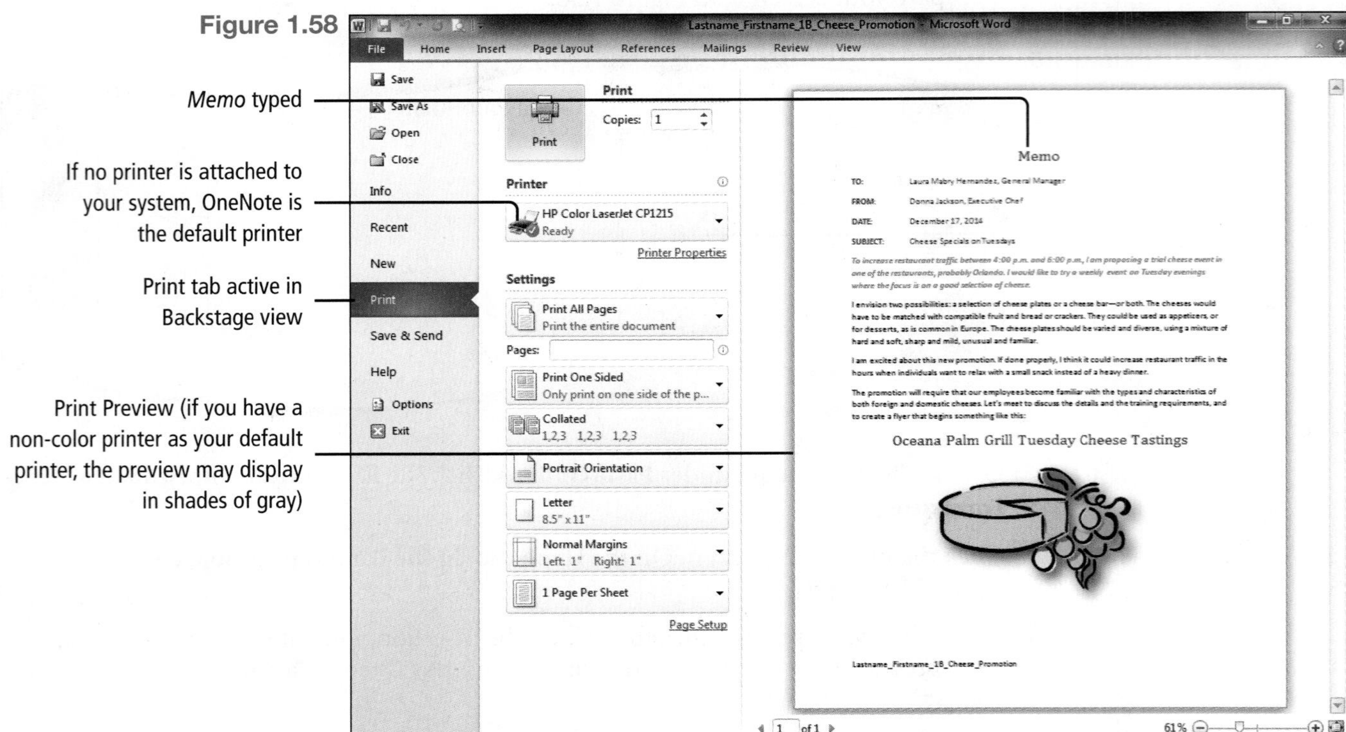

5 Examine the **Print Preview**. Under **Settings**, notice that in **Backstage** view, several of the same commands that are available on the Page Layout tab of the Ribbon also display.

For convenience, common adjustments to Page Layout display here, so that you can make last-minute adjustments without closing Backstage view.

6 If you need to make any corrections, click the Home tab to return to the document and make any necessary changes.

It is good practice to examine the Print Preview before printing or submitting your work electronically. Then, make any necessary corrections, re-save, and redisplay Print Preview.

7 If you are directed to do so, click Print to print the document; or, above the Info tab, click Close, and then submit your file electronically according to the directions provided by your instructor.

If you click the Print button, Backstage view closes and the Word window redisplays.

8 On the Quick Access Toolbar, point to the **Print Preview icon** you placed there, right-click, and then click **Remove from Quick Access Toolbar**.

If you are working on your own computer and you want to do so, you can leave the icon on the toolbar; in a lab setting, you should return the software to its original settings.

9 At the right end of the title bar, click the program **Close** button [X].

10 If a message displays asking if you want the text on the Clipboard to be available after you quit Word, click **No**.

This message most often displays if you have copied some type of image to the Clipboard. If you click Yes, the items on the Clipboard will remain for you to use.

Objective 11 | Use the Microsoft Office 2010 Help System

Within each Office program, the Help feature provides information about all of the program's features and displays step-by-step instructions for performing many tasks.

Activity 1.15 | Using the Microsoft Office 2010 Help System in Excel

In this activity, you will use the Microsoft Help feature to find information about formatting numbers in Excel.

> **Another Way**
> Press F1 to display Help.

1 **Start** the **Microsoft Excel 2010** program. In the upper right corner of your screen, click the **Microsoft Excel Help** button [?].

2 In the **Excel Help** window, click in the white box in upper left corner, type **formatting numbers** and then click **Search** or press Enter.

3 On the list of results, click **Display numbers as currency**. Compare your screen with Figure 1.59.

Figure 1.59

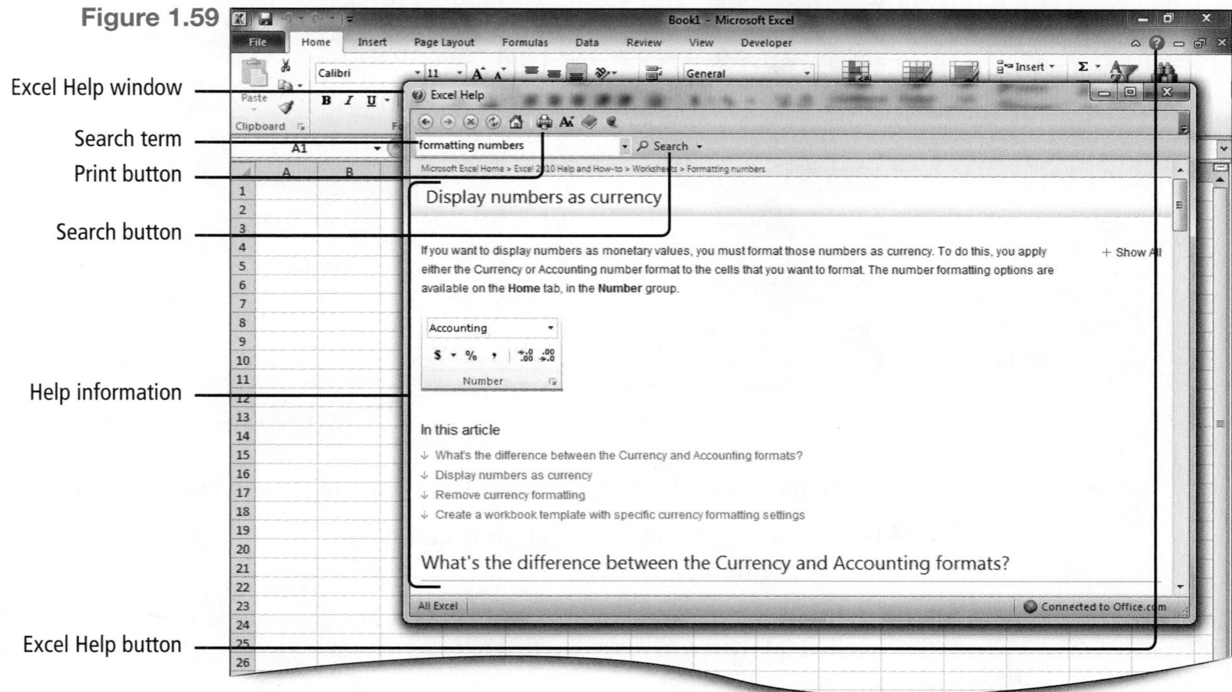

4 If you want to do so, on the toolbar at the top of the **Excel Help** window, click the Print [printer] button to print a copy of this information for your reference.

5 On the title bar of the Excel Help window, click the **Close** button [X]. On the right side of the Microsoft Excel title bar, click the **Close** button [X] to close Excel.

Objective 12 | Compress Files

A ***compressed file*** is a file that has been reduced in size. Compressed files take up less storage space and can be transferred to other computers faster than uncompressed files. You can also combine a group of files into one compressed folder, which makes it easier to share a group of files.

Activity 1.16 | Compressing Files

In this activity, you will combine the two files you created in this chapter into one compressed file.

1 On the Windows taskbar, click the **Start** button, and then on the right, click **Computer**.

2 On the left, in the **navigation pane**, click the location of your two files from this chapter—your USB flash drive or other location—and display the folder window for your **Common Features Chapter 1** folder. Compare your screen with Figure 1.60.

Figure 1.60

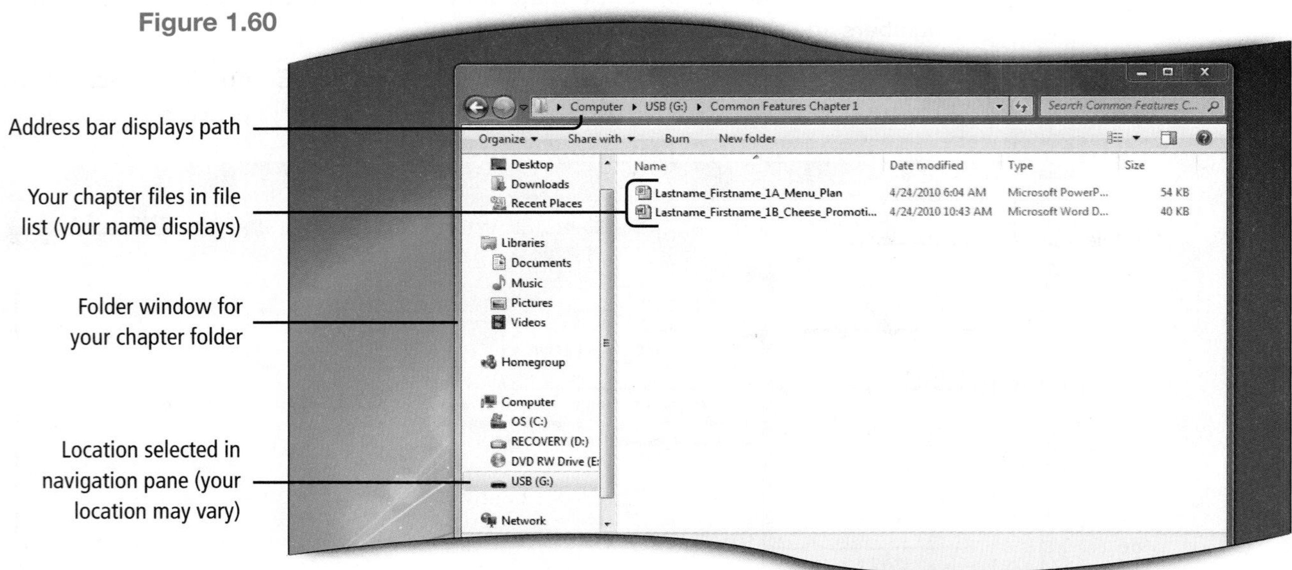

3 In the **file list**, click your **Lastname_Firstname_1A_Menu_Plan** file one time to select it.

4 Hold down Ctrl, and then click your **Lastname_Firstname_1B_Cheese_Promotion** file to select both files. Release Ctrl.

In any Windows-based program, holding down Ctrl while selecting enables you to select multiple items.

5 Point anywhere over the two selected files and right-click. On the shortcut menu, point to **Send to**, and then compare your screen with Figure 1.61.

Figure 1.61

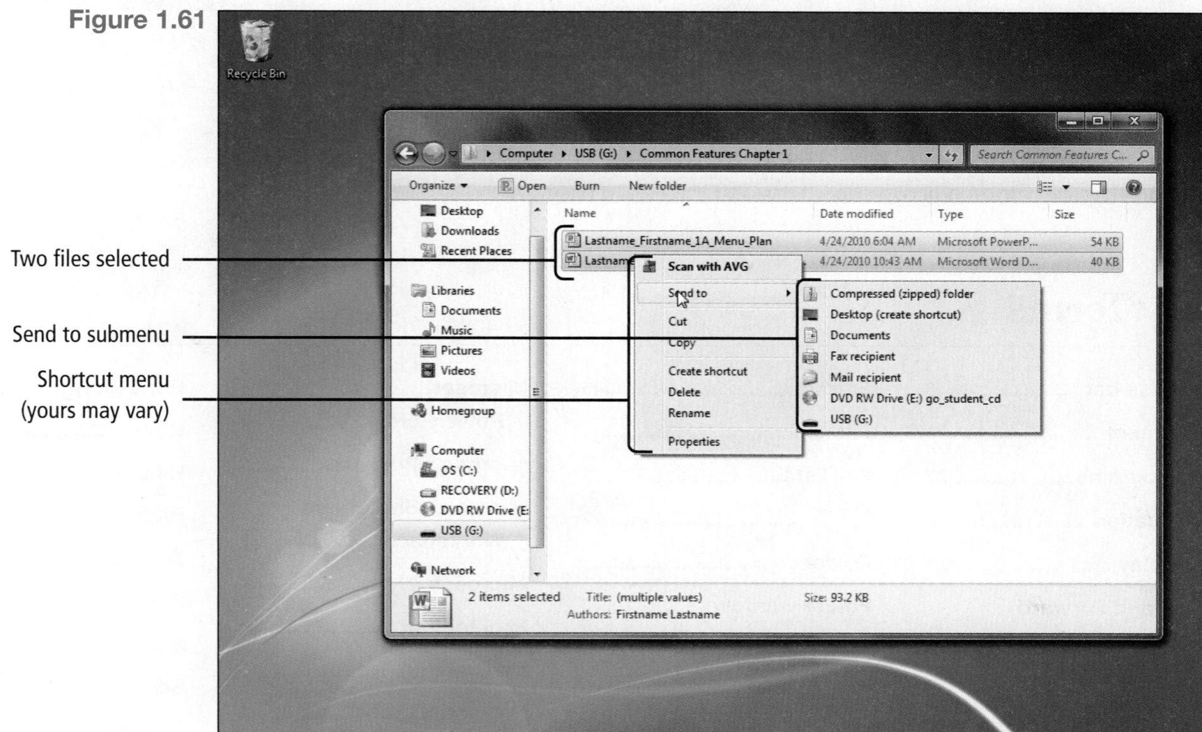

6 On the shortcut submenu, click **Compressed (zipped) folder**.

Windows creates a compressed folder containing a *copy* of each of the selected files. The folder name is the name of the file or folder to which you were pointing, and is selected—highlighted in blue—so that you can rename it.

7 Using your own name, type **Lastname_Firstname_Common_Features_Ch1** and press Enter.

The compressed folder is now ready to attach to an e-mail or share in some other electronic format.

8 **Close** [X] the folder window. If directed to do so by your instructor, submit your compressed folder electronically.

> **More Knowledge | Extracting Compressed Files**
>
> ***Extract*** means to decompress, or pull out, files from a compressed form. When you extract a file, an uncompressed copy is placed in the folder that you specify. The original file remains in the compressed folder.

End You have completed Project 1B

Content-Based Assessments

Summary

In this chapter, you used Windows Explorer to navigate the Windows file structure. You also used features that are common across the Microsoft Office 2010 programs.

Key Terms

Address bar 5
Alignment 34
All Programs 7
Application 6
AutoPlay 3
Back and Forward buttons 5
Backstage tabs 14
Backstage view 14
Center alignment 34
Click 4
Command 5
Common dialog boxes 22
Compressed file 44
Context sensitive command 11
Contextual tabs 30
Copy 38
Cut 38
Default 9
Deselect 29
Desktop 3
Details pane 5
Dialog box 11
Dialog Box Launcher 39
Document properties 14
Double-click 5
Drag 10
Edit 9
Ellipsis 11
Enhanced ScreenTip 28
Extract 45
File 3
File list 5
Fill 12
Folder 3
Folder window 4
Font 35
Font styles 36
Footer 33
Format Painter 37
Formatting 32
Formatting marks 25
Gallery 12
Groups 26
Header 33
Icons 5
Info tab 14
Insertion point 9
Keyboard shortcut 10
KeyTip 31
Landscape orientation 33
Library 4
Live Preview 31
Location 13
Metadata 14
Microsoft Access 7
Microsoft Excel 7
Microsoft InfoPath 7
Microsoft Office 2010 6
Microsoft OneNote 7
Microsoft Outlook 7
Microsoft PowerPoint 7
Microsoft Publisher 7
Microsoft SharePoint Workspace 7
Microsoft Word 7
Mini toolbar 10
Navigate 3
Navigation pane 5
Nonprinting characters 25
Office Clipboard 38
Open dialog box 22
Option button 12
Options dialog box 25
Paragraph symbol 28
Paste 38
Paste Options 40
PDF (Portable Document Format) file 20
Point 4
Pointer 9
Points 35
Portrait orientation 33
Preview pane button 5
Print Preview 18
Program 6
Program-level control buttons 8
Protected View 24
Pt 35
Quick Access Toolbar 27
Quick Commands 14
Read-Only 23
Ribbon 26
Ribbon tabs 8
Right-click 11
Sans serif 35
ScreenTip 12
Scroll bar 16
Scroll box 16
Search box 5
Select 10
Serif 35
Shortcut menu 11
Split button 5
Start button 4
Start menu 4
Status bar 8
Subfolder 3
Tabs 26
Tags 5
Task pane 28
Theme 35
Title bar 8
Toggle button 36
Triple-click 36
Trusted Documents 24
USB flash drive 6
Views button 5
Window 3
Windows Explorer 3
Windows taskbar 4
Zoom 18

Content-Based Assessments

Matching

Match each term in the second column with its correct definition in the first column by writing the letter of the term on the blank line in front of the correct definition.

_____ 1. A collection of information stored on a computer under a single name.
_____ 2. A container in which you store files.
_____ 3. A folder within a folder.
_____ 4. The program that displays the files and folders on your computer.
_____ 5. The Windows menu that is the main gateway to your computer.
_____ 6. In Windows 7, a window that displays the contents of the current folder, library, or device, and contains helpful parts so that you can navigate.
_____ 7. In Windows, a collection of items, such as files and folders, assembled from various locations that might be on your computer.
_____ 8. The bar at the top of a folder window with which you can navigate to a different folder or library, or go back to a previous one.
_____ 9. An instruction to a computer program that carries out an action.
_____ 10. Small pictures that represent a program, a file, a folder, or an object.
_____ 11. A set of instructions that a computer uses to perform a specific task.
_____ 12. A spreadsheet program used to calculate numbers and create charts.
_____ 13. The user interface that groups commands on tabs at the top of the program window.
_____ 14. A bar at the top of the program window displaying the current file and program name.
_____ 15. One or more keys pressed to perform a task that would otherwise require a mouse.

A Address bar
B Command
C File
D Folder
E Folder window
F Icons
G Keyboard shortcut
H Library
I Microsoft Excel
J Program
K Ribbon
L Start menu
M Subfolder
N Title bar
O Windows Explorer

Multiple Choice

Circle the correct answer.

1. A small toolbar with frequently used commands that displays when selecting text or objects is the:
A. Quick Access Toolbar **B.** Mini toolbar **C.** Document toolbar

2. In Office 2010, a centralized space for file management tasks is:
A. a task pane **B.** a dialog box **C.** Backstage view

3. The commands Save, Save As, Open, and Close in Backstage view are located:
A. above the Backstage tabs **B.** below the Backstage tabs **C.** under the screen thumbnail

4. The tab in Backstage view that displays information about the current file is the:
A. Recent tab **B.** Info tab **C.** Options tab

5. Details about a file, including the title, author name, subject, and keywords are known as:
A. document properties **B.** formatting marks **C.** KeyTips

6. An Office feature that displays a list of potential results is:
A. Live Preview **B.** a contextual tab **C.** a gallery

7. A type of formatting emphasis applied to text such as bold, italic, and underline, is called:
   A. a font style **B.** a KeyTip **C.** a tag

8. A technology showing the result of applying formatting as you point to possible results is called:
   A. Live Preview **B.** Backstage view **C.** gallery view

9. A temporary storage area that holds text or graphics that you select and then cut or copy is the:
   A. paste options gallery **B.** ribbon **C.** Office clipboard

10. A file that has been reduced in size is:
   A. a compressed file **B.** an extracted file **C.** a PDF file

Getting Started with PowerPoint

OUTCOMES

At the end of this chapter you will be able to:

OBJECTIVES

Mastering these objectives will enable you to:

PROJECT 1A
Create a new PowerPoint presentation.

PROJECT 1B
Edit and format a PowerPoint presentation.

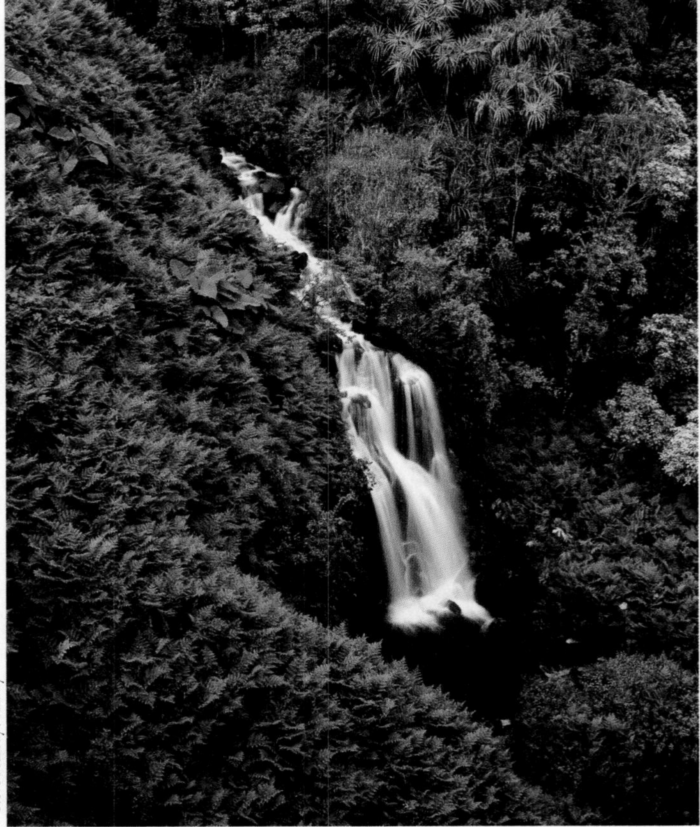

In This Chapter

In this chapter you will study presentation skills, which are among the most important skills you will learn. Good presentation skills enhance your communications—written, electronic, and interpersonal. In this technology-enhanced world, communicating ideas clearly and concisely is a critical personal skill. Microsoft PowerPoint 2010 is presentation software with which you create electronic slide presentations. Use PowerPoint to present information to your audience effectively. You can start with a new, blank presentation and add content, pictures, and themes, or you can collaborate with colleagues by inserting slides that have been saved in other presentations.

The projects in this chapter relate to **Lehua Hawaiian Adventures**. Named for the small, crescent-shaped island that is noted for its snorkeling and scuba diving, Lehua Hawaiian Adventures offers exciting but affordable adventure tours. Hiking tours go off the beaten path to amazing remote places on the islands. If you prefer to ride into the heart of Hawaii, try the cycling tours. Lehua Hawaiian Adventures also offers Jeep tours. Whatever you prefer—mountain, sea, volcano—our tour guides are experts in the history, geography, culture, and flora and fauna of Hawaii.

Project 1A Company Overview

Project Activities

In Activities 1.01 through 1.13, you will create the first four slides of a new presentation that Lehua Hawaiian Adventures tour manager Carl Kawaoka is developing to introduce the tour services that the company offers. Your completed presentation will look similar to Figure 1.1.

Project Files

For Project 1A, you will need the following files:

New blank PowerPoint presentation
p01A_Helicopter
p01A_Beach

You will save your presentation as:

Lastname_Firstname_1A_LHA_Overview

Project Results

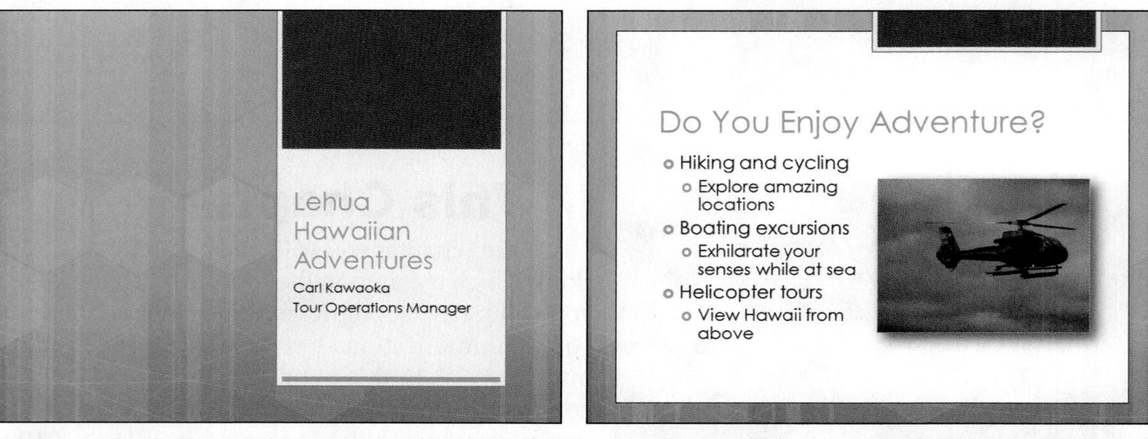

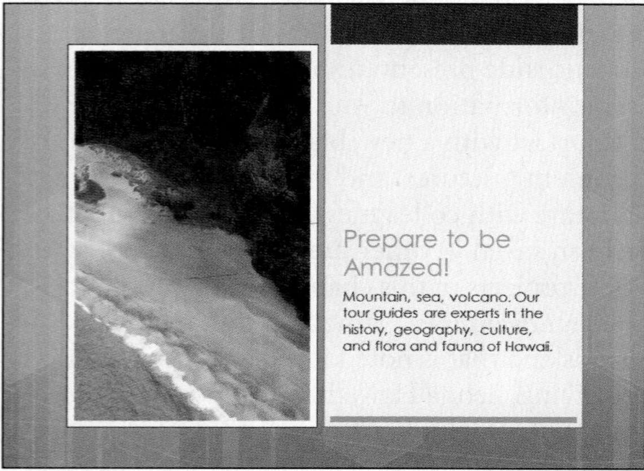

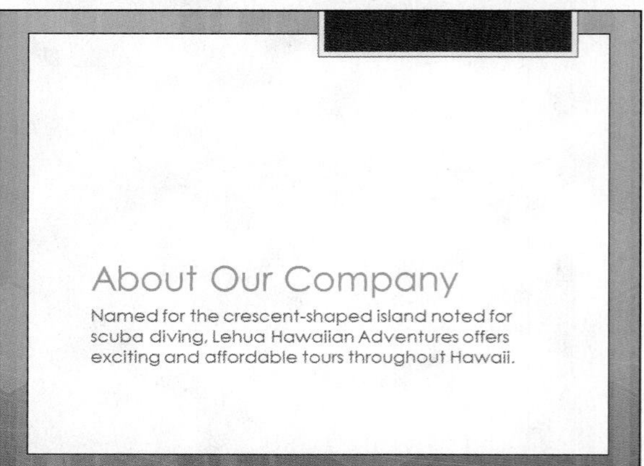

Figure 1.1
Project 1A LHA Overview

Objective 1 | Create a New Presentation

Microsoft PowerPoint 2010 is software with which you can present information to your audience effectively. You can edit and format a blank presentation by adding text, a presentation theme, and pictures.

Activity 1.01 | Identifying Parts of the PowerPoint Window

In this activity, you will start PowerPoint and identify the parts of the PowerPoint window.

1. **Start** PowerPoint to display a new blank presentation in Normal view, and then compare your screen with Figure 1.2.

   Normal view is the primary editing view in PowerPoint where you write and design your presentations. Normal view includes the Notes pane, the Slide pane, and the Slides/Outline pane.

Figure 1.2

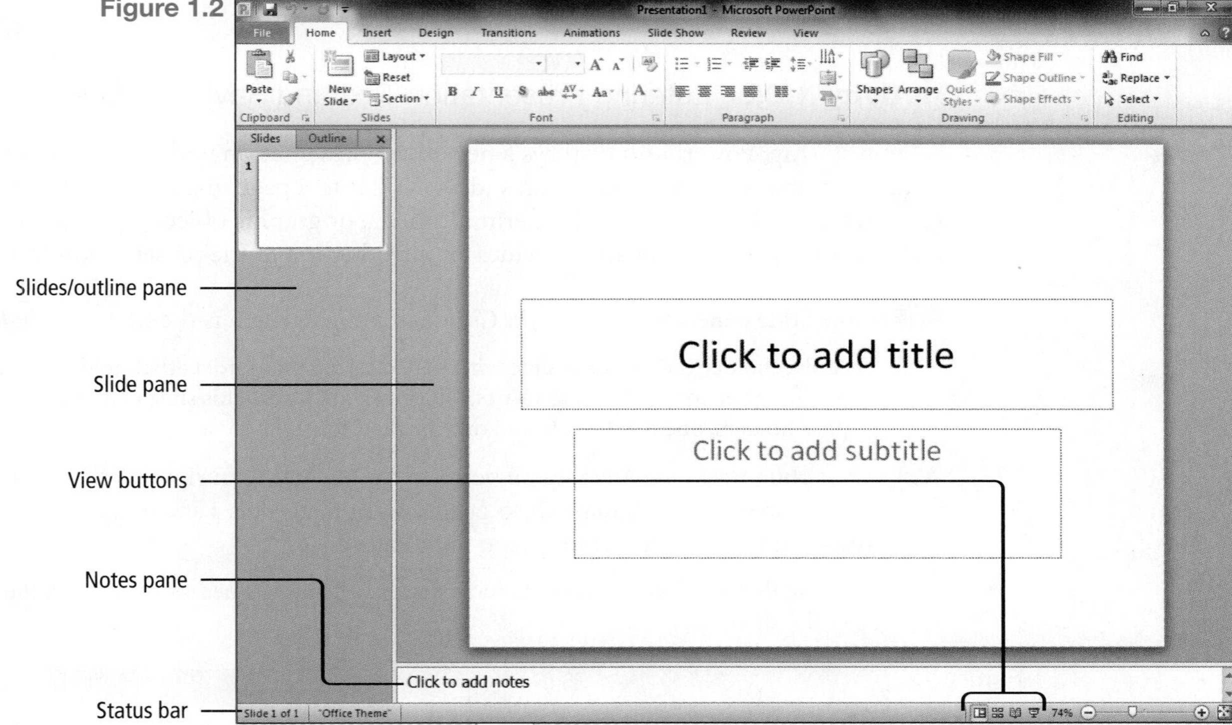

2. Take a moment to study the parts of the PowerPoint window described in the table in Figure 1.3.

Microsoft PowerPoint Screen Elements

Screen Element	Description
Notes pane	Displays below the Slide pane and provides space for you to type notes regarding the active slide.
Slide pane	Displays a large image of the active slide.
Slides/Outline pane	Displays either the presentation in the form of miniature images called ***thumbnails*** (Slides tab) or the presentation outline (Outline tab).
Status bar	Displays, in a horizontal bar at the bottom of the presentation window, the current slide number, number of slides in a presentation, theme, View buttons, Zoom slider, and Fit slide to current window button; you can customize this area to include additional helpful information.
View buttons	Control the look of the presentation window with a set of commands.

Figure 1.3

Activity 1.02 | Entering Presentation Text and Saving a Presentation

On startup, PowerPoint displays a new blank presentation with a single ***slide***—a ***title slide*** in Normal view. A presentation slide—similar to a page in a document—can contain text, pictures, tables, charts, and other multimedia or graphic objects. The title slide is the first slide in a presentation and provides an introduction to the presentation topic.

1 In the **Slide pane**, click in the text *Click to add title*, which is the title ***placeholder***.

A placeholder is a box on a slide with dotted or dashed borders that holds title and body text or other content such as charts, tables, and pictures. This slide contains two placeholders, one for the title and one for the subtitle.

2 Type **Lehua Hawaiian Adventures** point to *Lehua*, and then right-click. On the shortcut menu, click **Ignore All** so *Lehua* is not flagged as a spelling error in this presentation. Compare your screen with Figure 1.4.

Recall that a red wavy underline indicates that the underlined word is not in the Microsoft Office dictionary.

Figure 1.4

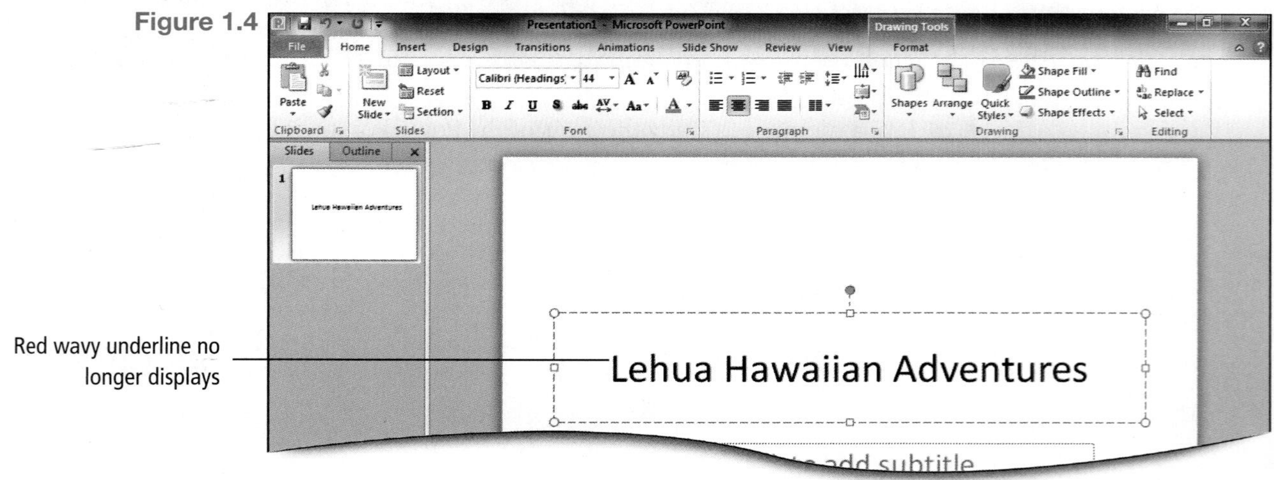

3 Click in the subtitle placeholder, and then type **Carl Kawaoka**

4 Press Enter to create a new line in the subtitle placeholder. Type **Tour Manager**

5 Right-click **Kawaoka**, and then on the shortcut menu, click **Ignore All**. Compare your screen with Figure 1.5.

Figure 1.5

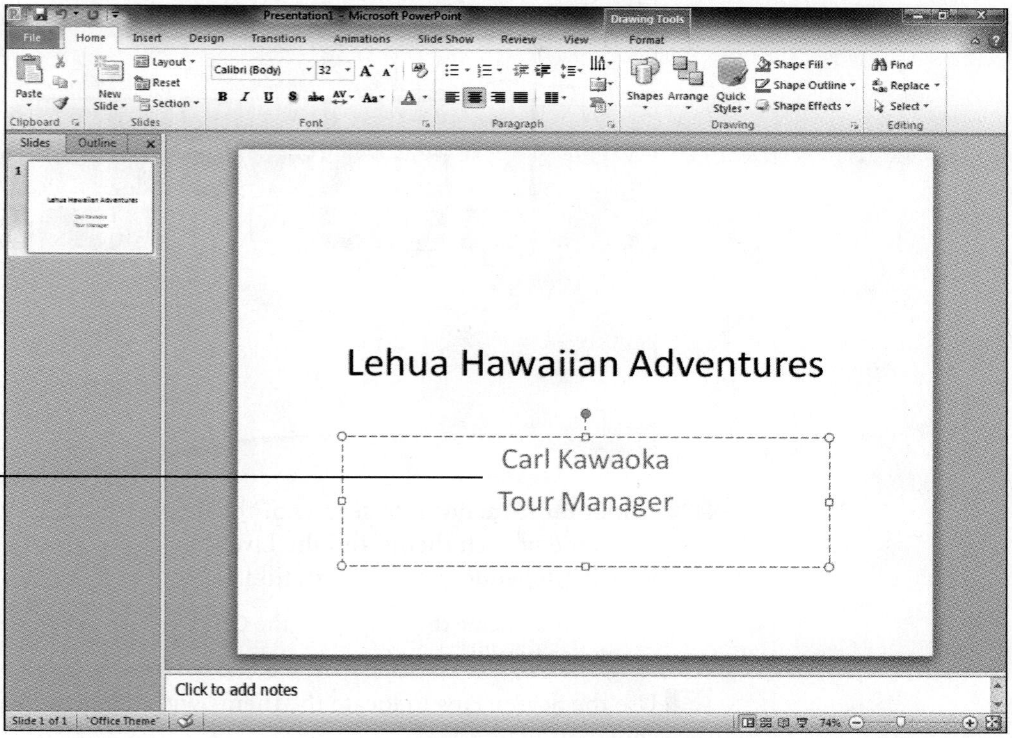

Text typed in subtitle placeholder

6 In the upper left corner of your screen, click the **File tab** to display **Backstage** view, click **Save As**, and then in the **Save As** dialog box, navigate to the location where you will store your files for this chapter. Create a new folder named **PowerPoint Chapter 1** In the **File name** box, replace the existing text with **Lastname_Firstname_1A_LHA_Overview** and then click **Save**.

Activity 1.03 | Applying a Presentation Theme

A ***theme*** is a set of unified design elements that provides a look for your presentation by applying colors, fonts, and effects.

1 On the Ribbon, click the **Design tab**. In the **Themes group**, click the **More** button [icon] to display the **Themes** gallery. Compare your screen with Figure 1.6.

Figure 1.6

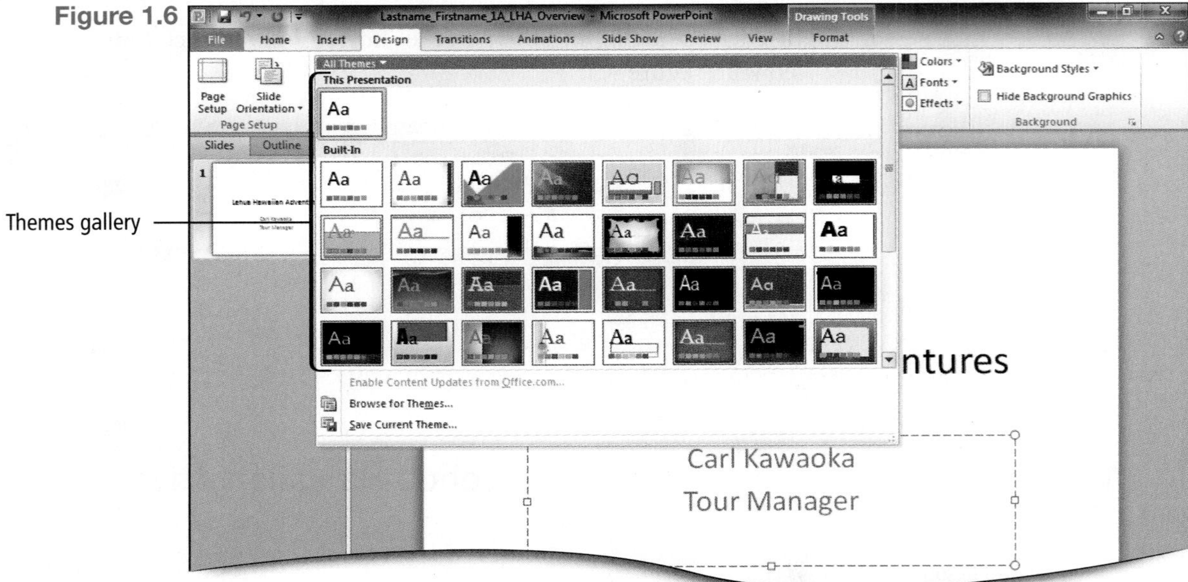

2 Under **Built-In**, point to several of the themes and notice that a ScreenTip displays the name of each theme and the Live Preview feature displays how each theme would look if applied to your presentation.

The first theme that displays is the Office theme. Subsequent themes are arranged alphabetically.

3 Use the ScreenTips to locate the theme with the green background—**Austin**—as shown in Figure 1.7.

Figure 1.7

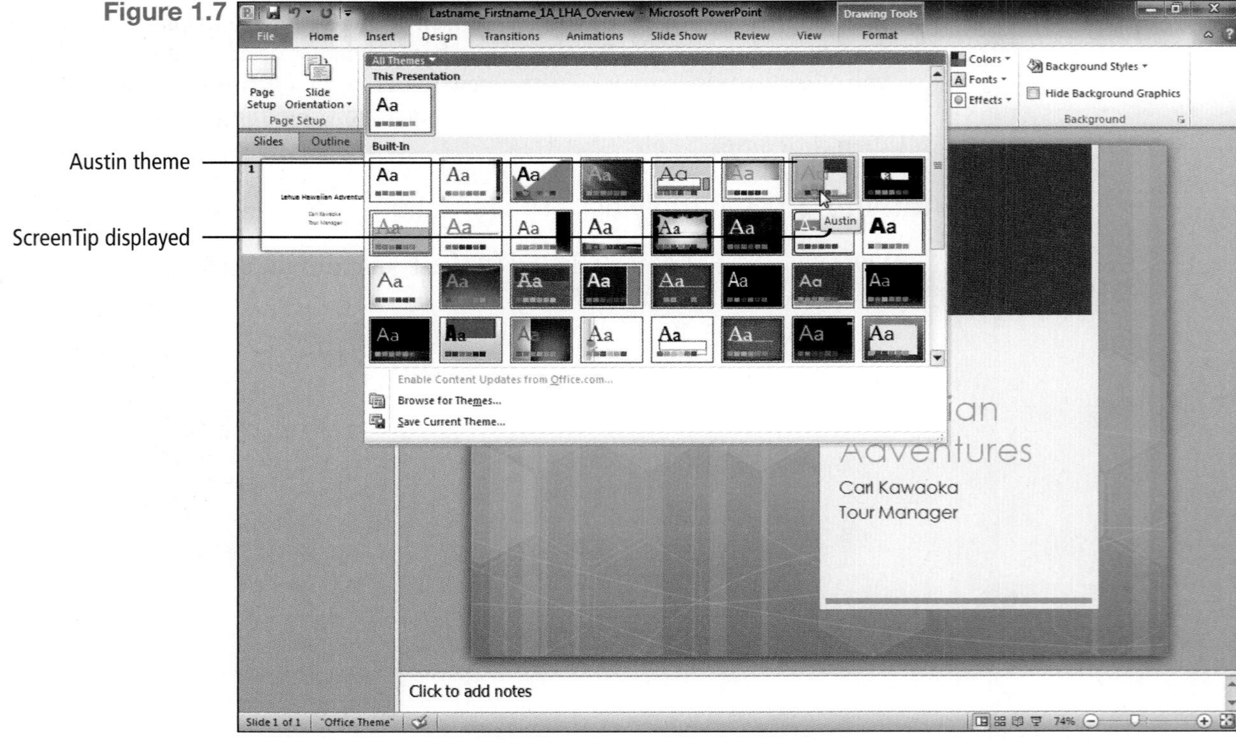

4 Click the **Austin** theme to change the presentation theme and then **Save** [icon] your presentation.

Objective 2 | Edit a Presentation in Normal View

Editing is the process of modifying a presentation by adding and deleting slides or by changing the contents of individual slides.

Activity 1.04 | Inserting a New Slide

To insert a new slide in a presentation, display the slide that will precede the slide that you want to insert.

1 On the **Home tab**, in the **Slides group**, point to the **New Slide** button. Compare your screen with Figure 1.8.

The New Slide button is a split button. Recall that clicking the main part of a split button performs a command and clicking the arrow opens a menu, list, or gallery. The upper, main part of the New Slide button, when clicked, inserts a slide without displaying any options. The lower part—the New Slide button arrow—when clicked, displays a gallery of slide ***layouts***. A layout is the arrangement of elements, such as title and subtitle text, lists, pictures, tables, charts, shapes, and movies, on a slide.

Figure 1.8

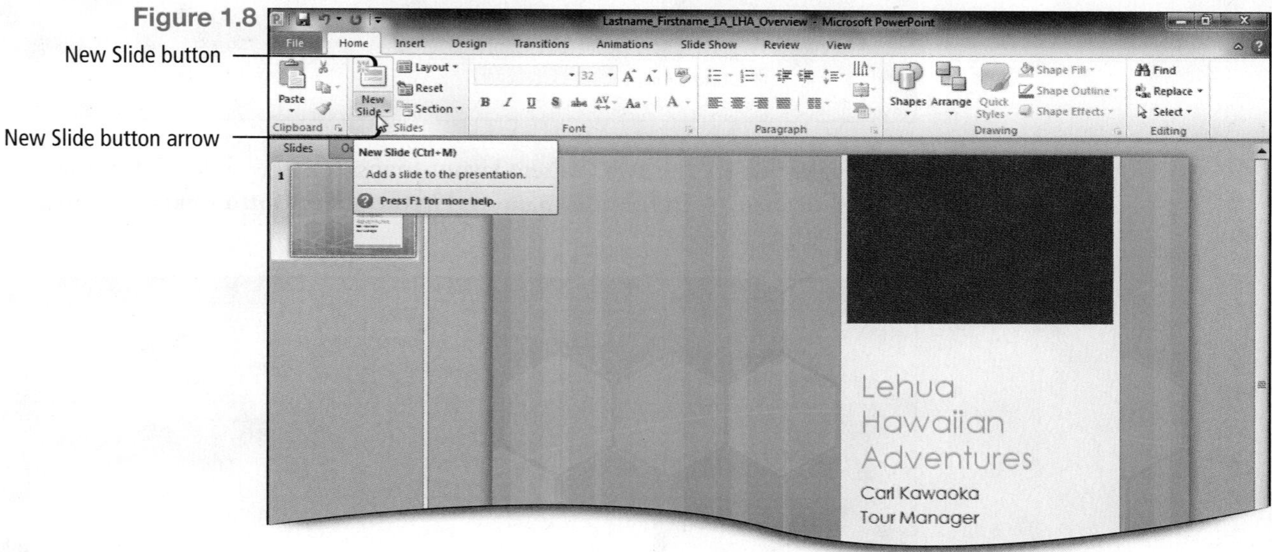

2 In the **Slides group**, click the lower portion of the New Slide button—the **New Slide button arrow**—to display the gallery, and then compare your screen with Figure 1.9.

Figure 1.9

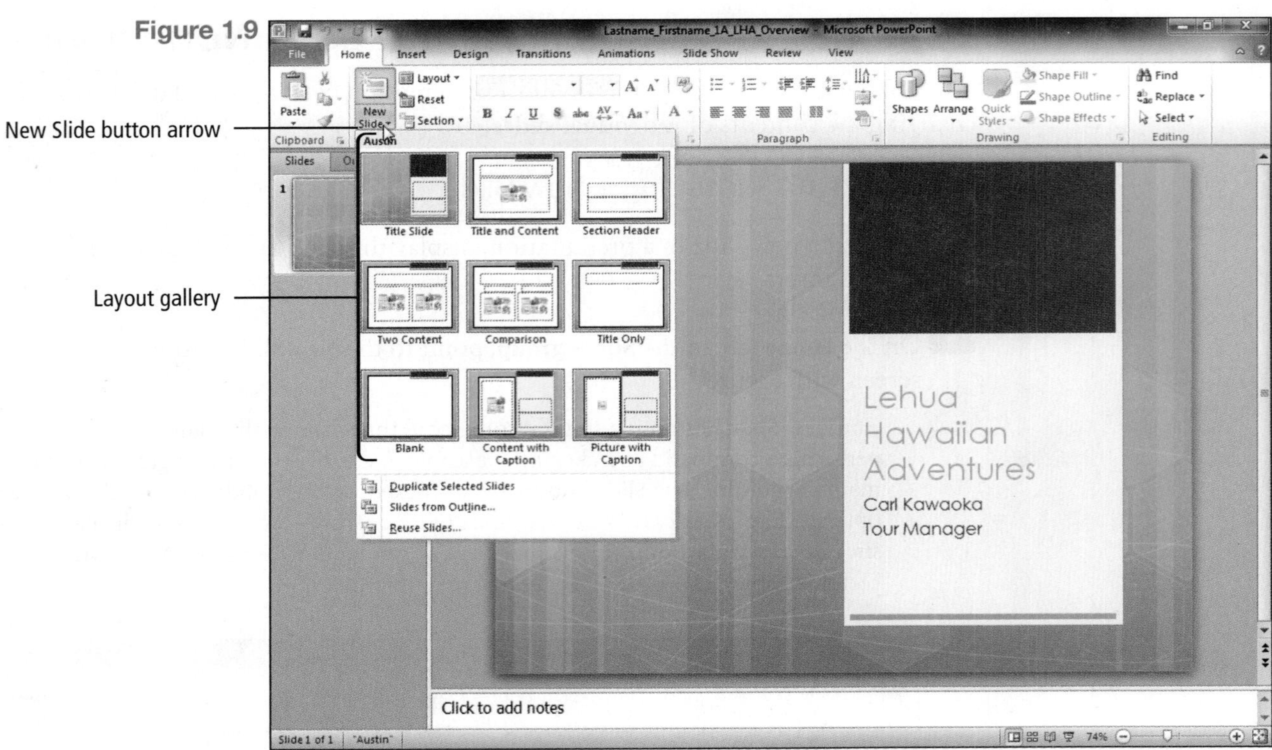

3 In the gallery, click the **Two Content** layout to insert a new slide. Notice that the new blank slide displays in the **Slide pane** and in the **Slides/Outline pane**. Compare your screen with Figure 1.10.

Figure 1.10

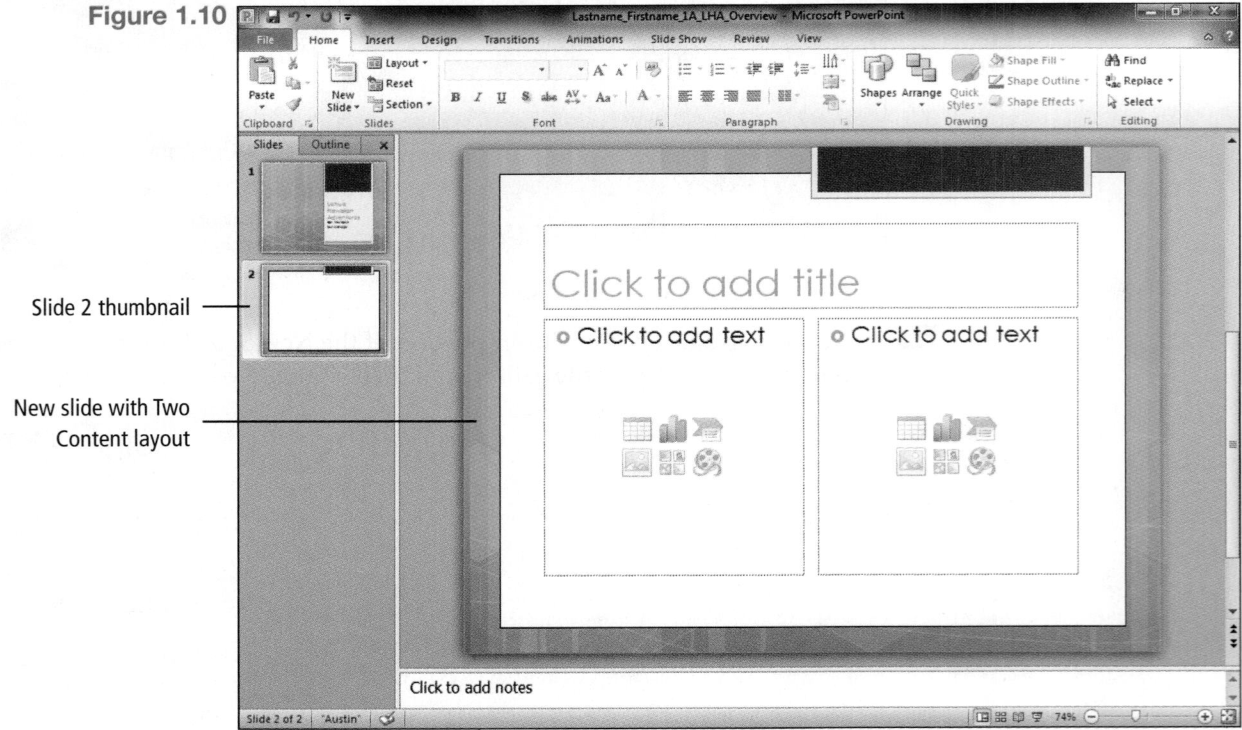

4 In the **Slide pane**, click the text *Click to add title*, and then type **Do You Enjoy Adventure?**

5 On the left side of the slide, click anywhere in the content placeholder. Type **Hiking and cycling** and then press Enter.

6 Type **Explore locations** and then compare your screen with Figure 1.11.

Figure 1.11

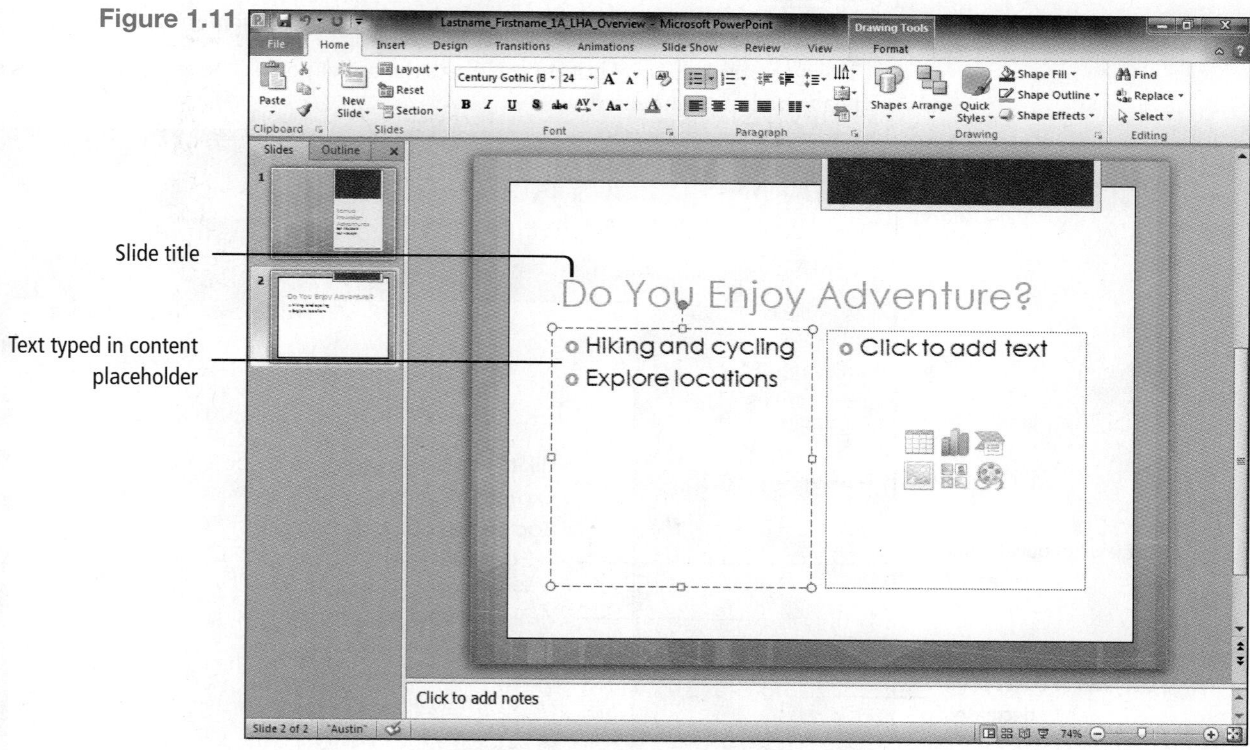

7 **Save** your presentation.

Activity 1.05 | Increasing and Decreasing List Levels

Text in a PowerPoint presentation is organized according to ***list levels***. List levels, each represented by a bullet symbol, are similar to outline levels. On a slide, list levels are identified by the bullet style, indentation, and the size of the text.

The first level on an individual slide is the title. Increasing the list level of a bullet point increases its indent and results in a smaller text size. Decreasing the list level of a bullet point decreases its indent and results in a larger text size.

1 On **Slide 2**, if necessary, click at the end of the last bullet point after the word *locations*, and then press Enter to insert a new bullet point.

2 Type **Boating excursions** and then press Enter.

3 Press Tab, and then notice that the green bullet is indented. Type **Exhilarate your senses while at sea**

By pressing Tab at the beginning of a bullet point, you can increase the list level and indent the bullet point.

4 Press Enter. Notice that a new bullet point displays at the same level as the previous bullet point. Then, on the **Home tab**, in the **Paragraph group**, click the **Decrease List Level** button. Type **Helicopter tours** and then compare your screen with Figure 1.12.

The Decrease List Level button promotes the bullet point. The text size increases and the text is no longer indented.

Figure 1.12

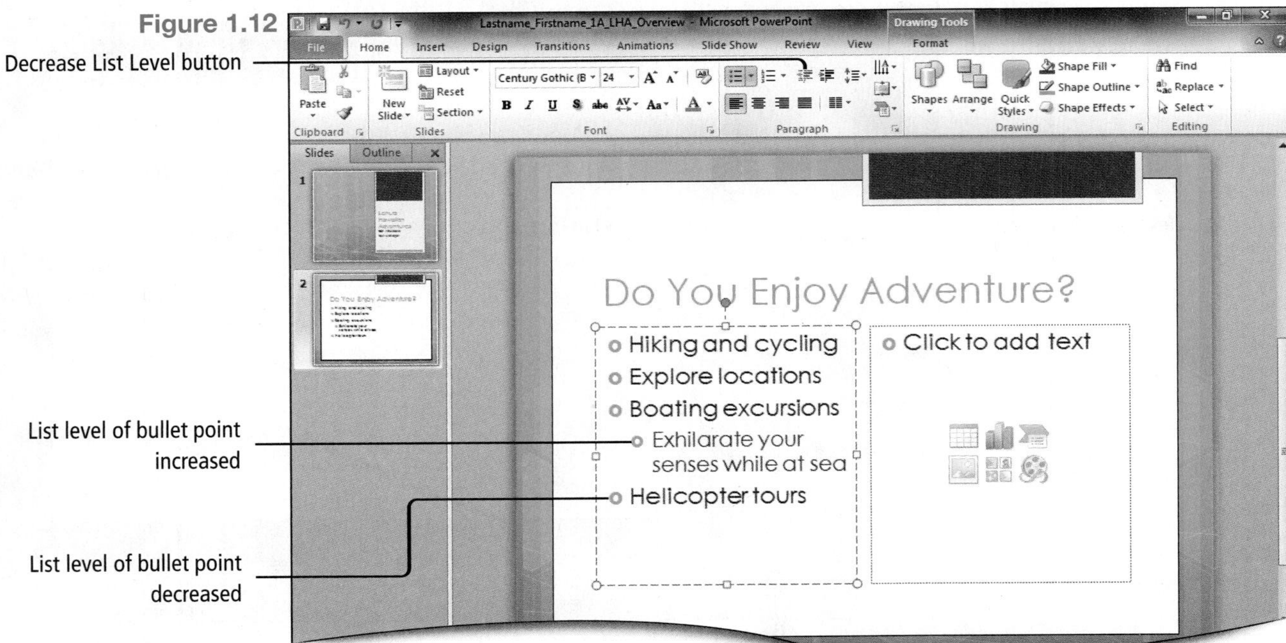

5 Press Enter, and then press Tab to increase the list level. Type **View Hawaii from above**

6 Click anywhere in the second bullet point—*Explore locations*. On the **Home tab**, in the **Paragraph group**, click the **Increase List Level** button. Compare your screen with Figure 1.13.

The bullet point is indented and the size of the text decreases.

Figure 1.13

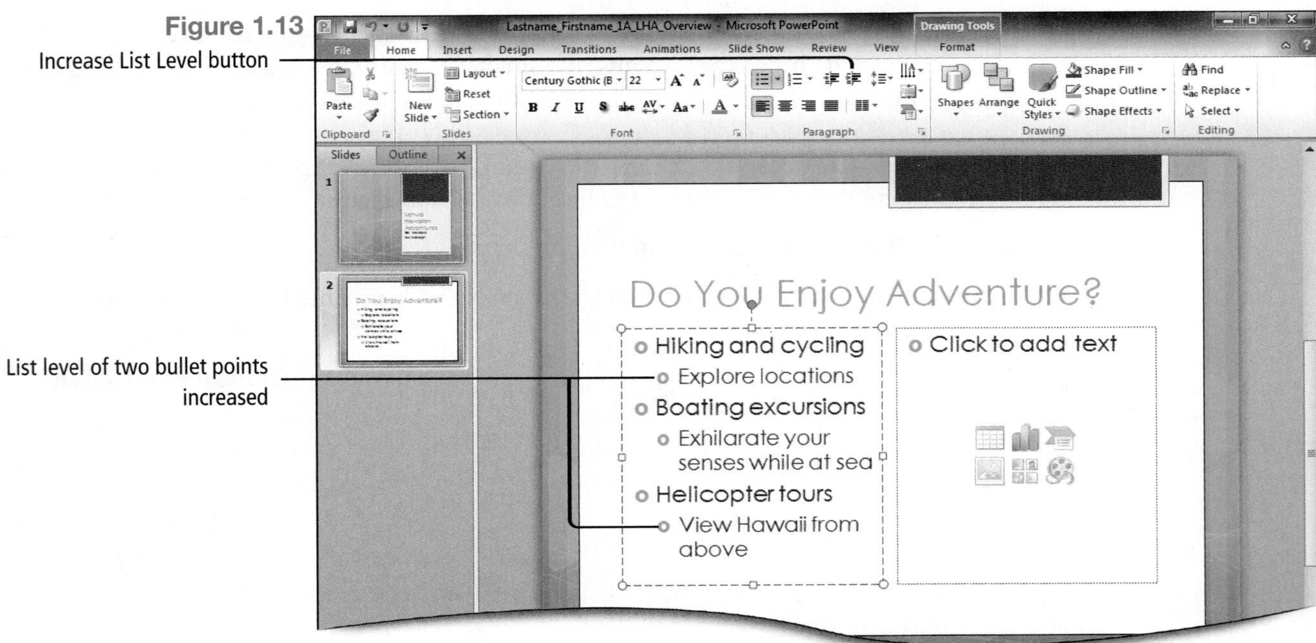

7 **Save** your presentation.

Activity 1.06 | Adding Speaker's Notes to a Presentation

Recall that when a presentation is displayed in Normal view, the Notes pane displays below the Slide pane. Use the Notes pane to type speaker's notes that you can print below a picture of each slide. Then, while making your presentation, you can refer to these printouts while making a presentation, thus reminding you of the important points that you want to discuss during the presentation.

1. With **Slide 2** displayed, on the **Home tab**, in the **Slides group**, click the **New Slide button arrow** to display the **Slide Layout** gallery, and then click **Section Header**.

   The section header layout changes the look and flow of a presentation by providing text placeholders that do not contain bullet points.

2. Click in the title placeholder, and then type **About Our Company**

3. Click in the content placeholder below the title, and then type **Named for the crescent-shaped island noted for scuba diving, Lehua Hawaiian Adventures offers exciting and affordable tours throughout Hawaii.** Compare your screen with Figure 1.14.

Figure 1.14

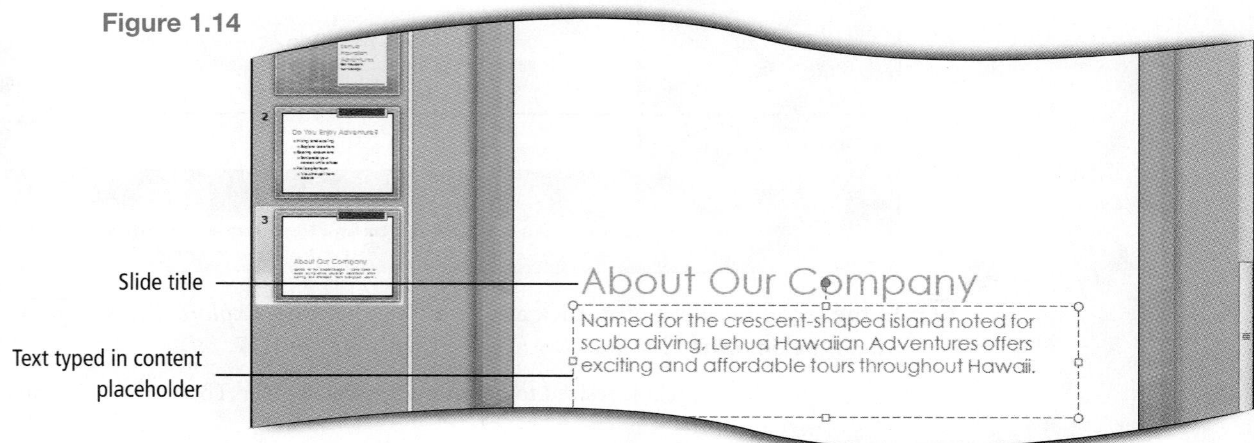

4. Below the slide, click in the **Notes pane**. Type **Lehua Hawaiian Adventures is based in Honolulu but has offices on each of the main Hawaiian islands.** Compare your screen with Figure 1.15, and then **Save** your presentation.

Figure 1.15

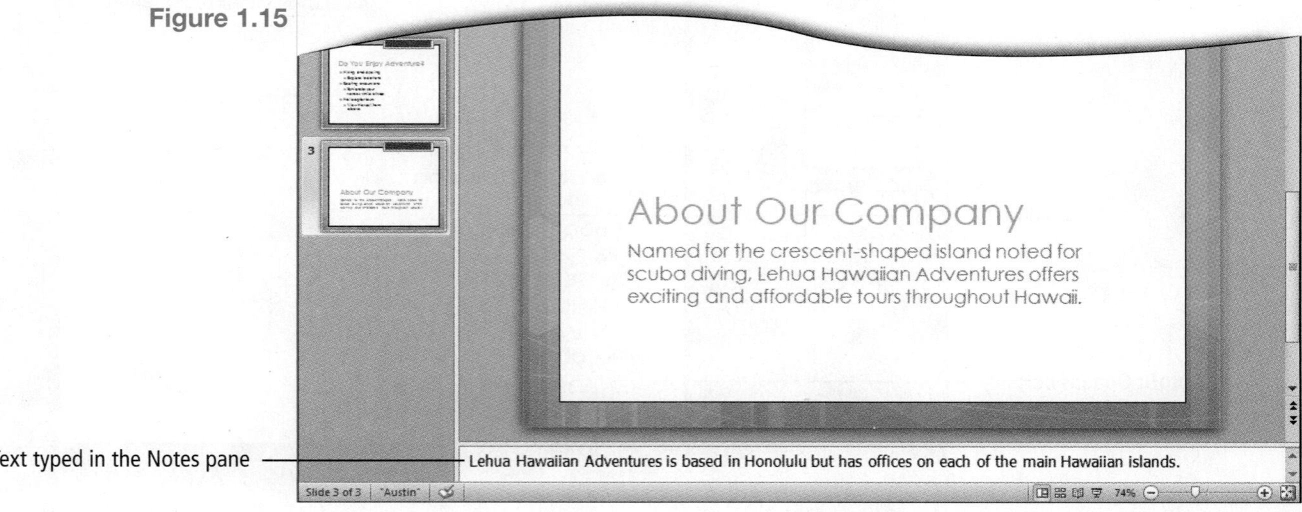

Activity 1.07 | Displaying and Editing Slides in the Slide Pane

To edit a presentation slide, display the slide in the Slide pane.

1 Look at the **Slides/Outline pane**, and then notice that the presentation contains three slides. At the right side of the PowerPoint window, in the vertical scroll bar, point to the scroll box, and then hold down the left mouse button to display a ScreenTip indicating the slide number and title.

2 Drag the scroll box up until the ScreenTip displays *Slide: 2 of 3 Do You Enjoy Adventure?* Compare your slide with Figure 1.16, and then release the mouse button to display **Slide 2**.

Figure 1.16

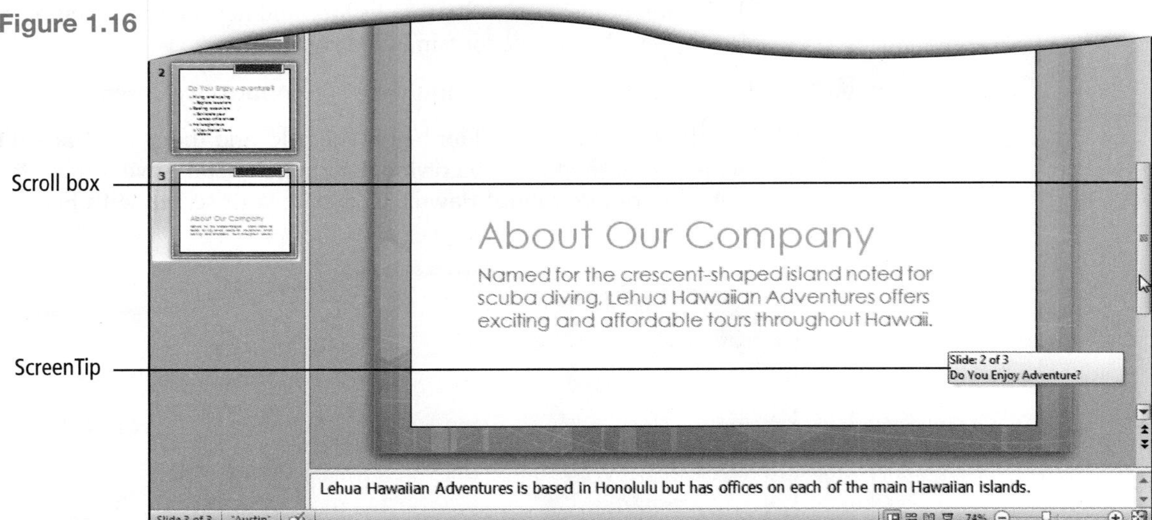

3 In the second bullet point, click at the end of the word *Explore*. Press Spacebar, and then type **amazing** Compare your screen with Figure 1.17.

The placeholder text is resized to fit within the placeholder. The AutoFit Options button displays.

Figure 1.17

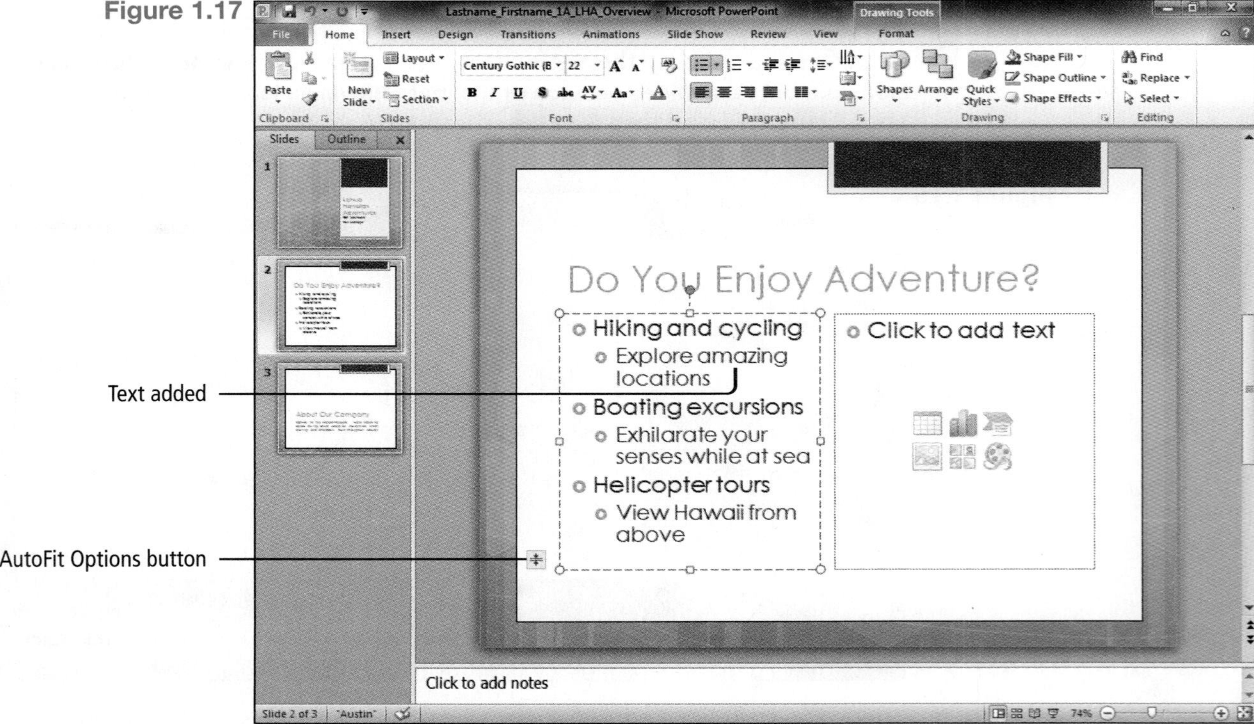

4 Click the **AutoFit Options** button, and then click **AutoFit Text to Placeholder**.

The *AutoFit Text to Placeholder* option keeps the text contained within the placeholder by reducing the size of the text. The *Stop Fitting Text to This Placeholder* option turns off the AutoFit option so that the text can flow beyond the placeholder border; the text size remains unchanged.

5 Below the vertical scroll bar, locate the **Previous Slide** and **Next Slide** buttons as shown in Figure 1.18.

Figure 1.18

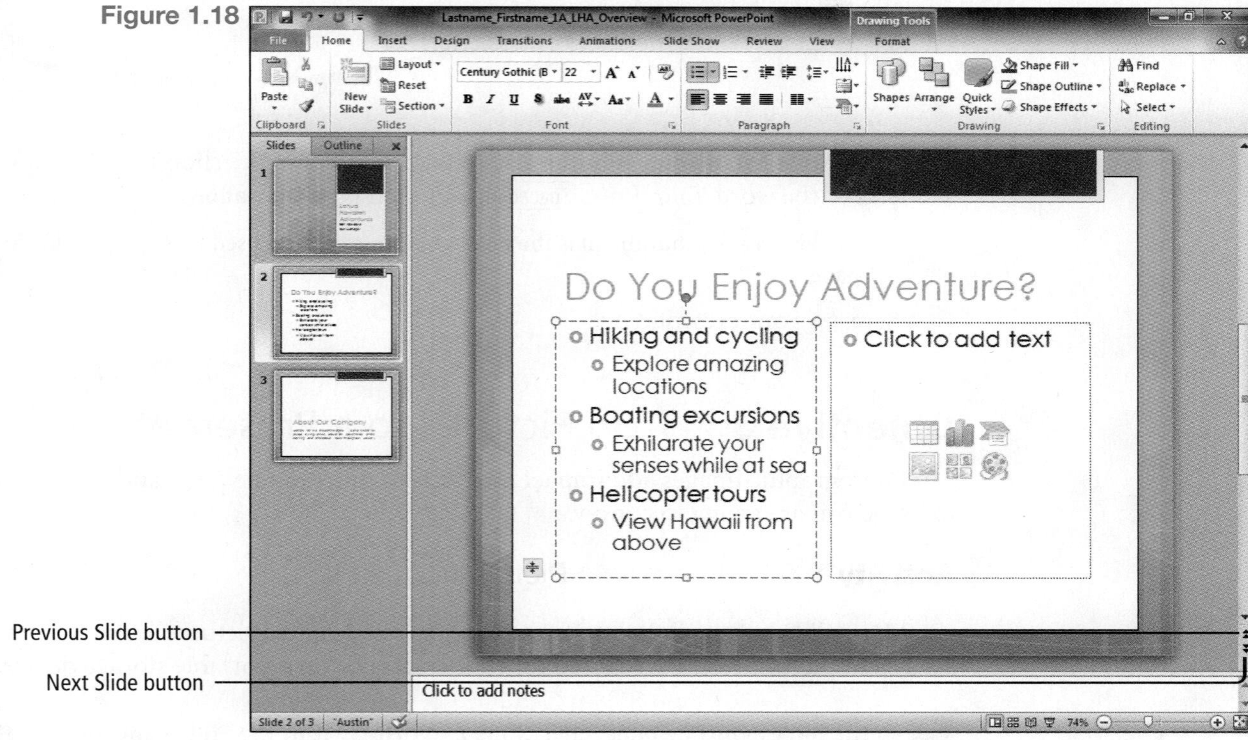

6 In the vertical scroll bar, click the **Previous Slide** button so that **Slide 1** displays. Then click the **Next Slide** button two times until **Slide 3** displays.

By clicking the Next Slide or the Previous Slide buttons, you can scroll through your presentation one slide at a time.

7 On the left side of the PowerPoint window, in the **Slides/Outline pane**, point to **Slide 1**, and then notice that a ScreenTip displays the slide title. Compare your screen with Figure 1.19.

In the Slides/Outline pane, the slide numbers display to the left of the slide thumbnails.

Figure 1.19

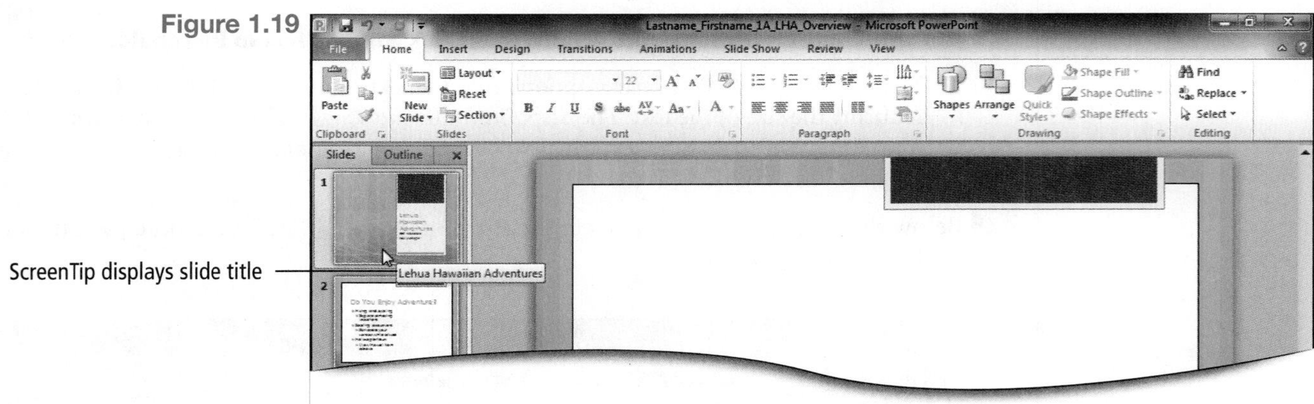

8 Click **Slide 1** to display it in the **Slide pane**, and then in the slide subtitle, click at the end of the word *Tour*. Press Spacebar, and then type **Operations**

Clicking a slide thumbnail is the most common method used to display a slide in the Slide pane.

9 **Save** your presentation.

Objective 3 | Add Pictures to a Presentation

Photographic images add impact to a presentation and help the audience visualize the message you are trying to convey.

Activity 1.08 | Inserting a Picture from a File

Many slide layouts in PowerPoint accommodate digital picture files so that you can easily add pictures you have stored on your system or on a portable storage device.

1 In the **Slides/Outline pane**, click **Slide 2** to display it in the **Slide pane**. On the **Home tab**, in the **Slides group**, click the **New Slide button arrow** to display the **Slide Layout** gallery. Click **Picture with Caption** to insert a new **Slide 3**. Compare your screen with Figure 1.20.

In the center of the large picture placeholder, the *Insert Picture from File* button displays.

Figure 1.20

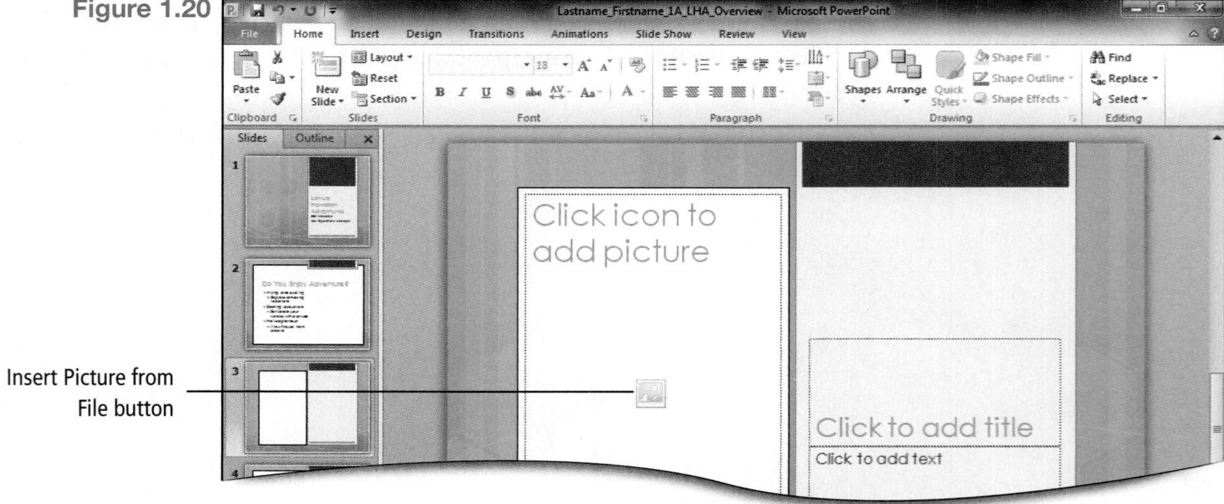

2 In the picture placeholder, click the **Insert Picture from File** button to open the **Insert Picture** dialog box. Navigate to the location in which your student files are stored, click **p01A_Beach**, then click **Insert** to insert the picture in the placeholder.

3 To the right of the picture, click in the title placeholder. Type **Prepare to be Amazed!**

4 Below the title, click in the caption placeholder, and then type **Mountain, sea, volcano. Our tour guides are experts in the history, geography, culture, and flora and fauna of Hawaii.** Compare your screen with Figure 1.21.

Figure 1.21

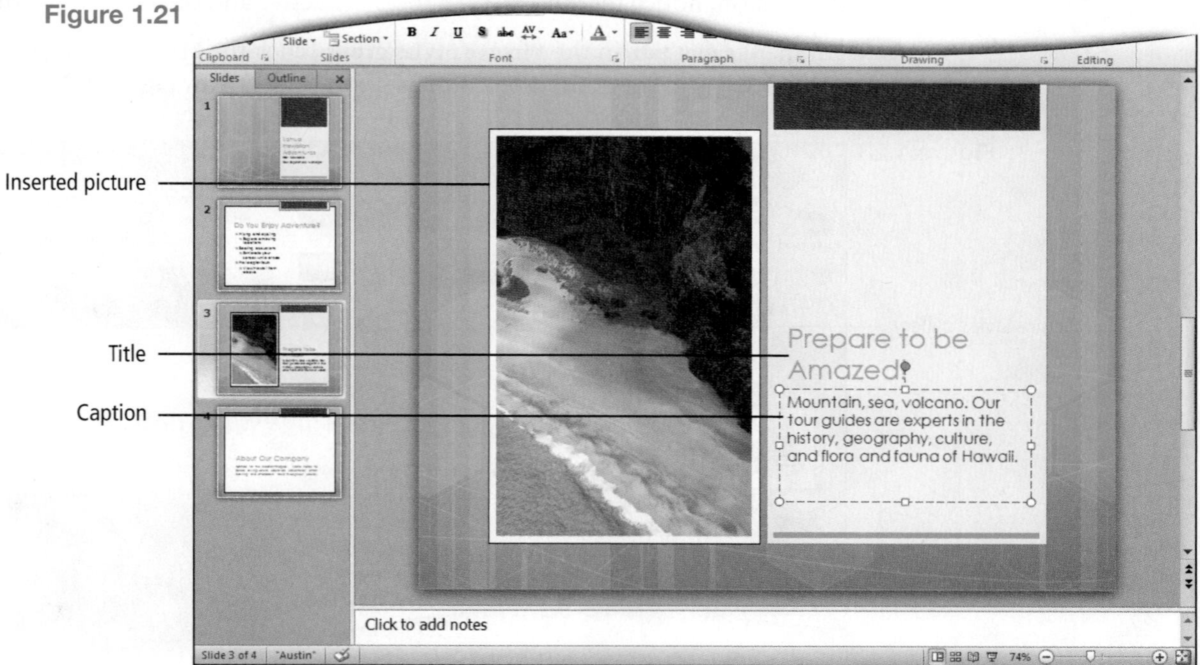

5 Display **Slide 2**. In the placeholder on the right side of the slide, click the **Insert Picture from File** button . Navigate to your student files, and then click **p01A_Helicopter**. Click **Insert**, and then compare your screen with Figure 1.22.

Small circles and squares—***sizing handles***—surround the inserted picture and indicate that the picture is selected and can be modified or formatted. The ***rotation handle***—a green circle above the picture—provides a way to rotate a selected image.

Figure 1.22

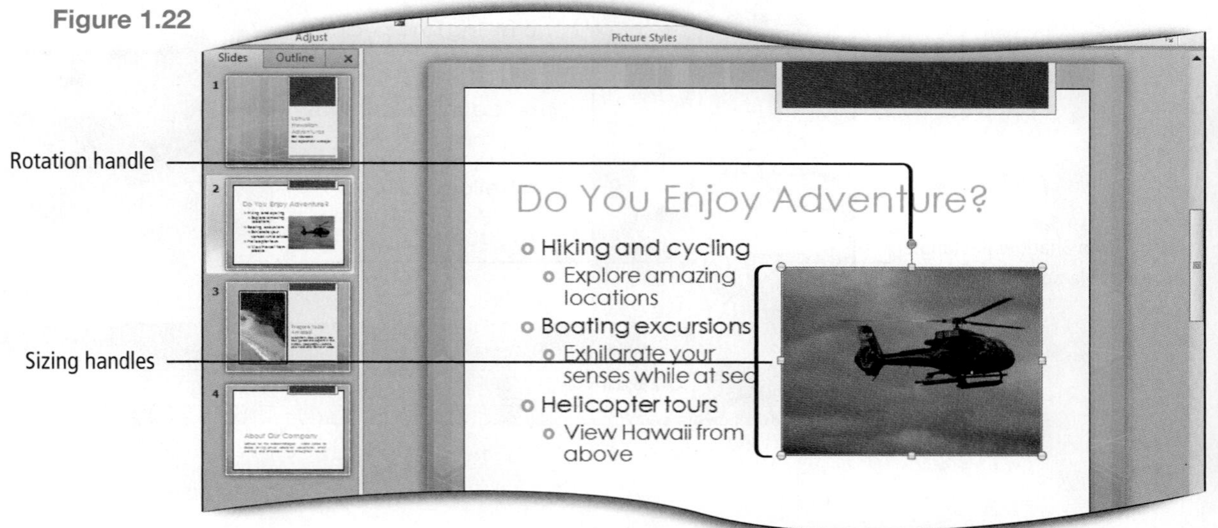

6 **Save** the presentation.

Activity 1.09 | Applying a Style to a Picture

The Picture Tools add the Format tab to the Ribbon, which provides numerous ***styles*** that you can apply to your pictures. A style is a collection of formatting options that you can apply to a picture, text, or an object.

1 With **Slide 2** displayed, if necessary, click the picture of the helicopter to select it. On the Ribbon, notice that the Picture Tools are active and the Format tab displays.

2 On the **Format tab**, in the **Picture Styles group**, click the **More** button to display the **Picture Styles** gallery, and then compare your screen with Figure 1.23.

Figure 1.23

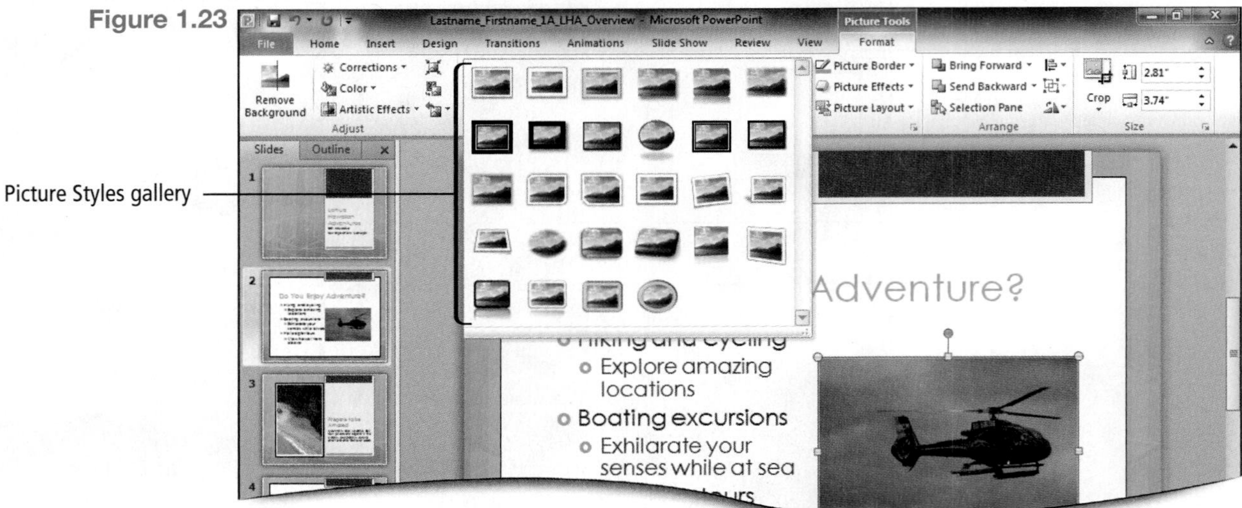

3 In the gallery, point to several of the picture styles to display the ScreenTips and to view the effect on your picture. In the first row, click **Drop Shadow Rectangle**.

4 Click in a blank area of the slide, and then compare your screen with Figure 1.24.

Figure 1.24

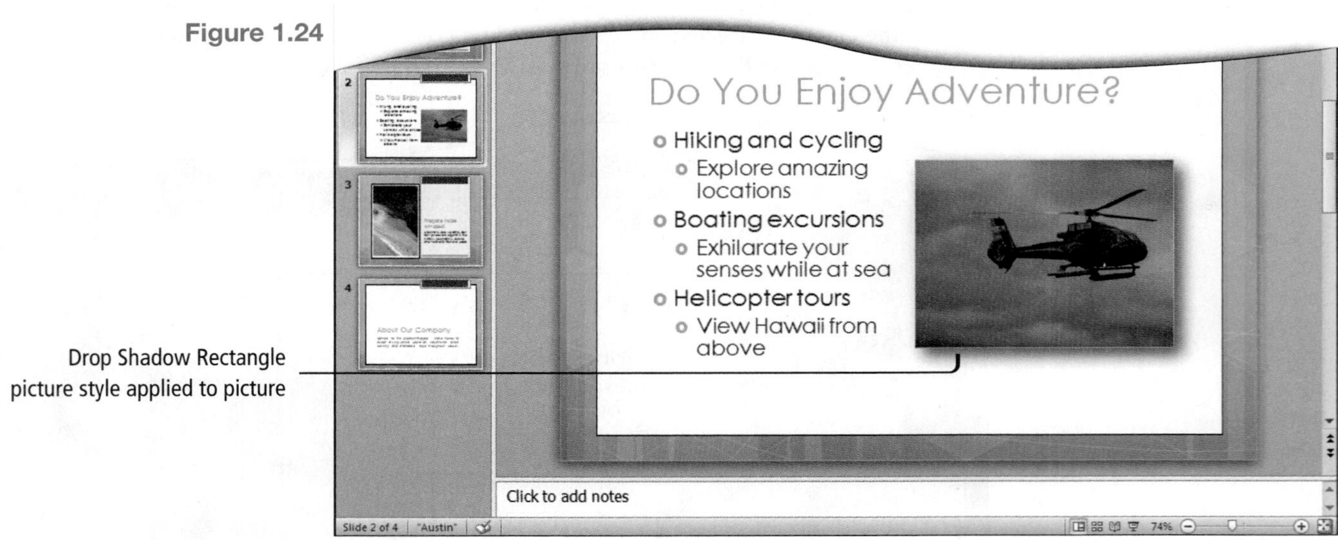

5 **Save** the presentation.

Activity 1.10 | Applying and Removing Picture Artistic Effects

Artistic effects are formats applied to images that make pictures resemble sketches or paintings.

1 With **Slide 2** displayed, select the picture of the helicopter.

2 Click the **Format tab**, and then in the **Adjust group**, click the **Artistic Effects** button to display the **Artistic Effects** gallery. Compare your screen with Figure 1.25.

Figure 1.25

3 In the gallery, point to several of the artistic effects to display the ScreenTips and to have Live Preview display the effect on your picture. Then, in the second row, click the **Paint Strokes** effect.

4 With the picture still selected, on the **Format tab**, in the **Adjust group**, click the **Artistic Effects** button to display the gallery. In the first row, click the first effect—**None**—to remove the effect from the picture and restore the previous formatting.

5 **Save** the presentation.

Objective 4 | Print and View a Presentation

Activity 1.11 | Viewing a Slide Show

When you view a presentation as an electronic slide show, the entire slide fills the computer screen, and an audience can view your presentation if your computer is connected to a projection system.

> **Another Way**
>
> Press F5 to start the slide show from the beginning. Or, display the first slide you want to show and click the Slide Show button on the lower right side of the status bar; or press Shift + F5.

1 On the Ribbon, click the **Slide Show tab**. In the **Start Slide Show group**, click the **From Beginning** button.

The first slide fills the screen, displaying the presentation as the audience would see it if your computer was connected to a projection system.

2 Click the left mouse button or press Spacebar to advance to the second slide.

3 Continue to click or press Spacebar until the last slide displays, and then click or press Spacebar one more time to display a black slide.

After the last slide in a presentation, a ***black slide*** displays, indicating that the presentation is over.

4 With the black slide displayed, click the left mouse button or press Spacebar to exit the slide show and return to the presentation.

Activity 1.12 | Inserting Headers and Footers

A ***header*** is text that prints at the top of each sheet of ***slide handouts*** or ***notes pages***. Slide handouts are printed images of slides on a sheet of paper. Notes pages are printouts that contain the slide image on the top half of the page and notes that you have created on the Notes pane in the lower half of the page.

In addition to headers, you can insert ***footers***—text that displays at the bottom of every slide or that prints at the bottom of a sheet of slide handouts or notes pages.

1 Click the **Insert tab**, and then in the **Text group**, click the **Header & Footer** button to display the **Header and Footer** dialog box.

2 In the **Header and Footer** dialog box, click the **Notes and Handouts tab**. Under **Include on page**, select the **Date and time** check box, and as you do so, watch the Preview box in the lower right corner of the Header and Footer dialog box.

The Preview box indicates the placeholders on the printed Notes and Handouts pages. The two narrow rectangular boxes at the top of the Preview box indicate placeholders for the header text and date. When you select the Date and time check box, the placeholder in the upper right corner is outlined, indicating the location in which the date will display.

3 If necessary, click the Update automatically option button so that the current date prints on the notes and handouts each time the presentation is printed.

4 If necessary, *clear* the Header check box to omit this element. Notice that in the **Preview** box, the corresponding placeholder is not selected.

5 Select the **Page number** and **Footer** check boxes, and then notice that the insertion point displays in the **Footer** box. Using your own name, type **Lastname_Firstname_1A_LHA_Overview** so that the file name displays as a footer, and then compare your dialog box with Figure 1.26.

Figure 1.26

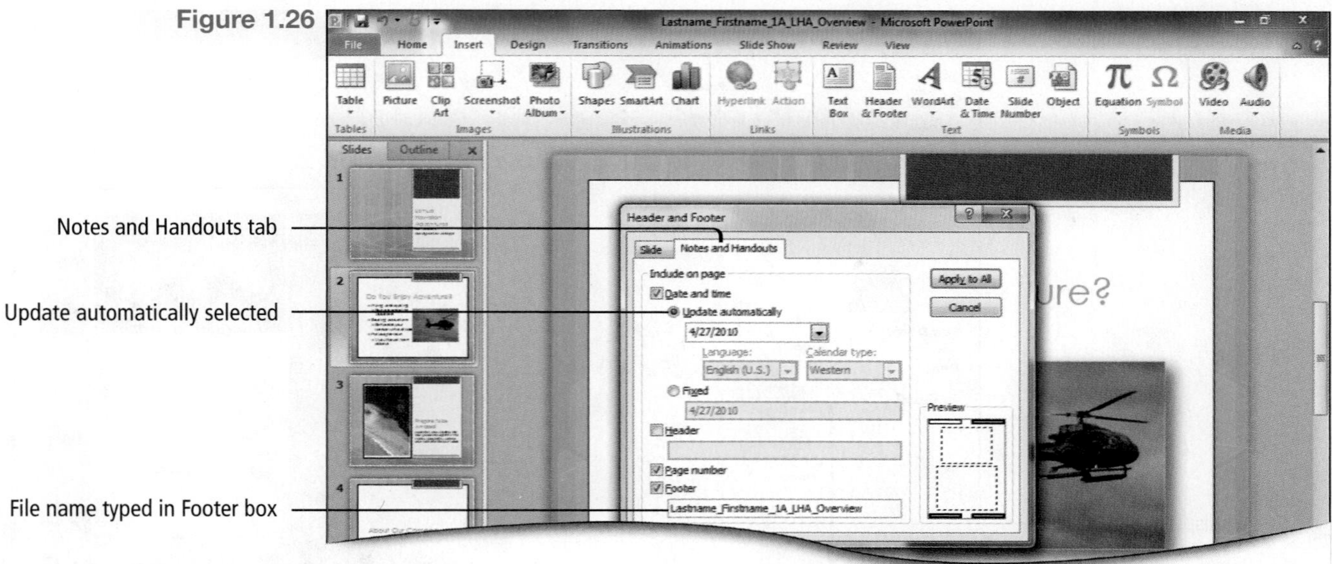

6 In the upper right corner of the dialog box, click **Apply to All**. **Save** your presentation.

> **More Knowledge | Adding Footers to Slides**
>
> You can also add footers to the actual slides, which will display during your presentation, by using the Slide tab in the Header and Footer dialog box. Headers cannot be added to individual slides.

Activity 1.13 | Printing a Presentation

Use Backstage view to preview the arrangement of slides on the handouts and notes pages.

1 Display **Slide 1**. Click the **File tab** to display **Backstage** view, and then click the **Print tab**.

The Print tab in Backstage view displays the tools you need to select your settings and also to view a preview of your presentation. On the right, Print Preview displays your presentation exactly as it will print.

2 In the **Settings group**, click **Full Page Slides**, and then compare your screen with Figure 1.27.

The gallery displays either the default print setting—Full Page Slides—or the most recently selected print setting. Thus, on your system, this button might indicate the presentation Notes Pages, Outline, or one of several arrangements of slide handouts—depending on the most recently used setting.

Figure 1.27

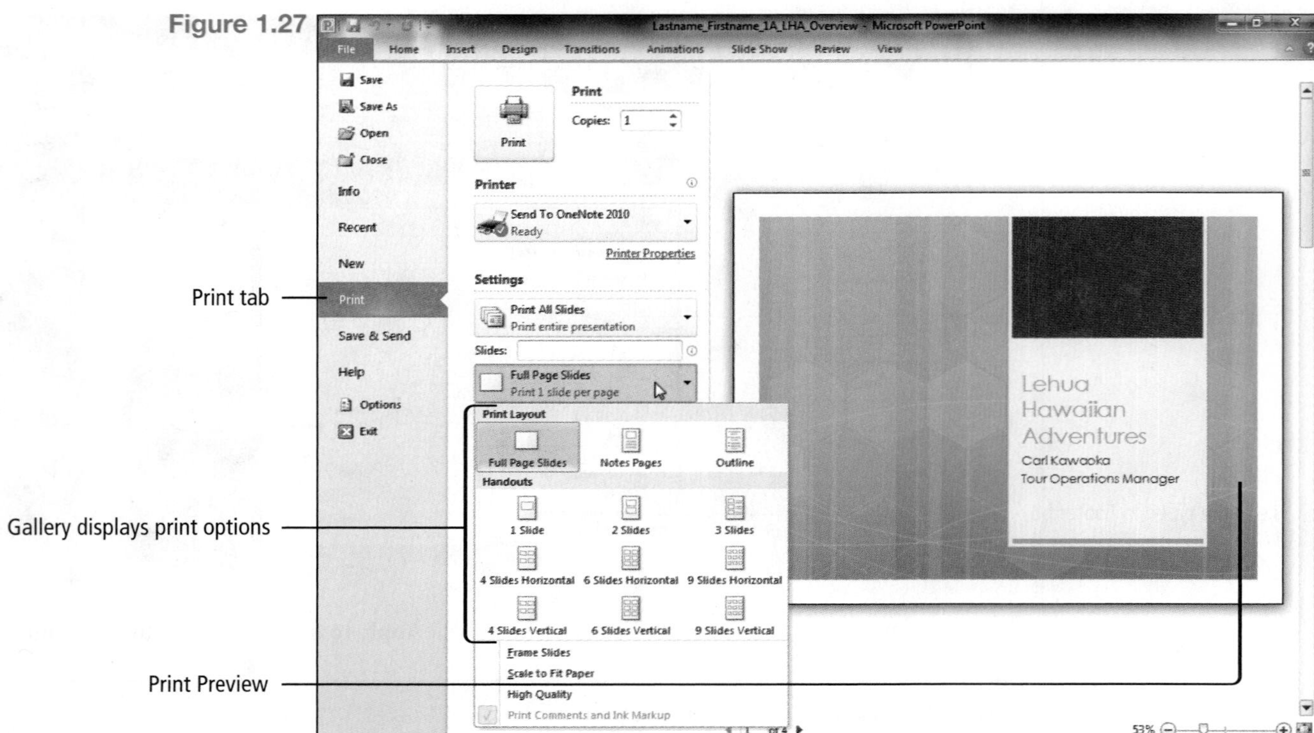

3 In the gallery, under **Handouts**, click **4 Slides Horizontal**. Notice that the **Print Preview** on the right displays the slide handout, and that the current date, file name, and page number display in the header and footer.

In the Settings group, the Portrait Orientation option displays so that you can change the print orientation from Portrait to Landscape. The Portrait Orientation option does not display when Full Page Slides is chosen.

4 To print your handout, be sure your system is connected to a printer, and then in the **Print group**, click the **Print** button.

The handout will print on your default printer—on a black and white printer, the colors will print in shades of gray. Backstage view closes and your file redisplays in the PowerPoint window.

5 Click the **File tab** to display **Backstage** view, and then click the **Print tab**. In the **Settings group**, click **4 Slides Horizontal**, and then under **Print Layout**, click **Notes Pages** to view the presentation notes for **Slide 1**; recall that you created notes for **Slide 4**.

Indicated below the Notes page are the current slide number and the number of pages that will print when Notes page is selected. You can use the Next Page and Previous Page arrows to display each Notes page in the presentation.

6 At the bottom of the **Print Preview**, click the **Next Page** button ▶ three times so that **Page 4** displays. Compare your screen with Figure 1.28.

The notes that you created for Slide 4 display below the image of the slide.

Figure 1.28

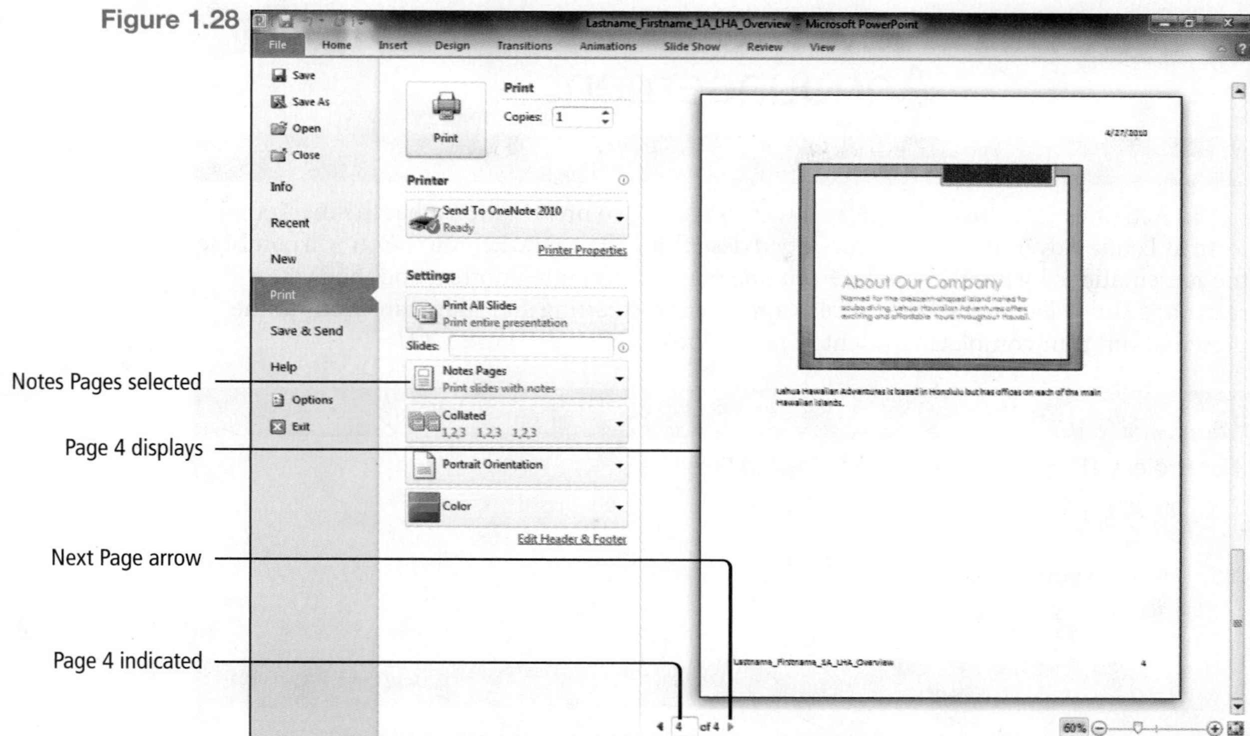

7 In the **Settings group**, click in the **Slides** box, and then type **4** so that only the Notes pages for **Slide 4** will print. In the **Settings group**, click **Notes Pages**, and then below the gallery, select **Frame Slides**. In the **Print group**, click the **Print** button to print the Notes page.

8 Click the **File tab** to redisplay **Backstage** view, be sure the **Info tab** is active, and then in the third panel, click **Properties**. Click **Show Document Panel**, and then in the **Author** box, delete any text and type your firstname and lastname.

9 In the **Subject** box, type your course name and section number. In the **Keywords** box, type **company overview** and then **Close** the Document Information Panel.

10 **Save** your presentation. On the right end of the title bar, click the **Close** button to close the presentation and close PowerPoint.

End You have completed Project 1A

Project 1B New Product Announcement

Project Activities

In Activities 1.14 through 1.23, you will combine two presentations that the marketing team at Lehua Adventure Travels developed describing their new Ecotours. You will combine the presentations by inserting slides from one presentation into another, and then you will rearrange and delete slides. You will also apply font formatting and slide transitions to the presentation. Your completed presentation will look similar to Figure 1.29.

Project Files

For Project 1B, you will need the following files:

p01B_Ecotours
p01B_Slides

You will save your presentation as:

Lastname_Firstname_1B_Ecotours

Project Results

Figure 1.29
Project 1B—Ecotours

Objective 5 | Edit an Existing Presentation

Recall that editing refers to the process of adding, deleting, and modifying presentation content. You can edit presentation content in either the Slide pane or the Slides/Outline pane.

Activity 1.14 | Displaying and Editing the Presentation Outline

You can display the presentation outline in the Slides/Outline pane and edit the presentation text. Changes that you make in the outline are immediately displayed in the Slide pane.

1 **Start** PowerPoint. From your student files, open **p01B_Ecotours**. On the **File tab**, click **Save As**, navigate to your **PowerPoint Chapter 1** folder, and then using your own name, save the file as **Lastname_Firstname_1B_Ecotours**

2 In the **Slides/Outline pane**, click the **Outline tab** to display the presentation outline. If necessary, below the Slides/Outline pane, drag the scroll box all the way to the left so that the slide numbers display. Compare your screen with Figure 1.30.

The outline tab is wider than the Slides tab so that you have additional space to type your text. Each slide in the outline displays the slide number, slide icon, and the slide title in bold.

Figure 1.30

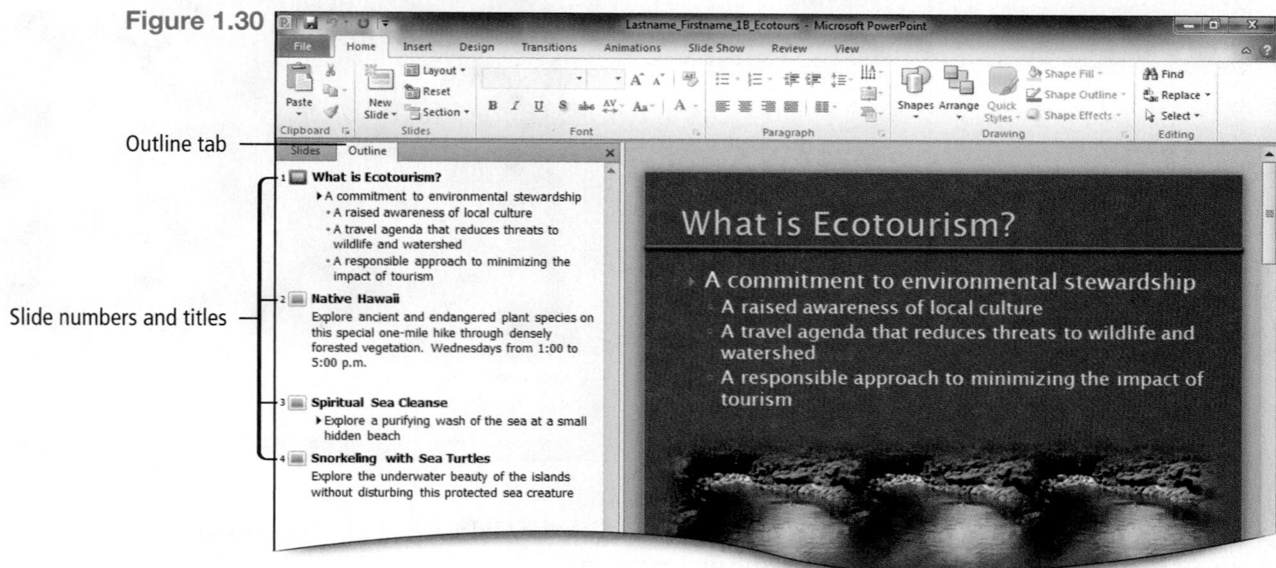

3 In the **Outline tab**, in **Slide 1**, select the last three bullet points, and then compare your screen with Figure 1.31.

Figure 1.31

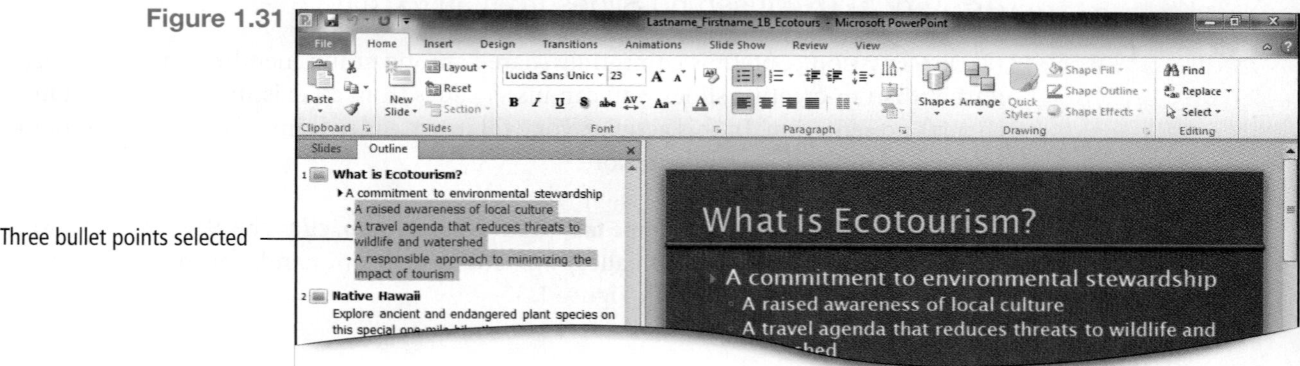

PowerPoint | Chapter 1

4 On the **Home tab**, in the **Paragraph group**, click the **Decrease List Level** button one time to decrease the list level of the selected bullet points.

When you type in the outline or change the list level, the changes also display in the Slide pane.

5 In the **Outline tab**, click anywhere in **Slide 3**, and then click at the end of the last bullet point after the word *beach*. Press Enter to create a new bullet point at the same list level as the previous bullet point. Type **Offered Tuesdays and Thursdays one hour before sunset, weather permitting**

6 Press Enter to create a new bullet point. Type **Fee: $30** and then compare your screen with Figure 1.32.

Figure 1.32

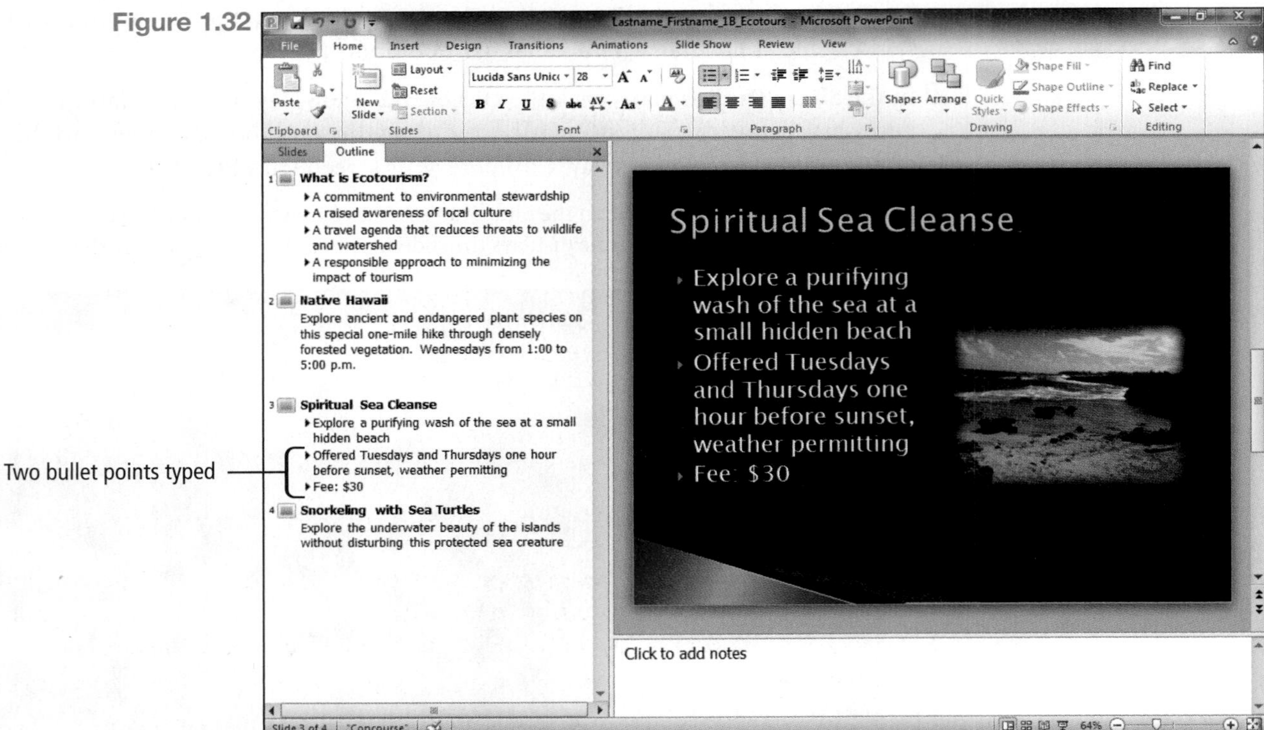

7 In the **Slides/Outline pane**, click the **Slides tab** to display the slide thumbnails, and then **Save** the presentation.

You can type text in the Slide tab or in the Outline tab. Displaying the Outline tab enables you to view the entire flow of the presentation.

Activity 1.15 | Inserting Slides from an Existing Presentation

Presentation content is commonly shared among group members in an organization. Rather than re-creating slides, you can insert slides from an existing presentation into the current presentation. In this activity, you will insert slides from an existing presentation into your 1B_Ecotours presentation.

1 Display **Slide 1**. On the **Home tab**, in the **Slides group**, click the **New Slide button arrow** to display the **Slide Layout** gallery and additional commands for inserting slides. Compare your screen with Figure 1.33.

Figure 1.33

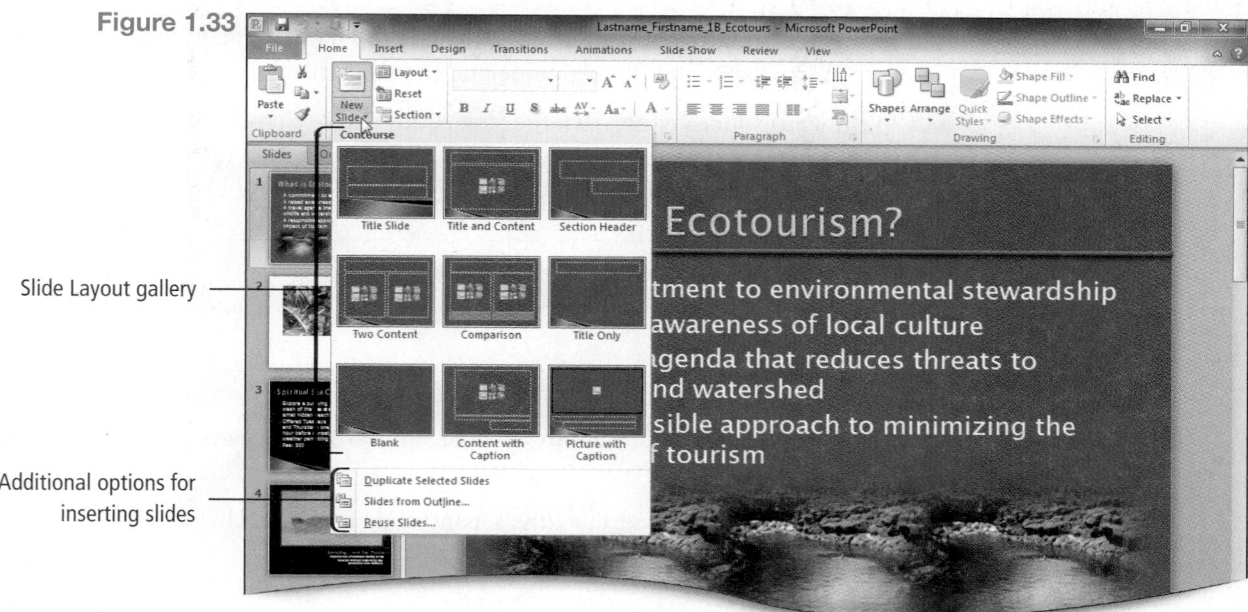

2 Below the gallery, click **Reuse Slides** to open the Reuse Slides pane on the right side of the PowerPoint window.

3 In the **Reuse Slides** pane, click the **Browse** button, and then click **Browse File**. In the **Browse** dialog box, navigate to the location where your student files are stored, and then double-click **p01B_Slides** to display the slides in the Reuse Slides pane.

4 At the bottom of the **Reuse Slides** pane, select the **Keep source formatting** check box, and then compare your screen with Figure 1.34.

By selecting the *Keep source formatting* check box, you retain the formatting applied to the slides when inserted into the existing presentation. When the *Keep source formatting* check box is cleared, the theme formatting of the presentation in which the slides are inserted is applied.

Figure 1.34

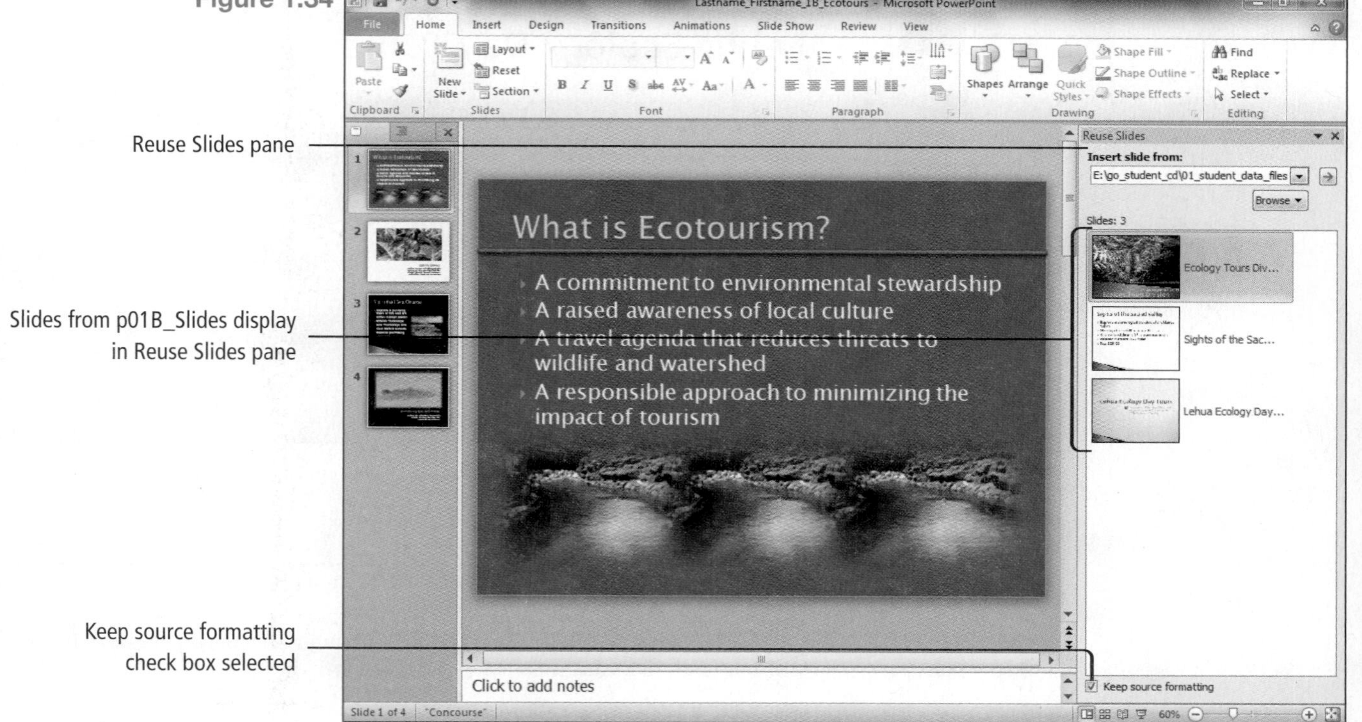

5 In the **Reuse Slides** pane, point to each slide to view a zoomed image of the slide and a ScreenTip displaying the file name and the slide title.

6 In the **Reuse Slides** pane, click the first slide—**Ecology Tours Division**—to insert the slide into the current presentation after Slide 1, and then notice that the original slide background formatting is retained.

> **Note** | Inserting Slides
>
> You can insert slides into your presentation in any order; remember to display the slide that will precede the slide that you want to insert.

7 In your **1B_Ecotours** presentation, in the **Slides/Outline pane**, click **Slide 5** to display it in the **Slide pane**.

8 In the **Reuse Slides** pane, click the second slide and then click the third slide to insert both slides after **Slide 5**.

Your presentation contains seven slides.

9 On **Slide 7**, point to *Lehua*, and then right-click to display the shortcut menu. Click **Ignore all**. Use the same technique to ignore the spelling of the word *Ecotour*. Compare your screen with Figure 1.35.

Figure 1.35

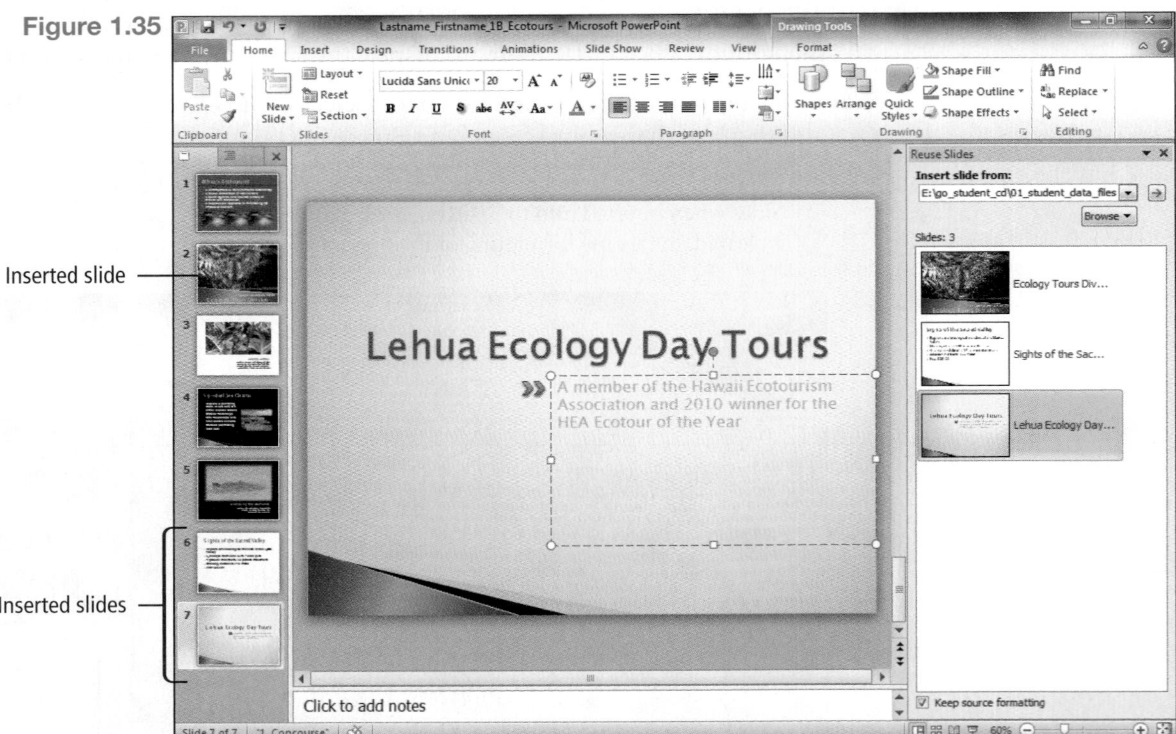

10 **Close** the **Reuse Slides** pane; click **Save**.

> **More Knowledge** | Inserting All Slides
>
> You can insert all of the slides from an existing presentation into the current presentation at one time. In the Reuse Slides pane, right-click one of the slides that you want to insert, and then click Insert All Slides.

Activity 1.16 | Finding and Replacing Text

The Replace command enables you to locate all occurrences of specified text and replace it with alternative text.

1 Display **Slide 1**. On the **Home tab**, in the **Editing group**, click the **Replace** button. In the **Replace** dialog box, in the **Find what** box, type **Ecology** and then in the **Replace with** box, type **Eco** Compare your screen with Figure 1.36.

Figure 1.36

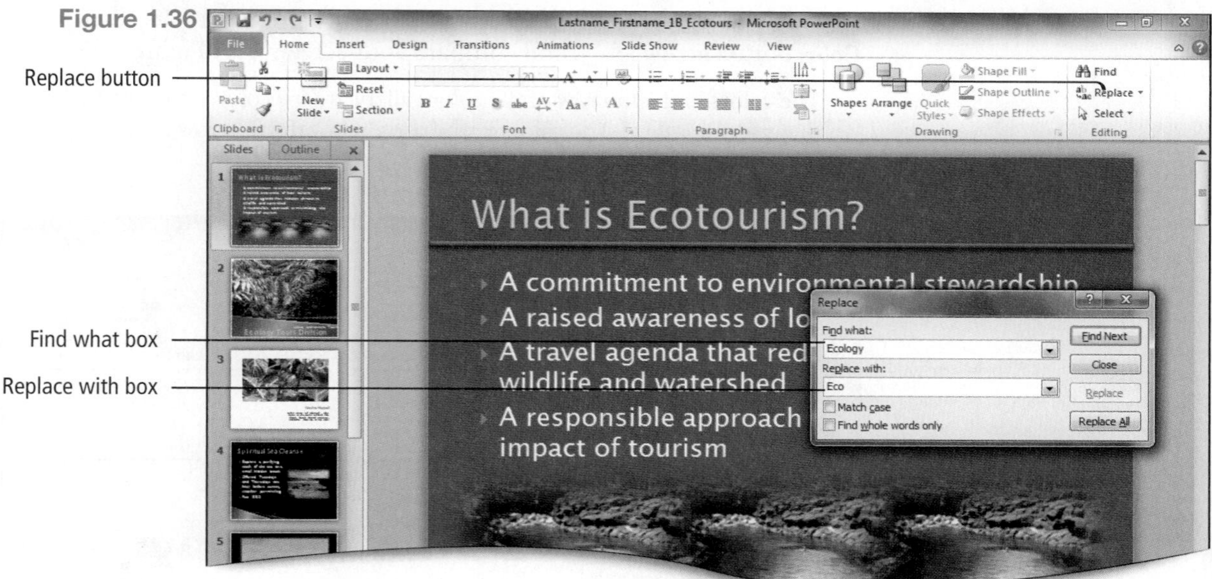

2 In the **Replace** dialog box, click the **Replace All** button.

A message box displays indicating the number of replacements that were made.

3 In the message box, click **OK**, **Close** the **Replace** dialog box, and then click **Save**.

Objective 6 | Format a Presentation

Formatting refers to changing the appearance of the text, layout, and design of a slide. You will find it easiest to do most of your formatting changes in PowerPoint in the Slide pane.

Activity 1.17 | Changing Fonts, Font Sizes, Font Styles, and Font Colors

Recall that a font is a set of characters with the same design and shape and that fonts are measured in points. Font styles include bold, italic, and underline, and you can apply any combination of these styles to presentation text. Font styles and font color are useful to provide emphasis and are a visual cue to draw the reader's eye to important text.

1 On the right side of the **Slides/Outline pane**, drag the scroll box down until **Slide 7** displays, and then click **Slide 7** to display it in the **Slides** pane.

When a presentation contains a large number of slides, a scroll box displays to the right of the slide thumbnails so that you can scroll and then select the thumbnails.

2 Select the title text—*Lehua Eco Day Tours.* Point to the Mini toolbar, and then click the **Font button arrow** to display the available fonts. Click **Arial Black.**

3 Select the light green text in the placeholder below the title, and then on the Mini toolbar, change the **Font** to **Arial Black** and the **Font Size** to **28**. Then, click the **Font Color button arrow** [A▾], and compare your screen with Figure 1.37.

The colors in the top row of the color gallery are the colors associated with the presentation theme—*Concourse.* The colors in the rows below the first row are light and dark variations of the theme colors.

Figure 1.37

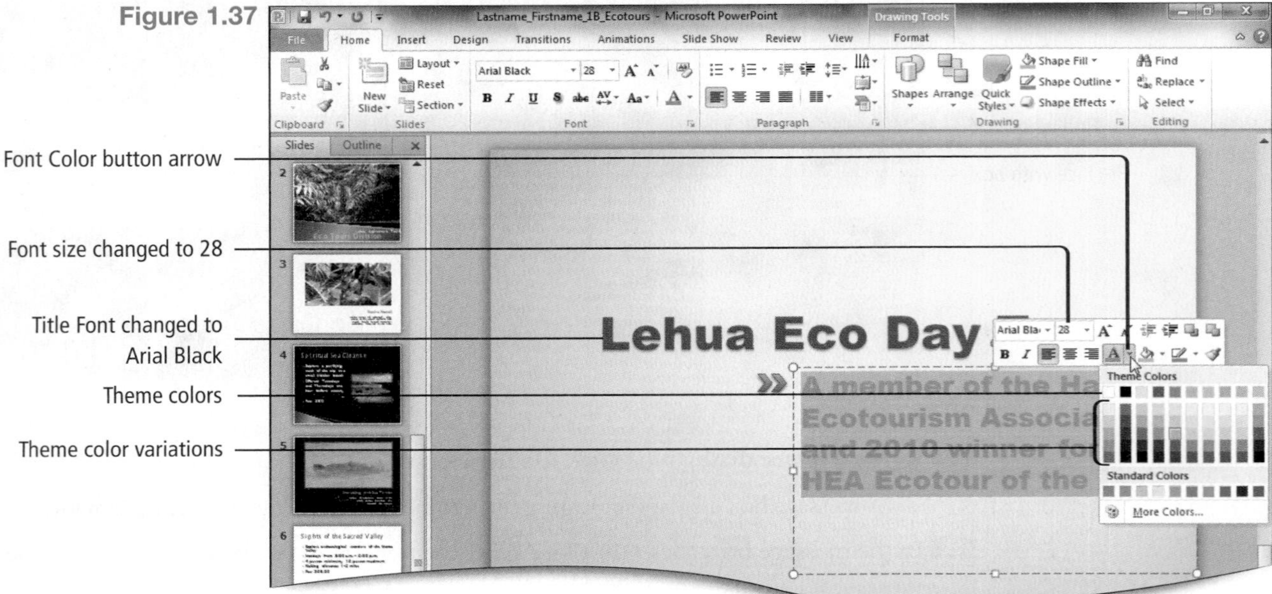

4 Point to several of the colors and notice that a ScreenTip displays the color name and Live Preview displays the selected text in the color to which you are pointing.

5 In the second column of colors, click the first color—**Black, Text 1**—to change the font color. Notice that on the Home tab and Mini toolbar, the lower part of the Font Color button displays the most recently applied font color—Black.

When you click the Font Color button instead of the Font Color button arrow, the color displayed in the lower part of the Font Color button is applied to selected text without displaying the color gallery.

6 Display **Slide 2**, and then select the title *Eco Tours Division.* On the Mini toolbar, click the **Font Color button** [A▾] to apply the font color **Black, Text 1** to the selection. Select the subtitle—*Lehua Adventure Tours*—and then change the **Font Color** to **Black, Text 1**. Compare your screen with Figure 1.38.

Figure 1.38

7 Display **Slide 3**, and then select the title—*Native Hawaii*. From the Mini toolbar, apply **Bold** [B] and **Italic** [I], and then **Save** your presentation.

Activity 1.18 | Aligning Text and Changing Line Spacing

In PowerPoint, ***text alignment*** refers to the horizontal placement of text within a placeholder. You can align left, centered, right, or justified.

1 Display **Slide 2**. Click anywhere in the title—*Eco Tours Division*.

2 On the **Home tab**, in the **Paragraph group**, click the **Align Text Right** button to right align the text within the placeholder.

3 Display **Slide 7**. Click anywhere in the text below the title. In the **Paragraph group**, click the **Line Spacing** button. In the list, click **1.5** to change from single-spacing between lines to one-and-a-half spacing between lines. **Save** your presentation, and then compare your screen with Figure 1.39.

Figure 1.39

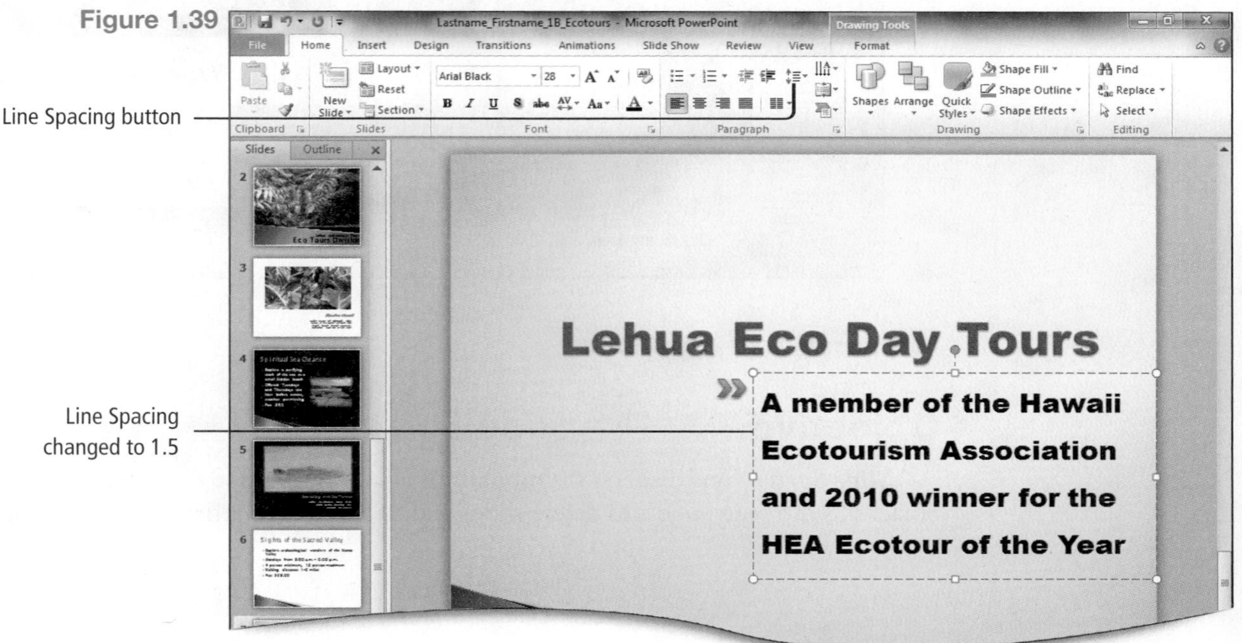

Activity 1.19 | Modifying Slide Layout

Recall that the slide layout defines the placement of the content placeholders on a slide. PowerPoint includes predefined layouts that you can apply to your slide for the purpose of arranging slide elements.

For example, a Title Slide contains two placeholder elements—the title and the subtitle. When you design your slides, consider the content that you want to include, and then choose a layout with the elements that will display the message you want to convey in the best way.

1 Display **Slide 3**. On the **Home tab**, in the **Slides group**, click the **Layout** button to display the **Slide Layout** gallery. Notice that *Content with Caption* is selected.

The selection indicates the layout of the current slide.

2 Click **Picture with Caption** to change the slide layout, and then compare your screen with Figure 1.40.

The Picture with Caption layout emphasizes the picture more effectively than the Content with Caption layout.

Figure 1.40

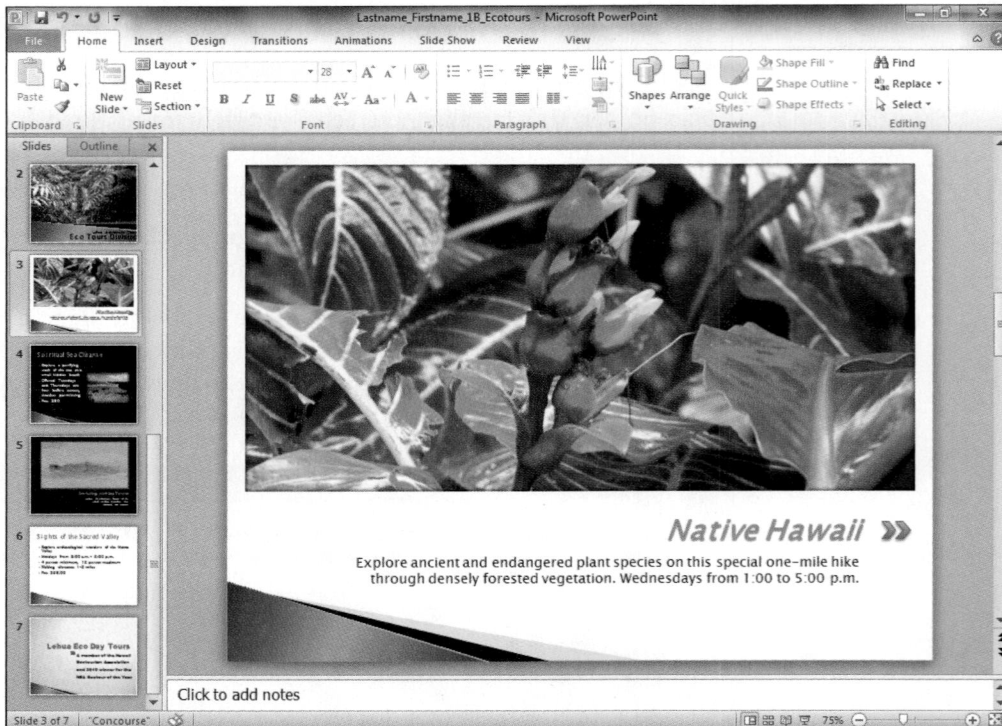

3 **Save** your presentation.

Objective 7 | Use Slide Sorter View

Slide Sorter view displays thumbnails of all of the slides in a presentation. Use Slide Sorter view to rearrange and delete slides and to apply formatting to multiple slides.

Activity 1.20 | Deleting Slides in Slide Sorter View

> **Another Way**
>
> On the Ribbon, click the View tab, and then in the Presentation Views group, click Slide Sorter.

1 In the lower right corner of the PowerPoint window, click the **Slide Sorter** button to display all of the slide thumbnails.

2 Compare your screen with Figure 1.41.

Your slides may display larger or smaller than those shown in Figure 1.41.

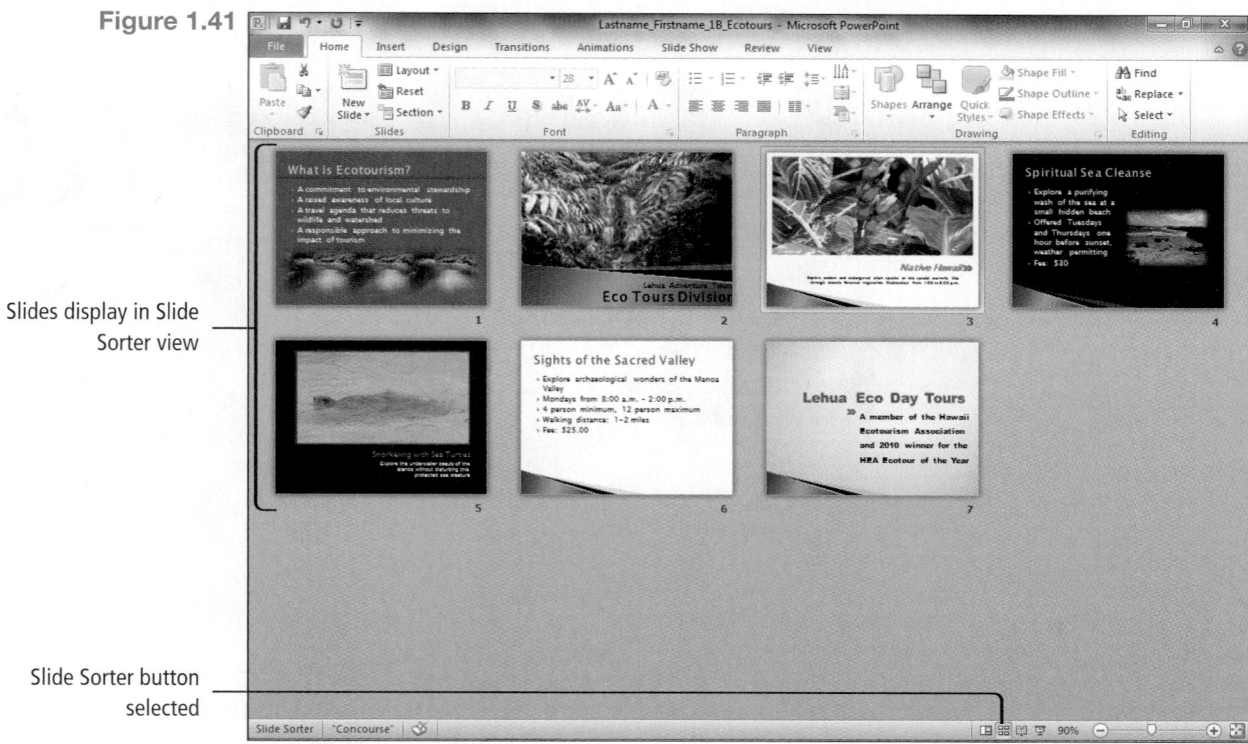

Figure 1.41

3 Click **Slide 6**, and notice that a thick outline surrounds the slide, indicating that it is selected. On your keyboard, press Del to delete the slide. Click **Save**.

Activity 1.21 | Moving Slides in Slide Sorter View

1 With the presentation displayed in Slide Sorter view, point to **Slide 2**. Hold down the left mouse button, and then drag the slide to the left until the vertical move bar and pointer indicating the position to which the slide will be moved is positioned to the left of **Slide 1**, as shown in Figure 1.42.

Figure 1.42

2 Release the mouse button to move the slide to the Slide 1 position in the presentation.

3 Click **Slide 4**, hold down Ctrl, and then click **Slide 5**. Compare your screen with Figure 1.43.

Both slides are outlined, indicating that both are selected. By holding down Ctrl, you can create a group of selected slides.

Figure 1.43

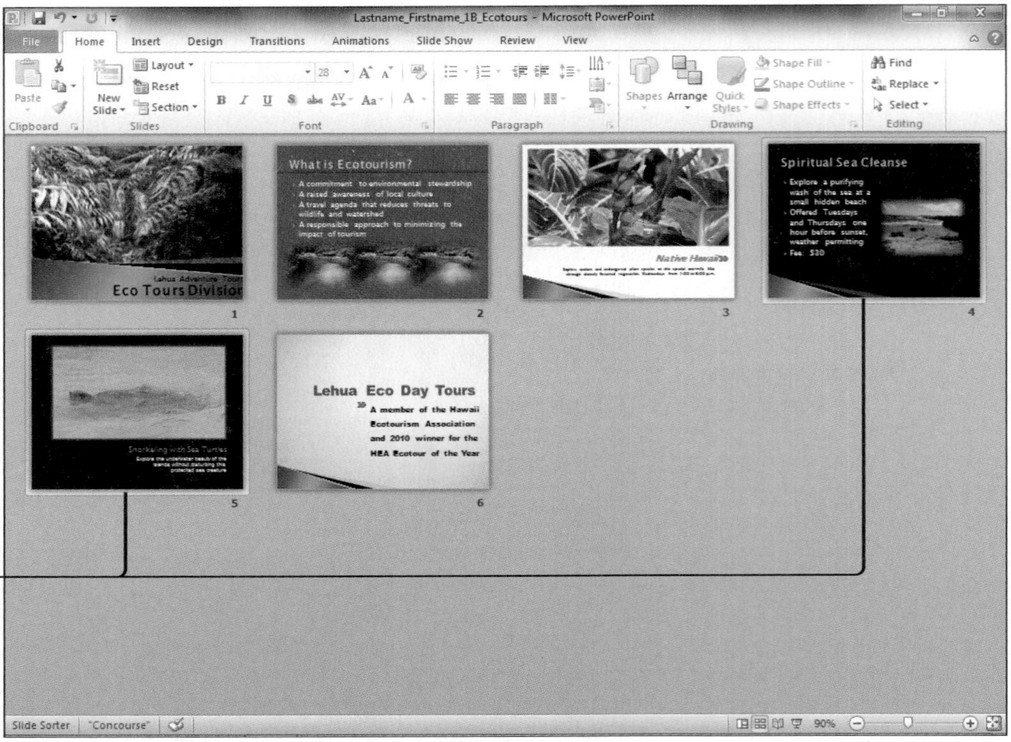

Two slides selected

4 Point to either of the selected slides, hold down the left mouse button, and then drag to position the vertical move bar to the left of **Slide 3**. Release the mouse button to move the two slides, and then compare your screen with Figure 1.44.

Figure 1.44

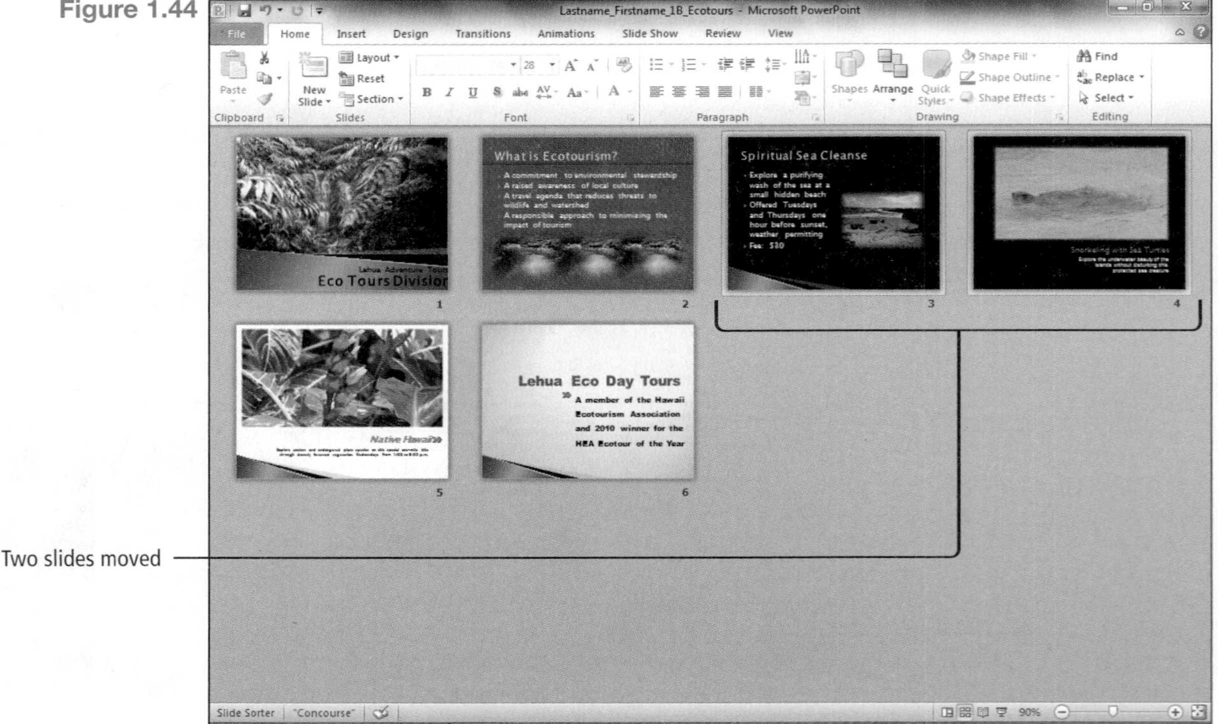

5 In the status bar, click the **Normal** button to return to Normal view. **Save** your presentation.

Objective 8 | Apply Slide Transitions

Slide transitions are the motion effects that occur in Slide Show view when you move from one slide to the next during a presentation. You can choose from a variety of transitions, and you can control the speed and method with which the slides advance.

Activity 1.22 | Applying Slide Transitions to a Presentation

1 Display **Slide 1**. On the **Transitions tab**, in the **Transition to This Slide group**, click the **More** button to display the **Transitions** gallery. Compare your screen with Figure 1.45.

Figure 1.45

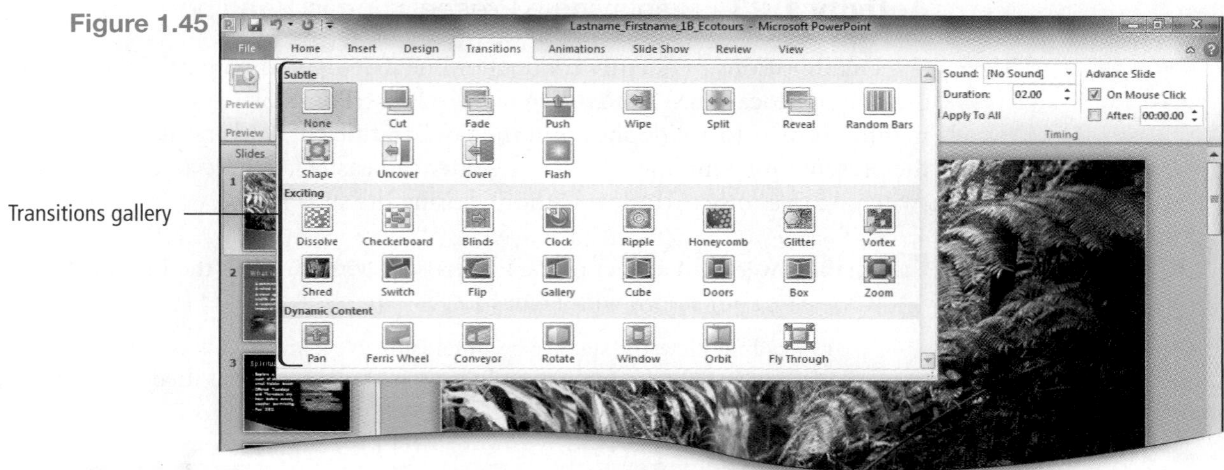

2 Under **Exciting**, click **Doors** to apply and view the transition. In the **Transition to This Slide group**, click the **Effect Options** button to display the directions from which the slide enters the screen. Click **Horizontal**.

The Effect Options vary depending upon the selected transition and include the direction from which the slide enters the screen or the shape in which the slide displays during the transition.

3 In the **Timing group**, notice that the **Duration** box displays *01.40*, indicating that the transition lasts 1.40 seconds. Click the **Duration** box **up spin arrow** two times so that *01.75* displays. Under **Advance Slide**, verify that the **On Mouse Click** check box is selected; select it if necessary. Compare your screen with Figure 1.46.

When the On Mouse Click option is selected, the presenter controls when the current slide advances to the next slide by clicking the mouse button or by pressing Spacebar.

Figure 1.46

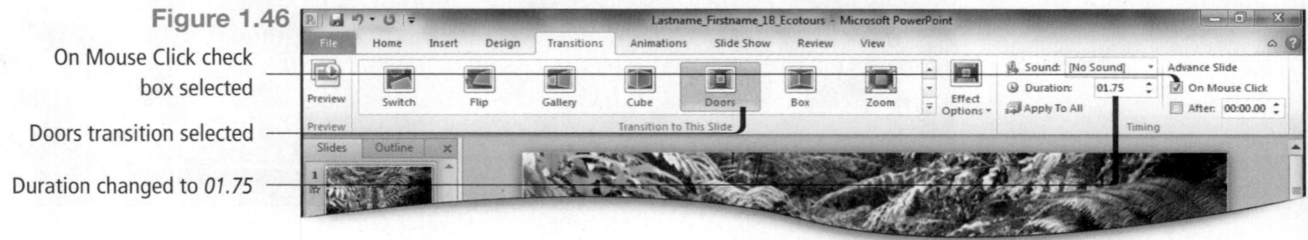

4 In the **Timing group**, click the **Apply To All** button so that the Doors, Horizontal with a Duration of 1.75 seconds transition is applied to all of the slides in the presentation. Notice that in the Slides/Outline pane, a star displays below the slide number providing a visual cue that a transition has been applied to the slide.

5 Click the **Slide Show tab**. In the **Start Slide Show group**, click the **From Beginning** button, and then view your presentation, clicking the mouse button to advance through the slides. When the black slide displays, click the mouse button one more time to display the presentation in Normal view. **Save** your presentation.

> **More Knowledge | Applying Multiple Slide Transitions**
>
> You can apply more than one type of transition in your presentation by displaying the slides one at a time, and then clicking the transition that you want to apply instead of clicking the Apply To All button.

Activity 1.23 | Displaying a Presentation in Reading View

Organizations frequently conduct online meetings when participants are unable to meet in one location. The ***Reading view*** in PowerPoint displays a presentation in a manner similar to a slide show but the taskbar, title bar, and status bar remain available in the presentation window. Thus, a presenter can easily facilitate an online conference by switching to another window without closing the slide show.

> **Another Way**
>
> On the View tab, in the Presentation Views group, click Reading View.

1 In the lower right corner of the PowerPoint window, click the **Reading View** button. Compare your screen with Figure 1.47.

In Reading View, the status bar contains the Next and Previous buttons, which are used to navigate in the presentation, and the Menu button which is used to print, copy, and edit slides.

Figure 1.47

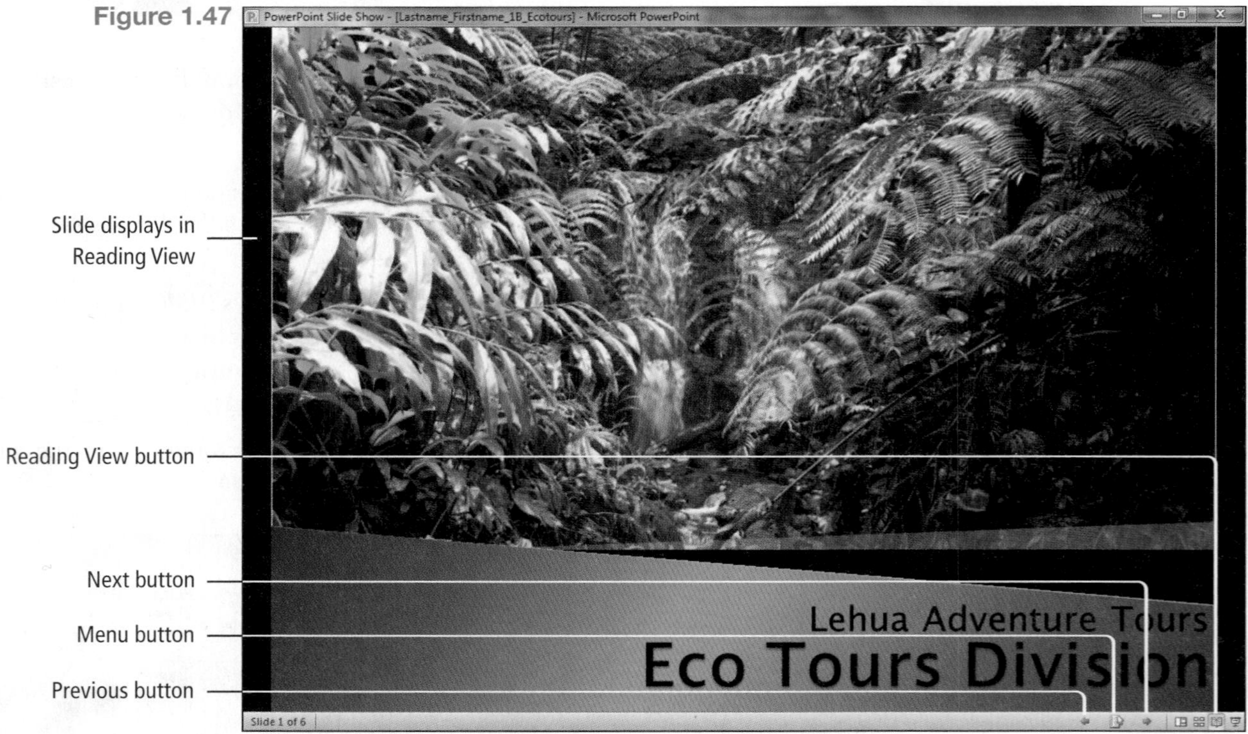

Another Way

Press Esc to exit Reading view and return to Normal view.

2 In the status bar, click the **Next** button to display **Slide 2**. Press Spacebar to display **Slide 3**. Click the left mouse button to display **Slide 4**. In the status bar, click the **Previous** button to display **Slide 3**.

3 In the status bar, click the **Menu** button to display the Reading view menu, and then click **End Show** to return to Normal view.

4 On the **Insert tab**, in the **Text group**, click the **Header & Footer** button, and then click the **Notes and Handouts tab**. Under **Include on page**, select the **Date and time** check box, and if necessary, select **Update automatically**. Clear the **Header** check box, and then select the **Page number** and **Footer** check boxes. In the **Footer** box, using your own name, type **Lastname_Firstname_1B_Ecotours** and then click **Apply to All**.

5 Display **Backstage** view, and then on the right, click **Properties**. Click **Show Document Panel**, and then in the **Author** box, delete any text and type your firstname and lastname. In the **Subject** box, type your course name and section number, and in the **Keywords** box, type **ecotours, ecotourism** **Close** the Document Information Panel.

6 **Save** your presentation. Submit your presentation electronically or print **Handouts, 6 Slides Horizontal**, as directed by your instructor.

7 **Close** the presentation and **Exit** PowerPoint.

More Knowledge | Broadcasting a Slide Show

You can broadcast a slide show to remote viewers by using the PowerPoint Broadcast Service or another broadcast service. To broadcast a slide show, on the Slide Show tab, in the Start Slide Show group, click Broadcast Slide Show, and then follow the instructions in the Broadcast Slide Show dialog box to start the broadcast.

End You have completed Project 1B

Content-Based Assessments

Summary

In this chapter, you created a new PowerPoint presentation and edited an existing presentation by reusing slides from another presentation. You entered, edited, and formatted text in Normal view; worked with slides in Slide Sorter view; and viewed the presentation as a slide show. You also added emphasis to your presentations by inserting pictures, applying font formatting, and modifying layout, alignment, and line spacing.

Key Terms

Matching

Match each term in the second column with its correct definition in the first column by writing the letter of the term on the blank line in front of the correct definition.

____ 1. The PowerPoint view in which the window is divided into three panes—the Slide pane, the Slides/Outline pane, and the Notes pane.

____ 2. A presentation page that can contain text, pictures, tables, charts, and other multimedia or graphic objects.

____ 3. The first slide in a presentation, the purpose of which is to provide an introduction to the presentation topic.

____ 4. A box on a slide with dotted or dashed borders that holds title and body text or other content such as charts, tables, and pictures.

____ 5. A set of unified design elements that provides a look for your presentation by applying colors, fonts, and effects.

____ 6. An outline level in a presentation represented by a bullet symbol and identified in a slide by the indentation and the size of the text.

____ 7. Small circles and squares that indicate that a picture is selected.

____ 8. A green circle located above a selected picture with which you can rotate the selected image.

____ 9. A collection of formatting options that can be applied to a picture, text, or object.

____ 10. A slide that displays at the end of every slide show to indicate that the presentation is over.

____ 11. Printed images of slides on a sheet of paper.

A Black slide
B Formatting
C List level
D Normal view
E Notes page
F Placeholder
G Rotation handle
H Sizing handles
I Slide
J Slide handouts
K Slide transitions
L Style
M Text alignment
N Theme
O Title slide

_____ 12. A printout that contains the slide image on the top half of the page and notes that you have created in the Notes pane on the lower half of the page.

_____ 13. The process of changing the appearance of the text, layout, and design of a slide.

_____ 14. The term that refers to the horizontal placement of text within a placeholder.

_____ 15. Motion effects that occur in Slide Show view when you move from one slide to the next during a presentation.

Multiple Choice

Circle the correct answer.

1. In Normal view, the pane that displays a large image of the active slide is the:
A. Slide pane **B.** Slides/Outline pane **C.** Notes pane

2. In Normal view, the pane that displays below the Slide pane is the:
A. Slide Sorter pane **B.** Slides/Outline pane **C.** Notes pane

3. The buttons in the lower right corner that control the look of the presentation window are the:
A. Normal buttons **B.** View buttons **C.** Thumbnails buttons

4. The process of modifying a presentation by adding and deleting slides or by changing the contents of individual slides is referred to as:
A. Editing **B.** Formatting **C.** Aligning

5. The arrangement of elements, such as title and subtitle text, lists, pictures, tables, charts, shapes, and movies, on a PowerPoint slide is referred to as:
A. Theme modification **B.** Editing **C.** Layout

6. Text that prints at the top of a sheet of slide handouts or notes pages is a:
A. Header **B.** Footer **C.** Page number

7. Text that displays at the bottom of every slide or that prints at the bottom of a sheet of slide handouts or notes.
A. Header **B.** Footer **C.** Page number

8. The command that locates all occurrences of specific text and replaces it with alternative text is:
A. Replace **B.** Find **C.** Edit

9. The view in which all of the slides in your presentation display in miniature is:
A. Slide Sorter view **B.** Normal view **C.** Reading view

10. A view similar to Slide Show view but that also displays the title bar, status bar, and taskbar is:
A. Slide Sorter view **B.** Normal view **C.** Reading view

Content-Based Assessments

Apply **1A** skills from these Objectives:

1. Create a New Presentation
2. Edit a Presentation in Normal View
3. Add Pictures to a Presentation
4. Print and View a Presentation

Skills Review | Project 1C Tour Hawaii

In the following Skills Review, you will create a new presentation by inserting content and pictures, adding notes and footers, and applying a presentation theme. Your completed presentation will look similar to Figure 1.48.

Project Files

For Project 1C, you will need the following files:

New blank PowerPoint presentation
p01C_Harbor
p01C_View

You will save your presentation as:

Lastname_Firstname_1C_Tour_Hawaii

Project Results

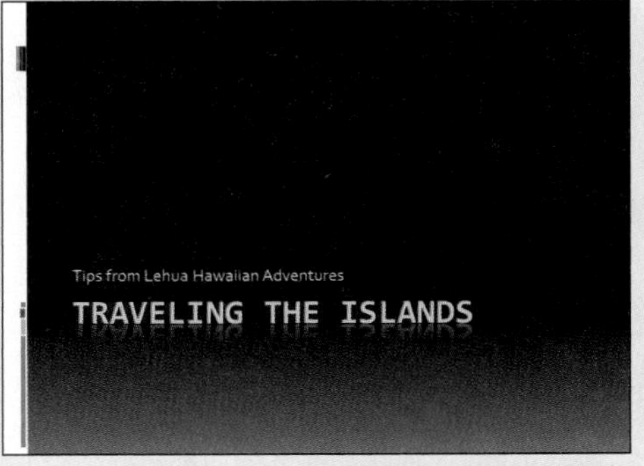

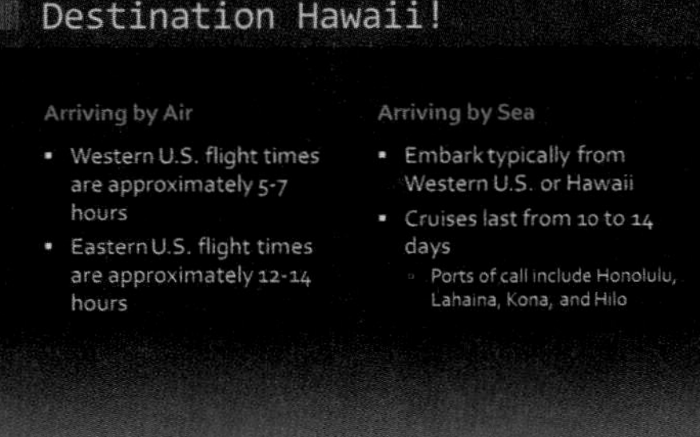

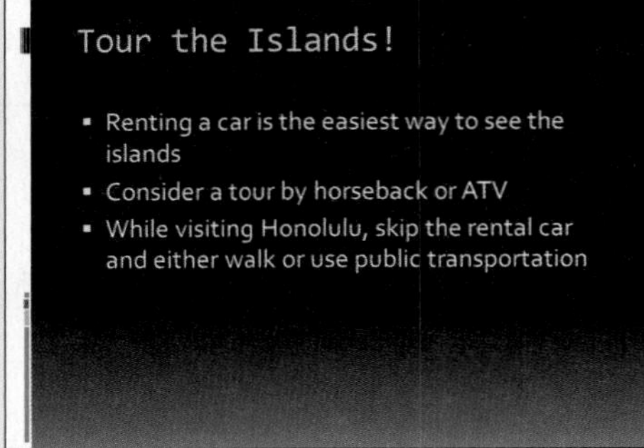

Figure 1.48

(Project 1C Tour Hawaii continues on the next page)

Skills Review | Project 1C Tour Hawaii (continued)

1 **Start** PowerPoint to display a new blank presentation in Normal view.

a. In the **Slide pane**, click in the title placeholder, which contains the text *Click to add title*. Type **Traveling the Islands**

b. Click in the subtitle placeholder, and then type **Tips from Lehua Hawaiian Adventures**

c. Right-click *Lehua*, and then on the shortcut menu, click **Ignore All**.

d. On the Ribbon, click the **Design tab**. In the **Themes group**, click the **More** button to display the **Themes gallery**. Recall that the themes display alphabetically. Using the ScreenTips, locate and then click **Metro** to apply the Metro theme to the presentation.

e. On the Quick Access Toolbar, click the **Save** button, navigate to your **PowerPoint Chapter 1** folder, and then **Save** the presentation as **Lastname_Firstname_1C_Tour_Hawaii**

2 On the **Home tab**, in the **Slides group**, click the **New Slide button arrow**. In the gallery, click the **Picture with Caption** layout to insert a new slide.

a. In the **Slide pane**, click the text *Click to add title*, and then type **Plan Ahead!**

b. Click in the text placeholder below the title, and then type **A little planning will go a long way toward creating a memorable and trouble-free vacation to the islands.**

c. In the picture placeholder, click the **Insert picture from File** button, and then navigate to your student data files. Click **p01C_View**, and then press Enter to insert the picture.

d. With the picture selected, on the **Format tab**, in the **Picture Styles group**, click the **More** button to display the **Picture Styles** gallery. Use the ScreenTips to locate, and then click the style **Soft Edge Oval**.

e. In the **Adjust group**, click the **Artistic Effects** button, and then in the fourth row, click the second effect—**Texturizer**.

3 On the **Home tab**, in the **Slides group**, click the **New Slide button arrow**. In the gallery, click the **Comparison** layout to insert a new slide. In the title placeholder, type **Destination Hawaii!**

a. Below the title, on the left side of the slide, click in the placeholder containing the pink words *Click to add text*. Type **Arriving by Air**

b. On the right side of the slide, click in the placeholder containing the pink words *Click to add text*. Type **Arriving by Sea**

c. On the left side of the slide, click in the content placeholder. Type **Western U.S. flight times are approximately 5–7 hours** and then press Enter. Type **Eastern U.S. flight times are approximately 12–14 hours**

d. On the right side of the slide, click in the content placeholder. Type **Embark typically from Western U.S. or Hawaii** and then press Enter. Type **Cruises last from 10 to 14 days**

e. Press Enter, and then on the **Home tab**, in the **Paragraph group**, click the **Increase List Level** button, and then type **Ports of call include Honolulu, Lahaina, Kona, and Hilo**

f. Right-click *Lahaina*, and then on the shortcut menu, click **Ignore All**. **Save** your presentation.

4 On the **Home tab**, in the **Slides group**, click the **New Slide button arrow**. In the gallery, click **Title and Content** to insert a new slide. In the title placeholder, type **Tour the Islands!**

a. In the content placeholder, type the following three bullet points:

Renting a car is the easiest way to see the islands

Consider a tour by horseback or ATV

While visiting Honolulu, skip the rental car and either walk or use public transportation

b. Below the slide, click in the **Notes pane**, and then type **Rental car company offices are located at each major airport.**

5 Insert a **New Slide** using the **Picture with Caption** layout.

a. In the title placeholder, type **Explore!** In the text placeholder, type **Regardless of the mode of transportation that you choose, explore Hawaii for an unforgettable vacation!**

b. In the center of the large picture placeholder, click the **Insert Picture from File** button. Navigate to your student files, and then insert **p01C_Harbor**.

c. With the picture selected, on the **Format tab**, in the **Picture Styles group**, click the **More** button to display the **Picture Styles** gallery. In the first row, click the sixth style—**Soft Edge Rectangle**.

(Project 1C Tour Hawaii continues on the next page)

Skills Review | Project 1C Tour Hawaii (continued)

6 On the Ribbon, click the **Slide Show tab**. In the **Start Slide Show group**, click the **From Beginning** button.

a. Click the left mouse button or press Spacebar to advance to the second slide. Continue to click or press Spacebar until the last slide displays, and then click or press Spacebar one more time to display a black slide.

b. With the black slide displayed, click the left mouse button or press Spacebar to exit the slide show and return to the presentation.

7 Click the **Insert tab**, and then in the **Text group**, click the **Header & Footer** button to display the **Header and Footer** dialog box.

a. In the **Header and Footer** dialog box, click the **Notes and Handouts tab**. Under **Include on page**, select the **Date and time** check box. If necessary, click the Update automatically option button so that the current date prints on the notes and handouts.

b. If necessary, clear the Header check box to omit this element. Select the **Page number** and **Footer** check boxes. In the **Footer** box, type **Lastname_Firstname_1C_Tour_Hawaii** and then click **Apply to All**.

c. Click the **File tab** to display **Backstage** view, and then on the right, click **Properties**. Click **Show Document Panel**, and then in the **Author** box, delete any text and type your firstname and lastname. In the **Subject** box, type your course name and section number, and in the **Keywords** box, type **travel tips, tour tips, trip planning Close** the Document Information Panel.

d. **Save** your presentation. Submit your presentation electronically or print **Handouts, 6 Slides Horizontal** as directed by your instructor. **Close** the presentation.

End **You have completed Project 1C**

Content-Based Assessments

Apply **1B** skills from these Objectives:

5 Edit an Existing Presentation
6 Format a Presentation
7 Use Slide Sorter View
8 Apply Slide Transitions

Skills Review | Project 1D Luau Information

In the following Skills Review, you will edit an existing presentation by inserting slides from another presentation, applying font and slide formatting, and applying slide transitions. Your completed presentation will look similar to Figure 1.49.

Project Files

For Project 1D, you will need the following files:

p01D_Luau_Information
p01D_History_of_Luaus

You will save your presentation as:

Lastname_Firstname_1D_Luau_Information

Project Results

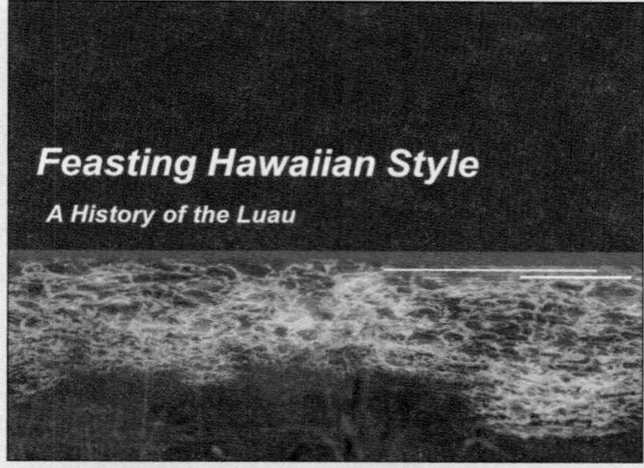

History of the Luau

- Luaus are traditional Hawaiian celebrations
  - Originally called 'aha 'aina, these celebrations became known as luaus about 150 years ago
- The term luau originates from the Hawaiian and other Hawaiian languages, and is the name for the taro leaf
  - Taro leaves are combined with others foods, such as chicken or fish, and then baked in coconut milk

The Modern Luau

- King Kamehameha II introduced the modern luau in 1819
- Luaus were celebrated when a child became of age, when a new canoe was launched, or when warriors returned home after long journeys
- Today, luaus celebrate events such as weddings, graduations, and first birthdays

Celebrating a Luau

- Traditional luau feasts were eaten on the ground and without utensils
- Mats were rolled out and held beautiful centerpieces made of leaves, ferns, and flowers
- Foods were cooked in an underground oven

Luau Delicacies

- Roasted pulled pork cooked in an imu
- Poi: Mashed taro root
- Laulau: Taro leaf tips and fish or chicken wrapped in ti leaves
- Lomi salmon: A salted fish marinated in lemon juice, tomatoes, and onions
- Plantain bananas, yams, fresh fruits

Experience Hawaiian Culture
On a Beautiful Hawaiian Beach

Contact Lehua Hawaiian Adventures for additional information about attending an authentic Hawaiian Luau

Figure 1.49

(Project 1D Luau Information continues on the next page)

Skills Review | Project 1D Luau Information (continued)

1 **Start** PowerPoint. From your student files, open **p01D_Luau_Information**. Click the **File tab** to display **Backstage** view, click **Save As**, navigate to your **PowerPoint Chapter 1** folder, and then using your own name, **Save** the file as **Lastname_Firstname_1D_Luau_Information** Take a moment to examine the content of the presentation.

- **a.** In the **Slides/Outline pane**, click the **Outline tab** to display the presentation outline.
- **b.** In the **Outline tab**, in **Slide 2**, click anywhere in the last bullet point, which begins with the text *Luaus were celebrated*.
- **c.** On the **Home tab**, in the **Paragraph group**, click the **Decrease List Level** button one time.
- **d.** In the **Outline tab**, click at the end of the second bullet after the word *journeys*. Press Enter to create a new bullet point at the same list level as the previous bullet point. Type **Today, luaus celebrate events such as weddings, graduations, and first birthdays**
- **e.** In the **Slides/Outline pane**, click the **Slides tab** to display the slide thumbnails.

2 Display **Slide 1**. On the **Home tab**, in the **Slides group**, click the **New Slide button arrow** to display the **Slide Layout** gallery and additional options for inserting slides.

- **a.** Below the gallery, click **Reuse Slides** to open the **Reuse Slides** pane on the right side of the PowerPoint window.
- **b.** In the **Reuse Slides** pane, click the **Browse** button, and then click **Browse File**. In the **Browse** dialog box, navigate to your student files, and then double-click **p01D_History_of_Luaus**.
- **c.** At the bottom of the **Reuse Slides** pane, select the **Keep source formatting** check box.
- **d.** In the **Reuse Slides** pane, click the first slide—*Luau Information*—to insert the slide into the current presentation after **Slide 1**. In the **Reuse Slides** pane, click the second slide—**Celebrating a Luau** to insert it as the third slide in your presentation.
- **e.** In your **1D_Luau_Information** presentation, in the **Slides/Outline pane**, click **Slide 5** to display it in the **Slide pane**.
- **f.** In the **Reuse Slides** pane, click the third slide—*History of the Luau*—and then click the fourth slide—*Luau Delicacies*—to insert both slides after **Slide 5**. In the **Reuse Slides** pane, click the **Close** button.

3 Display **Slide 1**, and then select the title—*Feasting Polynesian Style*.

- **a.** Point to the Mini toolbar, and then click the **Font arrow** to display the available fonts. Click **Arial**, and then click the **Font Size arrow**. Click **44** to change the font size. Use the Mini toolbar to apply **Bold** and **Italic** to the title.
- **b.** Select the subtitle—*A History of the Luau*. Use the Mini toolbar to change the **Font** to **Arial** and the **Font Size** to **28**.
- **c.** On the **Home tab**, in the **Editing group**, click the **Replace** button. In the **Replace** dialog box, click in the **Find what** box. Type **Polynesian** and then in the **Replace with** box, type **Hawaiian**
- **d.** In the **Replace** dialog box, click the **Replace All** button to replace three occurrences of *Polynesian* with *Hawaiian*. Click **OK** to close the message box, and then in the **Replace** dialog box, click the **Close** button.
- **e.** Display **Slide 6**, and then select the second bullet point, which begins *Originally*. On the Mini toolbar, click the **Font Color button arrow**. Under **Theme Colors**, in the sixth column, click the first color—**Teal, Accent 2**.
- **f.** Select the last bullet point, which begins *Taro leaves*. On the Mini toolbar, click the **Font Color button** to apply **Teal, Accent 2** to the selection.

4 With **Slide 6** displayed, click anywhere in the title.

- **a.** On the **Home tab**, in the **Paragraph group**, click the **Center** button to center the text within the placeholder.
- **b.** Display **Slide 7**, and then **Center** the slide title.
- **c.** Display **Slide 5**, and then click anywhere in the text in the lower portion of the slide. In the **Paragraph group**, click the **Line Spacing** button. In the list, click **1.5** to change from single-spacing between lines to one-and-a-half spacing between lines.
- **d.** Display **Slide 3**. On the **Home tab**, in the **Slides group**, click the **Layout** button to display the **Slide Layout** gallery. Click **Title and Content** to change the slide layout.

5 In the lower right corner of the PowerPoint window, in the **View** buttons, click the **Slide Sorter** button to display the slide thumbnails in Slide Sorter view.

(Project 1D Luau Information continues on the next page)

Skills Review | Project 1D Luau Information (continued)

a. Click **Slide 2**, and then notice that a thick outline surrounds the slide, indicating that it is selected. Press Del to delete the slide.

b. Point to **Slide 5**, hold down the mouse button, and then drag to position the vertical move bar to the left of **Slide 2**. Release the mouse button to move the slide.

c. Point to **Slide 5**, hold down the mouse button, and then drag so that the vertical move bar displays to the right of **Slide 6**. Release the mouse button to move the slide so that it is the last slide in the presentation.

d. Point to **Slide 4**, hold down the mouse button, and then drag so that the vertical move bar displays to the left of **Slide 3**. Release the mouse button to move the slide.

e. In the **View** buttons, click the **Normal** button to return the presentation to Normal view.

6 Display **Slide 1**. On the **Transitions tab**, in the **Transition to This Slide group**, click the **Wipe** button to apply the Wipe transition to the slide.

a. In the **Transition to This Slide group**, click the **Effect Options** button, and then click **From Top**.

b. In the **Timing group**, click the **Duration** box **up spin arrow** twice to change the Duration to *01.50*.

c. In the **Timing group**, under **Advance Slide**, verify that the **On Mouse Click** check box is selected, and select it if necessary.

d. In the **Timing group**, click the **Apply To All** button so that the transition settings are applied to all of the slides in the presentation.

e. Click the **Slide Show tab**. In the **Start Slide Show group**, click the **From Beginning** button, and then view your presentation, clicking the mouse button to advance through the slides. When the black slide displays, click the mouse button one more time to display the presentation in Normal view.

f. On the **Insert tab**, in the **Text group**, click the **Header & Footer** button to display the **Header and Footer** dialog box. Click the **Notes and Handouts tab**. Under **Include on page**, select the **Date and time** check box, and then if necessary, select Update automatically.

g. Clear the **Header** check box if necessary, and then select the **Page number** and **Footer** check boxes. In the **Footer** box, using your own name, type **Lastname_Firstname_1D_Luau_Information** and then click **Apply to All**.

h. Click the **File tab**, and then on the right side of the window, click **Properties**. Click **Show Document Panel**, and then in the **Author** box, delete any text and type your firstname and lastname. In the **Subject** box, type your course name and section number, and in the **Keywords** box, type **luau, Hawaiian history, Hawaiian culture Close** the Document Information Panel.

i. **Save** your presentation. Submit your presentation electronically or print **Handouts, 6 Slides Horizontal** as directed by your instructor. **Close** the presentation.

End **You have completed Project 1D**

Apply 1A skills from these Objectives:

1. Create a New Presentation
2. Edit a Presentation in Normal View
3. Add Pictures to a Presentation
4. Print and View a Presentation

Mastering PowerPoint | Project 1E Boat Tours

In the following Mastering PowerPoint project, you will create a new presentation describing the types of boat tours offered by Lehua Hawaiian Adventures. Your completed presentation will look similar to Figure 1.50.

Project Files

For Project 1E, you will need the following files:

New blank PowerPoint presentation
p01E_Catamaran
p01E_Raft

You will save your presentation as:

Lastname_Firstname_1E_Boat_Tours

Project Results

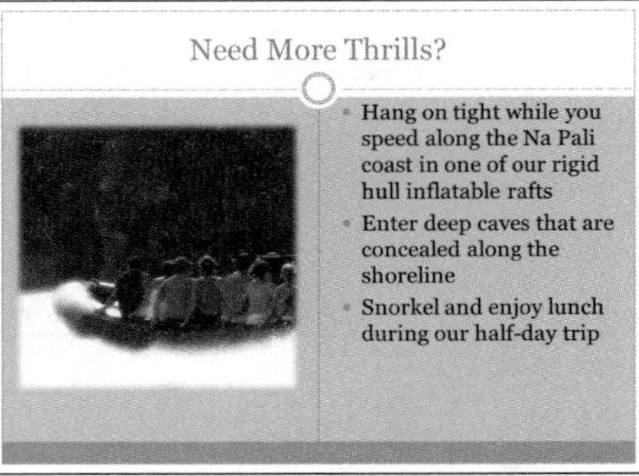

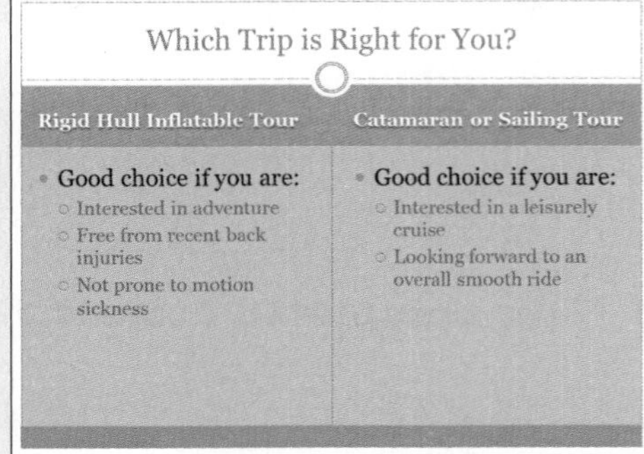

Figure 1.50

(Project 1E Boat Tours continues on the next page)

Mastering PowerPoint | Project 1E Boat Tours (continued)

1 **Start** PowerPoint to display a new blank presentation, and then change the **Design** by applying the **Civic** theme. As the title of this presentation type **Viewing Na Pali by Sea** and as the subtitle type **With Lehua Hawaiian Adventures**

2 Correct spelling errors on this slide by choosing the **Ignore All** option for the words *Pali* and *Lehua*. Save the presentation in your **PowerPoint Chapter 1** folder as **Lastname_Firstname_1E_Boat_Tours**

3 Insert a **New Slide** using the **Content with Caption** layout. In the title placeholder, type **Looking to Relax?** In the large content placeholder on the right side of the slide, from your student files, insert the picture **p01E_Catamaran**. Format the picture with the **Compound Frame, Black** picture style and the **Texturizer** artistic effect.

4 In the text placeholder, type **If an easy day of sailing is your style, consider a morning or sunset cruise on our forty-person catamaran. Our experienced crew will sail our vessel along the Na Pali coast for a view of waterfalls, caves, and beaches. Spinner dolphins often swim alongside and whales can be spotted January through March.**

5 Insert a **New Slide** using the **Two Content** layout. In the title placeholder, type **Need More Thrills?** In the content placeholder on the left side of the slide, from your student files, insert the picture **p01E_Raft**. Format the picture with the **Soft Edge Rectangle** picture style and the **Glow Diffused** artistic effect. In the content placeholder on the right side of the slide, type the following three bullet points:

Hang on tight while you speed along the Na Pali coast in one of our rigid hull inflatable rafts

Enter deep caves that are concealed along the shoreline

Snorkel and enjoy lunch during our half-day trip

6 Insert a **New Slide** using the **Comparison** layout. In the title placeholder, type **Which Trip is Right for You?** In the orange placeholder on the left side of the slide, type **Rigid Hull Inflatable Tour** and in the orange placeholder on the right side of the slide, type **Catamaran or Sailing Tour**

7 In the content placeholder on the left, type each of the following bullet points, increasing the list level for the last three bullet points as indicated:

Good choice if you are:

- **Interested in adventure**
- **Free from recent back injuries**
- **Not prone to motion sickness**

8 In the content placeholder on the right, type each of the following bullet points, increasing the list level for the last two bullet points as indicated:

Good choice if you are:

- **Interested in a leisurely cruise**
- **Looking forward to an overall smooth ride**

9 On **Slide 4**, type the following notes in the **Notes pane**: **If you need assistance deciding which boat tour is right for you, we'll be happy to help you decide.** Insert a **New Slide** using the **Section Header** layout. In the title placeholder, type **Book Your Trip Today!** In the text placeholder, type **Contact Lehua Hawaiian Adventures**

10 Insert a **Header & Footer** on the **Notes and Handouts**. Include the **Date and time** updated automatically, the **Page number**, and a **Footer**—using your own name—with the text **Lastname_Firstname_1E_Boat_Tours** and apply to all the slides.

11 Display the **Document Information Panel**. Replace the text in the **Author** box with your own firstname and lastname. In the **Subject** box, type your course name and section number, and in the **Keywords** box, type **Na Pali, boat tours, sailing** **Close** the Document Information Panel.

12 **Save** your presentation, and then view the slide show from the beginning. Submit your presentation electronically or print **Handouts, 6 Slides Horizontal** as directed by your instructor. **Close** the presentation.

You have completed Project 1E

Apply 1B skills from these Objectives:

- 5 Edit an Existing Presentation
- 6 Format a Presentation
- 7 Use Slide Sorter View
- 8 Apply Slide Transitions

Mastering PowerPoint | Project 1F Helicopter Tour

In the following Mastering PowerPoint project, you will edit a presentation describing the helicopter tours offered by Lehua Hawaiian Adventures. Your completed presentation will look similar to Figure 1.51.

Project Files

For Project 1F, you will need the following files:

p01F_Helicopter_Tour
p01F_Aerial_Views

You will save your presentation as:

Lastname_Firstname_1F_Helicopter_Tour

Project Results

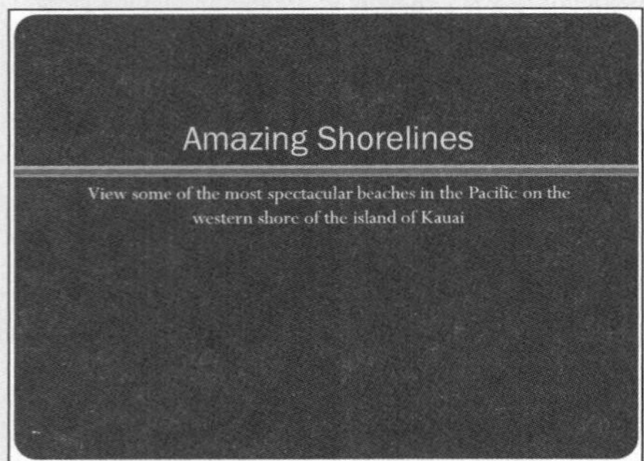

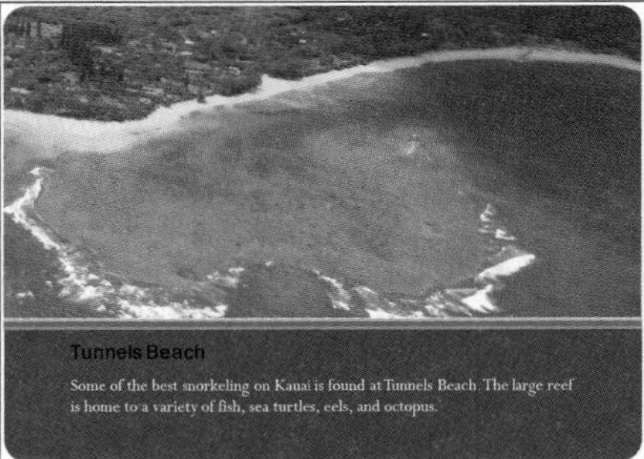

Figure 1.51

(Project 1F Helicopter Tour continues on the next page)

Mastering PowerPoint | Project 1F Helicopter Tour (continued)

1 **Start** PowerPoint, and then from your student data files, open the file **p01F_Helicopter_Tour**. In your **PowerPoint Chapter 1** folder, **Save** the file as **Lastname_Firstname_1F_Helicopter_Tour**

2 Display the presentation **Outline**. In the **Outline tab**, in **Slide 2**, increase the list level of the bullet point that begins *Formed by erosion*. In the **Outline tab**, click at the end of the second bullet point after the word *Kauai*. Press Enter, and then decrease the list level of the new bullet point. Type **Lava flows changed the canyon landscape over the course of centuries**

3 In the **Slides/Outline pane**, click the **Slides tab** to display the slide thumbnails, and then display **Slide 1**. Display the **Reuse Slides** pane, and then click the **Browse** button. Click **Browse File**, and then in the **Browse** dialog box, from your student files, open **p01F_Aerial_Views**. Select the **Keep source formatting** check box, and then from this group of slides, insert the first and second slides—*Aerial View of Kauai* and *Dramatic Overhead*.

4 In the **Slides/Outline pane**, click **Slide 4** to display it in the **Slide pane**, and then from the **Reuse Slides** pane, insert the third, fourth, fifth, and sixth slides—*Na Pali Coast*, *Honopu Beach*, *Amazing Shorelines*, *Tunnels Beach*. **Close** the **Reuse Slides** pane.

5 Display **Slide 1**, and then select the title—*Maui from the Sky*. Change the **Font** to **Arial**, and the **Font Size** to **44**. Change the **Font Color** to **White, Text 1**. Display the **Replace** dialog box. **Replace All** occurrences of the word **Maui** with **Kauai** and then **Close** the **Replace** dialog box.

6 Display **Slide 5**, and then select the paragraph in the content placeholder. Apply **Bold** and **Italic**, and then **Center** the text. Change the **Line Spacing** to **1.5**. Display **Slide 7**, and then change the **Slide Layout** to **Section Header**. **Center** the text in both placeholders.

7 In **Slide Sorter** view, delete **Slide 2**. Then select **Slides 6** and **7** and move both slides so that they are positioned after **Slide 3**. In **Normal** view, display **Slide 1**. Apply the **Split** transition and change the **Effect Options** to **Horizontal Out**. Apply the transition to all of the slides in the presentation. View the slide show from the beginning.

8 **Insert** a **Header & Footer** on the **Notes and Handouts**. Include the **Date and time** updated automatically, the **Page number**, and a **Footer** with the text **Lastname_Firstname_1F_Helicopter_Tour** Apply to all the slides.

9 Check spelling in the presentation. If necessary, select the Ignore All option if proper names are indicated as misspelled.

10 Display the **Document Information Panel**. Replace the text in the **Author** box with your own firstname and lastname. In the **Subject** box, type your course name and section number, and in the **Keywords** box, type **helicopter, Kauai** **Close** the Document Information Panel.

11 **Save** your presentation, and then submit your presentation electronically or print **Handouts, 4 Slides Horizontal** as directed by your instructor. **Close** the presentation.

End **You have completed Project 1F**

Apply **1A** and **1B** skills from these Objectives:

1. Create a New Presentation
2. Edit a Presentation in Normal View
3. Add Pictures to a Presentation
4. Print and View a Presentation
5. Edit an Existing Presentation
6. Format a Presentation
7. Use Slide Sorter View
8. Apply Slide Transitions

Mastering PowerPoint | Project 1G Volcano Tour

In the following Mastering PowerPoint project, you will edit an existing presentation that describes the tour of Volcanoes National Park offered by Lehua Hawaiian Adventures. Your completed presentation will look similar to Figure 1.52.

Project Files

For Project 1G, you will need the following files:

p01G_Crater_Information
p01G_Lava
p01G_Volcano_Tour

You will save your presentation as:

Lastname_Firstname_1G_Volcano_Tour

Project Results

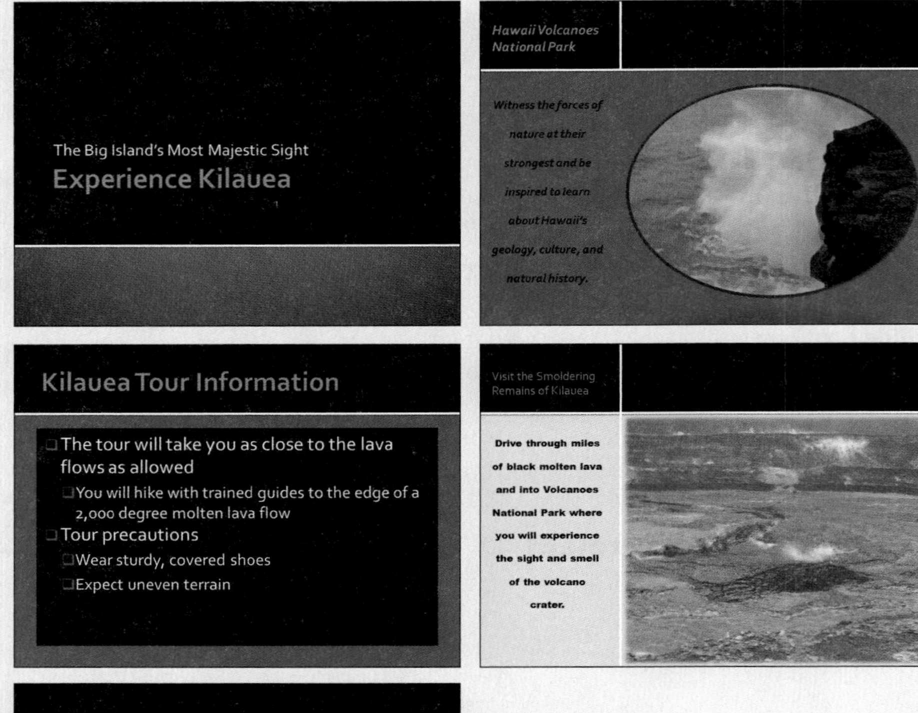

Figure 1.52

(Project 1G Volcano Tour continues on the next page)

Mastering PowerPoint | Project 1G Volcano Tour (continued)

1 **Start** PowerPoint, and then from your student files, open the file **p01G_Volcano_Tour**. In your **PowerPoint Chapter 1** folder, **Save** the file as **Lastname_Firstname_1G_Volcano_Tour**

2 Replace all occurrences of the text **Diamond Head** with **Kilauea** Display **Slide 3**, open the **Reuse Slides** pane, and then from your student files browse for and display the presentation **p01G_Crater_Information**. If necessary, clear the Keep source formatting check box, and then insert both slides from the **p01G_Crater_Information** file. **Close** the **Reuse Slides** pane.

3 Display the presentation outline, and then in **Slide 3**, increase the list level of the bullet point beginning *You will hike*. In either the **Slide pane** or the **Outline**, click at the end of the last bullet point after the word *flow*, and then insert a new bullet point. Decrease its list level. Type **Tour precautions** and then press Enter. Increase the list level, and then type the following two bullet points.

Wear sturdy, covered shoes

Expect uneven terrain

4 Display the slide thumbnails. In **Slide 1**, select the subtitle—*The Big Island's Most Majestic Sight*—and then change the **Font Color** to **White, Text 1** and the **Font Size** to **28**. On **Slide 2**, center the caption text located below the slide title and apply **Bold** and **Italic**. Change the **Line Spacing** to **2.0**. Click in the content placeholder on the right, and then from your student files, insert the picture **p01G_Lava**. Format the picture with the **Beveled Oval, Black** picture style and the **Paint Brush** artistic effect.

5 In **Slide Sorter** view, move **Slide 5** between **Slides 3** and **4**. In **Normal** view, on **Slide 5**, change the slide **Layout** to **Title Slide**, and then type the following notes in the **Notes pane**: **Recent volcanic activity at the national park site may result in changes to the tour itinerary.** Apply the **Uncover** transition and change the **Effect Options** to **From Top**. Change the **Timing** by increasing the **Duration** to **01.50**. Apply the transition effect to all of the slides. View the slide show from the beginning.

6 **Insert** a **Header & Footer** on the **Notes and Handouts**. Include the **Date and time** updated automatically, the **Page number**, and a **Footer**, using your own name, with the text **Lastname_Firstname_1G_Volcano_Tour**

7 Check spelling in the presentation. If necessary, select the Ignore All option if proper names are indicated as misspelled.

8 Display the **Document Information Panel**. Replace the text in the **Author** box with your own firstname and lastname. In the **Subject** box, type your course name and section number, and in the **Keywords** box, type **Kilauea, volcano** **Close** the Document Information Panel.

9 **Save** your presentation. Submit your presentation electronically or print **Handouts, 6 Slides Horizontal** as directed by your instructor. **Close** the presentation.

End **You have completed Project 1G**

Apply a combination of the 1A and 1B skills.

GO! Fix It | Project 1H Hawaii Guide

Project Files

For Project 1H, you will need the following files:

p01H_Hawaii_Guide
p01H_Islands

You will save your presentation as:

Lastname_Firstname_1H_Hawaii_Guide

In this project, you will edit a presentation prepared by Lehua Hawaiian Adventures that describes some of the activities on each of the Hawaiian Islands. From the student files that accompany this textbook, open the file p01H_Hawaii_Guide, and then save the file in your chapter folder as **Lastname_Firstname_1H_Hawaii_Guide**

To complete the project, you should know:

- All of the slides in the p01H_Islands presentation should be reused in this presentation and inserted after Slide 2. Correct two spelling errors and ignore all instances of proper names that are indicated as misspelled.
- The Opulent theme should be applied.
- Slides 3 through 8 should be arranged alphabetically according to the name of the island
- On the Maui and Molokai slides, the list level of the second bullet points should decreased.
- The Layout for Slide 2 should be Section Header, the slide should be moved to the end of the presentation, and the Flip transition using the Left effect option should be applied to all of the slides in the presentation.
- Document Properties should include your name, course name and section, and the keywords **guide, islands** A Header & Footer should be inserted on the Notes and Handouts that includes the Date and time updated automatically, the Page number, and a Footer with the text **Lastname_Firstname_1H_Hawaii_Guide**

Save your presentation and submit electronically or print Handouts, 4 Slides Horizontal as directed by your instructor. Close the presentation.

End You have completed Project 1H

Apply a combination of the 1A and 1B skills.

GO! Make It | Project 1I Dolphin Encounter

Project Files

For Project 1I, you will need the following files:

p01I_Dolphin_Encounters
p01I_Dolphin

You will save your presentation as:

Lastname_Firstname_1I_Dolphin_Encounters

From your student files, open p01I_Dolphin_Encounters, and then save it in your PowerPoint Chapter 1 folder as **Lastname_Firstname_1I_Dolphin_Encounters**

By using the skills you practiced in this chapter, create the slide shown in Figure 1.53 by inserting a new Slide 2 with the layout and text shown in the figure. The title font size is 36, and the font color is Black, Background 1. The caption text font is Arial, and the font size is 16 with bold and italic applied. To complete the slide, from your student files, insert the picture p01H_Dolphin. Insert the date and time updated automatically, the file name, and a page number in the Notes and Handouts footer. In the Document Information Panel, add your name and course information and the keyword **dolphin** Save your presentation, and then print or submit electronically as directed by your instructor.

Project Results

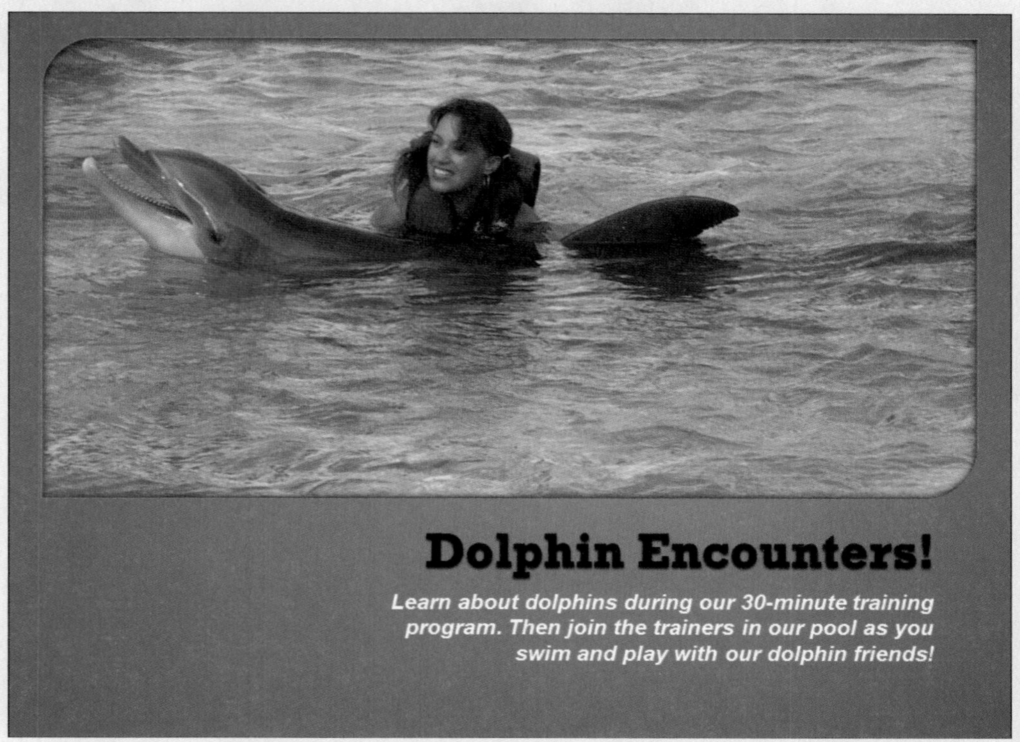

Figure 1.53

End **You have completed Project 1I**

Content-Based Assessments

Apply a combination of the 1A and 1B skills.

GO! Solve It | Project 1J Planning Tips

Project Files

For Project 1J, you will need the following file:

p01J_Planning_Tips

You will save your presentation as:

Lastname_Firstname_1J_Planning_Tips

Open the file p01J_Planning_Tips and save it as **Lastname_Firstname_1J_Planning_Tips** Complete the presentation by applying a theme and by correcting spelling errors. Format the presentation attractively by applying appropriate font formatting and by changing text alignment and line spacing. Change the layout of at least one slide to a layout that will accommodate a picture. Insert a picture that you have taken yourself, or use one of the pictures in your student data files that you inserted in other projects in this chapter. On the last slide, insert an appropriate picture, and then apply picture styles to both pictures. Apply slide transitions to all of the slides in the presentation, and then insert a header and footer that includes the date and time updated automatically, the file name in the footer, and the page number. Add your name, your course name and section number, and the keywords **planning, weather** to the Properties area. Save and print or submit as directed by your instructor.

Performance Elements	Performance Level: Exemplary: You consistently applied the relevant skills	Proficient: You sometimes, but not always, applied the relevant skills	Developing: You rarely or never applied the relevant skills
Apply a theme	An appropriate theme was applied to the presentation.	A theme was applied but was not appropriate for the presentation.	A theme was not applied.
Apply font and slide formatting	Font and slide formatting is attractive and appropriate.	Adequately formatted but difficult to read or unattractive.	Inadequate or no formatting.
Use appropriate pictures and apply styles attractively	Two appropriate pictures are inserted and styles are applied attractively.	Pictures are inserted but styles are not applied or are inappropriately applied.	Pictures are not inserted.

End **You have completed Project 1J**

Apply a combination of the **1A** and **1B** skills.

GO! Solve It | Project 1K Hikes

Project Files

For Project 1K, you will need the following file:

p01K_Hikes

You will save your presentation as:

Lastname_Firstname_1K_Hikes

Open the file p01K_Hikes and save it as **Lastname_Firstname_1K_Hikes** Complete the presentation by applying an appropriate theme. Move Slide 2 to the end of the presentation, and then change the layout to one appropriate for the end of the presentation. Format the presentation attractively by applying font formatting and by changing text alignment and line spacing. Review the information on Slide 3, and then increase list levels appropriately on this slide. Apply picture styles to the two pictures in the presentation and an artistic effect to at least one picture. Apply slide transitions to all of the slides. Insert a header and footer that includes the date and time updated automatically, the file name in the footer, and the page number. Add your name, your course name and section number, and the keywords **hiking Akaka Falls, Waimea Canyon** to the Properties area. Save and print or submit as directed by your instructor.

	Performance Level		
Performance Elements	**Exemplary:** You consistently applied the relevant skills	**Proficient:** You sometimes, but not always, applied the relevant skills	**Developing:** You rarely or never applied the relevant skills
Apply a theme	An appropriate theme was applied to the presentation.	A theme was applied but was not appropriate for the presentation.	A theme was not applied.
Apply appropriate formatting	Formatting is attractive and appropriate.	Adequately formatted but difficult to read or unattractive.	Inadequate or no formatting.
Apply appropriate list levels	List levels are applied appropriately.	Some, but not all, list levels are appropriately applied.	Changes to list levels were not made.

End **You have completed Project 1K**

Outcomes-Based Assessments

Rubric

The following outcomes-based assessments are *open-ended assessments*. That is, there is no specific correct result; your result will depend on your approach to the information provided. Make *Professional Quality* your goal. Use the following scoring rubric to guide you in *how* to approach the problem, and then to evaluate *how well* your approach solves the problem.

The *criteria*—Software Mastery, Content, Format and Layout, and Process—represent the knowledge and skills you have gained that you can apply to solving the problem. The *levels of performance*—Professional Quality, Approaching Professional Quality, or Needs Quality Improvements—help you and your instructor evaluate your result.

	Your completed project is of Professional Quality if you:	**Your completed project is Approaching Professional Quality if you:**	**Your completed project Needs Quality Improvements if you:**
1-Software Mastery	Choose and apply the most appropriate skills, tools, and features and identify efficient methods to solve the problem.	Choose and apply some appropriate skills, tools, and features, but not in the most efficient manner.	Choose inappropriate skills, tools, or features, or are inefficient in solving the problem.
2-Content	Construct a solution that is clear and well organized, contains content that is accurate, appropriate to the audience and purpose, and is complete. Provide a solution that contains no errors in spelling, grammar, or style.	Construct a solution in which some components are unclear, poorly organized, inconsistent, or incomplete. Misjudge the needs of the audience. Have some errors in spelling, grammar, or style, but the errors do not detract from comprehension.	Construct a solution that is unclear, incomplete, or poorly organized; contains some inaccurate or inappropriate content; and contains many errors in spelling, grammar, or style. Do not solve the problem.
3-Format and Layout	Format and arrange all elements to communicate information and ideas, clarify function, illustrate relationships, and indicate relative importance.	Apply appropriate format and layout features to some elements, but not others. Overuse features, causing minor distraction.	Apply format and layout that does not communicate information or ideas clearly. Do not use format and layout features to clarify function, illustrate relationships, or indicate relative importance. Use available features excessively, causing distraction.
4-Process	Use an organized approach that integrates planning, development, self-assessment, revision, and reflection.	Demonstrate an organized approach in some areas, but not others; or, use an insufficient process of organization throughout.	Do not use an organized approach to solve the problem.

Apply a combination of the 1A and 1B skills.

GO! Think | Project 1L Big Island

Project Files

For Project 1L, you will need the following files:

New blank PowerPoint presentation
p01L_Fishing
p01L_Monument

You will save your presentation as:

Lastname_Firstname_1L_Big_Island

Carl Kawaoka, Tour Operations Manager for Lehua Hawaiian Adventures, is developing a presentation describing sea tours on the Big Island of Hawaii to be shown at a travel fair on the mainland. In the presentation, Carl will be showcasing the company's two most popular sea excursions: The Captain Cook Monument Snorkeling Tour and the Kona Deep Sea Fishing Tour.

On the Captain Cook Monument Snorkeling Tour, guests meet at 8:00 a.m. at the Lehua Hawaiian Adventures Kona location and then board a 12-passenger rigid hull inflatable raft. Captained by a U.S. Coast Guard licensed crew, the raft is navigated along the Hawaii coastline, exploring sea caves, lava tubes, and waterfalls. Upon arrival at the Monument, guests snorkel in Hawaii's incredible undersea world of colorful fish, sea turtles, and stingrays. Lehua Hawaiian Adventures provides the lunch, snacks, drinks, and snorkeling equipment and asks that guests bring their own towels, sunscreen, swim suits, and sense of adventure. This tour lasts 5 hours and the fee is $85.

On the Kona Deep Sea Fishing Tour, guests meet at 7:00 a.m. at the Lehua Hawaiian Adventures Kona location and then board a 32-foot Blackfin fishing boat. The boat is captained by a U.S. Coast Guard licensed crew of three. A maximum of six guests are allowed on each trip, which sails, weather permitting, every Wednesday, Friday, and Saturday. For deep sea fishing, there is no better place than the Kona coast. On full-day adventures, it is common for guests to catch marlin, sailfish, ahi, ono, and mahi-mahi. This tour lasts 8 hours and the fee is $385.

Using the preceding information, create a presentation that Carl can show at the travel fair. The presentation should include four to six slides describing the two tours. Apply an appropriate theme and use slide layouts that will effectively present the content. From your student files, insert the pictures p01L_Fishing and p01L_Monument on appropriate slides and apply picture styles or artistic effects to enhance the pictures. Apply font formatting and slide transitions, and modify text alignment and line spacing as necessary. Save the file as **Lastname_Firstname_1L_Big_Island** and then insert a header and footer that include the date and time updated automatically, the file name in the footer, and the page number. Add your name, your course name and section number, and the keywords **sea tours, deep sea fishing, snorkeling tours** to the Properties area. Save and print or submit as directed by your instructor.

End **You have completed Project 1L**

Outcomes-Based Assessments

Apply a combination of the **1A** and **1B** skills.

GO! Think | Project 1M Beaches

Project Files

For Project 1M, you will need the following files:

New blank PowerPoint presentation
p01M_Black_Sand
p01M_Kite_Surf
p01M_Lithified_Cliffs
p01M_Reef
p01M_Tide_Pools

You will save your presentation as:

Lastname_Firstname_1M_Beaches

Katherine Okubo, President of Lehua Hawaiian Adventures, is making a presentation to groups of tourists at a number of hotels on the Hawaiian Islands. She would like to begin the presentation with an introduction to the beaches of Hawaii before discussing the many ways in which her company can assist tourists with selecting the places they would like to visit. The following paragraphs contain some of the information about the shorelines and beaches that Katherine would like to include in the presentation.

The shorelines of Hawaii vary tremendously, from black sand beaches with pounding surf to beaches of pink and white sand with calm waters perfect for snorkeling. Many of the shorelines provide picturesque hiking, shallow tide pools for exploring, beautiful reef where fish and turtles delight snorkelers, and waves that the most adventurous kite and board surfers enjoy. The terrain and the water make it easy for visitors to find a favorite beach in Hawaii.

The northern shore of Oahu is famous for its surfing beaches, while the southern shores of Kauai provide hikers with amazing views of the lithified cliffs formed by the power of the ocean. Black sand beaches are common on Hawaii, formed by the lava flows that created the islands. The reef that buffers many beaches from the open ocean is home to a wide variety of sea life that can be enjoyed while scuba diving and snorkeling.

Using the preceding information, create the first four to six slides of a presentation that Katherine can show during her discussion. Apply an appropriate theme and use slide layouts that will effectively present the content. Several picture files listed at the beginning of this project have been provided that you can insert in your presentation. Apply font formatting, picture styles, and slide transitions, and modify text alignment and line spacing as necessary. Save the file as **Lastname_Firstname_1M_Beaches** and then insert a header and footer that include the date and time updated automatically, the file name in the footer, and the page number. Add your name, your course name and section number, and the keywords **beaches, Black Sands beach, tide pools, lithified cliffs, scuba, snorkeling** to the Properties area. Save and print or submit as directed by your instructor.

End You have completed Project 1M

Outcomes-Based Assessments

Apply a combination of the **1A** and **1B** skills.

You and GO! | Project 1N Travel

Project Files

For Project 1N, you will need the following files:

New blank PowerPoint presentation

You will save your presentation as:

Lastname_Firstname_1N_Travel

Choose a place to which you have traveled or would like to travel. Create a presentation with at least six slides that describes the location, the method of travel, the qualities of the location that make it interesting or fun, the places you can visit, and any cultural activities in which you might like to participate. Choose an appropriate theme, slide layouts, and pictures, and then format the presentation attractively. Save your presentation as **Lastname_Firstname_1N_Travel** and submit as directed.

End **You have completed Project 1N**

Formatting PowerPoint Presentations

OUTCOMES

At the end of this chapter you will be able to:

OBJECTIVES

Mastering these objectives will enable you to:

PROJECT 2A

Format a presentation to add visual interest and clarity.

1. Format Numbered and Bulleted Lists (p. 109)
2. Insert Clip Art (p. 113)
3. Insert Text Boxes and Shapes (p. 118)
4. Format Objects (p. 122)

PROJECT 2B

Enhance a presentation with WordArt and diagrams.

5. Remove Picture Backgrounds and Insert WordArt (p. 131)
6. Create and Format a SmartArt Graphic (p. 136)

Nikolay Okhitin\Shutterstock

In This Chapter

A PowerPoint presentation is a visual aid in which well-designed slides help the audience understand complex information while keeping them focused on the message. Color is an important element that enhances your slides and draws the audience's interest by creating focus. When designing the background and element colors for your presentation, be sure that the colors you use provide contrast so that the text is visible on the background

Fascination Entertainment Group operates 15 regional theme parks across the United States, Mexico, and Canada. Park types include traditional theme parks, water parks, and animal parks. This year the company will launch three of its new "Fascination Parks" where attractions combine fun and the discovery of math and science information, and where teens and adults enjoy the free Friday night concerts.

Project 2A Employee Training Presentation

Project Activities

In Activities 2.01 through 2.14, you will format a presentation for Yuki Hiroko, Director of Operations for Fascination Entertainment Group, that describes important safety guidelines for employees. Your completed presentation will look similar to Figure 2.1.

Project Files

For Project 2A, you will need the following file:

p02A_Safety

You will save your presentation as:

Lastname_Firstname_2A_Safety

Project Results

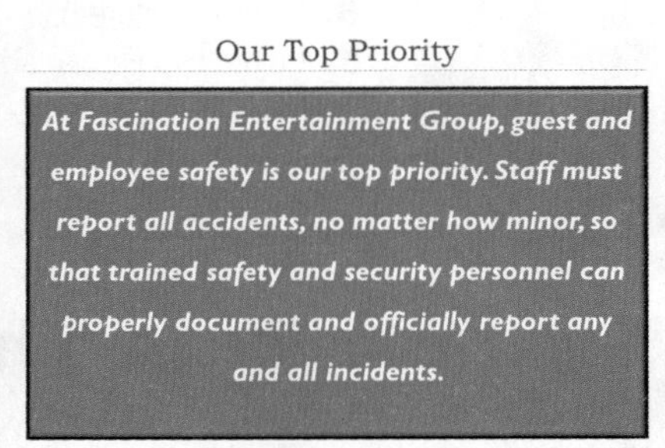

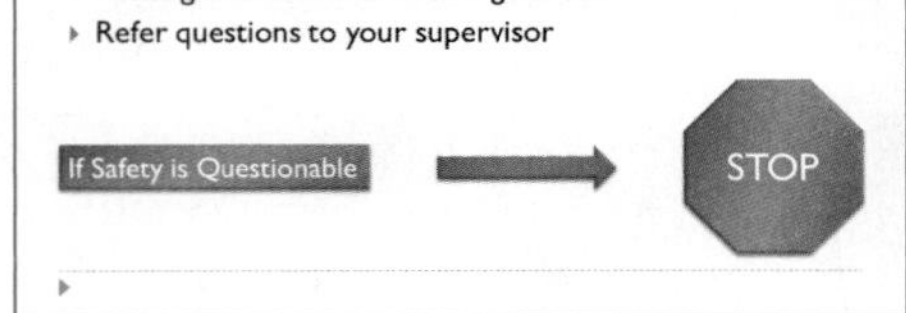

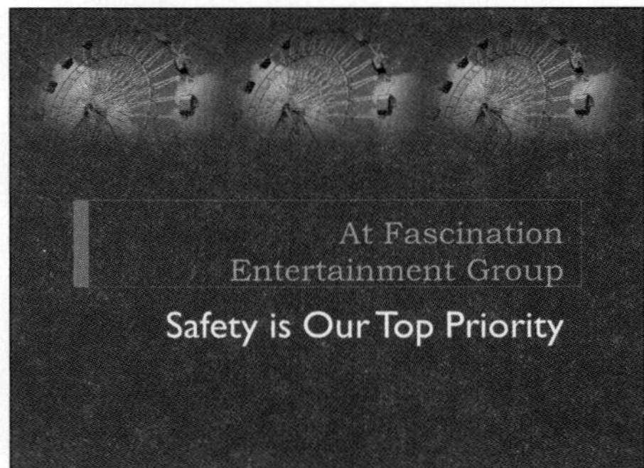

Figure 2.1
Project 2A Safety

Objective 1 | Format Numbered and Bulleted Lists

Recall that formatting is the process of changing the appearance of the text, layout, or design of a slide. You can format slide content by changing the bulleted and numbered list styles and colors.

Activity 2.01 | Selecting Placeholder Text

Recall that a placeholder is a box on a slide with dotted or dashed borders that holds title and body text or other content such as charts, tables, and pictures. You can format placeholder contents by selecting text or by selecting the entire placeholder.

1 **Start** PowerPoint. From the student files that accompany this textbook, locate and open **p02A_Safety**. On the **File tab**, click **Save As**, and then navigate to the location where you are storing your projects for this chapter. Create a new folder named **PowerPoint Chapter 2** and then in the **File name** box and using your own name, type **Lastname_Firstname_2A_Safety** Click **Save** or press Enter. Take a moment to view each slide and become familiar with the contents of this presentation.

2 Display **Slide 2**. Click anywhere in the content placeholder with the single bullet point, and then compare your screen with Figure 2.2.

A dashed border displays, indicating that you can make editing changes to the placeholder text.

Figure 2.2

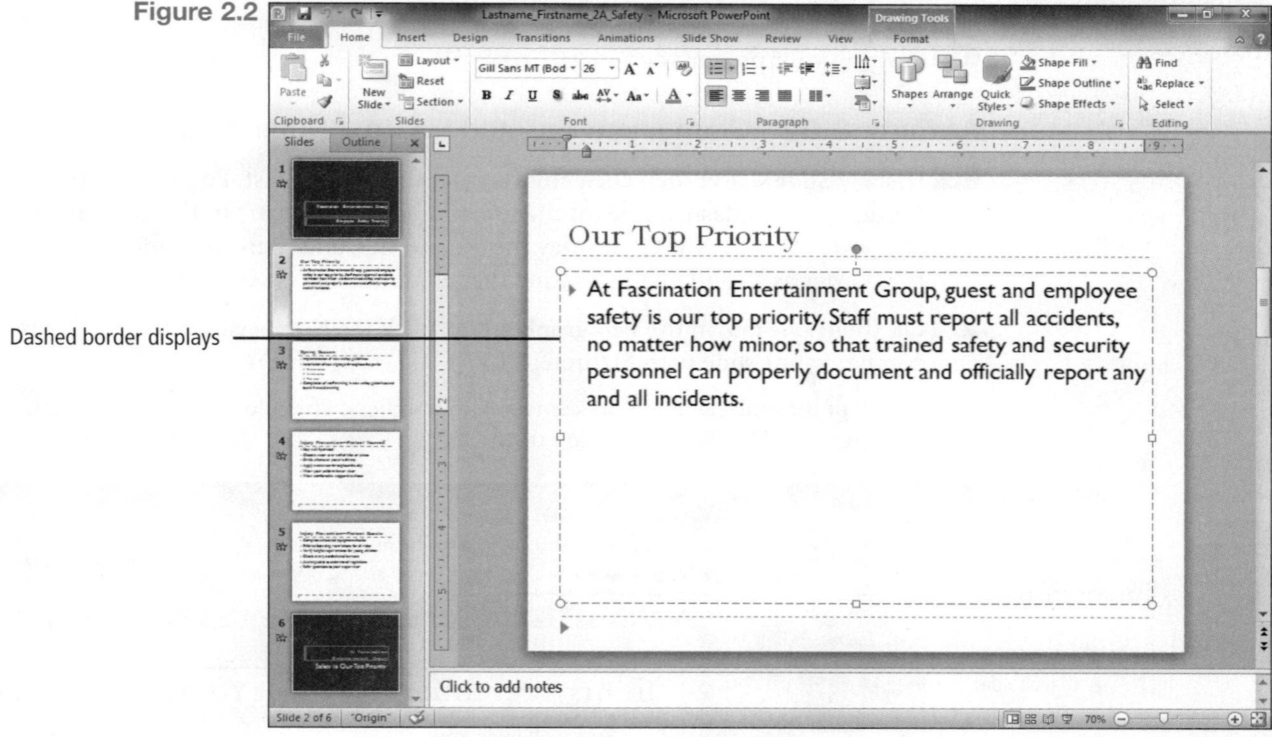

3 Point anywhere on the dashed border to display the [pointer] pointer, and then click one time to display the border as a solid line. Compare your screen with Figure 2.3.

When a placeholder's border displays as a solid line, all of the text in the placeholder is selected, and any formatting changes that you make will be applied to *all* of the text in the placeholder.

Figure 2.3

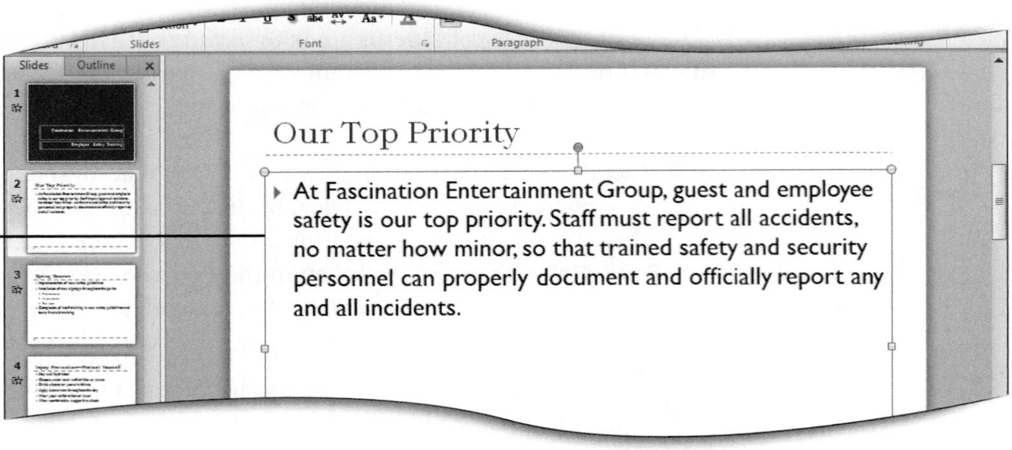

Solid border indicates that all placeholder text is selected

Our Top Priority

At Fascination Entertainment Group, guest and employee safety is our top priority. Staff must report all accidents, no matter how minor, so that trained safety and security personnel can properly document and officially report any and all incidents.

4 With the border of the placeholder displaying as a solid line, click in the **Font Size** box [44] to select the number, and then type **30** and press Enter. Notice that the font size of *all* of the placeholder text increases.

5 **Save** your presentation.

Activity 2.02 | Changing a Bulleted List to a Numbered List

1 Display **Slide 4**, and then click anywhere in the bulleted list. Point to the blue dashed border (the red dashed lines at the top and bottom are part of the decorative elements of the theme) to display the [pointer] pointer, and then click one time to display the border as a solid line indicating that all of the text is selected.

2 On the **Home tab**, in the **Paragraph group**, click the **Numbering** button [Numbering], and then compare your slide with Figure 2.4.

All of the bullet symbols are converted to numbers. The color of the numbers is determined by the presentation theme.

Figure 2.4

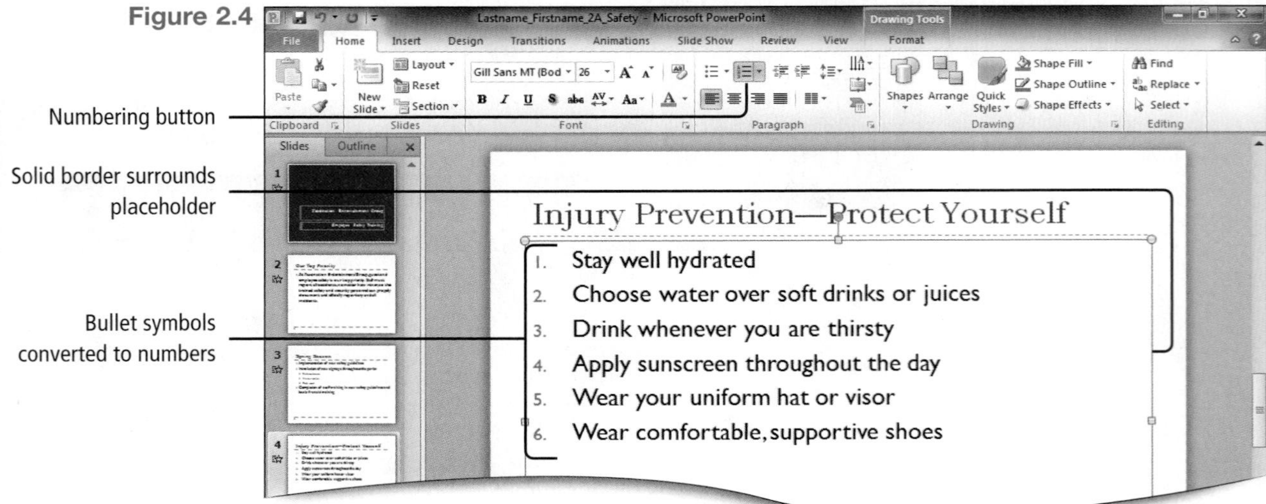
Numbering button
Solid border surrounds placeholder
Bullet symbols converted to numbers
Lastname_Firstname_2A_Safety - Microsoft PowerPoint
Injury Prevention—Protect Yourself
1. Stay well hydrated
2. Choose water over soft drinks or juices
3. Drink whenever you are thirsty
4. Apply sunscreen throughout the day
5. Wear your uniform hat or visor
6. Wear comfortable, supportive shoes

> **Alert!** | **Did You Display the Numbering Gallery?**
>
> If you clicked the Numbering button arrow instead of the Numbering button, the Numbering gallery displays. Click the Numbering button arrow again to close the gallery, and then click the Numbering button to convert the bullets to numbers.

3 **Save** your presentation.

Activity 2.03 | Modifying a Bulleted List Style

The presentation theme includes default styles for the bullet points in content placeholders. You can customize a bullet by changing its style, color, and size.

1 Display **Slide 3**, and then select the three second-level bullet points—*Ride entrances*, *Visitor center*, and *Rest areas*.

2 On the **Home tab**, in the **Paragraph group**, click the **Bullets button arrow** to display the **Bullets** gallery, and then compare your screen with Figure 2.5.

The Bullets gallery displays several bullet characters that you can apply to the selection.

Figure 2.5

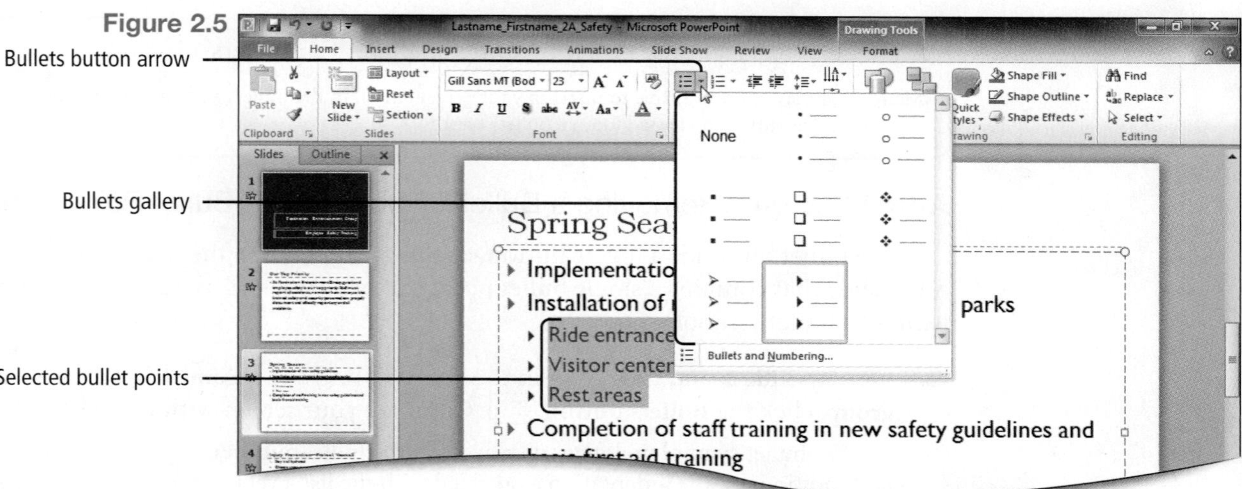

> **Alert!** | **Were the Bullets Removed?**
>
> If the bullets were removed, then you clicked the Bullets button instead of the Bullets button arrow. Click the Bullets button arrow, and then continue with Step 3.

3 At the bottom of the **Bullets** gallery, click **Bullets and Numbering**. In the **Bullets and Numbering** dialog box, point to each bullet style to display its ScreenTip. Then, in the second row, click **Star Bullets**. If the Star Bullets are not available, in the second row of bullets, click the second bullet style, and then click the Reset button.

4 Below the gallery, click the **Color** button. Under **Theme Colors**, in the sixth column, click the fifth color—**Red, Accent 2, Darker 25%**. In the **Size** box, select the existing number, type **100** and then compare your dialog box with Figure 2.6.

Figure 2.6

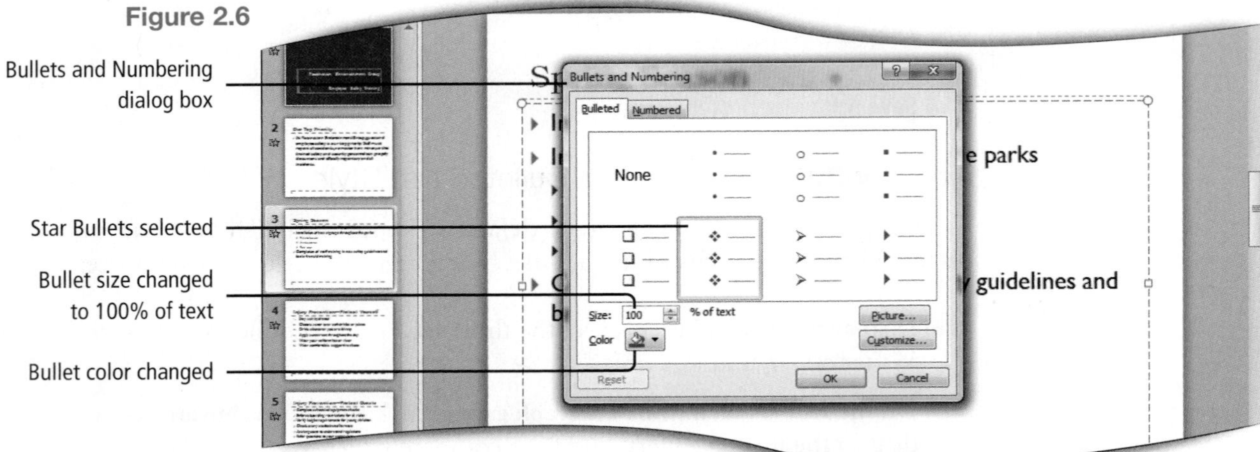

5 Click **OK** to apply the bullet style, and then **Save** your presentation.

> **More Knowledge | Using Other Symbols as Bullet Characters**
>
> Many bullets styles are available to insert in your presentation. In the Bullets and Numbering dialog box, click the Customize button to view additional bullet styles.

Activity 2.04 | Removing a Bullet Symbol from a Bullet Point

The Bullet button is a toggle button, enabling you to turn the bullet symbol on and off. A slide that contains a single bullet point can be formatted as a single paragraph *without* a bullet symbol.

1 Display **Slide 2**, and then click in the paragraph. On the **Home tab**, in the **Paragraph group**, click the **Bullets** button. Compare your screen with Figure 2.7.

The bullet symbol no longer displays, and the bullet button is no longer selected. Additionally, the indentation associated with the list level is removed.

2 **Center** the paragraph. On the **Home tab**, in the **Paragraph group**, click the **Line Spacing** button, and then click **1.5**.

Figure 2.7

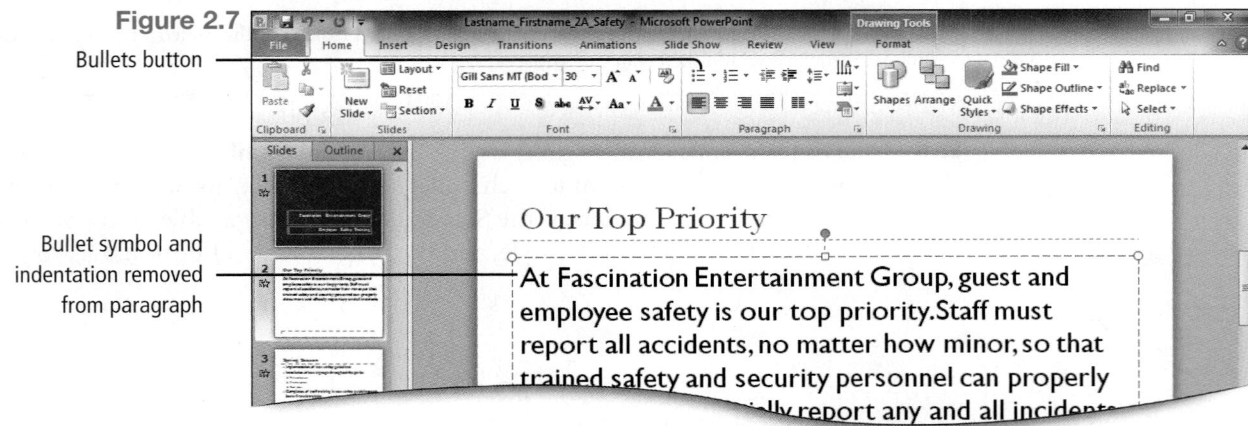

3 Click the dashed border to display the solid border and to select all of the text in the paragraph, and then apply **Bold** and **Italic**. Click in the slide title, and then click the **Center** button. **Save** your presentation.

Objective 2 | Insert Clip Art

There are many sources from which you can insert images into a presentation. One type of image that you can insert is a ***clip***—a single media file such as art, sound, animation, or a movie.

Activity 2.05 | Inserting Clip Art

1 Display **Slide 4**, and then on the **Home tab**, in the **Slides group**, click the **Layout** button. Click **Two Content** to change the slide layout.

2 In the placeholder on the right side of the slide, click the **Clip Art** button to display the **Clip Art** pane, and then compare your screen with Figure 2.8.

Figure 2.8

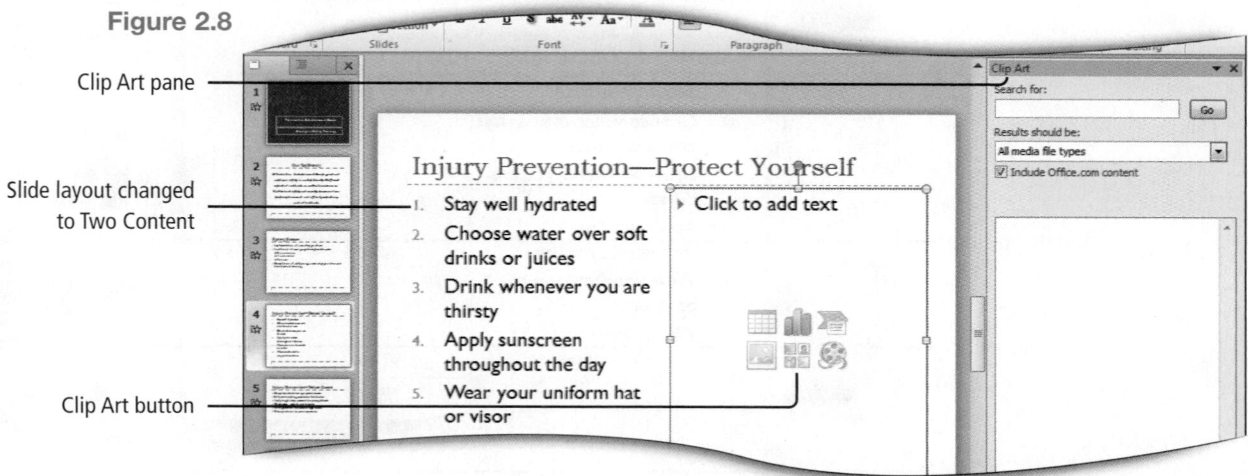

3 In the **Clip Art** pane, click in the **Search for** box, and then replace any existing text with **bottled water** so that PowerPoint can search for images that contain the keyword *bottled water*.

4 Click the **Results should be arrow**, and then click as necessary to *clear* the **Illustrations**, **Videos**, and **Audio** check boxes and to select only the **Photographs** check box. Compare your screen with Figure 2.9.

With the Photographs check box selected, PowerPoint will search for images that were created with a digital camera or a scanner.

Figure 2.9

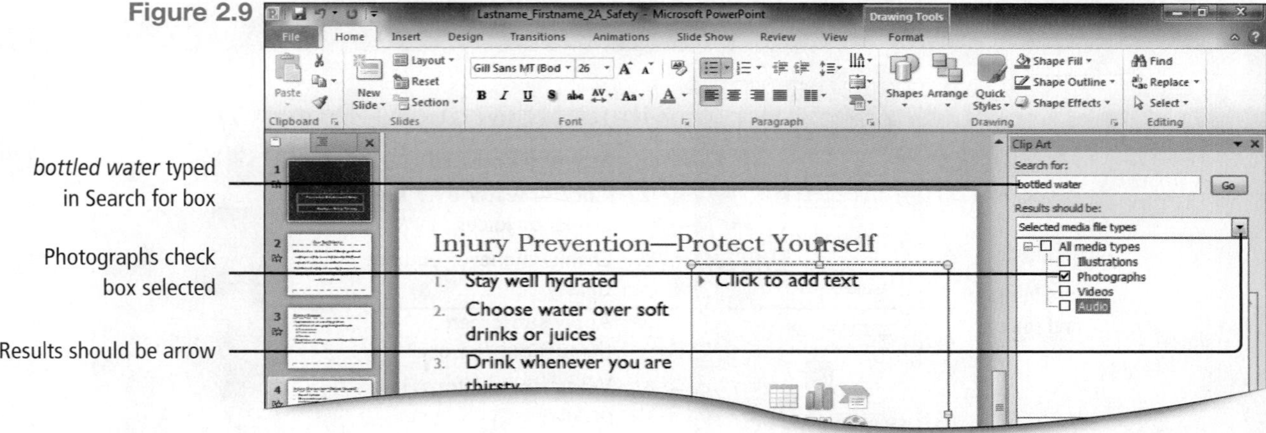

5 In the **Clip Art** pane, click the **Results should be arrow** to close the list. Then, if necessary, select the **Include Office.com content** check box so that images available on Office.com are included in the search.

6 In the **Clip Art** pane, click **Go** to display clips in the Clip Art pane. Scroll through the clips, and then locate and point to the image of the water pouring from a glass water bottle on a blue background. Compare your screen with Figure 2.10.

When you point to an image in the Clip Art pane, a ScreenTip displays the keywords and information about the size of the image.

Figure 2.10

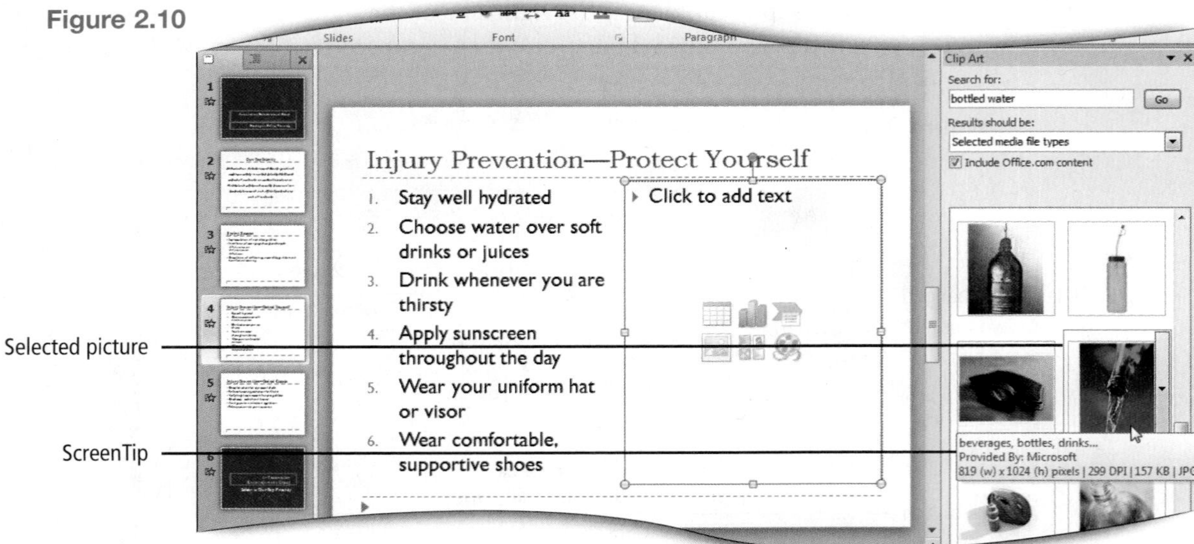

> **Alert! | Is the Water Bottle Picture Unavailable?**
>
> If you are unable to locate the suggested picture, choose another similar image.

7 Click the water bottle picture to insert it in the content placeholder on the right side of the slide. **Close** [X] the **Clip Art** pane, and then compare your slide with Figure 2.11.

On the Ribbon, the Picture Tools display, and the water bottle image is surrounded by sizing handles, indicating that it is selected.

Figure 2.11

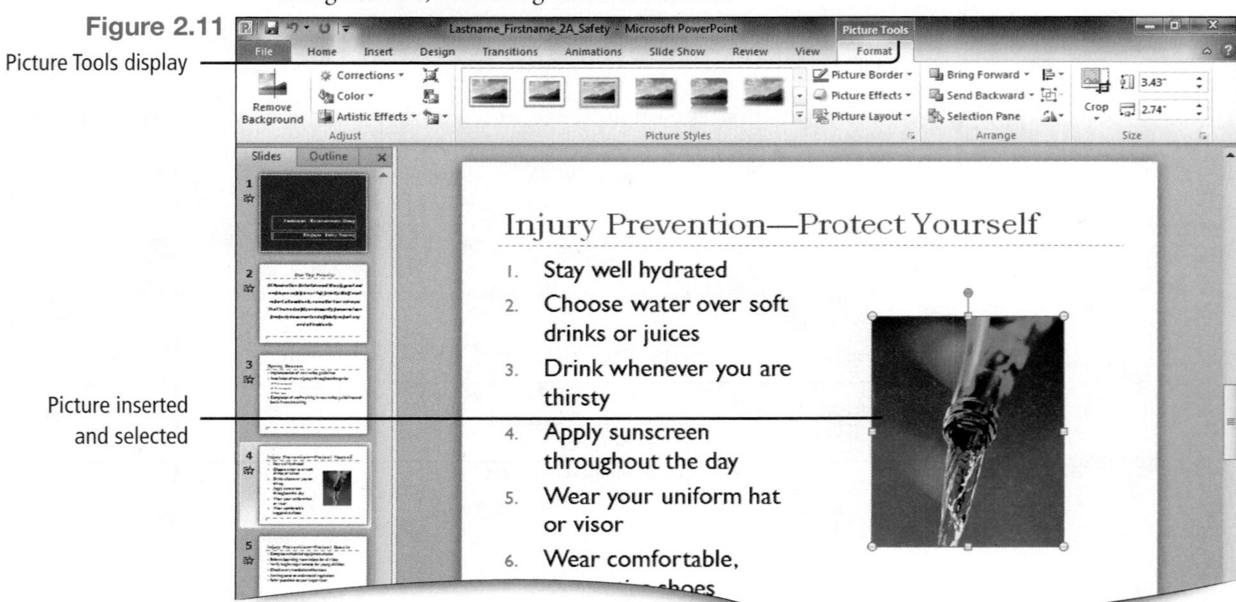

8 Display **Slide 1**. Click the **Insert tab**, and then in the **Images group**, click **Clip Art**.

9 In the **Clip Art** pane, in the **Search for** box, search for **red lights** and then click **Go**. Scroll as necessary to locate the picture of the single red warning light. Point to the picture, and then compare your screen with Figure 2.12.

If you cannot locate the picture, select another appropriate image.

Figure 2.12

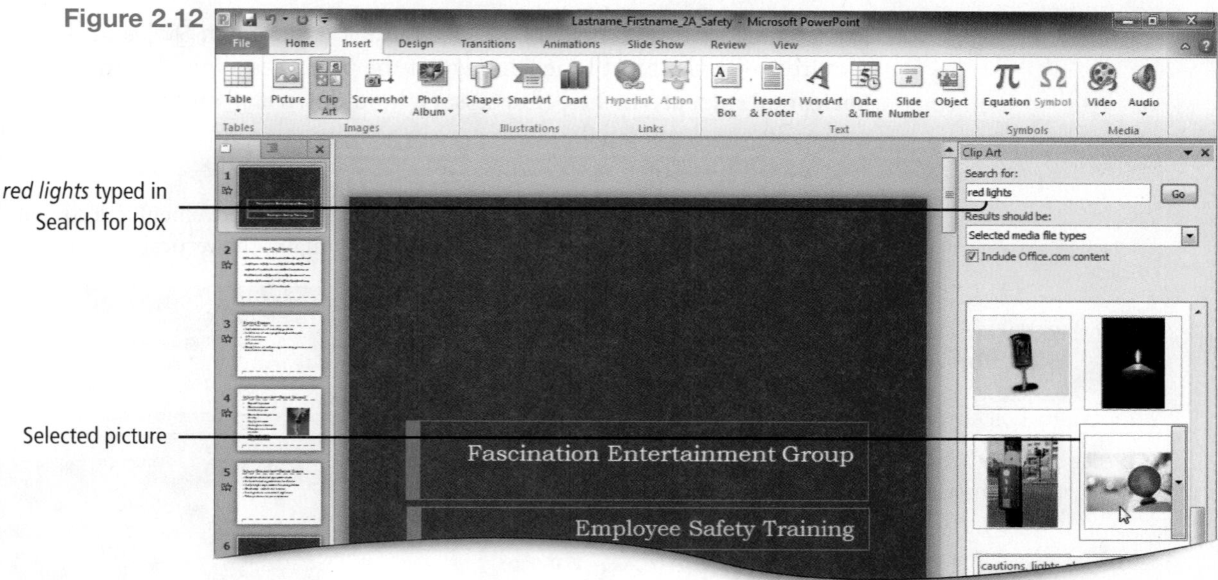

10 Click the **red light** picture to insert it in the center of the slide, and then **Close** the **Clip Art** pane. **Save** your presentation.

When you use the Clip Art command on the Ribbon instead of the Clip Art button in a content placeholder, PowerPoint inserts the image in the center of the slide.

Activity 2.06 | Moving and Sizing Images

Recall that when an image is selected, it is surrounded by sizing handles that you can drag to resize the image. You can also resize an image using the Shape Height and Shape Width boxes on the Format tab. When you point to the image, rather than pointing to a sizing handle, the move pointer—a four-headed arrow—displays, indicating that you can move the image.

> **Another Way**
>
> Alternatively, drag a corner sizing handle to resize an image proportionately.

1 If necessary, select the picture of the red light. On the **Format tab**, in the **Size group**, click in the **Shape Height** box, and then replace the selected number with **3.5**

2 Press Enter to resize the image. Notice that the picture is resized proportionately, and the **Width** box displays *5.26*. Compare your screen with Figure 2.13.

When a picture is resized in this manner, the width adjusts in proportion to the picture height.

Figure 2.13

3 Display the **View tab**. In the **Show group**, verify that the **Ruler** check box is selected and if necessary, select it. On the horizontal and vertical rulers, notice that *0* displays in the center.

Horizontally, the PowerPoint ruler indicates measurements from the center *out* to the left and to the right. Vertically, the PowerPoint ruler indicates measurements from the center up and down.

4 Point to the picture to display the pointer. Hold down Shift, and then drag the picture to the right until the left edge of the picture is aligned with the **left half of the horizontal ruler at 3 inches.** If necessary, hold down Ctrl and press an arrow key to move the picture in small increments in any direction for a more precise placement. Compare your screen with Figure 2.14.

Pressing Shift while dragging an object constrains object movement in a straight line either vertically or horizontally. Here, pressing Shift maintains the vertical placement of the picture.

Figure 2.14

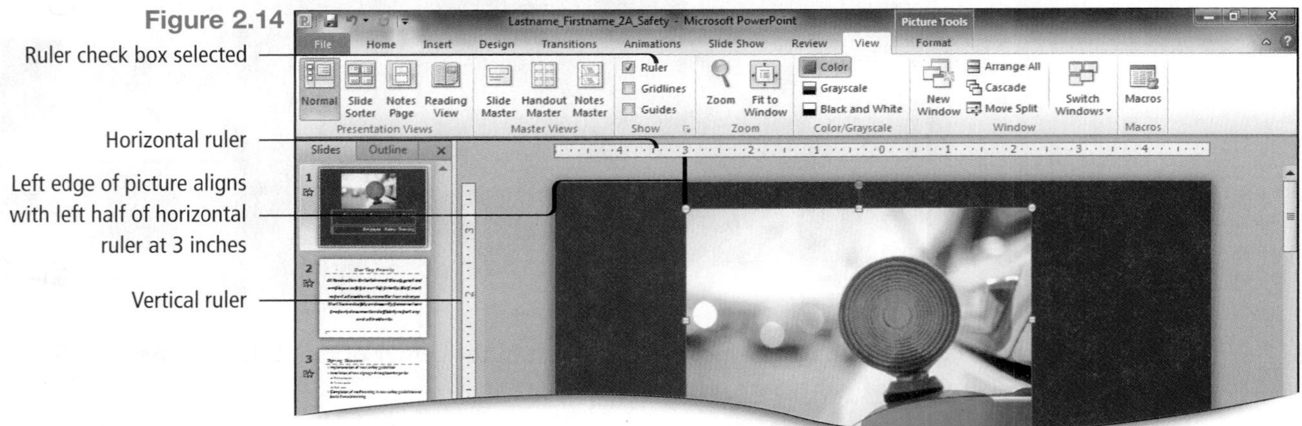

5 Display **Slide 6**. On the **Insert tab**, in the **Images group**, click the **Clip Art** button. In the **Clip Art** pane, search for **amusement park** and then click **Go**. Locate and click any picture of a ferris wheel, and then compare your slide with Figure 2.15.

Figure 2.15

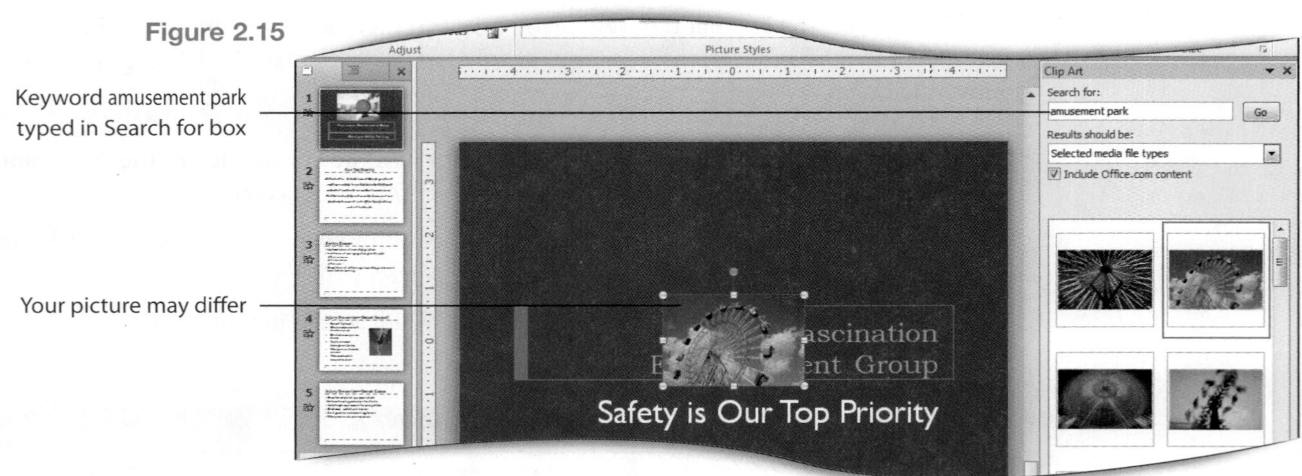

6 **Close** the **Clip Art** pane, and be sure that the picture is still selected. On the **Format tab**, in the **Size group**, click in the **Shape Height** box. Replace the displayed number with **2.5** and then press Enter to resize the picture. Compare your screen with Figure 2.16.

Figure 2.16

7 **Save** your presentation.

> **More Knowledge** | **Moving an Object by Using the Arrow Keys**
>
> You can use the directional arrow keys on your keyboard to move a picture, shape, or other object in small increments. Select the object so that its outside border displays as a solid line. Then, on your keyboard, hold down the Ctrl key and press the directional arrow keys to move the selected object in precise increments.

Activity 2.07 | Changing the Shape of a Picture

An inserted picture is rectangular in shape; however, you can modify a picture by changing its shape.

1 Display **Slide 1**, and then select the picture.

2 On the **Format tab**, in the **Size group**, *point* to the **Crop button arrow**, and then compare your screen with Figure 2.17.

The Crop button is a split button. The upper section—the Crop button—enables the ***crop*** feature, which reduces the size of a picture by removing vertical or horizontal edges. The lower section—the Crop arrow—displays cropping options, such as the option to crop a picture to a shape.

Figure 2.17

3 Click the **Crop button arrow**, and then point to **Crop to Shape** to display a gallery of shapes. Compare your screen with Figure 2.18.

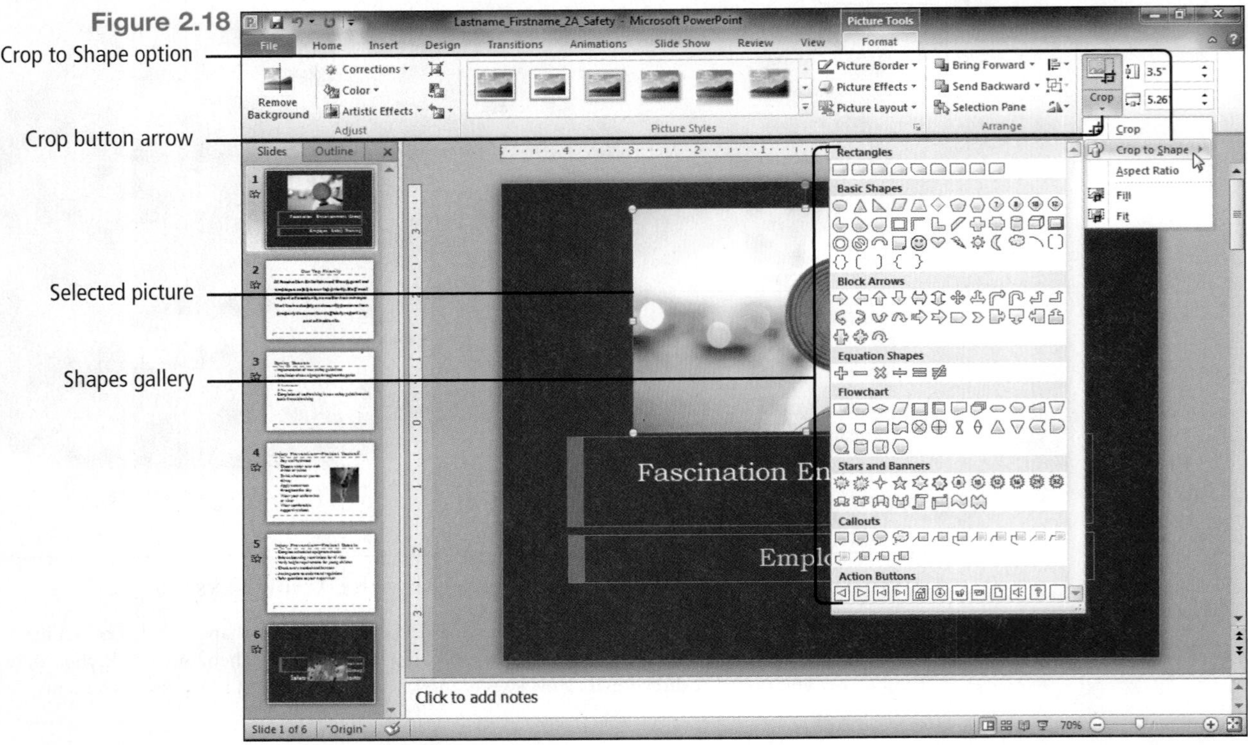

Figure 2.18

4 Under **Basic Shapes**, in the first row, click the first shape—**Oval**—to change the picture's shape to an oval. **Save** your presentation.

Objective 3 | Insert Text Boxes and Shapes

You can use objects, including text boxes and shapes, to draw attention to important information or to serve as containers for slide text. Many shapes, including lines, arrows, ovals, and rectangles, are available to insert and position anywhere on your slides.

Activity 2.08 | Inserting a Text Box

A ***text box*** is an object with which you can position text anywhere on a slide.

1 Display **Slide 5** and verify that the rulers display. Click the **Insert tab**, and then in the **Text group**, click the **Text Box** button.

2 Move the pointer to several different places on the slide, and as you do so, in the horizontal and vertical rulers, notice that ***ruler guides***—dotted vertical and horizontal lines that display in the rulers indicating the pointer's position—move also.

Use the ruler guides to help you position objects on a slide.

3 Position the pointer so that the ruler guides are positioned on the **left half of the horizontal ruler at 4.5 inches** and on the **lower half of the vertical ruler at 1.5 inches**, and then compare your screen with Figure 2.19.

Figure 2.19

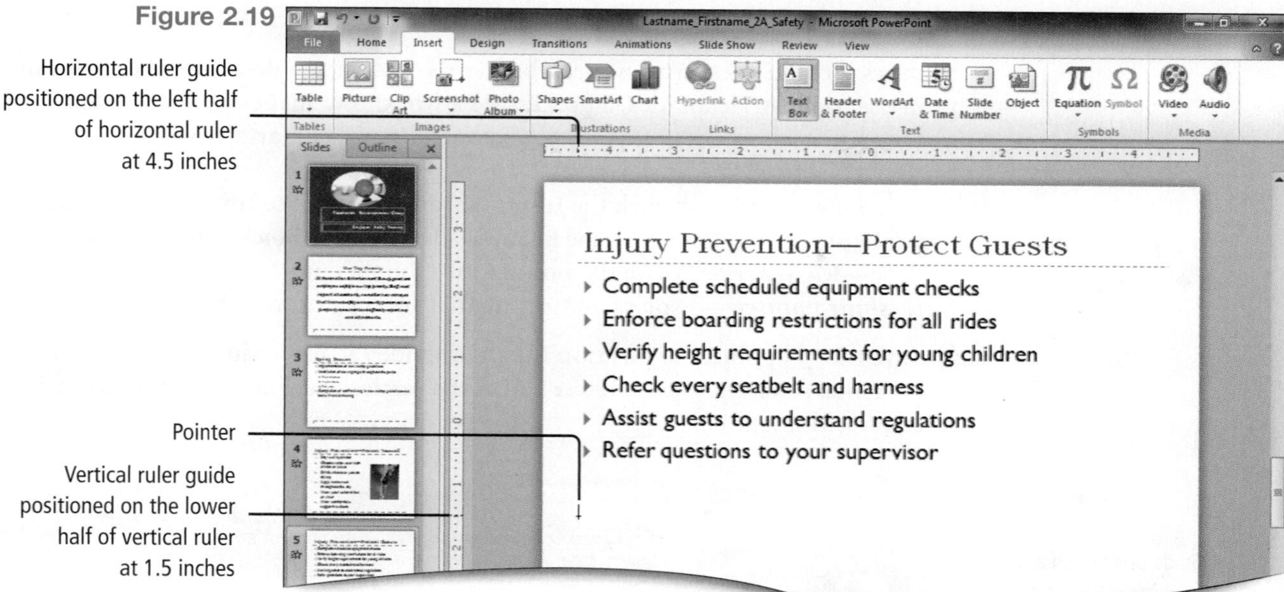

4 Click one time to create a narrow rectangular text box. With the insertion point blinking inside the text box, type **If Safety is Questionable** Notice that as you type, the width of the text box expands to accommodate the text. Compare your screen with Figure 2.20.

Do not be concerned if your text box is not positioned exactly as shown in Figure 2.20.

Figure 2.20

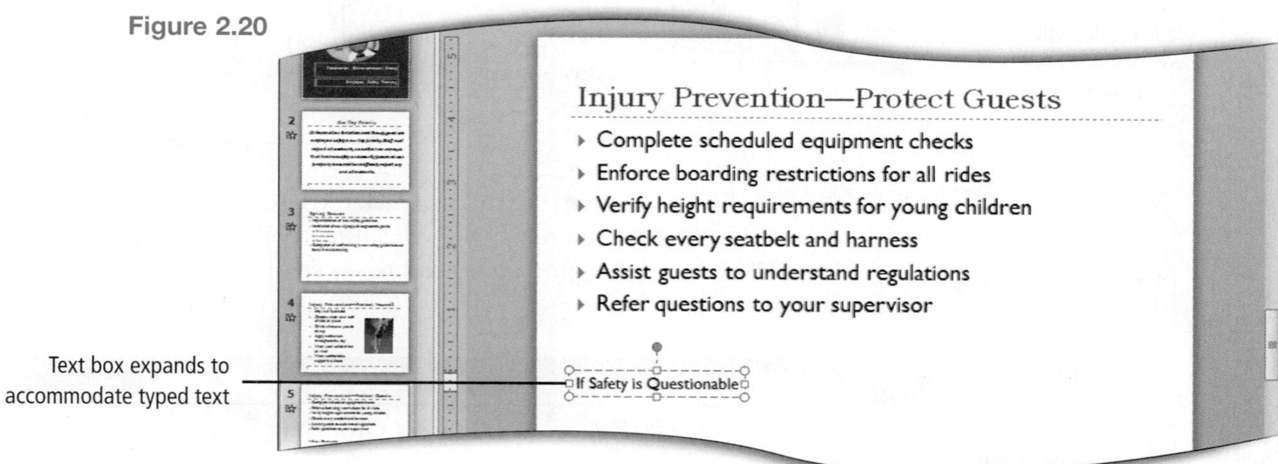

Alert! | Does the Text in the Text Box Display Vertically, One Character at a Time?

If you move the pointer when you click to create the text box, PowerPoint sets the width of the text box and does not widen to accommodate the text. If this happened to you, your text may display vertically instead of horizontally or it may display on two lines. Click Undo, and then repeat the steps again, being sure that you do not move the mouse when you click to insert the text box.

5 Select the text that you typed, change the **Font Size** to **24** and then **Save** your presentation.

You can format the text in a text box by using the same techniques that you use to format text in any other placeholder. For example, you can change the font, font style, font size, and font color.

Activity 2.09 | Inserting, Sizing, and Positioning Shapes

Shapes include lines, arrows, stars, banners, ovals, rectangles, and other basic shapes you can use to illustrate an idea, a process, or a workflow. Shapes can be sized and moved using the same techniques that you use to size and move clip art images.

1 With **Slide 5** displayed, click the **Insert tab**, and then in the **Illustrations group**, click the **Shapes** button to display the **Shapes** gallery. Under **Block Arrows**, click the first shape—**Right Arrow**. Move the pointer into the slide until the ⊞ pointer—called the ***crosshair pointer***—displays, indicating that you can draw a shape.

2 Move the ⊞ pointer to position the ruler guides at approximately **zero on the horizontal ruler** and on the **lower half of the vertical ruler at 1.5 inches**. Compare your screen with Figure 2.21.

Figure 2.21

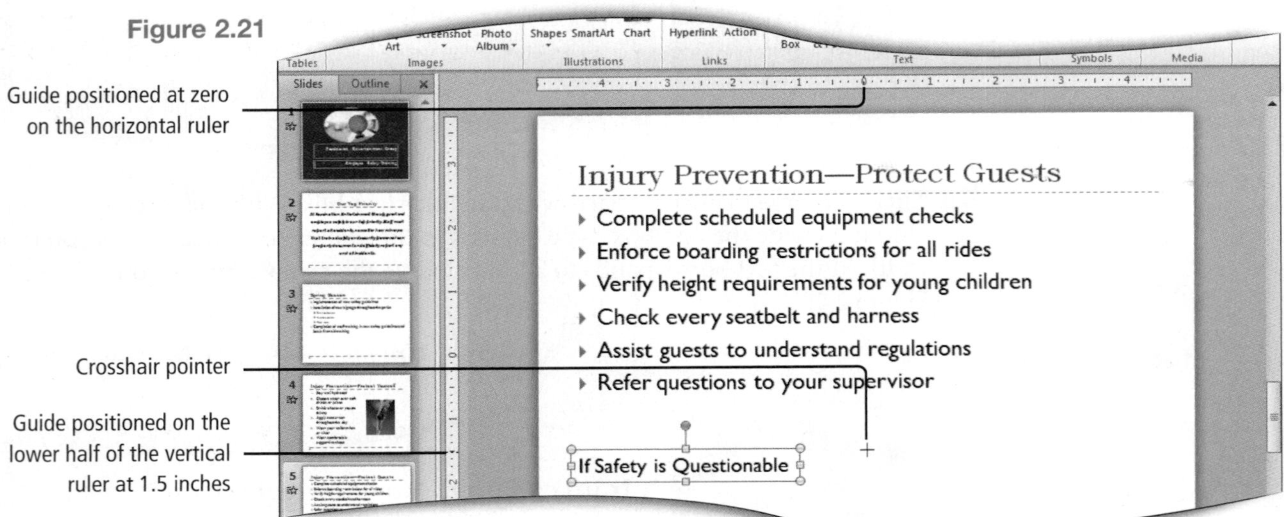

3 Click the mouse button to insert the arrow. Click the **Format tab**, and then in the **Size group**, click in the **Shape Height** box to select the number. Type **.5** and then click in the **Shape Width** box. Type **2** and then press Enter to resize the arrow. Compare your screen with Figure 2.22.

Figure 2.22

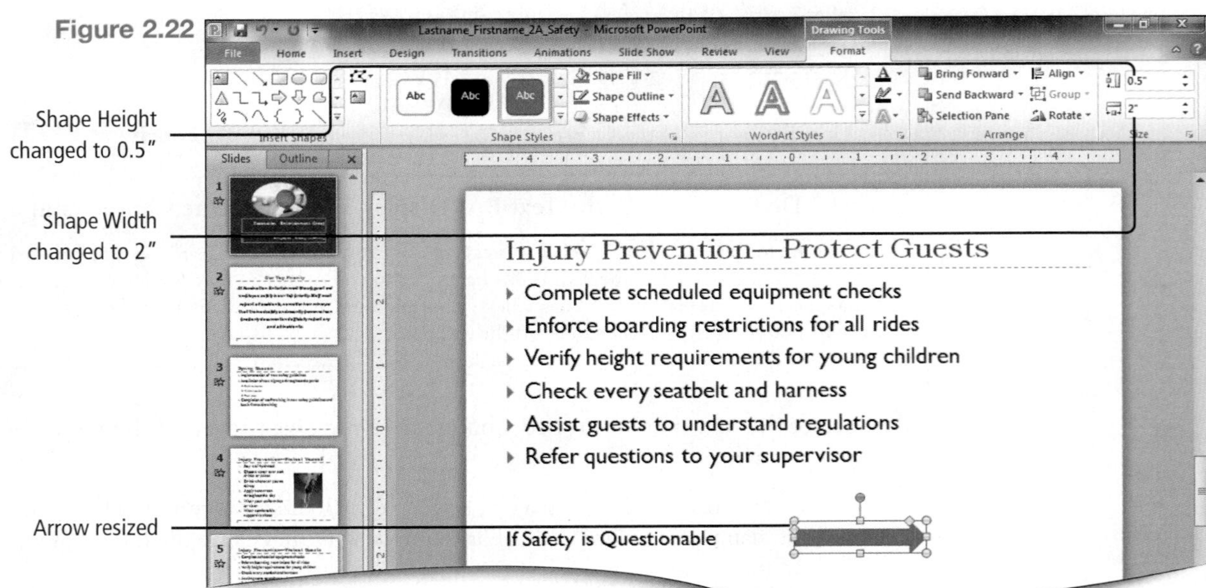

4 On the **Format tab**, in the **Insert Shapes group**, click the **More** button. In the gallery, under **Basic Shapes**, in the first row, click the second to last shape—**Octagon**.

5 Move the pointer to position the ruler guides on the **right half of the horizontal ruler at 2.5 inches** and on the **lower half of the vertical ruler at 1 inch**, and then click one time to insert an octagon.

6 On the **Format tab**, in the **Size group**, click in the **Shape Height** box to select the number. Type **2** and then click in the **Shape Width** box. Type **2** and then press Enter to resize the octagon. Compare your slide with Figure 2.23. Do not be concerned if your shapes are not positioned exactly as shown in the figure.

Figure 2.23

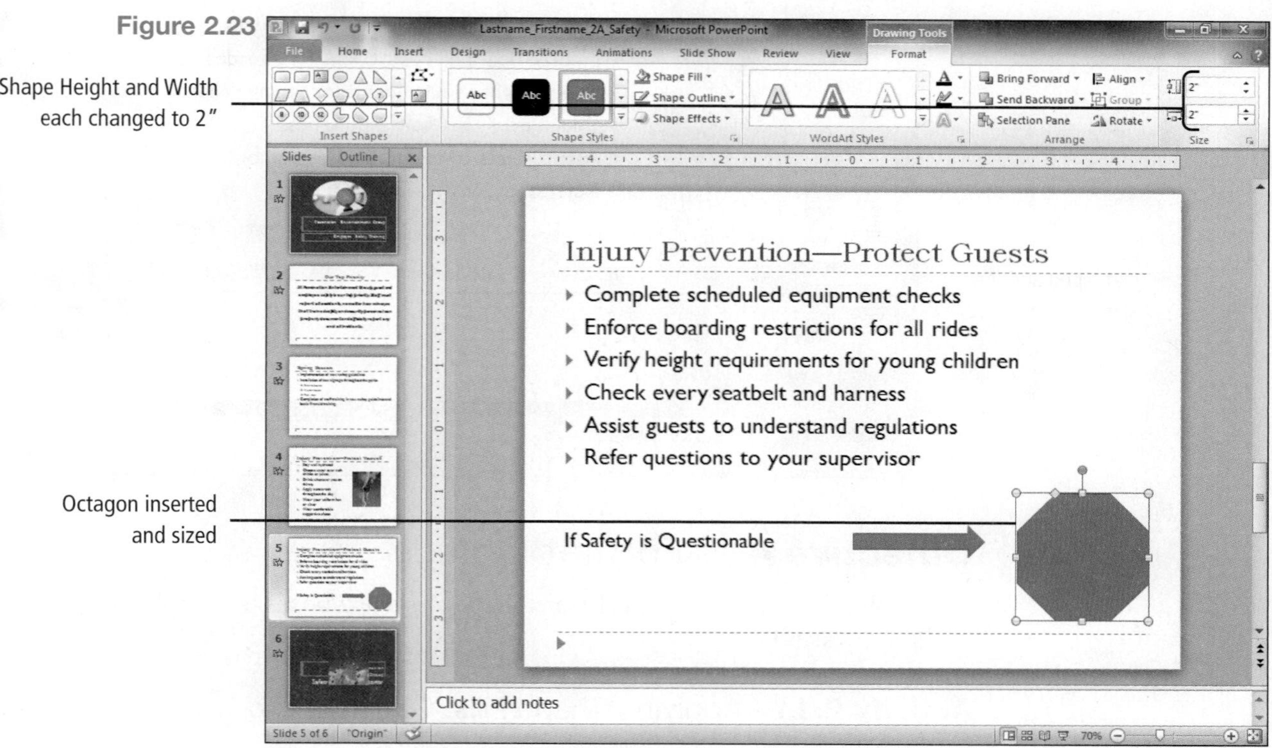

7 **Save** your presentation.

Activity 2.10 | Adding Text to Shapes

Shapes can serve as a container for text. After you add text to a shape, you can change the font and font size, apply font styles, and change text alignment.

1 On **Slide 5**, if necessary, click the octagon so that it is selected. Type **STOP** and notice that the text is centered within the octagon.

2 Select the text *STOP*, and then on the Mini toolbar, change the **Font Size** to **32**. Compare your screen with Figure 2.24, and then **Save** your presentation.

Figure 2.24

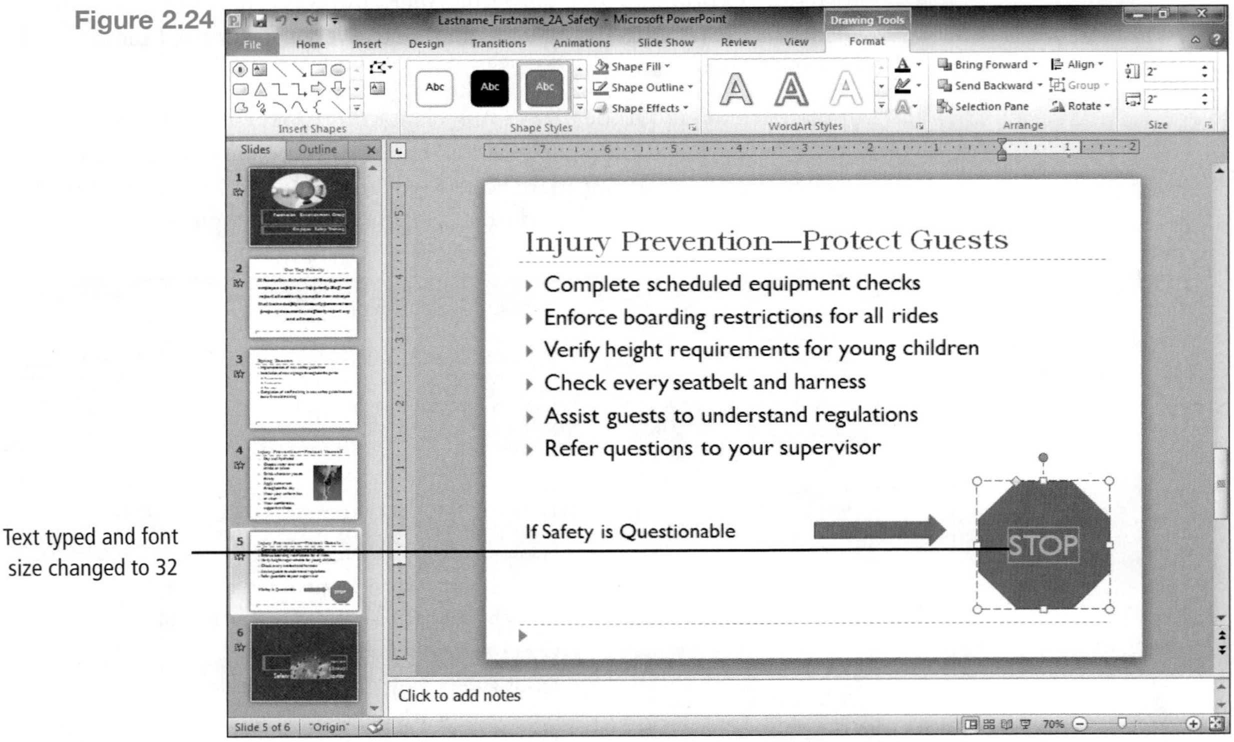

Text typed and font size changed to 32

Objective 4 | Format Objects

Apply styles and effects to clip art, shapes, and text boxes to complement slide backgrounds and colors.

Activity 2.11 | Applying Shape Fills, Outlines, and Styles

Changing the inside ***fill color*** and the outside line color is a distinctive way to format a shape. A fill color is the inside color of text or of an object. Use the Shape Styles gallery to apply predefined combinations of these fill and line colors and also to apply other effects.

1 On **Slide 5**, click anywhere in the text *If Safety is Questionable* to select the text box. On the **Format tab**, in the **Shape Styles group**, click the **More** button to display the **Shape Styles** gallery.

2 In the last row, click the third style—**Intense Effect - Red, Accent 2**. Select the **octagon** shape, and then apply the same style you applied to the text box—**Intense Effect - Red, Accent 2**.

3 Select the **arrow**, and then display the **Shape Styles** gallery. In the last row, click the second style—**Intense Effect - Blue, Accent 1**.

4 Click in a blank part of the slide so that no objects are selected, and then compare your screen with Figure 2.25.

Figure 2.25

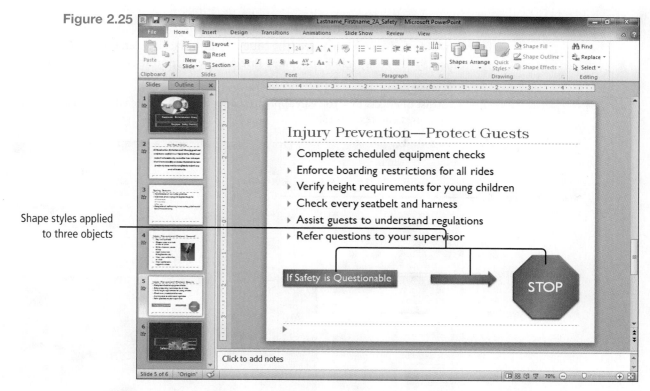

Shape styles applied to three objects

5 Display **Slide 2**, and then click anywhere in the paragraph of text to select the content placeholder.

6 On the **Format tab**, in the **Shape Styles group**, click the **Shape Fill** button, and then point to several of the theme colors and watch as Live Preview changes the inside color of the text box. In the fifth column, click the first color—**Blue, Accent 1**.

7 In the **Shape Styles group**, click the **Shape Outline** button. Point to **Weight**, click **3 pt**, and notice that a thick outline surrounds the text placeholder. Click in a blank area of the slide so that nothing is selected, and then compare your slide with Figure 2.26.

You can use combinations of shape fill, outline colors, and weights to format an object.

Figure 2.26

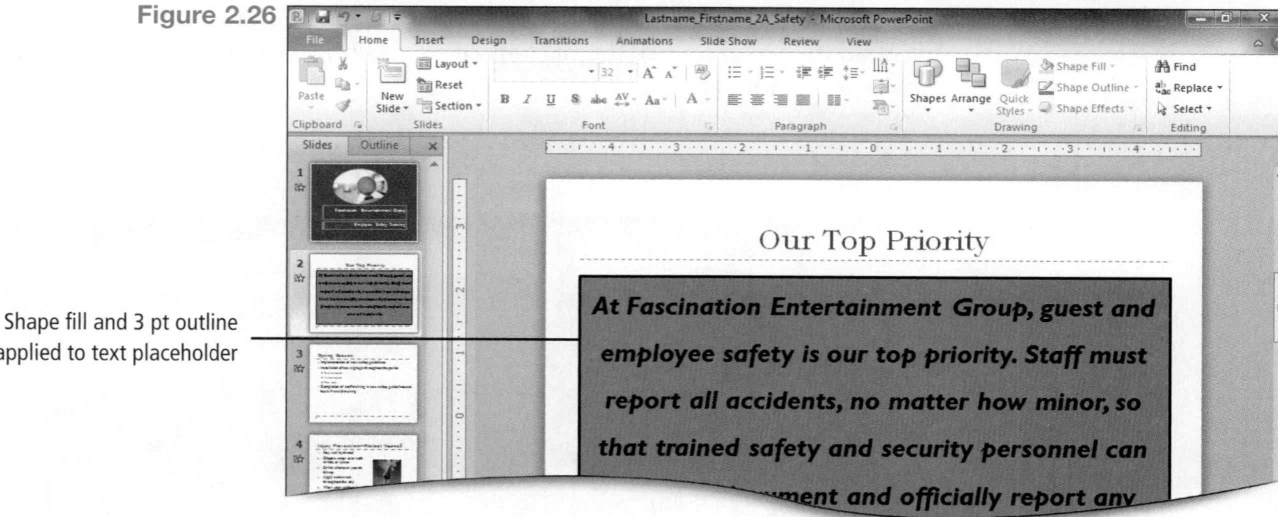

Shape fill and 3 pt outline applied to text placeholder

8 Click in the paragraph, and then press Ctrl + A to select all of the paragraph text, right-click in the selection to display the Mini toolbar, and then click the **Font Color button arrow** to display the **Theme Colors** gallery. Click the first color—**White, Background 1**. **Save** your presentation.

Activity 2.12 | Applying Shape and Picture Effects

1 On **Slide 2**, if necessary, select the blue content placeholder. On the **Format tab**, in the **Shape Styles group**, click the **Shape Effects** button, and then compare your screen with Figure 2.27.

A list of effects that you can apply to shapes displays. These effects can also be applied to pictures and text boxes.

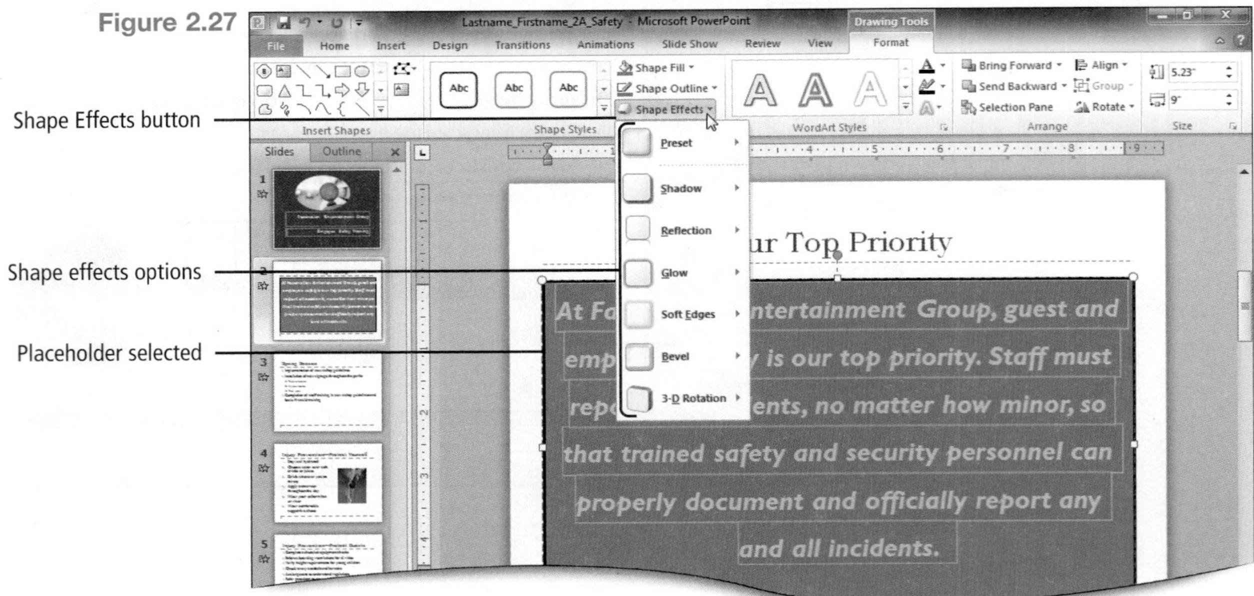

Figure 2.27

2 Point to **Bevel** to display the **Bevel** gallery. Point to each bevel to view its ScreenTip and to use Live Preview to examine the effect of each bevel on the content placeholder. In the last row, click the last bevel—**Art Deco**.

3 Display **Slide 1**, and then select the picture. On the **Format tab**, in the **Picture Styles group**, click the **Picture Effects** button.

4 Point to **Soft Edges**, and then in the **Soft Edges** gallery, point to each style to view its effect on the picture. Click the last **Soft Edges** effect—**50 Point**, and then compare your screen with Figure 2.28.

The soft edges effect softens and blurs the outer edge of the picture so that it blends into the slide background.

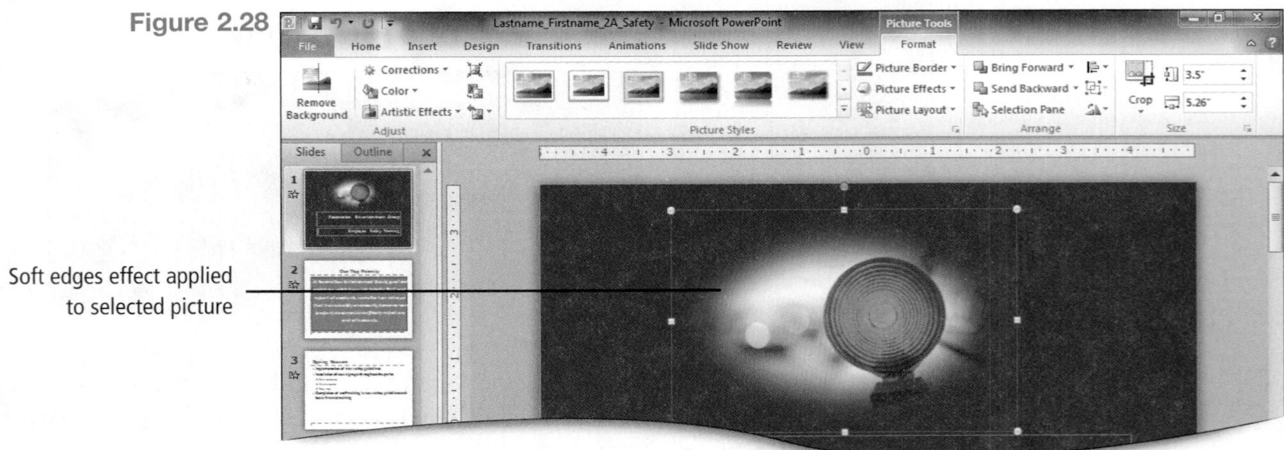

Figure 2.28

5 Display **Slide 4**, and then select the picture. On the **Format tab**, in the **Picture Styles group**, click the **Picture Effects** button, and then point to **Glow**.

6 Point to several of the effects to view the effect on the picture, and then under **Glow Variations**, in the second row, click the second glow effect—**Red, 8 pt glow, Accent color 2**. Click in a blank area of the slide to deselect the picture. Compare your slide with Figure 2.29, and then **Save** your presentation.

The glow effect applies a colored, softly blurred outline to the selected object.

Figure 2.29

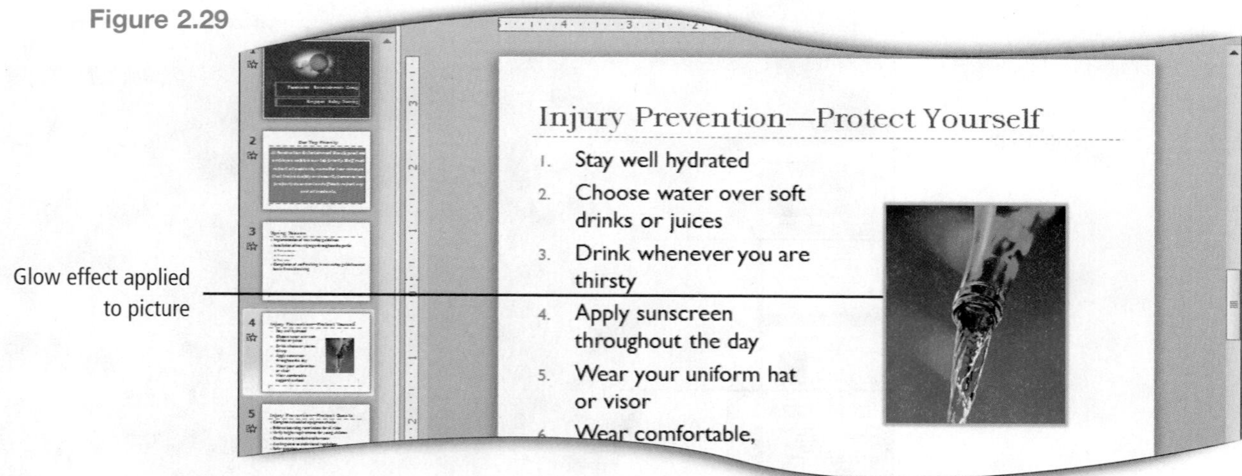

Activity 2.13 | Duplicating Objects

1 Display **Slide 6**, point to the picture to display the pointer, and then drag up and to the left so that the upper left corner of the picture aligns with the upper left corner of the slide.

2 Press and hold down Ctrl, and then press D one time. Release Ctrl.

A duplicate of the picture overlaps the original picture and the duplicated image is selected.

3 Point to the duplicated picture to display the pointer, and then drag down and to the right approximately 1 inch in both directions so that both pictures are visible. Compare your screen with Figure 2.30. Do not be concerned if your pictures are not positioned exactly as shown in the figure.

Figure 2.30

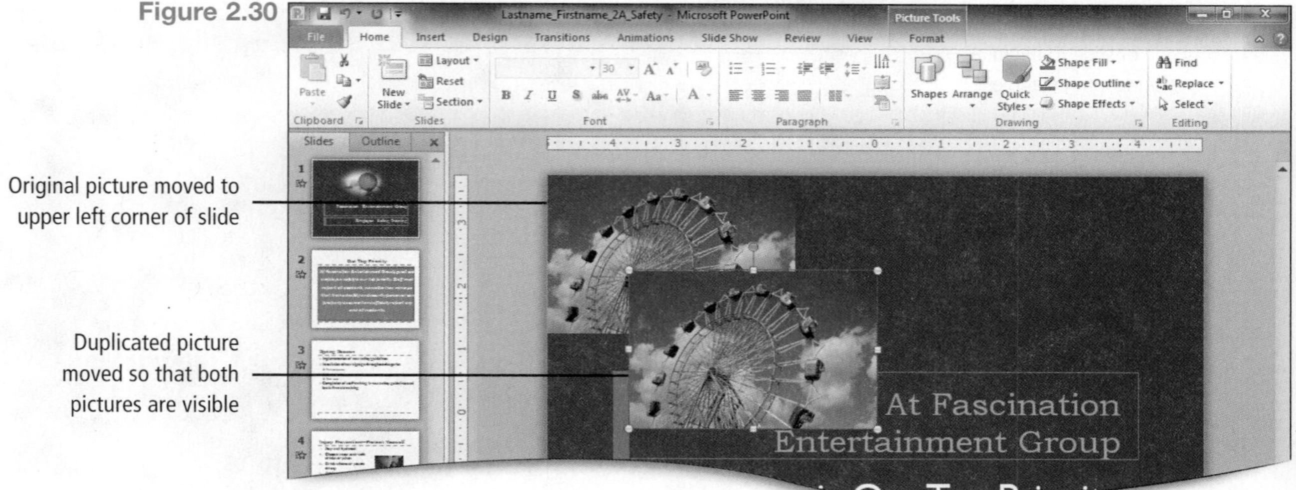

4 With the duplicated image selected, hold down Ctrl, and then press D to insert a third copy of the image.

5 Click anywhere on the slide so that none of the three pictures are selected. **Save** your presentation, and then compare your screen with Figure 2.31. Do not be concerned if your pictures are not positioned exactly as shown.

Figure 2.31

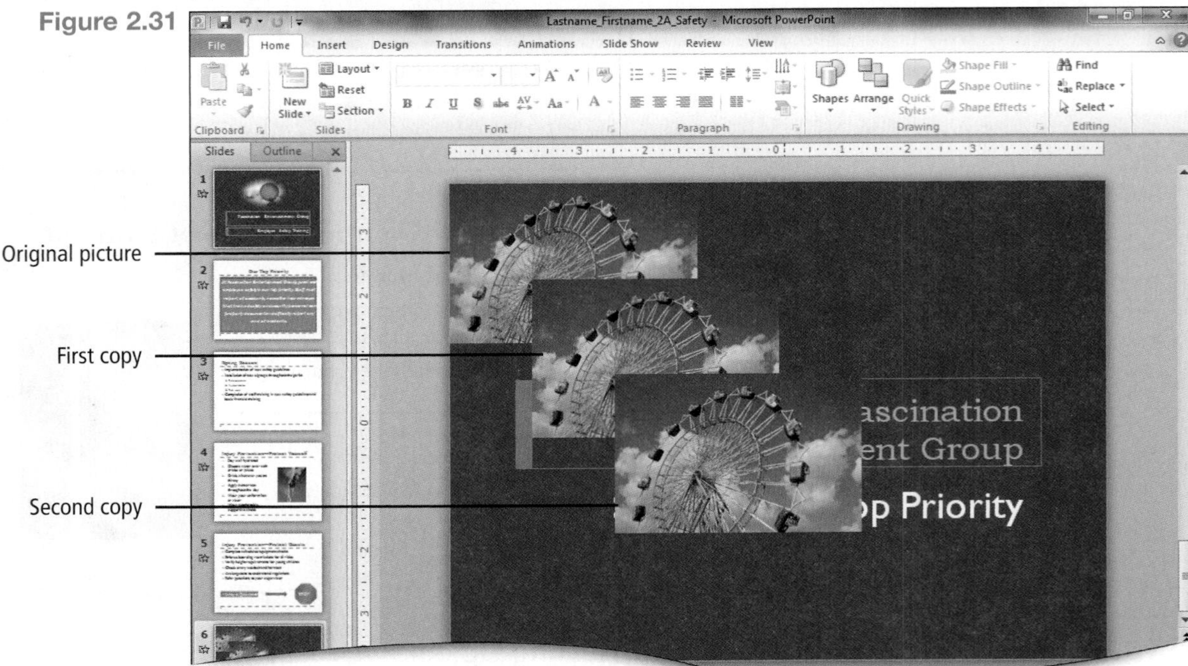

Activity 2.14 | Aligning and Distributing Objects

When you insert multiple objects on a slide, you can use commands on the Ribbon to align and distribute the objects precisely.

> **Another Way**
>
> Hold down Shift and click each object that you want to select.

1 With **Slide 6** displayed, position the pointer in the gray area of the Slide pane just outside the upper left corner of the slide to display the pointer. Drag down and to the right to draw a transparent blue rectangle that encloses the three pictures. Compare your slide with Figure 2.32.

Figure 2.32

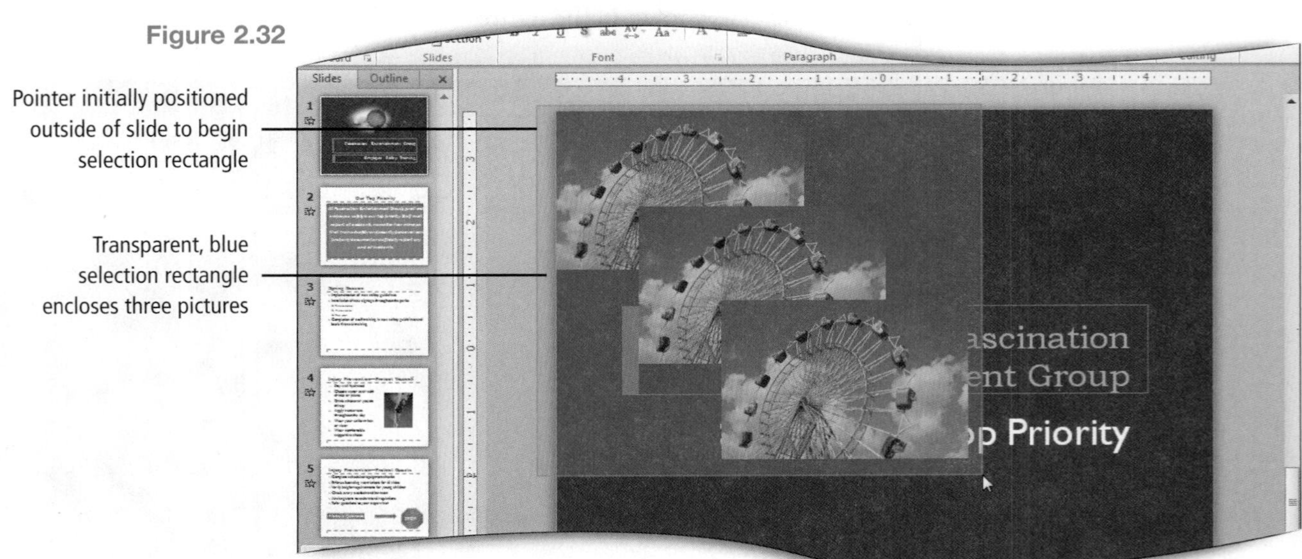

2 Release the mouse button to select the three objects, and then compare your screen with Figure 2.33.

Objects completely enclosed by a selection rectangle are selected when the mouse button is released.

Figure 2.33

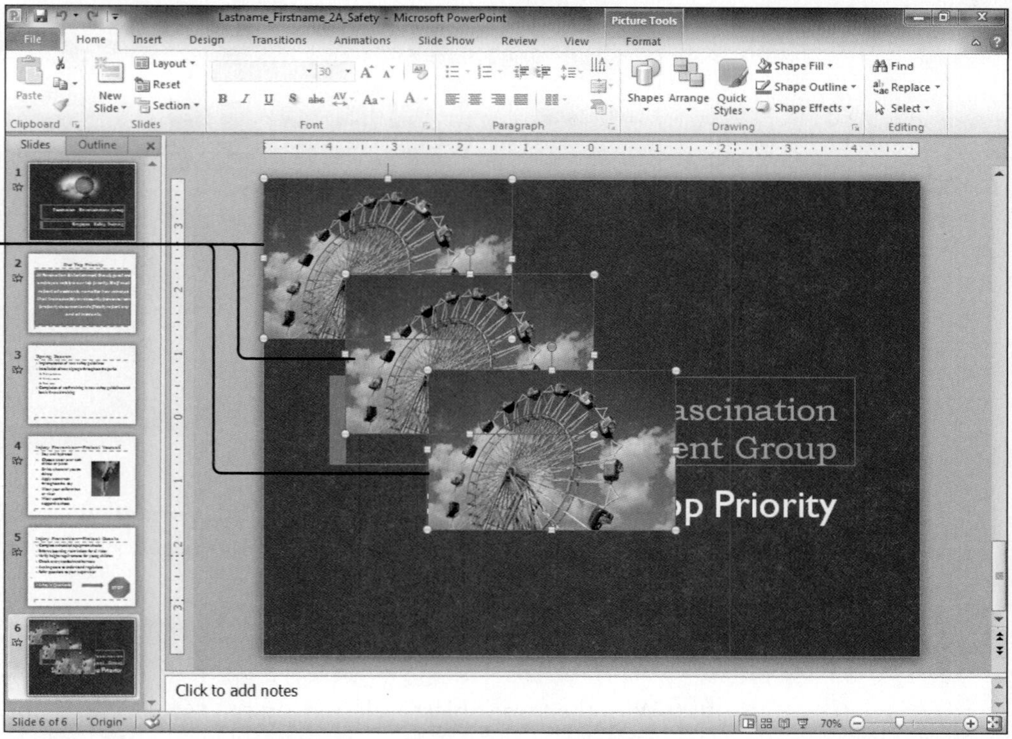

3 Click the **Format tab**, and then in the **Arrange group**, click the **Align** button. Toward the bottom of the menu, click **Align to Slide** to activate this setting.

When you select an alignment option, this setting will cause the objects to align with the edges of the slide.

4 On the **Format tab**, in the **Arrange group**, click the **Align** button again, and then click **Align Top**.

The top of each of the three pictures aligns with the top edge of the slide.

5 Click in a blank area of the slide so that nothing is selected. Then, click the third picture. Point to the picture so that the pointer displays, and then drag to the right so that its upper right corner aligns with the upper right corner of the slide.

6 Hold down Shift and click the remaining two pictures so that all three pictures are selected. On the **Format tab**, in the **Arrange group**, click the **Align** button. Click **Align Selected Objects** to activate this setting.

When you select an alignment option, this setting will cause the objects that you select to align relative to each other.

7. With the three pictures still selected, on the **Format tab**, in the **Arrange group**, click the **Align** button [icon] again, and then click **Distribute Horizontally**. Compare your screen with Figure 2.34.

   The three pictures are spaced and distributed evenly across the top of the slide and aligned with the top edge of the slide.

Figure 2.34

Pictures aligned with top edge of slide and distributed evenly across top edge of slide

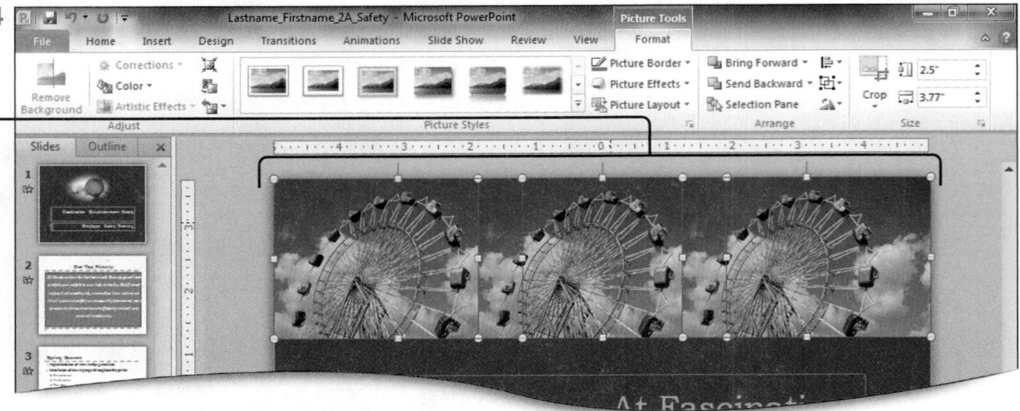

8. With the three pictures selected, on the **Format tab**, in the **Picture Styles group**, click the **Picture Effects** button. Point to **Soft Edges**, and then click **50 Point** to apply the picture effect to all three images.

9. Display **Slide 5**, hold down Shift, and then at the bottom of the slide, click the **text box**, the **arrow**, and the **octagon** to select all three objects.

10. With the three objects selected, on the **Format tab**, in the **Arrange group**, click the **Align** button [icon]. Be sure that **Align Selected Objects** is still active—a check mark displays to its left. Then, click **Align Middle**. Click the **Align** button again, and then click **Distribute Horizontally**.

    The midpoint of each object aligns and the three objects are distributed evenly.

11. Click anywhere on the slide so that none of the objects are selected, and then compare your screen with Figure 2.35.

Figure 2.35

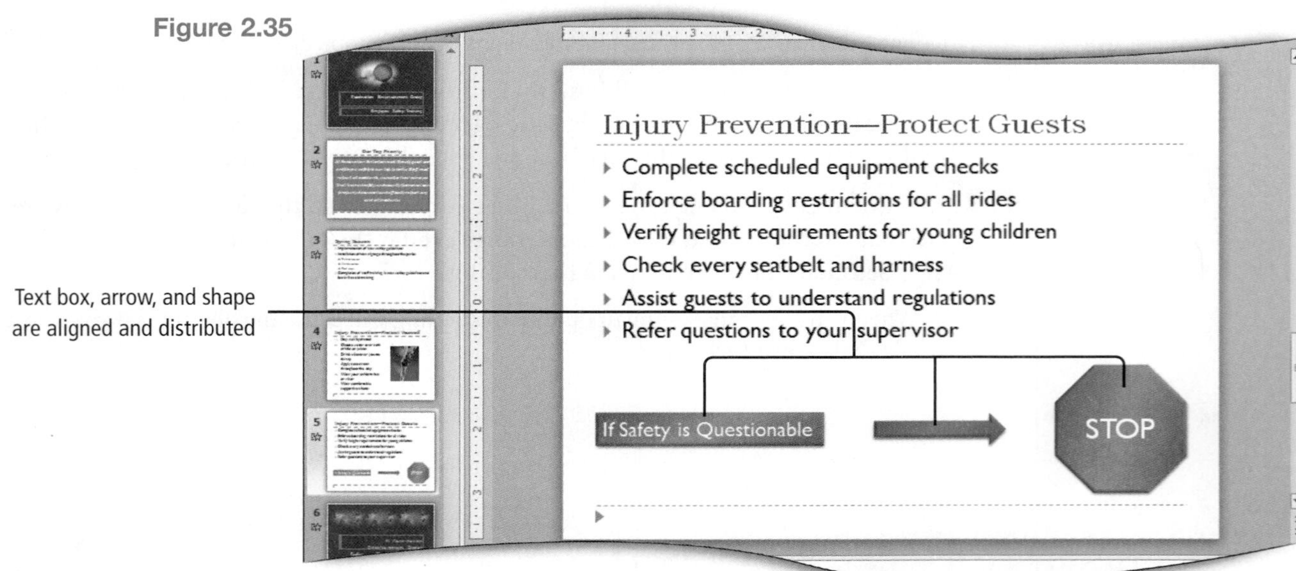

12 On the **Slide Show tab**, in the **Start Slide Show group**, click the **From Beginning** button, and then view the slide show. Press Esc when the black slide displays.

13 On the **Insert tab**, in the **Text group**, click the **Header & Footer** button to display the **Header and Footer** dialog box. Click the **Notes and Handouts tab**. Under **Include on page**, select the **Date and time** check box, and then select **Update automatically**. If necessary, clear the Header check box. Select the **Page number** and **Footer** check boxes. In the **Footer** box, using your own name, type **Lastname_Firstname_2A_Safety** and then click **Apply to All**.

14 Display the **Document Properties.** Replace the text in the **Author** box with your own firstname and lastname, in the **Subject** box, type your course name and section number, and in the **Keywords** box, type **safety, injury prevention** **Close** the **Document Information Panel**.

15 **Save** your presentation. Print **Handouts 6 Slides Horizontal**, or submit your presentation electronically as directed by your instructor.

16 **Close** the presentation and exit PowerPoint.

End You have completed Project 2A

Project 2B Event Announcement

Project Activities

In Activities 2.15 through 2.24, you will format slides in a presentation for the Fascination Entertainment Group Marketing Director that informs employees about upcoming events at the company's amusement parks. You will enhance the presentation using SmartArt and WordArt graphics. Your completed presentation will look similar to Figure 2.36.

Project Files

For Project 2B, you will need the following files:

p02B_Celebrations
p02B_Canada_Contact
p02B_Mexico_Contact
p02B_US_Contact

You will save your presentation as:

Lastname_Firstname_2B_Celebrations

Project Results

Figure 2.36
Project 2B Celebrations

Objective 5 | Remove Picture Backgrounds and Insert WordArt

To avoid the boxy look that results when you insert an image into a presentation, use ***Background Removal*** to flow a picture into the content of the presentation. Background Removal removes unwanted portions of a picture so that the picture does not appear as a self-contained rectangle.

WordArt is a gallery of text styles with which you can create decorative effects, such as shadowed or mirrored text. You can choose from the gallery of WordArt styles to insert a new WordArt object or you can customize existing text by applying WordArt formatting.

Activity 2.15 | Removing the Background from a Picture and Applying Soft Edge Options

1 **Start** PowerPoint. From your student files, open **p02B_Celebrations**. On the **View tab**, in the **Show group**, if necessary, select the Ruler check box. In your **PowerPoint Chapter 2** folder, save the file as **Lastname_Firstname_2B_Celebrations**

2 Display **Slide 6**. Notice how the picture is a self-contained rectangle and that it has a much darker black background than the presentation. Click the picture to select it, and then on the **Format tab**, in the **Adjust group**, click the **Remove Background** button. Compare your screen with Figure 2.37.

PowerPoint determines what portion of the picture is the foreground—the portion to keep—and which portion is the background—the portion to remove. The background is overlaid in magenta, leaving the remaining portion of the picture as it will look when the background removal is complete. A rectangular selection area displays that can be moved and sized to select additional areas of the picture. The Background Removal options display in the Refine group on the Ribbon.

Figure 2.37

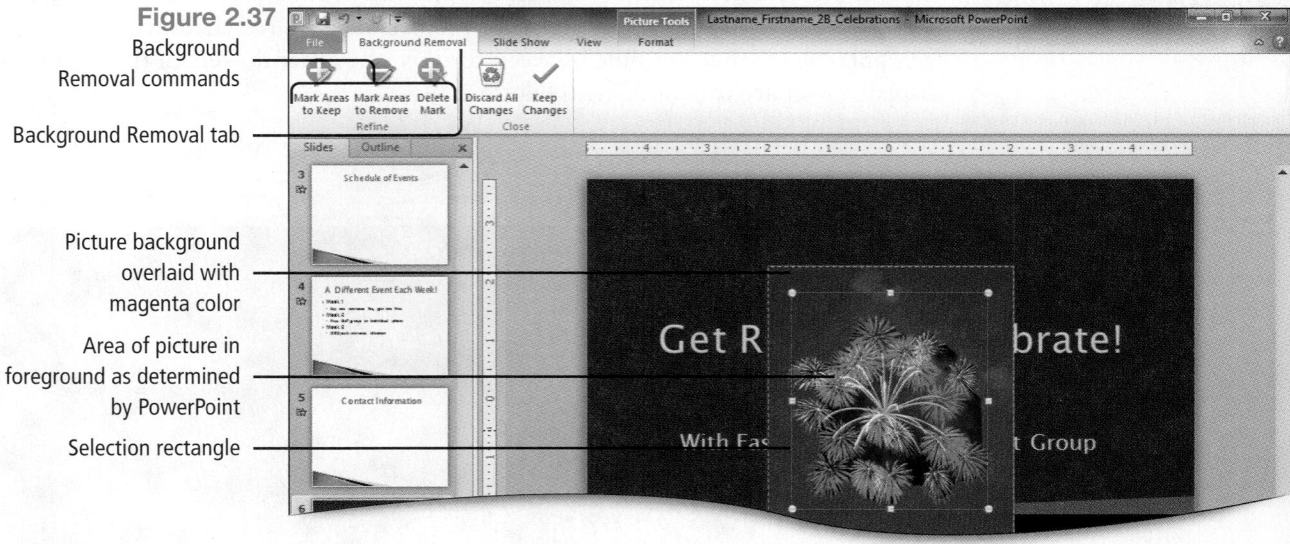

3 On the **selection rectangle**, point to the left center sizing handle to display the ↔ pointer, and then drag to the left so that the left edge of the selection area aligns with the dashed border surrounding the picture. Compare your screen with Figure 2.38.

When you move or size the selection area, the areas outside the selection are treated as background and are removed. Thus, you have control over which portions of the picture that you keep. Here, by resizing the selection area on the left, a larger area of each *flower* in the fireworks is included in the foreground of the picture. On the right side of the fireworks picture, some dark red shadowing is visible as part of the picture.

Figure 2.38

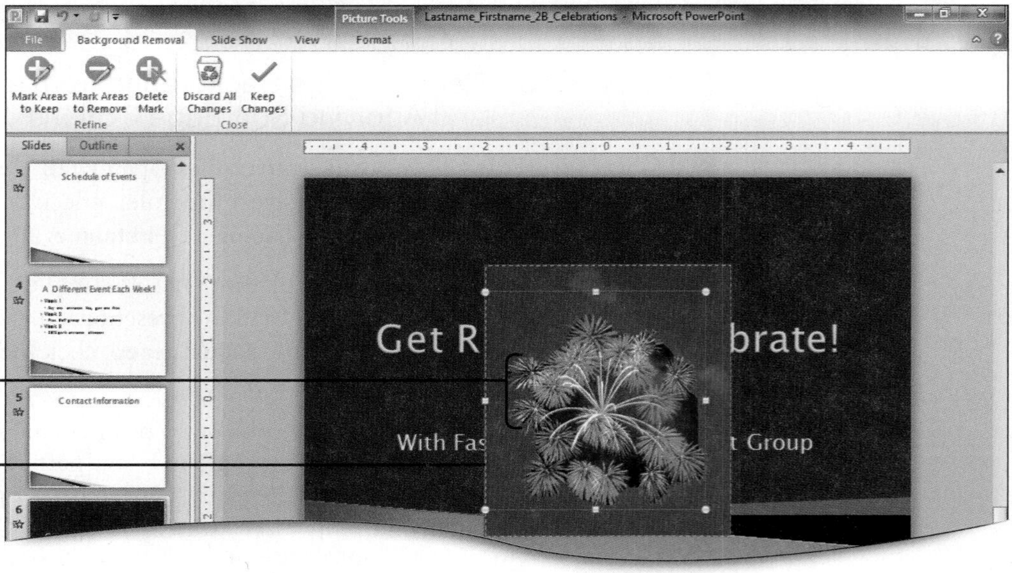

Additional portion of fireworks display as foreground

Selection rectangle aligns with dashed border

> **Another Way**
> In the status bar, use the Zoom Slider options to increase the Zoom to 100%.

4 On the **View tab**, in the **Zoom group**, click the **Zoom** button. In the **Zoom** dialog box, select **100%**, and then click **OK** to increase the size of the slide in the Slide pane. Notice on the right side of the fireworks picture the dark red shadowing in a triangular shape that is visible between some of the outer flowers of the fireworks display. Compare your slide with Figure 2.39.

Figure 2.39

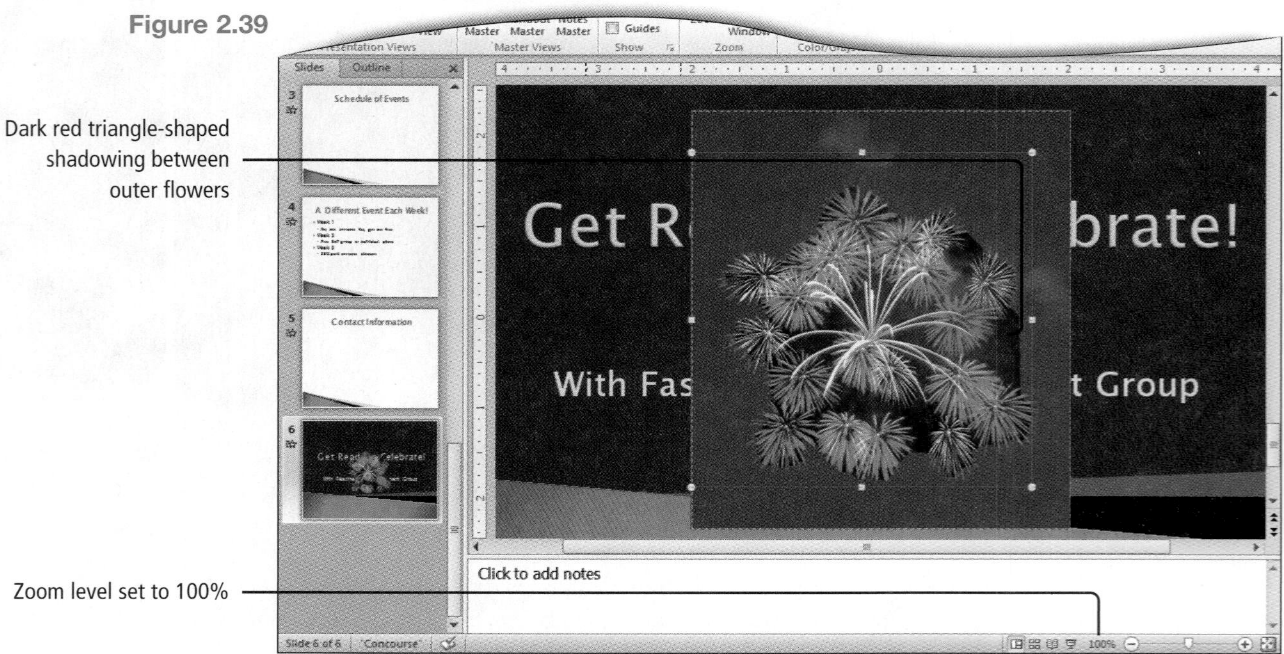

5 On the **Background Removal tab**, in the **Refine group**, click the **Mark Areas to Remove** button, and then position the pencil pointer so that the ruler guides align on the **right half of the horizontal ruler at 1 inch** and on the **lower half of the vertical ruler at 0.5 inch**. Click one time to insert a deletion mark, and then compare your screen with Figure 2.40. If your mark is not positioned as shown in the figure, click Undo and begin again.

You can surround irregular-shaped areas that you want to remove with deletion marks. Here, you can begin to surround the dark red shadow by placing a deletion mark in one corner of the red triangular area.

Figure 2.40

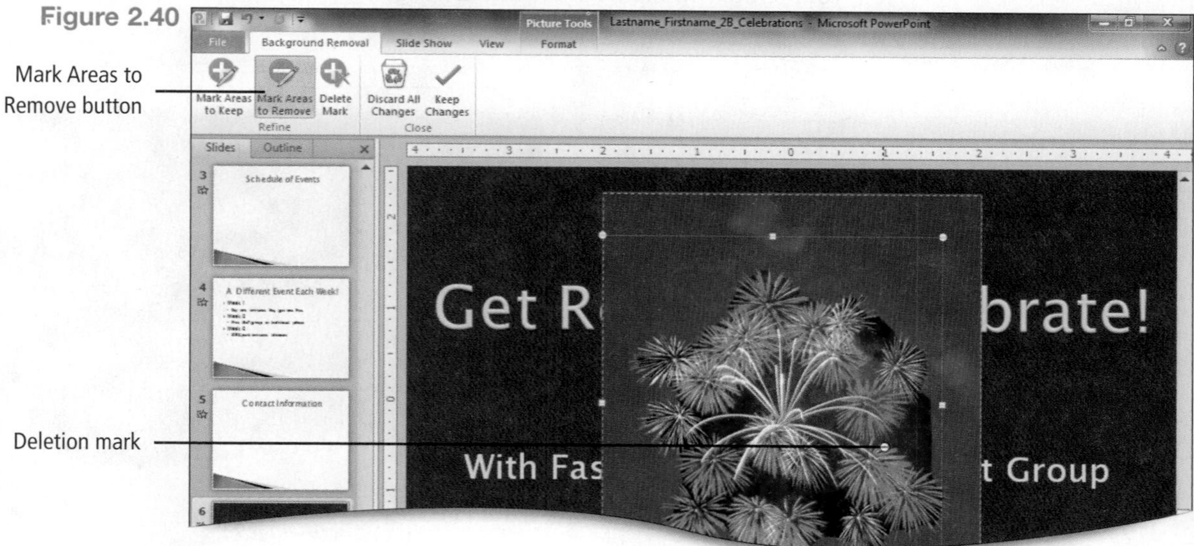

6 With the pencil pointer still active, position the pointer to align the ruler guides on the **right half of the horizontal ruler at approximately 1.5 inches** and on the **lower half of the vertical ruler to 0.75 inch** so that the pointer is aligned on the right edge of the dark red triangle. Click one time to insert another mark. Compare your screen with Figure 2.41.

The two inserted marks provide PowerPoint sufficient information to remove the triangular-shaped red and black shadowed area. If the area is not removed as shown in the figure, insert additional deletion marks as necessary.

Figure 2.41

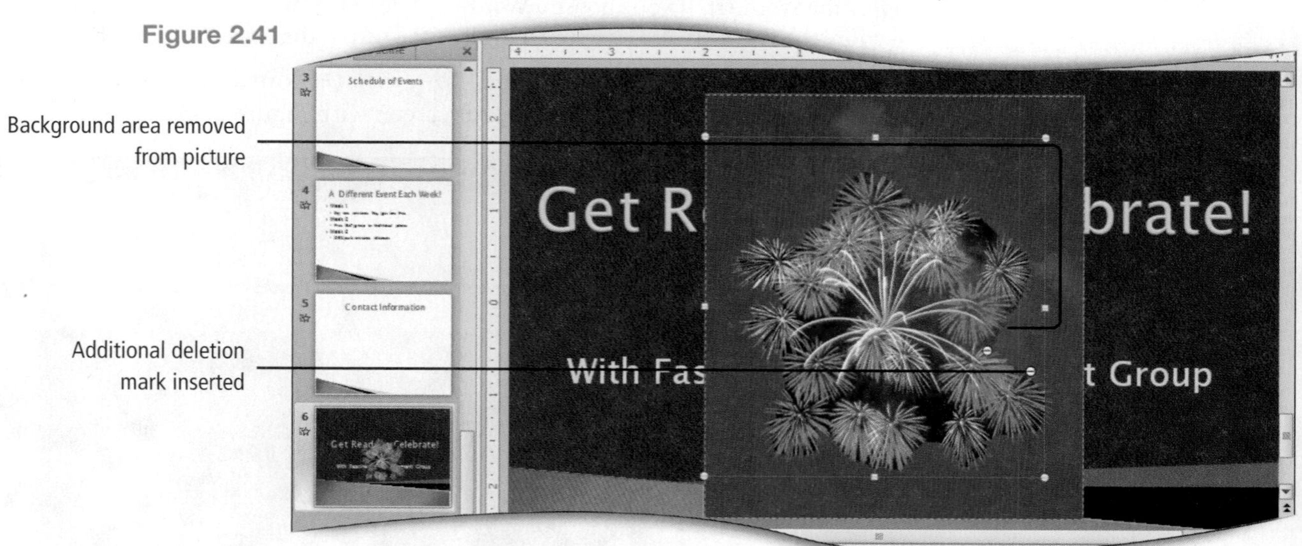

7 On the **Background Removal tab**, in the **Close group**, click the **Keep Changes** button to remove the background. On the far right edge of the status bar, click the **Fit slide to current window** button.

8 With the picture selected, on the **Format tab**, in the **Picture Styles group**, click the **Picture Effects** button, point to **Soft Edges**, and then click **50 Point**. In the **Adjust group**, click the **Artistic Effects** button, and then in the fourth row, click the third effect—**Crisscross Etching**.

9 In the **Size group**, click in the **Shape Height** box, replace the number with **3.5** and then press Enter. In the **Arrange group**, click the **Align** button, and then click **Align Center**. Click the **Align** button again, and then click **Align Middle**. Compare your slide with Figure 2.42, and then **Save** your presentation.

Figure 2.42

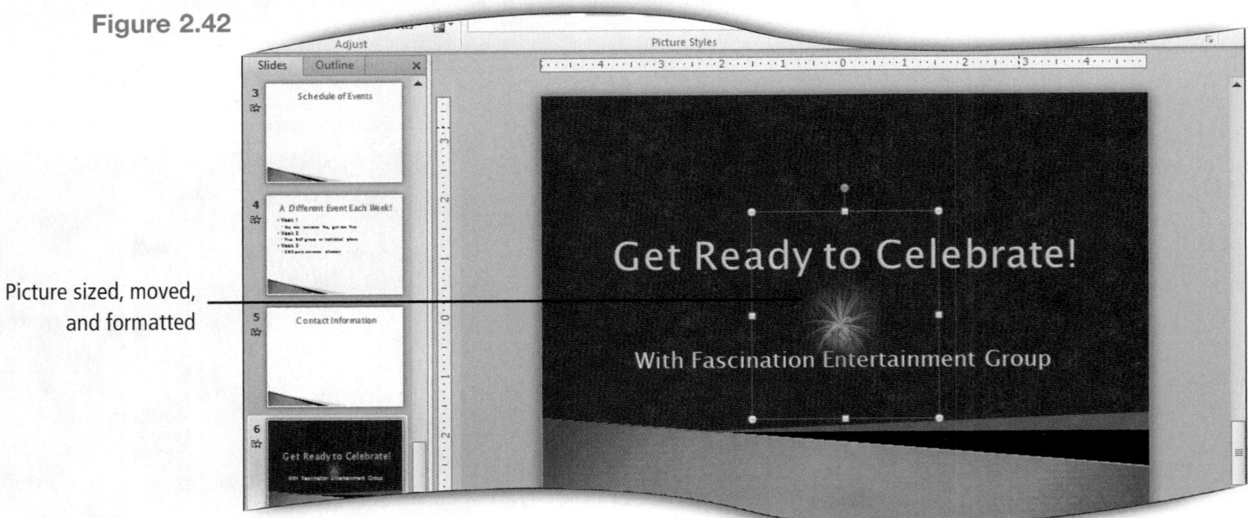

Activity 2.16 | Applying WordArt Styles to Existing Text

1 On **Slide 6**, click anywhere in the word *Get* to activate the title placeholder, and then select the title—*Get Ready to Celebrate*. Click the **Format tab**, and then in the **WordArt Styles group**, click the **More** button.

The WordArt Styles gallery displays in two sections. If you choose a WordArt style in the Applies to Selected Text section, you must first select all of the text to which you want to apply the WordArt. If you choose a WordArt style in the Applies to All Text in the Shape section, the WordArt style is applied to all of the text in the placeholder or shape.

2 Under **Applies to Selected Text**, in the first row, click the fourth style—**Fill – White, Outline – Accent 1**, and then compare your screen with Figure 2.43.

Figure 2.43

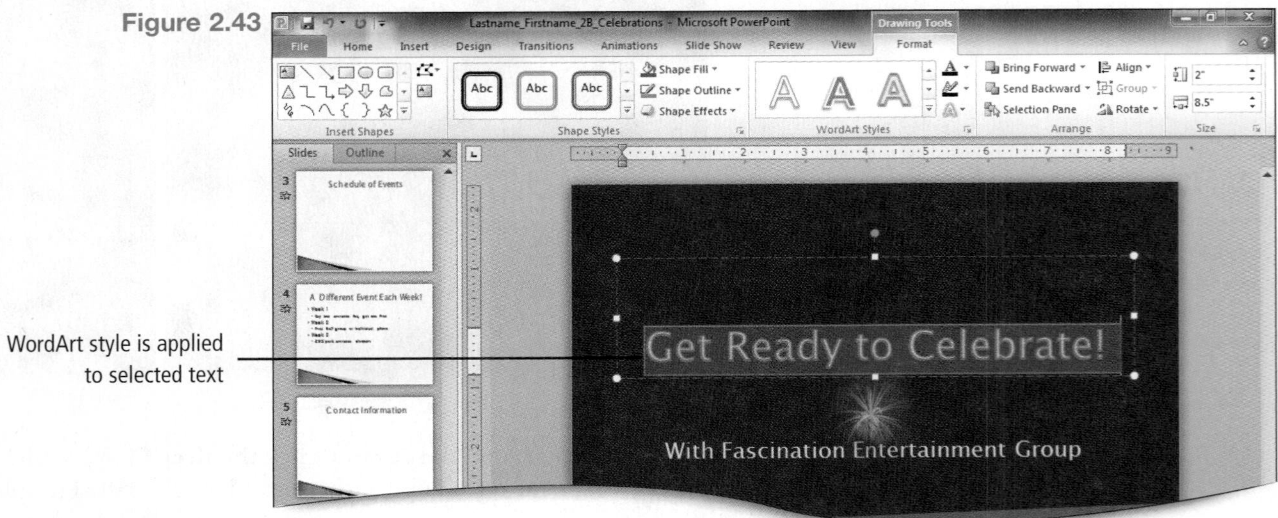

3 With the text still selected, in the **WordArt Styles group**, click the **Text Fill button arrow** [A]. Under **Theme Colors**, in the sixth column, click the fourth color—**Dark Red, Accent 2, Lighter 40%**, and then compare your screen with Figure 2.44.

Figure 2.44

4 Display **Slide 1**, and then click anywhere in the title—*Fascination Entertainment Group*.

5 Click the **Format tab**, and then in the **WordArt Styles group**, click the **More** button [▾] to display the **WordArt Styles** gallery. Under **Applies to All Text in the Shape**, in the first row, click the third style—**Fill – Dark Red, Accent 2, Warm Matte Bevel**, and then compare your screen with Figure 2.45.

Figure 2.45

6 **Save** [💾] your presentation.

Activity 2.17 | Inserting a WordArt Object

In addition to formatting existing text using WordArt, you can insert a new WordArt object anywhere on a slide.

1 Display **Slide 2**. Click the **Insert tab**, and then in the **Text group**, click the **WordArt** button. In the gallery, in the last row, click the third WordArt style—**Fill – Dark Red, Accent 2, Matte Bevel**.

In the center of your slide, a WordArt placeholder displays *Your text here*. Text that you type will replace this text and the placeholder will expand to accommodate the text. The WordArt is surrounded by sizing handles with which you can adjust its size.

2 Type **Get Ready for 2014!** to replace the WordArt placeholder text. Compare your screen with Figure 2.46.

Figure 2.46

3 Point to the WordArt border to display the pointer. Hold down Shift, and then drag down to position the WordArt between the picture and the text at the bottom of the slide and centered between the left and right edge of the slide. Use Ctrl + any of the arrow keys to move the WordArt in small increments. Compare your slide with Figure 2.47 and move the WordArt again if necessary.

Recall that holding down Shift when dragging an object constrains the horizontal and vertical movement so that the object is moved in a straight line.

Figure 2.47

4 **Save** your presentation.

Objective 6 | Create and Format a SmartArt Graphic

A ***SmartArt graphic*** is a visual representation of information that you create by choosing from among various layouts to communicate your message or ideas effectively. SmartArt graphics can illustrate processes, hierarchies, cycles, lists, and relationships. You can include text and pictures in a SmartArt graphic, and you can apply colors, effects, and styles that coordinate with the presentation theme.

Activity 2.18 | Creating a SmartArt Graphic from Bulleted Points

You can convert an existing bulleted list into a SmartArt graphic. When you create a SmartArt graphic, consider the message that you are trying to convey, and then choose an appropriate layout. The table in Figure 2.48 describes types of SmartArt layouts and suggested purposes.

Microsoft PowerPoint SmartArt Graphic Types

Graphic Type	Purpose of Graphic
List	Shows non-sequential information
Process	Shows steps in a process or timeline
Cycle	Shows a continual process
Hierarchy	Shows a decision tree or displays an organization chart
Relationship	Illustrates connections
Matrix	Shows how parts relate to a whole
Pyramid	Shows proportional relationships with the largest component on the top or bottom
Picture	Includes pictures in the layout to communicate messages and ideas

Figure 2.48

> **Another Way**
> Right-click on a bulleted list to display the shortcut menu, and then click **Convert to SmartArt**.

1. Display **Slide 4**, and then click anywhere in the bulleted list placeholder. On the **Home tab**, in the **Paragraph group**, click the **Convert to SmartArt** button. Below the gallery, click **More SmartArt Graphics**.

   Three sections comprise the Choose a SmartArt Graphic dialog box. The left section lists the SmartArt graphic types. The center section displays the SmartArt graphics according to type. The third section displays the selected SmartArt graphic, its name, and a description of its purpose.

2. On the left side of the **Choose a SmartArt Graphic** dialog box, click **List**. Use the ScreenTips to locate and then click **Vertical Bullet List**. Compare your screen with Figure 2.49.

Figure 2.49

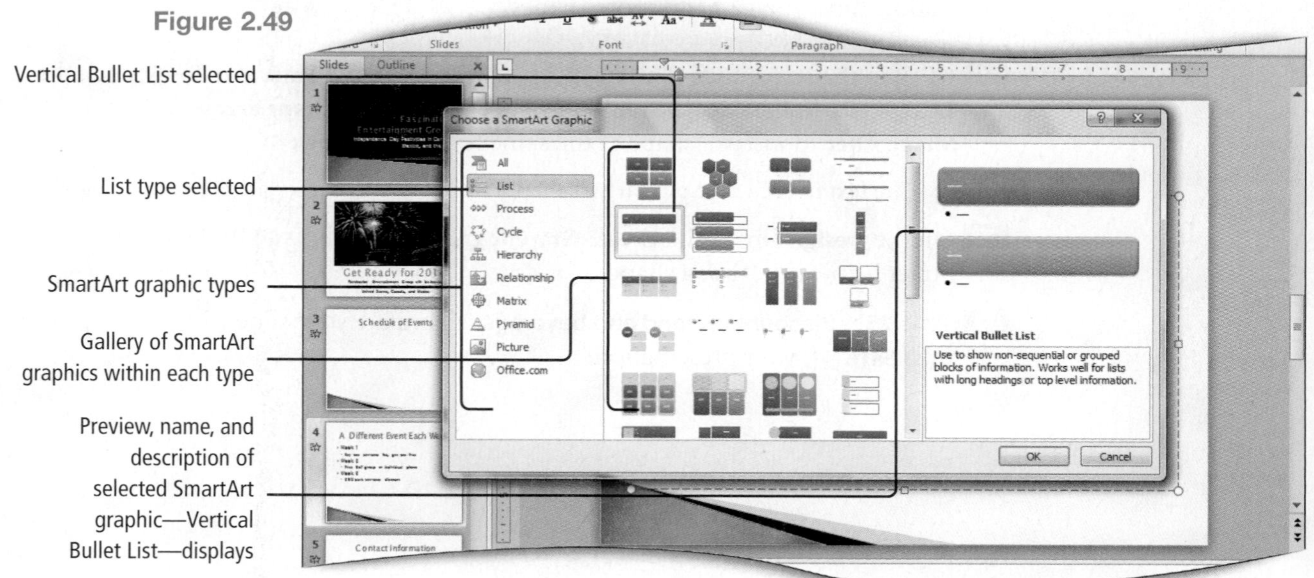

3 In the **Choose a SmartArt Graphic** dialog box, click **OK**. If the Text Pane displays to the right of the SmartArt graphic, click its Close button. Compare your screen with Figure 2.50, and then **Save** your presentation.

It is not necessary to select all of the text in the list. By clicking in the list, PowerPoint converts all of the bullet points to the selected SmartArt graphic. On the Ribbon, the SmartArt contextual tools display two tabs—Design and Format. The thick border surrounding the SmartArt graphic indicates that it is selected and displays the area that the object will cover on the slide.

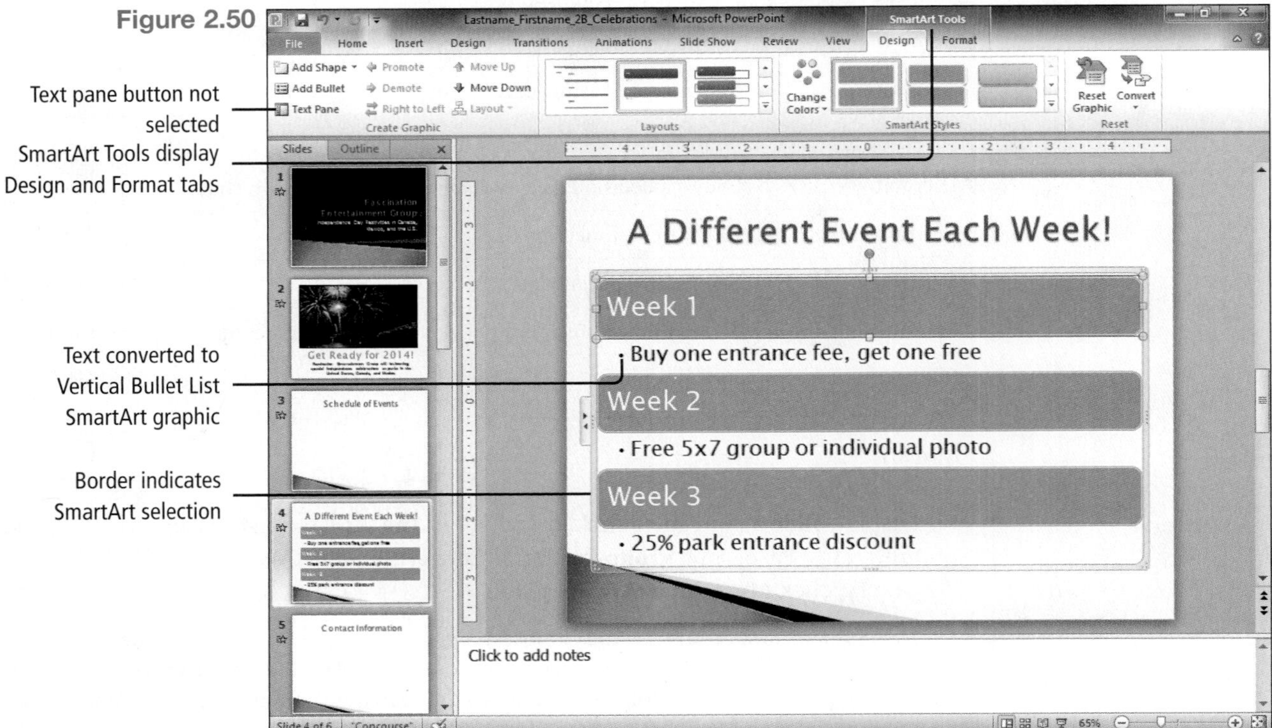

Figure 2.50

Activity 2.19 | Adding Shapes in a SmartArt Graphic

If a SmartArt graphic does not have enough shapes to illustrate a concept or display the relationships, you can add more shapes.

> **Another Way**
>
> Right-click the shape, point to **Add Shape**, and then click **Add Shape After**.

1 Click in the shape that contains the text *Week 3*. In the **SmartArt Tools**, click the **Design tab**. In the **Create Graphic group**, click the **Add Shape arrow**, and then click **Add Shape After** to insert a shape at the same level. Type **Week 4**

The text in each of the SmartArt shapes resizes to accommodate the added shape.

2 On the **Design tab**, in the **Create Graphic group**, click the **Add Bullet** button to add a bullet below the *Week 4* shape.

3 Type **25% discount on food and beverages** Compare your slide with Figure 2.51, and then **Save** your presentation.

Figure 2.51

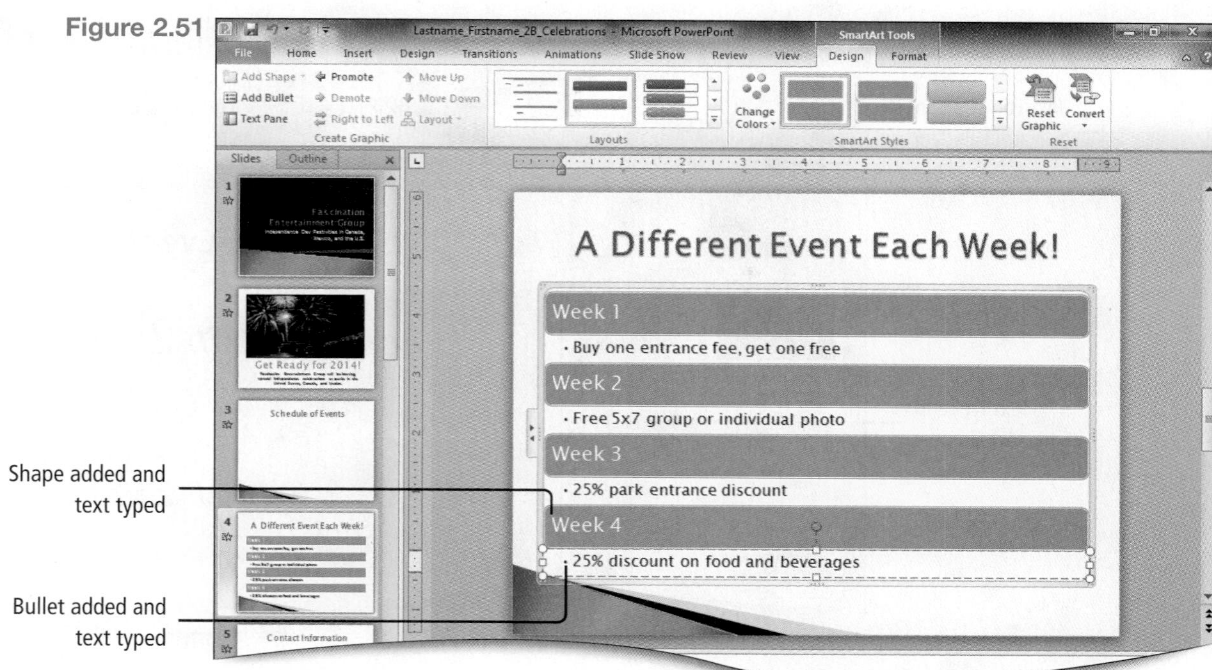

Activity 2.20 | Creating a SmartArt Graphic Using a Content Layout

1 Display **Slide 3**. In the center of the content placeholder, click the **Insert SmartArt Graphic** button to open the **Choose a SmartArt Graphic** dialog box.

2 On the left, click **Process**, and then scroll as necessary and use the ScreenTips to locate **Vertical Arrow List**. Click **Vertical Arrow List**. Compare your screen with Figure 2.52.

Figure 2.52

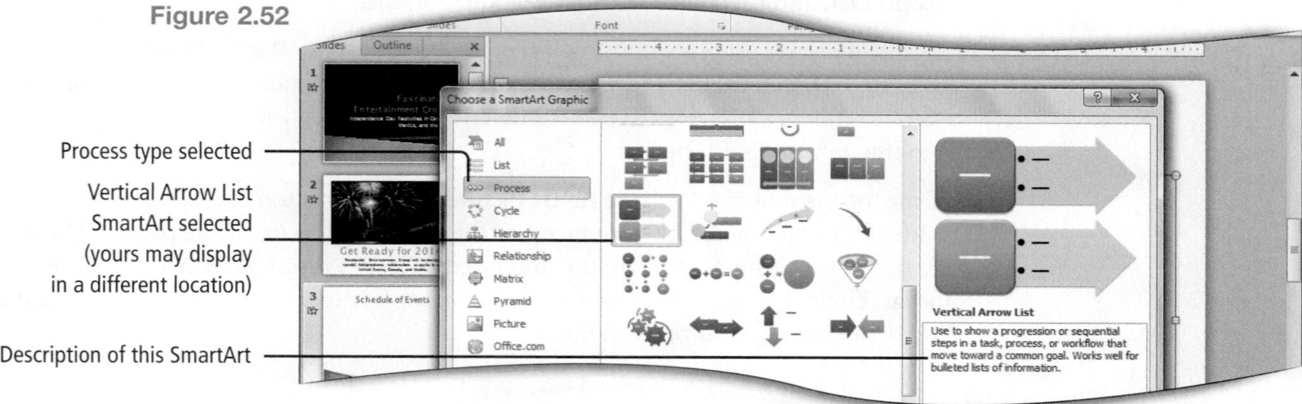

3 Click **OK** to insert the SmartArt graphic.

The SmartArt graphic displays with two rounded rectangle shapes and two arrow shapes. You can type text directly into the shapes or you can type text in the Text Pane, which may display to the left of your SmartArt graphic. You can display the Text Pane by clicking the Text Pane tab on the left side of the SmartArt graphic border, or by clicking the Text Pane button in the Create Graphic group. Depending on your software settings, the Text Pane may display.

4 In the SmartArt graphic, click in the first orange rectangle, and then type **Canada** In the arrow shape to the immediate right, click in the first bullet point. Type **July 2014** and then press Del to remove the second bullet point in the arrow shape.

5 Click in the second orange rectangle, and then type **U.S.** In the arrow shape to the immediate right, click in the first bullet point. Type **July 2014** and then press Del. Compare your slide with Figure 2.53.

Figure 2.53

6. Click in the *U.S.* rectangle. On the **Design tab**, in the **Create Graphic group**, click the **Add Shape arrow**. Click **Add Shape After** to insert a new rectangle and arrow. Type **Mexico** and then in the arrow shape to the right, type **September 2014**

7. Display **Slide 5**. In the center of the content placeholder, click the **Insert SmartArt Graphic** button. In the **Choose a SmartArt Graphic** dialog box, click **Picture**, and then scroll as necessary to locate **Vertical Picture Accent List**. Click **Vertical Picture Accent List**, and then click **OK** to insert the graphic.

8. In the SmartArt graphic, in the top rectangle shape, type **Rachel Lewis** and then press Enter. Type **United States** and then click in the middle rectangle shape. Type **Javier Perez** and then press Enter. Type **Mexico** and then click in the last rectangle shape, type **Annette Johnson** and then press Enter. Type **Canada**

9. In the top circle shape, click the **Insert Picture from File** button. Navigate to your student files, click **p02B_US_Contact**, and then press Enter to insert the picture. Using the technique you just practiced, in the middle circle shape, insert **p02B_Mexico_Contact**. In the last circle shape, insert **p02B_Canada_Contact**. Compare your screen with Figure 2.54, and then **Save** your presentation.

Figure 2.54

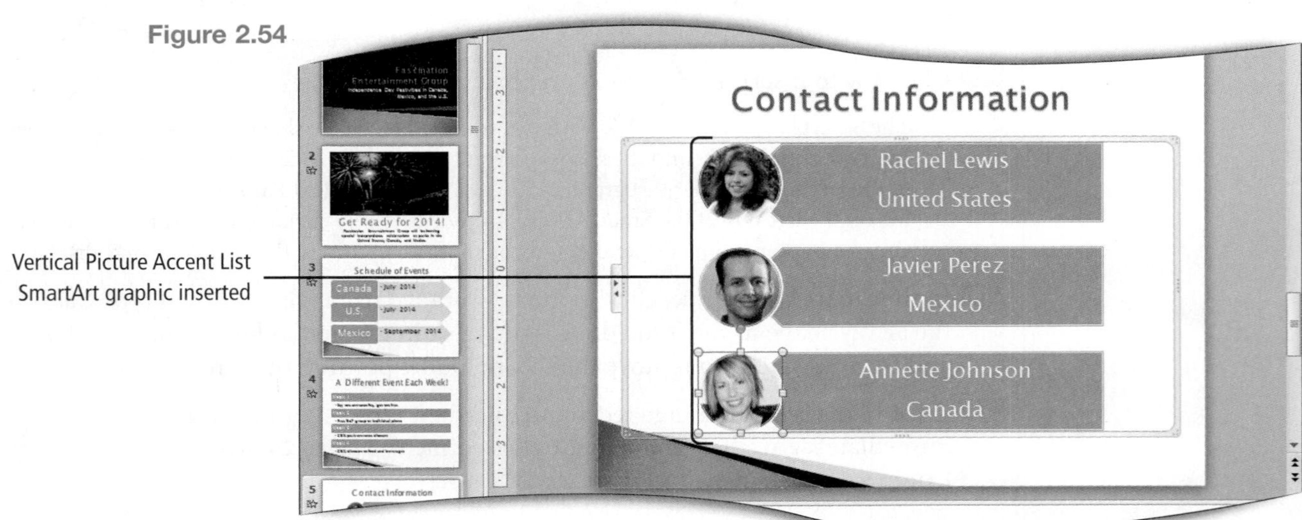

Activity 2.21 | Changing the SmartArt Layout

1 Display **Slide 3**, and then click anywhere in the SmartArt graphic. In the **SmartArt Tools**, click the **Design tab**. In the **Layouts group**, click the **More** button, and then click **More Layouts**. In the **Choose a SmartArt Graphic** dialog box, click **Hierarchy**. Locate and click **Hierarchy List**, and then click **OK**.

2 Compare your slide with Figure 2.55, and then **Save** the presentation.

Figure 2.55

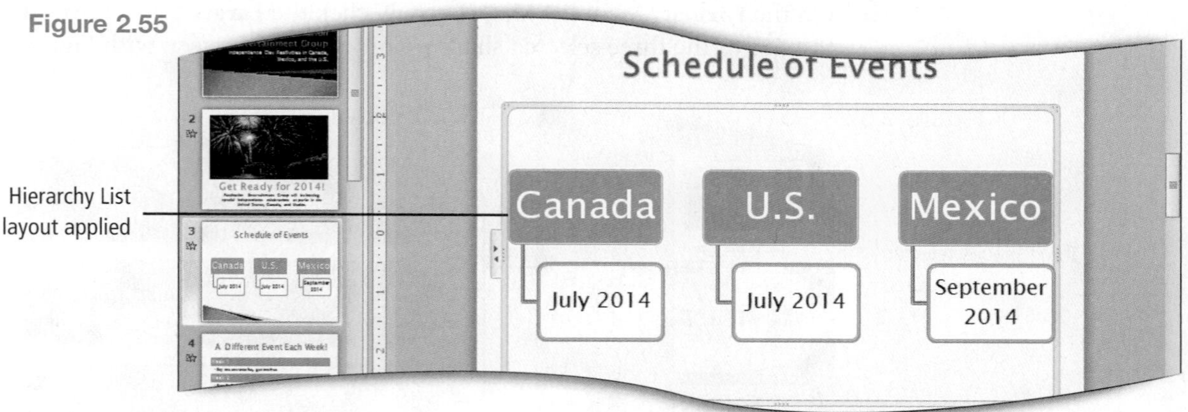

Activity 2.22 | Changing the Color and Style of a SmartArt Graphic

SmartArt Styles are combinations of formatting effects that you can apply to SmartArt graphics.

1 With **Slide 3** displayed and the SmartArt graphic selected, on the **Design tab**, in the **SmartArt Styles group**, click the **Change Colors** button. In the color gallery, under **Colorful**, click the first style—**Colorful - Accent Colors**—to change the color.

2 On the **Design tab**, in the **SmartArt Styles group**, click the **More** button to display the **SmartArt Styles gallery**. Under **3-D**, click the second style, **Inset**. Compare your slide with Figure 2.56.

Figure 2.56

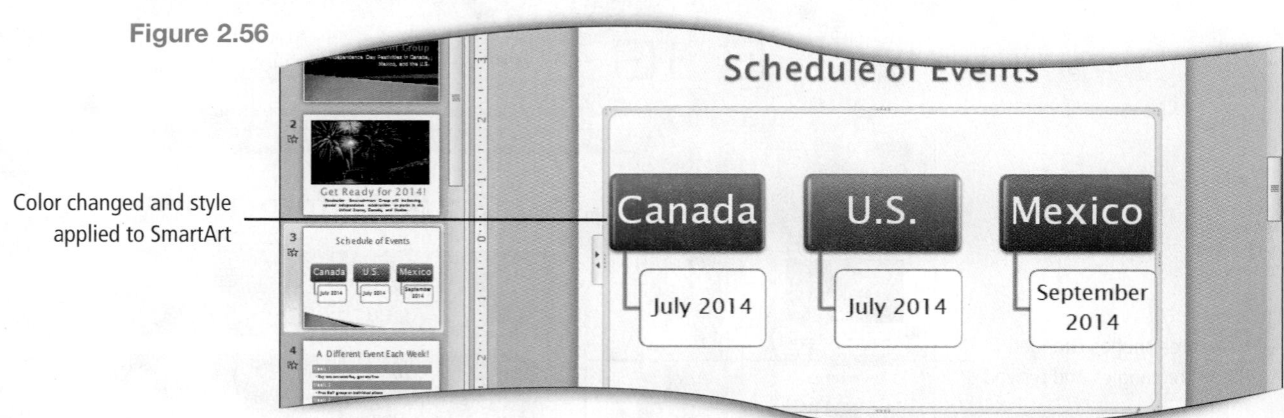

3 Display **Slide 5**, and select the SmartArt. On the **Design tab**, in the **SmartArt Styles group**, click the **Change Colors** button. Under **Accent 2**, click the second style—**Colored Fill - Accent 2**. On the **Design tab**, in the **SmartArt Styles group**, click the **More** button. Under **Best Match for Document**, click the last style, **Intense Effect**. **Save** the presentation.

Activity 2.23 | Customizing the Size and Shape of a SmartArt Graphic

You can select individual or groups of shapes in a SmartArt graphic and make them larger or smaller, and you can change selected shapes to another type of shape.

1. With **Slide 5** displayed, click in the upper red shape that contains the text *Rachel Lewis*. Hold down Shift, and then click in each of the two remaining red shapes containing the text *Javier Perez* and *Annette Johnson* so that all three text shapes are selected.
2. On the **Format tab**, in the **Shapes group**, click the **Larger** button two times to increase the size of the three selected shapes. Compare your screen with Figure 2.57.

Figure 2.57

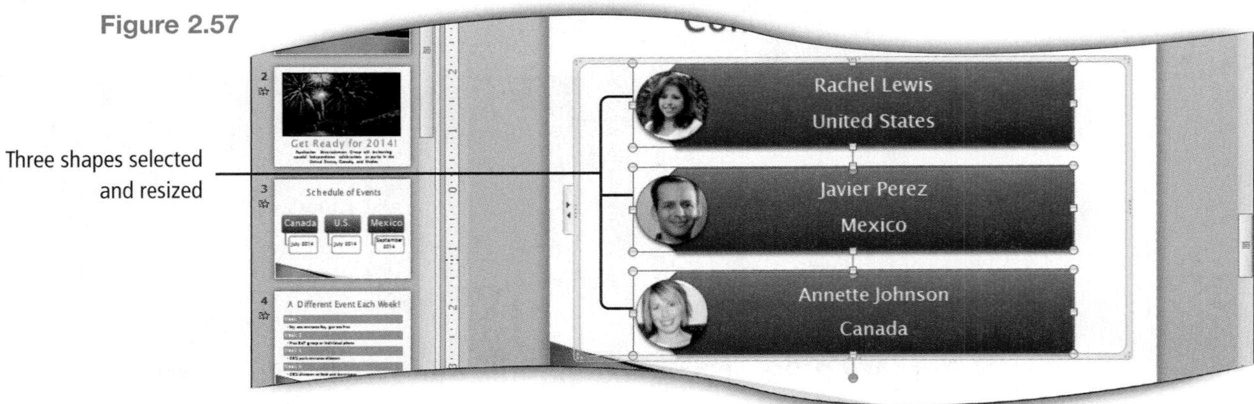

3. With the three shapes selected, on the **Home tab**, in the **Font group**, increase the **Font Size** to **28**.
4. Select the first circle picture, and then hold down Shift and click the remaining two circles so that all three circles are selected. In the **SmartArt Tools**, on the **Format tab**, in the **Shapes group**, click the **Change Shape** button. Under **Rectangles**, click the first shape—**Rectangle**—to change the circles to rectangles. With the three shapes selected, in the **Shapes group**, click the **Larger** button two times. Compare your screen with Figure 2.58, and then **Save** the presentation.

Figure 2.58

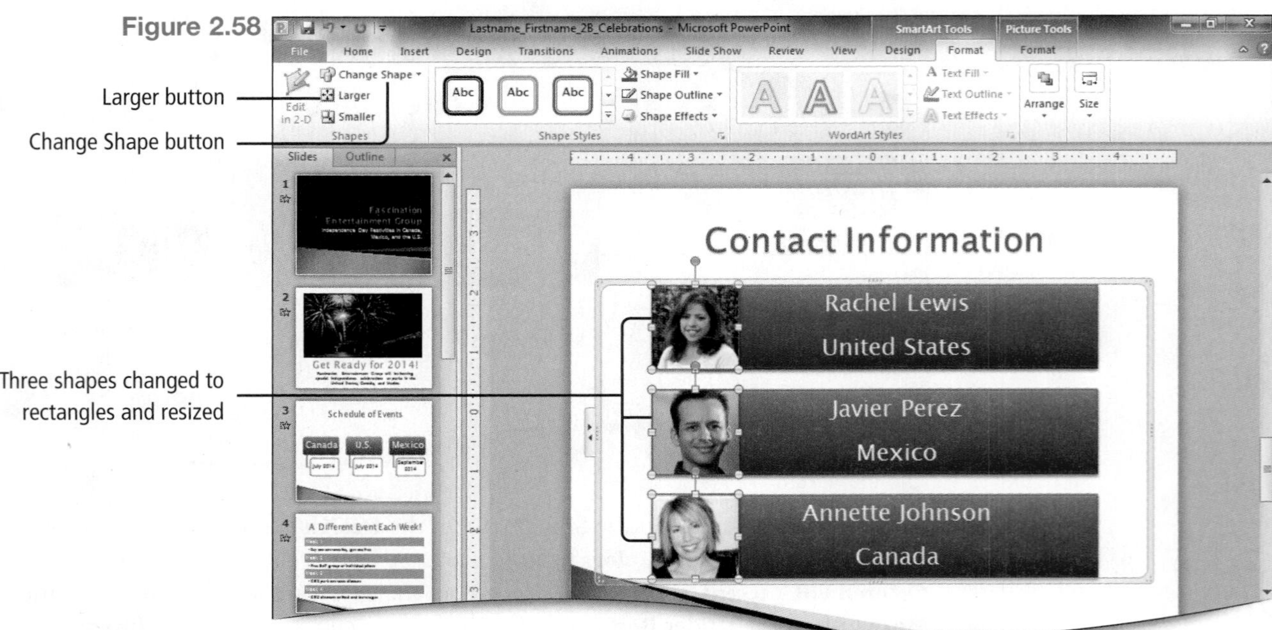

Activity 2.24 | Converting a SmartArt to Text

1 Display **Slide 4**, and then click anywhere in the SmartArt graphic. On the **Design tab**, in the **Reset group**, click the **Convert** button, and then click **Convert to Text** to convert the SmartArt graphic to a bulleted list. Compare your screen with Figure 2.59.

Figure 2.59

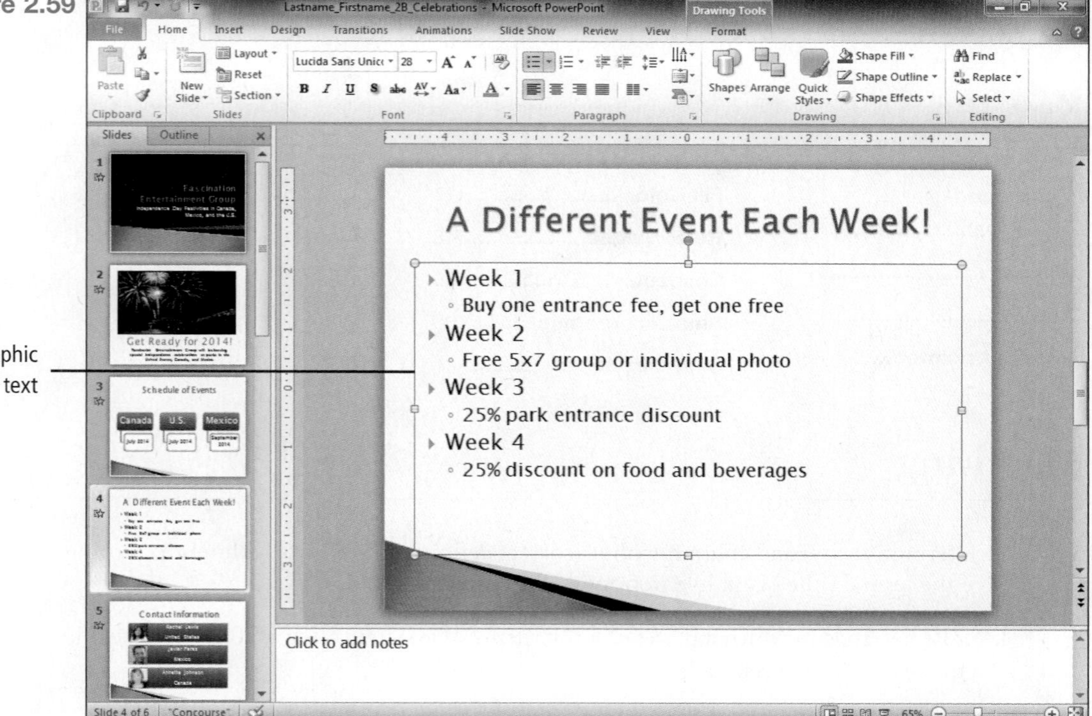

2 Display the **Document Properties**. Replace the text in the **Author** box with your own firstname and lastname, in the **Subject** box, type your course name and section number, and in the **Keywords** box, type **Independence day, celebrations Close** the **Document Information Panel**.

3 Insert a **Header & Footer** on the **Notes and Handouts**. Include the **Date and time updated automatically**, the **Page number**, and a **Footer** with the text **Lastname_Firstname_2B_Celebrations** Apply to all the slides. View the presentation from the beginning, and then make any necessary adjustments.

4 **Save** your presentation. Print **Handouts 6 Slides Horizontal**, or submit your presentation electronically as directed by your instructor.

5 **Close** the presentation.

End You have completed Project 2B

Content-Based Assessments

Summary

In this chapter, you formatted a presentation by changing the bullet style and by applying WordArt styles to text. You enhanced your presentations by inserting, sizing, and formatting shapes, pictures, and SmartArt graphics, resulting in a professional-looking presentation.

Key Terms

Matching

Match each term in the second column with its correct definition in the first column by writing the letter of the term on the blank line in front of the correct definition.

____ 1. The line style in which a placeholder border displays, indicating that all of the text in the placeholder is selected.

____ 2. A common format for a slide that contains a single point without a bullet symbol.

____ 3. A single media file, for example art, sound, animation, or a movie.

____ 4. A four-headed arrow-shaped pointer that indicates that you can reposition an object or image.

____ 5. An object within which you can position text anywhere on the slide.

____ 6. Vertical and horizontal lines that display in the rulers to provide a visual indication of the pointer position so that you can draw a shape.

____ 7. Lines, arrows, stars, banners, ovals, or rectangles used to illustrate an idea, a process, or a workflow.

____ 8. The pointer that indicates that you can draw a shape.

____ 9. The inside color of text or an object.

____ 10. A style gallery displaying predefined combinations of shape fill and line colors.

____ 11. A setting used to align selected objects.

____ 12. The command that reduces the size of a picture by removing vertical or horizontal edges.

____ 13. A gallery of text styles from which you can create shadowed or mirrored text.

____ 14. A visual representation of information that you create by choosing from among layouts to communicate your message or ideas.

____ 15. Combinations of formatting effects that are applied to SmartArt graphics.

A Align to Slide
B Clip
C Crop
D Crosshair pointer
E Fill color
F Move pointer
G Paragraph
H Ruler guides
I Shapes
J Shape Styles
K SmartArt graphic
L SmartArt Styles
M Solid
N Text box
O WordArt

Content-Based Assessments

Multiple Choice

Circle the correct answer.

1. The color of the numbers or bullet symbols in a list is determined by the:
   A. Slide layout   B. Presentation theme   C. Gallery
2. When you point to an image in the Clip Art pane, the screen element that displays the keywords and information about the size of the image is the:
   A. ScreenTip   B. Navigation bar   C. Menu
3. To horizontally or vertically position selected objects on a slide relative to each other, use the:
   A. Align tools   B. Distribute tools   C. Crop tools
4. The command that removes unwanted portions of a picture so that the picture does not appear as a self-contained rectangle is:
   A. Shape height   B. Picture adjust   C. Background removal
5. The SmartArt type that shows steps in a process or timeline is:
   A. Radial   B. Process   C. List
6. The SmartArt type that shows a continual process is:
   A. Hierarchy   B. Radial   C. Cycle
7. The SmartArt type with which you can show a decision tree or create an organization chart is:
   A. Matrix   B. Pyramid   C. Hierarchy
8. The SmartArt type that illustrates connections is:
   A. Picture   B. Radial   C. Relationship
9. The SmartArt type that shows how parts relate to a whole is:
   A. Matrix   B. Pyramid   C. Radial
10. The SmartArt type that shows proportional relationships with the largest component on the top or bottom is:
    A. Matrix   B. Pyramid   C. Relationship

Content-Based Assessments

Apply **2A** skills from these Objectives:

1. Format Numbered and Bulleted Lists
2. Insert Clip Art
3. Insert Text Boxes and Shapes
4. Format Objects

Skills Review | Project 2C Concerts

In the following Skills Review, you will format a presentation by inserting and formatting Clip Art, text boxes, and shapes, and by modifying bullets and numbering. Your completed presentation will look similar to Figure 2.60.

Project Files

For Project 2C, you will need the following file:

p02C_Concerts

You will save your presentation as:

Lastname_Firstname_2C_Concerts

Project Results

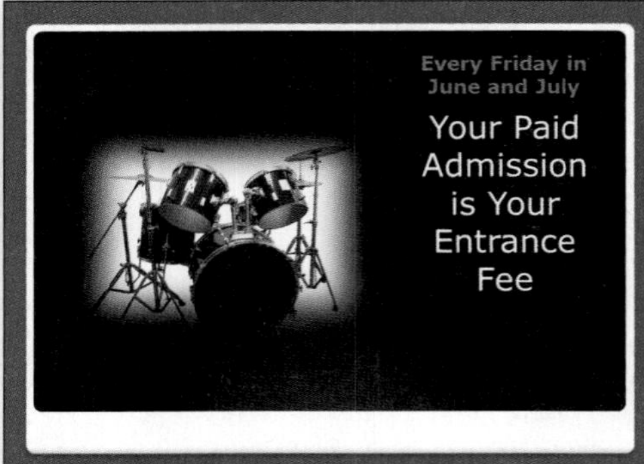

Every Friday in June and July
Your Paid Admission is Your Entrance Fee

- Located in the main plaza at each park
- Grandstand seating will be available
  - Seating is limited
  - Reserved seating is available through the information booth
- Concerts begin at 7:30 pm

Join Us as We Rock the Night!

1. Eighties Rock
2. Top Forty
3. Country Hits
4. Fifties and Sixties
5. Rhythm & Blues
6. Children's Favorites

A Different Band Each Week!

Figure 2.60

(Project 2C Concerts continues on the next page)

Skills Review | Project 2C Concerts (continued)

1 **Start** PowerPoint. From the student files that accompany this textbook, locate and open **p02C_Concerts**. **Save** the presentation in your **PowerPoint Chapter 2** folder as **Lastname_Firstname_2C_Concerts**

a. If necessary, display the Rulers. With **Slide 1** displayed, on the **Insert tab**, in the **Illustrations group**, click the **Shapes** button, and then under **Basic Shapes**, in the second row, click the fifth shape—**Frame**.

b. Move the pointer to align the ruler guides with the **left half of the horizontal ruler at 3 inches** and with the **upper half of the vertical ruler at 2.5 inches**, and then click to insert the Frame.

c. On the **Format tab**, in the **Size group**, click in the **Shape Height** box to select the number, and then type **1.7** Click in the **Shape Width** box. Replace the selected number with **5.5** and then press Enter to resize the shape.

d. With the frame selected, type **Fascination Entertainment Group Presents** and then change the **Font Size** to **24**. On the **Format tab**, in the **Shape Styles group**, click the **Shape Fill** button, and then under **Theme Colors**, in the fourth column, click the first color—**Lavender, Text 2**.

2 On the **Insert tab**, in the **Images group**, click the **Clip Art** button to display the **Clip Art** pane.

a. In the **Clip Art** pane, click in the **Search for** box and replace any existing text with **compositions musical notes** Click the **Results should be arrow**, and then click as necessary to so that only the **Photographs** check box is selected. Include Office.com content. Click **Go** to display the musical notes pictures.

b. Click the black and white picture of the two lines of music on a music sheet, and then **Close** the **Clip Art** pane. With the picture selected, on the **Format tab**, in the **Size group**, click in the **Shape Height** box. Replace the selected number with **2.5** and then press Enter to resize the image.

c. Point to the picture and then drag down and to the right so that it is centered just below the title—*Concerts in the Park*—and its top edge aligns with the lower edge of the black rounded rectangle.

d. With the picture selected, on the **Format tab**, in the **Size group**, click the **Crop arrow**, and then point to **Crop to Shape**. Under **Basic Shapes**, click the first shape—**Oval**. In the **Picture Styles group**, click the **Picture Effects** button, point to **Soft Edges**, and then click **25 Point**.

e. On the **Insert tab**, in the **Text group**, click the **Text Box** button. Move the pointer to position the ruler guides on the **horizontal ruler at 0 inches** and on the **lower half of the vertical ruler at 2.5 inches**, and then click to insert the text box.

f. On the **Format tab**, in the **Shape Styles group**, click the **More** button. In the first row, click the second style—**Colored Outline - Pink, Accent 1**. Type **Back by Popular Demand!**

g. With the text box selected, hold down Shift, and then click the frame shape, the title placeholder, and the picture so that all four objects are selected. Under **Drawing Tools**, on the **Format tab**, in the **Arrange group**, click the **Align** button, and then click **Align to Slide**. Click the **Align** button again, and then click **Align Center**. **Save** the presentation.

3 Display **Slide 2**, and then click in the title placeholder containing the text *Every Friday in June and July*.

a. On the **Home tab**, in the **Paragraph group**, click the **Bullets** button to remove the bullet symbol from the title.

b. On the left side of the slide, in the content placeholder, click the **Clip Art** button. In the **Clip Art** pane, in the **Search for** box, search for **cymbals** set the results to **Photographs**, include Office.com content, and then click **Go**. Insert the picture of the drum set on a white background.

c. On the **Format tab**, in the **Picture Styles group**, click the **Picture Effects** button, point to **Soft Edges**, and then click **50 Point**. **Close** the **Clip Art** pane.

4 Display **Slide 3**, and then select the third and fourth bullet points—the two, second-level bullet points.

a. On the **Home tab**, in the **Paragraph group**, click the **Bullets button arrow**, and then click **Bullets and Numbering**. In the first row of bullets, click the last style—**Filled Square Bullets**. Replace the number in the **Size** box with **125** and then click the **Color** button. In the eighth column, click the first color—**Gold, Accent 4**—and then click **OK** to change the bullet style.

b. Display **Slide 4**, and then click the bulleted list placeholder. Click the dashed border so that it displays as a solid line, and then on the **Home tab**, in the **Paragraph group**, click the **Numbering button** to change the bullets to numbers.

(Project 2C Concerts continues on the next page)

Skills Review | Project 2C Concerts (continued)

5 Display **Slide 5**. On the **Insert tab**, in the **Images group**, click the **Clip Art** button. In the **Clip Art** pane, in the **Search for** box, search for **electric guitar in monochrome** and then click **Go**. Insert the picture of the black electric guitar on the white, blue, and black background.

a. Change the picture **Height** to **4.5** and then drag the picture down and to the left so that its upper left corner aligns with the upper left corner of the black rectangle on the slide background. **Close** the **Clip Art** pane.

b. With the picture selected, on the **Format tab**, in the **Picture Styles group**, click **Picture Effects**, and then point to **Reflection**. Click the first reflection variation—**Tight Reflection, touching**.

c. With the picture selected, hold down Ctrl, and then press D to create a duplicate of the picture. Drag the duplicated picture to the right about 1 inch, and then hold down Ctrl and press D to create another duplicate.

d. Point to the third guitar picture that you inserted, and then drag to the right so that its upper right corner aligns with the upper right corner of the black rectangle on the slide background.

e. Hold down Shift, and then click the first two guitar pictures so that all three pictures are selected. On the **Format tab**, in the **Arrange group**, click the **Align** button, and then click **Align Selected Objects**. Click the **Align** button again, and then click **Align Top**. Click the **Align** button again, and then click **Distribute Horizontally**.

f. **Insert** a **Header & Footer** on the **Notes and Handouts**. Include the **Date and time updated automatically**, the **Page number**, and a **Footer** with the text **Lastname_Firstname_2C_Concerts** Click **Apply to All**.

g. Display the **Document Properties**. Replace the text in the **Author** box with your own firstname and lastname, in the **Subject** box, type your course name and section number, and in the **Keywords** box, type **concerts, summer events** **Close** the **Document Information Panel**.

h. View your slide show from the beginning, and then **Save** your presentation. Submit your presentation electronically or print **Handouts 6 Slides Horizontal** as directed by your instructor. **Close** the presentation and exit PowerPoint.

End **You have completed Project 2C**

Apply **2B** skills from these Objectives:

- **5** Remove Picture Backgrounds and Insert WordArt
- **6** Create and Format a SmartArt Graphic

Skills Review | Project 2D Corporate Events

In the following Skills Review, you will format a presentation by inserting and formatting WordArt and SmartArt graphics. Your completed presentation will look similar to Figure 2.61.

Project Files

For Project 2D, you will need the following file:

p02D_Corporate_Events

You will save your presentation as:

Lastname_Firstname_2D_Corporate_Events

Project Results

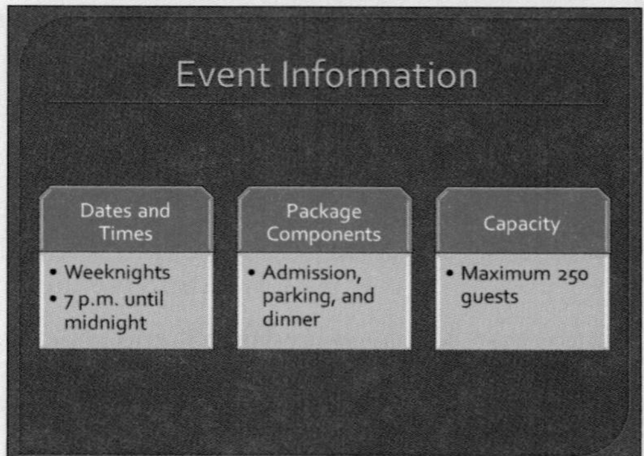

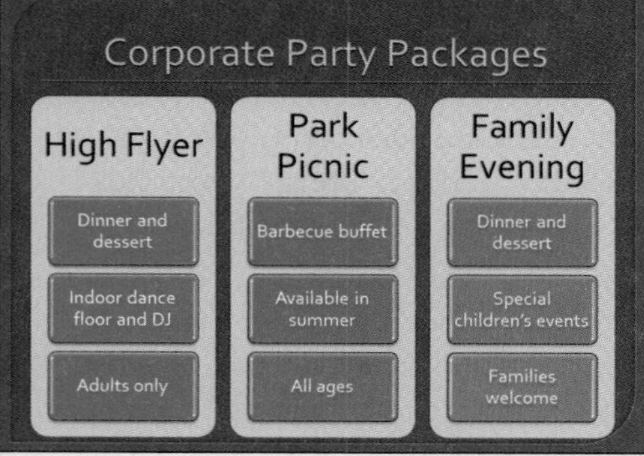

Figure 2.61

(Project 2D Corporate Events continues on the next page)

Content-Based Assessments

Skills Review | Project 2D Corporate Events (continued)

1 **Start** PowerPoint. From the student files that accompany this textbook, locate and open **p02D_Corporate_Events**. **Save** the presentation in your **PowerPoint Chapter 2** folder as **Lastname_Firstname_2D_Corporate_Events**

a. With **Slide 1** displayed, select the title—*Fascination Entertainment Group*. On the **Format tab**, in the **WordArt Styles group**, click the **More** button. Under **Applies to All Text in the Shape**, click the first style—**Fill - White, Warm Matte Bevel**. Change the **Font Size** to **40** so that all of the text displays on one line.

b. Display **Slide 2**. On the **Insert tab**, in the **Text group**, click the **WordArt** button. In the **WordArt** gallery, in the second row, click the second style—**Fill - Lime, Accent 6, Outline - Accent 6, Glow - Accent 6**. With the text *Your text here* selected, type **Corporate Events**

c. Point to the dashed, outer edge of the WordArt placeholder, hold down Shift, and drag straight down so that the WordArt is positioned between the picture and the text at the bottom of the slide.

d. With the WordArt selected, on the **Format tab**, in the **Arrange group**, click the **Align** button, and then click **Align Center** so that the WordArt is horizontally centered on the slide. **Save** the presentation.

2 Display **Slide 3**. In the center of the content placeholder, click the **Insert SmartArt Graphic** button to open the **Choose a SmartArt Graphic** dialog box. On the left, click **List**, and then use the ScreenTips to locate and then click **Vertical Bullet List**. Click **OK**.

a. In the SmartArt graphic, click *Text* in the first blue rectangle. Type **Dates and Times** and then click the bullet symbol below the first blue rectangle. Type **Weeknights** and then press Enter to insert a new bullet point. Type **7 p.m. until midnight**

b. Click in the second blue rectangle. Type **Package Components** and then click the bullet symbol below the second blue rectangle. Type **Admission, parking, and dinner**

c. Click in the *Package Components* rectangle, and then on the **SmartArt Tools Design tab**, in the **Create Graphic group**, click the **Add Shape arrow**. Click **Add Shape After** to insert a blue rectangle. Type **Capacity** and then on the **SmartArt Tools Design tab**, in the **Create Graphic group**, click the **Add Bullet** button. Type **Maximum 250 guests**

d. With the SmartArt selected, on the **SmartArt Tools Design tab**, in the **Layouts group**, click the **More** button, and then click **More Layouts**. On the left side of the dialog box, click **List**, and then in the center section of the dialog box, locate and click **Horizontal Bullet List**. Click **OK** to change the SmartArt layout.

e. On the **SmartArt Tools Design tab**, in the **SmartArt Styles group**, click the **More** button. Under **3-D**, in the first row, click the third style—**Cartoon**.

f. Hold down Shift, and then select the **Dates and Times**, **Package Components**, and **Capacity** rectangles. On the **Format tab**, in the **Shapes group**, click the **Change Shape** button, and then under **Rectangles**, click the fourth shape—**Snip Same Side Corner Rectangle**. **Save** the presentation.

3 Display **Slide 4**. In the content placeholder, right-click anywhere in the bulleted list. On the shortcut menu, point to **Convert to SmartArt**, and at the bottom of the gallery, click **More SmartArt Graphics**. On the left side of the **Choose a SmartArt Graphic** dialog box, click **Relationship**. Locate and click **Grouped List**, and then click **OK** to convert the list to a SmartArt graphic.

a. On the **SmartArt Tools Design tab**, in the **SmartArt Styles group**, click the **Change Colors** button. In the **Color** gallery, under **Accent 1**, click the last style—**Transparent Gradient Range - Accent 1**.

b. On the **Design tab**, in the **SmartArt Styles group**, click the **More** button to display the **SmartArt Styles gallery**. Under **3-D**, in the first row, click the third style—**Cartoon**. **Save** the presentation.

4 Display **Slide 5**, and if necessary, display the Rulers. On the **Insert tab**, in the **Text group**, click the **WordArt** button. In the **WordArt** gallery, in the first row, click the fourth style—**Fill - White, Outline - Accent 1**. With the text *Your text here* selected, type **Corporate_events@feg.com**

a. Point to the dashed, outer edge of the WordArt placeholder, and then drag down so that the top edge of the WordArt aligns with the **lower half of the vertical ruler at 1 inch**.

b. With the WordArt selected, on the **Format tab**, in the **Arrange group**, click the **Align** button, and then click **Align Center** so that the WordArt is horizontally centered on the slide.

(Project 2D Corporate Events continues on the next page)

Skills Review | Project 2D Corporate Events (continued)

c. **Insert** a **Header & Footer** on the **Notes and Handouts**. Include the **Date and time updated automatically**, the **Page number**, and a **Footer** with the text **Lastname_Firstname_2D_Corporate_Events** and **Apply to All**.

d. Display the **Document Properties**. Replace the text in the **Author** box with your own firstname and lastname, in the **Subject** box, type your course name and section number, and in the **Keywords** box, type **corporate events, group packages Close** the **Document Information Panel**. View the presentation from the beginning.

e. **Save** your presentation. Submit your presentation electronically or print **Handouts 6 Slides Horizontal** as directed by your instructor. **Close** the presentation and exit PowerPoint.

End You have completed Project 2D

Content-Based Assessments

Apply 2A skills from these Objectives:

1. Format Numbered and Bulleted Lists
2. Insert Clip Art
3. Insert Text Boxes and Shapes
4. Format Objects

Mastering PowerPoint | Project 2E Roller Coasters

In the following Mastering PowerPoint project, you will format a presentation describing new roller coaster attractions at the Fascination Entertainment Group theme parks. Your completed presentation will look similar to Figure 2.62.

Project Files

For Project 2E, you will need the following file:

p02E_Roller_Coasters

You will save your presentation as:

Lastname_Firstname_2E_Roller_Coasters

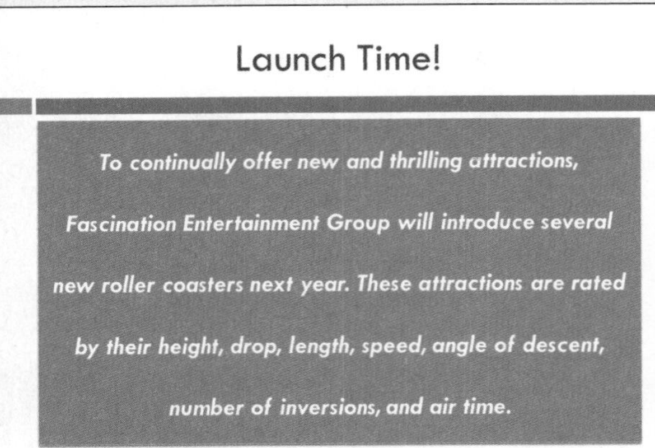

New Coasters for 2016

1. Intensity
   - 2,933 foot steel coaster
   - Scheduled for completion in March
   - Merrillville Park
2. Hang Time
   - 7,438 foot steel coaster
   - Scheduled for completion in May
   - Montreal Park
3. Last Chance
   - 4,564 foot steel coaster
   - Scheduled for completion in July
   - Atlanta Park

Hold Your Breath!

And Let the Excitement Begin!

Figure 2.62

(Project 2E Roller Coasters continues on the next page)

Mastering PowerPoint | Project 2E Roller Coasters (continued)

1 **Start** PowerPoint. From the student files that accompany this textbook, locate and open **p02E_Roller_Coasters**. In your **PowerPoint Chapter 2** folder, **Save** the file as **Lastname_Firstname_2E_Roller_Coasters**

2 On **Slide 2**, remove the bullet symbol from the paragraph. **Center** the paragraph, apply **Bold** and **Italic** to the text, and then set the **Line Spacing** to **2.0**. With the content placeholder selected, display the **Shape Styles** gallery, and then in the fifth row, apply the third style—**Moderate Effect - Red, Accent 2**.

3 On **Slide 3**, apply **Numbering** to the first-level bullet points—*Intensity, Hang Time,* and *Last Chance*. Under each of the numbered items, change all of the hollow circle bullet symbols to **Filled Square Bullets**, and then change the bullet color to **Dark Blue, Text 2**—the first color in the fourth column.

4 In the content placeholder on the right side of the slide, insert a **Clip Art** photograph by searching for **roller coaster** Insert the close-up picture of the roller coaster with the red cars on the blue sky background, as shown in Figure 2.62 at the beginning of this project. Crop the picture shape to **Rounded Rectangle**, and then modify the **Picture Effect** by applying the last **Bevel** style—**Art Deco**.

5 On **Slide 4**, insert the picture of the white looped roller coaster on the lighter blue sky background. Change the picture **Height** to **1.5** and then apply a **25 Point Soft Edges** effect. Drag the picture up and to the left to position it in the center of the red rectangle to the left of the slide title. Deselect the picture.

6 From the **Shapes** gallery, under **Block Arrows**, insert a **Down Arrow** aligned with the **left half of the horizontal ruler at 1 inch** and the **upper half of the vertical ruler at 0.5 inches**. On the **Format tab**, from the **Shape Styles** gallery, in the third row, apply the second style—**Light 1 Outline, Colored Fill - Blue, Accent 1**. Change the **Shape Height** to **2** and the **Shape Width** to **1**

7 Insert a **Text Box** aligned with the **left half of the horizontal ruler at 1.5 inches** and with the **lower half of the vertical ruler at 2 inches**. On the **Format tab**, from the **Shape Styles** gallery, in the last row, apply the third style—**Intense Effect - Red, Accent 2**. In the inserted text box, type **And Let the Excitement Begin!** Change the **Font Size** to **40**, and then if necessary, drag the text box so that its right edge aligns with the right edge of the slide. Select the arrow and the text box, and then apply **Align Left** alignment using the **Align Selected Objects** option.

8 Select the title, the arrow, and the text box. Distribute the objects vertically using the **Align Selected Objects** option. Apply the **Box** transition to all of the slides in the presentation, and then view the slide show from the beginning.

9 **Insert** a **Header & Footer** on the **Notes and Handouts**. Include the **Date and time updated automatically**, the **Page number**, and a **Footer** with the text **Lastname_Firstname_2E_Roller_Coasters** Apply to all.

10 Display the **Document Properties**. Replace the text in the **Author** box with your own firstname and lastname, in the **Subject** box, type your course name and section number, and in the **Keywords** box, type **roller coasters, new attractions Close** the **Document Information Panel**.

11 **Save** your presentation. Submit your presentation electronically or print **Handouts 4 Slides Horizontal** as directed by your instructor. **Close** the presentation and exit PowerPoint.

End **You have completed Project 2E**

Apply **2B** skills from these Objectives:

- 5 Remove Picture Backgrounds and Insert WordArt
- 6 Create and Format a SmartArt Graphic

Mastering PowerPoint | Project 2F Coaster Club

In the following Mastering PowerPoint project, you will format a presentation describing an event sponsored by Fascination Entertainment Group for roller coaster club members. Your completed presentation will look similar to Figure 2.63.

Project Files

For Project 2F, you will need the following file:

p02F_Coaster_Club

You will save your presentation as:

Lastname_Firstname_2F_Coaster_Club

Project Results

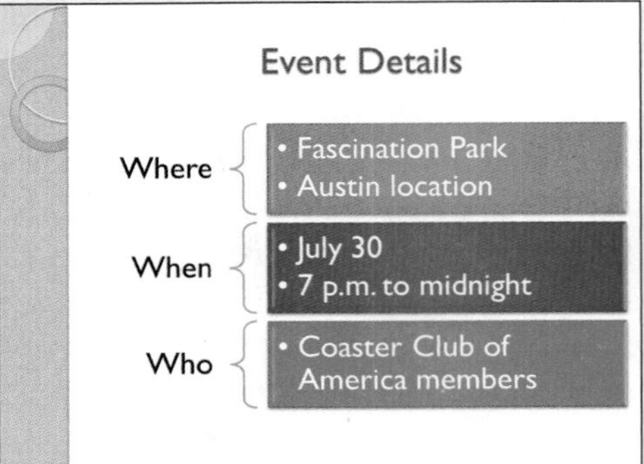

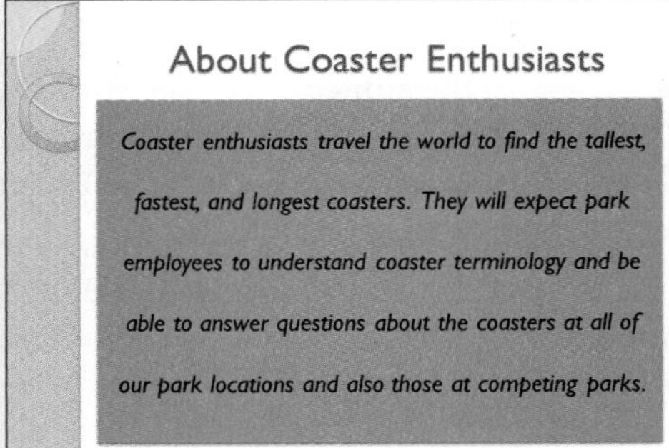

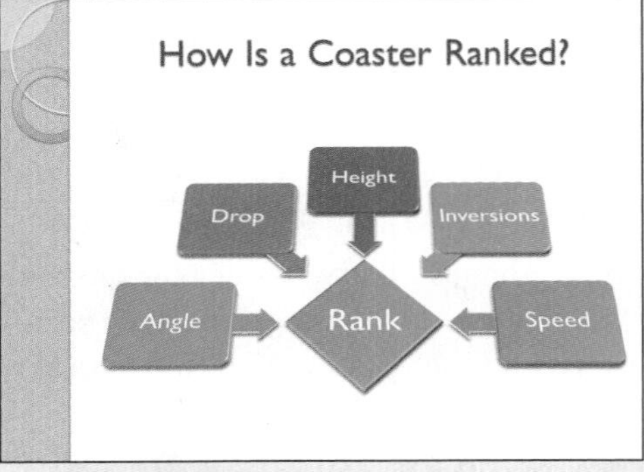

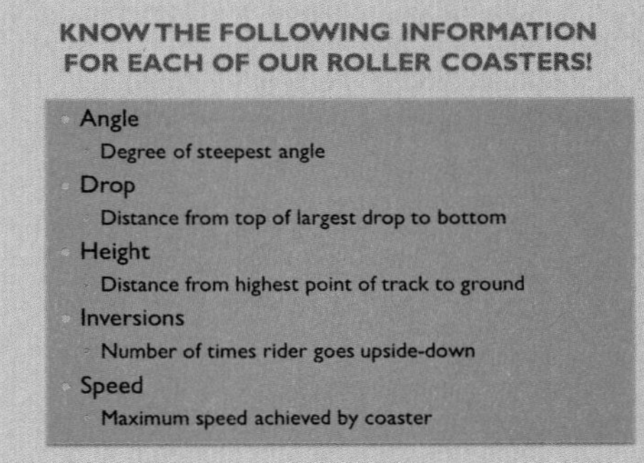

Figure 2.63

(Project 2F Coaster Club continues on the next page)

Mastering PowerPoint | Project 2F Coaster Club (continued)

1 **Start** PowerPoint. From the student files that accompany this textbook, open **p02F_Coaster_Club**, and then **Save** the file in your **PowerPoint Chapter 2** folder as **Lastname_Firstname_2F_Coaster_Club**

2 On **Slide 1**, select the title and display the **WordArt** gallery. In the last row, apply the third WordArt style—**Fill - Aqua, Accent 2, Matte Bevel**. On **Slide 2**, convert the bulleted list to a **SmartArt** graphic by applying the **Vertical Bracket List** graphic. Change the SmartArt color to **Colorful Range - Accent Colors 3 to 4**, and then apply the **Inset 3-D** style.

3 On **Slide 4**, in the content placeholder, insert a **Relationship** type **SmartArt** graphic—**Converging Radial**. In the circle shape, type **Rank** In the left rectangle, type **Angle** in the middle rectangle, type **Drop** and in the right rectangle type **Height** Add a shape after the *Height* rectangle, and then type **Inversions** Add a shape after the *Inversions* rectangle, and then type **Speed** so that your SmartArt contains five rectangular shapes pointing to the circle shape.

4 Change the SmartArt color to **Colorful Range - Accent Colors 3 to 4**, and then apply the **3-D Flat Scene** style. Change the circle shape to the **Diamond** basic shape. On the **Format tab**, in the **Shapes group**, click the **Larger** button two times to increase the size of the diamond.

5 On **Slide 5**, select the content placeholder, and then from the **Shape Styles** gallery, in the last row, apply the third style—**Intense Effect - Aqua, Accent 2**. Change the **Font Color** of all the text in the content placeholder to **Black, Text 1**.

6 On **Slide 6**, insert a **WordArt**—the third style in the last row—**Fill - Aqua, Accent 2, Matte Bevel**. Replace the WordArt text with **Mark Your Calendars!** Change the **Font Size** to **48**, and align the right edge of the WordArt placeholder with the right edge of the slide.

7 **Insert** a **Header & Footer** on the **Notes and Handouts**. Include the **Date and time updated automatically**, the **Page number**, and a **Footer** with the text **Lastname_Firstname_2F_Coaster_Club** Apply to all.

8 Display the **Document Properties**. Replace the text in the **Author** box with your own firstname and lastname, in the **Subject** box, type your course name and section number, and in the **Keywords** box, type **roller coasters, coaster club, events** **Close** the **Document Information Panel**.

9 **Save** your presentation, and then view the slide show from the beginning. Submit your presentation electronically or print **Handouts 6 Slides Horizontal** as directed by your instructor. **Close** the presentation and exit PowerPoint.

End **You have completed Project 2F**

Apply 2A and 2B skills from these Objectives:

1. Format Numbered and Bulleted Lists
2. Insert Clip Art
3. Insert Text Boxes and Shapes
4. Format Objects
5. Remove Picture Backgrounds and Insert WordArt
6. Create and Format a SmartArt Graphic

Mastering PowerPoint | Project 2G Orientation

In the following Mastering PowerPoint project, you will edit an existing presentation that is shown to Fascination Entertainment Group employees on their first day of a three-day orientation. Your completed presentation will look similar to Figure 2.64.

Project Files

For Project 2G, you will need the following files:

p02G_Orientation
p02G_Maya_Ruiz
p02G_David_Jensen
p02G_Ken_Lee

You will save your presentation as:

Lastname_Firstname_2G_Orientation

Project Results

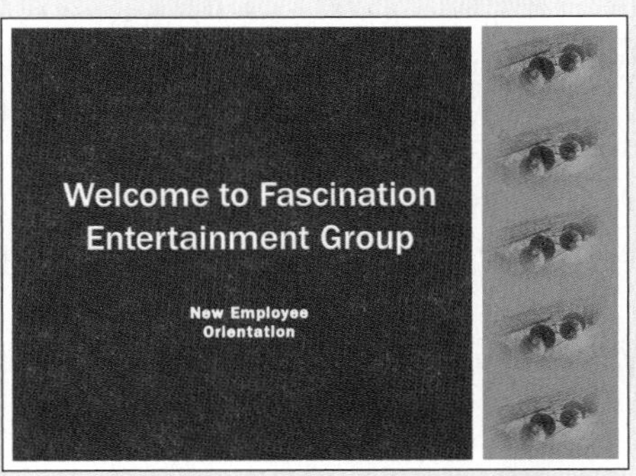

OUR GOAL IS TO ENSURE THAT ALL EMPLOYEES OF FASCINATION ENTERTAINMENT GROUP ARE AWARE OF OUR MISSION, VALUES, AND SAFETY PRACTICES.

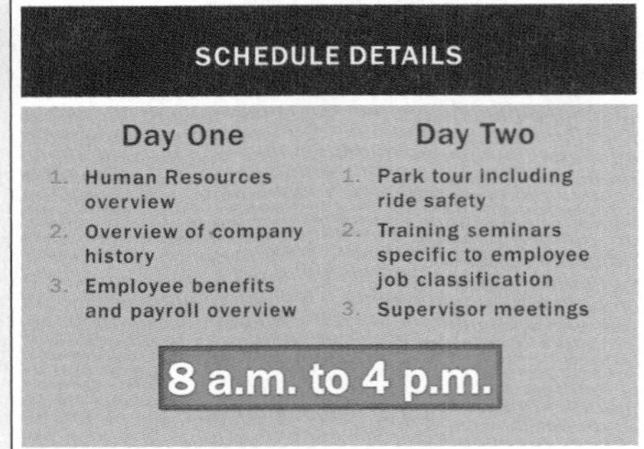

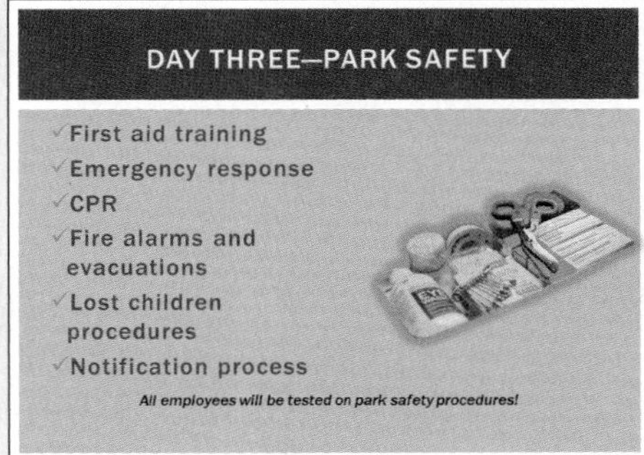

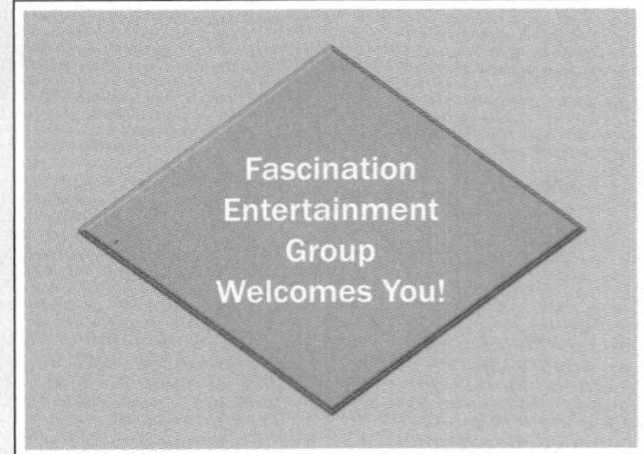

Figure 2.64

(Project 2G Orientation continues on the next page)

Content-Based Assessments

Mastering PowerPoint | Project 2G Orientation (continued)

1 **Start** PowerPoint, and then from your student data files, open the file **p02G_Orientation**. In your **PowerPoint Chapter 2** folder, **Save** the file as **Lastname_Firstname_2G_Orientation**

2 On **Slide 1**, format the title as a **WordArt** using the fourth style in the first row—**Fill - White, Outline - Accent 1**. Select the five pictures, and then using the **Align to Slide** option, align the pictures using the **Distribute Vertically** and **Align Right** commands. On **Slide 2**, change the **Shape Style** of the content placeholder to the second style in the last row—**Intense Effect - Tan, Accent 1**.

3 On **Slide 3**, convert the bulleted list to the **Picture** type **SmartArt** graphic—**Title Picture Lineup**. Change the color to **Colorful Range - Accent Colors 5 to 6**, and then apply the **3-D Inset** style. In the three picture placeholders, from your student files insert the following pictures: **p02G_Maya_Ruiz**, **p02G_David_Jensen**, and **p02G_Ken_Lee**.

4 On **Slide 4**, change the two bulleted lists to **Numbering**. Then, insert a **WordArt** using the **Fill - White, Drop Shadow** style with the text **8 a.m. to 4 p.m.** and position the WordArt centered below the two content placeholders. Apply a **Shape Style** to the WordArt using **Intense Effect - Tan, Accent 1**.

5 On **Slide 5**, change the bullet symbols to **Checkmark Bullets**, and then in the placeholder on the right, insert a **Clip Art** photograph by searching for **first aid kit** Insert the picture of the opened first aid box, and then remove the background from the picture so that only the items in the kit display. Mark areas to keep and remove as necessary. Change the **Shape Height** to **3.25** and then apply the **Brown, 18 pt glow, Accent color 4** picture effect.

6 On **Slide 5**, insert a **Text Box** aligned with the **left half of the horizontal ruler at 4 inches** and with the **lower half of the vertical ruler at 2.5 inches**. In the text box, type **All employees will be tested on park safety procedures!** Apply **Italic**, and then **Align Center** the text box using the **Align to Slide** option.

7 Insert a **New Slide** with the **Blank** layout. From the **Shapes** gallery, under **Basic Shapes**, insert a **Diamond** of any size anywhere on the slide. Then, resize the diamond so that its **Shape Height** is **6** and its **Shape Width** is **8** Using the **Align to Slide** option, apply the **Align Center**, and **Align Middle** alignment commands. Apply the **Moderate Effect - Tan, Accent 1** shape style to the diamond, and then in the diamond, type **Fascination Entertainment Group Welcomes You!** Change the **Font Size** to **40**, and then apply the **Art Deco Bevel** effect to the diamond shape.

8 **Insert** a **Header & Footer** on the **Notes and Handouts**. Include the **Date and time updated automatically**, the **Page number**, and a **Footer** with the text **Lastname_Firstname_2G_Orientation** Apply to all.

9 Display the **Document Properties**. Replace the text in the **Author** box with your own firstname and lastname, in the **Subject** box, type your course name and section number, and in the **Keywords** box, type **orientation, employee training** **Close** the **Document Information Panel**.

10 **Save** your presentation, and then view the slide show from the beginning. Submit your presentation electronically or print **Handouts 6 Slides Horizontal** as directed by your instructor. **Close** the presentation and exit PowerPoint.

End **You have completed Project 2G**

Apply a combination of the 2A and 2B skills.

GO! Fix It | Project 2H Summer Jobs

Project Files

For Project 2H, you will need the following file:

p02H_Summer_Jobs

You will save your presentation as:

Lastname_Firstname_2H_Summer_Jobs

In this project, you will edit several slides from a presentation prepared by the Human Resources Department at Fascination Entertainment Group regarding summer employment opportunities. From the student files that accompany this textbook, open the file p02H_Summer_Jobs, and then save the file in your chapter folder as **Lastname_Firstname_2H_Summer_Jobs**

To complete the project you should know:

- The Theme should be changed to Module and two spelling errors should be corrected.
- On Slide 1, the pictures should be aligned with the top of the slide and distributed horizontally.
- On Slide 2, the bulleted list should be converted to a Vertical Box List SmartArt and an attractive style should be applied. The colors should be changed to Colorful Range - Accent Colors 5 to 6.
- On Slide 3, the bulleted list should be formatted as a numbered list.
- On Slide 4, insert a Fill - White, Drop Shadow WordArt with the text **Apply Today!** and position the WordArt centered approximately 1 inch below the title placeholder.
- Document Properties should include your name, course name and section, and the keywords **summer jobs, recruitment** A Header & Footer should be inserted on the Notes and Handouts that includes the Date and time updated automatically, the Page number, and a Footer with the text **Lastname_Firstname_2H_Summer_Jobs**

Save and submit your presentation electronically or print Handouts 4 Slides Horizontal as directed by your instructor. Close the presentation.

End You have completed Project 2H

Apply a combination of the 2A and 2B skills.

GO! Make It | Project 2I Renovation Plans

Project Files

For Project 2I, you will need the following file:

New blank PowerPoint presentation

You will save your presentation as:

Lastname_Firstname_2I_Renovation_Plans

By using the skills you practiced in this chapter, create the first two slides of the presentation shown in Figure 2.65. Start PowerPoint to begin a new blank presentation, and apply the Urban theme and the Aspect color theme. Type the title and subtitle shown in Figure 2.65, and then change the background style to Style 12 and the title font size to 40. Apply the Fill - Black, Background 1, Metal Bevel WordArt style to the title. Save the file in your PowerPoint Chapter 2 folder as **Lastname_Firstname_2I_Renovation_Plans**

To locate the picture on Slide 1, search for a clip art photograph with the keyword **carnival rides** Resize the picture Height to **2** and then apply soft edges, duplicate, align, and distribute the images as shown in the figure.

Insert a new Slide 2 using the Content with Caption layout. Insert the Basic Matrix SmartArt layout shown in Figure 2.65 and change the color and style as shown. Type the title and caption text, changing the title Font Size to 28 and the caption text Font Size to 18. Modify line spacing and apply formatting to the caption text as shown in Figure 2.65. Insert the date, file name, and page number in the Notes and Handouts footer. In the Document Information Panel, add your name and course information and the Keywords **renovation, goals** Save, and then print or submit electronically as directed by your instructor.

Project Results

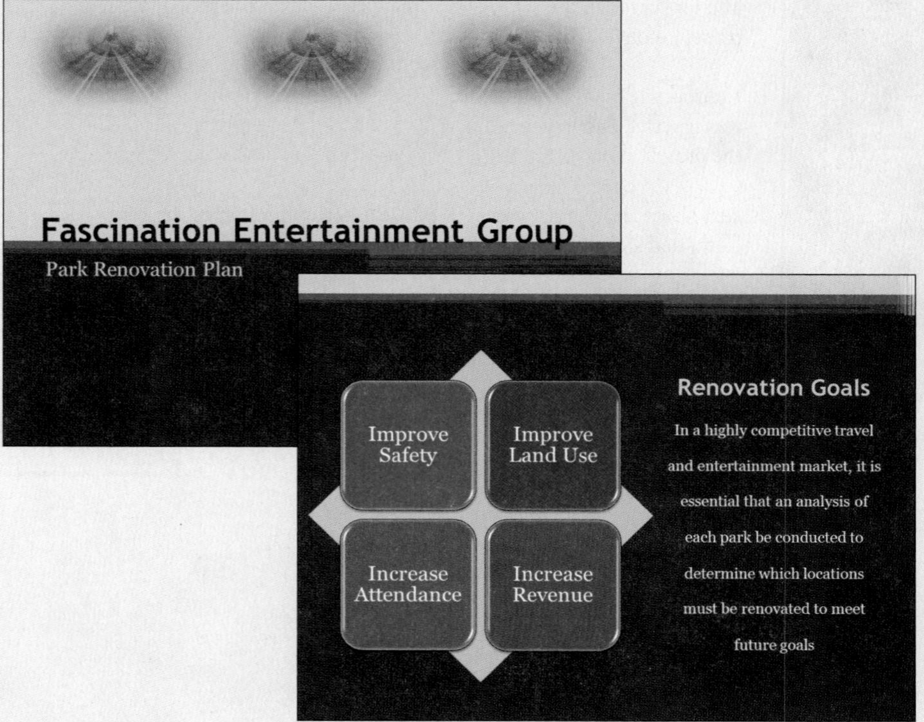

Figure 2.65

End You have completed Project 2I

Apply a combination of the 2A and 2B skills.

GO! Solve It | Project 2J Business Summary

Project Files

For Project 2J, you will need the following file:

p02J_Business_Summary

You will save your presentation as:

Lastname_Firstname_2J_Business_Summary

Open the file p02J_Business_Summary and save it in your chapter folder as **Lastname_Firstname_2J_Business_Summary** Format the presentation attractively by applying appropriate font formatting and by changing text alignment and line spacing. Insert at least one clip art image and change the picture shape and effect. On Slide 2, align and format the text box and shape attractively and insert a clip art image that can be duplicated, aligned, and distributed across the bottom edge of the slide. On Slide 3, insert an appropriate photo on the right. On Slide 4, convert the bulleted list to an appropriate SmartArt graphic and format the graphic appropriately. Apply slide transitions to all of the slides in the presentation and insert a header and footer that includes the date and time updated automatically, the file name in the footer, and the page number. Add your name, your course name and section number, and the keywords **business summary, revenue** to the Properties area. Save, and then print or submit electronically as directed by your instructor.

Performance Elements	Performance Level: Exemplary: You consistently applied the relevant skills	Proficient: You sometimes, but not always, applied the relevant skills	Developing: You rarely or never applied the relevant skills
Insert and format appropriate clip art	Appropriate clip art was inserted and formatted in the presentation.	Clip art was inserted but was not appropriate for the presentation or was not formatted.	Clip art was not inserted.
Insert and format appropriate SmartArt graphic	Appropriate SmartArt graphic was inserted and formatted in the presentation.	SmartArt graphic was inserted but was not appropriate for the presentation or was not formatted.	SmartArt graphic was not inserted.
Format text boxes and shapes attractively	Text boxes and shapes were formatted attractively.	Text boxes and shapes were formatted but the formatting was inappropriately applied.	Inadequate or no formatting.
Insert transitions	Appropriate transitions were applied to all slides.	Transitions were applied to some, but not all slides.	Transitions were not applied.

End **You have completed Project 2J**

Apply a combination of the 2A and 2B skills.

GO! Solve It | Project 2K Hotel

Project Files

For Project 2K, you will need the following file:

p02K_Hotel

You will save your presentation as:

Lastname_Firstname_2K_Hotel

Open the file p02K_Hotel and save it as **Lastname_Firstname_2K_Hotel** Complete the presentation by inserting a clip art image on the first slide and applying appropriate picture effects. On Slide 2, format the bullet point as a single paragraph, and then on Slide 3, convert the bulleted list to an appropriate SmartArt graphic. Change the SmartArt color and apply a style. On Slide 4, insert and attractively position a WordArt with the text **Save the Date!** Apply slide transitions to all of the slides. Insert a header and footer that includes the date and time updated automatically, the file name in the footer, and the page number. Add your name, your course name and section number, and the keywords **hotel, accommodations** to the Properties area. Save your presentation. Print or submit as directed by your instructor.

Performance Elements	Performance Level		
	Exemplary: You consistently applied the relevant skills	**Proficient:** You sometimes, but not always, applied the relevant skills	**Developing:** You rarely or never applied the relevant skills
Insert and format appropriate clip art	Appropriate clip art was inserted and formatted in the presentation.	Clip art was inserted but was not appropriate for the presentation or was not formatted.	Clip art was not inserted.
Insert and format appropriate SmartArt graphic	Appropriate SmartArt graphic was inserted and formatted in the presentation.	SmartArt graphic was inserted but was not appropriate for the presentation or was not formatted.	SmartArt graphic was not inserted.
Insert and format appropriate WordArt	Appropriate WordArt was inserted and formatted in the presentation.	WordArt was inserted but was not appropriate for the presentation or was not formatted.	WordArt was not inserted.
Insert transitions	Appropriate transitions were applied to all slides.	Transitions were applied to some, but not all slides.	Transitions were not applied.

End You have completed Project 2K

Outcomes-Based Assessments

Rubric

The following outcomes-based assessments are *open-ended assessments*. That is, there is no specific correct result; your result will depend on your approach to the information provided. Make *Professional Quality* your goal. Use the following scoring rubric to guide you in *how* to approach the problem, and then to evaluate *how well* your approach solves the problem.

The *criteria*—Software Mastery, Content, Format and Layout, and Process—represent the knowledge and skills you have gained that you can apply to solving the problem. The *levels of performance*—Professional Quality, Approaching Professional Quality, or Needs Quality Improvements—help you and your instructor evaluate your result.

	Your completed project is of Professional Quality if you:	Your completed project is Approaching Professional Quality if you:	Your completed project Needs Quality Improvements if you:
1-Software Mastery	Choose and apply the most appropriate skills, tools, and features and identify efficient methods to solve the problem.	Choose and apply some appropriate skills, tools, and features, but not in the most efficient manner.	Choose inappropriate skills, tools, or features, or are inefficient in solving the problem.
2-Content	Construct a solution that is clear and well organized, contains content that is accurate, appropriate to the audience and purpose, and is complete. Provide a solution that contains no errors in spelling, grammar, or style.	Construct a solution in which some components are unclear, poorly organized, inconsistent, or incomplete. Misjudge the needs of the audience. Have some errors in spelling, grammar, or style, but the errors do not detract from comprehension.	Construct a solution that is unclear, incomplete, or poorly organized; contains some inaccurate or inappropriate content; and contains many errors in spelling, grammar, or style. Do not solve the problem.
3-Format and Layout	Format and arrange all elements to communicate information and ideas, clarify function, illustrate relationships, and indicate relative importance.	Apply appropriate format and layout features to some elements, but not others. Overuse features, causing minor distraction.	Apply format and layout that does not communicate information or ideas clearly. Do not use format and layout features to clarify function, illustrate relationships, or indicate relative importance. Use available features excessively, causing distraction.
4-Process	Use an organized approach that integrates planning, development, self-assessment, revision, and reflection.	Demonstrate an organized approach in some areas, but not others; or, use an insufficient process of organization throughout.	Do not use an organized approach to solve the problem.

Outcomes-Based Assessments

Apply a combination of the **2A** and **2B** skills.

GO! Think | Project **2L** Interactive Ride

Project Files

For Project 2L, you will need the following file:

New blank PowerPoint presentation

You will save your presentation as:

Lastname_Firstname_2L_Interactive_Ride

As part of its mission to combine fun with the discovery of math and science, Fascination Entertainment Group is opening a new, interactive roller coaster at its South Lake Tahoe location. FEG's newest coaster is designed for maximum thrill and minimum risk. In a special interactive exhibit located next to the coaster, riders can learn about the physics behind this powerful coaster and even try their hand at building a coaster.

Guests will begin by setting the height of the first hill, which determines the coaster's maximum potential energy to complete its journey. Next they will set the exit path, and build additional hills, loops, and corkscrews. When completed, riders can submit their coaster for a safety inspection to find out whether the ride passes or fails.

In either case, riders can also take a virtual tour of the ride they created to see the maximum speed achieved, the amount of negative G-forces applied, the length of the track, and the overall thrill factor. They can also see how their coaster compares with other coasters in the FEG family, and they can e-mail the coaster simulation to their friends.

Using the preceding information, create a presentation that Marketing Director, Annette Chosek, will present at a travel fair describing the new attraction. The presentation should include four to six slides with at least one SmartArt graphic and one clip art image. Apply an appropriate theme and use slide layouts that will effectively present the content, and use text boxes, shapes, and WordArt if appropriate. Apply font formatting and slide transitions, and modify text alignment and line spacing as necessary. Save the file as **Lastname_Firstname_2L_Interactive_Ride** and then insert a header and footer that includes the date and time updated automatically, the file name in the footer, and the page number. Add your name, your course name and section number, and the keywords **roller coaster, new rides** to the Properties area. Print or submit as directed by your instructor.

You have completed Project 2L

Outcomes-Based Assessments

Apply a combination of the 2A and 2B skills.

GO! Think | Project 2M Research

Project Files

For Project 2M, you will need the following file:

New blank PowerPoint presentation

You will save your presentation as:

Lastname_Firstname_2M_Research

As the number of theme park vacations continues to rise, Fascination Entertainment Group is developing plans to ensure that its top theme parks are a true vacation destination. Fascination Entertainment Group research has verified that visitors use several factors in determining their theme park destinations: top attractions, overall value, and nearby accommodations.

Visitors, regardless of age, look for thrills and entertainment at a good value. Fascination Entertainment Group owns four of North America's top 15 coasters and two of its top 10 water parks, thus making the parks prime attraction destinations. Typical costs for visitors include park entrance fees, food and beverages, souvenirs, transportation, and lodging. Beginning this year, FEG will offer vacation packages. Package pricing will vary depending on number of adults, number of children, length of stay, and number of parks attended (i.e., theme park, water park, and zoo). Each park will continue to offer annual passes at a discount.

Research shows that visitors who travel more than 100 miles one way will consider the need for nearby accommodations. For its top 10 theme parks, Fascination Entertainment Group will open hotels at any parks that do not currently have them within the next two years. Until then, the company will partner with area hotels to provide discounts to theme park visitors.

Using the preceding information, create the first four slides of a presentation that the Fascination Entertainment Group marketing director can show at an upcoming board of directors meeting. Apply an appropriate theme and use slide layouts that will effectively present the content. Include clip art and at least one SmartArt graphic. Apply font and WordArt formatting, picture styles, and slide transitions, and modify text alignment and line spacing as necessary. If appropriate, insert and format a text box or a shape. Save the file as **Lastname_Firstname_2M_Research** and then insert a header and footer that includes the date and time updated automatically, the file name in the footer, and the page number. Add your name, your course name and section number, and the keywords **visitor preferences, research findings** to the Properties area. Print or submit as directed by your instructor.

End You have completed Project 2M

Outcomes-Based Assessments

Apply a combination of the 2A and 2B skills.

You and GO! | Project 2N Theme Park

Project Files

For Project 2N, you will need the following file:

New blank PowerPoint presentation

You will save your presentation as:

Lastname_Firstname_2N_Theme_Park

Research your favorite theme park and create a presentation with at least six slides that describes the park, its top attractions, nearby accommodations, and the reasons why you enjoy the park. Choose an appropriate theme, slide layouts, and pictures, and format the presentation attractively, including at least one SmartArt graphic and one WordArt object or shape. Save your presentation as Lastname_Firstname_2N_Theme_Park and submit as directed.

End You have completed Project 2N

Enhancing a Presentation with Animation, Video, Tables, and Charts

OUTCOMES
At the end of this chapter you will be able to:

OBJECTIVES
Mastering these objectives will enable you to:

PROJECT 3A
Customize a presentation with animation and video.

PROJECT 3B
Create a presentation that includes data in tables and charts.

Travis Houston/Shutterstock

In This Chapter

Recall that a presentation theme applies a consistent look to a presentation. You can customize a presentation by modifying the theme and by applying animation to slide elements, and you can enhance your presentations by creating tables and charts that help your audience understand numeric data and trends just as pictures and diagrams help illustrate a concept. The data that you present should determine whether a table or a chart would most appropriately display your information. Styles applied to your tables and charts unify these slide elements by complementing your presentation theme.

The projects in this chapter relate to **Golden Grove**, a growing city located between Los Angeles and San Diego. Just 10 years ago the population was under 100,000; today it has grown to almost 300,000. Community leaders have always focused on quality and economic development in decisions on housing, open space, education, and infrastructure, making the city a model for other communities its size around the United States. The city provides many recreational and cultural opportunities with a large park system, thriving arts, and a friendly business atmosphere.

Project 3A Informational Presentation

Project Activities

In Activities 3.01 through 3.11, you will edit and format a presentation that Mindy Walker, Director of Golden Grove Parks and Recreation, has created to inform residents about the benefits of using the city's parks and trails. Your completed presentation will look similar to Figure 3.1.

Project Files

For Project 3A, you will need the following files:

p03A_Park
p03A_Pets
p03A_Trails
p03A_Walking_Trails
p03A_Trails_Video

You will save your presentation as:

Lastname_Firstname_3A_Walking_Trails

Project Results

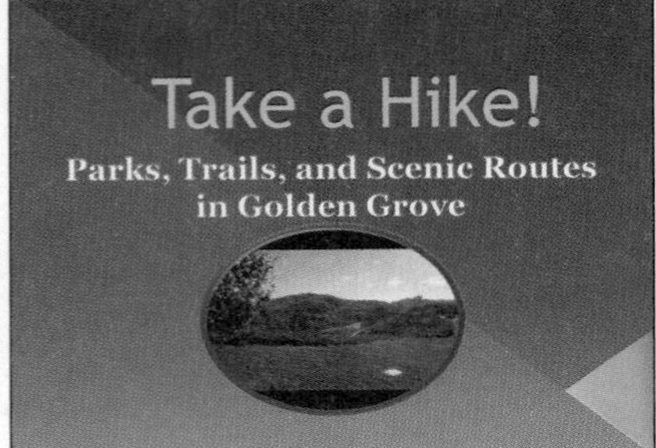

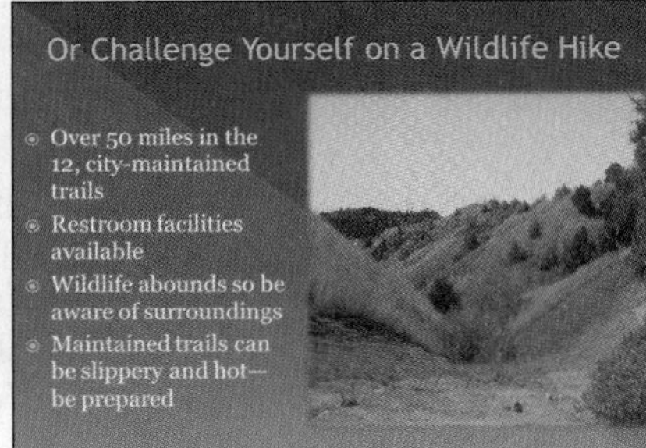

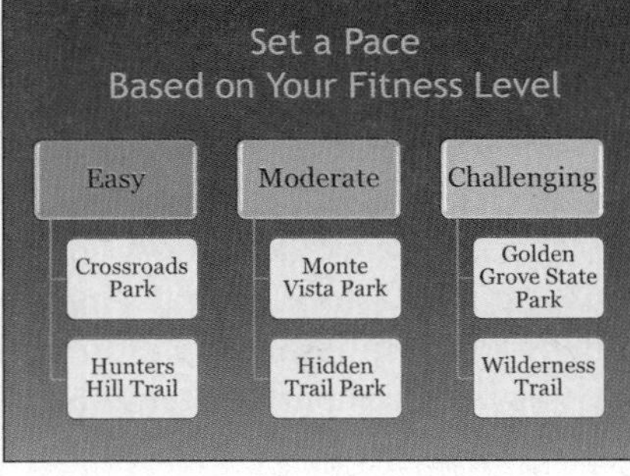

Figure 3.1
Project 3A Walking Trails

Objective 1 | Customize Slide Backgrounds and Themes

You have practiced customizing presentations by applying themes with unified design elements, backgrounds, and colors that provide a consistent look in your presentation. Additional ways to customize a slide include changing theme fonts and colors, applying a background style, modifying the background color, or inserting a picture on the slide background.

Activity 3.01 | Changing the Theme Colors and Theme Fonts

Recall that the presentation theme is a coordinated, predefined set of colors, fonts, lines, and fill effects. In this activity, you will open a presentation in which the Verve theme is applied, and then you will change the ***theme colors***—a set of coordinating colors that are applied to the backgrounds, objects, and text in a presentation.

In addition to theme colors, every presentation theme includes ***theme fonts*** that determine the font to apply to two types of slide text—headings and body. The ***Headings font*** is applied to slide titles and the ***Body font*** is applied to all other text. When you apply a new theme font to the presentation, the text on every slide is updated with the new heading and body fonts.

1 From the student files that accompany this textbook, locate and open **p03A_Walking_Trails**. Display **Backstage** view, click **Save As**, and then navigate to the location where you are storing your projects for this chapter. Create a new folder named **PowerPoint Chapter 3** and then in the **File name** box and using your own name, type **Lastname_Firstname_3A_Walking_Trails** Click **Save** or press Enter.

2 Click the **Design tab**, and then in the **Themes group**, click the **Colors** button to display the list of theme colors. Point to several themes and notice the color changes on **Slide 1**. Scroll the **Theme Colors** list, and then click **Metro** to change the theme colors.

Changing the theme colors does not change the overall design of the presentation. In this presentation, the *Verve* presentation theme is still applied to the presentation. By modifying the theme colors, you retain the design of the *Verve* theme. The colors of the *Metro* theme, which coordinate with the pictures in the presentation, are available as text, accent, and background colors.

3 With **Slide 1** displayed, click anywhere in the title placeholder. Click the **Home tab**, and then in the **Font group**, click the **Font button arrow**. Notice that at the top of the **Font** list, under **Theme Fonts**, Century Gothic (Headings) and Century Gothic (Body) display. Compare your screen with Figure 3.2.

Figure 3.2

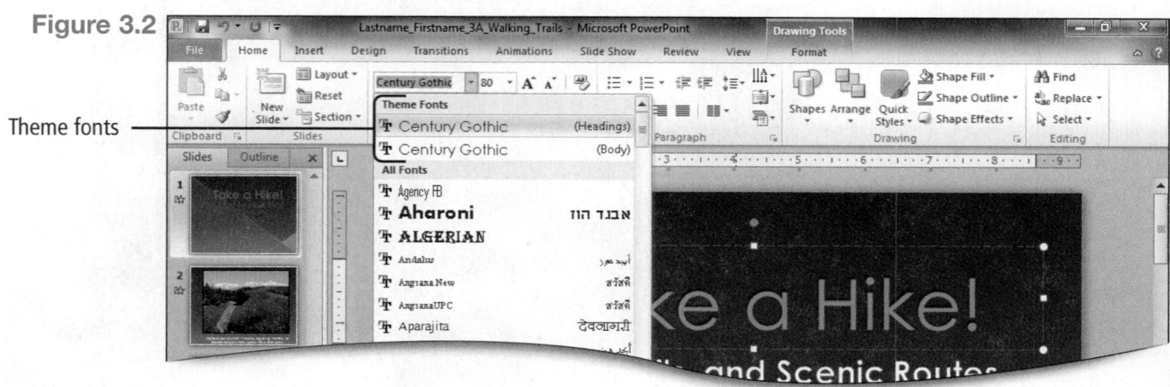

4 Click anywhere on the slide to close the Font list. Click the **Design tab**, and then in the **Themes group**, click the **Fonts** button.

This list displays the name of each theme and the pair of fonts in the theme. The first and larger font in each pair is the Headings font and the second and smaller font in each pair is the Body font.

5 Point to several of the themes and watch as Live Preview changes the title and subtitle text. Then, scroll to the bottom of the **Theme Fonts** list and click **Urban**. Compare your screen with Figure 3.3, and then **Save** your presentation.

Figure 3.3

Activity 3.02 | Applying a Background Style

1 With **Slide 1** displayed, on the **Design tab**, in the **Background group**, click the **Background Styles** button. Compare your screen with Figure 3.4.

A ***background style*** is a slide background fill variation that combines theme colors in different intensities or patterns.

Figure 3.4

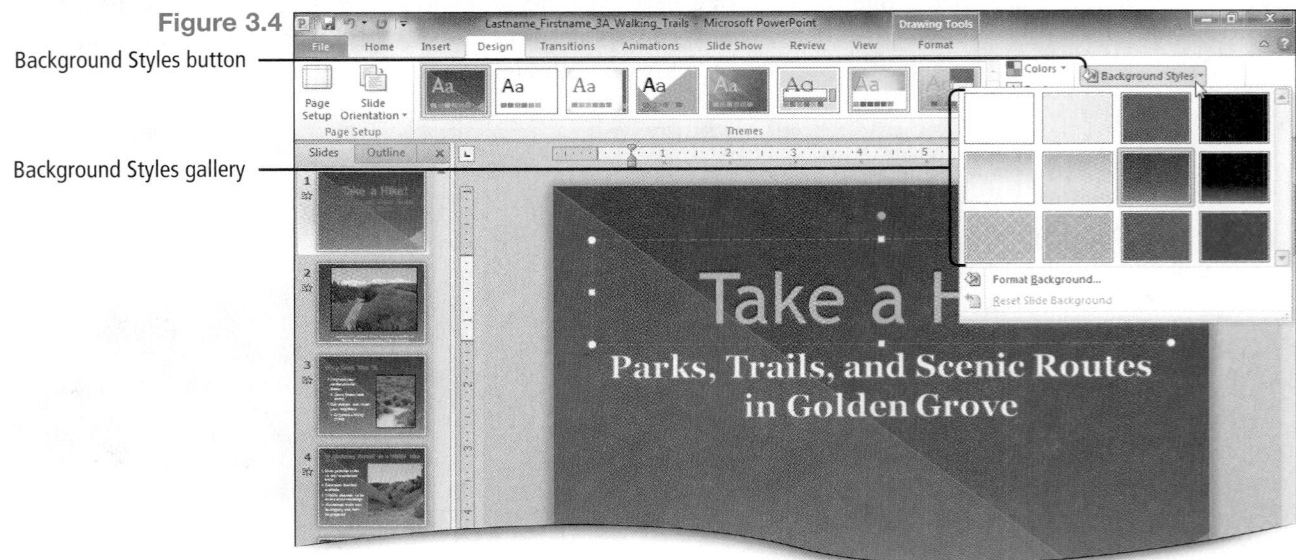

2 Point to each of the background styles to view the style on **Slide 1**. Then, in the first row, *right-click* **Style 2** to display the shortcut menu. Click **Apply to Selected Slides** and then compare your screen with Figure 3.5.

The background style is applied only to Slide 1.

3 **Save** your presentation.

Figure 3.5

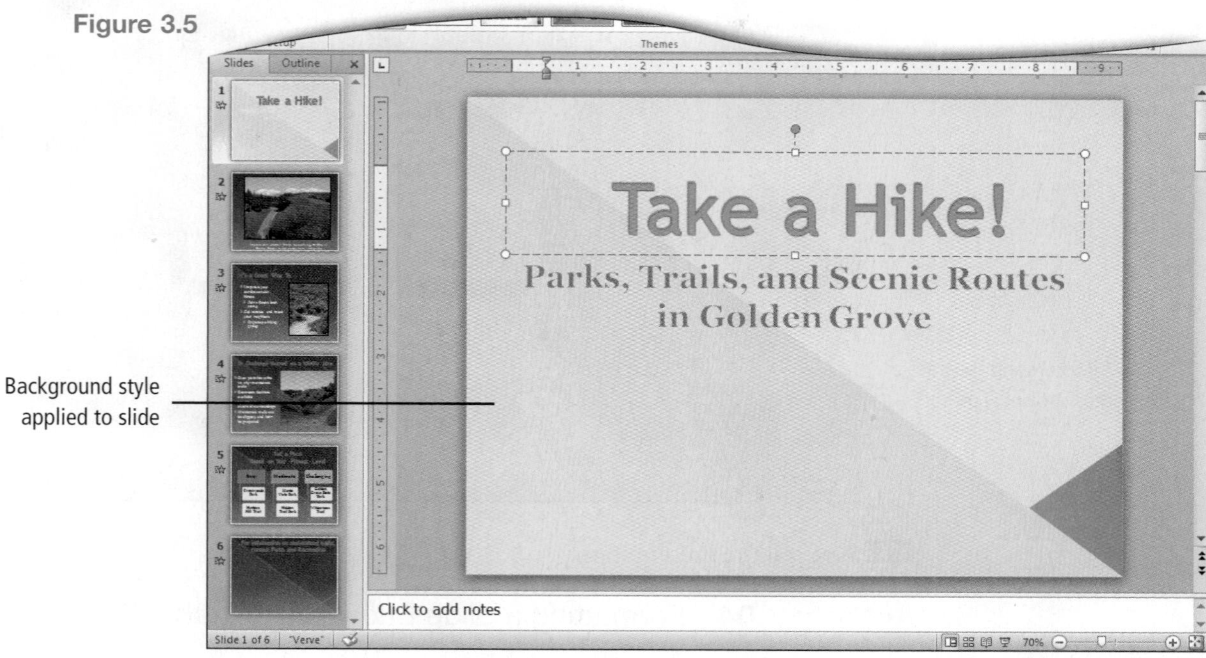

> **More Knowledge | Applying Background Styles to All Slides in a Presentation**
>
> To change the background style for all of the slides in the presentation, click the background style that you want to apply and the style will be applied to every slide.

Activity 3.03 | Hiding Background Graphics

Many of the PowerPoint 2010 themes contain graphic elements that display on the slide background. In the Verve theme applied to this presentation, the background includes a triangle and lines that intersect near the lower right corner of the slide. Sometimes the background graphics interfere with the slide content. When this happens, you can hide the background graphics.

1 Display **Slide 6**, and notice that on this slide, you can clearly see the triangle and lines on the slide background.

You cannot delete these objects because they are a part of the slide background; however, you can hide them.

2 Display **Slide 5**, and notice that the background graphics distract from the connecting lines on the diagram. On the **Design tab**, in the **Background group**, select the **Hide Background Graphics** check box, and then compare your slide with Figure 3.6.

The background objects no longer display behind the SmartArt diagram.

Figure 3.6

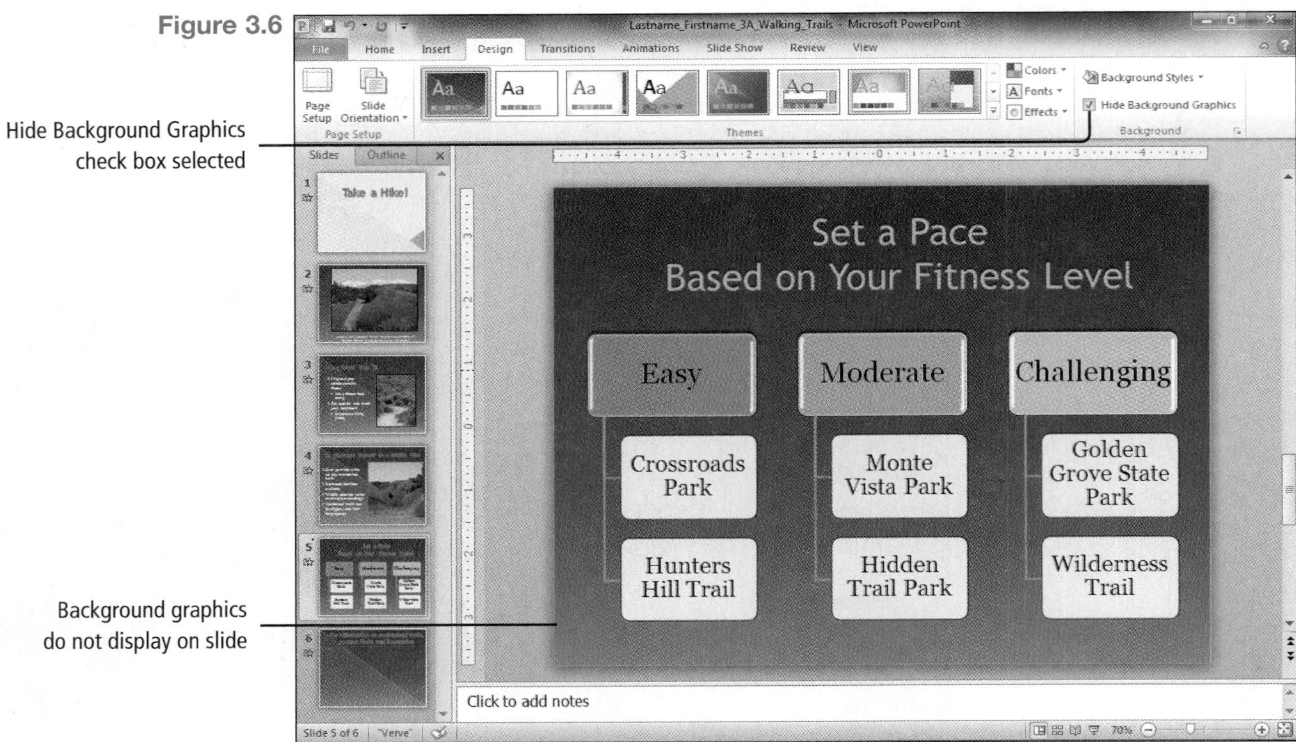

3 **Save** the presentation.

Activity 3.04 | Formatting a Slide Background with a Picture

You can insert a picture on a slide background so the image fills the entire slide.

1 Display **Slide 3**, and then click the **Home tab**. In the **Slides group**, click the **New Slide arrow**, and then click the **Title Only** layout to insert a new slide with the Title Only layout.

2 With the new **Slide 4** displayed, click the **Design tab**. In the **Background group**, select the **Hide Background Graphics** check box, and then click the **Background Styles** button. Below the displayed gallery, click **Format Background**.

In the Format Background dialog box, you can customize a slide background by changing the formatting options.

3 If necessary, on the left side of the dialog box, click Fill. On the right side of the dialog box, under **Fill**, click the **Picture or texture fill** option button, and then notice that on the slide background, a textured fill displays. Compare your screen with Figure 3.7.

Figure 3.7

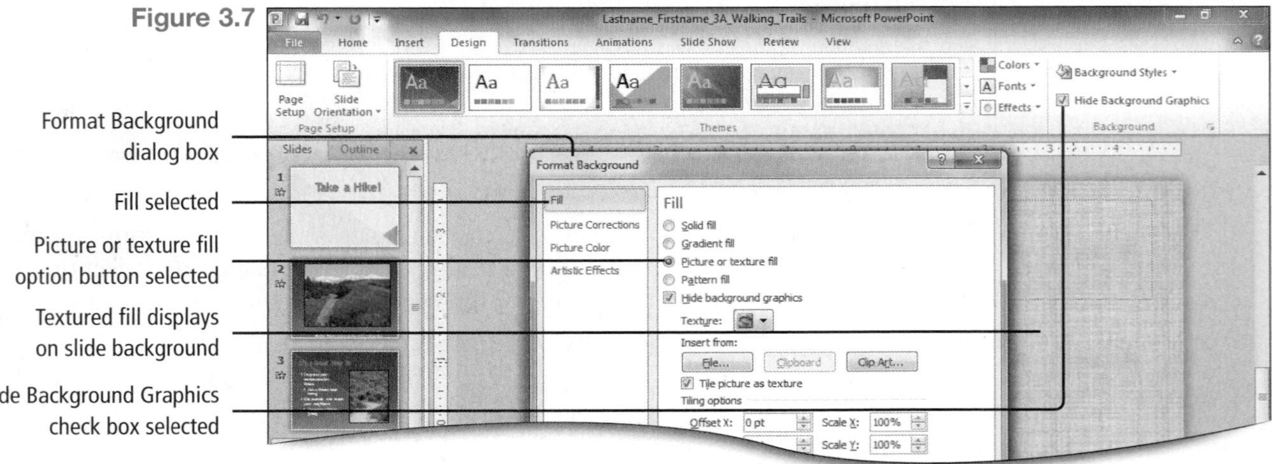

4 Under **Insert from**, click the **File** button to display the **Insert Picture** dialog box. Navigate to your student files, and then click **p03A_Pets**. Click **Insert**, and then at the bottom of the **Format Background** dialog box, click **Close**. Compare your slide with Figure 3.8 and notice that the picture displays as the background of Slide 4.

When a picture is applied to a slide background using the Format Background option, the picture is not treated as an object. The picture fills the background and you cannot move it or size it.

Figure 3.8

5 Click in the title placeholder, type **Find a Pet Friendly Trail** and then notice that the background picture does not provide sufficient contrast with the text to display the title effectively.

6 With your insertion point still in the title placeholder, click the **Format tab**. In the **Shape Styles group**, click the **Shape Fill button arrow**. In the fifth column, click the last color—**Green, Accent 1, Darker 50%**. Select the title text, and then on the **Format tab**, in the **WordArt Styles group**, in the first row, click the third style—**Fill - White, Drop Shadow**. **Center** the text.

The green fill color and the white WordArt style provide good contrast against the slide background so that the text is readable.

7 Point to the outer edge of the title placeholder to display the pointer, and then drag the placeholder up and to the left so that its upper left corner aligns with the upper left corner of the slide. Point to the center right sizing handle and drag to the right so that the placeholder extends to the right edge of the slide. Click outside of the placeholder, and then compare your slide with Figure 3.9.

Figure 3.9

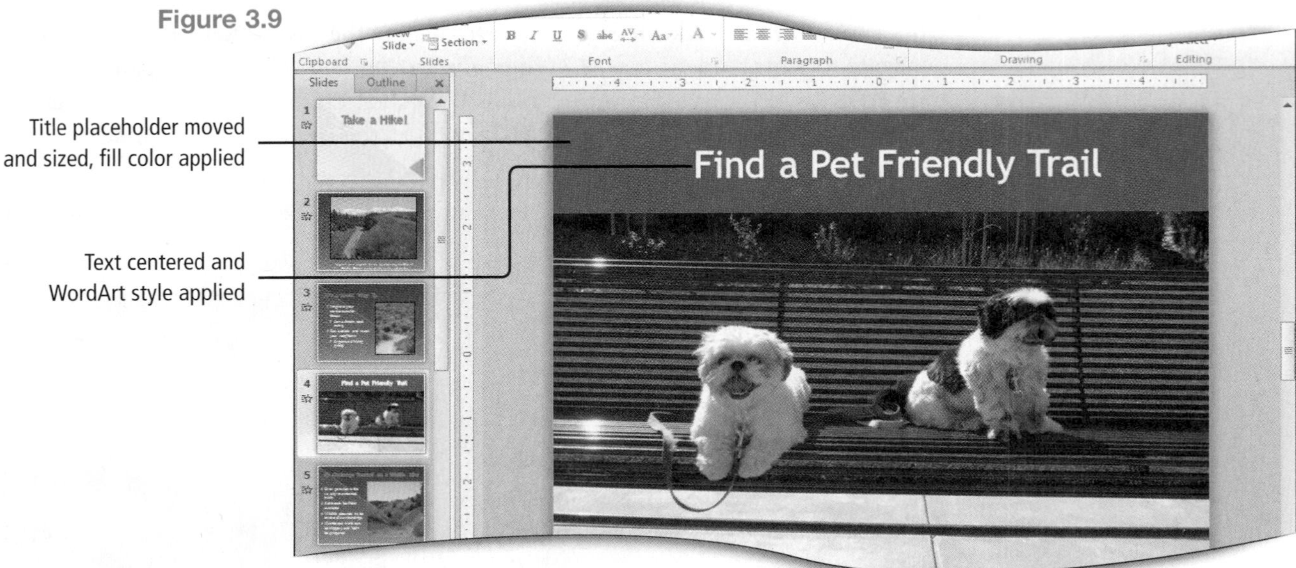

8 Display **Slide 5**, and then insert a **New Slide** with the **Title Only** layout. On the **Design tab**, in the **Background group**, select the **Hide Background Graphics** check box, and then click the **Background Styles** button. Click **Format Background**.

9 Under **Fill**, click the **Picture or texture fill** option button. Under **Insert from**, click **File**. Navigate to your student files, click **p03A_Trails**, click **Insert**, and then **Close** the dialog box. In the title placeholder, type **Get Outside! Get Fit! Get Walking!** and then **Center** the text.

10 Select the text, and then change the **Font Size** to **36**. Then, apply the same **Shape Fill** color and **WordArt** style to the title placeholder that you applied to the title on **Slide 4**. Size the placeholder so that it extends from the left edge of the slide to the right edge of the slide, and then drag the placeholder up so that its upper edge aligns with the upper edge of the slide. Click outside of the title so that it is not selected. Compare your slide with Figure 3.10.

The green fill color and white text provide good contrast with the slide background and complement the green color of the grass on the slide.

Figure 3.10

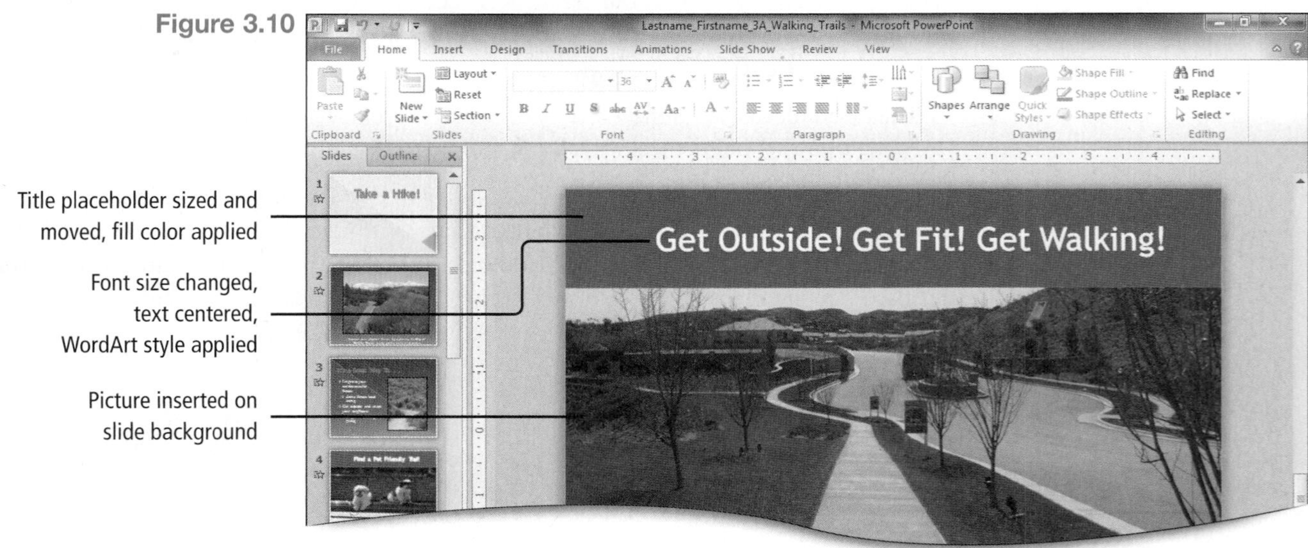

11 Display **Slide 8**, and then format the slide background with a picture from your student files—**p03A_Park**. On the **Design tab**, in the **Background group**, select the **Hide Background Graphics** check box.

12 Select the title placeholder. On the **Format tab**. In the **Shape Styles group**, click the **More** button. In the **Shape Styles** gallery, in the second row, click the sixth style—**Colored Fill – Periwinkle, Accent 5**.

13 Select the text, and then on the **Format tab**, in the **WordArt Styles group**, click the third style—**Fill - White, Drop Shadow**. Click outside of the placeholder, and then compare your slide with Figure 3.11. **Save** the presentation.

Figure 3.11

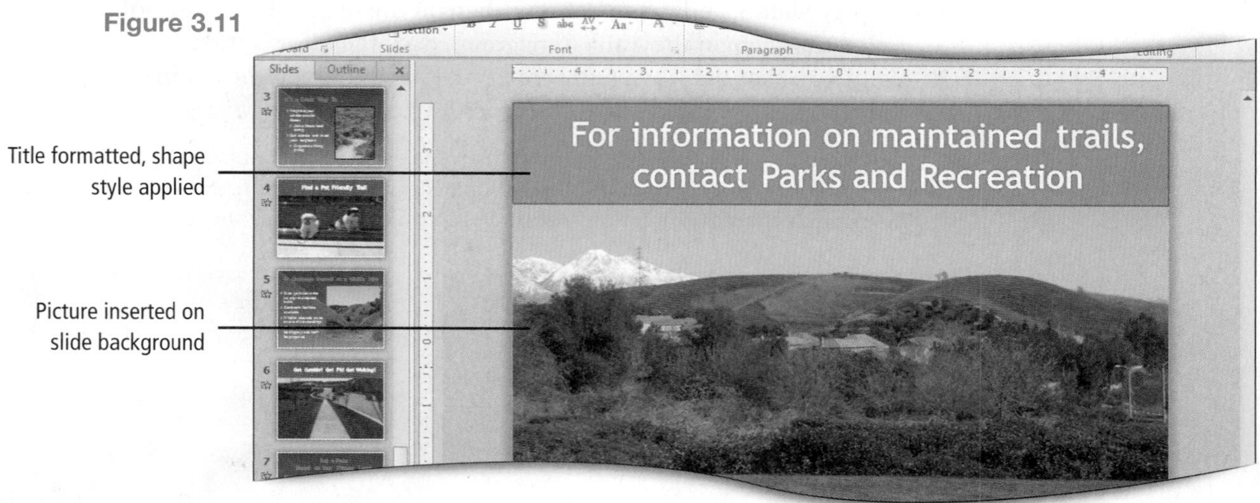

Activity 3.05 | Applying a Background Fill Color and Resetting a Slide Background

1 Display **Slide 1**, and then click the **Design tab**. In the **Background group**, click the **Background Styles** button, and then click **Format Background**.

2 In the **Format Background** dialog box, if necessary, click the Solid fill option button. Under **Fill Color**, click the **Color** button. Under **Theme Colors**, in the first column, click the last color—**White, Background 1, Darker 50%**. Click **Close**.

The solid fill color is applied to the slide background.

3 On the **Design tab**, in the **Background group**, click the **Background Styles** button. Below the gallery, click **Reset Slide Background**, and then **Save** the presentation.

After making many changes to a slide background, you may decide that the original theme formatting is the best choice for displaying the text and graphics on a slide. The Reset Slide Background feature restores the original theme and color theme formatting to a slide.

Objective 2 | Animate a Slide Show

Animation is a visual or sound effect added to an object or text on a slide. Animation can focus the audience's attention, providing the speaker with an opportunity to emphasize important points using the slide element as an effective visual aid.

Activity 3.06 | Applying Animation Entrance Effects and Effect Options

Entrance effects are animations that bring a slide element onto the screen. You can modify an entrance effect by using the animation Effect Options command.

1 Display **Slide 3**, and then click anywhere in the bulleted list placeholder. On the **Animations tab**, in the **Animation group**, click the **More** button [▾]. If necessary, scroll slightly so that the word *Entrance* displays at the top of the Animation gallery, and then compare your screen with Figure 3.12.

Recall that an entrance effect is animation that brings an object or text onto the screen. An ***emphasis effect*** is animation that emphasizes an object or text that is already displayed. An ***exit effect*** is animation that moves an object or text off the screen.

Figure 3.12

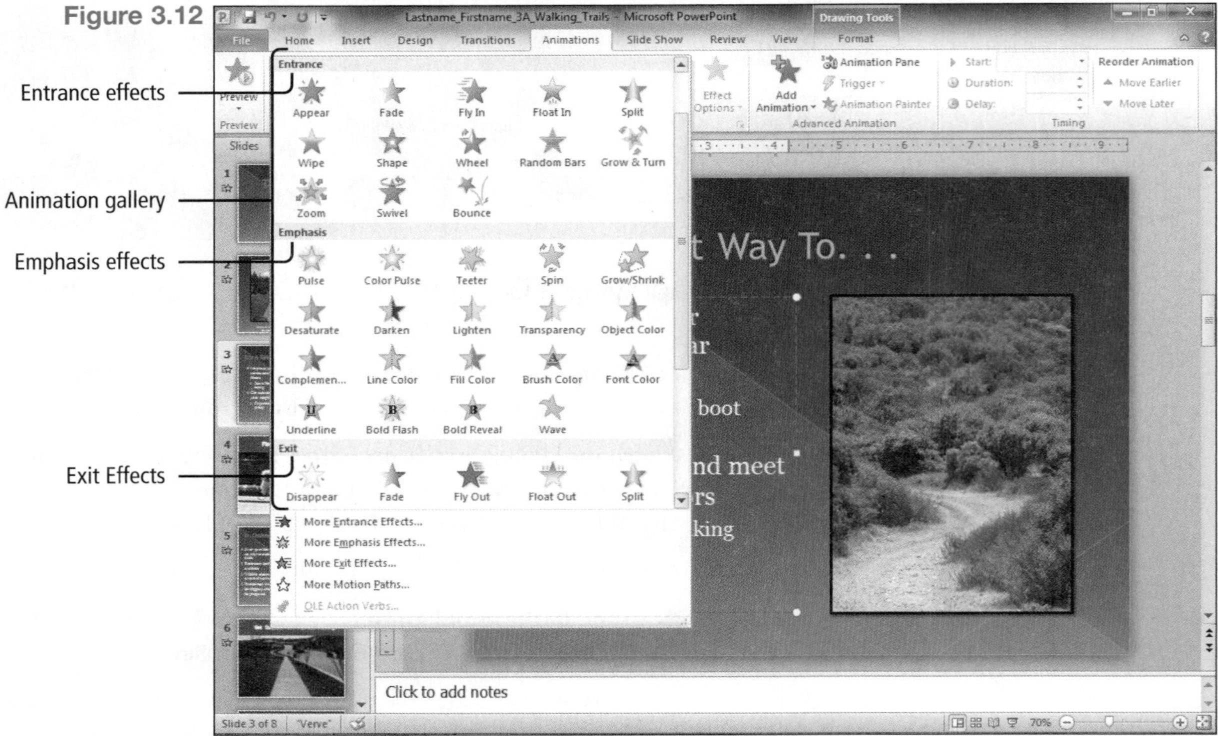

2 Under **Entrance**, click **Split**, and then notice the animation applied to the list. Compare your screen with Figure 3.13.

The numbers *1* and *2* display to the left of the bulleted list placeholder, indicating the order in which the bullet points will be animated during the slide show. For example, the first bullet point and its subordinate bullet are both numbered *1*. Thus, both will display at the same time.

Figure 3.13

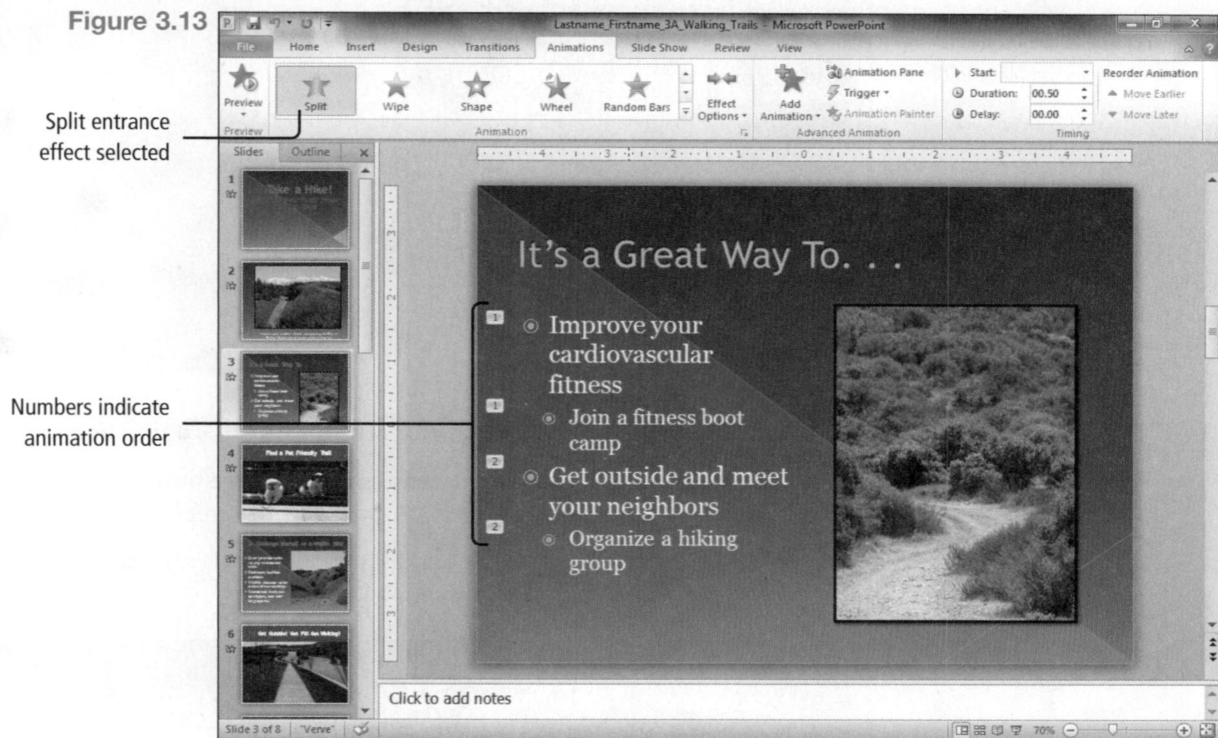

3 Select the bulleted text placeholder. In the **Animation group**, click the **Effect Options** button, and then compare your screen with Figure 3.14.

The Effect Options control the direction and sequence in which the animation displays. Additional options may be available with other entrance effects.

Figure 3.14

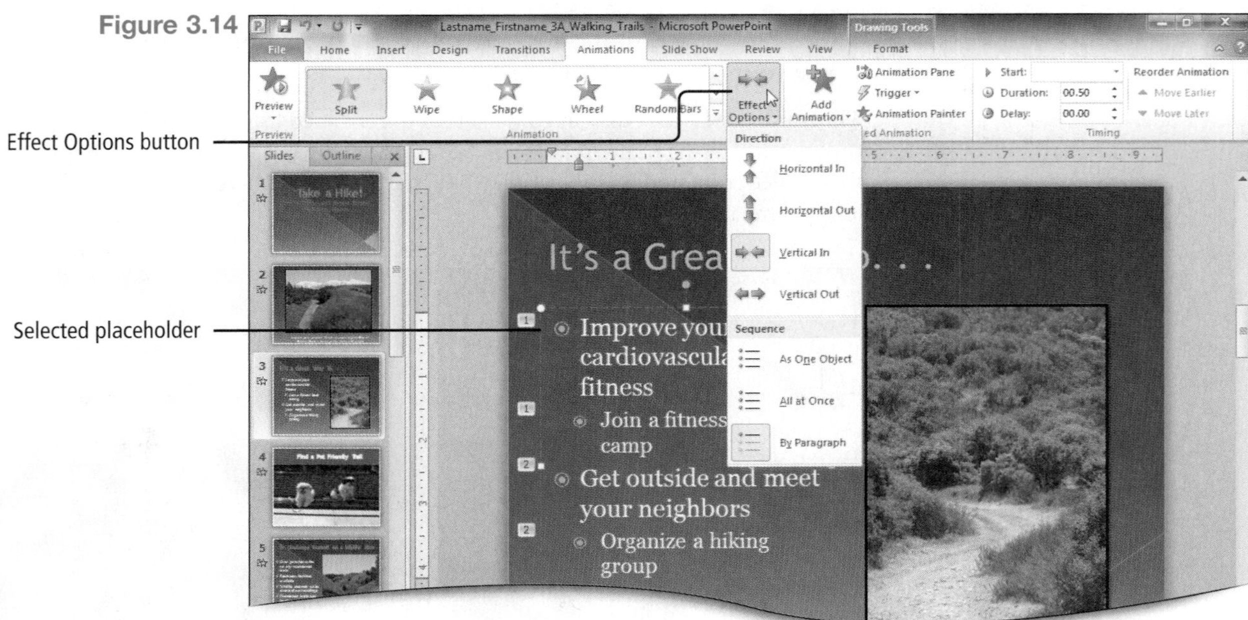

4 Click **Vertical Out** and notice the direction from which the animation is applied.

5 Select the picture. In the **Animation group**, click the **More** button, and then below the gallery, click **More Entrance Effects**. Compare your screen with Figure 3.15.

The Change Entrance Effect dialog box displays additional entrance effects grouped in four categories: Basic, Subtle, Moderate, and Exciting.

Figure 3.15

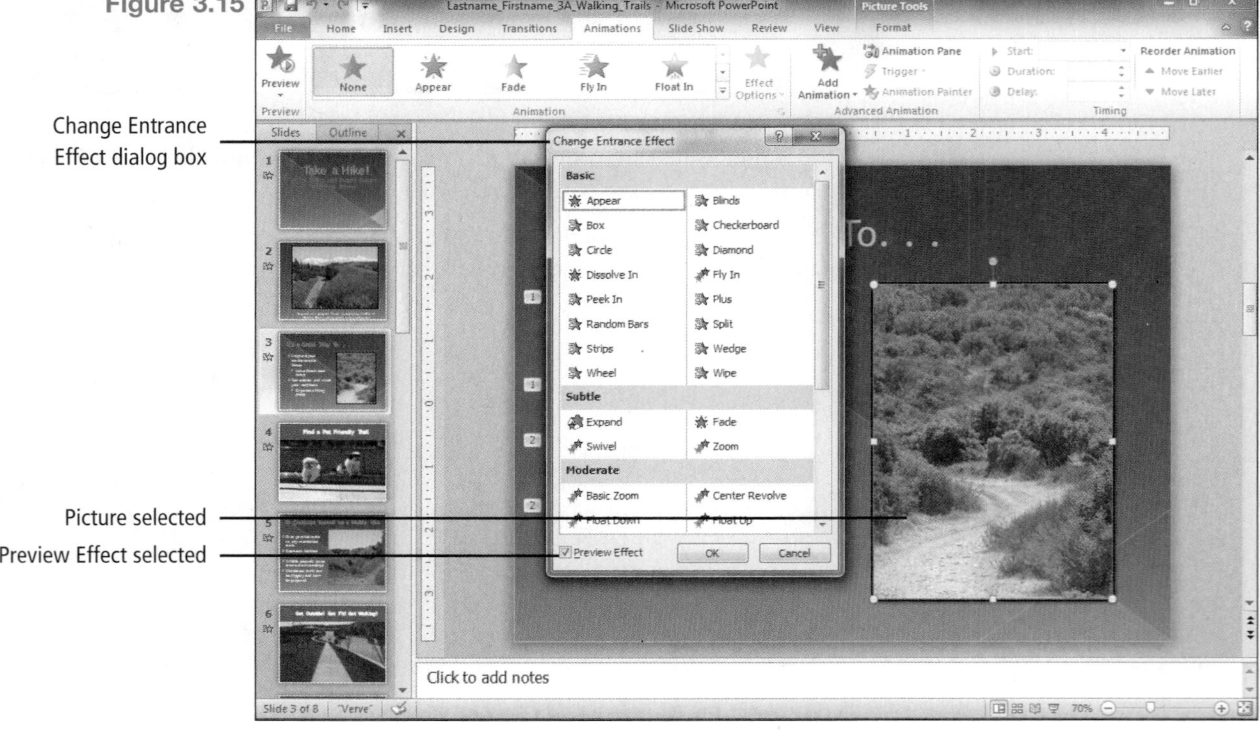

6 In the lower right corner of the **Change Entrance Effect** dialog box, verify that the **Preview Effect** check box is selected. Under **Basic**, click **Dissolve In**, and then watch as Live Preview displays the selected entrance effect. Click **OK**.

The number *3* displays next to the picture, indicating that it is third in the slide animation sequence.

7 Select the title. On the **Animations tab**, in the **Animation group**, click the **More** button, and then under **Entrance**, click **Split** to apply the animation to the title.

The number *4* displays next to the title, indicating that it is fourth in the slide animation sequence.

8 **Save** the presentation.

Activity 3.07 | Setting Animation Timing Options

Timing options control when animated items display in the animation sequence.

1 With **Slide 3** displayed, on the **Animations tab**, in the **Preview group**, click the **Preview** button.

The list displays first, followed by the picture, and then the title. The order in which animation is applied is the order in which objects display during the slide show.

2 Select the title. On the **Animations tab**, in the **Timing group**, under **Reorder Animation**, click the **Move Earlier** button two times, and then compare your screen with Figure 3.16.

To the left of the title placeholder, the number *1* displays. You can use the Reorder Animation buttons to change the order in which text and objects are animated during the slide show.

Figure 3.16

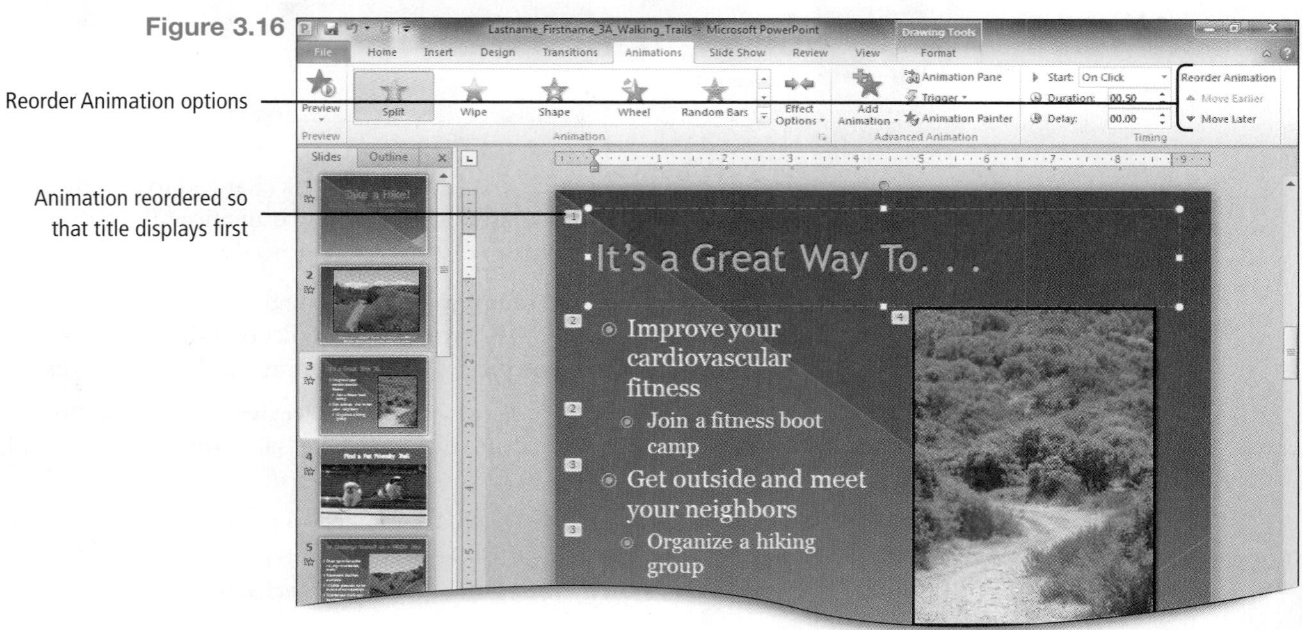

3. With the title selected, on the **Animations tab**, in the **Timing group**, click the **Start button arrow** to display three options—*On Click*, *With Previous*, and *After Previous*. Compare your screen with Figure 3.17.

   The ***On Click*** option begins the animation sequence for the selected slide element when the mouse button is clicked or the Spacebar is pressed. The ***With Previous*** option begins the animation sequence at the same time as the previous animation or slide transition. The ***After Previous*** option begins the animation sequence for the selected slide element immediately after the completion of the previous animation or slide transition.

Figure 3.17

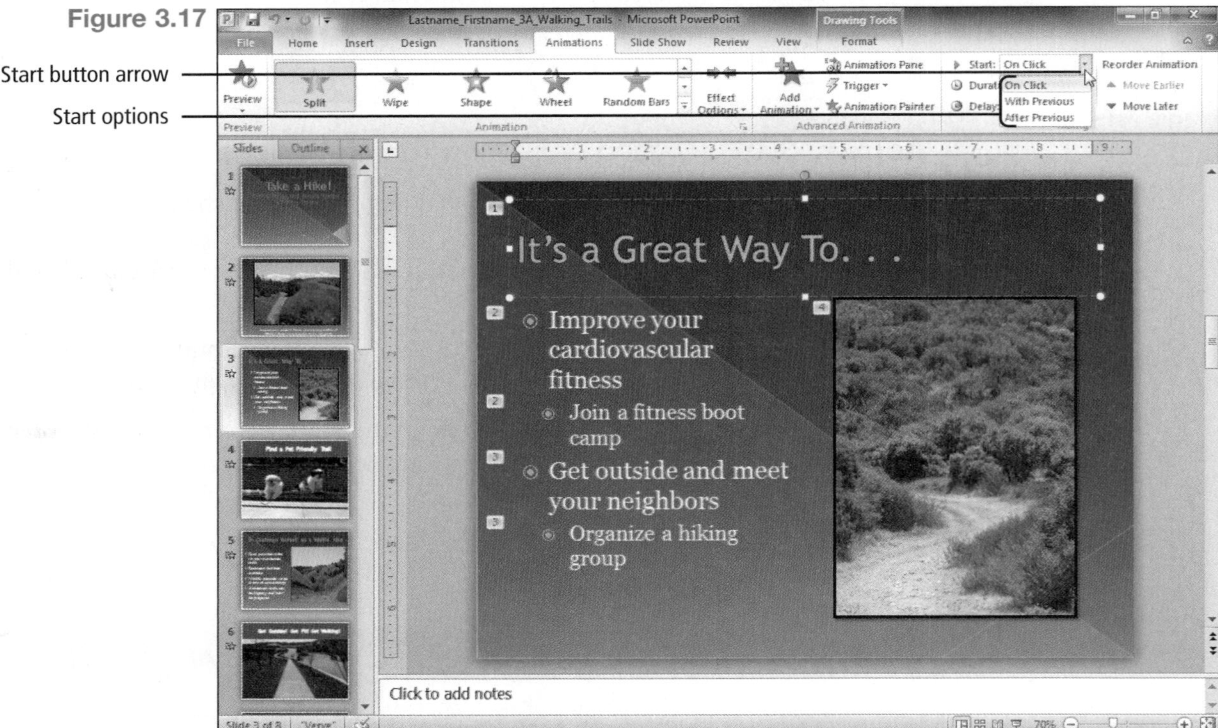

4. Click **After Previous**, and then notice that the number *1* is changed to *0*, indicating that the animation will begin immediately after the slide transition; the presenter does not need to click the mouse button or press Spacebar to display the title.
5. Select the picture, and then in the **Timing group**, click the **Start arrow**. Click **With Previous** and notice that the number is changed to *2*, indicating that the animation will begin at the same time as the second set of bullet points in the bulleted list.
6. On the **Animations tab**, in the **Preview group**, click the **Preview** button and notice that the title displays first, and that the picture displays at the same time as the second set of bullet points.
7. Display **Slide 1**, and then click in the title placeholder. On the **Animations tab**, in the **Animation group**, click the **Entrance** effect **Fly In**, and then click the **Effect Options** button. Click **From Top**. In the **Timing group**, click the **Start arrow**, and then click **After Previous**.

   The number *0* displays to the left of the title indicating that the animation will begin immediately after the slide transition.

8 With the title selected, in the **Timing group**, click the **Duration** down arrow so that *00.25* displays in the **Duration** box. Compare your screen with Figure 3.18.

Duration controls the speed of the animation. You can set the duration of an animation by typing a value in the Duration box, or you can use the spin box arrows to increase and decrease the duration in 0.25-second increments. When you decrease the duration, the animation speed increases. When you increase the duration, the animation is slowed.

Figure 3.18

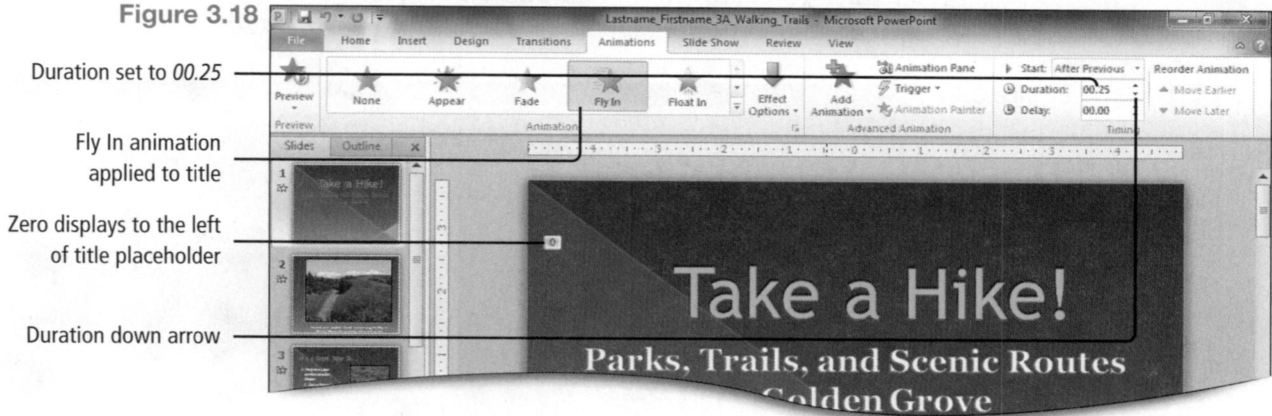

9 Select the subtitle, and then in the **Animation group**, apply the **Fly In** entrance effect. In the **Timing group**, click the **Start arrow**, and then click **After Previous**. In the **Timing group**, select the value in the **Delay** box, type **00.50** and then press Enter. Compare your screen with Figure 3.19.

You can use Delay to begin a selected animation after a specified amount of time has elapsed. Here, the animation is delayed by one-half of a second after the completion of the previous animation—the title animation. You can type a value in the Delay or Duration boxes, or you can use the up and down arrows to change the timing.

Figure 3.19

10 View the slide show from the beginning and notice the animation on Slides 1 and 3. When the black slide displays, press Esc to return to Normal view, and then **Save** the presentation.

Activity 3.08 | Using Animation Painter and Removing Animation

Animation Painter is a feature that copies animation settings from one object to another.

1 Display **Slide 3**, and then click anywhere in the bulleted list. On the **Animations tab**, in the **Advanced Animation group**, click the **Animation Painter** button. Display **Slide 5**, and then point anywhere in the bulleted list placeholder to display the Animation Painter pointer . Compare your screen with Figure 3.20.

Figure 3.20

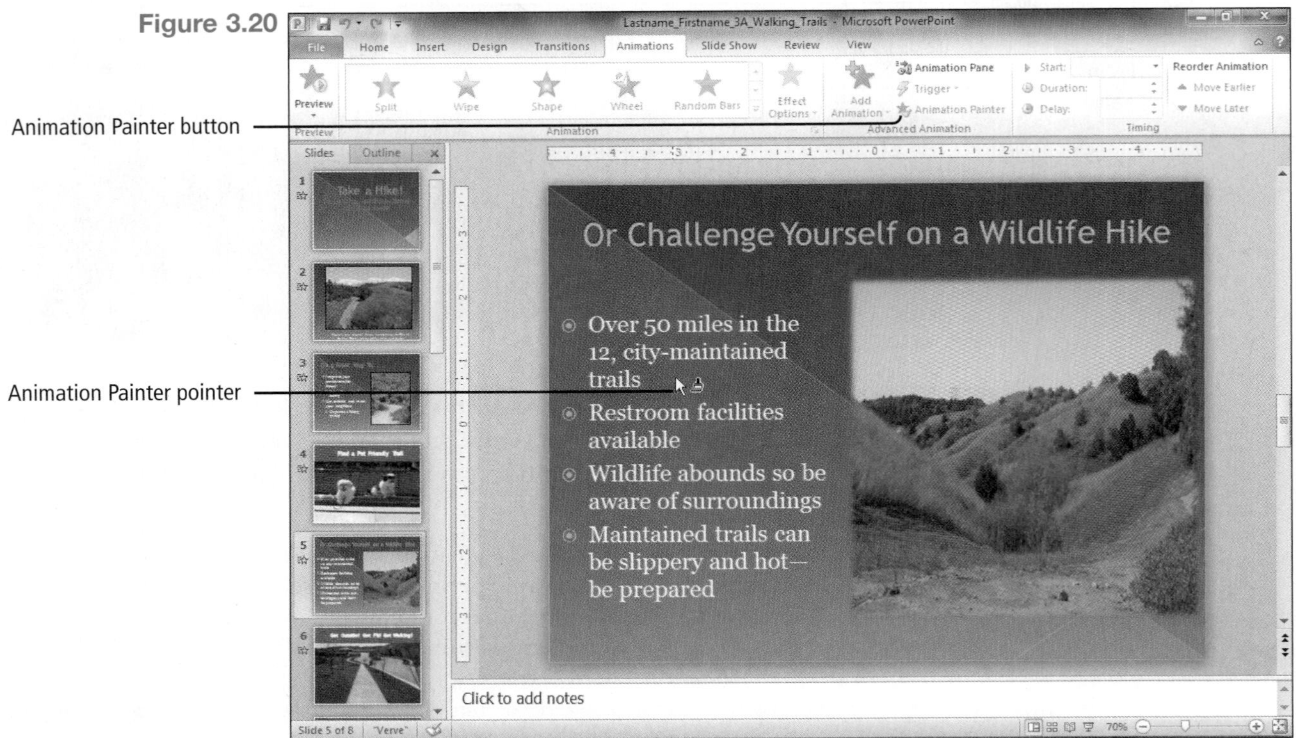

2 Click the bulleted list to copy the animation settings from the list on **Slide 3** to the list on **Slide 5**.

3 Display **Slide 3**, and then select the picture. Using the technique that you just practiced, use **Animation Painter** to copy the animation from the picture on **Slide 3** to the picture on **Slide 5**. With **Slide 5** displayed, compare your screen with Figure 3.21.

The numbers displayed to the left of the bulleted list and the picture indicate that animation is applied to the objects.

Figure 3.21

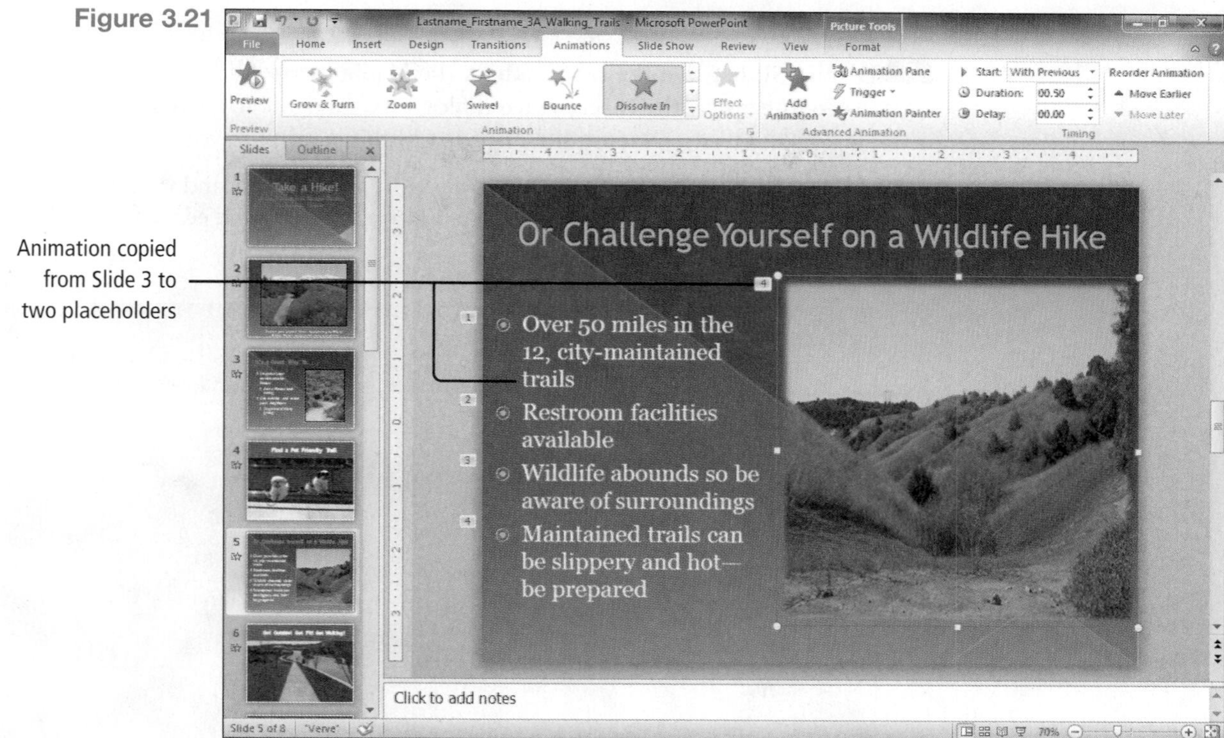

4 Display **Slide 3**, and then click in the title placeholder. On the **Animations tab**, in the **Animation group**, click the **More** button. At the top of the gallery, click **None** to remove the animation from the title placeholder. Compare your screen with Figure 3.22, and then **Save** the presentation.

Figure 3.22

Objective 3 | Insert a Video

You can insert, size, and move videos in a PowerPoint presentation, and you can format videos by applying styles and effects. Video editing features in PowerPoint 2010 enable you to trim parts of a video and to fade the video in and out during a presentation.

Activity 3.09 | Inserting a Video

1. Display **Slide 1**. On the **Insert tab**, in the **Media group**, click the upper part of the **Video** button. In the **Insert Video** dialog box, navigate to your student files, and then click **p03A_Trails_Video**. Click **Insert**, and then compare your screen with Figure 3.23.

   The video displays in the center of the slide, and playback and volume controls display in the control panel below the video. Video formatting and editing tools display on the Ribbon.

Figure 3.23

2. Below the video, on the control panel, click the **Play/Pause** button [▶] to view the video and notice that as the video plays, the control panel displays the time that has elapsed since the start of the video.

3. On the **Format tab**, in the **Size group**, click in the **Video Height** box. Type **3** and then press Enter. Notice that the video width adjusts proportionately.

4. Point to the video to display the pointer, and then drag the video down so that the top of the video is aligned at **zero on the vertical ruler**. On the **Format tab**, in the **Arrange group**, click the **Align** button, and then click **Align Center** to center the video horizontally on the slide. Compare your screen with Figure 3.24.

Figure 3.24

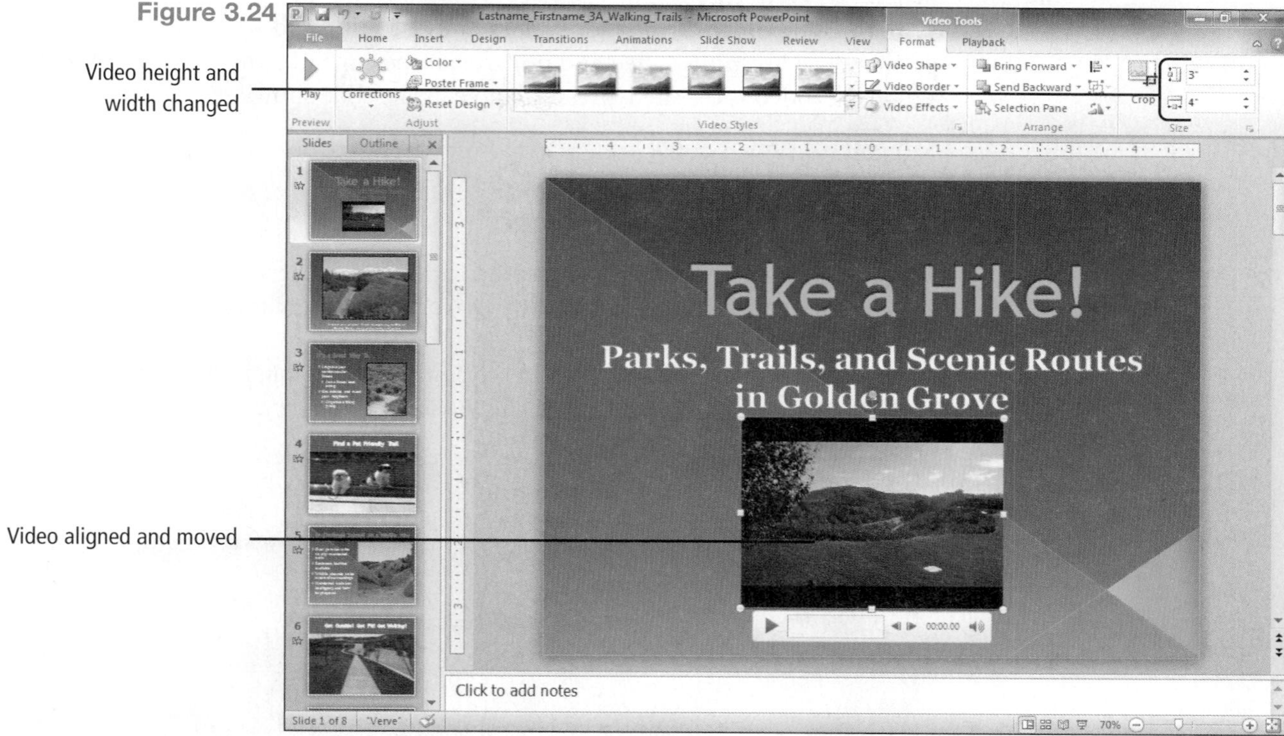

5 In the lower right corner of the PowerPoint window, in the **View** buttons, click the **Slide Show** button to display **Slide 1** in the slide show.

6 Point to the video to display the pointer, and then compare your screen with Figure 3.25.

When you point to the video during the slide show, the control panel displays.

Figure 3.25

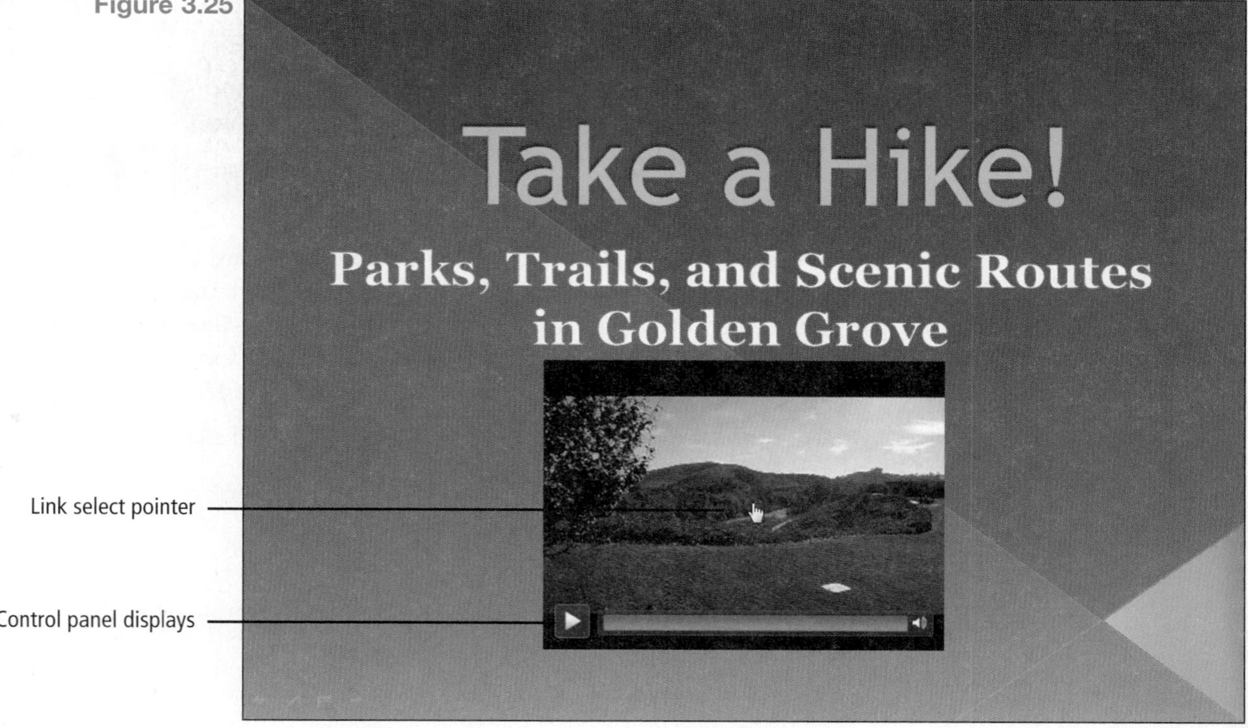

7 With the [pointer icon] pointer displayed, click the mouse button to view the video. Move the pointer away from the video and notice that the control panel no longer displays. When the video is finished, press Esc to exit the slide show.

8 **Save** [Save icon] the presentation.

Activity 3.10 | Formatting a Video

You can apply styles and effects to a video and change the video shape and border. You can also recolor a video so that it coordinates with the presentation theme.

1 With **Slide 1** displayed, select the video. On the **Format tab**, in the **Video Styles group**, click the **More** button [More icon] to display the **Video Styles** gallery.

2 Using the ScreenTips to view the style name, under **Moderate**, click the first style—**Compound Frame, Black**. Compare your screen with Figure 3.26.

Figure 3.26

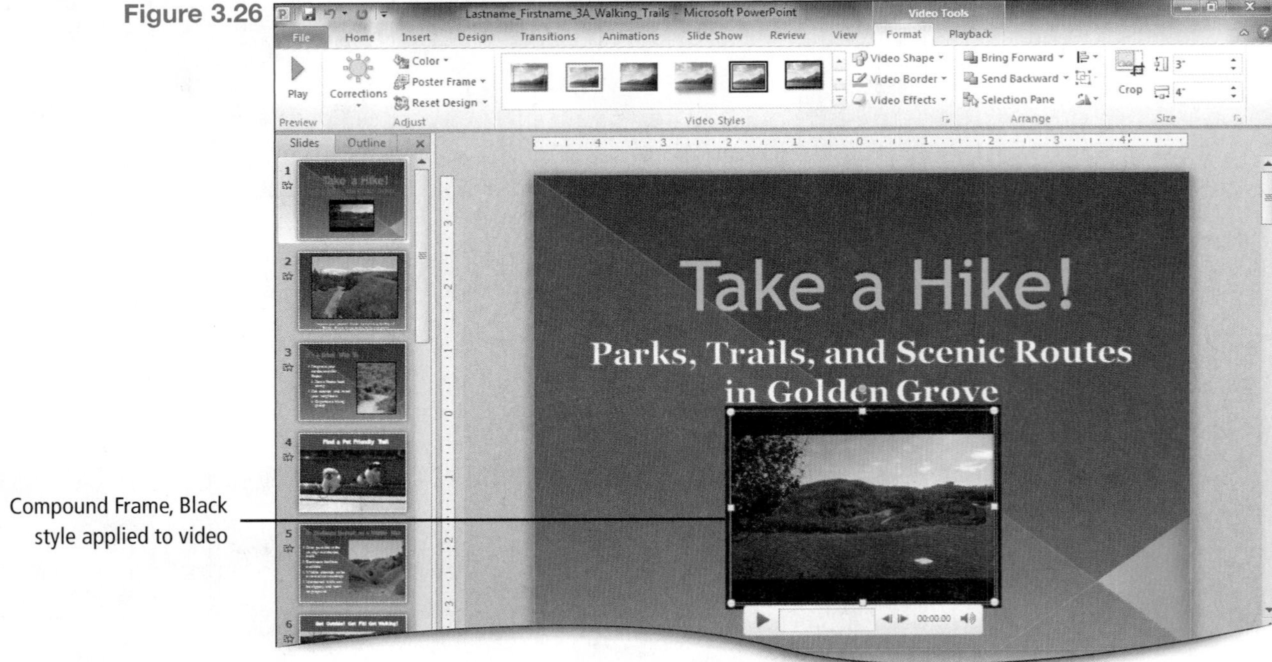

3 In the **Video Styles group**, click the **Video Shape** button, and then under **Basic Shapes**, click the first shape—**Oval**. In the **Video Styles group**, click the **Video Border** button, and then in the third column, click the fifth color—**Blue-Gray, Background 2, Darker 25%**. In the **Video Styles group**, click the **Video Effects** button, point to **Bevel**, and then click the last bevel—**Art Deco**. Compare your screen with Figure 3.27.

You can format a video with any combination of styles and effects.

Figure 3.27

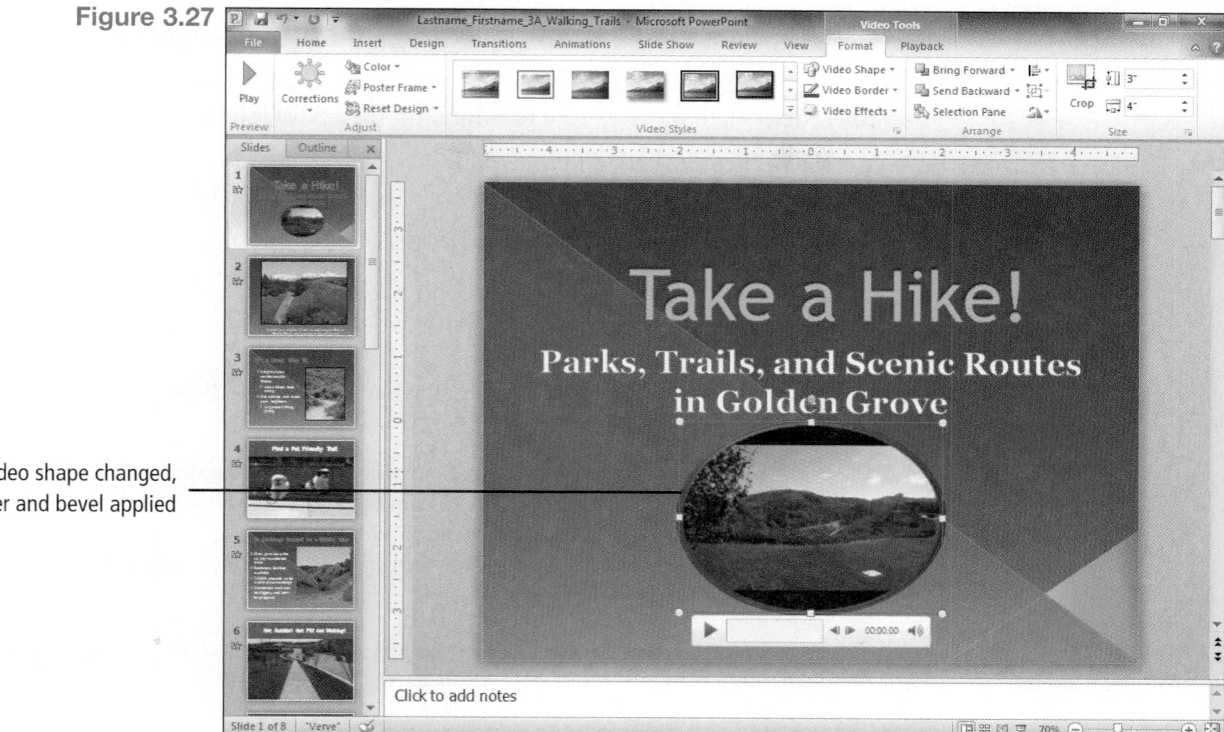

4 If necessary, select the video. On the **Format tab**, in the **Adjust group**, click the **Color** button to display the **Recolor** gallery.

The first row of the Recolor gallery displays options to recolor the video in grayscale, sepia, washout, or black and white variations. The remaining rows in the gallery display options to recolor the video in the theme colors.

5 In the **Recolor** gallery, in the second row, point to the first style—**Light Blue, Text color 2 Dark** and notice that Live Preview displays the video in the selected color. Compare your screen with Figure 3.28.

Figure 3.28

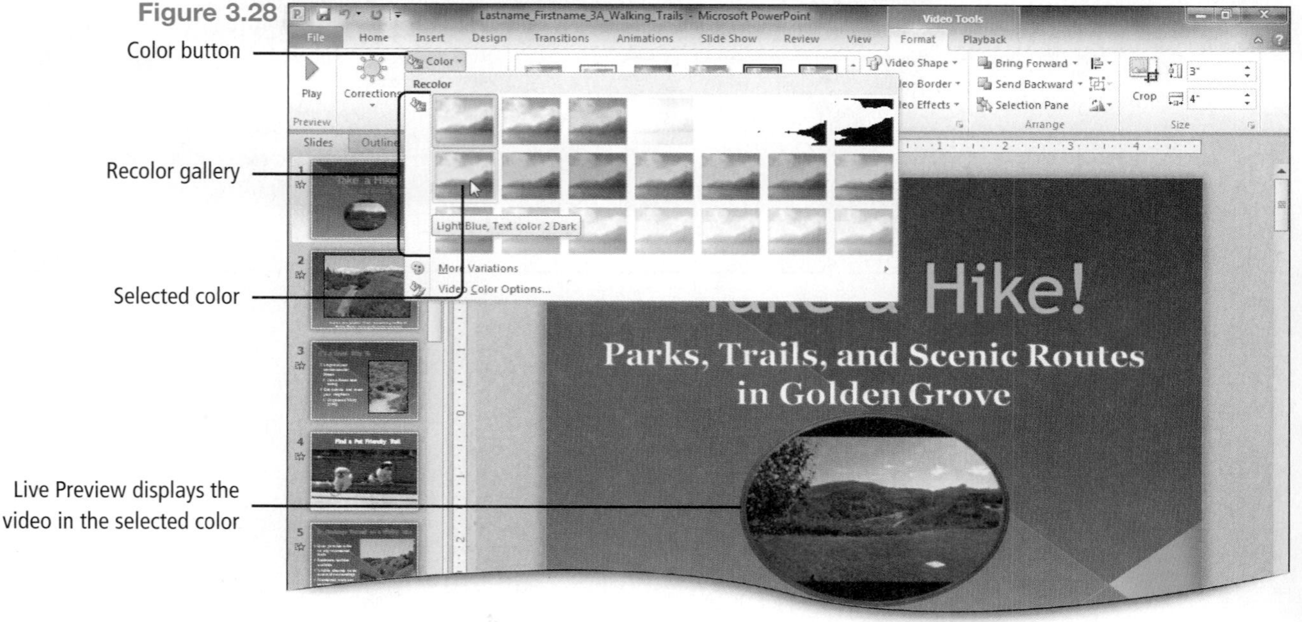

PowerPoint | Chapter 3

6. Click **Light Blue, Text color 2 Dark** to change the color of the video.
7. In the **Adjust group**, click the **Color** button to display the Recolor gallery. In the first row, click the first color—**No Recolor**, and then **Save** the presentation.

   The No Recolor option restores the video to its original color.

Activity 3.11 | Editing and Compressing a Video

You can ***trim***—delete parts of a video to make it shorter—and you can compress a video file to reduce the file size of your PowerPoint presentation.

1. If necessary, select the video. On the **Playback tab**, in the **Editing group**, click the **Trim Video** button, and then compare your screen with Figure 3.29.

   At the top of the displayed Trim Video dialog box, the file name and the video duration display. Below the video, a timeline displays with start and end markers indicating the video start and end time. Start Time and End Time boxes display the current start and end of the video. The Previous Frame and Next Frame buttons move the video forward and backward one frame at a time.

Figure 3.29

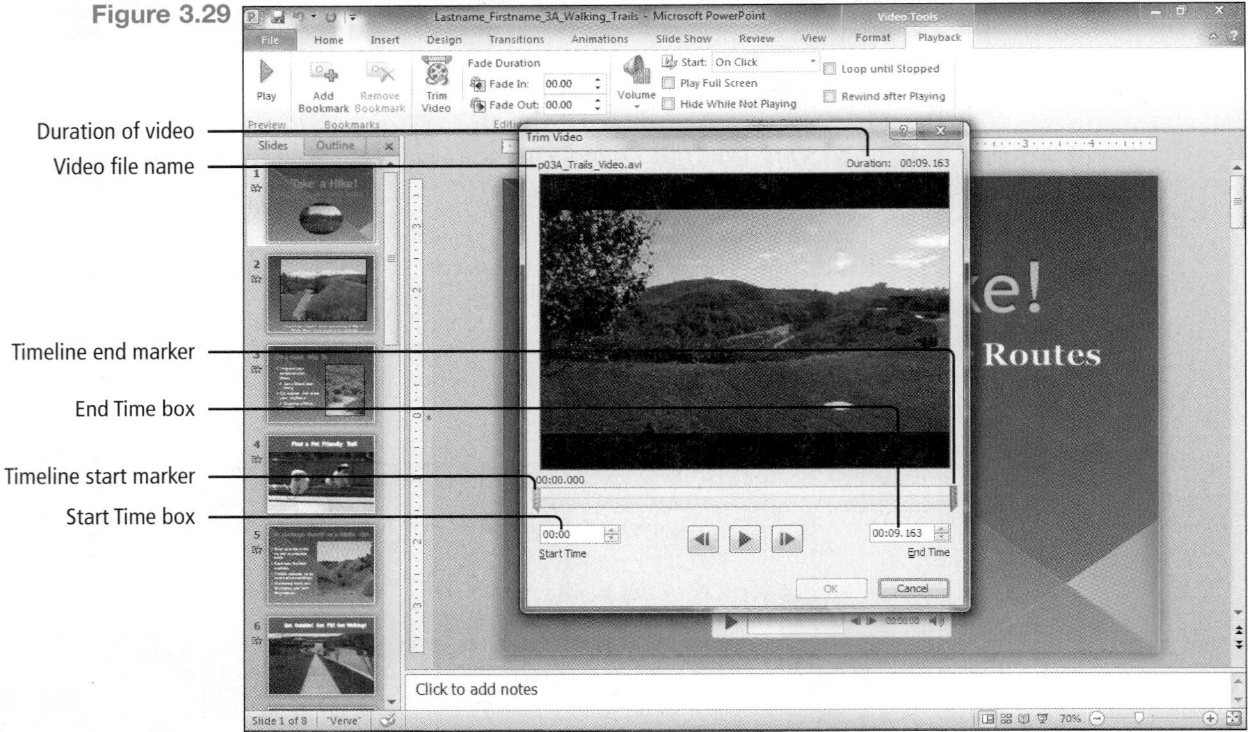

Another Way

Drag the red ending marking until its ScreenTip displays the ending time that you want; or type in the box.

2 Click in the **End Time** box, and then use the spin box arrows to set the End Time to **0:07.040**. Compare your screen with Figure 3.30.

The blue section of the timeline indicates the portion of the video that will play during the slide show. The gray section indicates the portion of the video that is trimmed.

Figure 3.30

3 Click **OK** to apply the trim settings.

4 Display **Backstage** view, and then on the **Info tab**, click the **Compress Media** button. Read the description of each video quality option, and then click **Low Quality.** Compare your screen with Figure 3.31.

The Compress Media dialog box displays the slide number on which the selected video is inserted, the video file name, the original size of the video file, and when compression is complete, the amount that the file size was reduced.

Figure 3.31

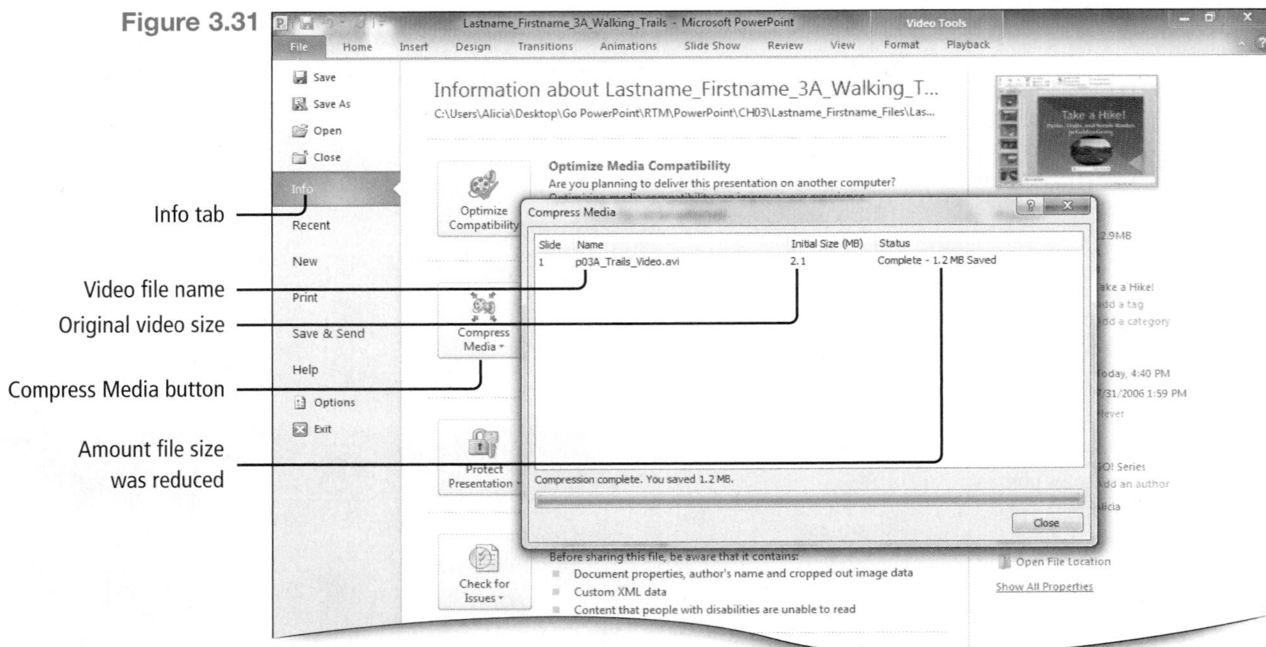

5 In the **Compress Media** dialog box, click **Close**, and then click the **Home tab** to return to **Slide 1**.

6 If necessary, select the video. On the **Playback tab**, in the **Video Options group**, click the **Start arrow**, and then click **Automatically** so that during the slide show, the video will begin automatically. Compare your screen with Figure 3.32.

Figure 3.32

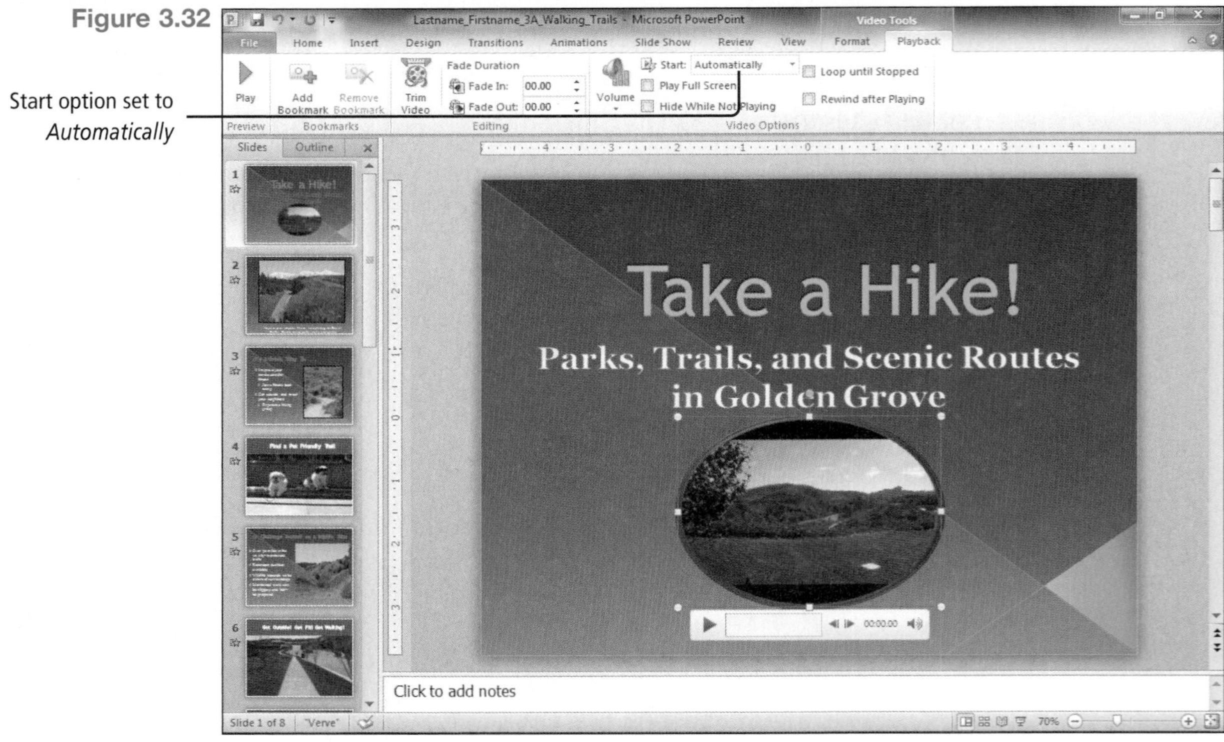

7 Click the **Slide Show tab**, in the **Start Slide Show group**, click the **From Beginning** button, and then view the slide show. Press Esc when the black slide displays.

> **Note** | Your Video May Look Blurry
>
> On playback, a compressed video may look slightly blurry. If you are certain that your presentation file will not be transmitted over the Internet, for example, in an e-mail message or in your learning management system, it is not necessary to compress the video.

8 On the **Insert tab**, in the **Text group**, click the **Header & Footer** button to display the **Header and Footer** dialog box. Click the **Notes and Handouts tab**. Under **Include on page**, select the **Date and time** check box, and then select **Update automatically**. If necessary, clear the **Header** check box, and then select the **Page number** and **Footer** check boxes. In the **Footer** box, using your own name, type **Lastname_Firstname_3A_Walking_Trails** and then click **Apply to All**.

9 Show the **Document Panel**. Replace the text in the **Author** box with your own firstname and lastname. In the **Subject** box, type your course name and section number, and in the **Keywords** box, type **trails, hiking Close** the **Document Information Panel**.

10 **Save** your presentation. Print **Handouts 4 Slides Horizontal**, or submit your presentation electronically as directed by your instructor.

11 **Close** the presentation and exit PowerPoint.

End 
You have completed Project 3A

Project 3B Summary and Analysis Presentation

Project Activities

In Activities 3.12 through 3.17, you will add a table and two charts to a presentation that Mindy Walker, Director of Parks and Recreation, is creating to inform the City Council about enrollment trends in Golden Grove recreation programs. Your completed presentation will look similar to Figure 3.33.

Project Files

For Project 3B, you will need the following file:

p03B_Recreation_Enrollment

You will save your presentation as:

Lastname_Firstname_3B_Recreation_Enrollment

Project Results

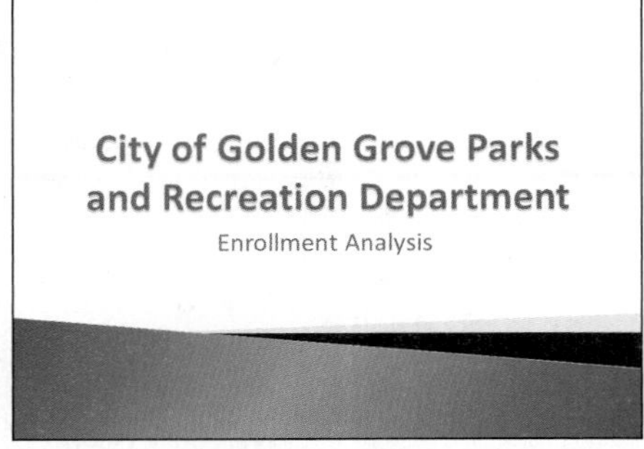

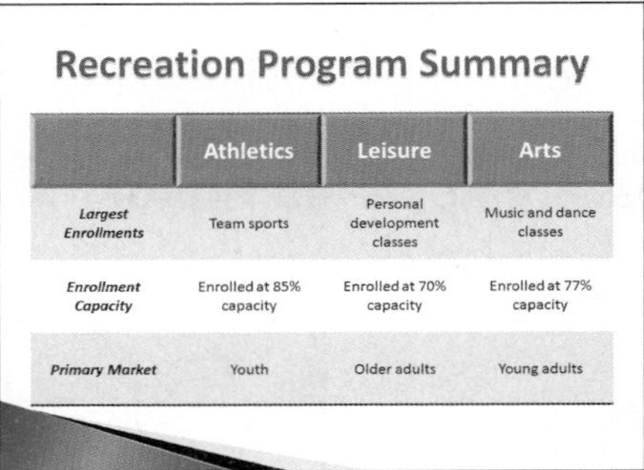

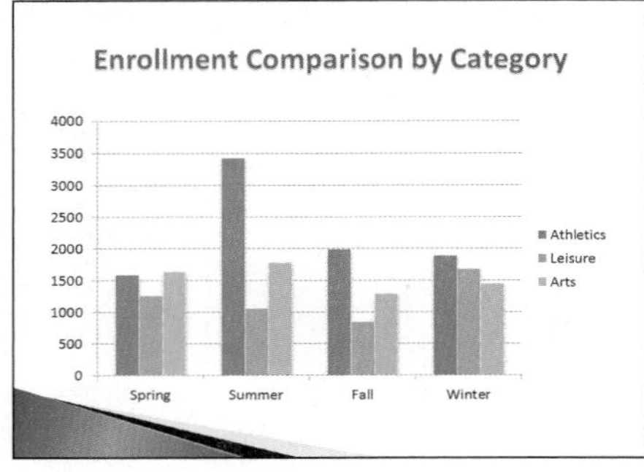

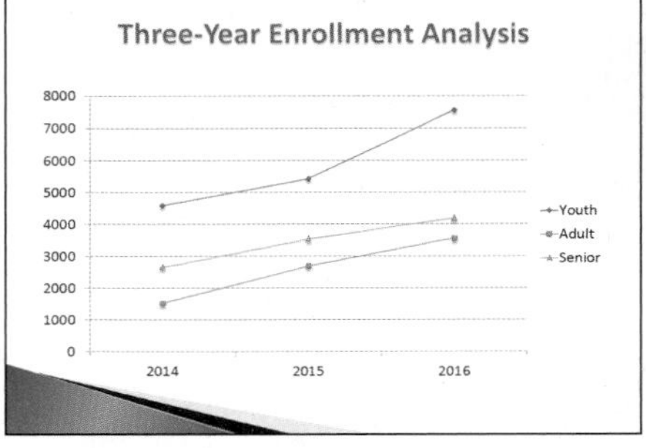

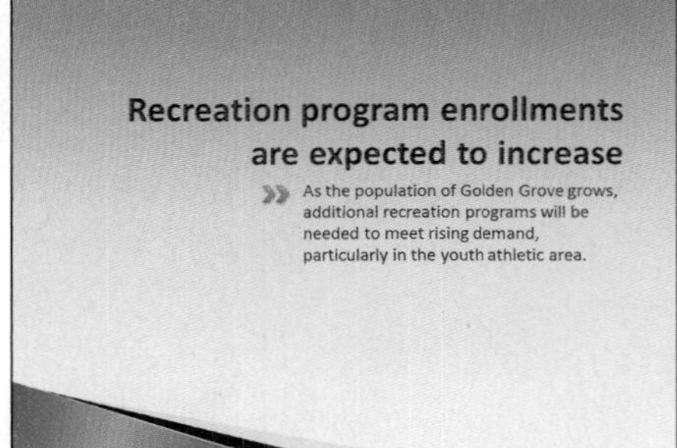

Figure 3.33
Project 3B Recreation Enrollment

Objective 4 | Create and Modify Tables

A ***table*** is a format for information that organizes and presents text and data in columns and rows. The intersection of a column and row is referred to as a ***cell*** and is the location in which you type text in a table.

Activity 3.12 | Creating a Table

There are several ways to insert a table in a PowerPoint slide. For example, you can use the Draw Table pointer, which is useful when the rows and columns contain cells of different sizes. Another way is to insert a slide with a Content Layout and then click the Insert Table button. Or, click the Insert tab and then click Table. In this activity, you will use a Content Layout to create a table.

1. **Start** PowerPoint. From your student files, open **p03B_Recreation_Enrollment**, and then **Save** the presentation in your **PowerPoint Chapter 3** folder as **Lastname_Firstname_3B_Recreation_Enrollment**

2. With **Slide 1** displayed, on the **Home tab**, in the **Slides group**, click the **New Slide** button to insert a slide with the **Title and Content** layout. In the title placeholder, type **Recreation Program Summary** and then **Center** the title.

3. In the content placeholder, click the **Insert Table** button to display the **Insert Table** dialog box. In the **Number of columns** box, type **3** and then press Tab. In the **Number of rows** box, type **2** and then compare your screen with Figure 3.34.

   Here you enter the number of columns and rows that you want the table to contain.

Figure 3.34

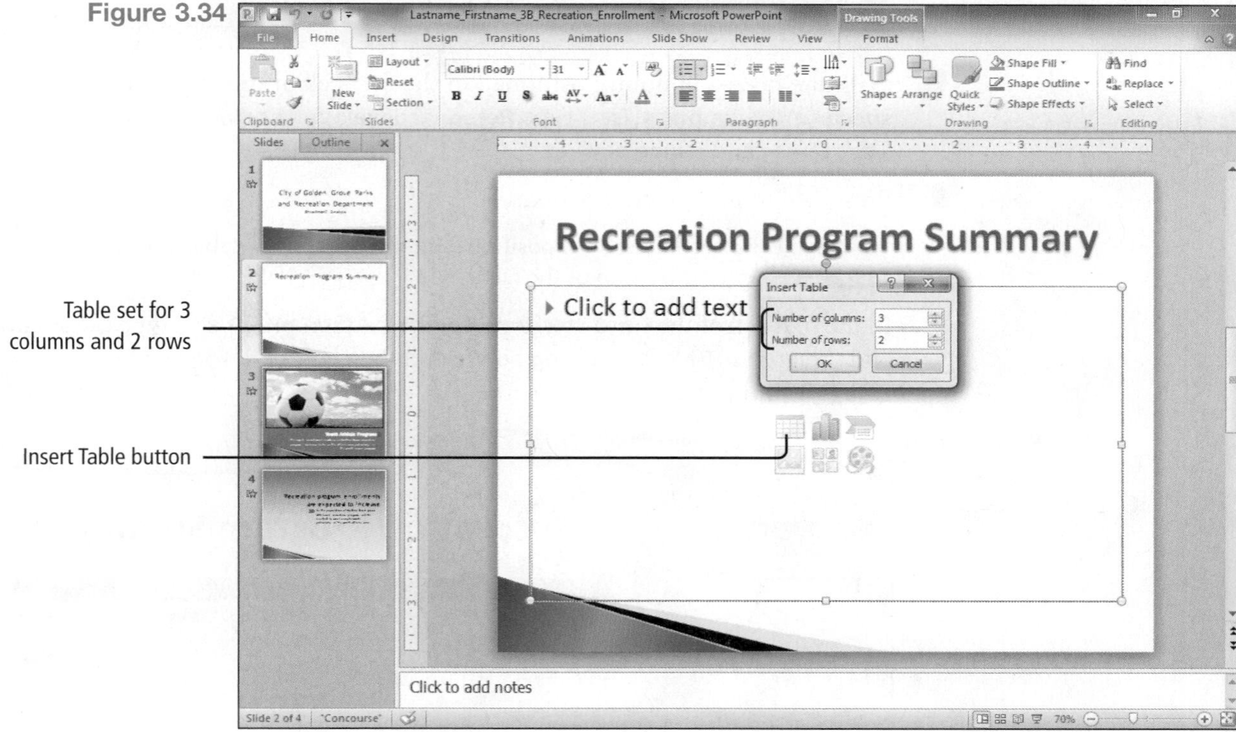

4. Click **OK** to create a table with three columns and two rows. Notice that the insertion point is blinking in the upper left cell of the table.

   The table extends from the left side of the content placeholder to the right side, and the three columns are equal in width. By default, a style is applied to the table.

5 With the insertion point positioned in the first cell of the table, type **Athletics** and then press Tab.

Pressing Tab moves the insertion point to the next cell in the same row. If the insertion point is positioned in the last cell of a row, pressing Tab moves the insertion point to the first cell of the next row.

> **Alert! | Did You Press Enter Instead of Tab?**
>
> In a table, pressing Enter creates another line in the same cell. If you press Enter by mistake, you can remove the extra line by pressing Backspace.

6 With the insertion point positioned in the second cell of the first row, type **Leisure** and then press Tab. Type **Arts** and then press Tab to move the insertion point to the first cell in the second row. Compare your table with Figure 3.35.

Figure 3.35

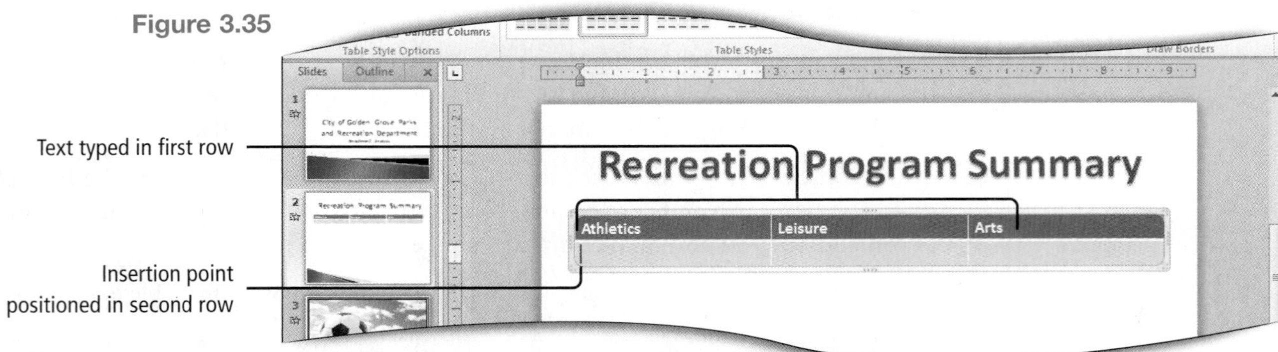

7 With the insertion point positioned in the first cell of the second row, type **Team sports** and then press Tab. Type **Personal development classes** and then press Tab. Type **Music and dance classes**

8 Press Tab to insert a new blank row.

When the insertion point is positioned in the last cell of a table, pressing Tab inserts a new blank row at the bottom of the table.

9 In the first cell of the third row, type **Youth** and then press Tab. Type **Older adults** and then press Tab. Type **Young adults** and then compare your table with Figure 3.36. **Save** your presentation.

Figure 3.36

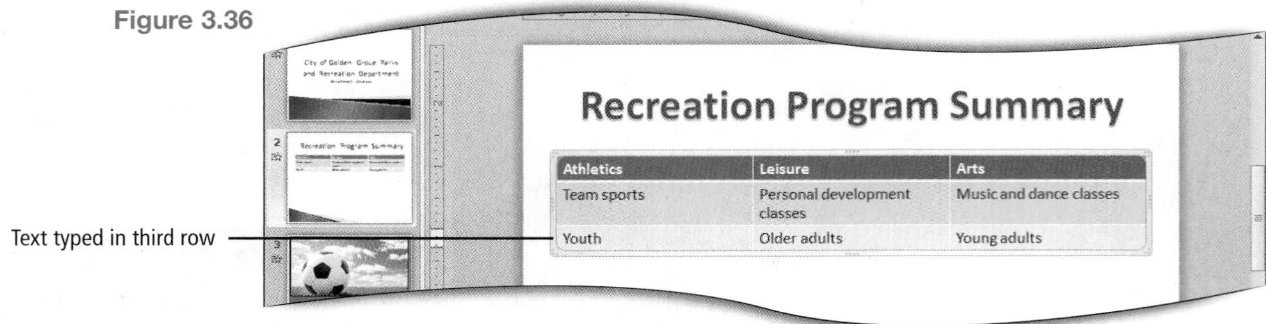

> **Alert! | Did You Add an Extra Row to the Table?**
>
> Recall that when the insertion point is positioned in the last cell of the table, pressing Tab inserts a new blank row. If you inadvertently inserted a blank row in the table, on the Quick Access Toolbar, click Undo.

Activity 3.13 | Modifying the Layout of a Table

You can modify the layout of a table by inserting or deleting rows and columns, changing the alignment of the text in a cell, adjusting the height and width of the entire table or selected rows and columns, and by merging multiple cells into one cell.

1 Click in any cell in the first column, and then click the **Layout tab**. In the **Rows & Columns group**, click the **Insert Left** button.

A new first column is inserted and the width of the columns is adjusted so that all four columns are the same width.

2 In the *second* row, click in the first cell, and then type **Largest Enrollments**

3 In the third row, click in the first cell, and then type **Primary Market** Compare your table with Figure 3.37.

Figure 3.37

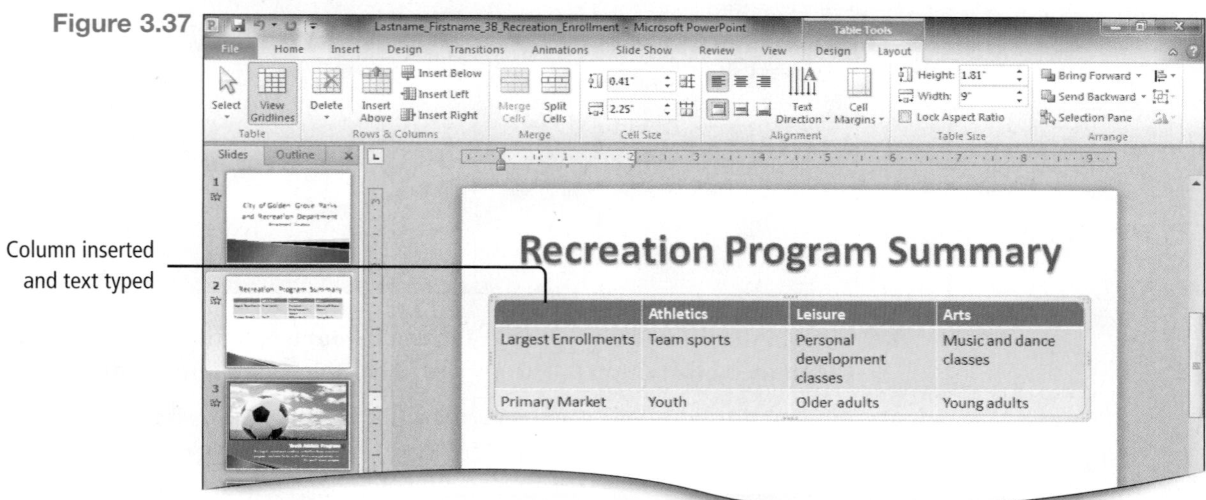

4 With the insertion point positioned in the third row, on the **Layout tab**, in the **Rows & Columns group**, click the **Insert Above** button to insert a new third row. In the first cell, type **Enrollment Capacity** and then press Tab. Type the remaining three entries, pressing Tab to move from cell to cell: **Enrolled at 85% capacity** and **Enrolled at 70% capacity** and **Enrolled at 77% capacity**

5 At the center of the lower border surrounding the table, point to the cluster of four dots—the sizing handle—to display the ↕ pointer. Compare your screen with Figure 3.38.

Figure 3.38

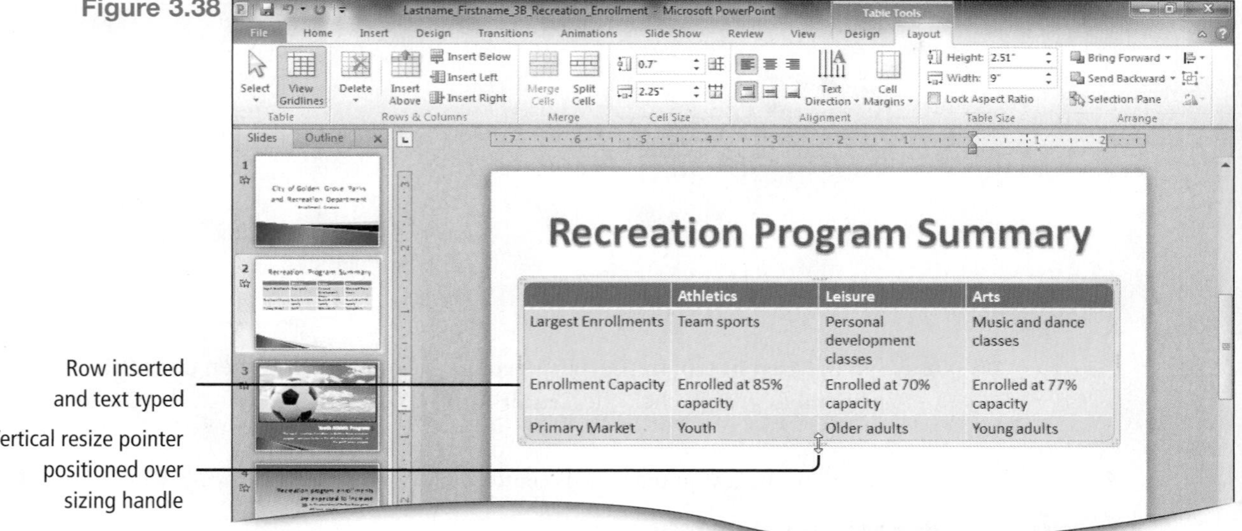

PowerPoint | Chapter 3

6 Drag down to resize the table until the lower left corner of the table outline is just above the graphic in the lower left corner of the slide. Compare your screen with Figure 3.39.

Figure 3.39

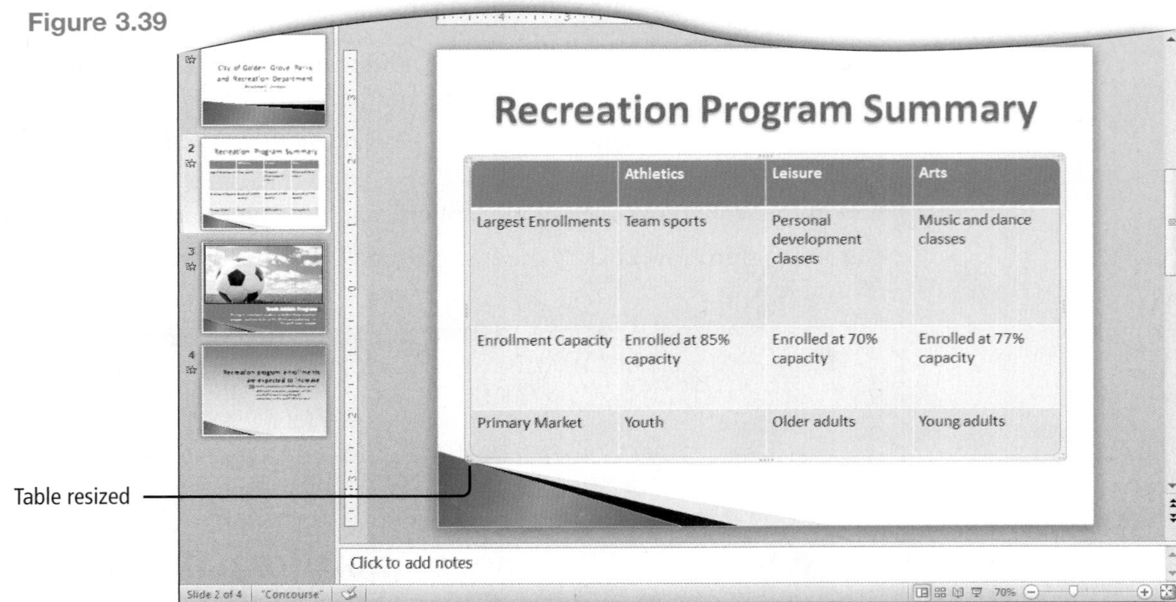

7 Click in the first cell of the table. On the **Layout tab**, in the **Cell Size group**, click the **Distribute Rows** button. Compare your table with Figure 3.40.

The Distribute Rows command adjusts the height of the rows in the table so that they are equal.

Figure 3.40

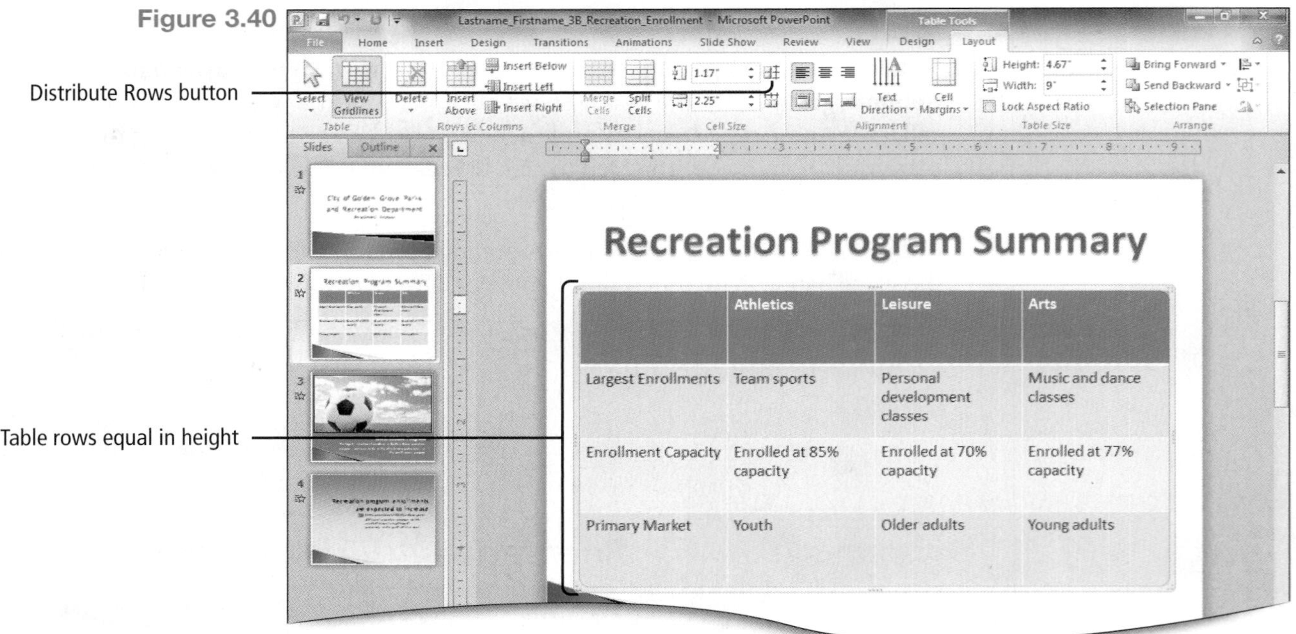

8 On the **Layout tab**, in the **Table group**, click **Select**, and then click **Select Table.** In the **Alignment group**, click the **Center** button, and then click the **Center Vertically** button.

All of the text in the table is centered horizontally and vertically within the cells.

9 **Save** your presentation.

> **More Knowledge | Deleting Rows and Columns**
>
> To delete a row or column from a table, click in the row or column that you want to delete. Click the Layout tab, and then in the Rows & Columns group, click Delete. In the displayed list, click Delete Columns or Delete Rows.

Activity 3.14 | Modifying a Table Design

You can modify the design of a table by applying a ***table style***. A table style formats the entire table so that it is consistent with the presentation theme. There are color categories within the table styles—Best Match for Document, Light, Medium, and Dark.

1. Click in any cell in the table. In the **Table Tools**, click the **Design tab**, and then in the **Table Styles group**, click the **More** button. In the displayed **Table Styles** gallery, point to several of the styles to view the Live Preview of the style.
2. Under **Medium**, scroll as necessary, and then in the third row, click the third button—**Medium Style 3 – Accent 2**—to apply the style to the table.
3. On the **Design tab**, in the **Table Style Options group**, clear the **Banded Rows** check box. Notice that each row except the header row displays in the same color.

   The check boxes in the Table Style Options group control where Table Style formatting is applied.
4. Select the **Banded Rows** check box.
5. Move the pointer outside of the table so that it is positioned to the left of the first row in the table to display the pointer, as shown in Figure 3.41.

Figure 3.41

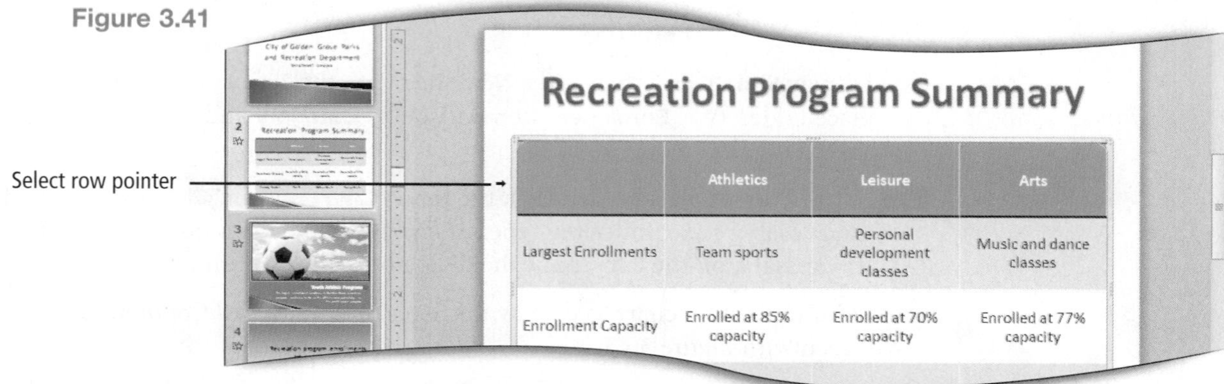

6. With the pointer pointing to the first row in the table, click the mouse button to select the entire row so that you can apply formatting to the selection. Move the pointer into the selected row, and then right-click to display the Mini toolbar and shortcut menu. On the Mini toolbar, change the **Font Size** to **28**.
7. With the first row still selected, in the **Table Tools**, on the **Design tab**, in the **Table Styles group**, click the **Effects** button. Point to **Cell Bevel**, and then under **Bevel**, click the first bevel—**Circle**.
8. Position the pointer above the first column to display the pointer, and then right-click to select the first column and display the shortcut menu. Click **Bold** and **Italic**.
9. Click in a blank area of the slide, and then compare your slide with Figure 3.42. **Save** the presentation.

Figure 3.42

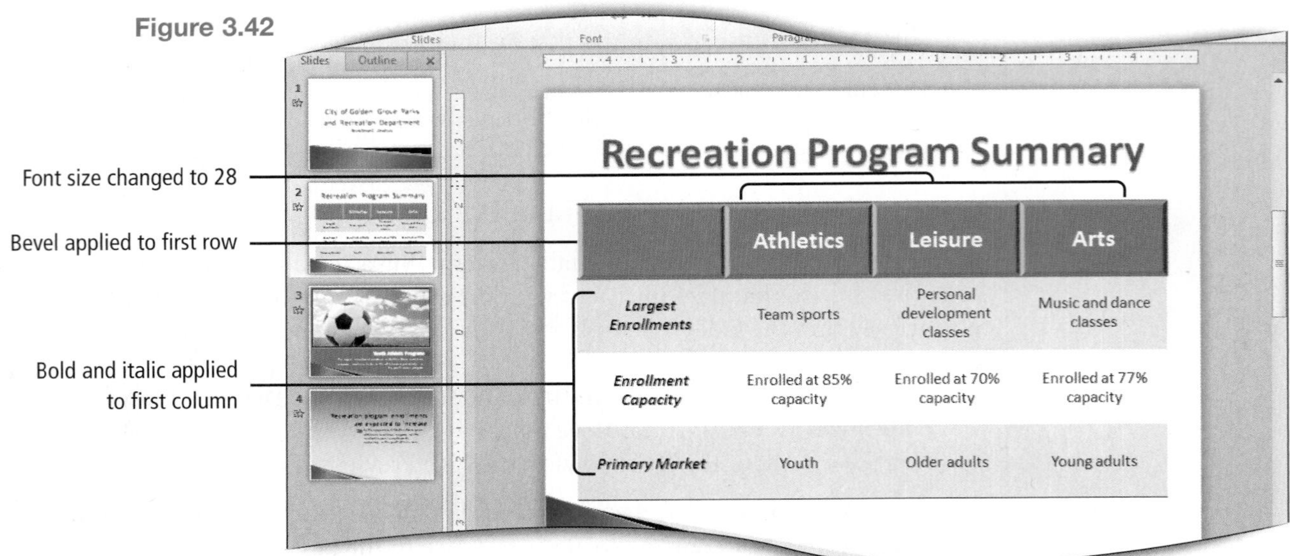

Objective 5 | Create and Modify Charts

A ***chart*** is a graphic representation of numeric data. Commonly used chart types include bar and column charts, pie charts, and line charts. A chart that you create in PowerPoint is stored in an Excel worksheet that is incorporated into the PowerPoint file.

Activity 3.15 | Creating a Column Chart and Applying a Chart Style

A ***column chart*** is useful for illustrating comparisons among related numbers. In this activity, you will create a column chart that compares enrollment in each category of recreation activities by season.

1. Display **Slide 3**, and then add a **New Slide** with the **Title and Content** layout. In the title placeholder, type **Enrollment Comparison by Category** and then **Center** the title and change the **Font Size** to **36**.
2. In the content placeholder, click the **Insert Chart** button to display the **Insert Chart** dialog box. Notice the types of charts that you can insert in your presentation. If necessary, on the left side of the dialog box, click Column.
3. Point to the first chart to display the ScreenTip *Clustered Column*. Compare your screen with Figure 3.43.

Figure 3.43

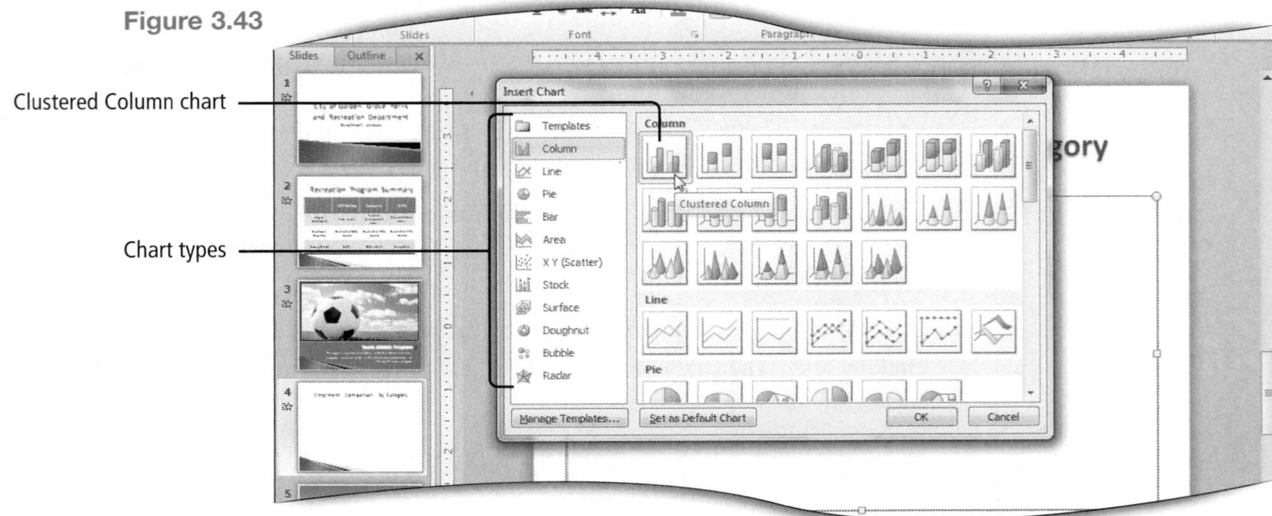

4 Click **Clustered Column**. Click **OK**, and then compare your screen with Figure 3.44.

The PowerPoint window displays a column chart on one side of your screen. On the other side of your screen, an Excel worksheet displays columns and rows. A cell is identified by the intersecting column letter and row number, forming the ***cell reference***.

The worksheet contains sample data in a data range outlined in blue, from which the chart in the PowerPoint window is generated. The column headings—*Series 1*, *Series 2*, and *Series 3* display in the chart ***legend*** and the row headings—*Category 1*, *Category 2*, *Category 3*, and *Category 4*—display as ***category labels***. The legend identifies the patterns or colors that are assigned to the data series in the chart. The category labels display along the bottom of the chart to identify the categories of data.

Figure 3.44

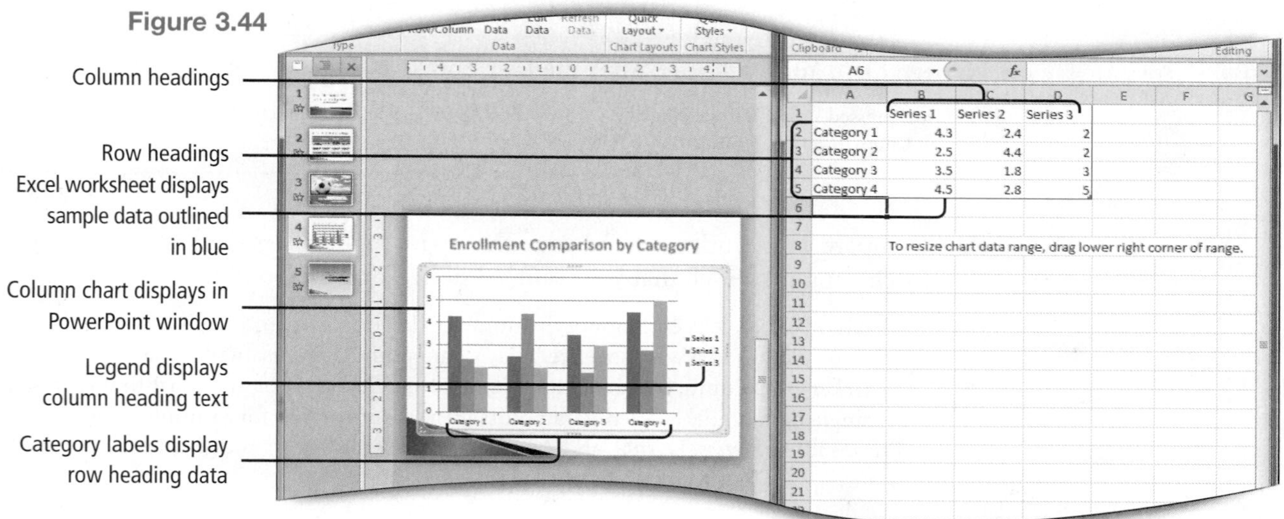

5 In the Excel window, click in cell **B1**, which contains the text *Series 1*. Type **Athletics** and then press Tab to move to cell **C1**.

The chart legend is updated to reflect the change in the Excel worksheet.

6 In cell **C1**, which contains the text *Series 2*, type **Leisure** and then press Tab to move to cell **D1**. Type **Arts** and then press Tab. Notice that cell **A2**, which contains the text *Category 1*, is selected. Compare your screen with Figure 3.45.

The blue box outlining the range of cells defines the area in which you are entering data. When you press Tab in the rightmost cell, the first cell in the next row becomes active.

Figure 3.45

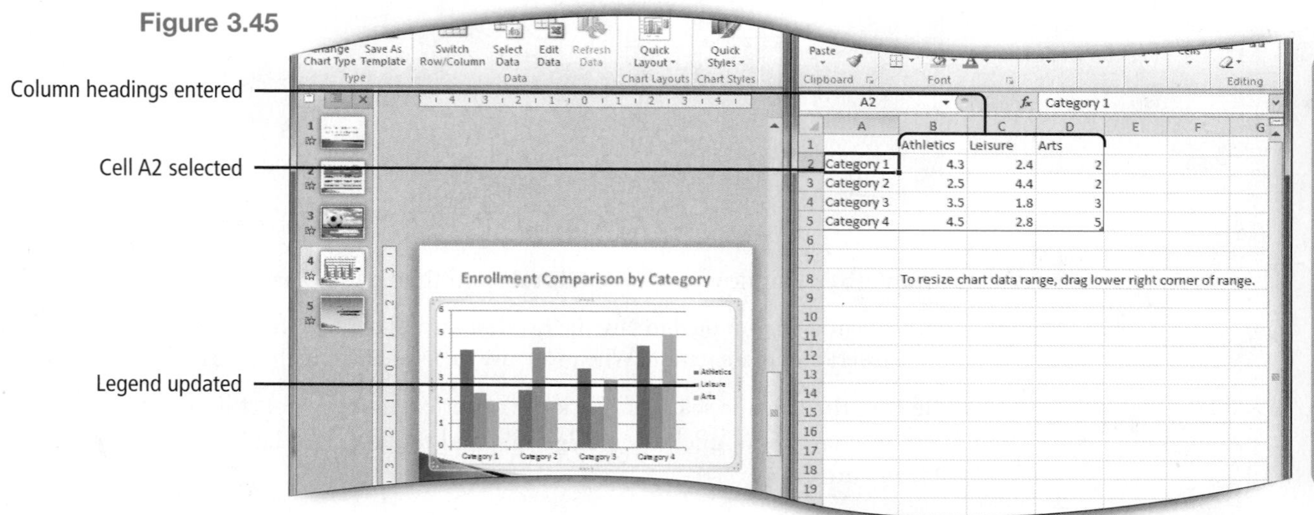

7 Beginning in cell **A2**, type the following data, pressing Tab to move from cell to cell.

	Athletics	Leisure	Arts
Spring	**1588**	**1263**	**1639**
Summer	**3422**	**1058**	**1782**
Fall	**1987**	**852**	**1293**
Winter	**1889**	**1674**	

8 In cell **D5**, which contains the value 5, type **1453** and then press Enter.

Pressing Enter in the last cell of the blue outlined area maintains the existing data range.

> **Alert! | Did You Press Tab After the Last Entry?**
>
> If you pressed Tab after entering the data in cell D5, you expanded the chart range. In the Excel window, click Undo.

9 Compare your worksheet and your chart with Figure 3.46. Correct any typing errors by clicking in the cell that you want to change, and then retype the data.

Each of the 12 cells containing the numeric data that you entered is a ***data point***—a value that originates in a worksheet cell. Each data point is represented in the chart by a ***data marker***—a column, bar, area, dot, pie slice, or other symbol in a chart that represents a single data point. Related data points form a ***data series***; for example, there is a data series for *Athletics*, *Leisure*, and *Arts*. Each data series has a unique color or pattern represented in the chart legend.

Figure 3.46

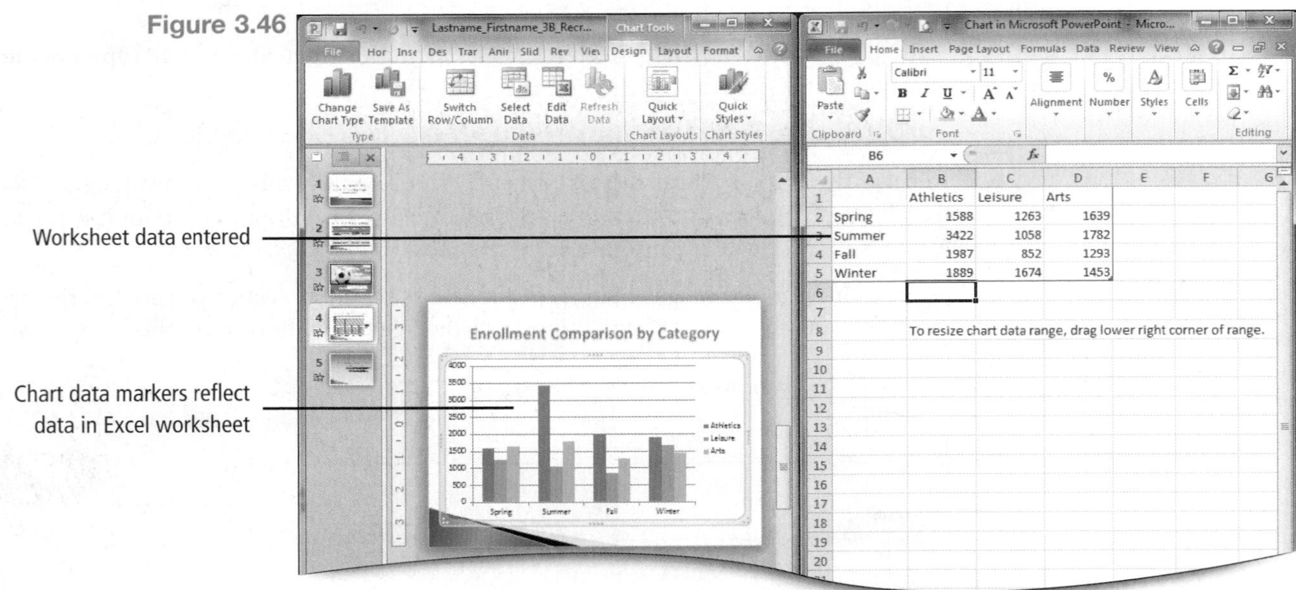

10 In the Excel window, click the **File tab**, and then click **Close**.

You are not prompted to save the Excel worksheet because the worksheet data is a part of the PowerPoint presentation. When you save the presentation, the Excel data is saved with it.

11 Be sure the chart is selected; click the outer edge of the chart if necessary to select it. In the **Chart Tools**, click the **Design tab**, and then in the **Chart Styles group**, click the **More** button.

12 In the **Chart Styles** gallery, the chart styles are numbered sequentially. Use ScreenTips to display the style numbers. Click **Style 10** to apply the style to the chart.

13 **Save** your presentation.

> **More Knowledge | Editing the Chart Data After Closing Excel**
>
> You can redisplay the Excel worksheet and make changes to the data after you have closed Excel. To do so, in PowerPoint, click the chart to select it, and then on the Design tab in the Data group, click Edit Data.

Activity 3.16 | Creating a Line Chart and Deleting Chart Data

To analyze and compare annual data over a three-year period, the presentation requires an additional chart. Recall that there are a number of different types of charts that you can insert in a PowerPoint presentation. In this activity, you will create a ***line chart***, which is commonly used to illustrate trends over time.

1 With **Slide 4** displayed, add a **New Slide** with the **Title and Content** layout. In the title placeholder, type **Three-Year Enrollment Analysis** and then **Center** the title and change the **Font Size** to **36**.

2 In the content placeholder, click the **Insert Chart** button. On the left side of the displayed **Insert Chart** dialog box, click **Line**, and then on the right, under **Line**, click the fourth chart—**Line with Markers**. Click **OK**.

3 In the Excel worksheet, click in cell **B1**, which contains the text *Series 1*. Type **Youth** and then press Tab. Type **Adult** and then press Tab. Type **Senior** and then press Tab.

4 Beginning in cell **A2**, type the following data, pressing Tab to move from cell to cell. If you make any typing errors, click in the cell that you want to change, and then retype the data.

	Youth	Adult	Senior
2014	**4586**	**1534**	**2661**
2015	**5422**	**2699**	**3542**
2016	**7565**	**3572**	**4183**

5 In the Excel window, position the pointer over **row heading 5** so that the pointer displays. Compare your screen with Figure 3.47.

Figure 3.47

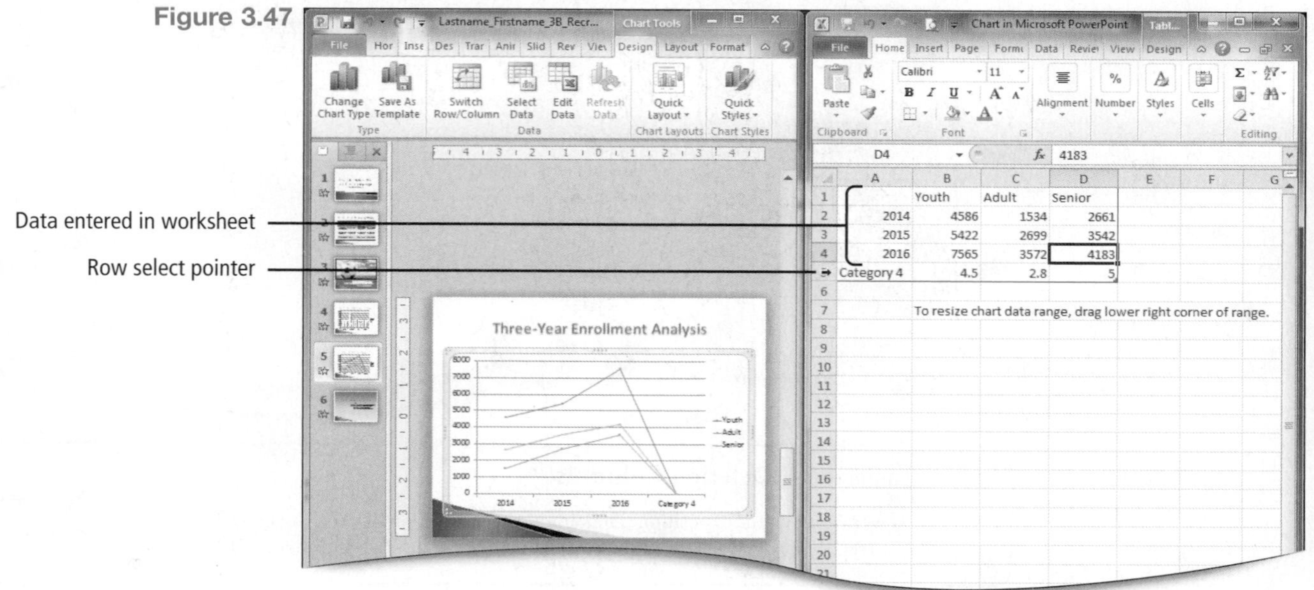

6 With the [→] pointer displayed, *right-click* to select the row and display the shortcut menu. On the shortcut menu, click **Delete** to delete the extra row from the worksheet, and then compare your screen with Figure 3.48.

The data in the worksheet contains four columns and four rows, and the blue outline defining the chart data range is resized. You must delete columns and rows that you do not want to include in the chart. You can add additional rows and columns by typing column and row headings and then entering additional data. When data is typed in cells adjacent to the chart range, the range is resized to include the new data.

Figure 3.48

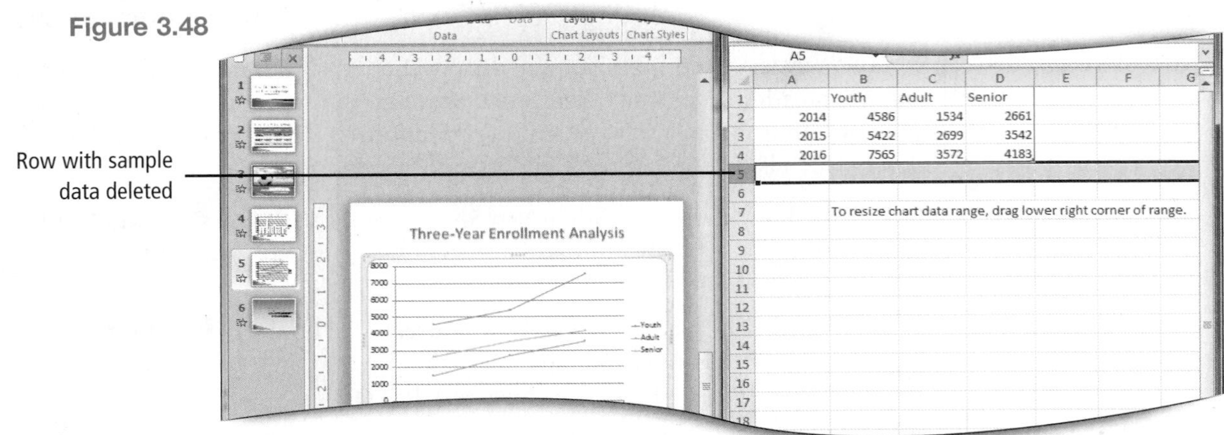

7 **Close** [X] the Excel window. In the **Chart Styles group**, click the **More** button [▾]. In the **Chart Styles** gallery, click **Style 26**, and then compare your slide with Figure 3.49. **Save** [💾] your presentation.

Figure 3.49

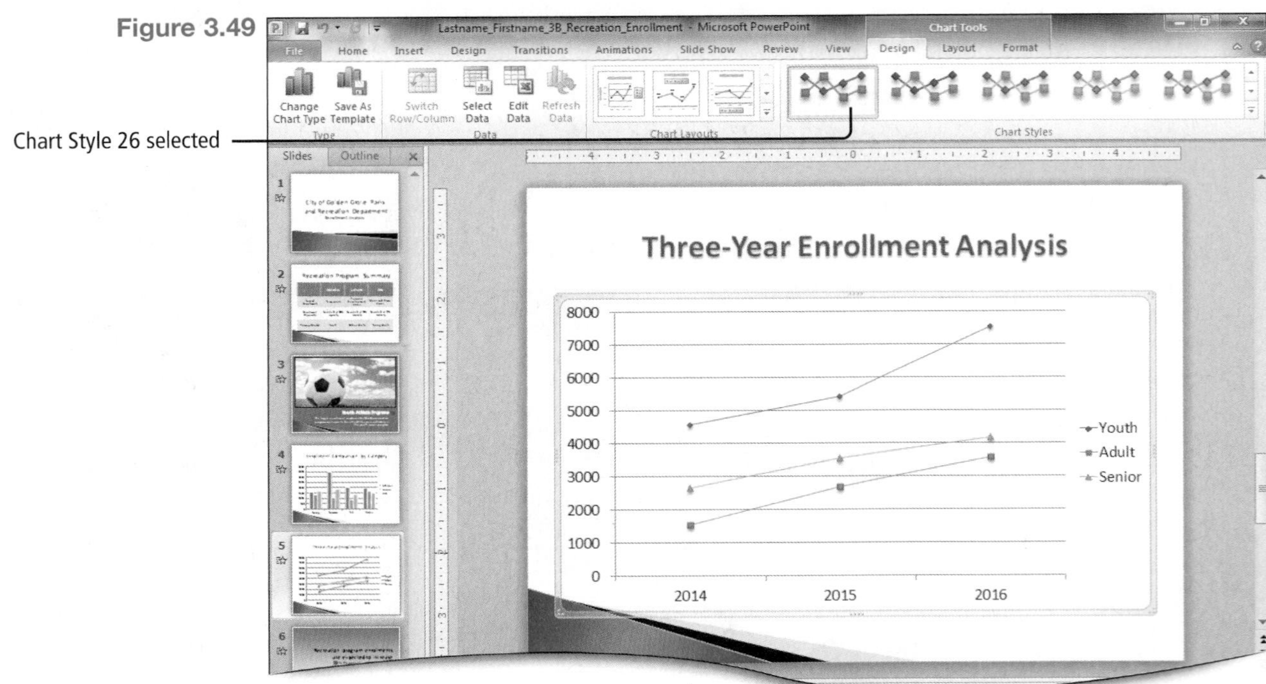

More Knowledge | Deleting Columns

To delete a worksheet column, position the pointer over the column letter that you want to select so that the [↓] pointer displays. Right-click to select the column and display the shortcut menu. Click Delete.

Activity 3.17 | Animating a Chart

1 Display **Slide 4**, and then click the column chart to select it. On the **Animations tab**, in the **Animation group**, click the **More** button, and then under **Entrance**, click **Split**.

2 In the **Animation group**, click the **Effect Options** button, and then under **Sequence**, click **By Series**. Compare your screen with Figure 3.50.

The By Series option displays the chart one data series at a time, and the numbers 1, 2, 3, and 4 to the left of the chart indicate the four parts of the chart animation sequence. The chart animation sequence includes the background, followed by the Athletics data series for each season, and then the Leisure series, and then the Arts series.

Figure 3.50

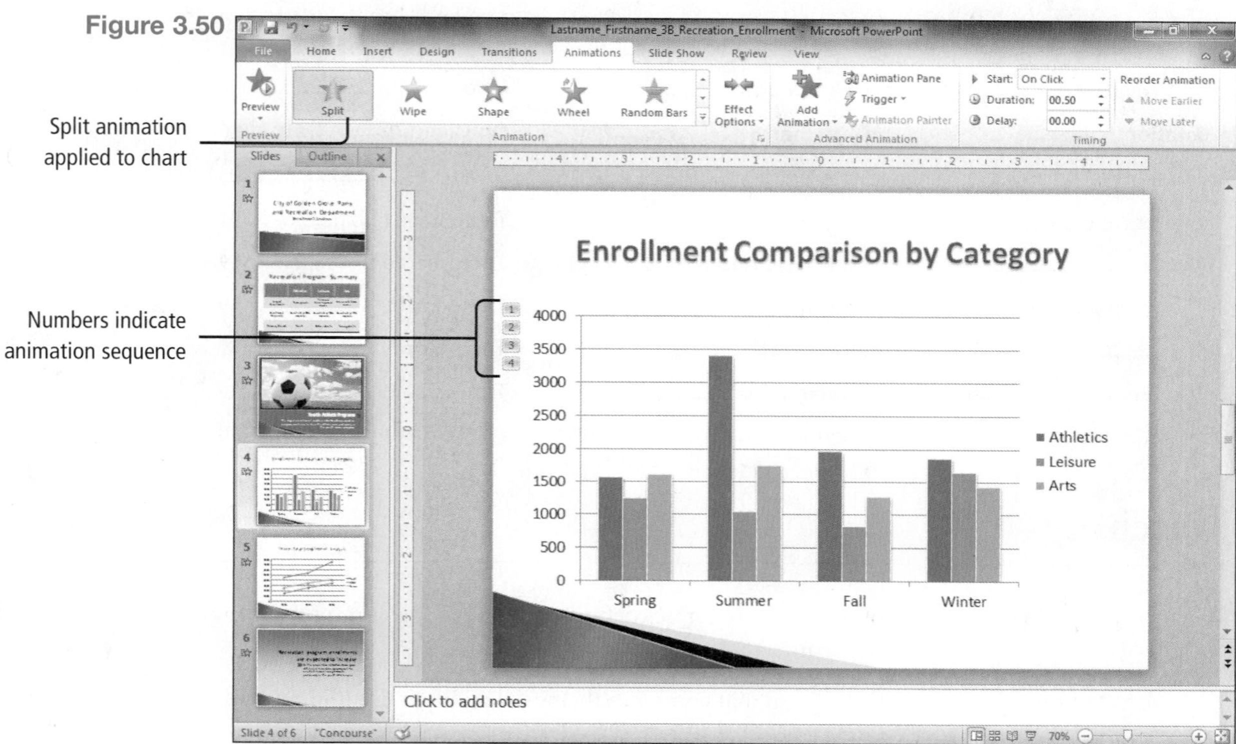

3 Click the **Slide Show tab**. In the **Start Slide Show group**, click **From Current Slide** to view the animation on **Slide 4**. Press Spacebar to display the legend and labels. Press Spacebar again to display the *Athletics* data.

4 Continue to press Spacebar to advance through the remaining animation effects. After the animations for Slide 4 are complete, press Esc to end the slide show and return to the presentation.

5 Insert a **Header & Footer** for the **Notes and Handouts**. Include the **Date and time updated automatically**, the **Page number**, and a **Footer** with the file name **Lastname_Firstname_3B_Recreation_Enrollment**

6 Show the **Document Panel**. Replace the text in the **Author** box with your own firstname and lastname. In the **Subject** box, type your course name and section number, and in the **Keywords** box, type **enrollment, recreation Close** the **Document Information Panel**.

7 **Save** your presentation. Print **Handouts 6 Slides Horizontal**, or submit your presentation electronically as directed by your instructor. **Close** the presentation and exit PowerPoint.

End You have completed Project 3B

Content-Based Assessments

Summary

In this chapter, you formatted a presentation by applying background styles, inserting pictures on slide backgrounds, and changing the theme fonts. You enhanced your presentation by inserting video, applying animation effects, and by changing effect and timing options. You practiced creating tables to present information in an organized manner, and you used charts to visually represent data.

Key Terms

Matching

Match each term in the second column with its correct definition in the first column by writing the letter of the term on the blank line in front of the correct definition.

____ 1. A slide background fill variation that combines theme colors in different intensities.

____ 2. A theme that determines the font applied to two types of slide text—headings and body.

____ 3. Of the two types of fonts in the theme font, the type that is applied to slide titles.

____ 4. Of the two types of fonts in the theme font, the type that is applied to all slide text except titles.

____ 5. A visual or sound effect added to an object or text on a slide.

____ 6. Animations that bring a slide element onto the screen.

____ 7. Animation that emphasizes an object or text that is already displayed.

____ 8. Animation that moves an object or text off the screen.

____ 9. A format for information that organizes and presents text and data in columns and rows.

____ 10. The intersection of a column and row.

____ 11. Formatting applied to an entire table so that it is consistent with the presentation theme.

____ 12. A graphic representation of numeric data.

____ 13. A type of chart used to compare data.

____ 14. A combination of the column letter and row number identifying a cell.

____ 15. A chart element that identifies the patterns or colors that are assigned to the each data series in the chart.

A Animation
B Background style
C Body font
D Cell
E Cell reference
F Chart
G Column chart
H Emphasis effect
I Entrance effect
J Exit effect
K Headings font
L Legend
M Table
N Table style
O Theme font

Content-Based Assessments

Multiple Choice

Circle the correct answer.

1. The set of coordinating colors applied to the backgrounds, objects, and text in a presentation is called:
   A. theme colors **B.** colors set **C.** coordinating colors
2. The command that is used to prevent background graphics from displaying on a slide is:
   A. Hide Background Styles **B.** Cover Background Graphics **C.** Hide Background Graphics
3. Animation options that control when animated items display in the animation sequence are called:
   A. timing options **B.** effect options **C.** sequence options
4. A feature that copies animation settings from one object to another is:
   A. copy **B.** format painter **C.** animation painter
5. The action of deleting parts of a video to make it shorter is referred to as:
   A. edit **B.** trim **C.** crop
6. A chart element that identifies categories of data is a:
   A. data marker **B.** category label **C.** category marker
7. A column, bar, area, dot, pie slice, or other symbol in a chart that represents a single data point is a:
   A. data marker **B.** data point **C.** data series
8. A chart value that originates in a worksheet cell is a:
   A. data marker **B.** data point **C.** data series
9. A group of related data points is called a:
   A. data marker **B.** data point **C.** data series
10. A type of chart that shows trends over time is a:
    A. pie chart **B.** column chart **C.** line chart

Content-Based Assessments

Apply **3A** skills from these Objectives:

1. Customize Slide Backgrounds and Themes
2. Animate a Slide Show
3. Insert a Video

Skills Review | Project 3C Lake

In the following Skills Review, you will format a presentation by applying slide background styles, colors, pictures, and animation. Your completed presentation will look similar to Figure 3.51.

Project Files

For Project 3C, you will need the following files:

p03C_Lake
p03C_Scenery
p03C_Lake_Video

You will save your presentation as:

Lastname_Firstname_3C_Lake

Project Results

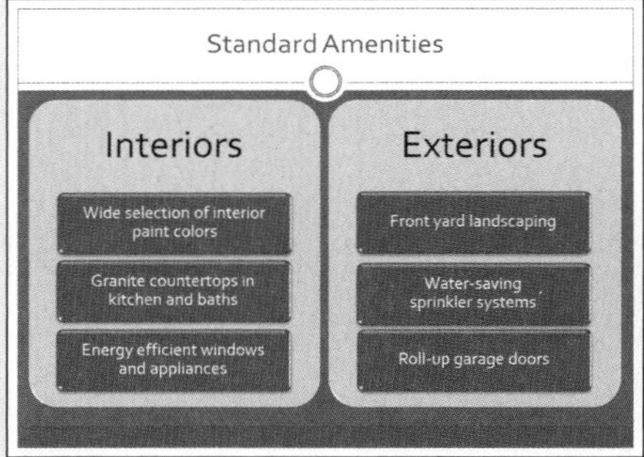

Figure 3.51

(Project 3C Lake continues on the next page)

Skills Review | Project 3C Lake (continued)

1 **Start** PowerPoint, from your student files open **p03C_Lake**, and then **Save** the presentation in your **PowerPoint Chapter 3** folder as **Lastname_Firstname_3C_Lake**

a. On the **Design tab**, in the **Themes group**, click the **Colors** button, and then click **Aspect** to change the theme colors. On the **Design tab**, in the **Themes group**, click the **Fonts** button, and then click **Module** to change the theme fonts.

b. Display **Slide 2**, and then on the **Home tab,** in the **Slides group**, click the **New Slide arrow**. Click **Title Only** to insert a new slide with the Title Only layout. On the **Design tab**, in the **Background group**, select the **Hide Background Graphics** check box. Click in the title placeholder, and then type **Enjoy the Lakeside Scenery**

c. On the **Design tab**, in the **Background group**, click the **Background Styles** button. Below the gallery, click **Format Background**, and then in the **Format Background** dialog box, verify that on the left side, **Fill** is selected. On the right side of the dialog box, under **Fill**, click the **Picture or texture fill** option button. Under **Insert from**, click the **File** button, and then navigate to your student data files. Click **p03C_Scenery**, and then click **Insert**. In the **Format Background** dialog box, click **Close** to format the slide background with the picture.

d. Click in the title placeholder. On the **Format tab**, in the **Shape Styles group**, click the **More** button, and then in the second row, click the fourth style—**Colored Fill - Dark Blue, Accent 3**.

e. Point to the outer edge of the title placeholder to display the [move] pointer, and then drag the placeholder up and to the left so that its top left corner aligns with the top left corner of the slide. Point to the center right sizing handle and drag to the right so that placeholder extends to the right edge of the slide.

2 Display **Slide 4**. On the **Design tab**, in the **Background group**, click the **Background Styles** button. In the second row, point to the third button—**Style 7**. *Right-click* to display the shortcut menu, and then click **Apply to Selected Slides** to apply the dark gray, patterned background to Slide 4.

a. Display **Slide 5**. On the **Design tab**, in the **Background group**, click the **Background Styles** button. Below the gallery, click **Format Background**.

b. In the **Format Background** dialog box, verify that on the left side, **Fill** is selected. On the right side, under **Fill**, click the **Solid Fill** option button, and then under **Fill Color**, click the **Color** button. In the seventh column, click the first color—**Dark Blue, Accent 3**, and then click **Close** to apply the background fill color to the slide.

3 Display **Slide 2**, and then on the **Insert tab**, in the **Media group**, click the **Video** button. Navigate to your student files, and then click **p03_Lake_Video**. Click **Insert** to insert the video.

a. With the video selected, on the **Format tab**, in the **Size group**, replace the value in the **Video Height** box with **3.25** and then press Enter.

b. Point to the video, and then hold down Shift and drag to the right so that its right edge aligns at **4.5 inches on the right side of the horizontal ruler**.

c. With the video selected, on the **Format tab**, in the **Video Styles group**, click the **Video Border** button, and then in the seventh column, click the first color—**Dark Blue, Accent 3**. Click the **Video Effects** button, point to **Bevel**, and then click the last style—**Art Deco**.

d. With the video selected, on the **Playback tab**, in the **Video Options group**, click the **Start arrow**, and then click **Automatically**. In the **Editing group**, click the **Trim Video** button. In the **Trim Video** dialog box, in the **End Time** box, use the spin box arrows to set the end time to **00:6.520** Click **OK**.

e. Display **Backstage** view. On the **Info page**, in the center panel, click the **Compress Media** button, and then click **Low Quality**. Recall that compressing in this manner facilitates sending your file over the Internet in an e-mail or in a learning management system, although it may make the video less clear when played. When the compression is complete, **Close** the **Compress Media** dialog box, and then click the **Home tab** to return to the presentation.

4 On **Slide 2**, click anywhere in the bulleted list placeholder. On the **Animations tab**, in the **Animation group**, click the **More** button, and then under **Entrance**, click **Split**.

a. In the **Animation group**, click the **Effect Options** button, and then click **Vertical Out**.

(Project 3C Lake continues on the next page)

Skills Review | Project 3C Lake (continued)

b. In the **Timing group**, click the **Start arrow**, and then click **With Previous** so that the list displays at the same time as the video begins to play.

c. In the **Timing group**, click the **Duration up arrow** two times so that *01.00* displays in the **Duration** box. Click the **Delay up arrow** one time so that *00.25* displays in the **Delay** box.

5 Display **Slide 5**, and then click in the title placeholder. On the **Animations tab**, in the **Animation group**, click the **More** button, and then under **Entrance**, click **Wipe**. In the **Timing group**, click the **Start arrow**, and then click **After Previous**.

a. Select the title, and then in the **Advanced Animation group**, click the **Animation Painter** button. Click the subtitle to apply the title animation effects to the subtitle.

b. Display **Slide 1**, and then select the title. On the **Animations tab**, in the **Animation group**, click the **More** button, and then click **None** to remove the animation from the title.

c. On the **Slide Show tab**, in the **Start Slide Show group**, click **From Beginning**, and then view your presentation, clicking the mouse button to advance through the slides.

d. Insert a **Header & Footer** for the **Notes and Handouts**. Include the **Date and time updated automatically**, the **Page number**, and a **Footer** with the file name **Lastname_Firstname_3C_Lake** Click **Apply to All**.

e. Show the **Document Panel**. Replace the text in the **Author** box with your own firstname and lastname. In the **Subject** box, type your course name and section number, and in the **Keywords** box, type **Gold Haven, lake** **Close** the **Document Information Panel**.

f. **Save** your presentation. Print **Handouts 6 Slides Horizontal**, or submit your presentation electronically as directed by your instructor. **Close** the presentation.

End **You have completed Project 3C**

Apply 3B skills from these Objectives:

- **4** Create and Modify Tables
- **5** Create and Modify Charts

Skills Review | Project 3D School Enrollment

In the following Skills Review, you will format a presentation by inserting and formatting a table, column chart, and line chart. Your completed presentation will look similar to Figure 3.52.

Project Files

For Project 3D, you will need the following file:

p03D_School_Enrollment

You will save your presentation as:

Lastname_Firstname_3D_School_Enrollment

Project Results

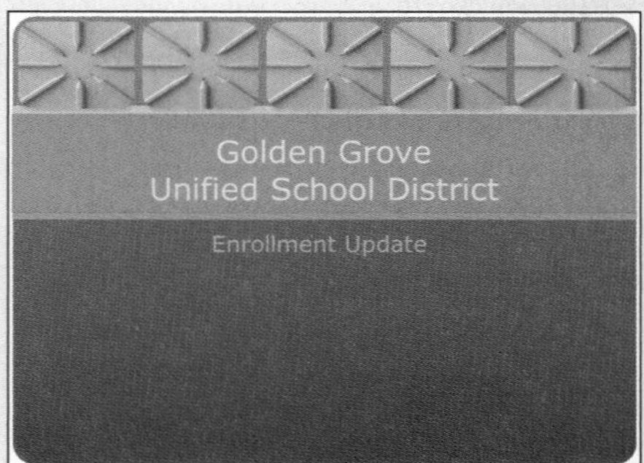

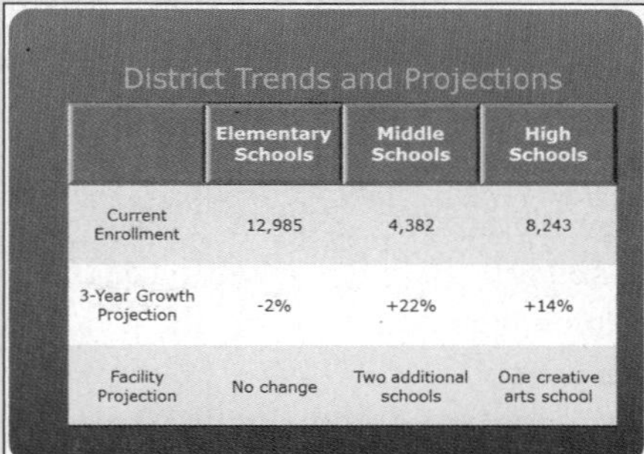
District Trends and Projections

	Elementary Schools	Middle Schools	High Schools
Current Enrollment	12,985	4,382	8,243
3-Year Growth Projection	-2%	+22%	+14%
Facility Projection	No change	Two additional schools	One creative arts school

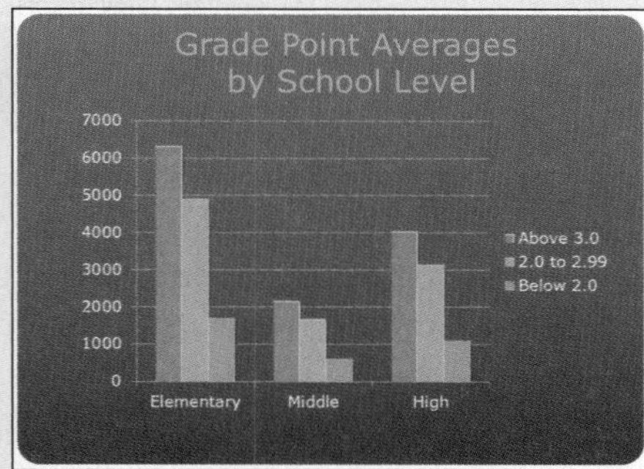

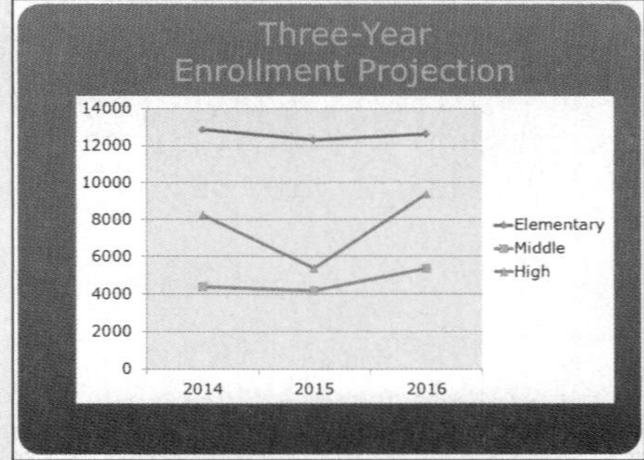

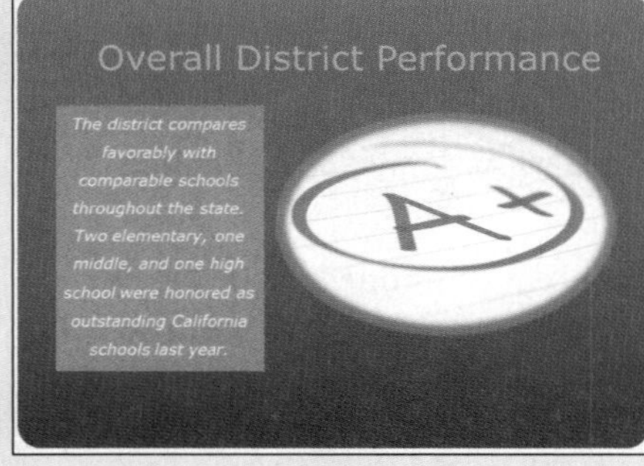

Figure 3.52

(Project 3D School Enrollment continues on the next page)

Content-Based Assessments

Skills Review | Project 3D School Enrollment (continued)

1 **Start** PowerPoint, from your student files open **p03D_School_Enrollment**, and then **Save** the presentation in your **PowerPoint Chapter 3** folder as **Lastname_Firstname_3D_School_Enrollment**

a. Display **Slide 2**. In the content placeholder, click the **Insert Table** button to display the **Insert Table** dialog box. In the **Number of columns** box, type **3** and then press Tab. In the **Number of rows** box, type **2** and then click **OK** to create the table.

b. In the first row of the table, click in the *second* cell. Type **Elementary Schools** and then press Tab. Type **High Schools** and then press Tab to move the insertion point to the first cell in the second row.

c. With the insertion point positioned in the first cell of the second row, type **Current Enrollment** and then press Tab. Type **12,985** and then press Tab. Type **8,243** and then press Tab to insert a new blank row. In the first cell of the third row, type **Facility Projection** and then press Tab. Type **No change** and then press Tab. Type **One creative arts school**

d. With the insertion point positioned in the last column, on the **Layout tab**, in the **Rows & Columns group**, click the **Insert Left** button. Click in the top cell of the inserted column, and then type **Middle Schools** In the second and third rows of the inserted column, type **4,382** and **Two additional schools**

e. With the insertion point positioned in the third row, on the **Layout tab**, in the **Rows & Columns group**, click the **Insert Above** button. Click in the first cell of the row you inserted, type **3-Year Growth Projection** and then press Tab. Type the remaining three entries in the row as follows: **-2%** and **+22%** and **+14%**

2 At the center of the lower border surrounding the table, point to the cluster of four dots—the sizing handle—and make the table larger by dragging down until the lower edge of the table aligns at **3 inches on the lower half of the vertical ruler.**

a. Click in the first cell of the table. On the **Layout tab**, in the **Cell Size group**, click the **Distribute Rows** button.

b. On the **Layout tab**, in the **Table group**, click **Select**, and then click **Select Table**. In the **Alignment group**, click the **Center** button, and then click the **Center Vertically** button.

c. Click in any cell in the table. In the **Table Tools**, click the **Design tab**, and then in the **Table Styles group**, click the **More** button. Under **Medium**, in the third row, click the second style—**Medium Style 3 – Accent 1**—to apply the style to the table.

d. Move the pointer outside of the table so that is positioned to the left of the first row in the table to display the → pointer, click one time to select the entire row. Click the **Design tab**, and then in the **Table Styles group**, click the **Effects** button. Point to **Cell Bevel**, and then under **Bevel**, click the first bevel—**Circle**. Change the **Font Size** of the text in the first row to **20**.

3 Display **Slide 3**. In the content placeholder, click the **Insert Chart** button to display the **Insert Chart** dialog box. Click the first chart—*Clustered Column*—and then click **OK**.

a. In the Excel window, click in cell **B1**, which contains the text *Series 1*. Type **Above 3.0** and then press Tab to move to cell **C1**.

b. In cell **C1**, which contains the text *Series 2*, type **2.0 to 2.99** and then press Tab to move to cell **D1**, which contains the text *Series 3*. Type **Below 2.0** and then press Tab.

c. Beginning in cell **A2**, type the following data, pressing Tab to move from cell to cell.

	Above 3.0	2.0 to 2.99	Below 2.0
Elementary	6318	4900	1676
Middle	2147	1665	596
High	4039	3132	1070

d. In the Excel window, position the pointer over **row heading 5** so that the → pointer displays. Then, *right-click* to select the row and display the shortcut menu. On the shortcut menu, click **Delete**. **Close** the Excel window.

e. If necessary, click the edge of the chart so that it is selected. In the **Chart Tools**, click the **Design tab**, and then in the **Chart Styles group**, click the **More** button. In the **Chart Styles** gallery, click **Style 10** to apply the style to the chart.

f. With the chart selected, click the **Animations tab**, and then in the **Animation group**, click the **More** button. Under **Entrance**, click **Split**. In the

(Project 3D School Enrollment continues on the next page)

Skills Review | Project 3D School Enrollment (continued)

Animation group, click the **Effect Options** button, and then under **Sequence**, click **By Series**.

4 Display **Slide 4**. In the content placeholder, click the **Insert Chart** button. On the left side of the displayed **Insert Chart** dialog box, click **Line**, and then under **Line**, click the fourth chart—**Line with Markers**. Click **OK**.

a. In the Excel worksheet, click in cell **B1**, which contains the text *Series 1*. Type **Elementary** and then press Tab. Type **Middle** and then press Tab. Type **High** and then press Tab.

b. Beginning in cell **A2**, type the following data, pressing Tab to move from cell to cell.

	Elementary	Middle	High
2014	**12895**	**4382**	**8243**
2015	**12322**	**4156**	**5346**
2016	**12637**	**5346**	**9397**

c. In the Excel window, position the pointer over **row heading 5** so that the ➡ pointer displays. Then, right-click to select the row and display the shortcut menu. On the shortcut menu, click **Delete**. **Close** the Excel window.

d. On the **Chart Tools Design tab**, in the **Chart Styles group**, click the **More** button. In the **Chart Styles** gallery, click **Style 34**.

e. Insert a **Header & Footer** for the **Notes and Handouts**. Include the **Date and time updated automatically**, the **Page number**, and a **Footer** with the file name **Lastname_Firstname_3D_School_Enrollment** Click **Apply to All**.

f. Show the **Document Panel**. Replace the text in the **Author** box with your own firstname and lastname. In the **Subject** box, type your course name and section number, and in the **Keywords** box, type **enrollment, schools** **Close** the **Document Information Panel**.

g. View the slide show from the beginning, and then **Save** your presentation. Print **Handouts 6 Slides Horizontal**, or submit your presentation electronically as directed by your instructor. **Close** the presentation and exit PowerPoint.

End **You have completed Project 3D**

Content-Based Assessments

Apply **3A** skills from these Objectives:

1 Customize Slide Backgrounds and Themes
2 Animate a Slide Show
3 Insert a Video

Mastering PowerPoint | Project 3E Spotlight Neighborhood

In the following Mastering PowerPoint project, you will format a presentation created by the Golden Grove Public Relations department that announces the winner of the Spotlight Neighborhood award. Your completed presentation will look similar to Figure 3.53.

Project Files

For Project 3E, you will need the following files:

p03E_Spotlight_Neighborhood
p03E_Neighborhood
p03E_Neighborhood_Video

You will save your presentation as:

Lastname_Firstname_3E_Spotlight_Neighborhood

Project Results

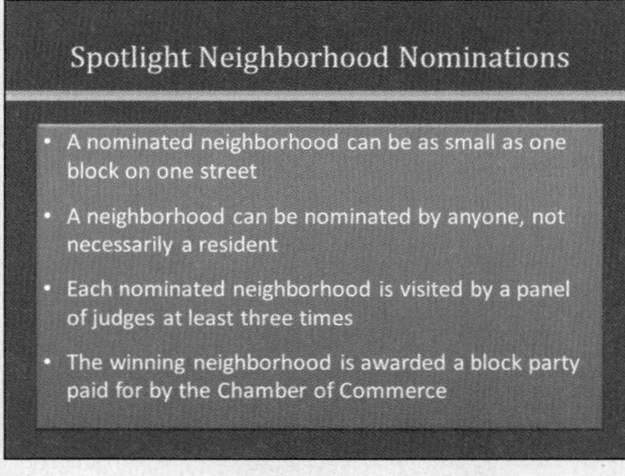

Figure 3.53

(Project 3E Spotlight Neighborhood continues on the next page)

Mastering PowerPoint | Project 3E Spotlight Neighborhood (continued)

1 **Start** PowerPoint. From the student files that accompany this textbook, locate and open **p03E_Spotlight_Neighborhood**. Change the **Theme Colors** for the presentation to **Office**, and the **Theme Fonts** to **Adjacency**. **Save** the presentation in your **PowerPoint Chapter 3** folder as **Lastname_Firstname_3E_Spotlight_Neighborhood**

2 On **Slide 1**, hide the background graphics, and then format the slide background by inserting a picture from your student files—**p03E_Neighborhood**. To the title, apply the first **WordArt** style—**Fill - Tan Text 2, Outline - Background 2**.

3 On **Slide 2**, display the **Background Styles** gallery, right-click **Background Style 12**, and then apply the style to this slide only. Select the paragraph on the left side of the slide, and then change the **Font Color** to **White, Text 1**. With the paragraph selected, apply the **Split** entrance effect, and then change the **Effect Options** to **Horizontal Out**. Change the **Start** setting to **After Previous**, and then change the **Duration** to **01.00**. Animate the **SmartArt** graphic by applying the **Fade** entrance effect and so that it starts **With Previous**.

4 On **Slide 3**, format the **Background Style** by applying a **Solid fill—Dark Blue, Text 2**. Change the **Font Color** of the title text to **White, Background 1**. Remove the entrance effect from the title.

5 On **Slide 4**, hide the background graphics, and then apply background **Style 12**. From your student files, insert the video **p03E_Neighborhood_Video**. Change the **Video Height** to **4** and **Align Center** the video. Format the video by applying, from the **Video Styles** gallery, an **Intense** style—**Monitor, Gray**. Change the **Start** setting to **Automatically**.

6 Display **Slide 2**, and then use **Animation Painter** to apply the animation from the paragraph on the left side of the slide to the bulleted list on **Slide 3**.

7 **Insert** a **Header & Footer** on the **Notes and Handouts**. Include the **Date and time updated automatically**, the **Page** number, and a **Footer** with the text **Lastname_Firstname_3E_Spotlight_Neighborhood**

8 Update the **Document Properties** with your name, course name and section number, and the **Keywords** **spotlight neighborhood** **Close** the **Document Information Panel**.

9 **Save** your presentation, and then view the slide show from the beginning. Submit your presentation electronically, or print **Handouts 4 Slides Horizontal** as directed by your instructor. **Close** the presentation.

End **You have completed Project 3E**

Content-Based Assessments

Apply 3B skills from these Objectives:

4 Create and Modify Tables

5 Create and Modify Charts

Mastering PowerPoint | Project 3F Water Conservation

In the following Mastering PowerPoint project, you will format a presentation that the Golden Grove Chief Water Engineer will present at a community forum. Your completed presentation will look similar to Figure 3.54.

Project Files

For Project 3F, you will need the following file:

p03F_Water_Conservation

You will save your presentation as:

Lastname_Firstname_3F_Water_Conservation

Project Results

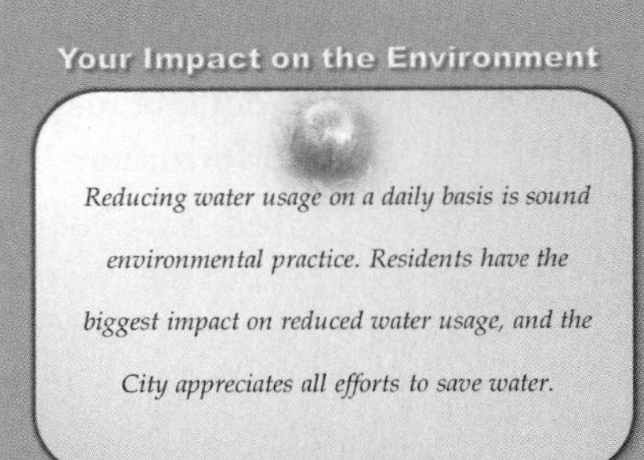

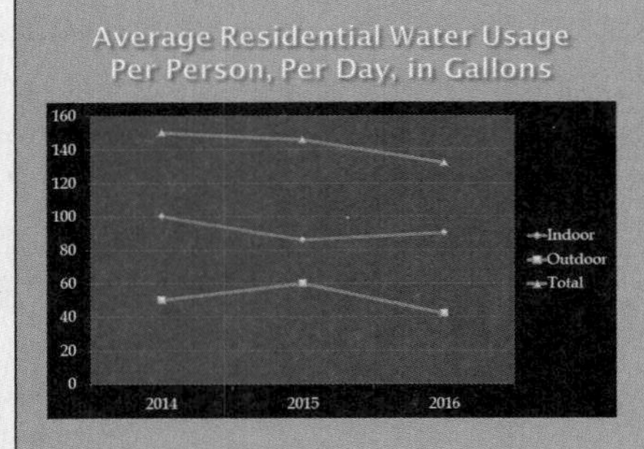

Every Drop Counts

- Reduce water consumption by watering outdoor plants and yards early in the day
- Water infrequently but deeply to reduce water use and encourage deep rooting
- Use a drip or micro-irrigation system
- Mulch around plants to maintain soil water

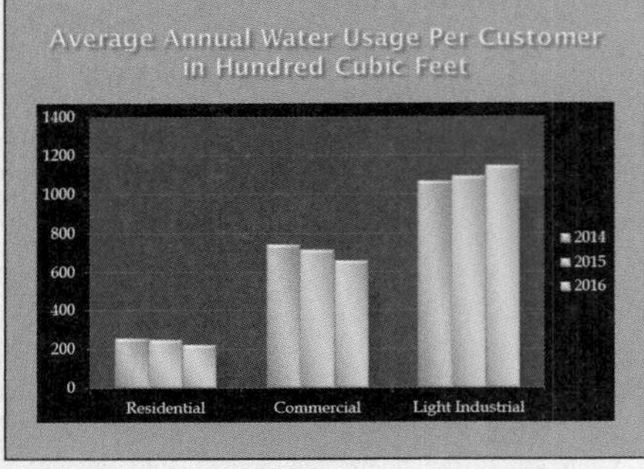

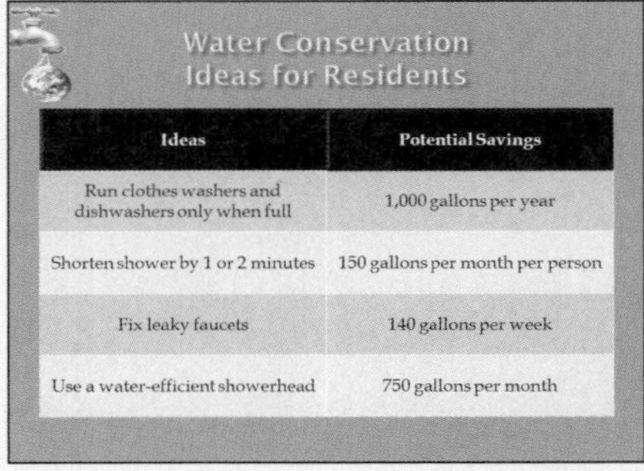

Ideas	Potential Savings
Run clothes washers and dishwashers only when full	1,000 gallons per year
Shorten shower by 1 or 2 minutes	150 gallons per month per person
Fix leaky faucets	140 gallons per week
Use a water-efficient showerhead	750 gallons per month

Figure 3.54

(Project 3F Water Conservation continues on the next page)

Mastering PowerPoint | Project 3F Water Conservation (continued)

1 **Start** PowerPoint. From your student files open **p03F_Water_Conservation**, and then **Save** the presentation in your **PowerPoint Chapter 3** folder as **Lastname_Firstname_3F_Water_Conservation**

2 On **Slide 3**, in the content placeholder, insert a **Line with Markers** chart. In the Excel worksheet, in cell **B1**, type **Indoor** and then enter the following data:

	Indoor	Outdoor	Total
2014	100	50	150
2015	86	60	146
2016	90	42	132

3 In the Excel window, delete **row 5**, and then **Close** the Excel window. Apply **Chart Style 42** to the chart, and then apply the **Wipe** entrance effect to the chart.

4 On **Slide 5**, in the content placeholder, insert a **Clustered Column** chart. In the Excel worksheet, in cell **B1**, type **2014** and then enter the following data:

	2014	2015	2016
Residential	256	249	225
Commercial	746	718	660
Light Industrial	1065	1092	1146

5 In the Excel window, delete **row 5**, and then **Close** the Excel window. Apply **Chart Style 42** to the chart, and then apply the **Wipe** entrance effect to the chart. Change the **Effect Options** so that the animation is applied **By Series**. Change the **Timing** so that the animation starts **After Previous**.

6 On **Slide 6**, in the content placeholder, insert a **Table** with **2 columns** and **5 rows**, and then type the text in **Table 1** at the bottom of the page.

7 Resize the table so that its lower edge extends to **3 inches on the lower half of the vertical ruler**, and then distribute the table rows. Align the table text so that it is centered horizontally and vertically within the cells. Apply table style **Medium Style 2**, and then apply a **Circle Bevel** to the first row. Change the table text **Font Size** to **20**.

8 Insert a **Header & Footer** for the **Notes and Handouts**. Include the **Date and time updated automatically**, the **Page number**, and a **Footer** with the file name **Lastname_Firstname_3F_Water_Conservation** Update the **Document Properties** with your name, course name and section number, and the **Keywords water conservation Close** the **Document Information Panel**.

9 View the slide show from the beginning, and then **Save** your presentation. Print **Handouts 4 Slides Horizontal**, or submit your presentation electronically as directed by your instructor. **Close** the presentation.

Table 1

Ideas	Potential Savings
Run clothes washers and dishwashers only when full	1,000 gallons per year
Shorten shower by 1 or 2 minutes	150 gallons per month per person
Fix leaky faucets	140 gallons per week
Use a water-efficient showerhead	750 gallons per month

(Return to Step 7)

End **You have completed Project 3F**

Content-Based Assessments

Apply **3A** and **3B** skills from these Objectives:

1. Customize Slide Backgrounds and Themes
2. Animate a Slide Show
3. Insert a Video
4. Create and Modify Tables
5. Create and Modify Charts

Mastering PowerPoint | Project 3G Restaurants

In the following Mastering PowerPoint project, you will format a presentation that the Golden Grove Public Relations Director will show at a meeting of the National Restaurant Owners Association to encourage new restaurant and catering business in the city. Your completed presentation will look similar to Figure 3.55.

Project Files

For Project 3G, you will need the following files:

p03G_Restaurants
p03G_Town_Center
p03G_Catering

You will save your presentation as:

Lastname_Firstname_3G_Restaurants

Project Results

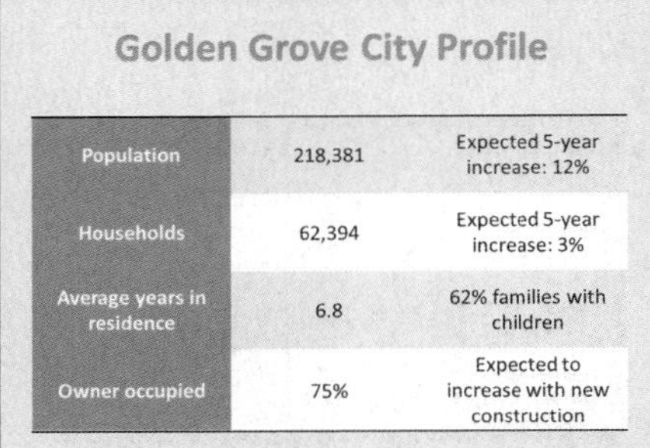

Population	218,381	Expected 5-year increase: 12%
Households	62,394	Expected 5-year increase: 3%
Average years in residence	6.8	62% families with children
Owner occupied	75%	Expected to increase with new construction

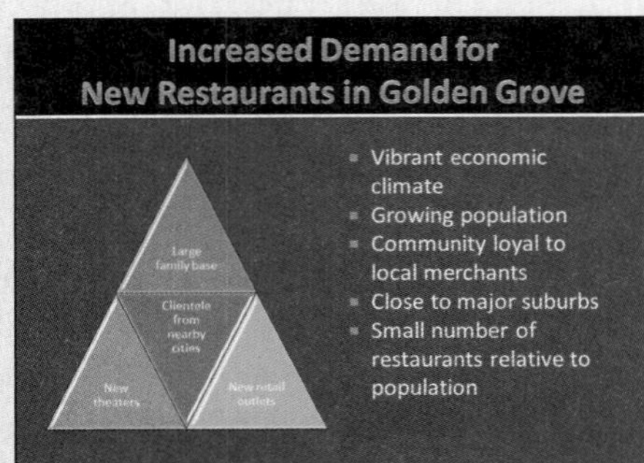

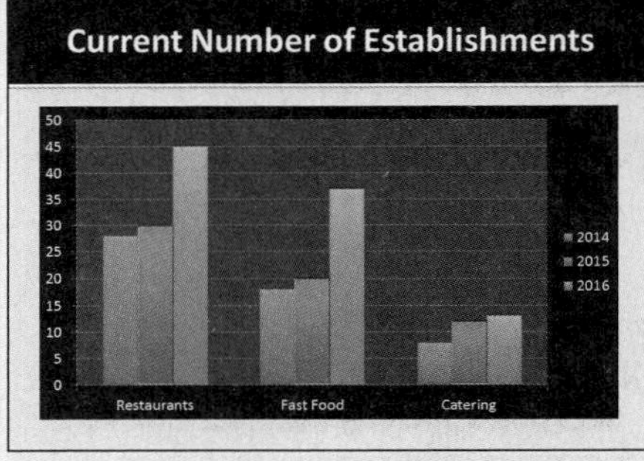

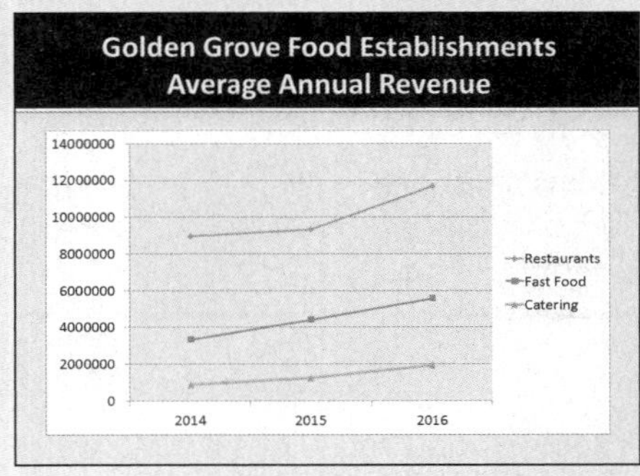

Figure 3.55

(Project 3G Restaurants continues on the next page)

Mastering PowerPoint | Project 3G Restaurants (continued)

1 **Start** PowerPoint. From the student files that accompany this textbook, locate and open **p03G_Restaurants**. Change the **Theme Colors** for the presentation to **Apothecary**, and the **Theme Fonts** to **Composite**. **Save** the presentation in your **PowerPoint Chapter 3** folder as **Lastname_Firstname_3G_Restaurants**

2 On **Slide 2**, insert a **Table** with **3 columns** and **4 rows**. Apply table style **Medium Style 3 - Accent 2**, and then type the information in **Table 1**, shown at the bottom of this page, into the inserted table.

3 On the **Design tab**, in the **Table Style Options group**, select *only* the **First Column** and **Banded Rows** check boxes. Resize the table so that its lower edge extends to **3 inches on the lower half of the vertical ruler**, and then distribute the table rows. Align the table text so that it is centered horizontally and vertically within the cells, and then change the **Font Size** of all of the table text to **24**.

4 On **Slide 3**, display the **Background Styles** gallery, right-click **Background Style 3**, and then apply the style to this slide only. Animate the **SmartArt** graphic using the **Wipe** entrance effect starting **After Previous**. Apply the **Split** entrance effect to the bulleted list placeholder, and then change the **Effect Options** to **Vertical Out**.

5 On **Slide 4**, insert a **Clustered Column** chart. In the Excel worksheet, in cell **B1** type **2014** and then enter the following data:

	2014	2015	2016
Restaurants	28	30	45
Fast Food	18	20	37
Catering	8	12	13

6 In the Excel window, delete **row 5**, and then **Close** the Excel window. Apply **Chart Style 42** to the chart, and then apply the **Wipe** entrance effect to the chart.

7 On **Slide 5**, from your student files, insert the video **p03G_Town_Center**. Change the **Video Height** to **3** and then drag the video down so that its top edge aligns at **zero on the vertical ruler**. Apply the **Align Center** alignment option, display the **Video Styles** gallery, and then apply the first **Moderate** style—**Compound Frame, Black**. Change the **Video Border** to **Gray-50%, Accent 1, Darker 50%**—in the fifth column, the last color.

8 On the **Playback tab**, change the **Video Options** to **Start** the video **Automatically**. **Trim** the video so that the **End Time** is **00:05.560**

9 On **Slide 6**, in the content placeholder, insert a **Line with Markers** chart. In the Excel worksheet, in cell **B1**, type **Restaurants** and then enter the following data:

	Restaurants	Fast Food	Catering
2014	8956231	3284680	856700
2015	9326852	4369571	1235640
2016	11689730	5526895	1894325

10 In the Excel window, delete **row 5**, and then **Close** the Excel window. Apply **Chart Style 34** to the chart, and then use **Animation Painter** to copy the animation from the column chart on **Slide 4** to the line chart on **Slide 6**.

11 On **Slide 7**, hide the background graphics. Format the slide background by inserting a picture from your student files—**p03G_Catering**. Change the title placeholder **Shape Fill** color to **Black, Text 1**, and then change the **Font Color** to **Red, Accent 2**. Size the placeholder so that it extends from the left edge of the slide to the right edge of the slide, and then position it so that its lower edge aligns with the lower edge of the slide. **Center** the text.

12 Insert a **Header & Footer** for the **Notes and Handouts**. Include the **Date and time updated automatically**, the **Page number**, and a **Footer** with the file name **Lastname_Firstname_3G_Restaurants** Update the **Properties** with your name, course name and section number, and the **Keywords catering, restaurants Close** the **Document Information Panel**.

13 View the slide show from the beginning, and then **Save** your presentation. Print **Handouts 4 Slides Horizontal**, or submit your presentation electronically as directed by your instructor. **Close** the presentation.

Table 1

Population	218,381	Expected 5-year increase: 12%
Households	62,394	Expected 5-year increase: 3%
Average years in residence	6.8	62% families with children
Owner occupied	75%	Expected to increase with new construction

---> (Return to Step 3)

You have completed Project 3G

Content-Based Assessments

Apply a combination of the 3A and 3B skills.

GO! Fix It | Project 3H Housing Developments

Project Files

For Project 3H, you will need the following file:

p03H_Housing_Developments

You will save your presentation as:

Lastname_Firstname_3H_Housing_Developments

In this project, you will edit several slides from a presentation prepared by the Golden Grove Planning Department regarding real estate developments in the city. From the student files that accompany this textbook, open the file p03H_Housing_Developments, and then save the file in your chapter folder as **Lastname_Firstname_3H_Housing_Developments**

To complete the project, you should know:

- The Theme Colors should be changed to Module and the Theme Fonts should be changed to Apex.
- The titles on Slides 2 and 3 should be centered.
- On Slide 2, the table style Light Style 2 - Accent 2 should be applied and a column should be added to right of the last column in the table. In the inserted column, the following text should be entered in the three cells: **Bering** and **37%** and **August 2016**
- On Slides 3 and 4, the charts should be animated with the Wipe entrance effect.
- Document Properties should include your name, course name and section, and the keywords **property tax, housing** A Header & Footer should be inserted on the Notes and Handouts that includes the Date and time updated automatically, the Page number and a Footer with the text **Lastname_Firstname_3H_Housing_Developments**

Save and submit your presentation electronically or print Handouts 4 Slides Horizontal as directed by your instructor. Close the presentation.

End You have completed Project 3H

Apply a combination of the 3A and 3B skills.

GO! Make It | Project 3I Arboretum

Project Files

For Project 3I, you will need the following files:

New blank PowerPoint presentation
p03I_Flowers

You will save your presentation as:

Lastname_Firstname_3I_Arboretum

Start PowerPoint to begin a new blank presentation, and apply the Opulent theme. Save the file in your PowerPoint Chapter 3 folder as **Lastname_Firstname_3I_Arboretum**

By using the skills you practiced in this chapter, create the first two slides of the presentation shown in Figure 3.56. The layout for Slide 1 is Title Only, and the background is formatted with the picture from your student data file— p03I_Flowers. The title Shape Fill color is Purple, Accent 2, Darker 50%. On Slide 2, insert and format the table as shown. Change the Font Size of the text in the first row to 32. Insert the file name, date, and page number in the Notes and Handouts footer. In the Document Information Panel, add your name and course information and the Keywords **arboretum, events** Save, and then print or submit electronically as directed by your instructor.

Project Results

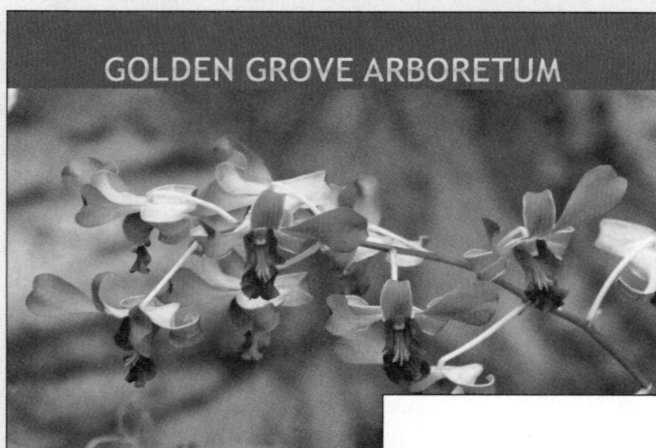

UPCOMING EVENTS

Event	Description	Dates
Festival of Flowers	A presentation of annual spring blooms	May 1-7
Landscaping 101	A four-day course on selecting appropriate flora for your yard	Every Saturday in June and July
Summer Nature Adventure	A botanical discovery camp for children ages 8 to 12	August 1 - 14

Figure 3.56

End **You have completed Project 3I**

Content-Based Assessments

Apply a combination of the 3A and 3B skills.

GO! Solve It | Project 3J Aquatic Center

Project Files

For Project 3J, you will need the following file:

p03J_Aquatic_Center

You will save your presentation as:

Lastname_Firstname_3J_Aquatic_Center

Open the file p03J_Aquatic_Center and save it as **Lastname_Firstname_3J_Aquatic_Center** Complete the presentation by changing the Theme Fonts and then formatting the slide background of at least one of the slides using a Background Style or Solid Fill color. On Slide 4, insert and format a table with the following information regarding the fee schedule for swim passes.

Membership	Monthly	Seasonal
Youth	$10	$25
Adult	$25	$50
Senior	$15	$30

Apply appropriate animation and slide transitions to the slides. Insert a header and footer that includes the date and time updated automatically, the file name in the footer, and the page number. Add your name, your course name and section number, and the keywords **aquatic center, swim program** to the Properties area. Save and then print, or submit it as directed by your instructor.

Performance Elements	Performance Level: Exemplary: You consistently applied the relevant skills	Proficient: You sometimes, but not always, applied the relevant skills	Developing: You rarely or never applied the relevant skills
Format slide with a background style	Slide background style was applied to at least one slide and text displayed with good contrast against the background.	Slide background was formatted but text did not display well against the chosen background.	Slide background was not formatted with a background style.
Insert and format appropriate table	Appropriate table was inserted and formatted.	A table was inserted but was not appropriately formatted.	Table was not inserted.
Apply appropriate animation	Appropriate animation was applied to the presentation.	Animation was applied but was not appropriate for the presentation.	Animation was not applied.

End **You have completed Project 3J**

Apply a combination of the 3A and 3B skills.

GO! Solve It | Project 3K Power

Project Files

For Project 3K, you will need the following files:

p03K_Power
p03K_Tower

You will save your presentation as:

Lastname_Firstname_3K_Power

Open the file p03K_Power and save it as **Lastname_Firstname_3K_Power** Complete the presentation by applying a theme and then formatting the slide background of one of the slides with the picture found in your student files—p03K_Tower. Adjust the size, position, fill color, and font color of the slide titles as necessary so that the title text displays attractively against the background picture. Format the background of at least one other slide using a Background Style or Solid Fill color. Insert a new Slide 3 that includes an appropriate title and a table with the following information regarding the power sources that the City uses.

Power Sources	Percent Used by City
Natural gas	32%
Hydroelectric	17%
Renewables	18%
Coal	23%
Nuclear	10%

On Slide 4, insert and format an appropriate chart to demonstrate the revenue collected from residential power sales over the past three years. Revenue in 2014 was 35.5 million dollars, in 2015 revenue was 42.6 million dollars, and in 2016 revenue was 48.2 million dollars. Apply appropriate animation and slide transitions to the slides. Insert a header and footer that includes the date and time updated automatically, the file name in the footer, and the page number. Add your name, your course name and section number, and the keywords **power sources, revenue** to the Properties area. Save and then print or submit the presentation as directed by your instructor.

Performance Elements	Performance Level: Exemplary: You consistently applied the relevant skills	Proficient: You sometimes, but not always, applied the relevant skills	Developing: You rarely or never applied the relevant skills
Format two slide backgrounds with pictures and styles	Two slide backgrounds were formatted attractively and text displayed with good contrast against backgrounds.	Slide backgrounds were formatted but text did not display well against the chosen background, or only one slide background was formatted.	Slide backgrounds were not formatted with pictures or styles.
Insert and format appropriate table and chart	Appropriate table and chart were inserted and formatted and the entered data was accurate.	A table and a chart were inserted but were not appropriate for the presentation or either a table or a chart was omitted.	Table and chart were not inserted.
Apply appropriate animation	Appropriate animation was applied to the presentation.	Animation was applied but was not appropriate for the presentation.	Animation was not applied.

End **You have completed Project 3K**

Outcomes-Based Assessments

Rubric

The following outcomes-based assessments are *open-ended assessments*. That is, there is no specific correct result; your result will depend on your approach to the information provided. Make *Professional Quality* your goal. Use the following scoring rubric to guide you in *how* to approach the problem, and then to evaluate *how well* your approach solves the problem.

The *criteria*—Software Mastery, Content, Format and Layout, and Process—represent the knowledge and skills you have gained that you can apply to solving the problem. The *levels of performance*—Professional Quality, Approaching Professional Quality, or Needs Quality Improvements—help you and your instructor evaluate your result.

	Your completed project is of Professional Quality if you:	**Your completed project is Approaching Professional Quality if you:**	**Your completed project Needs Quality Improvements if you:**
1-Software Mastery	Choose and apply the most appropriate skills, tools, and features and identify efficient methods to solve the problem.	Choose and apply some appropriate skills, tools, and features, but not in the most efficient manner.	Choose inappropriate skills, tools, or features, or are inefficient in solving the problem.
2-Content	Construct a solution that is clear and well organized, contains content that is accurate, appropriate to the audience and purpose, and is complete. Provide a solution that contains no errors in spelling, grammar, or style.	Construct a solution in which some components are unclear, poorly organized, inconsistent, or incomplete. Misjudge the needs of the audience. Have some errors in spelling, grammar, or style, but the errors do not detract from comprehension.	Construct a solution that is unclear, incomplete, or poorly organized; contains some inaccurate or inappropriate content; and contains many errors in spelling, grammar, or style. Do not solve the problem.
3-Format and Layout	Format and arrange all elements to communicate information and ideas, clarify function, illustrate relationships, and indicate relative importance.	Apply appropriate format and layout features to some elements, but not others. Overuse features, causing minor distraction.	Apply format and layout that does not communicate information or ideas clearly. Do not use format and layout features to clarify function, illustrate relationships, or indicate relative importance. Use available features excessively, causing distraction.
4-Process	Use an organized approach that integrates planning, development, self-assessment, revision, and reflection.	Demonstrate an organized approach in some areas, but not others; or, use an insufficient process of organization throughout.	Do not use an organized approach to solve the problem.

Apply a combination of the 3A and 3B skills.

GO! Think | Project 3L Animal Sanctuary

Project Files

For Project 3L, you will need the following file:

New blank PowerPoint presentation

You will save your presentation as:

Lastname_Firstname_3L_Animal Sanctuary

The Golden Grove Animal Sanctuary, a non-profit organization, provides shelter and care for animals in need, including dogs, cats, hamsters, and guinea pigs. The Sanctuary, which celebrates its tenth anniversary in July, has cared for more than 12,000 animals since it opened and is a state-of-the-art facility. Funding for the Sanctuary comes in the form of business sponsorships, individual donations, and pet adoption fees. The following table indicates revenue generated by the Sanctuary during the past three years.

	Fees	Donations	Sponsorships
2014	125,085	215,380	175,684
2015	110,680	256,785	156,842
2016	132,455	314,682	212,648

In addition to shelter services, the Sanctuary offers community service and training programs, veterinarian services, and vaccine clinics. Examples of these services include Canine Obedience classes, microchipping ($25 fee), and the Healthy Pet Hotline (free). Canine Obedience classes are for puppies and adult dogs to improve obedience, socialization, and behavior. Classes last two, three, or four months and cost $150 to $250.

Using the preceding information, create the first five slides of a presentation that the director of the Golden Grove Animal Sanctuary will show at an upcoming pet fair. Apply an appropriate theme and use slide layouts that will effectively present the content. Include a line chart with the revenue data, a table with the community service programs information, and at least one slide formatted with a dog or cat on the slide background. Apply styles to the table and chart, and apply animation and slide transitions to the slides. Use the techniques that you practiced in this chapter so that your presentation is professional and attractive. Save the file as **Lastname_Firstname_3L_Animal_Sanctuary** and then insert a header and footer that includes the date and time updated automatically, the file name in the footer, and the page number. Add your name, your course name and section number, and the keywords **animals, pets** to the Properties area. Save and then print or submit the presentation as directed by your instructor.

End **You have completed Project 3L**

Outcomes-Based Assessments

Apply a combination of the 3A and 3B skills.

GO! Think | Project 3M Water Sources

Project Files

For Project 3M, you will need the following file:

New blank PowerPoint presentation

You will save your presentation as:

Lastname_Firstname_3M_Water_Sources

The Golden Grove Department of Water and Power operations are financed solely through sales of water and electric services. A portion of capital expenditures are funded through the sale of municipal bonds. The city's water supply is generated from a number of sources, with 35% from the Sierra Nevada aqueduct system, 42% from water districts, 18% from groundwater, and 5% from recycled sources. This supply provides water for the City's residents and commercial and industrial customers.

In the past three years, the Department has renovated several reservoirs and pump stations, resulting in better reserves and emergency preparedness capacity. The following table details the in-city reservoir capacities over the past three years. Water capacity is measured in acre feet, in which one acre foot is equal to approximately 325,000 gallons. Years in which zero or low capacity is specified indicates years in which the reservoir was undergoing renovation.

	2014	2015	2016
Elkhart Reservoir	350	1250	2243
Gold Lake Reservoir	3685	865	2865
Diamond Canyon Reservoir	2650	3850	4635

Using the preceding information, create a title slide and four additional slides of a presentation that the Golden Grove Chief Water Engineer can show at an upcoming City Council meeting. Apply an appropriate theme and use slide layouts that will effectively present the content. Include a table that details the water supply sources, and a column chart with the reservoir information. Apply animation and slide transitions and use the techniques that you practiced in this chapter so that your presentation is professional and attractive. Save the file as **Lastname_Firstname_3M_Water_Sources** and then insert a header and footer that includes the date and time updated automatically, the file name in the footer, and the page number. Add your name, your course name and section number, and the keywords **reservoirs, water capacity** to the Properties area. Save, and then print or submit the presentation as directed by your instructor.

End You have completed Project 3M

Outcomes-Based Assessments

Apply a combination of the **3A** and **3B** skills.

You and GO! | Project 3N Recreation Programs

Project Files

For Project 3N, you will need the following file:

New blank PowerPoint presentation

You will save your presentation as:

Lastname_Firstname_3N_Recreation_Programs

Research the recreation programs available in the city in which you live, and then create a presentation about the program. Include a table that describes some of the activities, the location in which they are held, and the fees. Choose an appropriate theme, slide layouts, and pictures, and format the presentation attractively, including at least one slide with a picture on the slide background. Save your presentation as **Lastname_Firstname_3N_Recreation_Programs** and submit as directed.

End **You have completed Project 3N**

Business Running Case

Razvan CHIRNOAGA/Shutterstock

This project relates to **Front Range Action Sports**, which is one of the country's largest retailers of sports gear and outdoor recreation merchandise. The company has large retail stores in Colorado, Washington, Oregon, California, and New Mexico, in addition to a growing online business. Major merchandise categories include fishing, camping, rock climbing, winter sports, action sports, water sports, team sports, racquet sports, fitness, golf, apparel, and footwear.

In this project, you will apply skills you practiced from the Objectives in PowerPoint Chapters 1 through 3. You will develop a presentation that Irene Shviktar, Vice President of Marketing, will show at a corporate marketing retreat that summarizes the company's plans to expand the winter sports product line. Your completed presentation will look similar to Figure 1.1.

Project Files

For Project BRC1, you will need the following files:

pBRC1_Company_Overview
pBRC1_Heights
pBRC1_Lake
pBRC1_Mountain
pBRC1_Skiing
pBRC1_Winter_Products

You will save your presentation as:
Lastname_Firstname_BRC1_Winter_Products

Project Results

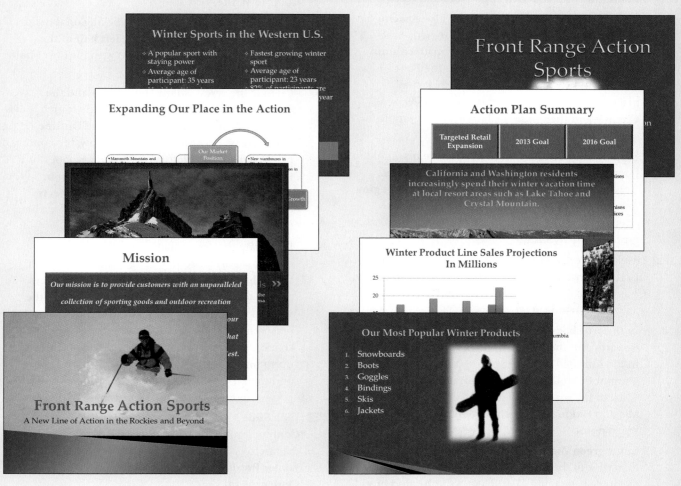

Figure 1.1

Business Running Case

Front Range Action Sports (continued)

1 **Start** PowerPoint. From the student files that accompany this textbook, locate and open **pBRC1_Winter_Products**. In the location where you are storing your projects, create a new folder named **Front Range Action Sports** or navigate to this folder if you have already created it. **Save** the presentation as **Lastname_Firstname_BRC1_ Winter_Products**

a. Display **Slide 1**. Change the presentation theme to **Concourse**, and then change the **Theme Colors** to **Office**. Change the **Theme Fonts** to **Elemental**. On **Slide 1**, format the background with a picture from your student files—**pBRC1_Skiing**.

b. Display the **Reuse Slides** pane. Browse your student files, and display in the **Reuse Slides** pane **pBRC1_ Company_Overview**. Insert the second slide—**Mission**—as **Slide 2**, and then **Close** the **Reuse Slides** pane. Remove the bullet symbol from the paragraph, **Center** the text, and then apply **Bold** and **Italic**.

c. With **Slide 2** displayed, change the **Line Spacing** of the content placeholder text to **2.0**. Change the **Shape Fill** to the first color in the fourth column—**Dark Blue, Text 2**, and then change the **Font Color** to **White, Background 1**. Format the placeholder with the first **Bevel** shape effect—**Circle**—and then hide the background graphics on the slide.

d. Display **Slide 3**, and then in the picture placeholder, from your student files insert **pBRC1_Heights**. Apply the first **Glow** picture effect—**Blue, 5 pt glow, Accent color 1**. Format the slide background by applying **Style 12**, being sure to apply the background only to **Slide 3**.

2 Display **Slide 4**, and then in the content placeholder, insert the **Process** SmartArt graphic **Alternating Flow**. Change the color to **Colorful - Accent Colors**, and then apply **3-D Cartoon** style.

a. In the **red shape**, type **Washington and California Resorts** and then click in the first bullet point in the rounded rectangle above the red shape. Type **Mammoth Mountain and Lake Tahoe in California** Click in the second bullet point, and then type **Mission Ridge and Crystal Mountain in Washington**

b. In the **green shape**, type **Our Market Position** and then click in the first bullet point in the rounded rectangle below the green shape. Type **Trusted brand name in the sporting world** In the second bullet point, type **Winter sports product line not fully marketed in the Western United States**

c. In the **purple shape**, type **Poised for Growth** and then click in the first bullet point in the rounded rectangle above the purple shape. Type **New warehouses in Washington** In the second bullet point, type **Proposed retail division in Northern California**

d. Animate the SmartArt by applying the **Wipe** entrance effect. Change the **Start** option so that the SmartArt animation begins **After Previous**.

3 Display **Slide 5**, and then apply background **Style 3** to the slide. In both content placeholders, change the bullet symbol to **Star Bullets**, and then change the bullet **Color** to **Olive Green, Accent 3**. In the **blue shapes** at the bottom of the slide, change the **Font Color** to **White, Text 1**.

a. Insert a **Down Arrow** shape by clicking on the slide with the guides aligned with the **left half of the horizontal ruler at 3 inches** and with the **lower half of the vertical ruler at 1 inch**.

b. Change the arrow **Shape Height** to **1** and the **Shape Width** to **0.5** and then apply the fourth **Shape Style** in the first row—**Colored Outline - Olive Green, Accent 3**. Select the arrow, the content placeholder on the left, and the *Skiing* shape, and then on the **Format tab**, in the **Arrange group**, click the **Align** button. Click **Align Selected Objects**. Click the **Align** button again, and then click **Align Center**.

c. Duplicate the arrow shape, and then drag the duplicated arrow so that its left edge aligns with the **right half of the horizontal ruler at 2 inches** and its top edge aligns with the **lower half of the vertical ruler at 1 inch**. Select the arrow, the content placeholder on the right, and the *Snowboarding* shape, and then using the **Align Selected Objects** option apply **Align Center**. Select the two arrows, and then using the **Align Selected Objects** option, apply **Align Top** to the two arrow shapes.

4 With **Slide 5** displayed, insert a **New Slide** with the **Two Content** layout and then apply background **Style 3** to the inserted slide. Type the slide title **Our Most Popular Winter Products** Change the **Font Size** to **32** and then **Center** the title.

(Business Running Case: Front Range Action Sports continues on the next page)

Front Range Action Sports (continued)

a. In the content placeholder on the left, type the following six bullet points:

Snowboards
Boots
Goggles
Bindings
Skis
Jackets

b. Change the bulleted list to **Numbering**, and then change the number **Color** to **White, Text 1**.

c. In the placeholder on the right, insert a **Clip Art** by searching for a **Photograph** with the keyword **snowboard** Insert the black and white silhouette picture of the person holding a snowboard behind his back. If you cannot locate the picture, choose another image, and then **Close** the Clip Art pane.

d. Change the **Height** of the picture to **5** and then move the picture so that its upper left corner aligns with **zero on the horizontal ruler** and with the **upper half of the vertical ruler at 2.5 inches**. Apply a **Soft Edges** picture effect of **25 Point**.

e. Display **Slide 7**, and then in the content placeholder, insert a **Clustered Column** chart. In the **Excel** worksheet, enter the following data.

	Oregon	Colorado	British Columbia
2012	12.2	17.5	6.5
2013	14.5	19.2	8.7
2014	11.9	18.6	10.6
2015	17.6	22.4	11.3

f. **Close** the Excel worksheet. Apply **Chart Style 26**, and then animate the chart by applying the **Wipe** entrance effect.

5 Display **Slide 8**, and then hide the background graphics on the slide. Format the background with a picture from your student files—**pBRC1_Lake**.

a. Select the title placeholder, and then using the **Align to Slide** option, align the title using the **Align Top** and **Align Center** options.

b. Display **Slide 9**, and then in the content placeholder, insert a **Table** with **3** columns and **3** rows. Type the following text in the table.

Targeted Retail Expansion	2013 Goal	2016 Goal
Northern California	Three new franchises with rental services	Four new franchises
Central and Eastern Washington	Four new franchises with rental services and lessons	Eight new franchises with rental services

c. Apply the **Light Style 2 - Accent 1** table style, and then resize the table so that its lower left corner touches the graphic in the lower left corner of the slide. Distribute the table rows.

d. To the first row, apply the first **Cell Bevel** effect—**Circle**, and then change the **Font Size** to **24**. Center all of the text in the table horizontally and vertically, and then apply the **Wipe** entrance effect to the table.

6 Display **Slide 10**. Apply background **Style 3** to the slide, and then hide the background graphics. To the title, apply the fourth **WordArt** style in the first row **Fill - White, Outline -Accent 1**.

a. With **Slide 10** displayed, from your student files, insert the picture **pBRC1_Mountain**. Change the picture **Height** to **2.5** and then apply a **Soft Edges** picture effect of **25 Point**. Use the **Crop to Shape** option to change the picture shape to the tenth **Basic Shape** in the third row—**Cloud**. **Align Center** and **Align Middle** the picture using the **Align to Slide** option.

b. On **Slide 10**, insert a **WordArt** using the fourth **WordArt** style in the first row **Fill - White, Outline - Accent 1**. Type **Moving to the Top of the Winter Sports Action** and then change the **Font Size** to **28**. Drag the WordArt down so that its top edge aligns with the **lower half of the vertical ruler at 1 inch**. Select the title placeholder, picture, and WordArt, and then using the **Align to Slide** option, apply **Align Center**.

c. To all of the slides in the presentation, apply the **Box** transition, and then change the **Effect Options** to **From Top**. Display **Slide 6**, and then apply the **Split** entrance effect to the numbered list.

d. Display **Slide 3**. In the **Notes pane**, type **The key elements necessary to achieve our 2016 goals are the expansion of the winter sports product line, an aggressive marketing campaign, and new retail locations in California and Washington.**

(Business Running Case: Front Range Action Sports continues on the next page)

Front Range Action Sports (continued)

e. Insert a **Header & Footer** for the **Notes and Handouts**. Include the **Date and time** updated automatically, the **Page number**, and a **Footer** with the file name **Lastname_Firstname_BRC1_Winter_Products**

f. Display the **Document Properties**. Add your name, your course name and section, and the keywords **winter products, goals Close** the **Document Information Panel**.

g. View the slide show from the beginning, and then **Save** your presentation. Print **Handouts 6 Slides Horizontal**, or submit your presentation electronically as directed by your instructor. **Close** the presentation.

End **You have completed Business Running Case 1**

Creating Templates and Reviewing, Publishing, and Protecting Presentations

OUTCOMES At the end of this chapter you will be able to:	**OBJECTIVES** Mastering these objectives will enable you to:
PROJECT 4A Create and apply a custom template.	1. Create a Custom Template by Modifying Slide Masters (p. 233) 2. Apply a Custom Template to a Presentation (p. 247)
PROJECT 4B Review, publish, and protect presentations.	3. Create and Edit Comments (p. 256) 4. Prepare a Presentation for Distribution (p. 261) 5. Protect a Presentation (p. 268)

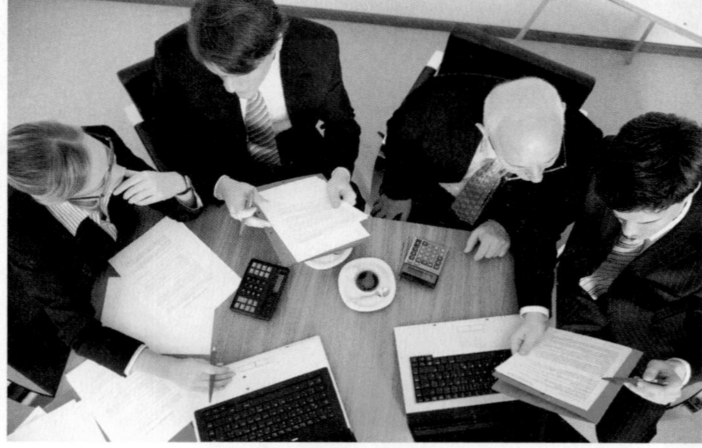

Kzenon\Shutterstock

In This Chapter

Microsoft Office PowerPoint provides built-in templates that contain layouts and formatting to use when creating a new presentation. You can create your own customized templates and reuse them. Tastefully designed templates ensure that presentations using the template maintain a consistent look.

PowerPoint also enables you to review and comment on the content of a presentation by inserting and editing comments in the file. It also provides a variety of ways to share presentations with others: converting to PDF or XPS format or printing handouts. PowerPoint also enables you to check a presentation for compatibility with other versions of PowerPoint and protect the presentation from further editing by marking it as Final.

Attorneys at **DeLong Grant Law Partners** counsel their clients on a wide variety of issues including contracts, licensing, intellectual property, and taxation, with emphasis on the unique needs of the entertainment and sports industries. Entertainment clients include production companies, publishers, talent agencies, actors, writers, artists—anyone involved in creating or doing business in the entertainment industry. Sports clients include colleges and universities, professional sports teams, athletes, and venue operators. Increasingly, amateur and community sports coaches and organizations with concerns about liability are also seeking the firm's specialized counsel.

Project 4A Instructional Presentation

Project Activities

In Activities 4.01 through 4.09, you will design a template for the DeLong Grant Law Partners to use to create presentations for meetings with the partners and clients. The template will contain formatting for the slide masters and shapes and images to add interest. Then you will use the template to create a presentation. You will also edit slide masters in an existing presentation in order to maintain uniformity in the slide designs. Your completed presentation will look similar to Figure 4.1.

Project Files

For Project 4A, you will need the following files:

New blank PowerPoint presentation
p04A_Law1.jpg

You will save your presentation as:

Lastname_Firstname_4A_Meeting_Template.potx
Lastname_Firstname_4A_Filing_Procedures.pptx

Project Results

Referencing Number System

- Include these three parts in the number:
  - Client last name
  - Date file opened
  - Date file completed (if applicable)
- Example: DeLong_01-15-2014_10-14-2016

Hardcopy filing

- Include the reference number on all pages of the legal document.
  - Place the number in the upper right corner.
  - Add the date completed when the case is closed.
- Retain a copy of the document for your personal file.

Digital Filing

- Use the reference number for the file name.
- Save a copy of the file to the company database.
  - Require authorized employees to use a Login to view the file.
  - Lock the file after any changes are made.

Summary

All changes are effective immediately. Direct questions to the support team.

Figure 4.1
Project 4A Filing Procedures

Objective 1 | Create a Custom Template by Modifying Slide Masters

A PowerPoint ***template*** is a predefined layout for a group of slides and is saved as a .potx file. You use a template to standardize the design of the slides in a presentation. A ***slide master*** is part of a template that stores information about the formatting and text that displays on every slide in a presentation. The stored information includes such items as the placement and size of text and object placeholders.

For example, if your company or organization has a logo that should be displayed on all slides of a presentation, the logo can be inserted one time on the slide master. That logo will then display in the same location on all slides of the presentation.

There are several approaches to creating a template. You can create a template from a new blank presentation, modify an existing template, or modify master slides in an existing presentation.

Activity 4.01 | Displaying and Editing Slide Masters

In this activity, you will change the Office Theme Slide Master background and the Title Slide Layout font and font size. You will start with a blank PowerPoint file.

1 **Start** PowerPoint to display a new blank presentation. On the Ribbon, click the **View tab**. In the **Master Views group**, point to, but do not click, the **Slide Master** button. Read the ScreenTip: *Slide Master View Open Slide Master view to change the design and layout of the master slides*. Compare your screen with Figure 4.2.

In the Master Views group, notice the three views available—Slide Master, Handout Master, and Notes Master.

Figure 4.2

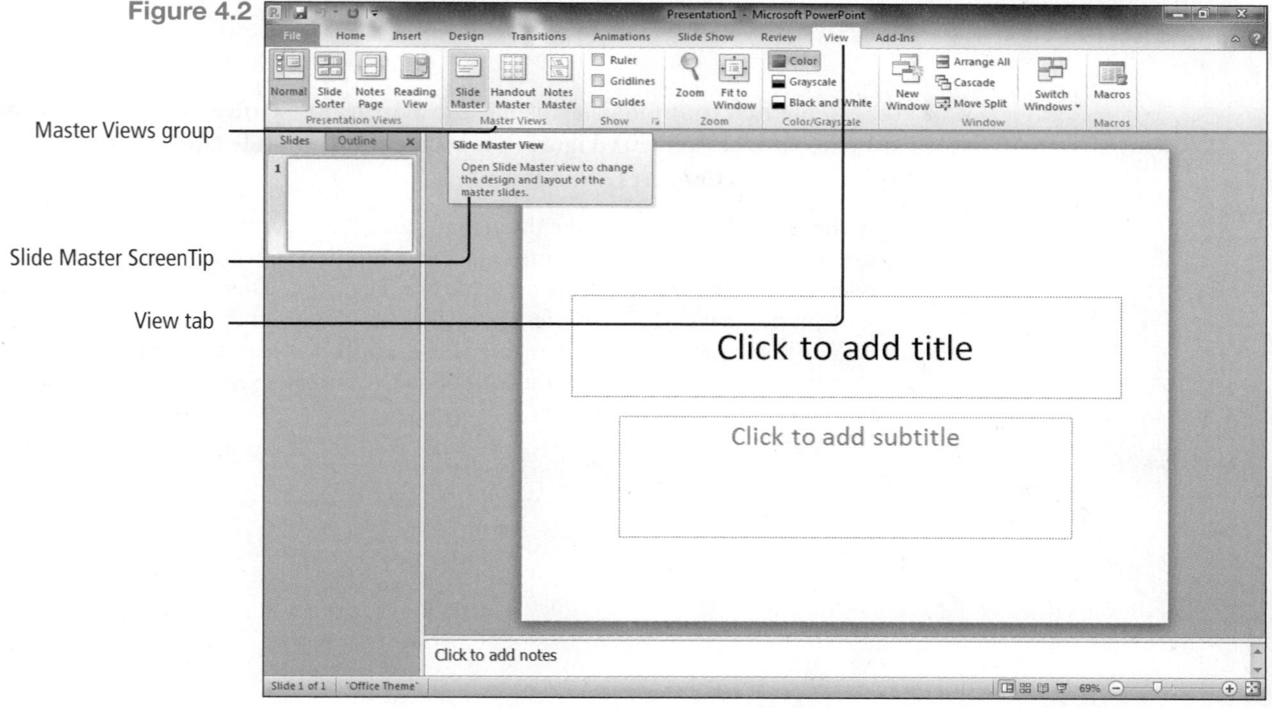

2 Click the **Slide Master** button. Take a moment to study the options associated with the Slide Master tab, as described in the table shown in Figure 4.3.

You are already familiar with editing themes, fonts, and colors by using the Edit Theme group, customizing a background by using the Background group, and modifying page setup and orientation by using the Page Setup group. From the Slide Master tab, you can apply these changes to certain layouts or to the entire theme.

Options on the Slide Master Tab

Screen Element	Description
Edit Master group	Enables you to:
Insert Slide Master	Add a new Slide Master to the presentation.
Insert Layout	Add a custom layout.
Delete	Delete a layout not in use by the presentation.
Rename	Rename a custom layout. This layout will become part of the layout gallery and will be visible when adding new slides to the presentation.
Preserve	Preserve the master slide so that it remains with the presentation, even if it is not used.
Master Layout group	Enables you to:
Master Layout	Choose which elements you want to include on the master layout.
Insert Placeholder	Add placeholders for content, text, pictures, charts, tables, SmartArt, media, and clip art.
Title	Show or hide the title placeholder.
Footers	Show or hide the placeholders for footers.

Figure 4.3

3 Point to the first thumbnail to display the ScreenTip—**Office Theme Slide Master**. Compare your screen with Figure 4.4. Locate the **Title Slide Layout**, **Title and Content Layout**, and **Two Content Layout** thumbnails.

In the Slide Master view, in the thumbnail pane, the larger slide image represents the slide master, and the associated layouts are smaller, positioned beneath it. The slide master is referred to as the ***Office Theme Slide Master***. The Office Theme Slide Master is a specific slide master that contains the design, such as the background, that displays on all slide layouts in the presentation. Changes made to it affect all slides in the presentation. Other common slide layouts include the Title Slide Layout, the Title and Content Layout, and the Two Content Layout.

Figure 4.4

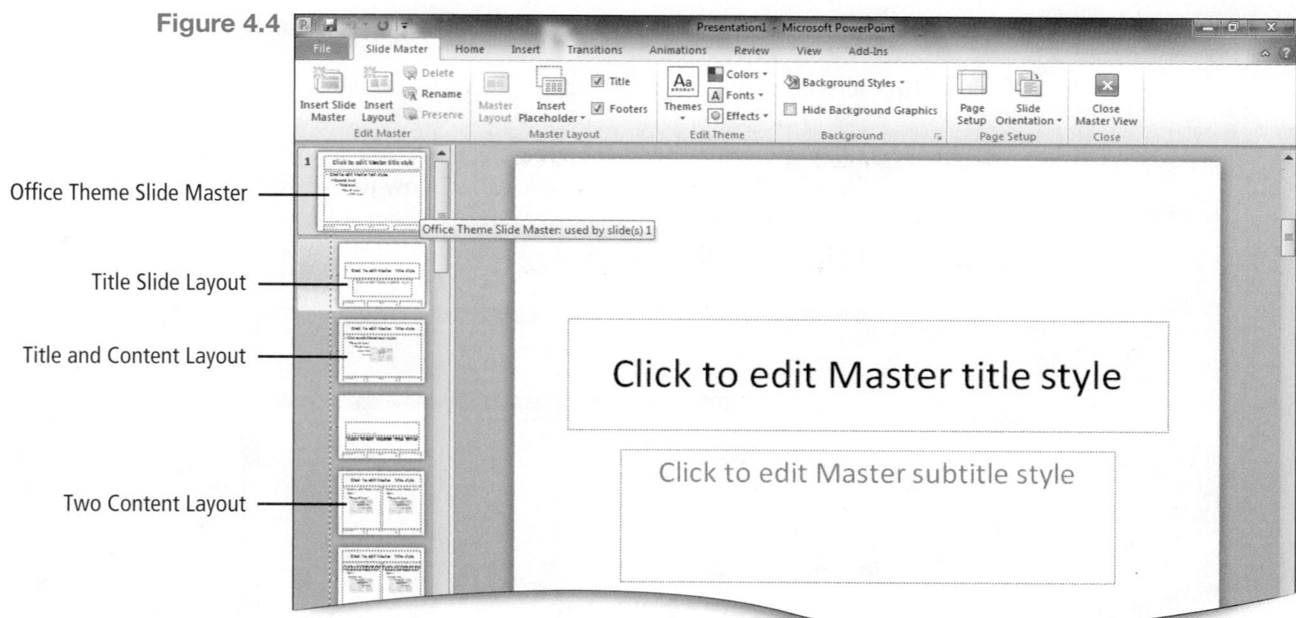

4 Click the first thumbnail—**Office Theme Slide Master**. In the **Background group**, click the **Background Styles** button. In the **Background Styles gallery**, scroll until you locate **Style 10**, and then click it.

Notice that all slide layouts display with the same background style.

> **Another Way**
>
> You can also triple-click the text in the Master title style placeholder to select the text.

5 Click the second thumbnail—**Title Slide Layout**. On the slide, click anywhere on the dashed border on the Master title style placeholder to display the border as a solid line. Click the **Home tab**. In the **Font group**, change the font to **Lucida Sans Unicode**. Change the font size to **40**. Compare your screen with Figure 4.5.

The font and font size change affects only the Title Slide.

Figure 4.5

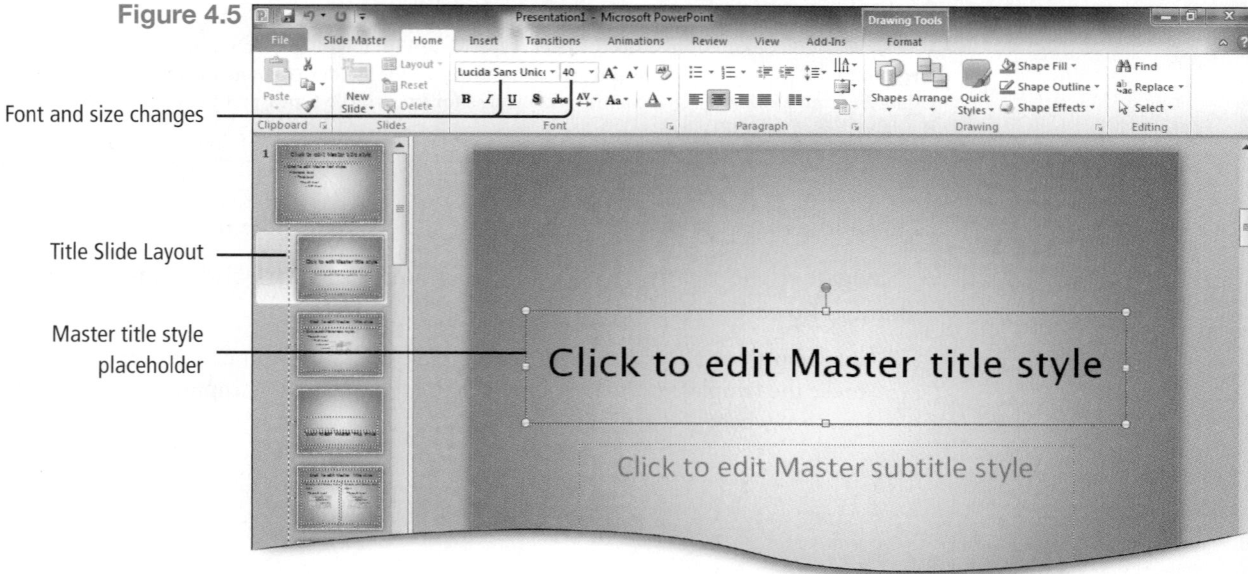

Activity 4.02 | Saving a Presentation as a Template

In this activity, you will save your design as a template.

1 Display **Backstage** view, and then click **Save As** to display the **Save As** dialog box. At the right side of the **Save as type** box, click the arrow to display the file types. Point to, but do not click, **PowerPoint Template (*.potx)**. Compare your screen with Figure 4.6. Your display may differ slightly.

Figure 4.6

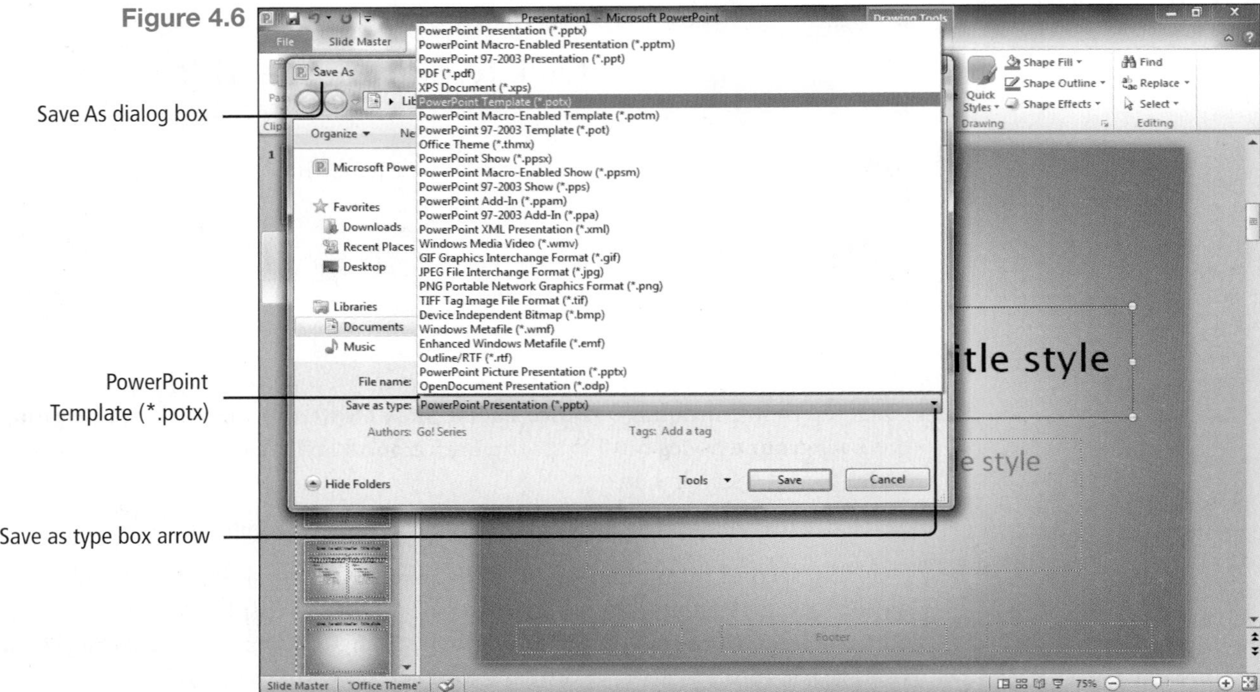

> **Note | Displaying File Extensions in Windows Explorer**
>
> If the extension does not display after the file type, go to Windows Explorer. On the Windows menu bar, click **Organize**, and then click **Folder and search options**. In the **Folder Options** dialog box, click the **View tab**. Under **Files and Folders**, scroll to **Hide extensions for known file types**, and then remove the check mark in the check box. Click **OK**.

2 From the displayed list of file types, click **PowerPoint Template (*.potx)**.

3 Navigate to the location where you are saving your work and create a new folder named **PowerPoint Chapter 4**

By default, templates are saved in a template folder on your computer's hard drive. To make the template portable so you can use it on another computer, change the drive to the location where you are saving your files.

4 Type the file name **Lastname_Firstname_4A_Meeting_Template** and then click **Save**. On the **Title bar**, look for ***.potx***, which is the file extension for templates.

The file extension .potx is automatically added to your file name. When working with templates, it is best to have the extensions displaying so you can tell the difference between a template and a presentation file.

> **More Knowledge | Modifying a Template**
>
> To make changes to a PowerPoint template, start PowerPoint, display Backstage view, click Open, navigate to the folder where the template is saved, click the file name, and then click Open.
>
> You can also open it from Windows Explorer. Navigate to the file, display Backstage view, and then click Open. Do not double-click on the file name because that action will display a copy of the template, not the template itself.

Activity 4.03 | Formatting a Slide Master with a Gradient Fill

In this activity, you will add a gradient fill to the slide master background. A ***gradient fill*** is a gradual progression of several colors blending into each other or shades of the same color blending into each other. A ***gradient stop*** allows you to apply different color combinations to selected areas of the background.

1 To the left of the Slide pane, click the **Office Theme Slide Master** thumbnail—the first thumbnail.

2 Click the **Slide Master tab**. In the **Background group**, click the **Background Styles** button to display the **Background Styles gallery**, and then click **Format Background**. In the **Format Background** dialog box, click **Fill**, if necessary. At the right, under **Fill**, click **Gradient fill**, if necessary. Click the **Type arrow** to display the list, and then click **Linear**.

> **Another Way**
>
> Instead of clicking the Add gradient stop button, you can click anywhere on the slider to add a gradient stop.

3 Under **Gradient stops**, at the right side, click the **Add gradient stop** button once. On the slider, drag the **gradient stop** to the left and then to the right and observe how the background changes on the slide and the percentage of gradation change in the Position box. Position the stop at **60%**.

> **Another Way**
>
> You can position the gradient stop by typing the value or using the spin arrows in the Position spin box.

4 Click the **Add gradient stop** button again to add another gradient stop, and then position it at **25%**. Click the **Color button arrow**, and then, click **Dark Blue, Text 2, Lighter 60%**, which is in the third row, fourth column. Compare your screen with Figure 4.7.

Applying a gradient stop to the background makes the color vary smoothly from a darker to a lighter shade. The additional stop with a different color provides more interest.

Figure 4.7

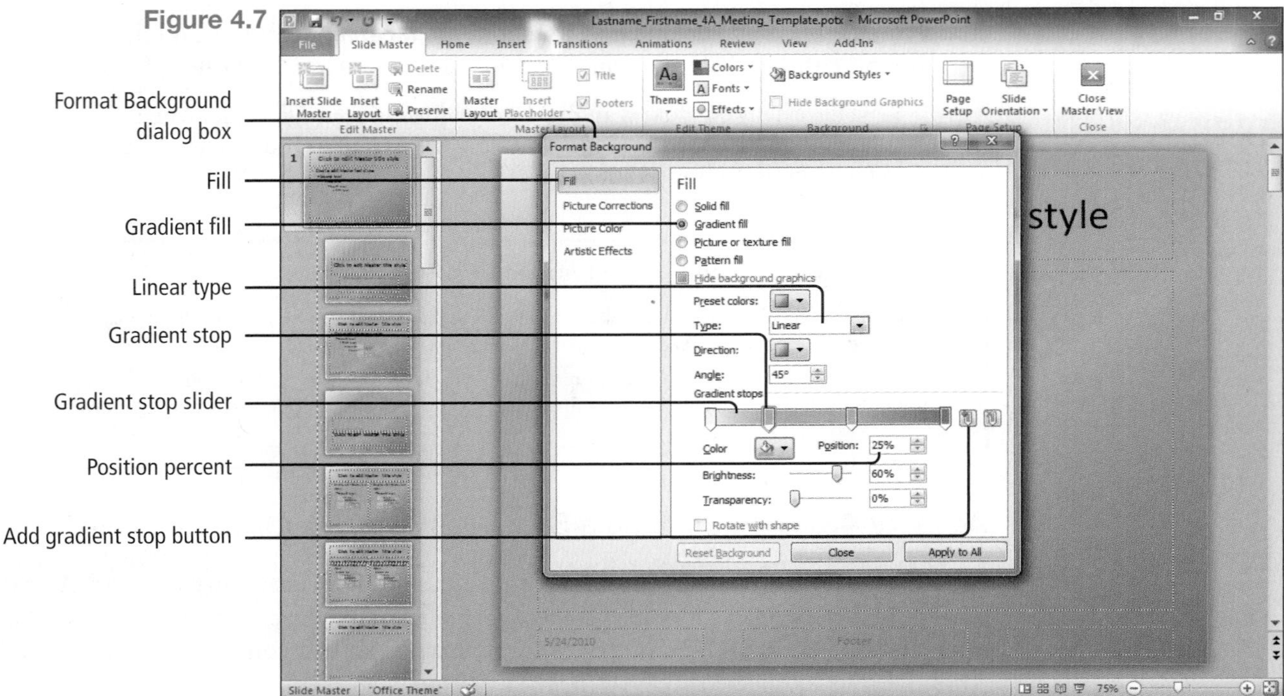

5 In the **Format Background** dialog box, click **Apply to All**. Click **Close**.

All slide layout thumbnails are displayed with the gradient fill.

6 **Save** the template.

Activity 4.04 | Formatting Slide Masters by Adding Pictures and Shapes

In this activity, you will add and format a shape and then insert a picture into the shape. Then you will duplicate the shape, move the copied shape to a different slide layout, and resize it.

1 Click the **Title Slide Layout** thumbnail—the second thumbnail—to make the **Title Slide Layout** master the active slide layout.

2 On the **View tab**, in the **Show group**, click the **Ruler** check box to display the horizontal and vertical rulers (if necessary). Click the **Insert tab**. In the **Illustrations group**, click the **Shapes** button. From the displayed list, under **Basic Shapes**, click the **Oval** shape. Position the pointer at **2 inches on the right side of the horizontal ruler** and **3 inches on the upper half of the vertical ruler**, and then click to insert the shape. It may look like a circle.

When you insert a shape, a Drawing Tools tab is displayed above the Ribbon tabs. A context-sensitive Format tab is displayed under the Drawing Tools tab. When you deselect the shape, the Drawing Tools and Format tabs disappear.

3 With the shape still selected, on the Ribbon, under **Drawing Tools**, click the **Format tab**. In the **Shapes Styles group**, click the **Shape Effects** button. From the displayed list, click **Bevel**. Point to some of the effects and note the changes made to the oval. In the first row, click the first effect— **Circle**. In the **Shapes Styles group**, click the **Shape Outline** button, and then click **No Outline**.

Removing the border softens the appearance of the shape.

4 With the oval still selected, in the **Size group**, change the **Shape Height** to **2"** and the **Shape Width** to **2"**. Compare your screen with Figure 4.8. If the placement of your oval does not match, click on the shape, and then move it to match the position shown in the figure.

Figure 4.8

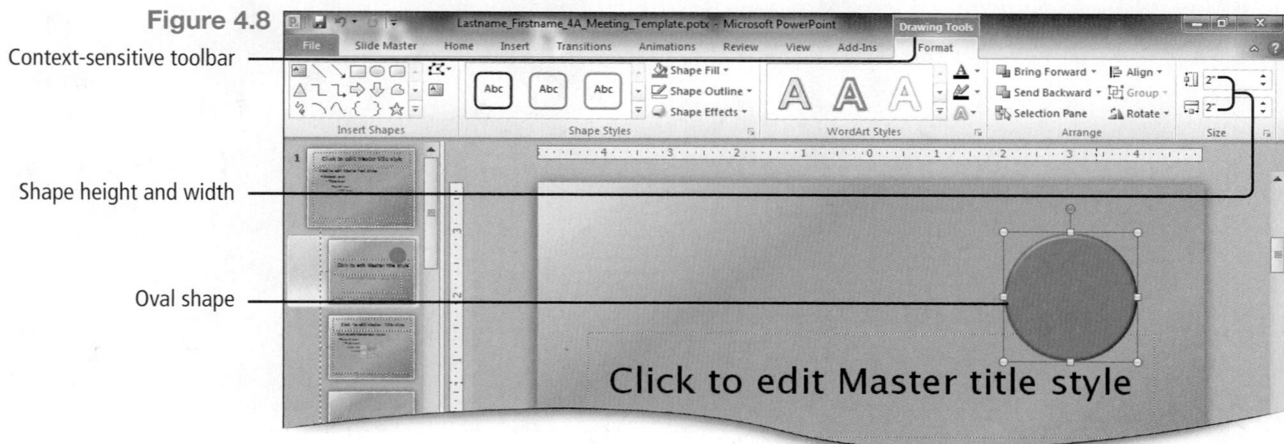

5 Click the **Format tab**. In the **Shape Styles group**, click the **Shape Fill** button, and then point to **Picture** to read the ScreenTip.

6 Click **Picture**. Navigate to the location where your data files are stored, and then click **p04A_Law1.jpg**. Click the **Insert** button.

The picture fills only the shape. When you add a picture inside the shape, a Picture Tools tab displays above the Ribbon tabs with a Format tab beneath it. One Format tab is for the Drawing Tools for the shape. The other Format tab is for the Picture Tools for the picture you inserted. When you deselect the shape, both the Drawing Tools and Picture Tools tabs disappear.

7 With the shape still selected, in the **Arrange group**, click the **Align** button to see the alignment options. Click **Align Center**. Click the **Align** button again, and then click **Align Bottom**. Deselect the shape to see it better. Click on the shape once again to select it.

The shape with the picture aligns in the horizontal center at the bottom of the slide.

8. On the Ribbon, under **Picture Tools**, click the **Format tab**. In the **Adjust Group**, click the **Color** button. Under **Recolor**, in the second row, click the second color—**Blue, Accent color 1 Dark**. Compare your screen with Figure 4.9.

Figure 4.9

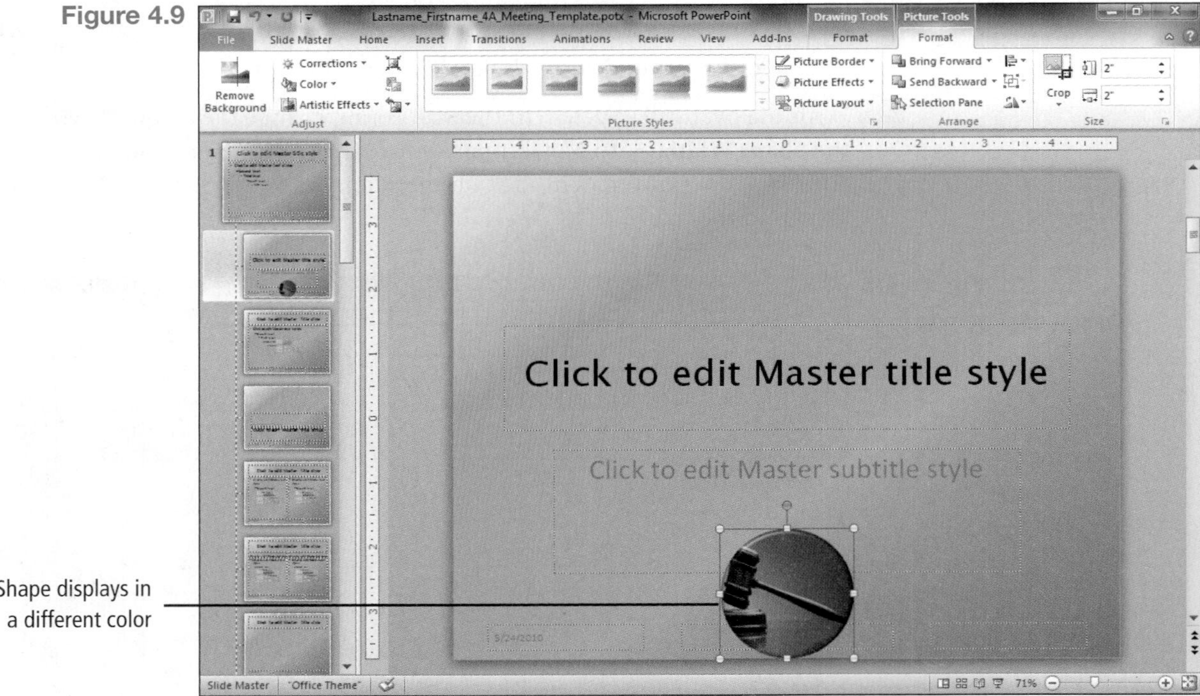

9. With the shape still selected, on the **Home tab**, in the **Clipboard group**, click the **Copy** button. Click the **Title and Content Layout** thumbnail, which is the third thumbnail. In the **Clipboard group**, click the **Paste** button.

   The copied shape maintains the same format and position.

10. On the Ribbon, under **Drawing Tools**, click the **Format tab**. In the **Size group**, change the **Shape Height** to **1"** and the **Shape Width** to **1"**.

11. With the shape still selected, hold down the Shift key, and then click in the text placeholder. In the **Arrange group**, click the **Align** button, and then click **Align Right**. Click the **Align** button again, and then click **Align Bottom.** Compare your screen with Figure 4.10.

   The logo now appears on the first slide of your presentation and then displays in a smaller format on slides using the title and content layout. If you wanted to have the logo on other slide layouts, you could copy the small logo to those layouts as well.

Figure 4.10

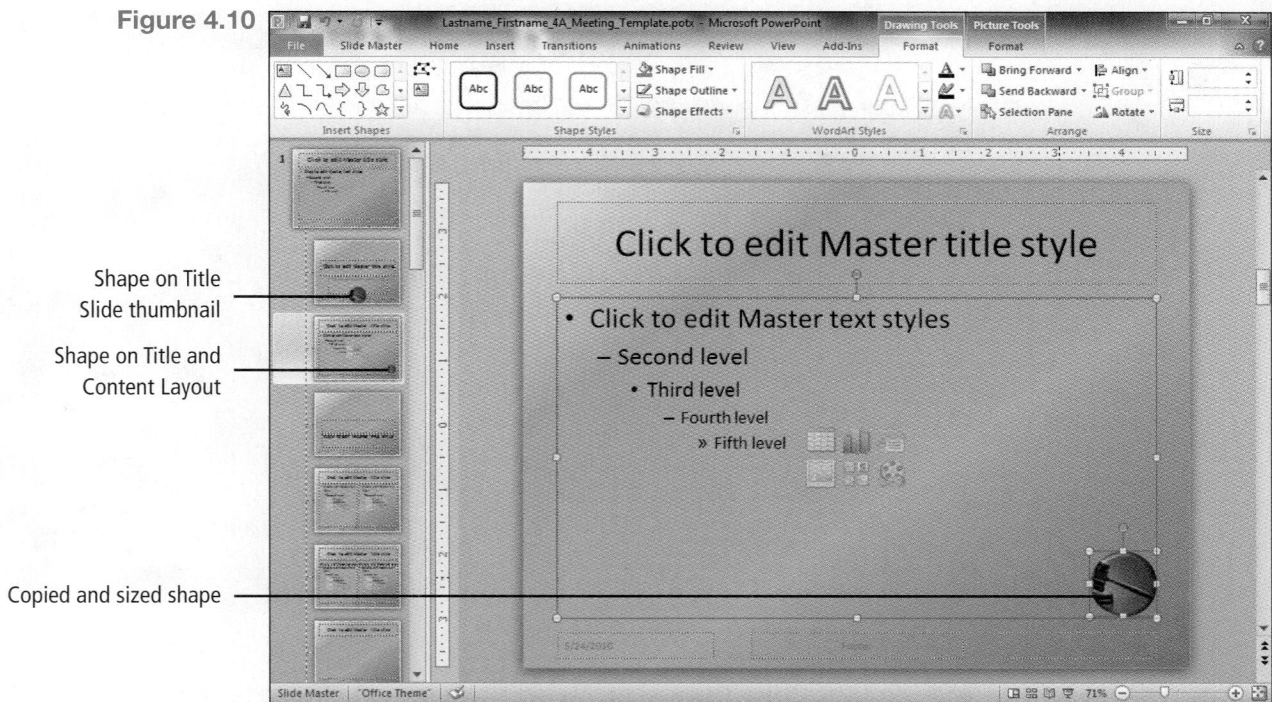

12 **Save** the template.

Activity 4.05 | Customizing Placeholders on a Slide Master

In this activity, you will change the size and position of the placeholders on the Title Slide master, format the Footer placeholder, and then change the bullet types on the Title and Content Slide master.

1 Click the **Title Slide Layout** thumbnail to make it the active slide. Click anywhere on the dashed border for the **title placeholder**, hold down the Shift key, and then drag the entire placeholder so the top border is at **3 inches on the upper half of the vertical ruler**. Release the Shift key. Click anywhere on the dashed border for the **subtitle placeholder**, hold down the Shift key, and then drag the entire placeholder so the top border is at **1 inch on the upper half of the vertical ruler**.

Moving a placeholder does not change the size of it. Using the Shift key while dragging the placeholder keeps the placeholder from moving to the left or right.

2 With the **subtitle placeholder** still selected, drag the **bottom middle sizing handle** to **.5 inches on the lower half of the vertical ruler** to decrease the size of the placeholder. Compare your screen with Figure 4.11.

Using the sizing handle changes the size of the placeholder.

Figure 4.11

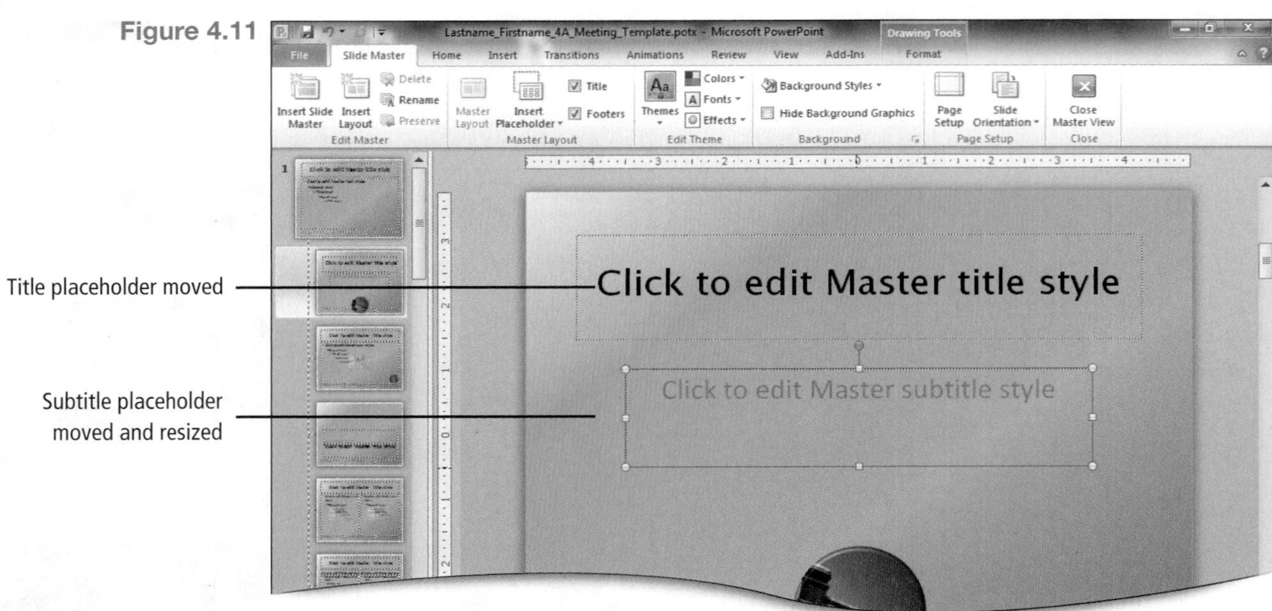

3 Click the **Office Theme Slide Master** thumbnail to make it the active slide. Click anywhere in the first bulleted line. On the **Home tab**, in the **Paragraph group**, click the **Bullets button arrow**, and then click **Bullets and Numbering**. In the **Bullets and Numbering** dialog box, click the **Bulleted tab** if necessary. Click **Arrow Bullets**. At the bottom left, click the **Color button arrow**. Under **Theme Colors**, in the last column, click the last color—**Orange, Accent 6, Darker 50%**. Compare your screen with Figure 4.12. Click **OK**.

Figure 4.12

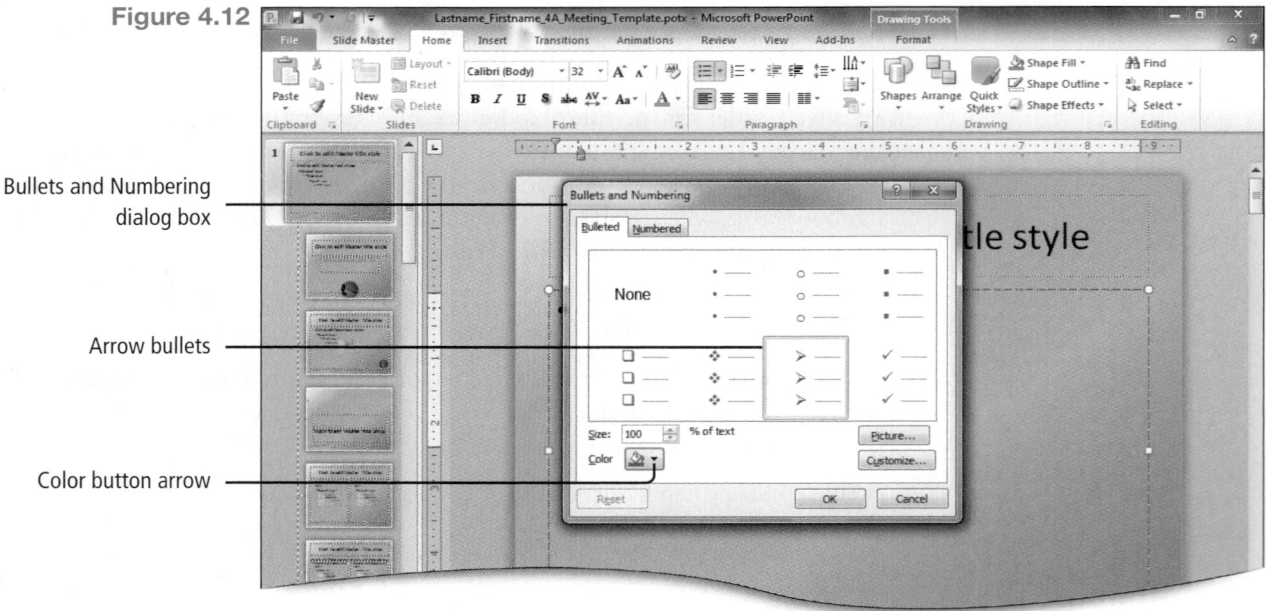

4 Click anywhere in the second bulleted line. Using the procedure that you used for the first bulleted line, display the **Bullets and Numbering** dialog box. Click the **Filled Square Bullets**. Click the **Color button arrow**, and then in the last row, last column, click **Orange, Accent 6, Darker 50%**. Click **OK**. Compare your screen with Figure 4.13.

All slides in the presentation will automatically display these custom bullets for the first two levels of the outline. If you intend to have more levels in your outline, you can continue customizing them.

Figure 4.13

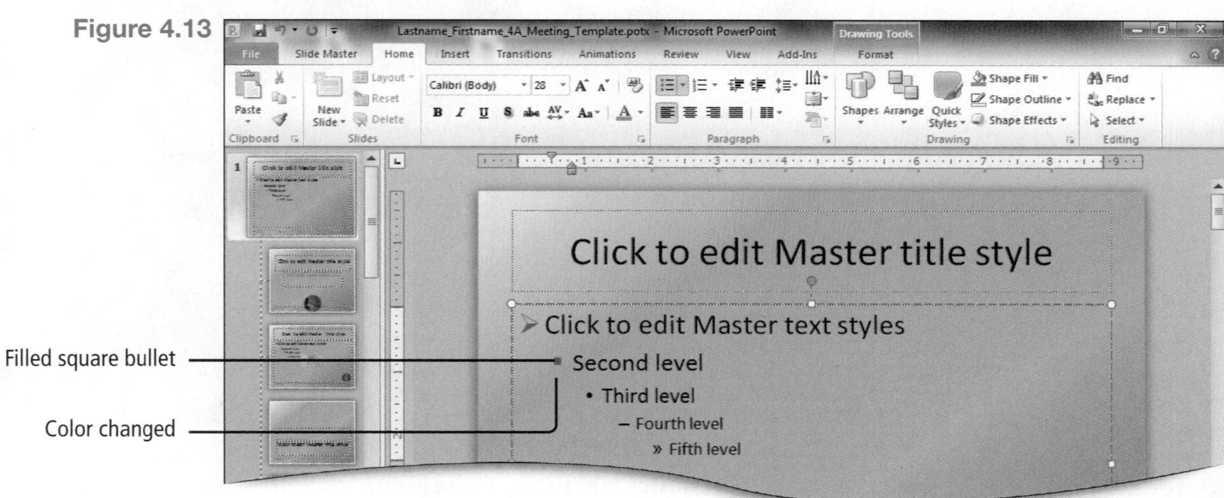

> **More Knowledge | Customizing Bullets on Different Slide Masters**
>
> When you customize the bullets on the Office Theme Slide Master, the customized bullets are available on all slides. If you want different bullets on some of the slide masters, customize the slide masters separately. For example, you could change the bullets on the Title and Content Layout and then change the bullets on the Two Content Layout.

> **Another Way**
>
> Highlight the date to select the date placeholder.

5 Click the first thumbnail, the **Office Theme Slide Master**. At the bottom left on the **Office Theme Master Slide**, click anywhere on the dashed border for the date placeholder to select the date. On the **Home tab**, change the **font size** to **10**.

Changing the font size on the Office Theme Slide Master will affect all slide layouts in the presentation.

6 Click the **Title Slide Layout** thumbnail. Select and drag the entire shape up so the top aligns at **1 inch on the lower half of the vertical ruler**. Under **Drawing Tools**, on the **Format tab**, in the **Arrange group**, click the **Align** button, and then select **Align Center**. Click outside to deselect the shape. Compare your screen with Figure 4.14.

When you drag a shape, you might change the alignment by accident, so set the alignment again. The shape now clears the area reserved for the footer.

Figure 4.14

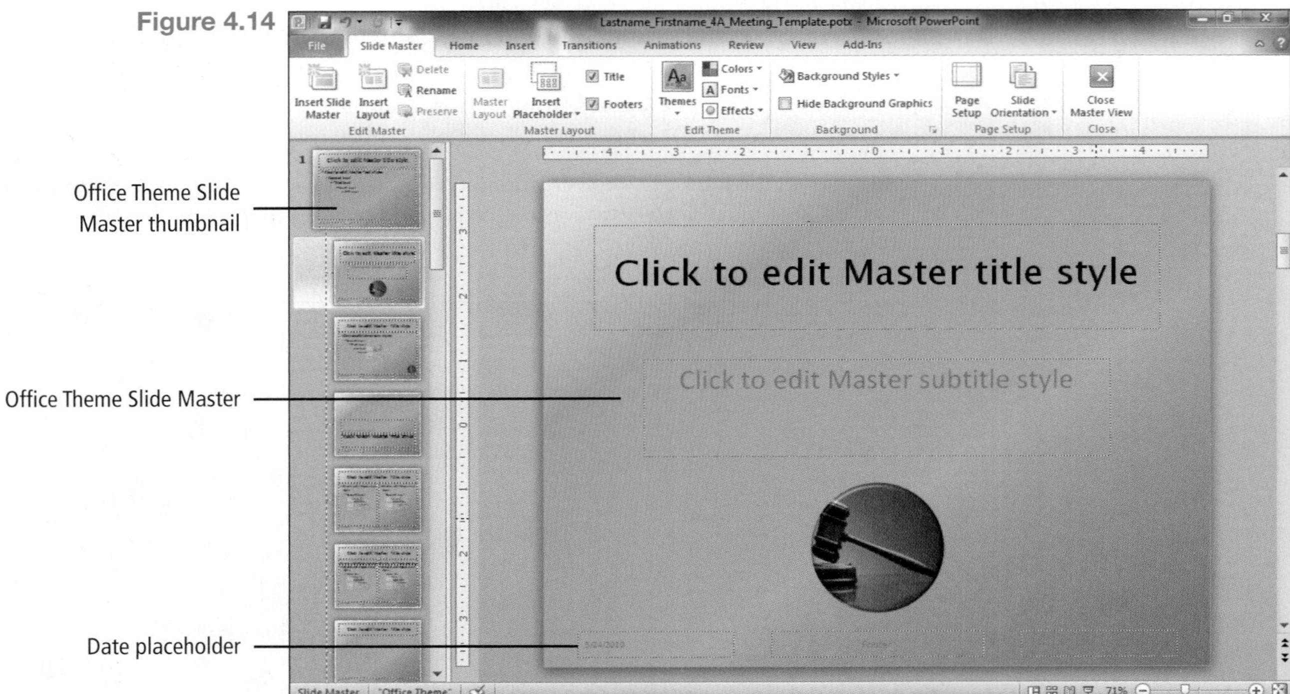

Another Way

On the status bar, click the Normal button to close the Master View.

7 Click the **Slide Master tab**. In the **Close group**, click the **Close Master View** button.

8 **Save** the template.

Activity 4.06 | Displaying and Editing the Handout Master

In this activity, you will edit the handout master for the meeting template you are building for the DeLong Grant Law Partners. You can print your presentation in the form of handouts that your audience can use to follow along as you give your presentation or keep for future reference. The ***Handout Master*** specifies the design of presentation handouts for an audience. You will learn how to change from landscape to portrait orientations, set the number of slides on a page, and specify whether you want to include the header, footer, date, and page number placeholders. Because you are working in a template file rather than a presentation file, the changes to the master affect presentations created from this template. You may change the settings in each presentation if you wish.

1 Open **Lastname_Firstname_4A_ Meeting_Template**, if necessary. Click the **View tab**. In the **Master View group**, click **Handout Master**. In the **Page Setup group**, click the **Handout Orientation** button, and then notice that the default orientation is **Portrait**. Click the **Slide Orientation** button, and then notice that the default orientation is **Landscape**. Leave the settings as they are. Compare your screen with Figure 4.15.

The Portrait handout orientation means that the slides will print on paper that is 8.5" wide by 11" long. The Landscape handout orientation means that the slides will print on paper that is 11" wide by 8.5" long.

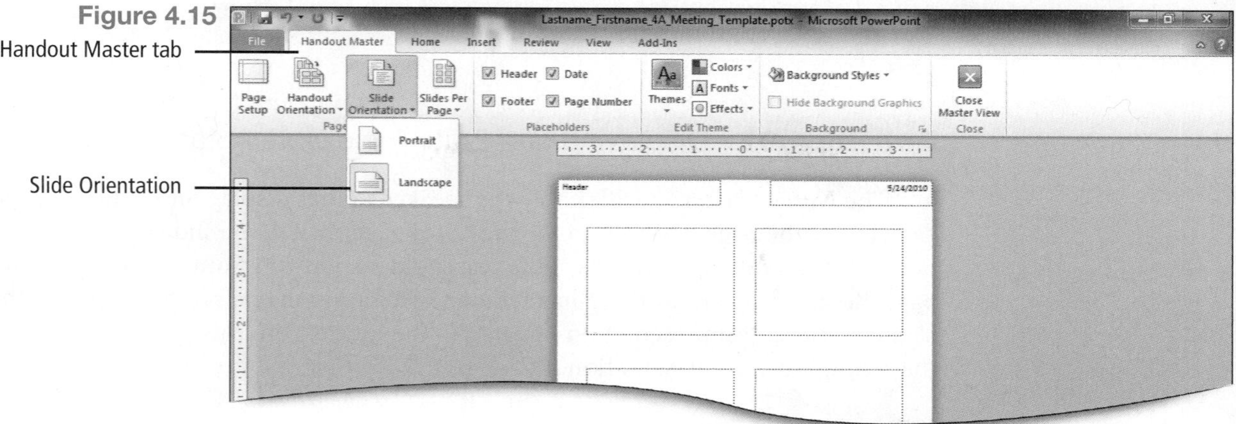

Figure 4.15

2 In the **Page Setup group**, click the **Slides Per Page** button. Click **3 Slides**. Compare your screen with Figure 4.16.

You can print the handouts with 1, 2, 3, 4, 6, or 9 slides per page.

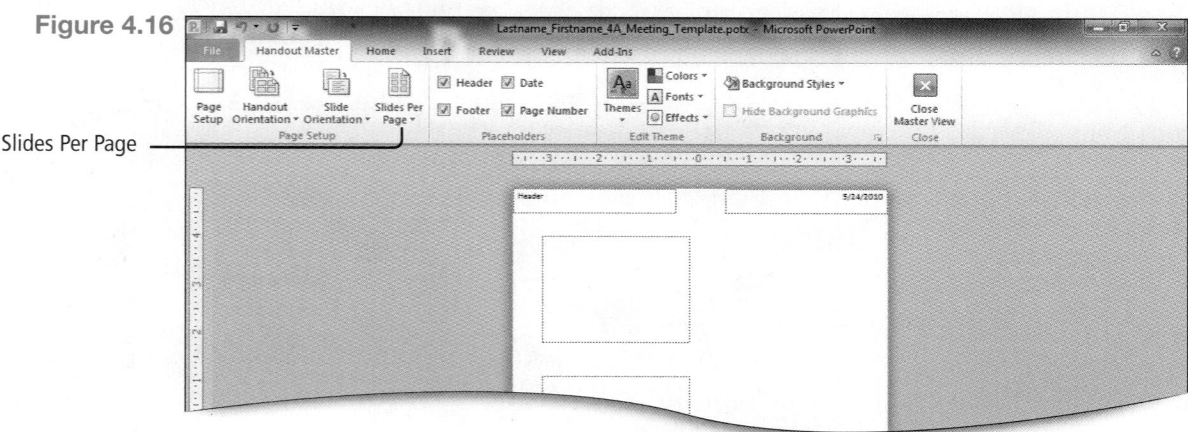

Figure 4.16

3 In the **Placeholders group**, click **Header** to remove the check mark. Compare your screen with Figure 4.17.

Notice that the Header placeholder disappeared. The placeholders for the notes master include Header, Footer, Date, and Page Number.

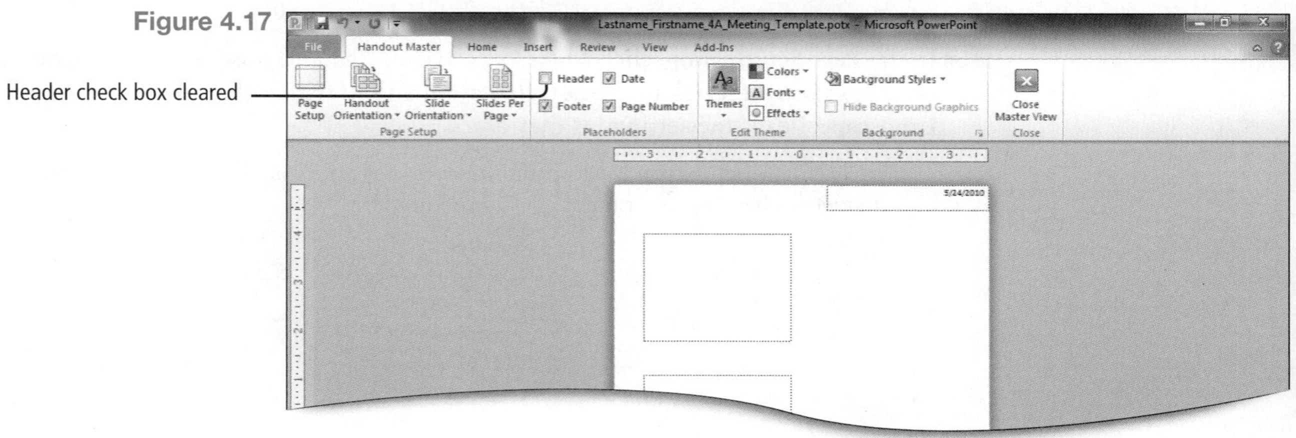

Figure 4.17

4 In the **Close group**, click **Close Master View**.

5 **Save** the template.

Activity 4.07 | Displaying and Editing the Notes Master

The ***Notes Master*** specifies how the speaker's notes display on the printed page. You can choose the page orientation for the notes page, switch the slide orientation between portrait and landscape, and select the placeholders that you want to display on the printed page. Because you are working in a template file rather than a presentation file, the changes to the master affect presentations created in the future from this template. You may change the settings in each presentation if you wish.

1 On the **View tab**, in the **Master Views group**, click the **Notes Master** button. Compare your screen with Figure 4.18.

Recall that the Notes page shows a picture of the slide as well as appropriate notes to assist the speaker when delivering the presentation to a group.

Figure 4.18

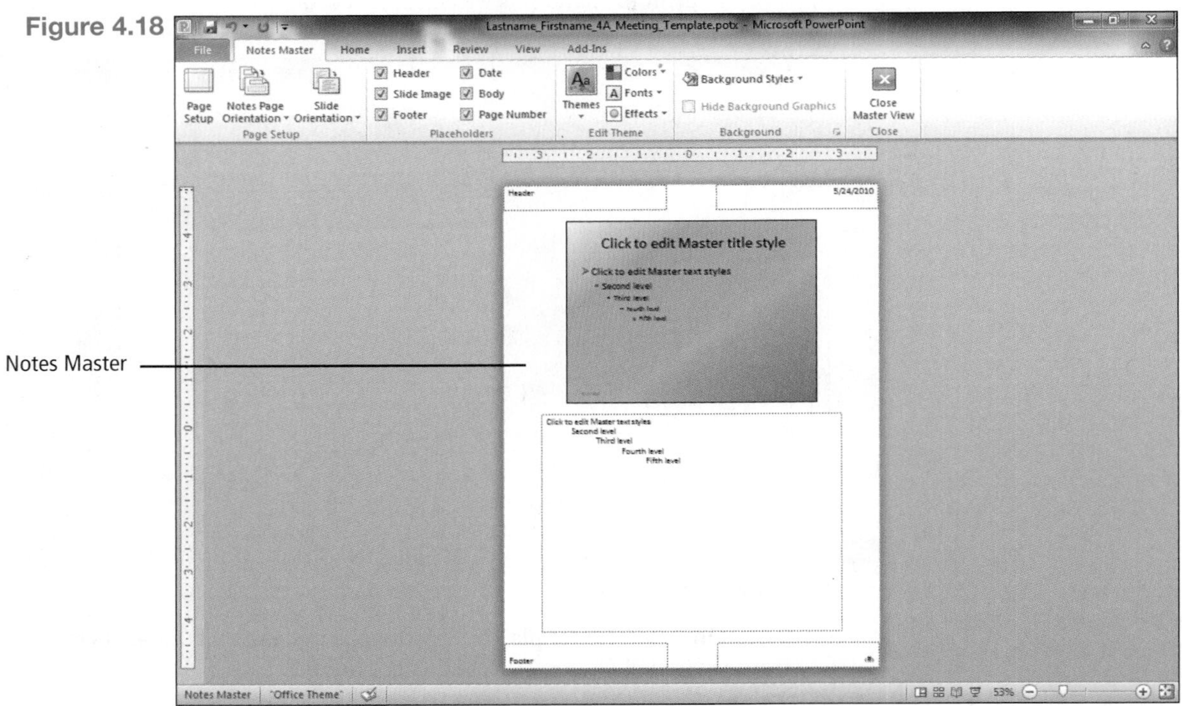

Notes Master

2 In the **Page Setup group**, click **Notes Page Orientation** and observe that the orientation is set for **Portrait.** Click the **Slide Orientation** and note that the orientation is set for **Landscape**. Leave the settings as they are.

The orientation that you use to print the notes page is a matter of personal preference and what works best for the content of the presentation.

3 In the **Placeholders group**, click **Header** to remove the Header placeholder. Compare your screen with Figure 4.19.

Notice that the Header placeholder disappears. The placeholders for the notes master include Header, Slide Image, Footer, Date, Body, and Page Number.

Figure 4.19

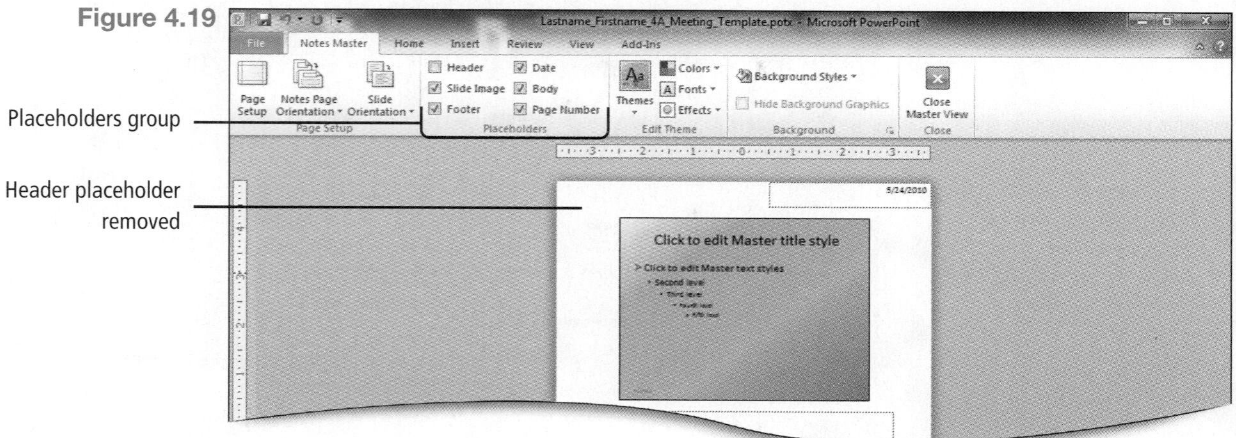

4 In the **Close group**, click **Close Master View**.

5 **Save** the presentation, and then close the template file.

Objective 2 | Apply a Custom Template to a Presentation

Activity 4.08 | Applying a Template to a Presentation

In this activity, you will use the meeting template to create a slide presentation that explains the new filing procedures to the law partners. Recall that templates you design are, by default, saved in a templates folder on the computer. You, however, are saving your template in your Chapter 4 folder.

1 **Start** PowerPoint if necessary. Display **Backstage** view, and then click **New**. Under **Available Templates and Themes**, you see several categories listed in the **Home group**. Compare your screen with Figure 4.20. For complete descriptions of the templates and themes, see Figure 4.21.

Recall that a PowerPoint template is a file that contains layouts, theme colors, theme fonts, theme effects, background styles, and content. It contains the complete blueprint for slides pertaining to a specific kind of presentations. A theme includes coordinated colors and matched backgrounds, fonts, and effects.

Figure 4.20

Available Templates and Themes

Available Templates and Themes

Available Templates and Themes	Description
Blank presentation	Default template that contains no content or design.
Recent templates	Templates that you have used recently.
Sample templates	Templates designed for specific uses, such as a photo album, quiz show, or training.
Themes	Templates with themes already added.
My templates	Templates that you have saved on your computer in the default template folder.
New from existing	Templates that you have created and saved.

Figure 4.21

2 Under **Available Templates and Themes**, click **New from existing**. Navigate to the location where you are saving your files. Locate **Lastname_Firstname_4A_Meeting Template.potx**. Click the file name one time, and then compare your screen with Figure 4.22.

Recall that the extension for a PowerPoint template is .potx and the extension for a PowerPoint file or presentation is ***.pptx***. The Open button changes to Create New.

Figure 4.22

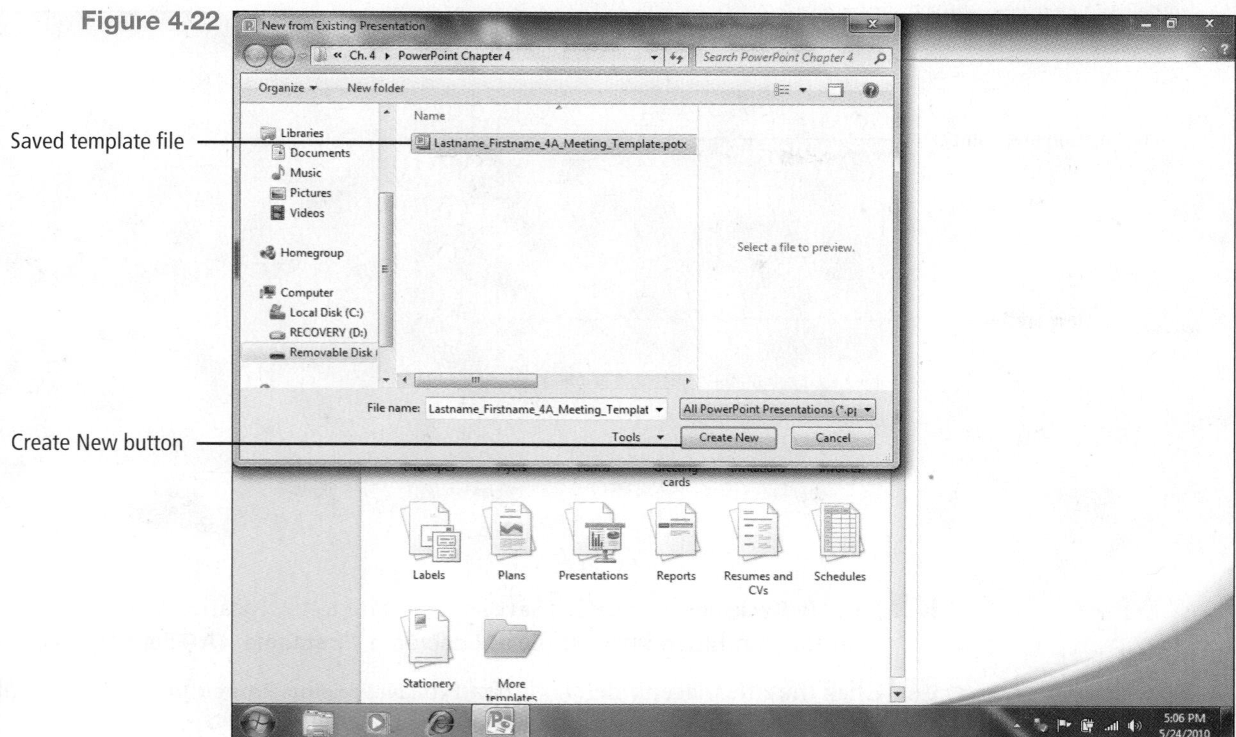

Alert! | Did You Display the File Extensions?

If the file extension does not display on the Title bar, go to Windows Explorer. On the Windows menu bar, click **Organize**, and then click **Folder and search options**. In the **Folder Options** dialog box, click the **View tab**. Under **Files and Folders**, scroll to **Hide extensions for known file types**, and then remove the check mark in the check box. Click **OK**.

3 At the lower right of the window, click the **Create New** button to display a copy of the template with the Title slide active. Compare your screen with Figure 4.23

The file name on the Title Bar displays as Presentation2 – Microsoft PowerPoint (the presentation number may vary).

More Knowledge | Opening a Template

If you need to edit a template, start PowerPoint. Display Backstage view, click Open, navigate to your storage location, and then open the file. You can also open a template by navigating to it in Windows Explorer, right-clicking the file name, and then clicking Open. Make sure that you see the .potx at the end of the file name in the Title bar. To open a template saved in the Template folder on your computer, you have to know the path to the template.

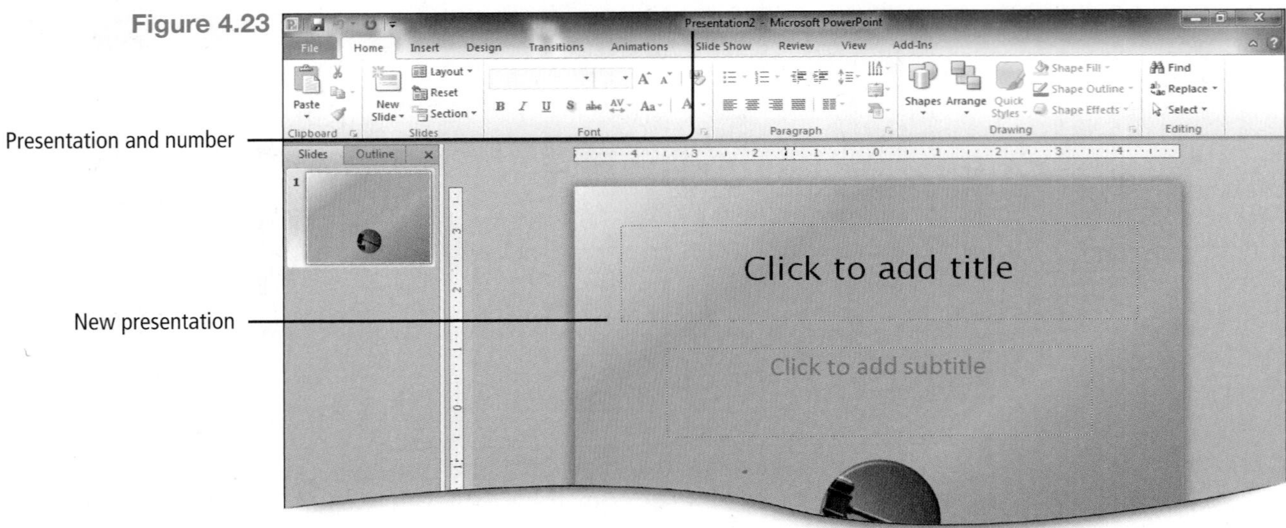

Figure 4.23

4 Display **Backstage** view, click **Save As**. Navigate to the location where you are saving your files, and then save the file as **Lastname_Firstname_4A_Filing_Procedures**

> **Another Way**
>
> Press the keyboard shortcut Ctrl + Enter to move to the subtitle placeholder.

5 Click the title placeholder, and then type **New Filing Procedures** Click the subtitle placeholder, and then type **DeLong Grant Law Partners**

6 On the **Home tab**, in the **Slides group**, click the **New Slide button arrow**. The displayed gallery shows the formatting you created for the slide layouts. Compare your screen with Figure 4.24.

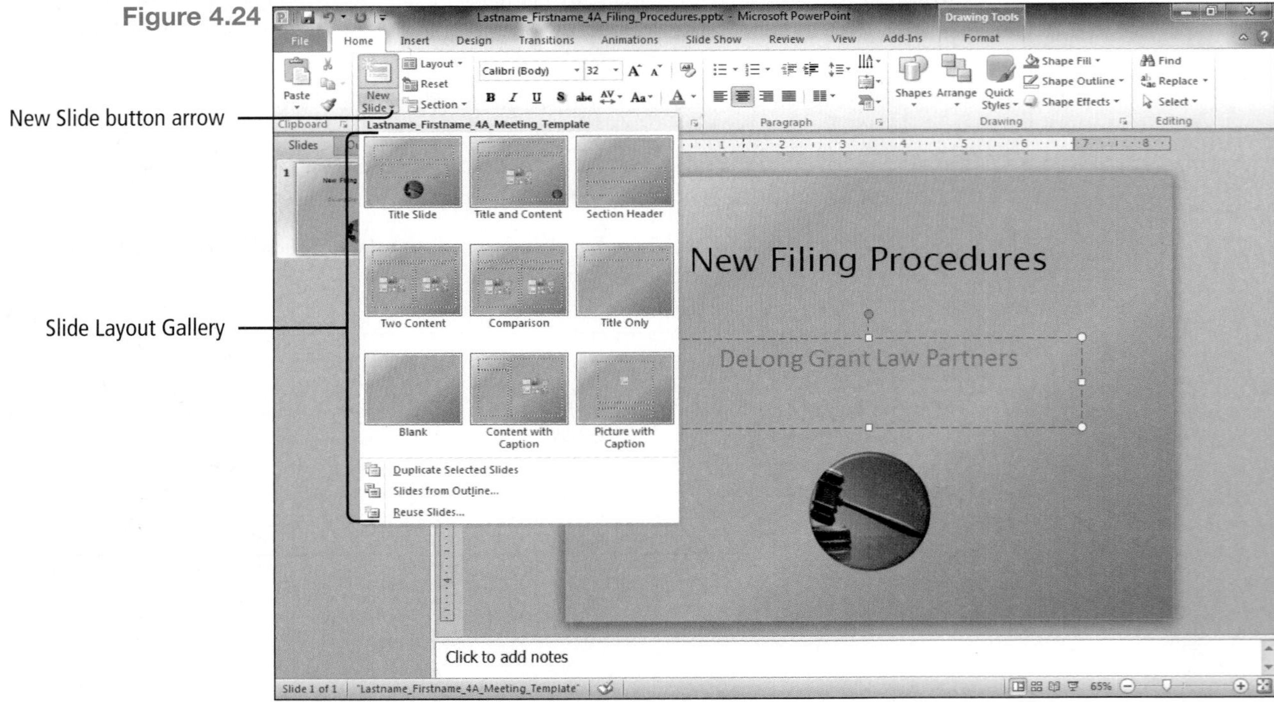

Figure 4.24

> **Another Way**
>
> Use the Tab to increase the outline level. Use the Shift + Tab key combination to decrease the outline level.

7 Click **Title and Content** to add the slide and make it the active slide. In the title placeholder, type **Referencing Number System** Press Ctrl + Enter. In the content placeholder, type **Include these three parts in the number:** and then press Enter. In the **Paragraph group**, click the **Increase List Level** button to increase the outline level. Type **Client last name** Press Enter, and then type **Date file opened** Press Enter, type **Date file completed (if applicable)** and then press Enter.

When you increase an outline level, the text moves to the right. When you press Enter, the same outline level continues.

8 In the **Paragraph group**, click the **Decrease List Level** button to decrease the outline level. Type **Example: DeLong_01-15-2014_10-14-2016**

To move the text to the left, you need to decrease the outline level.

> **Another Way**
>
> To add a slide with the same layout as the previous slide, you can click the New Slide Button without displaying the gallery.

9 In the **Slides group**, click the **New Slide button arrow**, and then click **Title and Content** to add a third slide. In the title placeholder, type **Hardcopy Filing** and then press Ctrl + Enter. Following the procedure explained for the previous slide, type the following bulleted items for the Hardcopy Filing slide in the content placeholder.

Include the reference number on all pages of the legal document.

Place the number in the upper right corner.

Add the date completed when the case is closed.

Retain a copy of the document for your personal file.

10 In the **Notes pane**, type **The ending date is the actual date that the case is closed. Until then, leave the ending date blank.** Compare your screen with Figure 4.25.

Figure 4.25

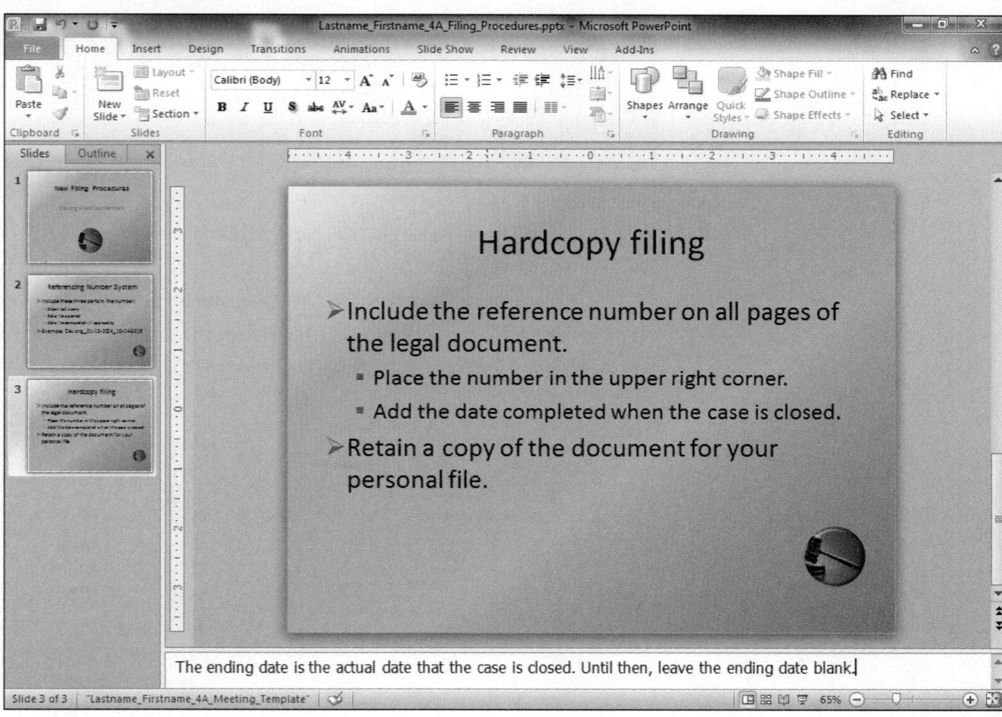

PowerPoint | Chapter 4

11 Add another **Title and Content** slide. In the title placeholder, type **Digital Filing** and then press Ctrl + Enter. In the content placeholder, type the following bulleted items. Compare your screen with Figure 4.26.

Use the reference number for the file name.

Save a copy of the file to the company database.

> **Require authorized employees to use a Login to view the file.**
>
> **Lock the file after any changes are made.**

Figure 4.26

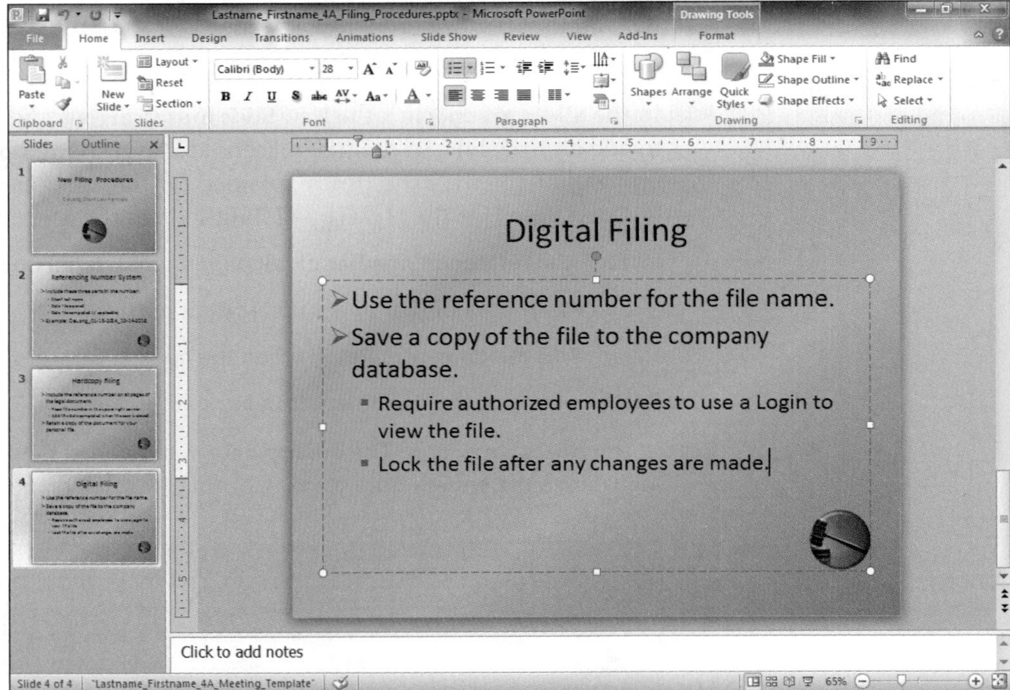

12 In the **Slides group**, click the **New Slide button arrow**, and then click **Title and Content** to add another slide. In the title placeholder, type **Summary** In the content placeholder, type **All changes are effective immediately. Direct questions to the support team.** On the **Home tab**, in the **Paragraph group**, click the **Bullets** button to remove the bullet. In the **Paragraph group**, click the **Center** button.

13 On the left side of the content placeholder, click the **middle sizing handle**, and then drag the sizing handle to **3 inches on the left side of the horizontal ruler**. On the right side of the content placeholder, drag the **middle sizing handle** to **3 inches on the right side of the horizontal ruler**. With the content placeholder still selected, at the bottom of the content placeholder, drag the **middle sizing handle** to **1.5 inches on the lower half of the vertical ruler** to reduce the size of the placeholder. Hold down the Shift key, and then click the top border of the content placeholder. Drag the entire placeholder down so the top is aligned at **1.5 inches on the upper half of the vertical ruler**. In the **Paragraph group**, click the **Line Spacing** button, and then click **1.5**. Compare your screen with Figure 4.27.

Figure 4.27

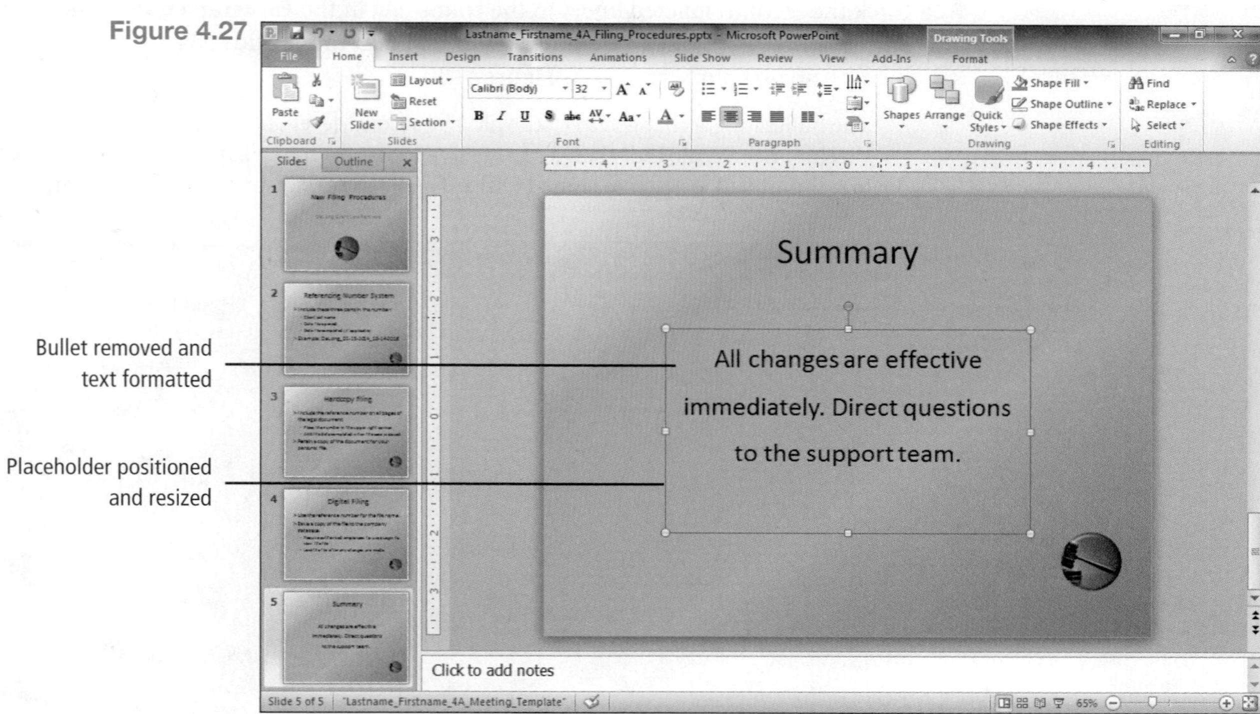

14 On the **Insert tab**, in the **Text group**, click the **Header & Footer** button to display the **Header and Footer** dialog box. Click the **Notes and Handouts tab**. Under **Include on page**, select the **Date and time** check box, and then select **Fixed.** If necessary, clear the **Header** check box, and then select the **Page number** and **Footer** check boxes. In the **Footer** box, using your own name, type **Lastname_Firstname_4A_Filing_Procedures** and then click **Apply to All**.

15 Display **Backstage** view, click **Properties**, and then click **Show Document Panel**. Replace the text in the **Author** box with your own first and last name. In the **Subject** box, type your course name and section number. In the **Keywords** box, type **filing, number, system Close** the **Document Information Panel**.

16 **Save** the presentation.

Activity 4.09 | Editing Slide Masters in an Existing Presentation

Occasionally, you might want to change the master design for a presentation created from your custom template. In this activity, you will change the bullet style on the Title and Content Layout slide master.

1 Open **Lastname_Firstname_4A_Filing_Procedures** if necessary. On the **View tab**, in the **Master View group**, click **Slide Master**.

2 Click the first thumbnail—**Lastname_Firstname_4A_Meeting...Slide Master**. On the **Slide Master tab**, in **Edit theme group**, click the **Fonts** button, and then click **Office 2**.

3 Click the second bulleted line. On the **Home tab**, in the **Paragraph group**, click the **Bullets button arrow**. Click **Checkmark Bullets**. Point to the Slide Master thumbnail, and then compare your screen with Figure 4.28.

The bullet font is changed to Cambria. The second-level bullets are now displayed as checkmarks. Recall, that changes made to the first thumbnail affect all slides. Notice that the first thumbnail, originally named Office Theme, is now displayed with the name of the file.

Figure 4.28

Another Way
Press F5 to start a slide show from the beginning.

4 On the **Slide Master tab**, in the **Close group**, click the **Close Master View** button. On the **Slide Show tab**, in the **Start Slide Show group**, click the **From Beginning** button. View the entire slide presentation.

Because you changed the second-level bullet to checkmarks on the slide master, all slides have checkmarks instead of square bullets. Changing the bullet style on the master slide saved you the time it would take to change the bullets on each slide.

5 **Save** your presentation. Print **Handouts 3 Slides**, or submit your presentation electronically as directed by your instructor.

The change that you made to the bullets affects only this presentation. The original meeting template still uses the square bullets. If you want the change to be permanent on the template, you should open the template and make the change in that file.

6 **Close** the presentation, and then **Exit** PowerPoint.

7 Submit **Lastname_Firstname_4A_Meeting_Template** and **Lastname_Firstname_4A_Filing_Procedures** as directed by your instructor.

End You have completed Project 4A

Project 4B Commented Presentation

Project Activities

In Activities 4.10 through 4.16, you will use reviewing comments to provide feedback to a presentation created by a colleague at the DeLong Grant Law Partners firm. Then you will publish your presentation in both PDF and XPS formats. These formats preserve the document formatting and enable file sharing. You will save the presentation as Word handouts for the audience. Finally, you will check your presentation for compatibility with previous versions of PowerPoint and mark the presentation as final. Your completed presentation will look similar to Figure 4.29.

Project Files

For Project 4B, you will need the following file:

p04B_Entertainment_Basics.pptx

You will save your presentation as:

Lastname_Firstname_4B_Entertainment_Basics.pptx
Lastname_Firstname_4B_Entertainment_Basics.pdf
Lastname_Firstname_4B_Entertainment_Basics.xps
Lastname_Firstname_4B_Entertainment_Basics.docx

Project Results

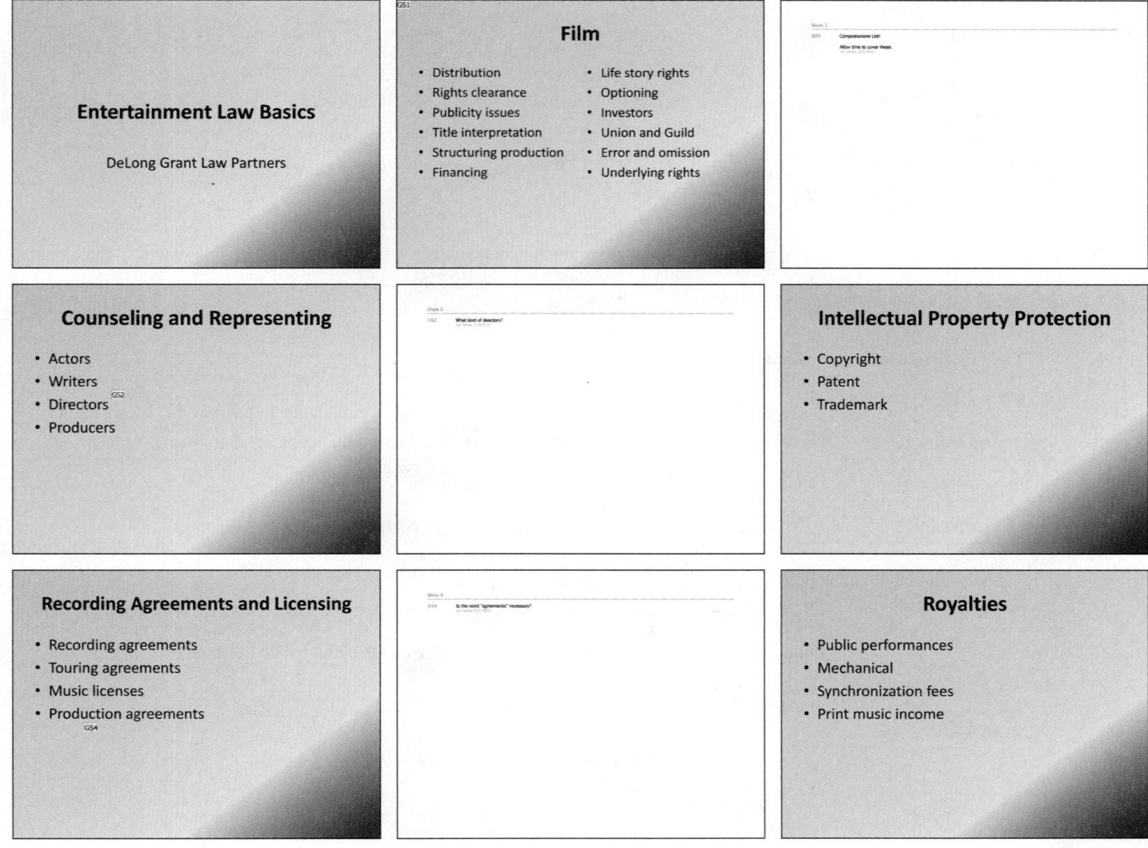

Figure 4.29
Project 4B Commented Presentation

Objective 3 | Create and Edit Comments

A ***comment*** is a note that you can attach to a letter or word on a slide or to an entire slide. People use comments to provide feedback on a presentation. A ***reviewer*** is someone who adds comments to the presentation to provide feedback.

Activity 4.10 | Adding Comments

In this activity, you will add comments to your meeting presentation. Comments may be added by the person who created the presentation or other persons who are invited to provide suggestions.

1. **Start** PowerPoint. Locate and open the file **p04B_Entertainment_Basics.pptx**. Navigate to the location where you are storing your folders and projects for this chapter, and then **Save** the file as **Lastname_Firstname_4B_Entertainment_Basics**

2. Make **Slide 2** the active slide. Click the **Review tab**. In the **Comments group**, point to each of the buttons and read the ScreenTips. Compare your screen with Figure 4.30. For a complete explanation of each of these buttons, see Figure 4.31.

Figure 4.30

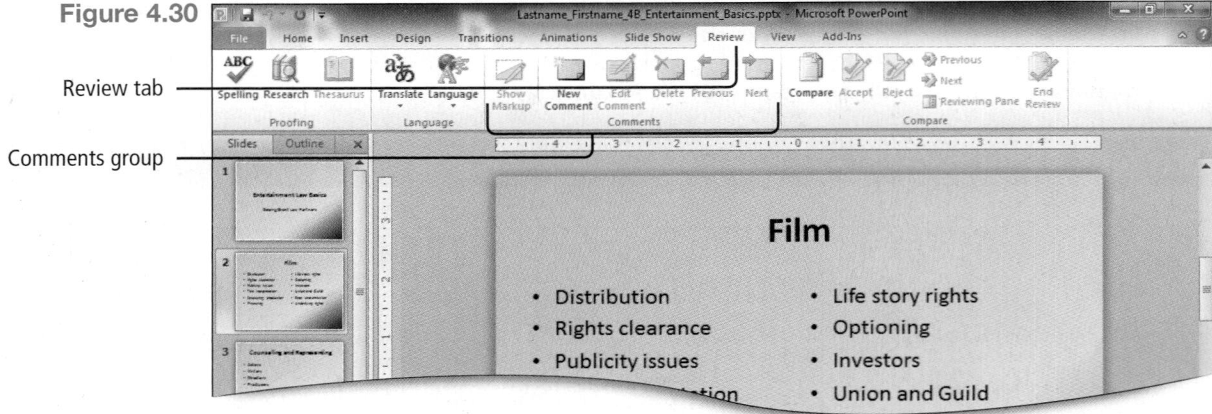

Reviewing Elements

Screen Element	**Description**
Comments Group	
Show Markup	Displays the comments and other annotations so you can see them.
New Comment	Displays a new comment so you can enter a note.
Edit Comment	Allows a reviewer to make changes to a comment.
Delete	Removes the comment.
Previous	Displays the content of the comment before the position of the insertion point.
Next	Displays the content of the comment after the position of the insertion point.

Figure 4.31

3 In the **Comments group**, click the **New Comment** button. In the space provided, type **Comprehensive List!** In the **Comments group**, all buttons in the Comments group become active. Compare your screen with Figure 4.32.

When there are no comments in the file, the only button in the Comments group that is active is the New Comment button. On other slides, the Edit button is active only when there is a comment on that slide. When a comment is added, the relevant buttons become active. When no placeholder or text is selected before adding a comment, by default the comment displays at the upper left corner of the slide. The person's name displays at the upper left and the date at the upper right in the comment.

Figure 4.32

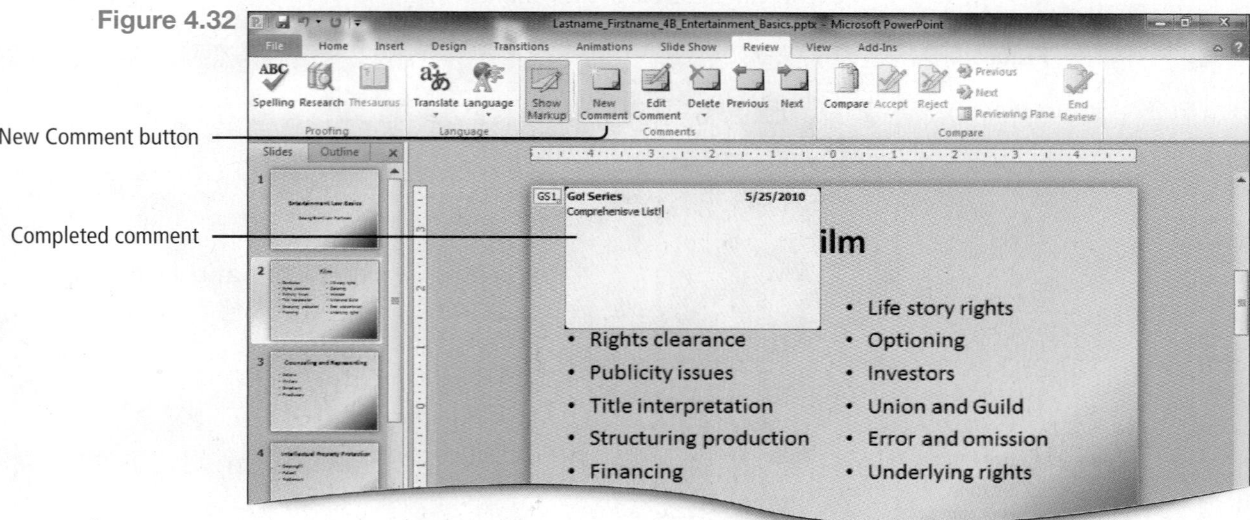

4 Make **Slide 3** the active slide. Click at the end of the third bulleted item, after *Directors*. In the **Comments group**, click **New Comment**. Type **What kind of directors?** Click outside the comment to close it. Compare your screen with Figure 4.33.

Placing the insertion point within a specific area of the slide will position the comment box at that place.

Figure 4.33

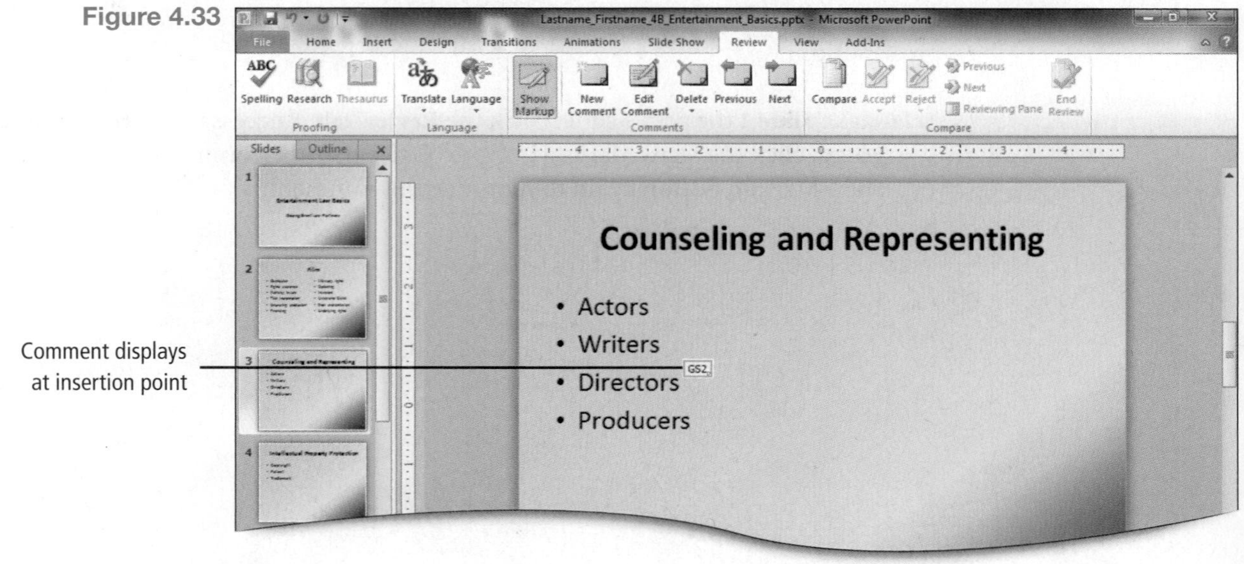

PowerPoint | Chapter 4

5 Make **Slide 4** the active slide. Select the word *Copyright*. Use the procedure explained in the previous steps to add this comment: **Add short definitions.** Click outside the comment to close it.

When you add a comment to selected text, the comment is displayed near the selected text.

6 Select **Slide 5**, and then enter this comment: **Is the word "agreements" necessary?** Click outside the comment. Drag the comment so it is positioned directly below the last bulleted line, under the word *Production*. Compare your screen with Figure 4.34.

You can drag a comment box to any position on the slide. Note that bold, underline, and italic are not available in the comment box.

Figure 4.34

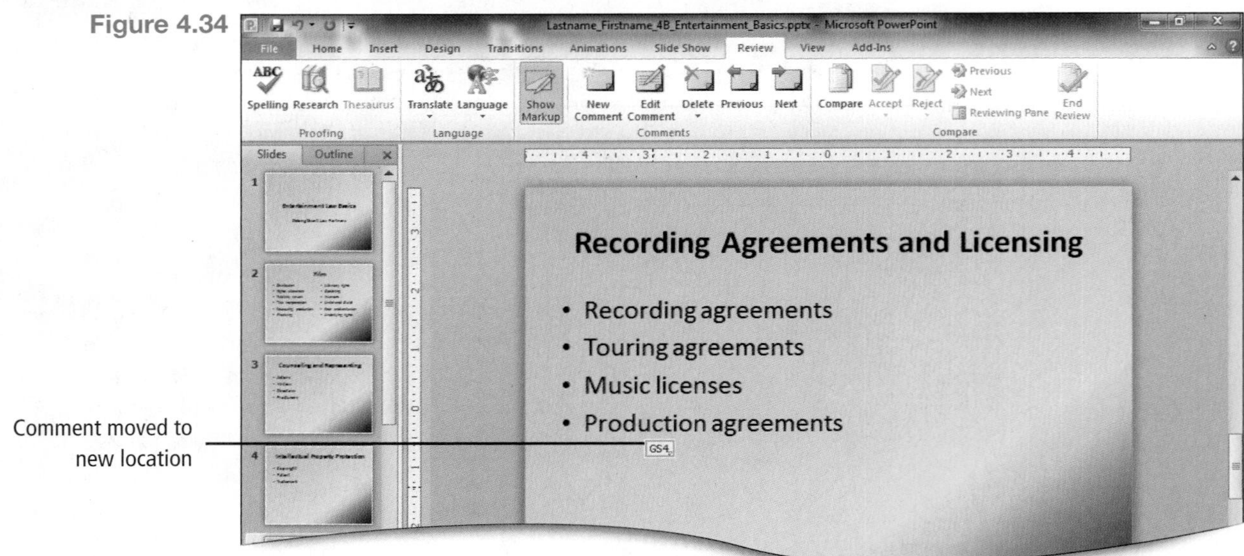

7 **Save** the presentation.

Activity 4.11 | Reading Comments

In this activity, you will learn how to navigate among the comments entered in a presentation.

1 Make **Slide 2** the active slide. Click the **Review tab** if necessary. In the **Comments group**, click the **Show Markup** button. Notice that the comment disappears. Click the **Show Markup** button again to redisplay the comment.

Another Way

You can also point to a closed comment to reveal the message.

2 Make **Slide 1** the active slide. In the **Comments group**, click the **Next** button. The first comment displays so you can read it. Click the **Next** button again to read the second comment, which is on **Slide 3**. Continue clicking the **Next button** until you see the message *PowerPoint reached the end of all changes. Do you want to continue from the beginning of the change list?* Compare your screen with Figure 4.35. Click **Cancel**.

Comments are numbered consecutively in the order they were added.

Figure 4.35

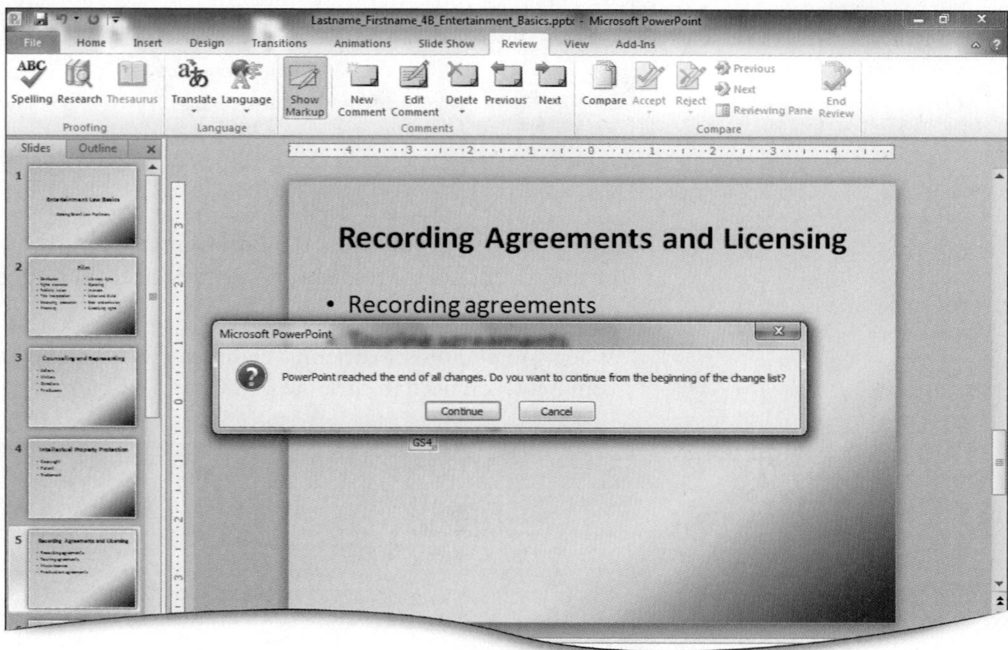

3 In the **Comments group**, click the **Previous** button to read the previous comment. Continue clicking **Previous** until you receive this message: *PowerPoint reached the beginning of all changes. Do you want to continue from the end of the change list?* Click **Cancel**.

Use the Next and Previous buttons to read the comments in your presentation.

Activity 4.12 | Editing Comments

In this activity, you will learn how to edit a comment and how to delete a comment.

1 Make **Slide 2** the active slide, if necessary. At the upper left corner of the slide, click the comment. The text in the comment displays so you can read it, but you cannot edit it. See Figure 4.36.

Figure 4.36

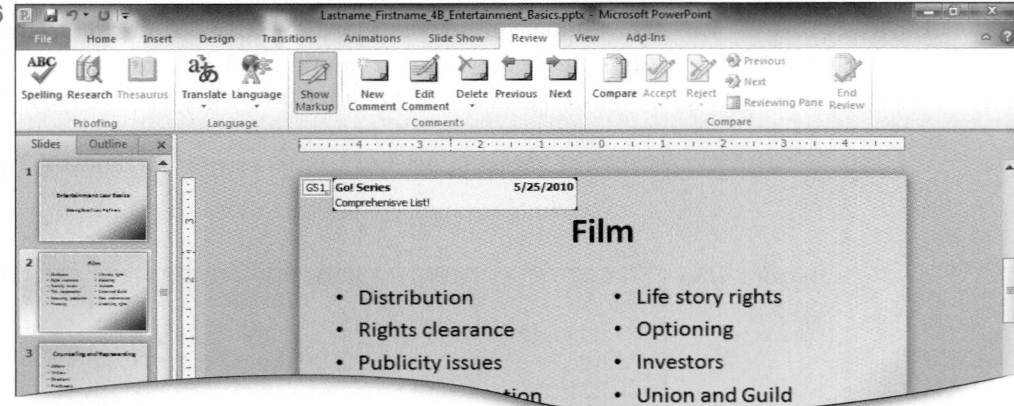

> **Another Way**
>
> You can double-click the comment box to edit the content. Also, you can right-click in the comment and click Edit Comment.

2 In the **Comments group**, click the **Edit Comment** button and notice the insertion point at the end of the text. Press Enter two times, and then type **Allow time to cover these.** Compare your screen with Figure 4.37.

When you point to or click on a comment, you can only read the message. To edit the comment, you need to click the Edit Comment button.

Figure 4.37

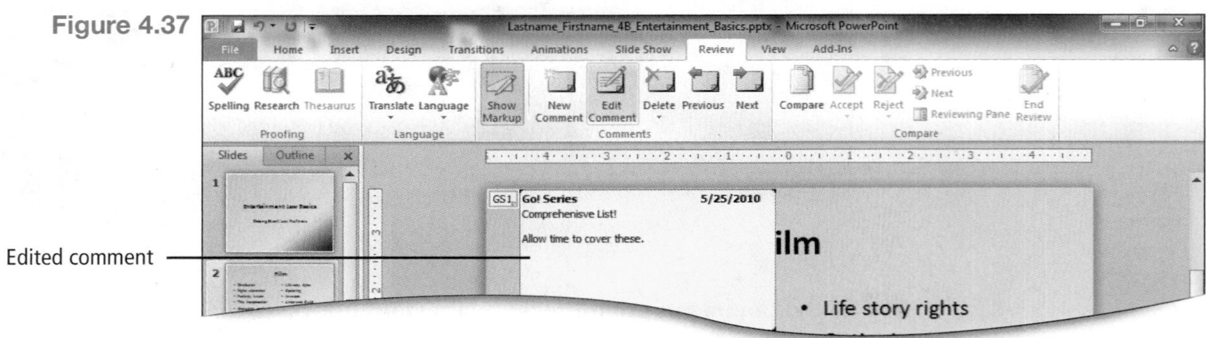

3 Click the **Next** button until you reach the comment on **Slide 4**. In the **Comments group**, click the **Delete button arrow**, and then read the three options: *Delete*, *Delete All Markup on the Current Slide*, and *Delete All Markup in this Presentation*. Compare your screen with Figure 4.38.

Figure 4.38

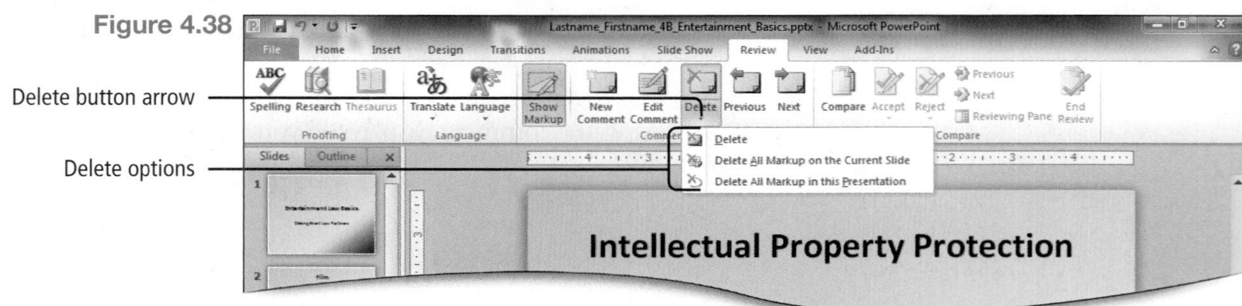

Another Way

To delete a comment, you can also right-click the comment and then click Delete Comment.

4 Click **Delete** to remove this comment. Click the **Next** and **Previous** buttons to see how comments are numbered.

Recall that comments are numbered consecutively in the order that they are inserted. When you delete a comment, the numbering of the rest of the comments does not change.

5 **Save** the presentation.

Objective 4 | Prepare a Presentation for Distribution

PowerPoint offers several ways to share, or distribute, a presentation. A common way is to create a PDF document that people who have Adobe Reader installed on their computers can read. You can also create an XPS document that people who have an XPS viewer can read. Another way to share a presentation is to create handouts in Microsoft Word.

Activity 4.13 | Publishing a Presentation in PDF and XPS Format

In this activity, you will save a presentation in PDF and XPS file formats. Adobe's ***Portable Document Format (PDF)*** preserves document formatting and enables file sharing. The PDF format is also useful if you intend to use commercial printing methods. ***XML Paper Specification (XPS)*** is Microsoft's electronic paper format, an alternative to the PDF format, that also preserves document formatting and enables file sharing. When an XPS or PDF file is viewed online or printed, it retains the format that you intended, and the data in the file cannot be easily changed.

1 Open **Lastname_Firstname_4B_Entertainment_Basics**, if necessary. On the **Insert tab**, in the **Text group**, click the **Header & Footer** button to display the **Header and Footer** dialog box. Click the **Notes and Handouts tab**. Under **Include on page**, select the **Date and time** check box, and then select **Fixed**. If necessary, clear the **Header** check box, and then select the **Page number** and **Footer** check boxes. In the **Footer** box, using your own name, type **Lastname_Firstname_4B_Entertainment_Basics** and then click **Apply to All**.

2 Make **Slide 1** active. Display **Backstage** view, and then click **Save & Send**. Under **File Types**, click **Create PDF/XPS Document**. At the right side of your screen, read the explanation of a PDF/XPS document. Compare your screen with Figure 4.39.

Presentations saved as a PDF/XPS document are saved in a fixed format. The document looks the same on most computers. Fonts, formatting, and images are preserved. Because content cannot be easily changed, your document is more secure. To view a PDF or XPS file, you must have a reader installed on your computer. Free viewers are available on the Web to view PDF and XPS documents.

Figure 4.39

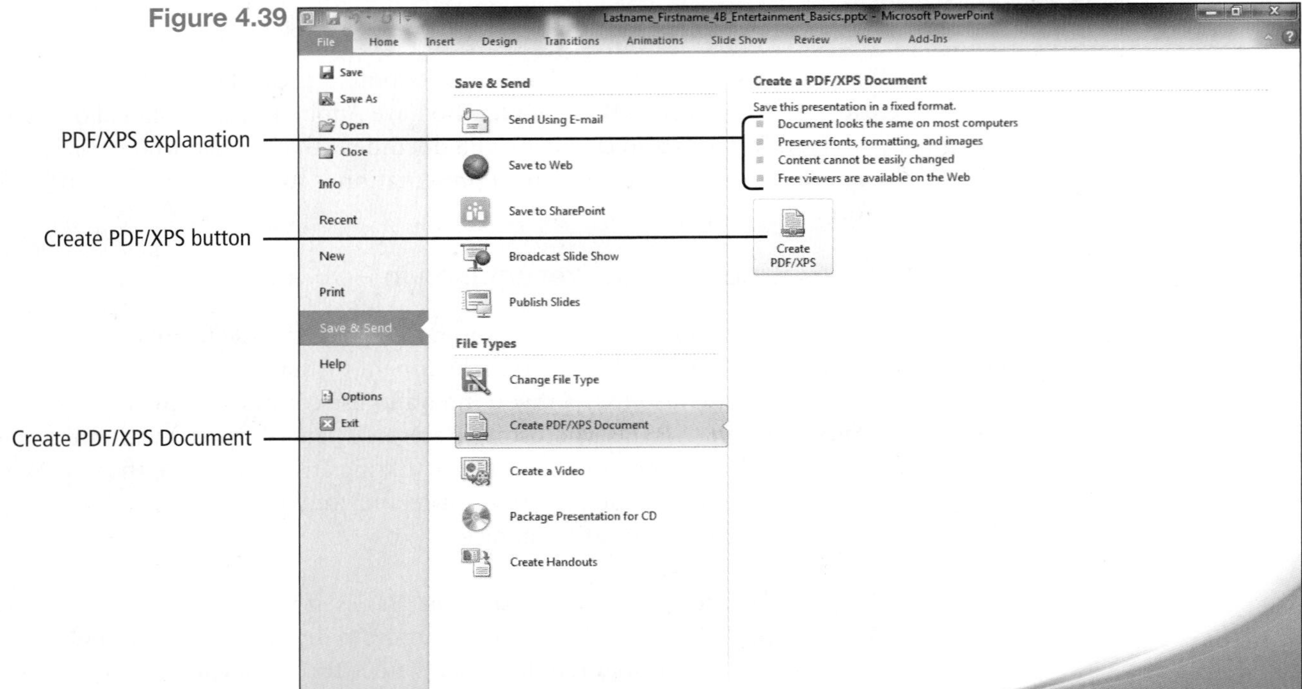

3 Click the **Create PDF/XPS** button. Click the **Save as type arrow** to see the two file formats—PDF (*.pdf) and XPS Document (*.xps). Click **PDF(*.pdf)**. If necessary, click the check boxes for **Open file after publishing** and **Standard (publishing online and printing)** to open the file after saving and to select the print quality. Compare your screen with Figure 4.40.

Opening a file after publishing allows you to see the document in the chosen format. Choose Standard (publishing online and printing) if the presentation requires high print quality. If the file size is more important than the print quality, click Minimum size (publishing online).

Figure 4.40

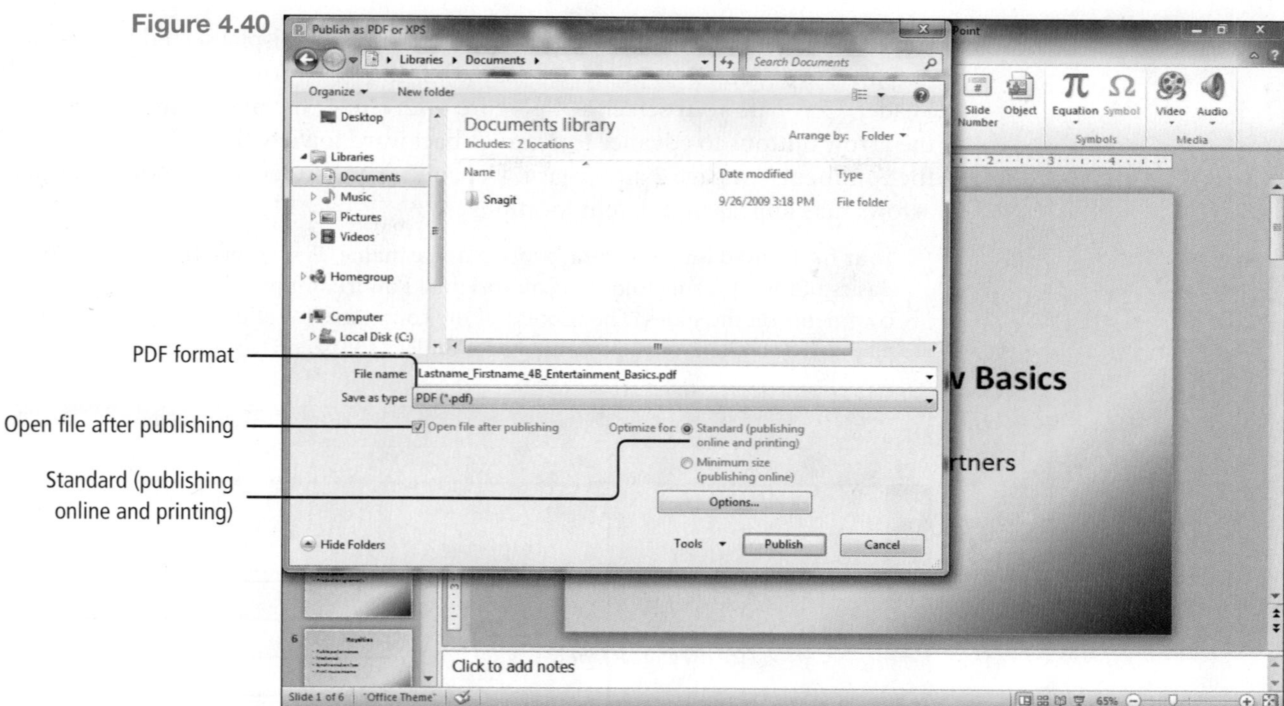

4 On the **Publish as PDF or XPS** window, click the **Options** button located just below the Standard and Minimum size choices. In the **Options** dialog box under **Publish options**, click **Include comments and ink markup**.

The options to publish a presentation to a PDF file are the same as the options to print the file.

Another Way

Enter the page number in the text box to change pages in the PDF.

5 Click the **Publish what arrow** to see the choices—Slides, Handouts, Notes pages, and Outline view. Click **Handouts**, and then click the **Slides per page arrow**. Click **3**, and then view the preview showing how the printed page will look. Compare your screen with Figure 4.41.

Figure 4.41

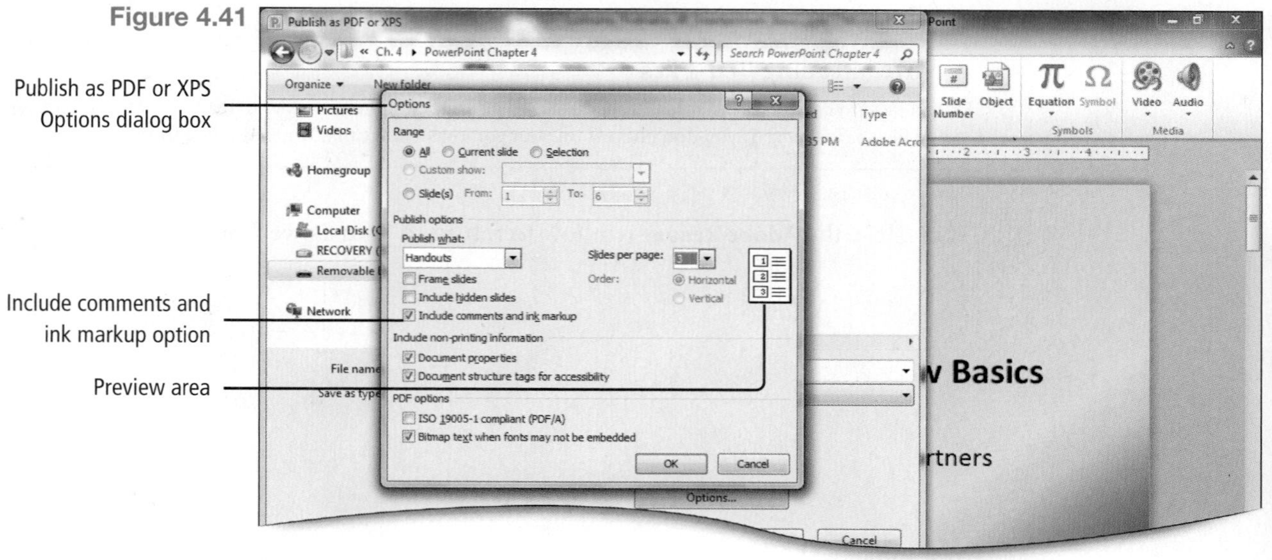

6 Click **OK**. Click **Publish**. If a license agreement message displays, read it, and then click **Accept**. The document is published (saved) in the PDF format and opens in Adobe Reader. Compare your screen with Figure 4.42. Under the **menu bar** at the top, click the arrow buttons to advance forward or backward to view the slides. Be sure to view the comments on page 2 and page 4. Depending on the version of Adobe Reader, the arrows may appear in different locations.

Your file is saved on your storage media as Lastname_Firstname_4B_Entertainment_Basics.pdf in the same folder as your original PowerPoint presentation file. Notice the comments on the slides. The content of the comments for Slides 1-3 (page 1) appear on page 2. The content of the comments for Slides 4-6 (page 3) appear on page 4.

Figure 4.42

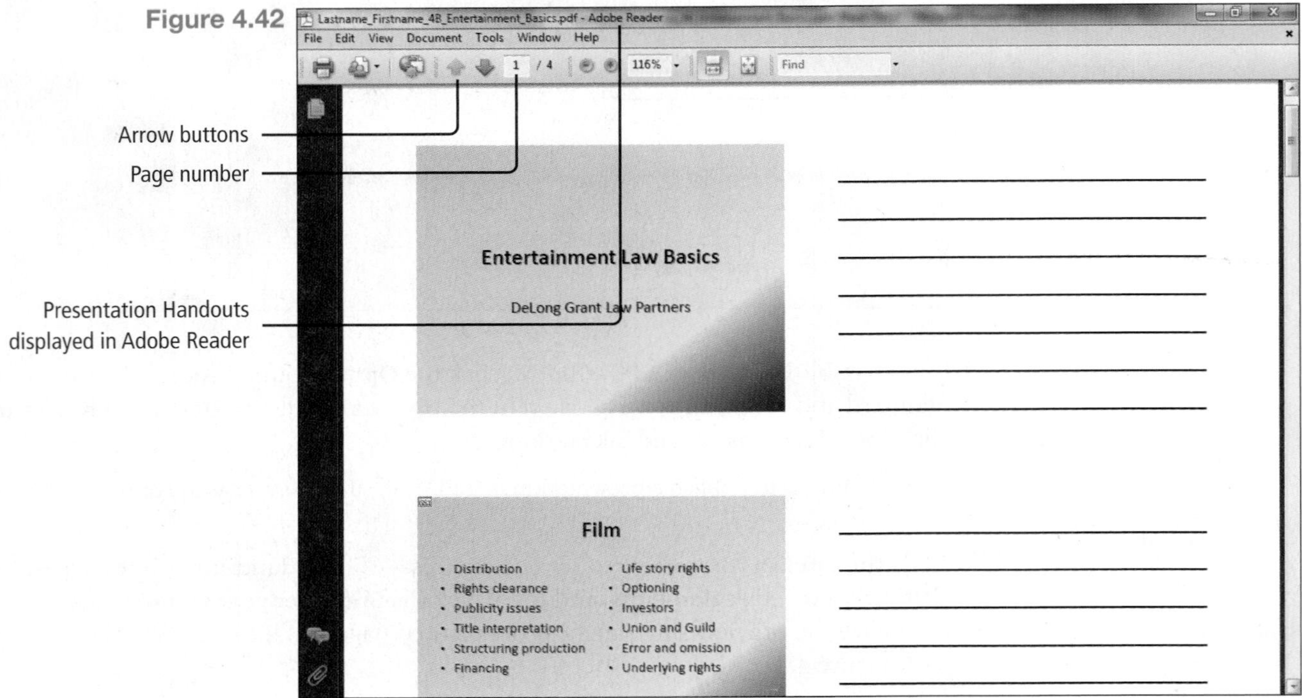

Note | Reading PDF Files

You need to have Adobe Acrobat Reader installed on your computer in order to read PDF files. Most people have the Reader installed. If you don't have it on your computer, you can download it free from www.adobe.com.

7 Close the **Adobe Reader** window to return to your PowerPoint presentation window.

8 Display **Backstage** view. Click **Save & Send**, and then click **Create PDF/XPS Document**. Click the **Create PDF/XPS** button. Change the file type to **XPS Document (*.xps)**. Click the **Options** button, and then click **Include comments and ink markup**. Click the **Publish what arrow**, and then click **Handouts**. Click **OK**, and then click **Publish**. The presentation is saved as an XPS document and opens in the XPS Viewer. Maximize your window if necessary. The menu bar on the XPS Viewer provides options to set permissions and digitally sign a document. Scroll to the bottom of page 1 so you can also see page 2. Compare your screen with Figure 4.43.

The handouts are displayed 6 slides per page. The comment numbers are displayed on the slides, and the comment content is displayed on the second page. Your file is saved on your storage media as Lastname_Firstname_4B_Entertainment_Basics.xps in the same folder as your original PowerPoint presentation file. You can only view XPS documents with an XPS Viewer, such as the one provided in Microsoft Windows. You can also download a free copy of the Viewer at www.microsoft.com. Only presentations formatted in PowerPoint 2000 or later versions can be saved and viewed in the Viewer.

Figure 4.43

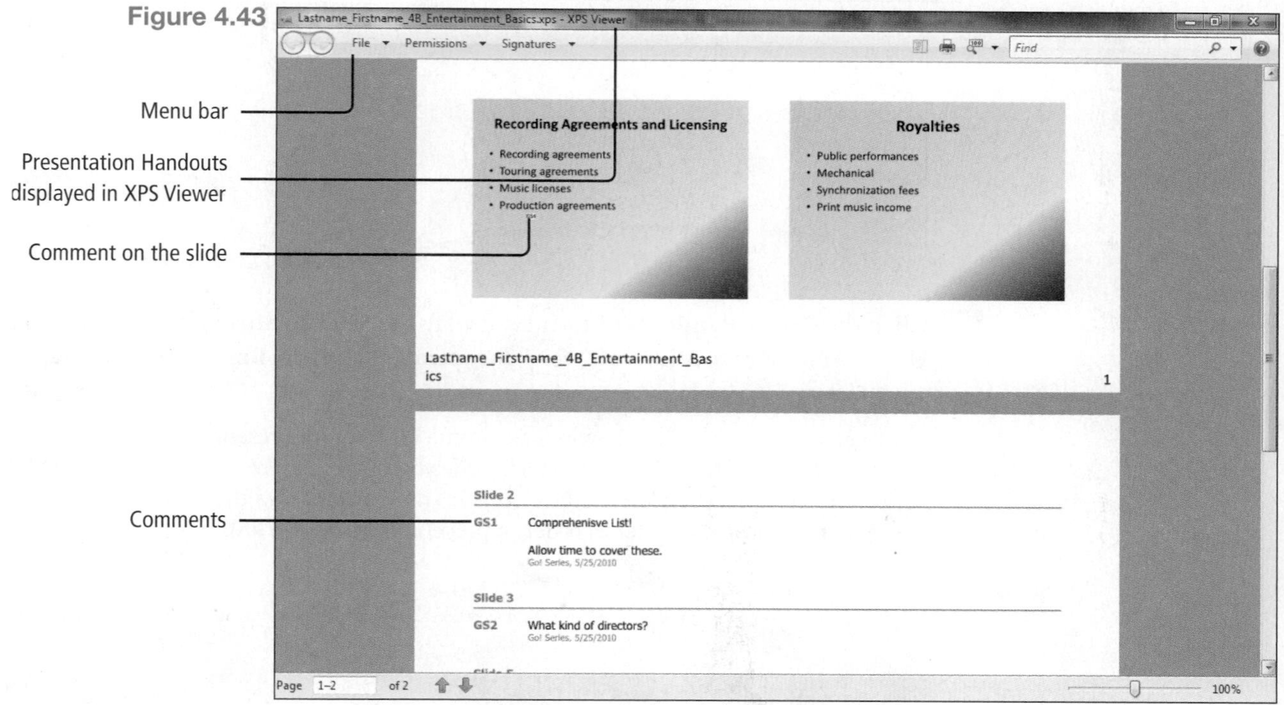

> **Another Way**
> To close the file and the viewer, press Alt + F4.

9 Click **File**, and then click **Exit** to close the XPS file and viewer.

Activity 4.14 | Creating Handouts in Microsoft Word

In this activity, you will create handouts that open in Microsoft Word.

1 Display **Backstage** view. Click **Save & Send**. Under **File Types**, click **Create Handouts**. At the right, under **Create Handouts in Microsoft Word**, read the explanation. Compare your screen with Figure 4.44.

The handouts are a document that contains the slides and notes from the presentation. You can use Word to change the layout and format and even add additional content to the handouts. If you link the handout file to your presentation, changes in your presentation will automatically update the handout content.

Figure 4.44

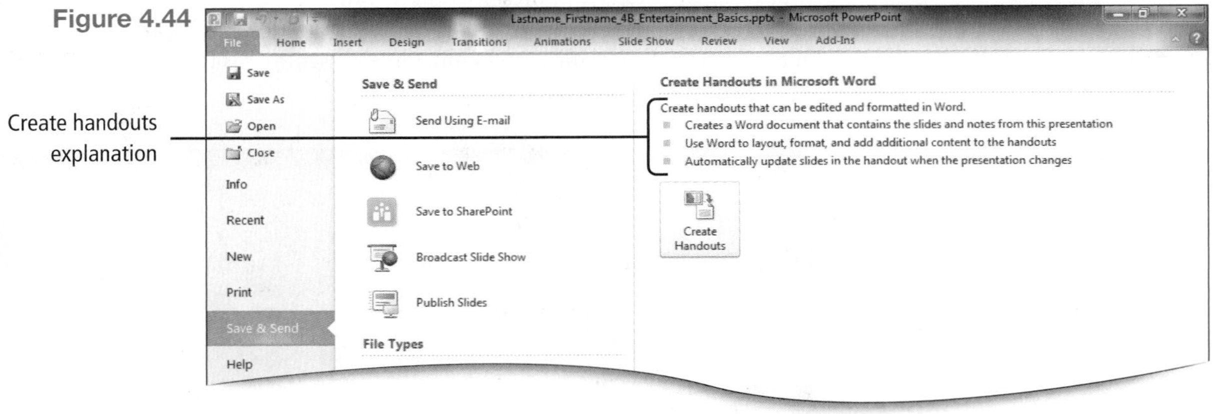

Create handouts explanation

Create Handouts in Microsoft Word

Create handouts that can be edited and formatted in Word.

- Creates a Word document that contains the slides and notes from this presentation
- Use Word to layout, format, and add additional content to the handouts
- Automatically update slides in the handout when the presentation changes

2 Click the **Create Handouts** button to display the **Send To Microsoft Word** dialog box. Under **Add slides to Microsoft Word document**, click **Paste link**. Compare your screen with Figure 4.45.

To ensure that any changes you make to the PowerPoint presentation are reflected in the Word document, use Paste link. Each time you open the Word document, you will be prompted to accept or reject the changes. The Word file and the PowerPoint file must remain in the same folder in order to prevent breaking the link.

Figure 4.45

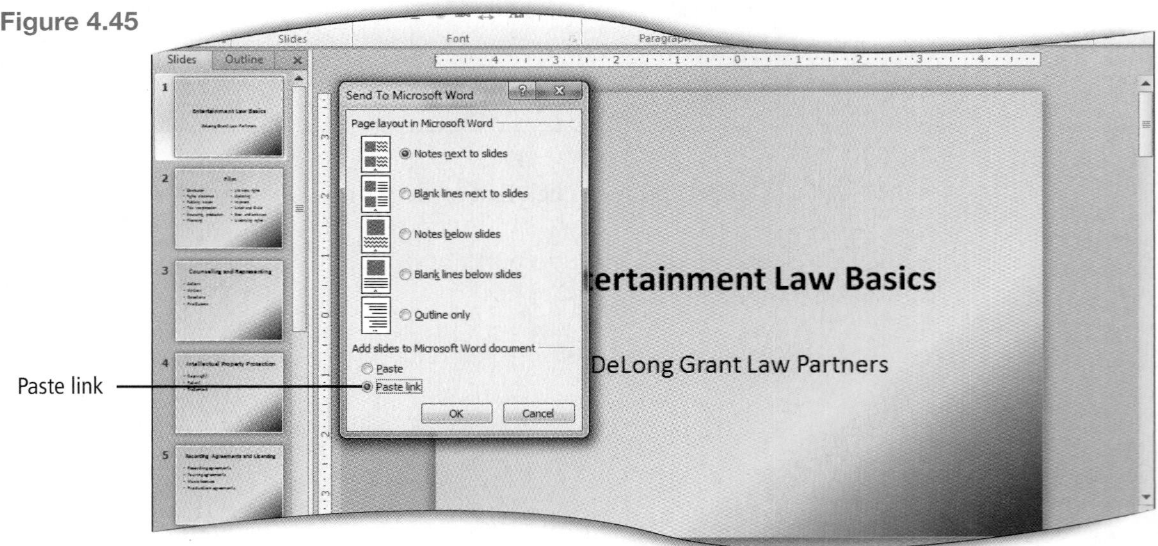

3 Click **OK**. Click **Word** on the taskbar to see the presentation slides displayed in a new Word document. Compare your screen with Figure 4.46.

Figure 4.46

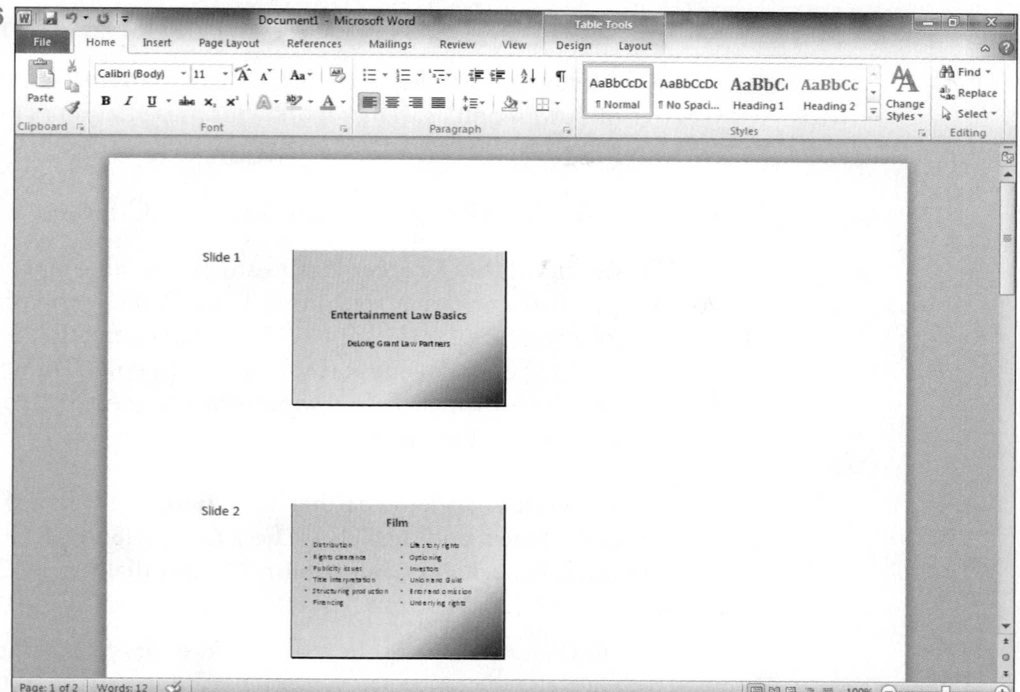

4 In the **Word document**, click the **Insert tab**. In the **Header & Footer group**, click the **Footer** button, and then click **Edit Footer**. At the left, type **Lastname_Firstname_4B_Entertainment_Basics** Press the Tab key two times, and then type the current date. On the **Design tab**, in the **Close group**, click **Close Header and Footer.**

5 Display **Backstage** view, and then click **Save As**. Navigate to the location where you are saving your work, and then save the Word file as **Lastname_Firstname_4B_Entertainment_Basics** **Close** the Word document and return to the presentation file.

6 Display **Backstage** view, click **Properties**, and then click **Show Document Panel.** Replace the text in the **Author** box with your own first and last name; in the **Subject** box, type your course name and section number; and then in the **Keywords** box, type **mission, agreements, licensing, film, royalties** **Close** the **Document Information Panel.**

7 **Save** the presentation.

PowerPoint | Chapter 4

Objective 5 | Protect a Presentation

In the following activities, you will check the compatibility of your file with previous versions of PowerPoint as well as mark your presentation as final and then save it as read-only.

Activity 4.15 | Using the Compatibility Checker

The ***Compatibility Checker*** locates any potential compatibility issues between PowerPoint 2010 and earlier versions of PowerPoint. It will prepare a report to help you resolve any issues. PowerPoint 2010 files are compatible with 2007 files; however, PowerPoint 2010 does not support saving files to PowerPoint 95 or earlier. If necessary, you can save the presentation in ***compatibility mode***, which means to save it as a PowerPoint 97-2003 Presentation.

1 Display **Backstage** view, and then click **Info**. To the left of **Prepare for Sharing**, click **Check for Issues**, and then click **Check Compatibility**. Read the report displayed in the **Microsoft PowerPoint Compatibility Checker** dialog box. Compare your screen with Figure 4.47.

The Compatibility Checker summary identifies parts of the presentation that cannot be edited in earlier versions because those features are not available.

Figure 4.47

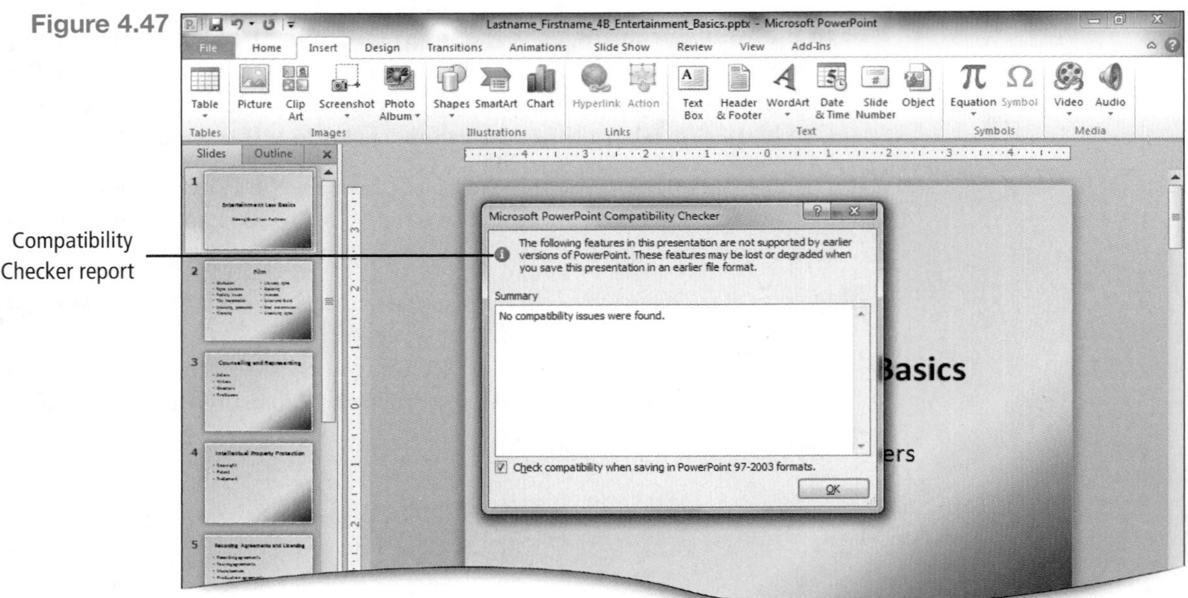

2 Click **OK**.

> **More Knowledge | Saving Presentations in Other File Formats**
>
> If you exchange PowerPoint presentations with other people, you may save the presentation in different formats. Display Backstage view, click Save & Send, click Change File Type, and then you may change the file type to PowerPoint 97-2003 Presentation. Other options include PowerPoint Show and PowerPoint Picture Presentation.

Activity 4.16 | Marking a Presentation as Final

In this activity, you will use the ***Mark as Final*** command to make your presentation document read-only in order to prevent changes to the document. Additionally, the Status property of the document is set to Final.

1 Display **Backstage** view, and then click **Info**. To the left of **Permissions**, click **Protect Presentation**. Notice that the current Permissions are: *Anyone can open, copy, and change any part of this presentation*. Examine the Protect Presentation options. Compare your screen with Figure 4.48.

The options to protect a presentation are Mark as Final, Encrypt with Password, Restrict Permission by People, and Add a Digital Signature.

Figure 4.48

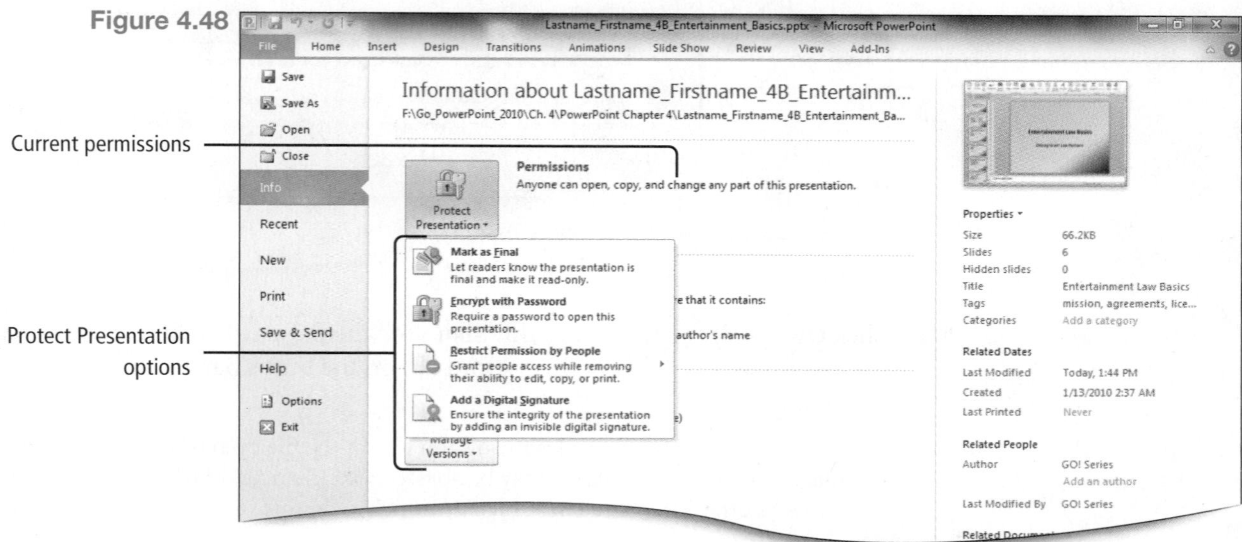

2 Click **Mark as Final**. Notice the message that the presentation will be marked as final and then saved. Compare your screen with Figure 4.49.

The Mark as Final command helps prevent reviewers or readers from accidentally making changes to the document. Because the Mark as Final command is not a security feature, anyone who receives an electronic copy of a document that has been marked as final can edit that document by removing Mark as Final status from the document.

Figure 4.49

3 Click **OK**. A message displays that reminds you that the document will be saved as final. The message also tells you that a **Mark As Final** icon will display in the status bar. Compare your screen with Figure 4.50.

Figure 4.50

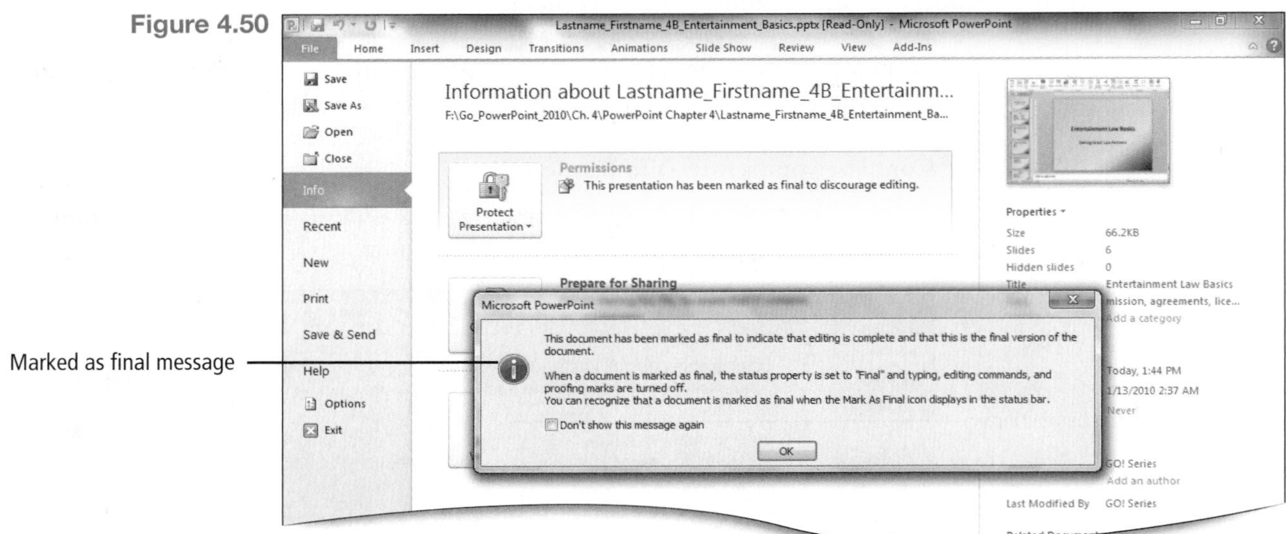

4 Click **OK**. Click the **Home tab**, and then note the information bar at the top and the **Marked as Final** icon at the bottom left on the status bar. Compare your screen with Figure 4.51.

The information bar provides the option to edit the file even though you marked it as final, so be aware that others may be able to make changes. Marking the presentation as final tells others that you encourage them not to do this.

Figure 4.51

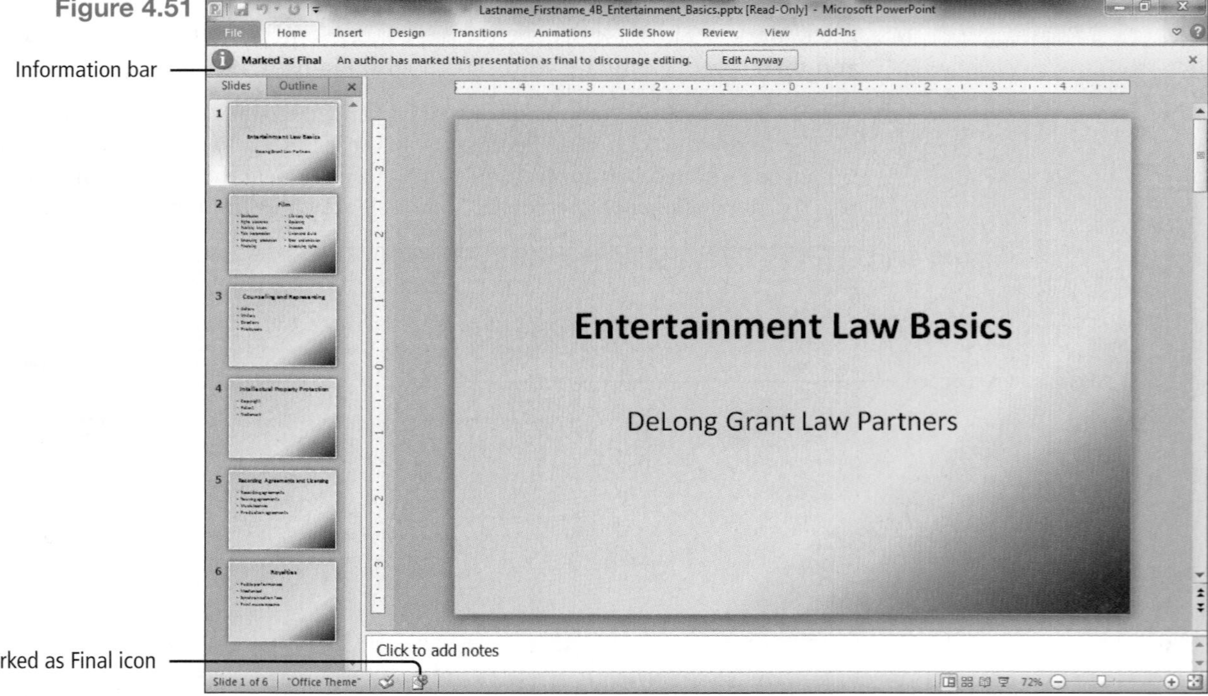

5 On the information bar, click the **Edit Anyway** button.

You are free to make changes to the document.

6 **Save** your presentation. Display **Backstage** view, click **Print**, and then under **Slides**, click the **Full Page Slides button arrow** to display the **Print Layout** dialog box. Click **Handouts 3 Slides**. Display the Print Layout dialog box again, if necessary, and then check **Print Comments and Ink Markup**. Print the slides. If requested, submit your presentation electronically as directed by your instructor instead of printing.

7 **Close** the presentation, and then **Exit** PowerPoint.

End
You have completed Project 4B

Content-Based Assessments

Summary

In this chapter, you designed a PowerPoint template containing formats, shapes, and images on the master pages. You then created a presentation based on this template and entered the text for a meeting. You edited Handout and Notes Masters. You added comments into the presentation and practiced navigating through the presentation to read, edit, and delete comments. You prepared a presentation for distribution by publishing it in PDF and XPS formats. You created PowerPoint handouts in Microsoft Word and linked the Word content to the presentation file so any updates in the presentation file will be reflected in the Word file. You checked the compatibility of the file with other versions of PowerPoint and marked your presentation as Final to discourage anyone from changing your file.

Key Terms

Matching

Match each term in the second column with its correct definition in the first column by writing the letter of the term on the blank line in front of the correct definition.

____ 1. A person who inserts comments into a presentation to provide feedback.
____ 2. A predefined layout for a group of slides saved as a .potx file.
____ 3. File extension for a PowerPoint presentation.
____ 4. Includes the specifications for the design of presentation handouts.
____ 5. A note that you can attach to a letter or word on a slide or to an entire slide.
____ 6. File extension for a PowerPoint template.
____ 7. Contains templates that you have saved on your computer in the default template folder.
____ 8. A universal file format commonly associated with Microsoft Viewer.
____ 9. Contains various slide master layouts.
____ 10. A universal file format commonly associated with Adobe Reader.
____ 11. A specific slide master that contains the design, such as the background, that displays on all slide layouts in the presentation.
____ 12. Displays a logo on every slide that uses a title and only one column of bullet items.
____ 13. Makes a presentation file read-only and discourages others from making changes to it.
____ 14. Identifies features that potentially are not supported by earlier versions of PowerPoint.
____ 15. Contains templates that you have saved in your chapter folder.

A Comment
B Compatibility Checker
C Handout Master
D Mark as Final
E My templates
F New from existing
G Office Theme Slide Master
H Portable Document Format (PDF)
I Reviewer
J Slide Master
K Template
L Title and Content Layout Slide Master
M XML Paper Specification (XPS)
N .potx
O .pptx

Content-Based Assessments

Multiple Choice

Circle the correct answer.

1. To ensure that a PowerPoint presentation can be viewed as a slide show on computers using earlier versions of PowerPoint, save the presentation in:
   A. compatibility mode **B.** Word handouts **C.** read-only format

2. To avoid having to use the same color and design of bullets on every slide in a presentation, make the changes on the:
   A. Handout Master **B.** Slide Master **C.** Title slide

3. Apply a Background Style for all slide layouts in a template on the:
   A. Office Theme Slide Master **B.** Title slide layout **C.** Title slide in normal view

4. The file extension for a PowerPoint 2010 template is:
   A. .pptx **B.** .pdf **C.** .potx

5. To make the background color vary smoothly from darker to lighter shades in more than one color combination, set a gradient:
   A. fill **B.** stop **C.** shape

6. Unless changed, the default location for saving templates is the:
   A. computer hard drive **B.** online server **C.** portable storage device

7. To change the content of a comment, click the ______ button.
   A. New Comment **B.** Review **C.** Edit Comment

8. To apply a template that is saved on your portable storage, in which location under Available Templates and Themes will you find it?
   A. New from existing **B.** My templates **C.** Sample templates

9. When dragging a placeholder up or down, what key should you use to prevent the placeholder from moving to the left or right?
   A. Ctrl **B.** Shift **C.** Alt

10. You can print the comments in a presentation by clicking which of these options?
    A. Print comments **B.** High quality **C.** Include comments and ink markup

Content-Based Assessments

Apply 4A skills from these Objectives:

1. Create a Custom Template by Modifying Slide Masters
2. Apply a Custom Template to a Presentation

Skills Review | Project 4C Night Owls

In the following Skills Review, you will create a template that DeLong Grant Law Partners will use to prepare presentations for the initial meeting with a client. You will use the template to create a presentation for the musical group Billy and the Night Owls. Your completed presentation will look similar to Figure 4.52.

Project Files

For Project 4C, you will need the following files:

New blank PowerPoint presentation
p04C_Contract.jpg

You will save your presentation as:

Lastname_Firstname_4C_Contract_Template.potx
Lastname_Firstname_4C_Night_Owls.pptx

Project Results

Performance Contract Basics

- A contract includes a:
  - Performance agreement outline.
  - Document of agreement.
- The contractee is the party for whom the performance service is provided.
- The contractor is the party that performs the service.

Cross Licensing

- Cross licensing is a legal agreement.
- Two or more parties may share rights to a performance.
- A royalty fee exchange may be included.
- Performance recording rights may be included.

Figure 4.52

(Project 4C Night Owls continues on the next page)

Skills Review | Project 4C Night Owls (continued)

1 **Start** PowerPoint to display a new blank presentation. Display **Backstage** view, and then click **Save As**. Click the **Save as type box arrow**, and then click **PowerPoint Template (*.potx)**. Navigate to the location where you are saving your work, and then save your file as **Lastname_Firstname_4C_Contract_Template**

2 Click the **View tab**. In the **Master Views group**, click the **Slide Master** button.

a. Click the first thumbnail—**Office Theme Slide Master**. In the **Background group**, click the **Background Styles** button. In the **Background Styles gallery**, select **Style 9**.

b. Click the second thumbnail—**Title Slide Layout**. Click the dashed border on the Master title style placeholder, and then change the font size to **48 point**.

3 Click the **Office Theme Slide Master** thumbnail.

a. On the **Slide Master tab**, in the **Background group**, click the **Background Styles** button, and then click **Format Background**. Under **Fill**, click **Gradient fill**. Click the **Type arrow**, and then click **Radial**.

b. Click the **Add gradient stop** button once, and then position the stop at **80%**.

c. Click the **Color arrow**, and then in the eighth column in the second row, click **Purple, Accent 4, Lighter 80%**.

d. Click **Apply to All**. Click **Close.**

4 Click the **Title Slide Layout** thumbnail.

a. Click the **View tab**. In the **Show group**, click the **Ruler** checkbox to display the horizontal and vertical rulers (if necessary).

b. Click the **Insert tab**. In the **Illustrations group**, click the **Shapes** button. Under **Basic Shapes**, click the **Diamond** shape. At **2 inches on the right side of the horizontal ruler** and **3 inches on the upper half of the vertical ruler**, click to insert the shape.

c. On the Ribbon, under **Drawing Tools**, click the **Format tab**. In the **Shapes Styles group**, click the **Shape Effects** button, click **Preset**, and then click **Preset 2**. In the **Shapes Styles group**, click the **Shape Outline button arrow**, and then click **No Outline**.

d. With the diamond still selected, in the **Size group**, change the **Shape Height** to **1.5"** and the **Shape Width** to **1.5"**.

e. In the **Shape Styles group**, click the **Shape Fill** button, and then click **Picture**. Navigate to the location where your data files are stored and select **p04C_Contract.jpg**. Click the **Insert** button.

f. With the shape still selected, in the **Arrange group**, click the **Align** button. Click **Align Center**. Click the **Align button** again, and then click **Align Bottom**.

g. On the Ribbon, under **Picture Tools**, click the **Format tab**. In the **Adjust Group**, click the **Color** button. Under **Recolor**, click **Purple, Accent color 4 Dark**.

h. With the shape still selected, on the **Home tab**, in the **Clipboard group**, click the **Copy** button. Click the **Title and Content Layout** thumbnail. In the **Clipboard group**, click the **Paste** button.

i. Under the **Drawing Tools**, click the **Format tab**. In the **Size group**, change the **Shape Height** to **1"** and the **Shape Width** to **1"**.

j. With the shape still selected, press the Shift key, and then click the content placeholder. In the **Arrange group**, click the **Align** button, and then select **Align Right**. Click the **Align** button, and then select **Align Top**.

5 Click the **Title Slide** thumbnail.

a. Press the Shift key, and then drag the Master title placeholder up so the top aligns at **2.5 inches on the upper half of the vertical ruler**. Click outside the placeholder. Press the Shift key, and then drag the Master subtitle placeholder up so the top aligns with **.5 inch mark on the upper half of the vertical ruler**.

b. With the subtitle placeholder still selected, drag the bottom middle sizing handle to **1 inch on the lower half of the vertical ruler**.

c. Click the shape, and then drag the entire shape so the top aligns with **1.5 inches on the lower half of the vertical ruler**. Under **Drawing Tools**, on the **Format tab**, in the **Arrange group**, click the **Align** button, and then click **Align Center**.

6 Click the **Title and Content** thumbnail.

a. Click anywhere in the first bulleted line. Click the **Home tab**. In the **Paragraph group**, click the **Bullets button arrow**, and then click **Bullets and Numbering**. In the **Bullets and Numbering** dialog box, click the **Bulleted tab** if necessary. Click **Star Bullets**. Then click the **Color button arrow**. Under **Standard Colors**, click **Purple**. Click **OK**.

b. Click anywhere in the second bulleted line. Display the **Bullets and Numbering** dialog box. Click the

(Project 4C Night Owls continues on the next page)

Skills Review | Project 4C Night Owls (continued)

Filled Square Bullets. Click the **Color button arrow**. Under **Standard Colors**, click **Purple**. Click **OK**.

7 Click the first thumbnail, the **Office Theme Slide Master**.

a. At the bottom left on the **Office Theme Slide**, click anywhere on the dashed border of the date placeholder.

b. Click the **Home tab**, and then change the **font size** to **10**.

c. Click the **Slide Master tab**. In the **Close group**, click the **Close Master View** button.

8 On the **Insert tab**, in the **Text group**, click the **Header & Footer** button to display the **Header and Footer** dialog box. Click the **Notes and Handouts tab**. Under **Include on page**, select the **Date and time** check box, and then select **Fixed**. If necessary, clear the **Header** check box, and then select the **Page number** and **Footer** check boxes. In the **Footer** box, using your own name, type **Lastname_Firstname_4C_Contract_Template** and then click **Apply to All**.

9 Display **Backstage** view, click **Properties**, and then click **Show Document Panel**. Replace the text in the **Author** box with your own first and last name; in the **Subject** box, type your course name and section number; and then in the **Keywords** box, type **template Close** the **Document Information Panel**.

10 Print **Handouts 4 Slides Horizontal**, or submit your presentation electronically as directed by your instructor.

11 **Save** the template. **Close** the template.

12 Display **Backstage** view, click **New**, and then click **New from existing**.

a. Navigate to the location where you are saving your files. Click **Lastname_Firstname_4C_Contract_Template.potx** and then click **Create New**.

b. Save the file as **Lastname_Firstname_4C_Night_Owls** in your storage location.

13 Click **Slide 1**. In the title placeholder, type **Billy and the Night Owls** In the subtitle placeholder, type **DeLong Grant Law Partners**

a. On the **Home tab**, in the **Slides group**, click the **New Slide button arrow**, and then click **Title and Content**.

b. In the title placeholder, type **Performance Contract Basics**

c. In the content placeholder, type the following bulleted items, using the **Increase and Decrease List Level** buttons as needed:

A contract includes a:

Performance agreement outline.

Document of agreement.

The contractee is the party for whom the performance service is provided.

The contractor is the party that performs the service.

14 In the **Slides group**, click the **New Slide button arrow**, and then click **Title and Content** to add a third slide.

a. In the title placeholder, type **Cross Licensing** and then press Ctrl + Enter.

b. Type the following bulleted items in the content placeholder:

Cross licensing is a legal agreement.

Two or more parties may share rights to a performance.

A royalty fee exchange may be included.

Performance recording rights may be included.

15 **Save** your presentation.

16 Click the **View tab**. In the **Master Views group**, click **Handout Master**. In the **Page Setup group**, click the **Slides Per Page** button. Click **3 Slides**.

17 Click the **View tab**. In the **Master Views group**, click **Notes Master**. In the **Placeholders group**, remove the **Body**.

18 In the **Close group**, click **Close Master View**.

19 On the **Insert tab**, in the **Text group**, click the **Header & Footer** button to display the **Header and Footer** dialog box. Click the **Notes and Handouts tab**. In the **Footer** box, change the name to: **Lastname_Firstname_4C_Night_Owls** and then click **Apply to All**.

20 Display **Backstage** view, click **Properties**, and then click **Show Document Panel**. Replace the text in the **Author** box with your own first and last name. In the **Keywords** box, remove the existing content, and then type **cross licensing, royalty, rights Close** the **Document Information Panel**.

21 Print **Handouts 4 Slides Horizontal**, or submit your presentation electronically as directed by your instructor.

22 **Save** the presentation. **Exit** PowerPoint.

End You have completed Project 4C

Content-Based Assessments

Apply 4B skills from these Objectives:

3 Create and Edit Comments

4 Prepare a Presentation for Distribution

5 Protect a Presentation

Skills Review | Project 4D Nagursky Taxes

In the following Skills Review, you will modify a presentation created by DeLong Grant Law Partners as a brief overview of taxation issues to present to Finley Nagursky, who is a professional football player. You will add comments to the presentation, prepare the document for distribution, and then protect it. Your completed presentation will look similar to Figure 4.53.

Project Files

For Project 4D, you will need the following file:

p04D_Athlete_Taxes.pptx

You will save your presentation as:

Lastname_Firstname_4D_Nagursky_Taxes.pptx
Lastname_Firstname_4D_Nagursky_Taxes.pdf
Lastname_Firstname_4D_Nagursky_Taxes.xps

Project Results

Taxation Issues for Athletes

DeLong Grant Law Partners

GS1

Direct Taxes

- Definition
  - Levied directly on athletes
- Examples
  - Performance income tax
  - Athletic property tax

Indirect Taxes

- Definition
  - Tax imposed on performance rights
  - Tax on athletic property
- Examples
  - Personal property tax
  - Sales tax on commission income GS2
  - Value-added tax on half-time entertainment

Jock Tax

- Definition
  - Income tax imposed on visitors who earn money in other cities or states
  - Targeted are wealthy, high-profile professional athletes
- Examples
  - Tax on earned income per state/venue
  - Tax on paid public appearances
  - Deductions for charity appearances

Figure 4.53

(Project 4D Nagursky Taxes continues on the next page)

Skills Review | Project 4D Nagursky Taxes (continued)

1 **Start** PowerPoint. Locate and open the file **p04D_Athlete_Taxes.pptx**. Navigate to the location where you are storing your folders and projects for this chapter, and then **Save** the file as **Lastname_Firstname_4D_Nagursky_Taxes**

2 Make **Slide 2** the active slide. Click the **Review tab**. In the **Comments group**, click the **New Comment** button. In the space provided, type **It would be a good idea to add a couple more examples.**

3 Make **Slide 3** the active slide. Click at the end of the bulleted item that ends with *commission income*. In the **Comments group**, click **New Comment**. Type **I am glad you added this one.** Click outside the comment to close it.

4 Make **Slide 4** the active slide. In the last bulleted item, select the word *Deductions*. Use the procedure explained in the previous steps to add this comment: **Is this clear enough for the client to understand?** Click outside the comment to close it.

5 Make **Slide 2** the active slide. At the upper left corner of the slide, click the **Comment**. In the **Comments group**, click the **Edit Comment** button and notice the insertion point at the end of the text.

6 Press Enter two times, and then type **Ask sports agents for more examples.**

7 Click the **Next** button until you reach the comment on **Slide 3**. In the **Comments group**, click **Delete** to remove this comment.

8 On the **Insert tab**, in the **Text group**, click the **Header & Footer** button to display the **Header and Footer** dialog box. Click the **Notes and Handouts tab**. Under **Include on page**, select the **Date and time** check box, and then select **Fixed**. If necessary, clear the **Header** check box, and then select the **Page number** and **Footer** check boxes. In the **Footer** box, using your own name, type **Lastname_Firstname_4D_Nagursky_Taxes** and then click **Apply to All**.

9 Display **Backstage** view, click **Properties**, and then click **Show Document Panel**. Replace the text in the **Author** box with your own first and last name. In the **Subject** box, type your course name and section number, and then in the **Keywords** box, type **direct taxes, jock tax, indirect taxes Close** the **Document Information Panel**.

10 Print **Handouts 4 Slides Horizontal**, or submit your presentation electronically as directed by your instructor.

11 Display **Backstage** view, and then click **Save & Send**. Under **File Types**, click **Create PDF/XPS Document**.

- **a.** Click **Create PDF/XPS**. Click the **Save as type**, and then click **PDF(*.pdf)**. If necessary, click the check boxes for **Open file after publishing** and **Standard (publishing online and printing)**.
- **b.** Click the **Options** button. Click the **Publish what arrow**, and then select **Handouts**. Click the **Slides per page arrow**, and then select **4**. Click the check box for **Include comments and ink markup**. Click **OK**.
- **c.** Click **Publish**. In Adobe Reader, scroll through the slides to see the comments on page 2.
- **d.** **Close** the Adobe Reader window to return to your PowerPoint presentation window.

12 Display **Backstage** view, Click **Save & Send**, and then click **Create PDF/XPS Document**.

- **a.** Click **Create PDF/XPS**. Change the file type to **XPS Document (*.xps)**.
- **b.** Click the **Options** button. Click the **Publish what arrow**, and then select **Handouts**. Click the **Slides per page arrow**, and then select **4**. Click the check box for **Include comments and ink markup**. Click **OK**.
- **c.** Click **Publish**. In the XPS Viewer, scroll through the slides to see the comments on page 2.
- **d.** Close the XPS file and viewer.

13 Display **Backstage** view, click **Info**. Click **Protect Presentation**, and then select **Mark as Final**.

14 **Exit** PowerPoint.

15 Submit the printed work for:

Lastname_Firstname_4D_Nagursky_Taxes.pptx
Lastname_Firstname_4D_Nagursky_Taxes.pdf
Lastname_Firstname_4D_Nagursky_Taxes.xps

or submit your presentations electronically as directed by your instructor.

End **You have completed Project 4D**

Content-Based Assessments

Apply 4A skills from these Objectives:

1. Create a Custom Template by Modifying Slide Masters
2. Apply a Custom Template to a Presentation

Mastering PowerPoint | Project 4E Sports Law

In the following Mastering PowerPoint project, you will edit a presentation you already prepared to explain the aspects of Title IX in Collegiate Sports Law and then save it as a template. You will use the template to personalize it for a presentation to Hugh Appleton, who is a college athletic director. Your completed presentation will look similar to Figure 4.54.

Project Files

For Project 4E, you will need the following files:

p04E_Sports_Law.pptx
p04E_Sports1.jpg

You will save your presentation as:

Lastname_Firstname_4E_Sports_Template.potx
Lastname_Firstname_4E_Sports_Law.pptx

Project Results

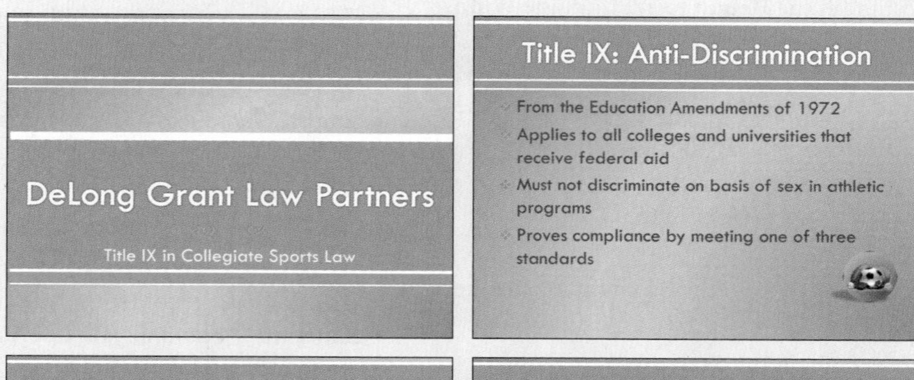

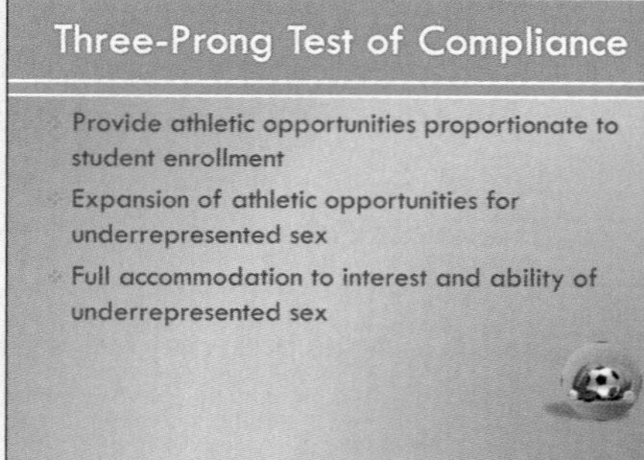

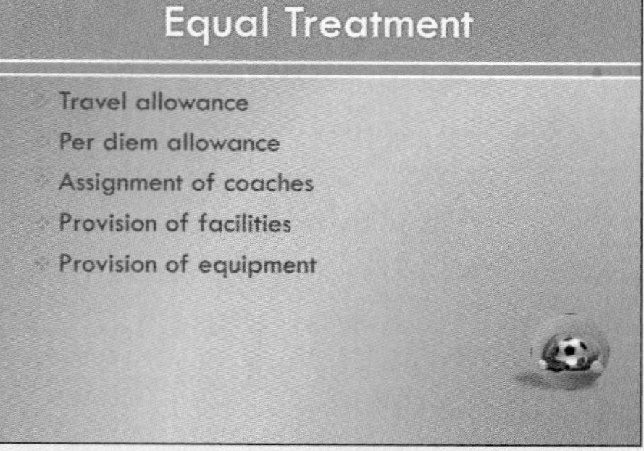

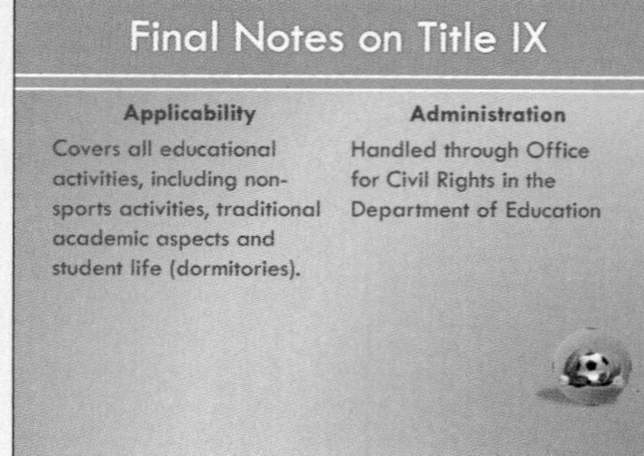

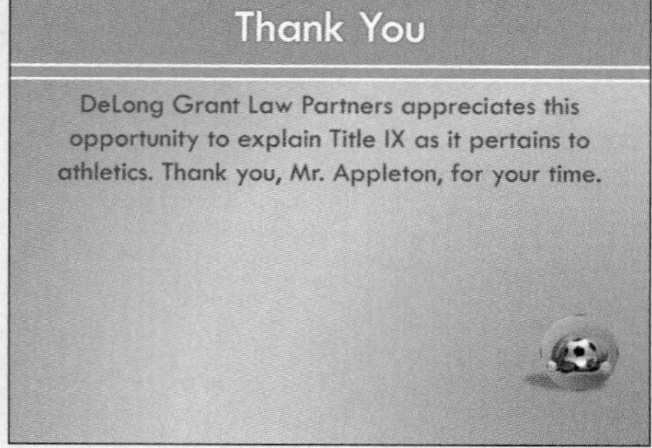

Figure 4.54

(Project 4E Sports Law continues on the next page)

Mastering PowerPoint | Project 4E Sports Law (continued)

1 **Start** PowerPoint. Locate and open the file **p04E_Sports_Law.pptx**. Save the file as a **PowerPoint Template** in your chapter folder, using the file name **Lastname_Firstname_4E_Sports_Template**

2 Edit the **Office Theme Slide Master**. In the **Edit Theme group**, in the **Themes group**, under **From Office.com**, use the **Decatur** theme. Within that theme, use the **Median** theme font. Apply Background **Style 6**. Format the background with a **Radial Gradient fill**, and then apply it to all slides. On the first bulleted item, change the font size to **32**.

3 On the **Title Slide Layout** thumbnail, change the Master title style placeholder **font size** to **60 pts**. Change the Master subtitle style placeholder **font size** to **32 pts**.

4 On the **Title and Content Layout** thumbnail, insert an **Oval** shape and set the **Height** to **1.2"** and the **Width** to **1.2"**. Apply a **Shadow Shape Effect** of **Perspective Diagonal Upper Left**. Fill the shape with **p04E_Sports1 .jpg**. Remove the **Shape Outline**, and then position the shape at the bottom right corner of the content placeholder.

5 Copy the shape to the **Two Content Layout** thumbnail.

6 Remove the Header from the **Handout Master**, and then close the Master View.

7 On the **Insert tab**, in the **Text group**, click the **Header & Footer** button to display the **Header and Footer** dialog box. Click the **Notes and Handouts tab**. Under **Include on page**, select the **Date and time** check box, and then select **Fixed**. If necessary, clear the **Header** check box, and then select the **Page number** and **Footer** check boxes. In the **Footer** box, using your own name, type **Lastname_ Firstname_4E_Sports_Template** and then click **Apply to All**.

8 Revise the document properties. Replace the text in the **Author** box with your own first and last name. In the **Subject** box, type your course name and section number, and then in the **Keywords** box, type **Title IX, discrimination**

9 **Save** the template. Print **Handouts 6 Slides Horizontal**, or submit your presentation electronically as directed by your instructor.

10 **Close** the template.

11 Create a **new presentation** using your template. Save the file as **Lastname_Firstname_4E_Sports_Law** in your storage location.

12 On **Slide 5**, in the left column, remove the bullet, center *Applicability*, and then add bold. Repeat the formatting for *Administration* in the second column.

13 Add a **Title and Content** slide. In the title placeholder, type **Thank You** In the content placeholder, type **DeLong Grant Law Partners appreciates this opportunity to explain Title IX as it pertains to athletics. Thank you, Mr. Appleton, for your time.** Remove the bullet and center the text.

14 On the **Slide Master**, change the first-level bullets to **Star Bullets**. Close the Master View.

15 Change the footer on the handouts to include **Lastname_Firstname_4E_Sports_Law** and then click **Apply to All**.

16 Edit the document properties. Replace the text in the **Author** box with your own first and last name.

17 **Save** the presentation. Print **Handouts 6 Slides Horizontal**, or submit your presentation electronically as directed by your instructor.

18 **Close** the presentation.

End You have completed Project 4E

Content-Based Assessments

Apply **4B** skills from these Objectives:

- **3** Create and Edit Comments
- **4** Prepare a Presentation for Distribution
- **5** Protect a Presentation

Mastering PowerPoint | Project 4F Contract Aspects

In the following Mastering PowerPoint project, you will complete a presentation that covers various aspects of contracts in the entertainment industry, including royalties, minors, and advances. You will review the presentation and add comments before preparing it for distribution. Your completed presentation will look similar to Figure 4.55.

Project Files

For Project 4F, you will need the following file:

p04F_Contract_Aspects.pptx

You will save your presentation as:

Lastname_Firstname_4F_Contract_Aspects.pptx
Lastname_Firstname_4F_Contract_Aspects.pdf
Lastname_Firstname_4F_Contract_Aspects.xps

Project Results

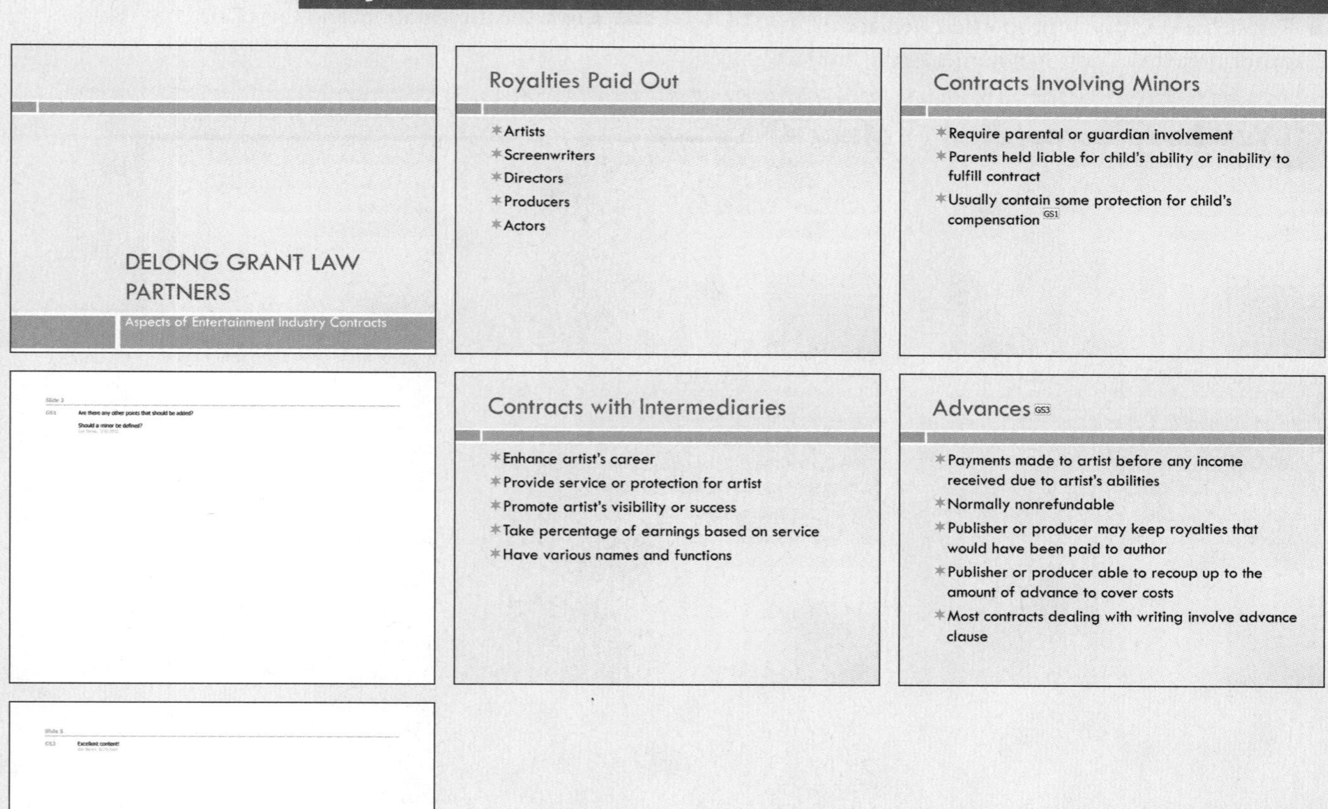

Figure 4.55

(Project 4F Contract Aspects continues on the next page)

Mastering PowerPoint | Project 4F Contract Aspects (continued)

1 **Start** PowerPoint. Locate and open the file **p04F_Contract_Aspects**. Save the file as **Lastname_Firstname_4F_Contract_Aspects**

2 Make **Slide 3** the active slide. At the end of the last bulleted item, insert a comment, and then type **Are there any other points that should be added?**

3 On **Slide 4**, select *Intermediaries*, and then add this comment: **I think this term needs to be defined.**

4 On **Slide 5**, add this comment: **Excellent content!** Drag the comment so it is positioned right after *Advances*.

5 Edit the comment on **Slide 3**. Press Enter two times, and then type **Should a minor be defined?**

6 Delete the comment on **Slide 4**.

7 Insert a footer on Notes and Handouts that includes the fixed date and time, page number, and file name.

8 Revise the document properties. Replace the text in the **Author** box with your own name. In the **Subject** box, type your course name and section number, and then in the **Keywords** box, type **entertainment, royalties, minors, advances**

9 **Save** the presentation.

10 **Save** the presentation as a **PDF** file. As you do, display the **Options** dialog box and specify **Include comments and ink markup**, **Handouts**, **6 slides per page**, and **Horizontal**.

11 **Print** the PDF file, or submit your presentation electronically as directed by your instructor

12 **Save** the presentation as an **XPS** file following the same instructions for saving the PDF file. **Print** the XPS file, or submit your presentation electronically as directed by your instructor.

13 Mark your presentation as **Final**, and then **Save**.

14 **Close** the presentation, and then **Exit** PowerPoint.

End **You have completed Project 4F**

Content-Based Assessments

Apply 4A and 4B skills from these Objectives:

1. Create a Custom Template by Modifying Slide Masters
2. Apply a Custom Template to a Presentation
3. Create and Edit Comments
4. Prepare a Presentation for Distribution
5. Protect a Presentation

Mastering PowerPoint | Project 4G Film Production

In the following Mastering PowerPoint project, you will open a presentation explaining the legal aspects of film production and modify the slide masters. Frequently, DeLong Grant Law Partners presents this information to college classes, so you will save the presentation as a template. Then you will create a presentation from the template and personalize it for the Film Production course at the local university. You will add some comments for other partners to see and save the presentation as a PDF file for the participants. Your completed presentation will look similar to Figure 4.56.

Project Files

For Project 4G, you will need the following file:

p04G_Film_Production.pptx

You will save your presentation as:

Lastname_Firstname_4G_Film_Template.potx
Lastname_Firstname_4G_Film_Production.pptx
Lastname_Firstname_4G_Film_Production.xps

Project Results

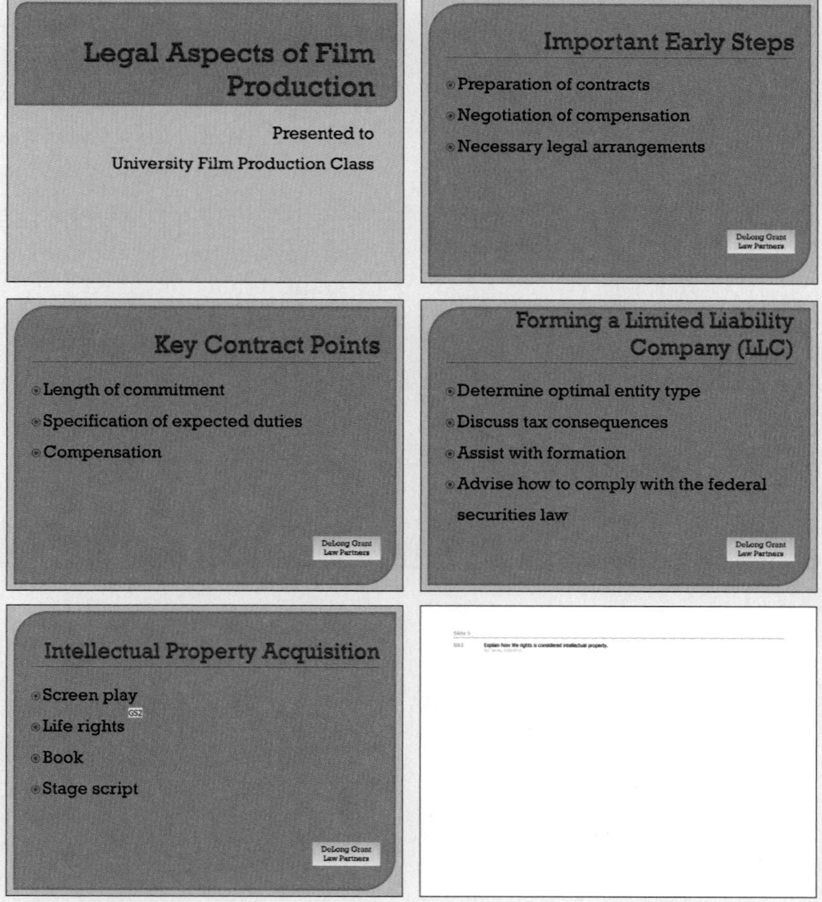

Figure 4.56

(Project 4G Film Production continues on the next page)

Mastering PowerPoint | Project 4G Film Production (continued)

1 **Start** PowerPoint. Locate and open the file **p04G_Film_Production.pptx**, and then save it as a template with the name **Lastname_Firstname_4G_Film_Template**

2 In the **Slide Master View**, click the **Foundry Slide Master** thumbnail. Change the theme colors to **Elemental**, and then change the background to **Style 2**. Change the color of the first bulleted item to **Blue, Accent 1, Darker 50%**.

3 Click the **Title Slide Layout** thumbnail, and then change font size of the Master title style placeholder to **54**.

4 Click the **Title and Content Layout** thumbnail. Under **Basic Shapes**, insert a **Text Box** shape anywhere on the right side of the content placeholder. Inside the shape, type **DeLong Grant** Press Enter, and then type **Law Partners** Change the font size to **14 pt**, and then center the text. Select the text, and then change the **Height** to **.6"** and the **Width** to **1.6"**. Use **Shape Fill** to add a **Gradient** with a **Light Variation** of **Linear Down**. Then position the text box shape in the lower right corner of the content placeholder.

5 Remove the Header on the **Handout Master**, and then close the **Master View**.

6 Insert the **Header & Footer**. On the **Notes and Handouts tab**, include a **Fixed** date and the **Page number** and **Footer**. In the **Footer** box, using your own name, type **Lastname_Firstname_4G_Film_Template** and then click **Apply to All**.

7 Revise the document properties. Replace the text in the **Author** box with your own first and last name. In the **Subject** box, type your course name and section number, and then in the **Keywords** box, type **film production, LLC, intellectual property**

8 Print **Handouts 6 Slides Horizontal**, or submit your presentation electronically as directed by your instructor.

9 **Save** the template. **Close** the template.

10 Create a new document from existing template **Lastname_Firstname_4G_Film_Template.potx**, and then save it as **Lastname_Firstname_4G_Film_Production.pptx**

11 On **Slide 1**, after *Presented to,* press Enter, then and type **University Film Production Class**

12 On the **Foundry Slide Master**, select all of the text in the first bulleted item, change the line spacing to **1.5**, and then close the Master View.

13 On **Slide 4**, after the third bulleted item, add this comment: **Maybe clarify that you mean the formation of an LLC.**

14 On **Slide 5**, select *Life rights*, and then add this comment: **Explain how life rights is considered intellectual property.**

15 Delete the first comment.

16 Update the filename in the Notes and Handouts footer to **Lastname_Firstname_4G_Film_Production** and then update the Properties with your name as the Author.

17 Print **Handouts 6 Slides Horizontal**, or submit your presentation electronically as directed by your instructor.

18 **Save** the presentation.

19 **Save** the presentation as an **XPS file**, including the comments and ink markup and specifying handouts 6 slides per page. **Print** the XPS file, or submit the file electronically as directed by your instructor. **Close** the **XPS Viewer**.

20 Mark the presentation as **Final**, and then **Close** it. **Exit** PowerPoint.

End You have completed Project 4G

Apply a combination of the 4A and 4B skills.

GO! Fix It | Project 4H Labor Issues

Project Files

For Project 4H, you will need the following file:

p04H_Labor_Template.potx

You will save your presentation as:

Lastname_Firstname_4H_Labor_Template.potx
Lastname_Firstname_4H_Labor_Issues.pptx
Lastname_Firstname_4H_Labor_Issues.pdf

In this project, you will edit a template for the DeLong Grant Law Partners regarding labor issues in sports. From the student files that accompany this textbook, open the file **p04H_Labor_Template.potx**, and then save the file in your **PowerPoint Chapter 4** folder as **Lastname_Firstname_4H_Labor_Template.potx** After completing the template, you will create a presentation from the template and name it **Lastname_Firstname_4H_Labor_Issues.pptx** You will also save the presentation as PDF Handouts 6 slides per page including comments.

To complete the project, you must correct these errors:

In the master slide view:

- The Gradient type should be Linear and the Gradient stop positioned at 70%. The color should Aqua, Accent 5.
- First-level bullets on all slides should be Arrow Bullets.
- Line spacing for the first-level bullets on the Title and Content Layout should be changed to 1.5.
- The shape should be at the lower right of the Title and Content Layout content placeholder.
- Properties should include your name, course name and section, and the keywords **labor, sports, agent, bargaining**
- A header and footer should be inserted on the Notes and Handouts that includes a fixed date and time, the page number, and a footer with the text **Lastname_Firstname_4H_Labor_Template** applied to all slides.

In a new presentation named **Lastname_Firstname_4H_Labor_Issues** created from the template:

- The title slide should be personalized for the Association of Sports Agents.
- Slide 2 should have a comment after *Wages* with this text: **This is always a tough topic to cover.**
- The comment on Slide 4 should be deleted.
- The Notes and Handouts footer should include the file name.
- Your name should be the author in the properties.
- PDF Handouts 6 slides per page including comments should be prepared.

Submit your presentation files electronically, or print out the PDF file of handouts and submit it as directed by your instructor. Close the presentation and exit PowerPoint.

You have completed Project 4H

Apply a combination of the 4A and 4B skills.

GO! Make It | Project 4I Consignment Contracts

Project Files

For Project 4I, you will need the following files:

p04I_Consignment_Contracts.pptx
p04I_Contract.jpg

You will save your presentation as:

Lastname_Firstname_4I_Consignment_Template.potx
Lastname_Firstname_4I_Consignment_Contracts.pptx
Lastname_Firstname_4I_Consignment_Contracts.pdf

Start PowerPoint, and then open p04I_Consignment_Contracts. Save the file in your PowerPoint Chapter 4 folder as **Lastname_Firstname_4I_Consignment_Template.potx** Modify the Slide Master in the template. Apply the Background Style 11, and then format the background with a Rectangular Gradient Fill and a Gradient Stop positioned at 90%. Add Bold to the Master title style, and then change the bullets as shown in Figure 4.57. Change the first-level bullet line spacing to 1.5. On the Title and Content Layout, insert and position the Plaque shape at the bottom right of the placeholder with p04I_Contract.jpg as the fill.

Insert a header on the notes and handouts that includes the page number and a fixed date and time and a footer with the text **Lastname_Firstname_4I_Consignment_Template** applied to all slides. Properties should include your name, the course name and section, and the keywords **financial, claim**

Create a new presentation from the template, and then save the file in your PowerPoint Chapter 4 folder as **Lastname_Firstname_4I_Consignment_Contracts** Refer to Figure 4.57 for the information for a new Slide 3. Add this comment to the right of . . . *each piece* on Slide 2: **How do you assess the market value?** Update the notes and handouts footer with the correct file name, and then change the author in Properties to your name.

Save the presentation as Handouts 3 slides per page in a PDF file, including the comments. Print the PDF file or submit electronically as directed by your instructor. Save the presentation, and then mark the presentation as final. Print the template file and the presentation file as Handouts 3 slides per page or submit electronically as directed by your instructor.

Project Results

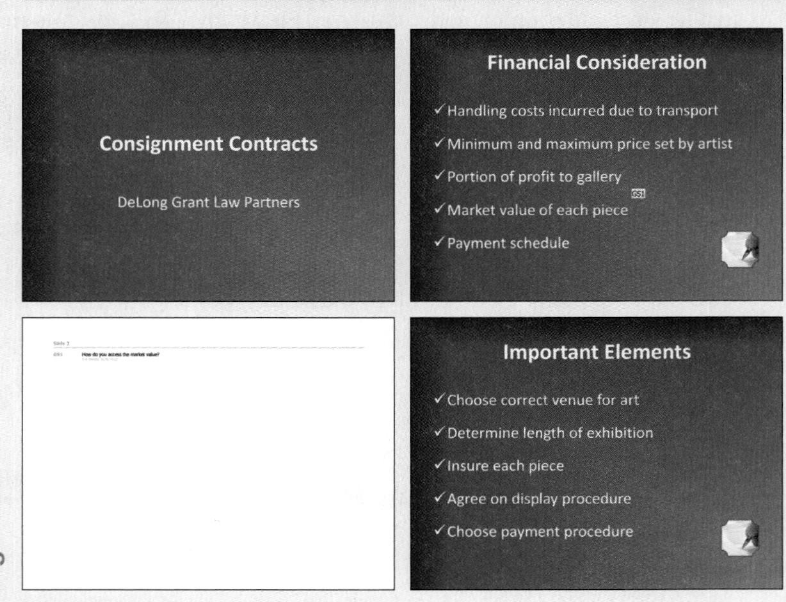

Figure 4.57

End **You have completed Project 4I**

Apply a combination of the 4A and 4B skills.

GO! Solve It | Project 4J Legal Guide

Project Files

For Project 4J, you will need the following file:

p04J_Legal_Guide.pptx

You will save your presentation as:

Lastname_Firstname_4J_Legal_Template.potx
Lastname_Firstname_4J_Legal_Guide.pptx
Lastname_Firstname_4J_Legal_Guide.pdf

Open p04J_Legal_Guide, and then save it as **Lastname_Firstname_4J_Legal_Template.potx** Format the slide master with a Background Style, and then format the Background with two gradient stops applying a fill color at each gradient stop. Change the bullets on the appropriate slide master so they all display with a different bullet style. Change font formatting and bullet color to maintain good contrast with the background. Insert the fixed date and time, the page number, and the file name applied in the Notes and Handouts. Add your name, your course name and section number, and the keywords **athlete, legal, agent** to the Properties.

Create a new presentation from the template. Save the file in your PowerPoint Chapter 4 folder as **Lastname_Firstname_4J_Legal_Guide.pptx** On Slide 1, on the line below *Prepared for*, type **Association of Sports Agents** On Slide 4, insert a comment. Update the Notes and Handouts footer and the Properties. Save the presentation as Handouts 6 slides per page in a PDF file, including the comments. Mark the PowerPoint presentation as final, and then save the presentation.

Print the PDF or submit it electronically, and print the template file and the presentation file as Handouts 6 slides per page or submit electronically as directed by your instructor.

		Performance Level		
	Performance Element	Exemplary: You consistently applied the relevant skills.	Proficient: You sometimes, but not always, applied the relevant skills.	Developing: You rarely or never applied the relevant skills.
Performance Criteria	Formatted Office Theme Slide Master with a background style and applied a fill color to two Gradient stops.	Slide background style was applied to the slide master and applied color to two Gradient stops.	Slide background style and added color to two Gradient stops, but did not apply them on the slide master.	Slide background style and color on two Gradient stops were not applied in the template.
	Changed bullet style on the Office Theme Slide Master.	Bullet style changed for all bullets on the slide master. Good contrast with the background.	Bullet style was not changed on the template slide master. Contrast may not be appropriate.	Bullet style was not changed in the template.
	Created and personalized a presentation based on the template.	Presentation file was created correctly; Subtitle and comment were inserted correctly.	Presentation file was created, but the subtitle information and/or the comment were entered in the template.	No presentation file was created from the template.
	Saved presentation as PDF handouts with comments and marked as Final.	Presentation was saved correctly as PDF file and marked as Final.	Presentation was not saved correctly as PDF or not marked as Final.	Presentation was not saved as PDF and not marked as Final.

End You have completed Project 4J

Content-Based Assessments

Apply a combination of the **4A** and **4B** skills.

GO! Solve It | Project 4K Actor Advice

Project Files

For Project 4K, you will need the following files:

p04K_Actor_Advice.pptx
p04K_Cinema.jpg

You will save your presentation as:

Lastname_Firstname_4K_Actor_Template.potx
Lastname_Firstname_4K_Actor_Advice.pptx
Lastname_Firstname_4K_Actor_Advice.pdf

Open p04K_Actor_Advice and save it as a template **Lastname_Firstname_4K_Actor_Template** Examine the slide content, and then modify the appropriate slide master with a background style or a theme. Adjust colors and fonts as needed. Change the bullet style for levels of bullets that are used. Insert a shape on the appropriate slide master so the shape displays only on Slide 1. Insert p04K_Cinema.jpg in the shape. On the Notes and Handouts, insert the fixed date and time, page number, and a footer with the file name. Add your name, your course name and section number, and the keywords **contracts, paparazzi, media** to the Properties.

Create a new presentation based on the template. Personalize the presentation for Julia Simpson. Save the presentation as **Lastname_Firstname_4K_Actor_Advice.pptx** On Slide 2, insert a comment. Update the Notes and Handouts footer with the correct file name, and then change the author in the Properties. Save the presentation in a PDF file as handouts, including the comments. Mark the presentation as final and save it. Print or submit electronically as directed by your instructor.

Performance Criteria	Performance Level: Exemplary: You consistently applied the relevant skills	Proficient: You sometimes, but not always, applied the relevant skills	Developing: You rarely or never applied the relevant skills
Customized Office Theme Slide Master with a background/ theme and bullet styles.	Slide master was customized correctly with a background or theme and with bullet styles. Maintained good contrast.	Slide master was not customized with a background or theme and with bullet styles. Customization done on other slide masters.	No slide master customization was completed.
Inserted a shape with the picture on the Title Slide Layout master.	Shape was inserted on the slide master and was sized and placed in an appropriate position.	The shape was not inserted on the appropriate slide master.	The shape was not inserted.
Created and personalized a presentation. Saved presentation as PDF with comments and marked as Final.	Presentation file was created, personalized, and included comments. Saved as PDF handouts with comments and marked as Final.	Presentation file was created, but was not personalized. Presentation may or may not have been saved as PDF and marked as Final.	A presentation file was not created from the template.

End You have completed Project 4K

Outcomes-Based Assessments

Rubric

The following outcomes-based assessments are *open-ended assessments*. That is, there is no specific correct result; your result will depend on your approach to the information provided. Make *Professional Quality* your goal. Use the following scoring rubric to guide you in *how* to approach the problem and then to evaluate *how well* your approach solves the problem.

The *criteria*—Software Mastery, Content, Format and Layout, and Process—represent the knowledge and skills you have gained that you can apply to solving the problem. The *levels of performance*—Professional Quality, Approaching Professional Quality, or Needs Quality Improvements—help you and your instructor evaluate your result.

	Your completed project is of Professional Quality if you:	**Your completed project is Approaching Professional Quality if you:**	**Your completed project Needs Quality Improvements if you:**
1-Software Mastery	Choose and apply the most appropriate skills, tools, and features and identify efficient methods to solve the problem.	Choose and apply some appropriate skills, tools, and features, but not in the most efficient manner.	Choose inappropriate skills, tools, or features, or are inefficient in solving the problem.
2-Content	Construct a solution that is clear and well organized, contains content that is accurate, appropriate to the audience and purpose, and is complete. Provide a solution that contains no errors in spelling, grammar, or style.	Construct a solution in which some components are unclear, poorly organized, inconsistent, or incomplete. Misjudge the needs of the audience. Have some errors in spelling, grammar, or style, but the errors do not detract from comprehension.	Construct a solution that is unclear, incomplete, or poorly organized; contains some inaccurate or inappropriate content; and contains many errors in spelling, grammar, or style. Do not solve the problem.
3-Format and Layout	Format and arrange all elements to communicate information and ideas, clarify function, illustrate relationships, and indicate relative importance.	Apply appropriate format and layout features to some elements, but not others. Overuse features, causing minor distraction.	Apply format and layout that does not communicate information or ideas clearly. Do not use format and layout features to clarify function, illustrate relationships, or indicate relative importance. Use available features excessively, causing distraction.
4-Process	Use an organized approach that integrates planning, development, self-assessment, revision, and reflection.	Demonstrate an organized approach in some areas, but not others; or, use an insufficient process of organization throughout.	Do not use an organized approach to solve the problem.

Outcomes-Based Assessments

Apply a combination of the 4A and 4B skills.

GO! Think | Project 4L Venue Risks

Project Files

For Project 4L, you will need the following file:

New blank PowerPoint presentation

You will save your presentation as:

Lastname_Firstname_4L_Venue_Template.potx
Lastname_Firstname_4L_Venue_Risks.pptx
Lastname_Firstname_4L_Venue_Risks.pdf

In this project, you will create a PowerPoint template for DeLong Grant Law Partners to educate colleges, universities, and other sports venues about safety and security.

Create a template named **Lastname_Firstname_4L_Venue_Template.potx** Customize the slide masters, applying formatting as needed. In the Notes and Handouts, include the fixed date and time, page number, and file name in the footer. Add your name, course name and section number, and the keywords **venue, sports, risk** to the Properties.

Create a new presentation based on the template that addresses safety and security concerns. Save the presentation as **Lastname_Firstname_4L_Venue_Risks.pptx**. Create three slides, each using a different layout. Add two comments. Update the Notes and Handouts footer with the new file name and the author name in the Properties. Save the presentation as Handouts 6 slides per page in a PDF file, including the comments. Mark the PowerPoint presentation as final. Print or submit electronically as directed by your instructor.

End You have completed Project 4L

Apply a combination of the 4A and 4B skills.

GO! Think | Project 4M Intellectual Property

Project Files

For Project 4M, you will need the following files:

New blank PowerPoint presentation
p04M_Intellectual_Property.jpg

You will save your presentation as:

Lastname_Firstname_4M_Property_Template.potx
Lastname_Firstname_4M_Intellectual_Property.pptx
Lastname_Firstname_4M_Intellectual_Property.xps

In this project, you will create a PowerPoint presentation for DeLong Grant Law Partners that provides an overview of intellectual property concepts.

Create a template and customize the appropriate slide masters. Insert a shape on the slides and fill it with p04M_Intellectual_Property.jpg. Design the appropriate master slides for an effective template. In the Notes and Handouts, include the date and time fixed, the page number, and the file name in the footer. Add your name, course name and section number, and the keywords **intellectual, property** to the Properties area.

Create a four-slide presentation based on your template. Update the Notes and Handouts footer and the Document Properties. Prepare XPS handouts with four slides per page, including the comments. Print or submit electronically as directed by your instructor.

End You have completed Project 4M

Apply a combination of the 4A and 4B skills.

You and GO! | Project 4N Copyright

Project Files

For Project 4N, you will need the following files:

New blank PowerPoint presentation
p04N_Copyright.jpg

You will save your presentation as:

Lastname_Firstname_4N_Copyright_Template.potx
Lastname_Firstname_4N_Copyright.pptx
Lastname_Firstname_4N_Copyright.pdf

Research the copyright law as it pertains to the exclusive right to copy literary, musical, artistic, or other original creations. Create a PowerPoint template, and then name it **Lastname_Firstname_4N_Copyright_Template** Customize the slide master, title slide, title and content, and two content layouts. Select an appropriate theme or background, and then customize the bullets. Insert a shape, and then fill it with p04N_Copyright.jpg. Apply appropriate formats.

In the Notes and Handouts, include the date and time fixed, the page number, and the template file name in the footer. Add your name, your course name and section number, and the keywords **copyright, art, music** to the Properties.

Then create a presentation that explains copyright and what it protects based on the template. Include four slides—one title slide, two title and content slides, and one two-content slide. Name the presentation **Lastname_Firstname_4N_Copyright** Focus on one area, such as literary or music copyrights.

Include comments on two slides in the presentation. Update the footer and properties as needed. Prepare PDF handouts with four slides per page, including comments. Mark the presentation as Final. Print or submit electronically as directed by your instructor.

End You have completed Project 4N

Applying Advanced Graphic Techniques and Inserting Audio and Video

OUTCOMES

At the end of this chapter you will be able to:

OBJECTIVES

Mastering these objectives will enable you to:

PROJECT 5A

Edit and format pictures and add sound to a presentation.

1. Use Picture Corrections (p. 295)
2. Add a Border to a Picture (p. 302)
3. Change the Shape of a Picture (p. 306)
4. Add a Picture to a WordArt Object (p. 307)
5. Enhance a Presentation with Audio and Video (p. 310)

PROJECT 5B

Create and edit a photo album and crop pictures.

6. Create a Photo Album (p. 322)
7. Edit a Photo Album and Add a Caption (p. 324)
8. Crop a Picture (p. 328)

Dudarev Mikhail/Shutterstock

In This Chapter

Microsoft Office PowerPoint provides a variety of methods for formatting and enhancing graphic elements. You have practiced using some of the tools that change the style and add an effect to a picture or a graphic. PowerPoint also provides sophisticated tools for changing the brightness, contrast, and shape of a picture; adding a border; and cropping a picture to remove unwanted areas. These tools eliminate the need to use a separate program to format a picture.

PowerPoint also allows you to include audio and video effects in presentations, although the resulting files are quite large. For example, you might want to introduce a slide with an audio effect or music, or have an audio effect or music play when the slide or a component on the slide, such as text or a graphic, is clicked. The inclusion of audio and video can significantly enhance the overall presentation when used properly.

Cross Oceans Music produces and distributes recordings of innovative musicians from every continent in genres that include Celtic, jazz, New Age, reggae, flamenco, calypso, and unique blends of all styles. Company scouts travel the world attending world music festivals, concerts, and small local venues to find their talented roster of musicians. These artists create new music using traditional and modern instruments and technologies. Cross Oceans' customers are knowledgeable about music and demand the highest quality digital recordings provided in state-of-the-art formats.

Project 5A Overview Presentation

Project Activities

In Activities 5.01 through 5.10, you will change the sharpness or softness and the brightness and contrast of pictures. You will also add borders and change the outline shape of pictures. You will insert linked video files and add a trigger to the audio and video. Your completed presentation will look similar to Figure 5.1.

Project Files

For Project 5A, you will need the following files:

p05A_Cross_Oceans.pptx
p05A_Building.jpg
p05A_Island2.jpg
p05A_MP3.jpg
p05A_Smooth_Jazz.wav
p05A_NewAge.wav

You will save your presentation as:

Lastname_Firstname_5A_Cross_Oceans.pptx

Project Results

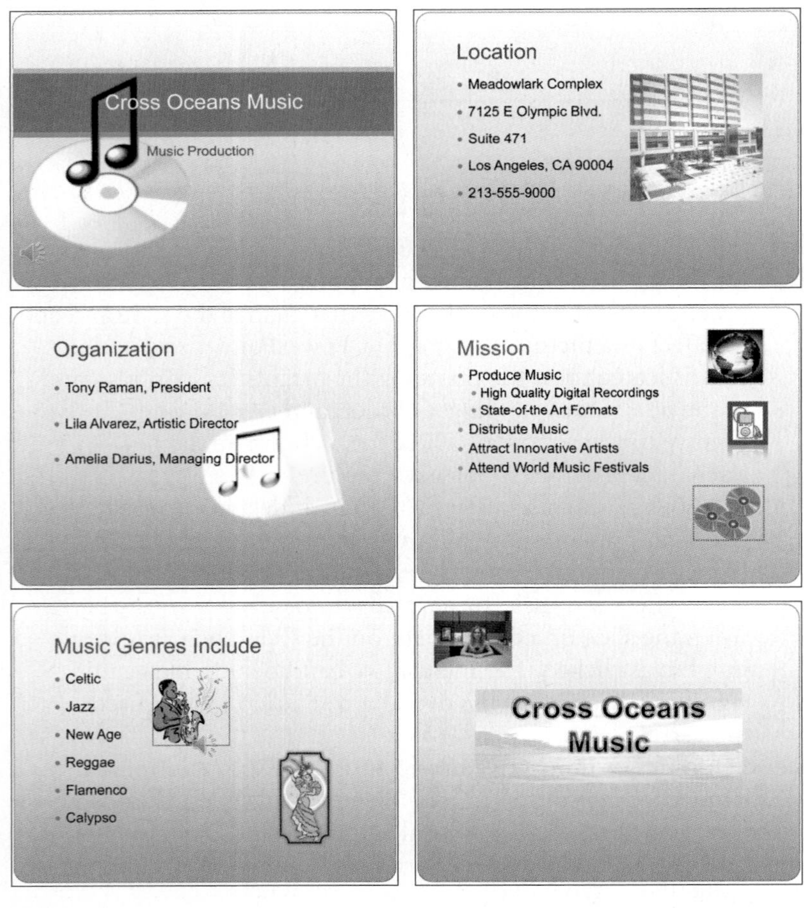

Figure 5.1
Project 5A Cross Oceans Music

Objective 1 | Use Picture Corrections

Pictures can be corrected to improve the brightness, contrast, or sharpness. For example, you can use Sharpen and Soften to enhance picture details or make a picture more appealing by removing unwanted blemishes. When you ***sharpen*** an image, the clarity of an image increases. When you ***soften*** an image, the picture becomes fuzzier. You can use Presets to choose common, built-in blurriness adjustments from a gallery. You can also use a slider to adjust the amount of blurriness, or you can enter a number in the box next to the slider.

Another way to correct pictures is to use Brightness and Contrast. ***Brightness*** is the relative lightness of a picture, and ***contrast*** is the difference between the darkest and lightest area of a picture. You can use **Presets** to choose common, built-in brightness and contrast combinations from a gallery, or you can use a slider to adjust the amount of brightness and contrast separately.

When you change the overall lightening and darkening of the image, you change the individual pixels in an image. ***Pixel*** is short for *picture element* and represents a single point in a graphic image. To increase brightness, more light or white is added to the picture by selecting positive percentages. To decrease brightness, more darkness or black is added to the image by selecting negative percentages.

Changing the contrast of a picture changes the amount of gray in the image. Positive percentages increase the intensity of a picture by removing gray; negative percentages decrease intensity by adding more gray.

When you ***recolor*** a picture, you change all colors in the image into shades of one color. This effect is often used to stylize a picture or make the colors match a background.

Activity 5.01 | Using Sharpen and Soften on a Picture

In this activity, you will change the sharpness of a picture so the text on the slide will have greater emphasis. You will also use the Presets, which allows you to apply one of five standard settings.

1 **Start** PowerPoint. Locate and open the file **p05A_Cross_Oceans** Display **Backstage** view, click **Save As**, and then navigate to the location where you are storing your projects for this chapter. Create a new folder named **PowerPoint Chapter 5** and then in the File name box and using your own name, save the file as **Lastname_Firstname_5A_Cross_Oceans** Click **Save** or press Enter.

2 Make **Slide 1** the active slide, if necessary, and then click to select the image.

3 Under **Picture Tools**, click the **Format tab**. In the **Arrange group**, click the **Send Backward button arrow**, and then click **Send to Back**.

The slide title and subtitle words are now displayed in front of the picture so you can read the words. When you click the Send Backward button, there are two options. Send Backward moves the image behind the title text. Send to Back moves the image behind both the title and subtitle text.

Another Way

To move a picture behind all components on the slide, right-click the picture, click Send to Back.

Alert! | **Is the Text Visible?**

If you cannot read the text in front of a picture that has been sent to the back, move the picture or change the text color.

4 Compare your screen with Figure 5.2, and then take a moment to study the descriptions of the picture adjustment settings, as shown in the table in Figure 5.3.

Figure 5.2

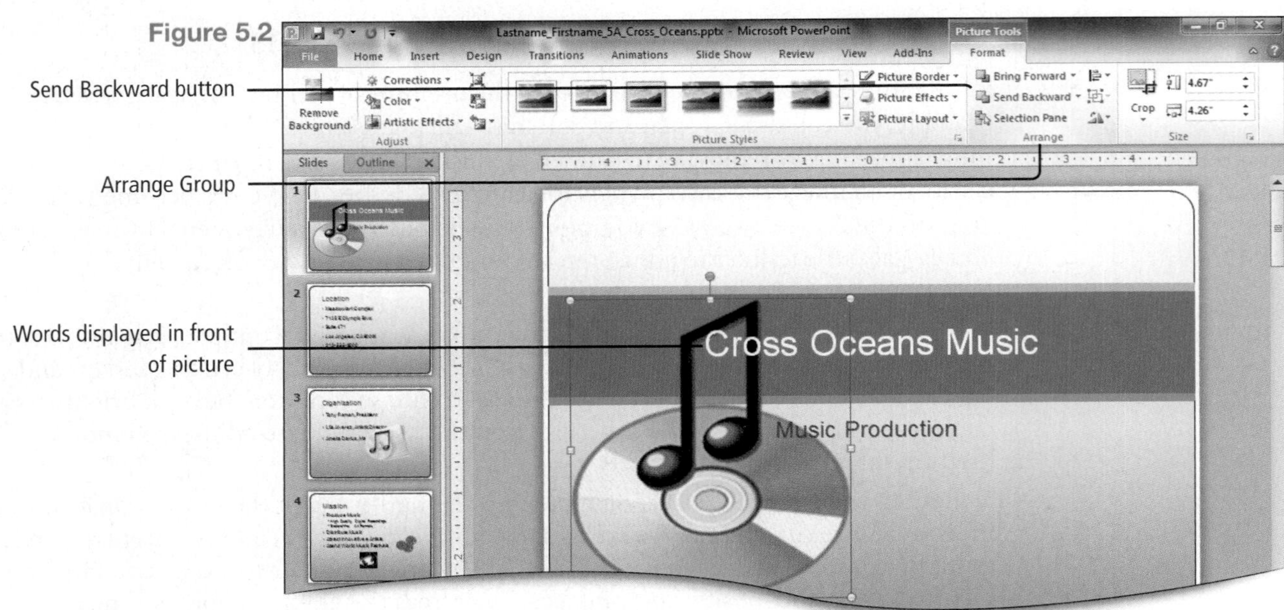

Picture Adjustment Options

Screen Element	Description
Remove Background	Removes unwanted portions of a picture. If needed, use marks to indicate areas to keep or remove from the picture.
Corrections	Improves the appearance of a picture by adjusting the: Brightness of the picture. Contrast between the darkest and lightest areas of a picture. Sharpness, or blurriness, of a picture.
Color	Adjusts the color intensity, color dominance, and color effects of a picture through the use of: Color saturation (intensity): A higher saturation makes a picture look more vivid. A lower saturation turns the colors toward gray. Color tone (temperature): The higher the temperature, the more orange is added to the picture. The lower the number, the more blue is added to the picture. These changes improve the appearance of a picture taken by a camera that did not measure the color temperature correctly. Recolor: A built-in stylized effect, such as grayscale or a color combination compatible with your picture, may be applied.
Artistic Effects	Adds an artistic effect to a picture to make it look like a sketch or painting. You can access the Artistic Effects Options from this menu.
Compress Pictures	Reduces the color format of the image to make the file size smaller. Compressing a picture makes the color take up fewer bits per pixel with no loss of quality. There are two compression options: The default is to compress the selected picture, but you can uncheck this option to compress all pictures in the document. If you have cropped a picture, you can delete the cropped area to reduce the file size. However, if you want to undo the cropping, you have to insert the picture again. Provides four target output methods: Print (220 ppi): Excellent quality on most printers and screens (selected by default). Screen (150 ppi): Good for Web pages and projectors. E-mail (96 ppi): Minimizes the document size for use when sharing the document through an e-mail attachment. Use document resolution: This option uses the resolution set on the File tab. By default this is set to Print or 220 ppi (pixels per inch), but you can change this default picture resolution.
Change Picture button	Allows you to select and insert a different picture to replace the current picture. The new picture maintains the formatting and size of the original picture.
Reset Picture button	Discards all formatting changes made to the picture.

Figure 5.3

5. In the **Adjust group**, click the **Corrections** button, and then click **Picture Corrections Options** to display the **Format Picture** dialog box. Drag the **Format Picture** dialog box to the side to make the picture visible, if necessary. Under **Sharpen and Soften**, drag the slider to the left to **-100%** and observe the fuzzy effect on the picture. Drag the slider to the right to **100%** and notice the sharpness of the picture.

6. Under **Sharpen and Soften**, click the **Presets** button. Compare your screen with Figure 5.4.

   The ScreenTip for the Sharpen and Soften Presets button is Sharpen & Soften.

Figure 5.4

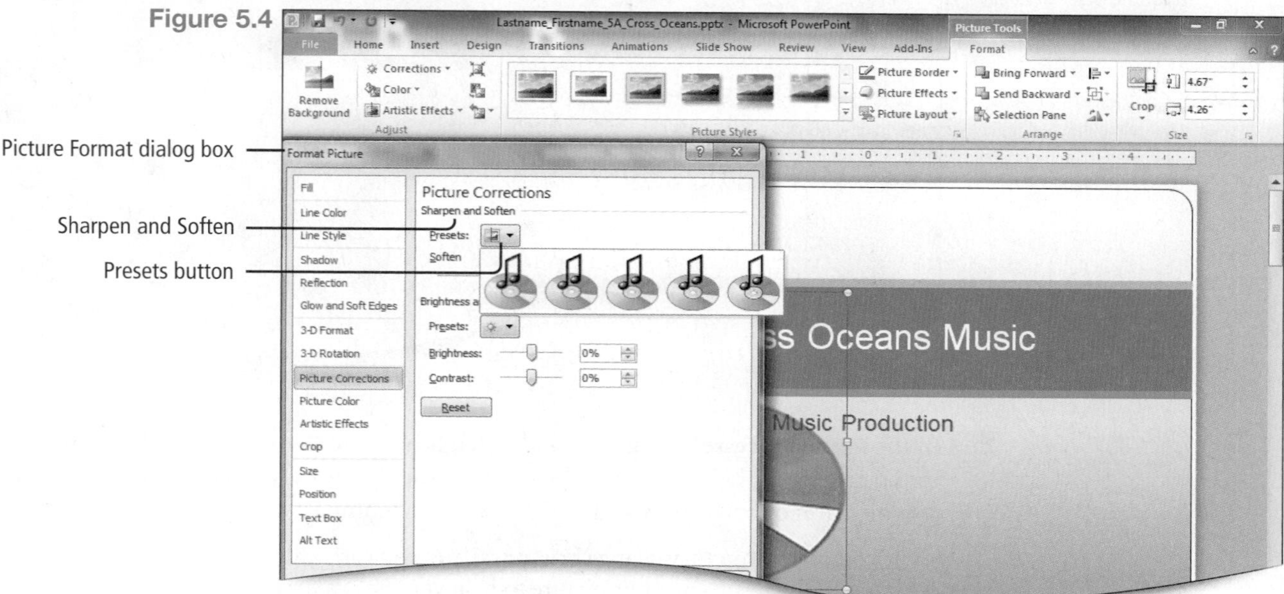

7. Click the first option—**Soften: 50%**.

   The slider is now set at -50%, meaning that the picture is fuzzier than the text.

> **More Knowledge | Using Picture Presets**
>
> The default for Sharpen and Soften is 0%. The Presets range from Soften: 50% to Sharpen: 50%. The slider settings range from -100% to +100%. Soften: 50% in Presets is the same as -50% on the slider.

8. Click **Close** to close the **Format Picture** dialog box. **Save** the presentation.

Activity 5.02 | Changing the Brightness and Contrast of a Picture

In this activity, you will change the brightness and the contrast of a picture. You will also use the Presets, which allows you to select a combination of brightness and contrast settings.

1. With the image still selected, on the **Format tab**, in the **Adjust group**, click the **Corrections** button, and then click **Picture Corrections Options** to display the **Format Picture** dialog box again. Under **Brightness and Contrast**, drag the **Brightness** slider to the left and then to the right. Watch how the picture brightness changes. Type **20%** in the **Brightness** box.

2. Under **Brightness and Contrast**, drag the **Contrast** slider to the left and then to the right. Watch how the picture contrast changes. Type **40%** in the **Contrast** box. Compare your screen with Figure 5.5.

   The picture is enhanced so the slide title displays with more prominence than the picture.

Figure 5.5

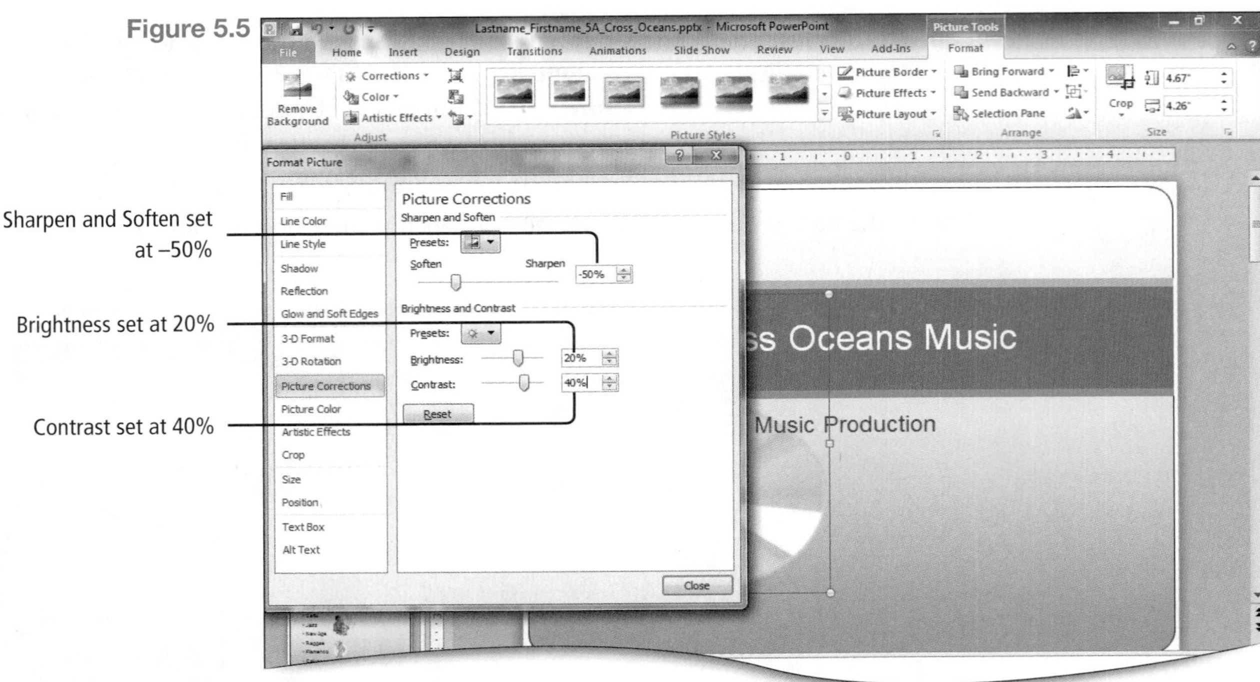

3 In the **Format Picture** dialog box, under **Brightness and Contrast**, click the **Presets** button. In the gallery, in the bottom row locate **Brightness: +20% Contrast: +40%**, which is the combination of brightness and contrast you set. Compare your screen with Figure 5.6.

If you prefer, you may change brightness and contrast with one of the presets. The gallery displays the results on your picture to help you make a decision.

Figure 5.6

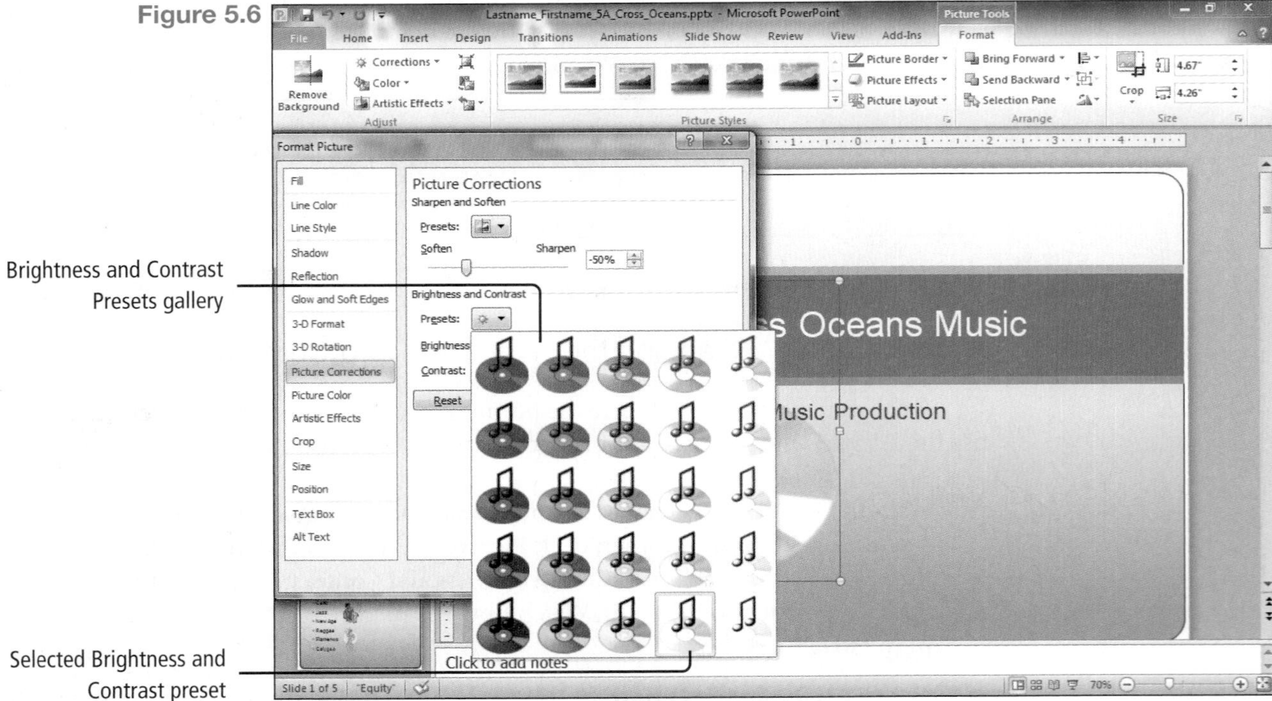

4 Click outside the **Brightness and Contrast** gallery to collapse it. Click **Close**.

5 **Save** your changes.

Activity 5.03 | Recoloring a Picture

In this activity, you will recolor a picture.

> **Another Way**
>
> To display the gridlines, on the View tab, in the Show group, click a check mark in the Gridlines check box.

1 With the picture on **Slide 1** selected, under **Picture Tools**, click the **Format tab** if necessary. In the **Arrange group**, click the **Align** button, and then click **View Gridlines.** Click outside the picture to deselect it. Compare your screen with Figure 5.7.

The gridlines help you align objects at specific locations on the ruler.

Figure 5.7

2 Make **Slide 2** the active slide. Click the **Insert tab**. In the **Images group**, click the **Picture** button. Navigate to the location where your student files are stored, and then insert the picture **p05A_Building.jpg**.

3 Move the entire picture so that the right edge aligns with the **4 inches on the right side of the horizontal ruler** and the **2 inches on the upper half of the vertical ruler**. Compare your screen with Figure 5.8.

Figure 5.8

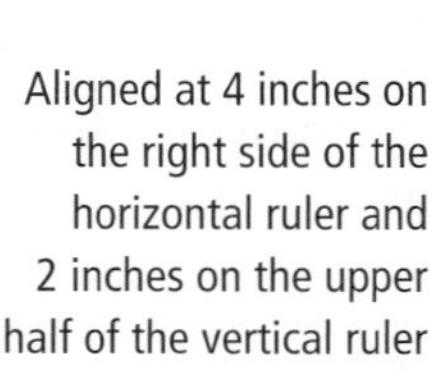

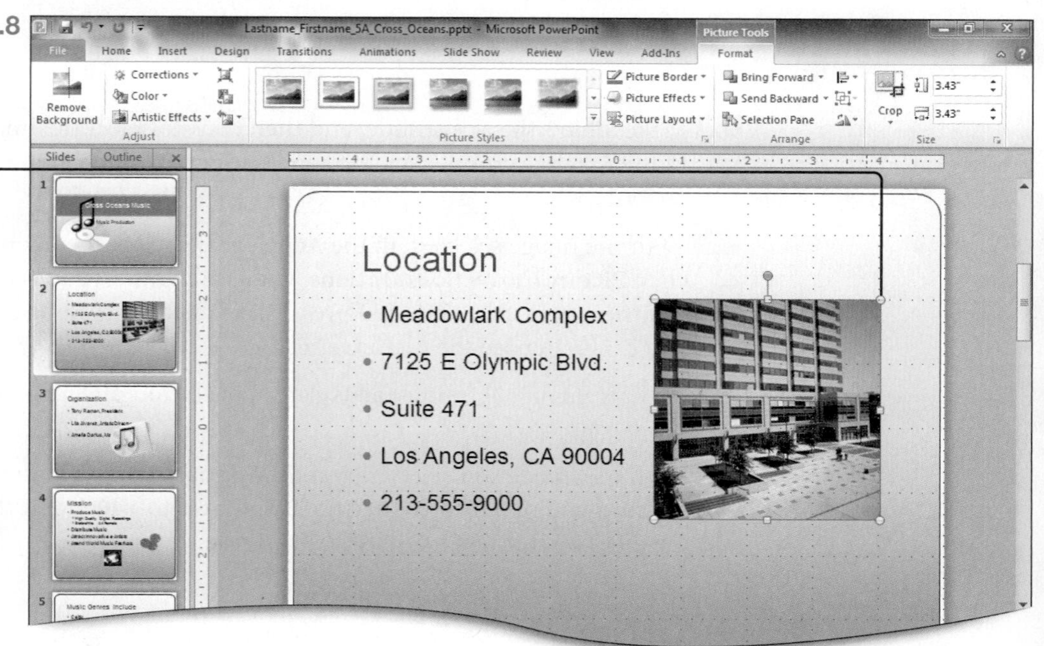

PowerPoint | Chapter 5

Another Way

To display the Format Picture dialog box, right-click the picture, and then click Format Picture.

4 With the picture still selected, on the **Format tab**, in the **Adjust group**, click the **Color** button. Click **Picture Color Options** to display the **Format Picture** dialog box. At the right, under **Recolor**, click the **Presets** button. In the third row, second column, locate **Blue, Accent color 1 Light**, and then click it. Do not close the **Format Picture** dialog box yet.

5 On the left side of the **Format Picture** dialog box, click **Picture Corrections**. Change the **Brightness** to **20%**. Compare your screen with Figure 5.9.

This effect increases the brightness of the picture and adds visual interest. Notice that you were able to access both the Picture Color and Picture Corrections without closing the Format Picture dialog box.

Figure 5.9

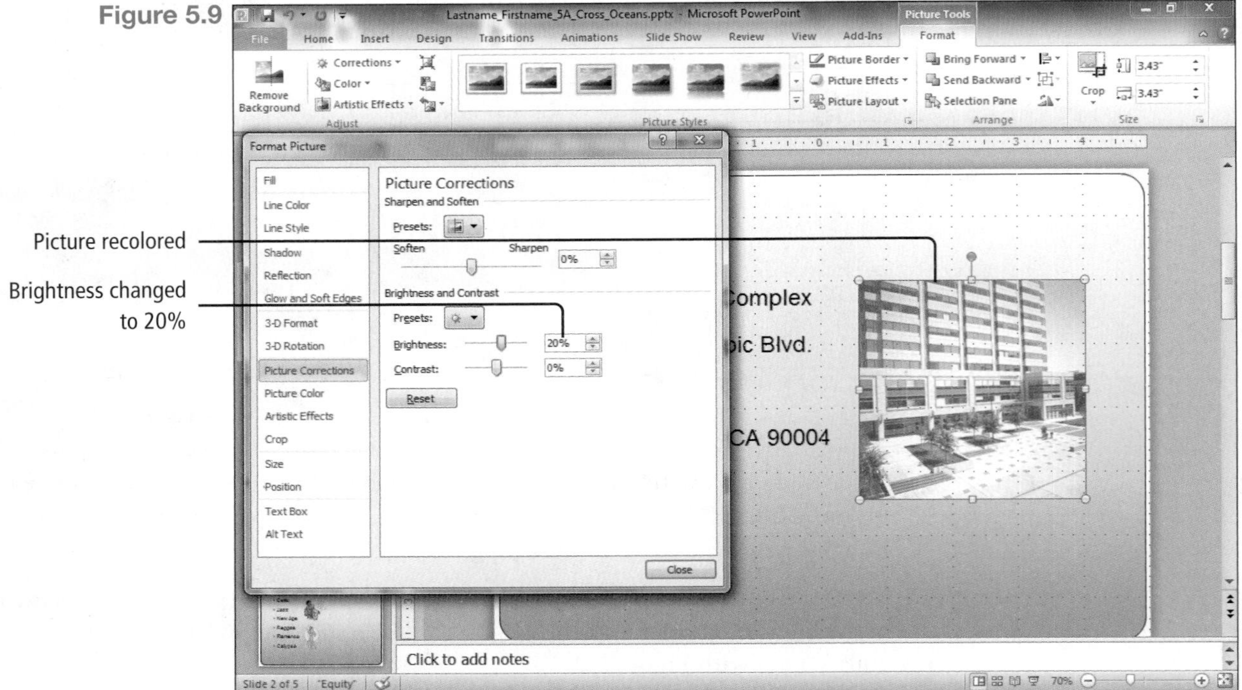

6 Click **Close**.

7 Make **Slide 3** the active slide, and then click to select the image. On the **Format tab**, in the **Arrange group**, click the **Send Backward button arrow**, and then click **Send to Back**.

8 With the image selected, in the **Adjust group**, click the **Corrections** button, and then click **Picture Corrections Options**. Under **Brightness and Contrast**, in the box next to **Contrast**, type **30%** and then press Tab. If necessary, drag the dialog box to the side so you can better see the picture effect.

This amount of contrast adds glare to the picture and makes the bulleted items difficult to read.

9 With the image still selected and the **Format Picture** window still displaying, use the method you prefer to change the **Brightness** to **+40**% and the **Contrast** to **+40**%. Change the softness to **-100%.** Click **Close**.

10 In the **Arrange group**, click the **Selection Pane** button to display the **Selection and Visibility pane**. Compare your screen with Figure 5.10. Click **Content Placeholder 2** to select the content placeholder including the three names. Click **Title 1** to select the title placeholder—*Organization*. Click **Picture 4** to select the picture on the slide.

The Selection and Visibility pane displays the shapes on the slide, making it easy to select the desired shape.

Figure 5.10

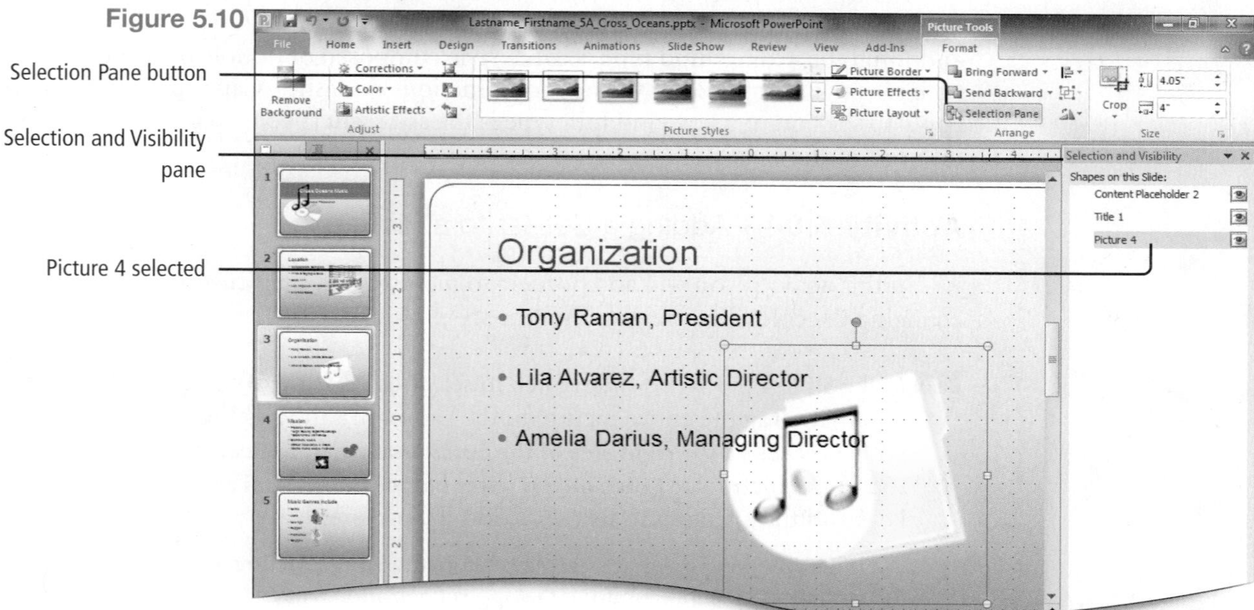

Another Way

On the Selection and Visibility pane, click the Close button to close the Selection Pane.

11 With the picture selected, drag it so the left side is aligned at **0 on the horizontal ruler** and the top edge of the picture aligns with **1.5 on the upper half of the vertical ruler**. On the **Format tab**, in the **Arrange group**, click the **Selection Pane** to close it. Click to the left of *Organization* to deselect the picture, and then compare your screen with Figure 5.11.

Reducing the contrast and softness of the picture makes the picture fade into the background, allowing the content of the bulleted items to appear more prominently. Repositioning the picture makes the words easier to read.

Figure 5.11

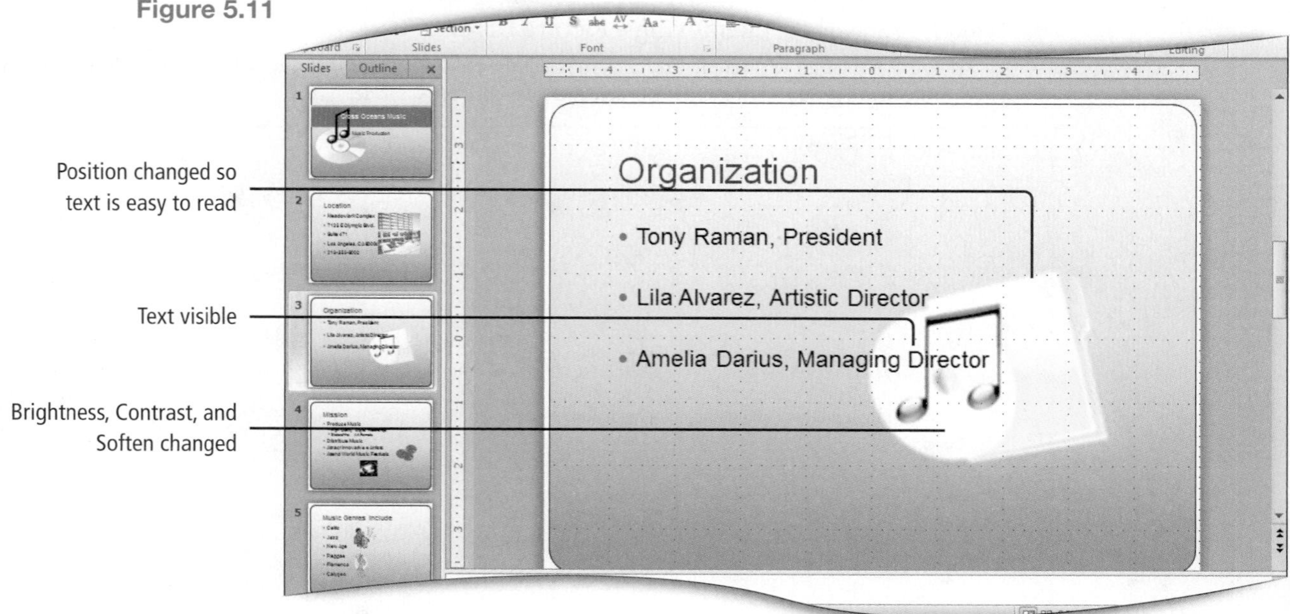

12 **Save** your changes.

Objective 2 | Add a Border to a Picture

After you have inserted a picture into a slide, you can add a ***border***, which is actually a frame, around the picture. It is possible to edit the color of the border and the line weight. The ***line weight*** is the thickness of the line measured in points (abbreviated as pt), similar to font sizes. It is sometimes also called line width.

You can also select the ***line style***, which is how the line displays, such as a solid line, dots, or dashes. You can also change Line Width, Compound type, Dash type, Cap type, and Join type. Compound type is a line style composed of double or triple lines. Dash type is a style composed of various combinations of dashes. Cap type is the style you apply to the end of a line, and Join type is the style you specify to be used when two lines intersect at the corner.

Activity 5.04 | Adding a Border to a Picture

In this activity, you will add borders to pictures and then customize those borders by changing the color, line weight, and line style.

1 Make **Slide 4** the active slide. Click to select the picture of the CDs. Hold down Shift, and then drag the entire picture to the right until the right edge of the picture aligns with **4 inches on the right side of the horizontal ruler**. Repeat the procedure to align the top of the picture at **1 inch on the lower half of the vertical ruler**. Use the Ctrl + arrow keys and the gridlines to help position the picture.

When you hold down the Shift key before dragging a picture, you can move the picture without accidentally shifting the opposite position. For example, if you start moving the picture to the right, you cannot drag it up or down at the same time.

2 With the picture still selected, click the **Format tab**. In the **Picture Styles group**, click the **Picture Border** button, and then in the first row, click the fourth color—**Dark Blue, Text 2**. Click **Picture Border**, click **Weight**, and then click **2 1/4 pt**. Click **Picture Border**, click **Dashes**, and then click **Round Dot**. Deselect the picture, and then compare your screen with Figure 5.12.

The picture displays with a border. The color, style, and weight have all been set.

> **More Knowledge | Removing a Picture Border**
>
> To remove the border on a picture, click to select the picture. Under Picture Tools, click the Format tab. In the Picture Styles group, click Picture Border, and then click No Outline.

Figure 5.12

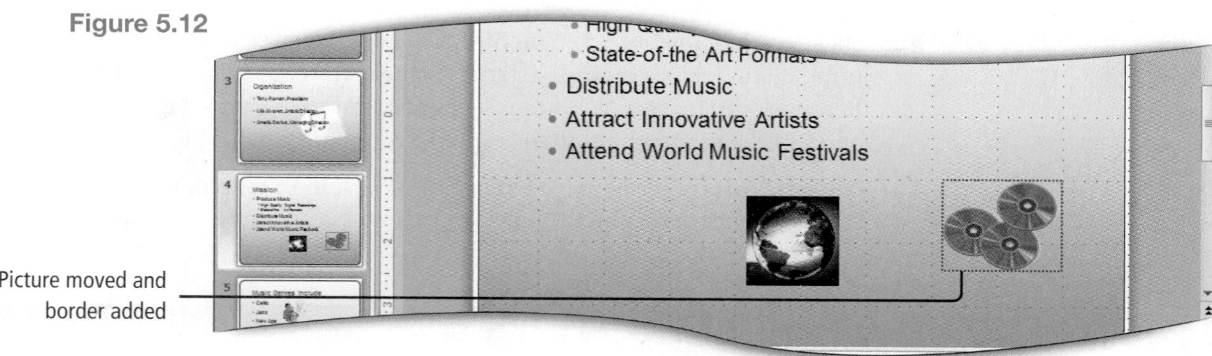

> **Another Way**
> To size a picture proportionately, select the picture, and then drag a corner diagonally to the desired height or width.

3 Click the **Insert tab**. In the **Images group**, click the **Picture** button. Navigate to the location where your student files are stored, and then insert the picture **p05A_MP3.jpg**. On the **Format tab**, in the **Size group**, click the **Shape Height** box, type **1** and then press Enter.

The picture is sized proportionately.

4 Drag the entire picture so the top edge aligns at **1 inch on the upper half of the vertical ruler** and the right edge of the picture aligns at **4 inches on the right side of the horizontal ruler**.

5 With the picture still selected, on the **Format tab**, in the **Picture Styles group**, click the **Picture Border** button, and then in the last row, click the fifth color—**Blue, Accent 1, Darker 50%**. Click **Picture Border**. Point to **Weight**, and then click **More Lines** to display the **Format Picture** dialog box.

Recall that the Format Picture dialog box displays the picture formatting types. The Line Style option is selected because you displayed the Picture Border first and then clicked More Lines.

6 In the **Width** spin box, increase the line width to **9 pt**. In the **Join type** box, click the **down arrow**, and then click **Miter**. Compare your screen with Figure 5.13.

A ***mitered*** border has corners that are square. The default is rounded corners. The Format Picture dialog box allows you to enter borders wider than the maximum 6 pt listed when you click the Picture Border button and select Weight.

Figure 5.13

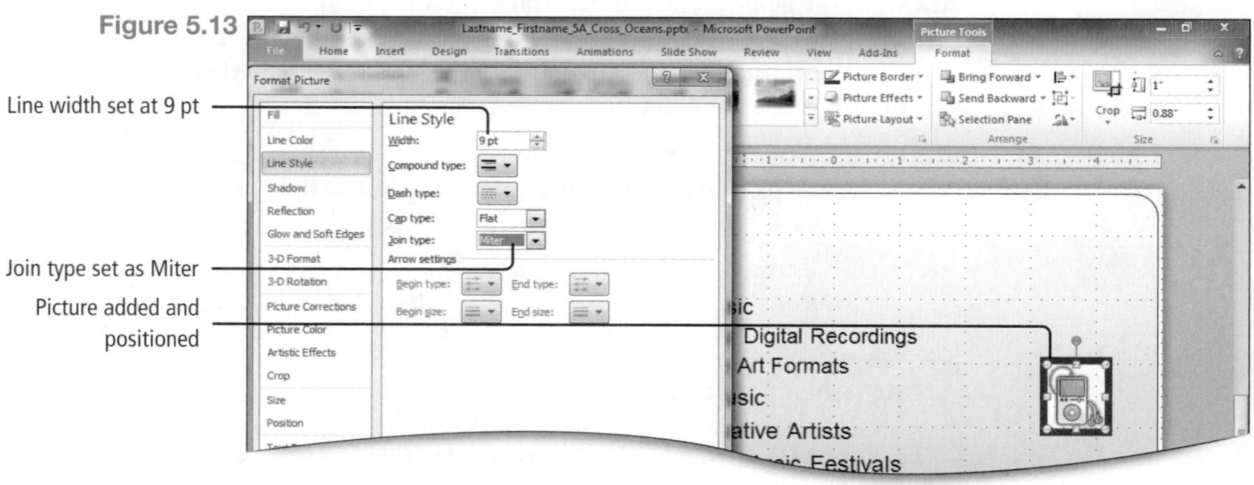

7 Click **Close**.

8 Click to select the bordered picture of the MP3 player if necessary. On the **Format tab**, in the **Picture Styles group**, click the **Picture Effects** button, point to **Reflection**, and then under **Reflection Variations**, click the first variation—**Tight Reflection, touching**. Deselect the picture, and then compare your screen with Figure 5.14

The corners of the border are mitered borders, and a reflection is displayed below the picture. The border on the right side extends beyond the 4-inch mark on the horizontal ruler.

Figure 5.14

9 Click to select the picture of the globe. Drag the entire picture so the top edge aligns at **3 inches on the upper half of the vertical ruler** and the right edge aligns at **4 inches on the right side of the horizontal ruler.**

10 With the globe picture still selected, on the **Format tab**, in the **Picture Styles group**, click the **Picture Border** button, and then under **Standard Colors**, click **Yellow**. Click the **Picture Border** button, point to **Weight**, and then click **3 pt**.

11 Click the globe picture, if necessary, and then hold down Shift, and then click the other two pictures. All three pictures should be selected. On the **Format tab**, in the **Arrange group**, click the **Align** button, and then click **Align Right**. Click anywhere off the slide to deselect the pictures.

12 Click the picture of the MP3 player. Hold down Ctrl, and then press ← a few times to nudge the picture border so it aligns at **4 inches on the right side of the horizontal ruler**. Deselect the picture, and then compare your screen with Figure 5.15.

Because the MP3 player picture has a wide border, it is now aligned better with the other pictures.

> **Note | Aligning Pictures**
>
> Use the alignment options on the Format tab in the Arrange group to align pictures evenly. When you select Align Right, the selected pictures will align at the right side of the picture that is farthest to the right. Make sure that all pictures are selected before applying the alignment. The border size is not included in the alignment.

Figure 5.15

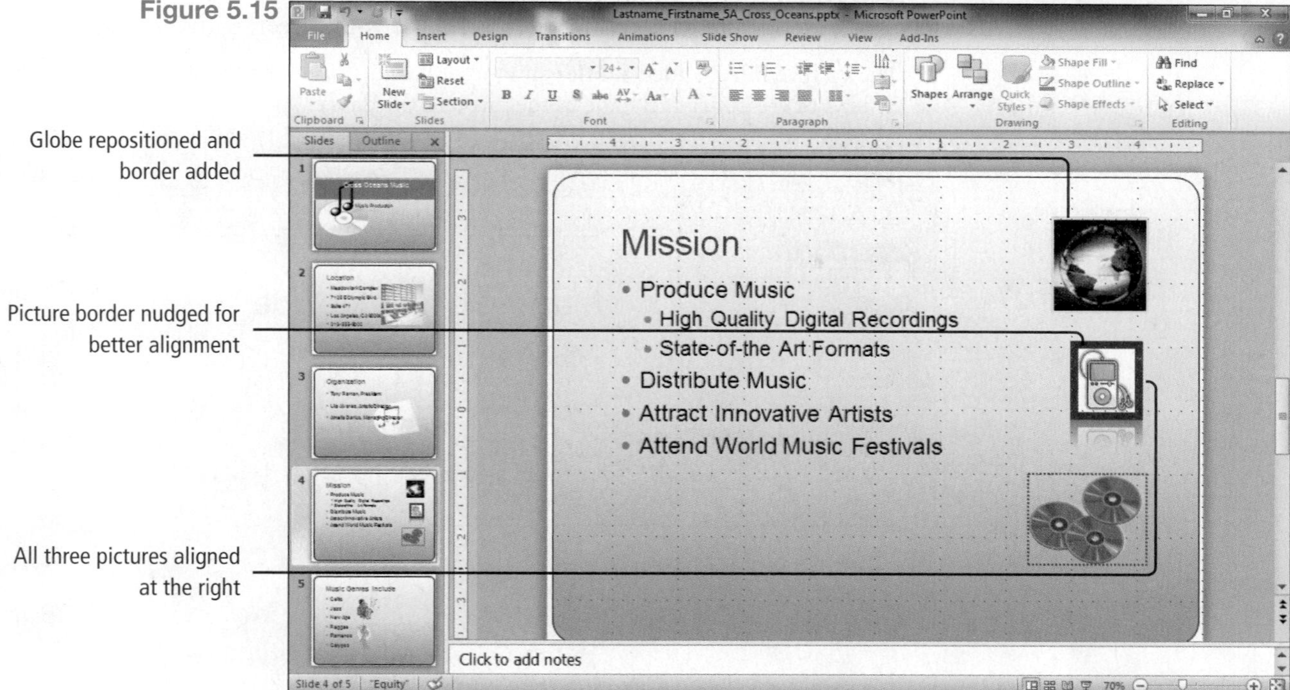

13 Make **Slide 5** the active slide, and then click to select the picture of the saxophone musician. Click the **Format tab**. In the **Picture Styles group**, click the **Picture Border** button. Under **Theme Colors**, in the last row, click the fifth color—**Blue, Accent 1, Darker 50%**.

14 Click the **Picture Border** button, point to **Weight**, and then click **1 pt**. Click outside the picture to deselect it, and then compare your screen with Figure 5.16.

Figure 5.16

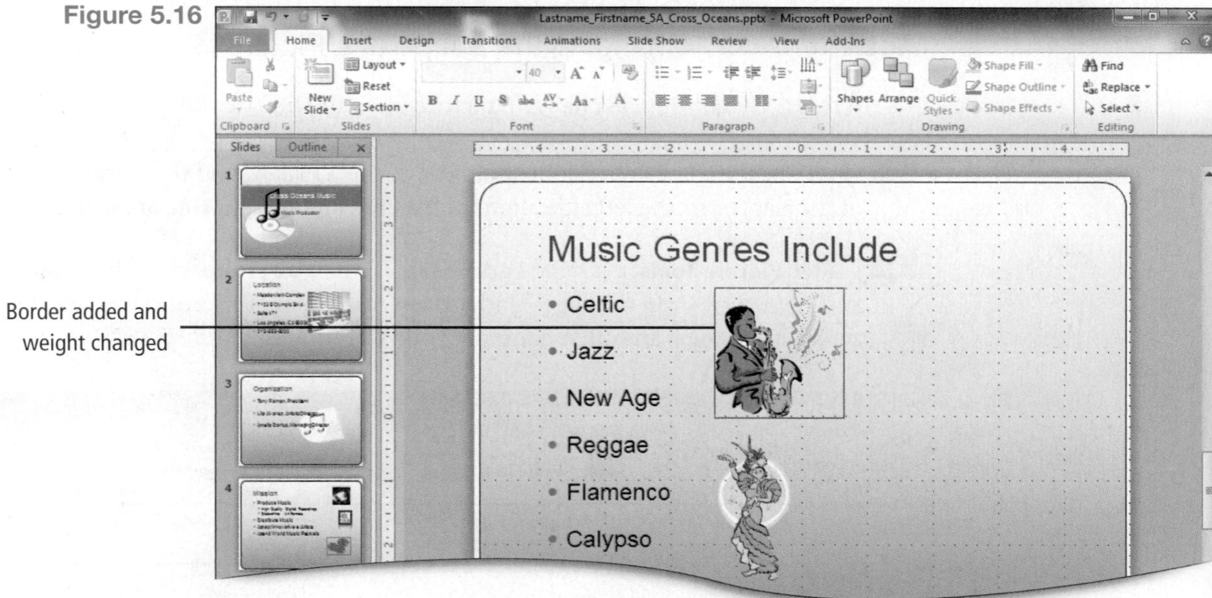

15 Click to select the picture of the Calypso dancer. On the **Format tab**, In the **Picture Styles group**, click the **Picture Effects** button, point to **Glow**, and then under **Glow Variations**, in the second row, click the first selection—**Blue, 8 pt glow, Accent color 1**.

16 Click to deselect the picture, and then compare your screen with Figure 5.17.

The Picture Effect added a different kind of border. It defined the shape of the picture instead of creating a rectangle border around the dancer.

Figure 5.17

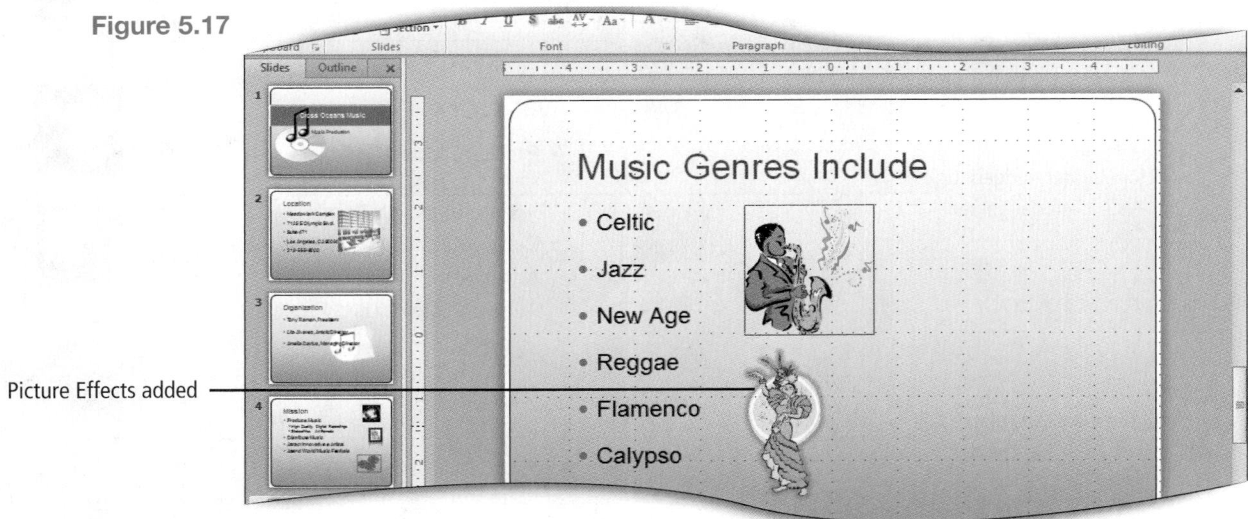

17 **Save** your changes.

Objective 3 | Change the Shape of a Picture

After you have inserted a picture, you can change the outline shape of the image. This is possible with or without the addition of a border. A large selection of shapes is available in PowerPoint. We apply several formatting techniques in this project so you can experiment with different options. Keep in mind, however, that applying too many formatting techniques can distract from the content of the presentation.

Activity 5.05 | Changing the Shape of a Picture

In this activity, you will change a picture on your slide to a shape and then add a border.

1 With **Slide 5** as the active slide, hold down the Shift key, and then drag the entire picture of the dancer so the left side aligns at **2 inches on the right side of the horizontal ruler**.

2 Under **Picture Tools**, click the **Format tab**. In the **Size group**, click the **Crop button arrow**, and then click **Crop to Shape**. Under **Basic Shapes**, in the second row, locate the ninth symbol—**Plaque**, and then compare your screen with Figure 5.18.

Figure 5.18

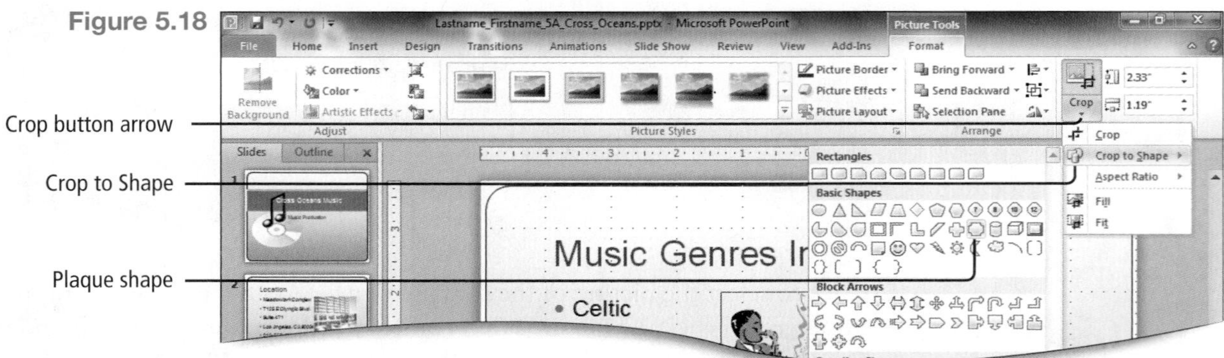

3 Click the **Plaque** shape. Click the **Picture Border** button, and then in the sixth row, click the fifth color—**Blue, Accent 1, Darker 50%**. Click **Picture Border**, point to **Weight**, and then click **3 pt**. Click to deselect the picture, and then compare your screen with Figure 5.19.

Without the border, applying the shape is confusing. Adding the border emphasized the shape.

Figure 5.19

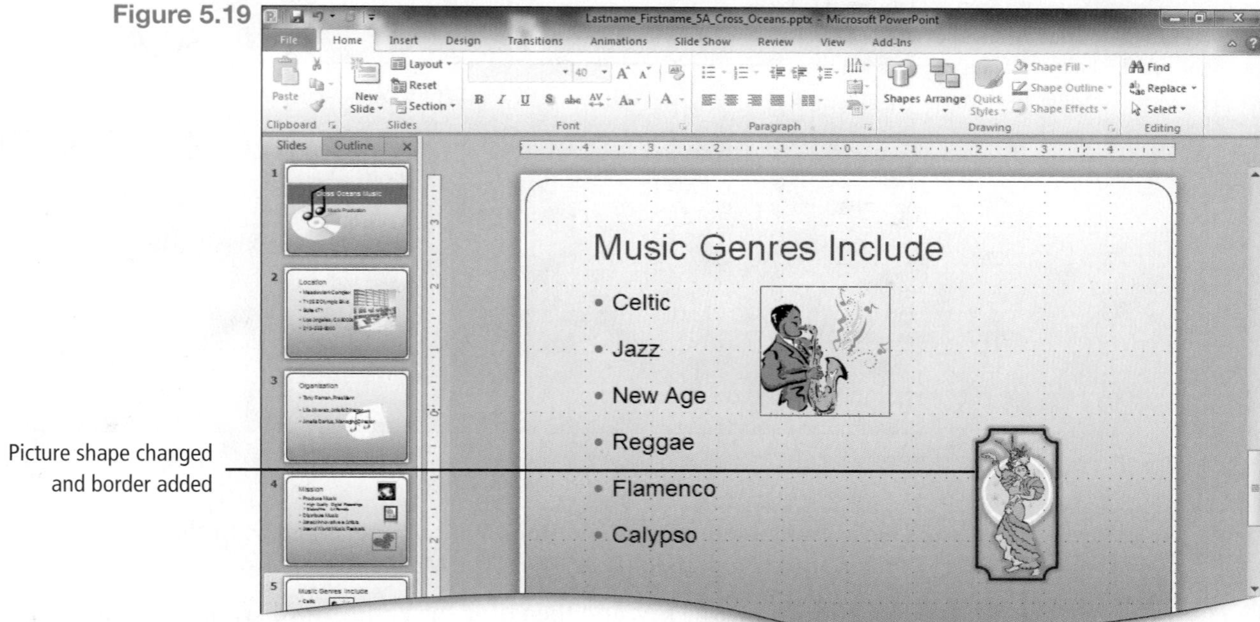

4 Click the **View tab**. In the **Show group**, deselect the **Gridlines** check box.

5 **Save** your changes.

Objective 4 | Add a Picture to a WordArt Object

A WordArt object may have a picture fill to add interest to a presentation. After adding the WordArt text, insert a picture fill that complements the WordArt message.

Activity 5.06 | Adding a WordArt Object and Embedding a Picture

In this activity, you will insert a new blank slide and add a WordArt object containing text. Then you will insert a picture as a fill for the object. You will also recolor the picture.

1 Click **Slide 5**. On the **Home tab**, in the **Slides group**, click the **New Slide button arrow**, and then click **Blank** to add a new slide.

2 On **Slide 6**, click the **Insert tab**. In the **Text group**, click the **WordArt** button. In the fourth row, in the third column, locate **Gradient Fill – Black, Outline – White, Outer Shadow**, and then compare your screen with Figure 5.20.

Figure 5.20

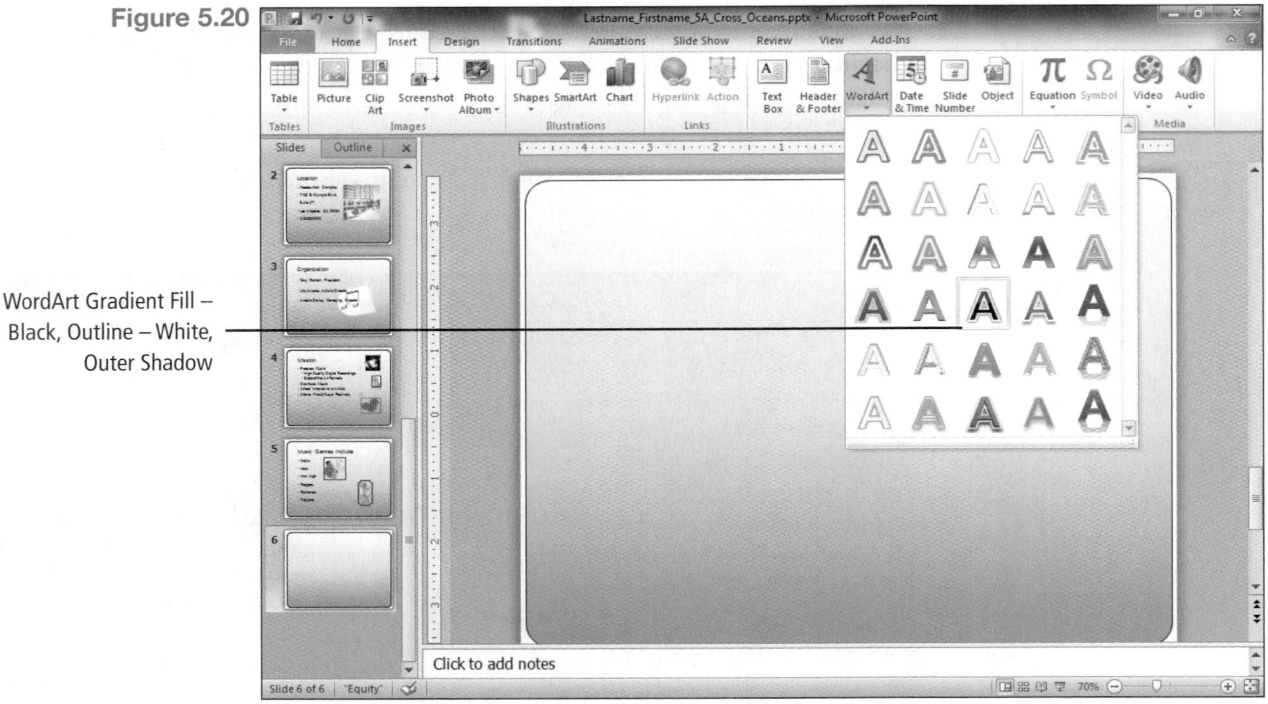

WordArt Gradient Fill – Black, Outline – White, Outer Shadow

3 Click **Gradient Fill – Black, Outline – White, Outer Shadow**. In the **WordArt** object, type **Cross Oceans** and then press Enter. Type **Music** on the second line.

4 Hold down the Shift key, and then drag the entire WordArt up so the top edge of the picture is aligned at **1.5 inches on the upper half of the vertical ruler**. Compare your screen with Figure 5.21.

Figure 5.21

5 With the **WordArt** object still selected, click the **Format tab**. In the **Shape Styles group**, click the **Shape Fill** button, and then click **Picture**. In the location where you are storing your files, click **p05A_Island2.jpg**, and then click **Insert**. Compare your screen with Figure 5.22.

Figure 5.22

6 With the **WordArt** object still selected, under **Picture Tools**, click the **Format tab**. In the **Adjust group**, click the **Color** button. Under **Recolor**, in the first row, in the fourth column, click **Washout**.

7 In the **Size group**, click the **Size & Position** button. Under **Scale**, click the **Lock aspect ratio** check box to select it. Under **Size and rotate**, change the **Height** to **2.5″**. Compare your screen with Figure 5.23.

When ***Lock aspect ratio*** is selected, you can change one dimension (height or width) of an object, such as a picture, and the other dimension will automatically be changed to maintain the proportion.

Figure 5.23

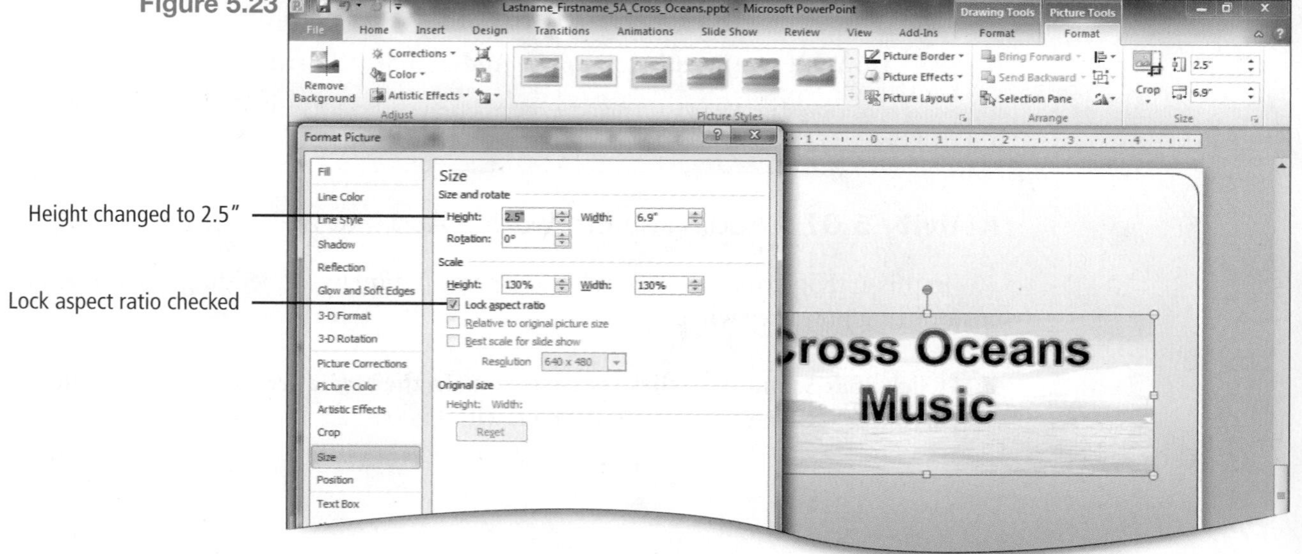

8 Click **Close**. In the **Arrange group**, click the **Align** button, and then select **Align Center**. Deselect the WordArt, and then compare your screen with Figure 5.24

Figure 5.24

9 **Save** your changes.

Objective 5 | Enhance a Presentation with Audio and Video

To further enhance a presentation, you can add audio and video to the presentation. After you have applied audio and/or video to a presentation, you can control how you would like the files to play. A file can be set to play one time and then stop, or to ***loop***, meaning the audio or video file will play repeatedly from start to finish until it is stopped manually. A ***track***, or song, from a CD can also play during a slide show. Audio and video can be embedded or linked to the presentation. To ***embed*** is to save a presentation so that the audio or video file becomes part of the presentation file. To ***link*** is to save a presentation so that the audio or video file is saved separately from the presentation. Be sure to obtain permission to link or embed audio and video to a presentation to avoid violating the copyright.

> **Alert! | Do You Have Permission to Use Audio in the Classroom?**
>
> If you are not allowed to play audio in your classroom or lab, use a headset for these activities. If you do not have a headset, ask your instructor how to proceed.

Activity 5.07 | Adding an Embedded Audio to a Presentation

In this activity, you will add audio to a presentation by embedding audio files and customizing how they will play.

1 Click **Slide 5**, and then click the **Insert tab**. In the **Media group**, click the **Audio button arrow**, and then compare your screen with Figure 5.25

Figure 5.25

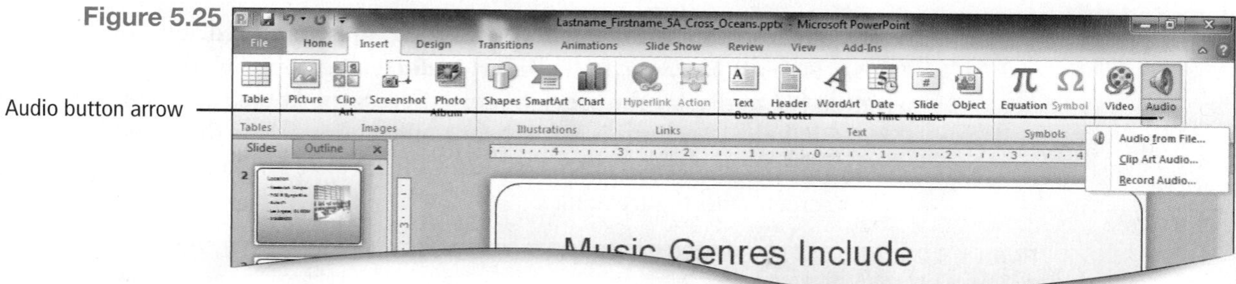

2 Take a moment to study the options available for inserting audio into a presentation, as shown in the table in Figure 5.26.

Sound Options

Screen Element	Description
Audio from File	Enables you to insert audio clips such as music, narration, or audio bites. Compatible audio file formats include .mid or .midi, .mp3, and .wav.
Clip Art Audio	Displays the Clip Art pane so that you can search for audio files in the Microsoft Office collection, both locally and online.
Record Audio	Enables you to insert audio by recording the audio through a microphone and then naming and inserting the recorded audio.

Figure 5.26

3 From the displayed menu, click **Audio from File** to display the **Insert Audio** dialog box.

4 Above the **Cancel** button, click the **Audio Files down arrow** to display the audio files supported by PowerPoint, and then compare your screen with Figure 5.27. Click the **Show preview pane** button if necessary.

The preview pane button in Windows Explorer is a toggle button. If the preview pane is not displaying, the button ScreenTip is *Show preview pane.* If the preview pane is displaying, the button ScreenTip is *Hide preview pane.*

Figure 5.27

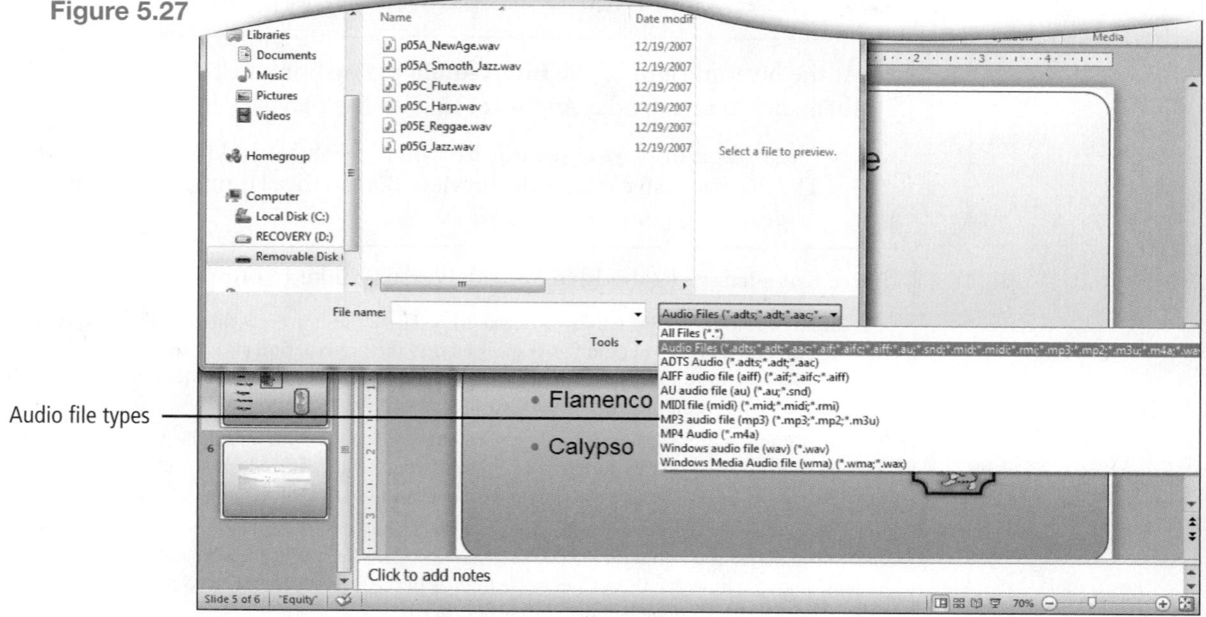

5 Navigate to the location where your student files are stored, click once on **p05A_Smooth_Jazz.wav**. In the **Insert Audio** dialog box, click the **Show the preview pane** button to display the preview area if necessary. At the right side, in the preview area, click the **Play** button to hear to the audio. While the audio is playing, the **Play** button changes to a **Pause** button. Click **Pause** to stop the audio. Compare your screen with Figure 5.28.

Figure 5.28

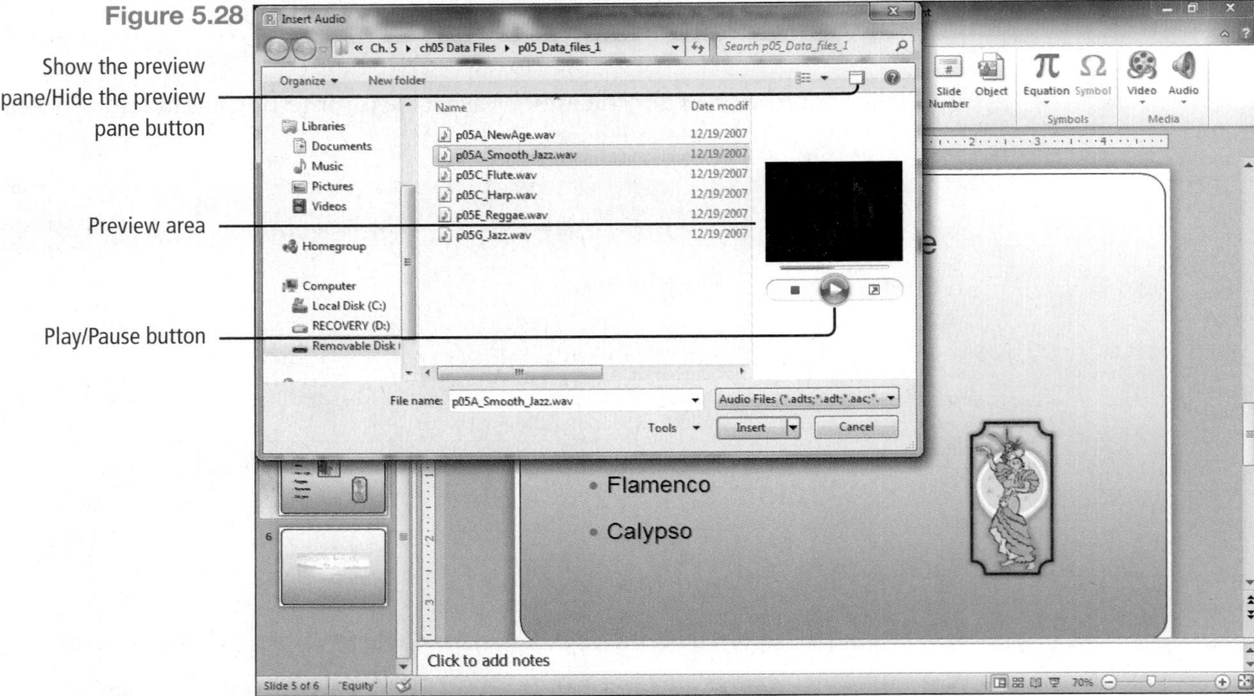

> **Alert! | Is the Audio Not Audible?**
>
> Your PC may not have audio capability. If you know for a fact that your PC has audio capability, open the Control Panel by clicking the Start button and then click Control Panel. In Control Panel, click Hardware and Sound. Under Sound, click Adjust system volume, and then drag the Speakers slider up to increase the volume. Make sure that the audio has not been muted. If the audio is muted, there will be a red stop symbol beside the speaker icon. Click the speaker icon and unmute the audio. Finally make sure that you have your speakers turned on.

6 At the bottom right of the **Insert Audio** dialog box, click the **Insert button arrow**, and then click **Insert**. Under **Audio Tools**, click the **Playback tab**.

Audio Tools displays in the title bar with the Format and Playback tabs located under it. The Playback tab contains the Preview, Bookmarks, Editing, and Audio Options groups. A speaker icon displays on the slide.

> **More Knowledge | Embedded Sounds Versus Linked Sounds**
>
> The audio files used in this activity are .wav files. These files are embedded in the PowerPoint presentation, meaning that the object, or audio file, is inserted into the presentation and becomes part of the saved presentation file. Because the audio is stored within the presentation file, this guarantees that the audio will play from any audio-enabled computer that you use to show the presentation.
>
> The other method of inserting audio into a presentation is to link the audio file. When you link the audio file, it is stored outside the presentation. If your presentation includes linked files, you must copy both the presentation file and the linked files to the same folder if you want to show the presentation on another computer.
>
> By default, the only files that may be embedded in a PowerPoint presentation are ***.wav*** *(waveform audio data)* audio files under 100 kilobytes in size. You may increase the size of the embedded .wav file to a maximum of 50,000 kilobytes; however, this will increase the size of the presentation file and may slow down its performance. Other audio file types must be linked regardless of size.

Another Way

To adjust the audio volume, on the taskbar, on the right side, click the Speakers icon, and then adjust the volume.

7 In the **Audio Options group**, click the **Hide During Show** check box. Click the **Volume button arrow**, and then click **Medium**. Click the **Start arrow**, and then click **Automatically**. Compare your screen with Figure 5.29.

Figure 5.29

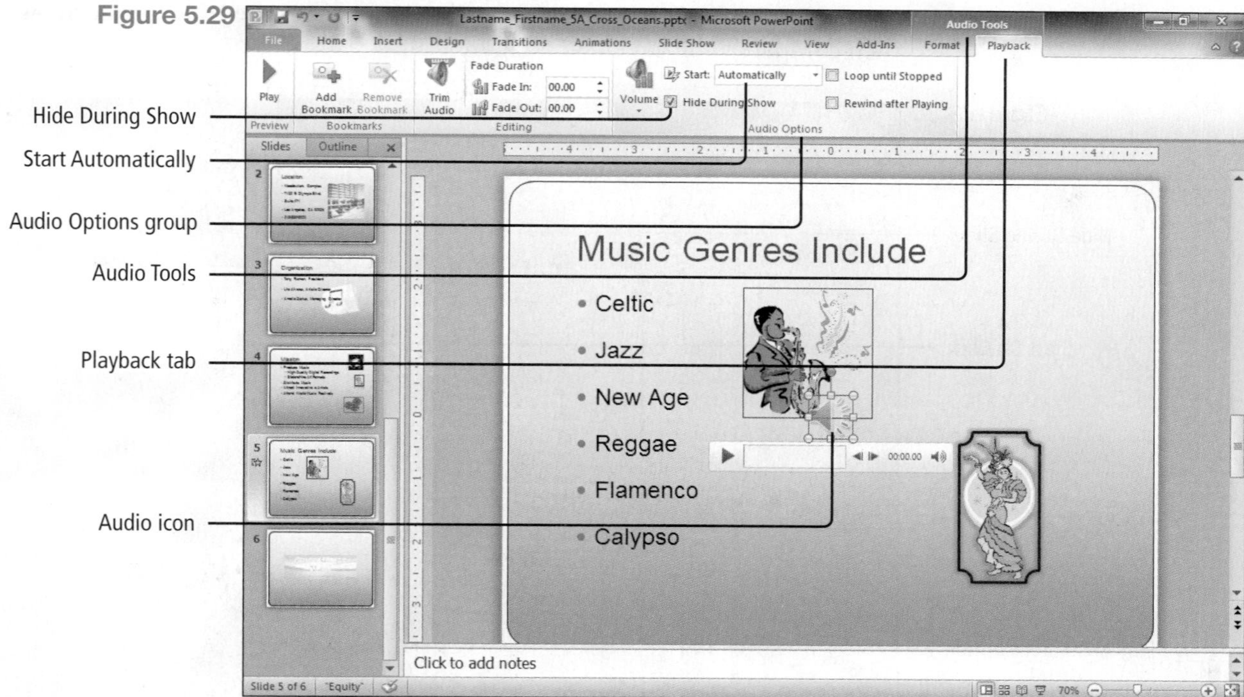

8 With **Slide 5** as the active slide, click the **Slide Show tab**. In the **Start Slide Show group**, click **From Current Slide**.

During a slide show presentation, the audio starts automatically when the slide displays. The audio plays one time and then stops. Because the audio icon is hidden, it does not display on the slide during the presentation of a slide show.

You can stop the audio by clicking the slide, by pressing Enter to advance to the next slide, or by pressing Esc.

9 Press Esc to end the slide show and return to **Normal** view.

It is possible to play sounds in Normal view. In the Slides pane, a small star-shaped icon displays to the left of the slide thumbnail. This is the ***Play Animations button***. Click this small button to play the sound.

10 Make **Slide 1**, the title slide, the active slide. Click the **Insert tab**, and then in the **Media group**, click the **Audio button arrow**. Click **Audio from File**. Navigate to the location where your student files are stored, click **p05A_NewAge.wav**, and then click **Insert**. Drag the audio icon to the lower left corner so the top edge aligns at **2.5 inches on the lower half of the vertical ruler** and the left edge aligns at **4.5 inches on the left side of the horizontal ruler**.

Note | Moving the Audio Icon

You can move the audio icon away from the main content of the slide so that the icon is easier for the presenter to locate. Avoid placing the icon where it interferes with the text the audience is viewing.

11 Under **Audio Tools**, click the **Playback tab**. Click the **Start arrow**, and then click **On Click**. On the slide, on the **Sound Control Panel**, click **Play** to listen to the audio clip.

> **Alert!** | **Is the Sound Control Panel Missing?**
>
> If you cannot see the Sound Control Panel, click the audio icon.

12 On the **Playback tab**, in the **Audio Options group**, click the **Hide During Show** box, and then compare your screen with Figure 5.30.

Figure 5.30

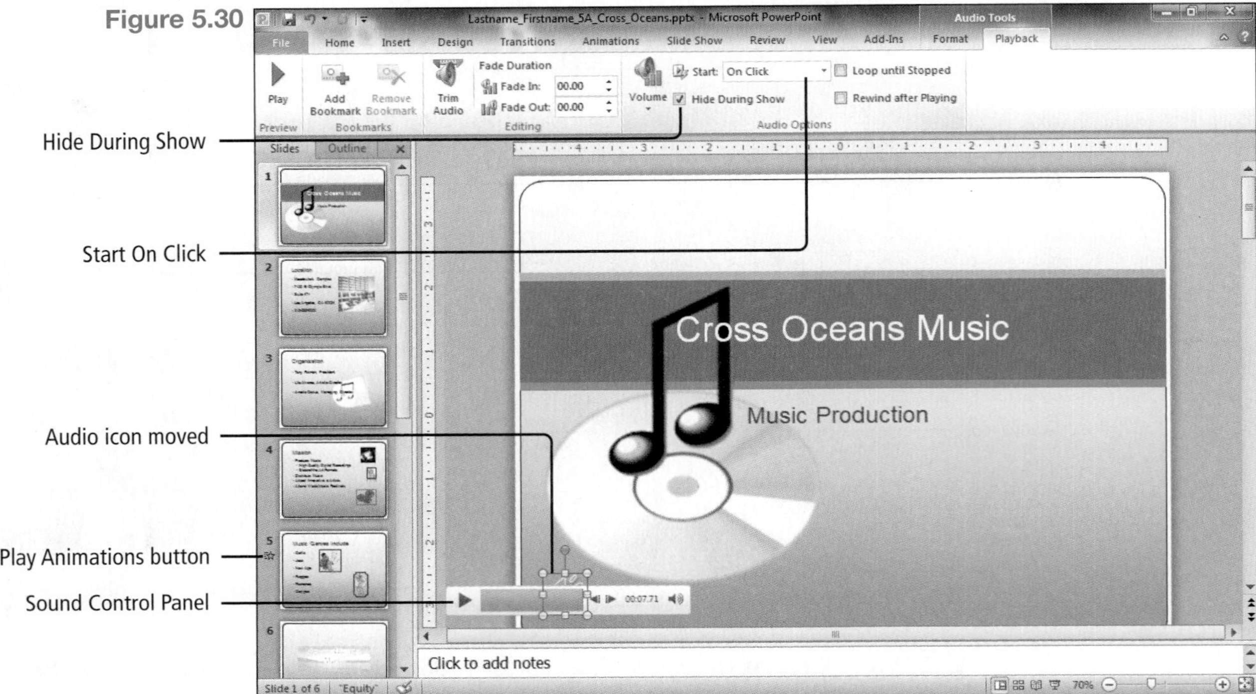

13 Click the **Slide Show tab**. In the **Start Slide Show group**, click **From Beginning**. Click the slide, and notice that no audio plays. Instead, it takes you to the next slide.

> **Note** | **Hiding the Audio Icon During a Slide Show**
>
> Hiding the audio icon during the slide show works only when the audio is set to play Automatically. If you select When Clicked, the icon must display. If you select Hide During Show, the audio will not play when you click the slide, unless you create a specific trigger.

14 Press Esc to end the slide show and return to **Normal** view.

15 Click **Slide 1**. Click to select the speaker icon. Under **Audio Tools**, click the **Playback tab**.

16 In the **Audio Options group**, deselect the **Hide During Show** check box. Click the **Slide Show tab**. In the **Start Slide Show group**, click the **From Current Slide** button. Point to the **Audio** icon. On the control panel, click the **Play** button. Alternatively, you can click the top part of the speaker icon to hear the sound.

After the slide show is started, there may be a delay before the mouse pointer becomes active.

17 Press Esc.

18 **Save** your changes.

Activity 5.08 | Setting a Trigger for an Embedded Audio in a Presentation

In this activity, you will set a trigger for an embedded audio. A ***trigger*** is a portion of text, a graphic, or a picture that, when clicked, causes the audio or video to play. You will display the Animation Pane to help you locate the trigger. The ***Animation Pane*** is an area used for adding and removing effects.

1 With **Slide 1** as the active slide, click to select the audio icon.

2 Click the **Animations tab**. In the **Advanced Animations group**, click **Animation Pane** to display the Animation Pane on the right side of the window. In the Animation Pane, the audio filename is displayed in the list.

> **Alert! | Did the Audio Filename Not Display in the Animation Pane?**
>
> If the name of the audio file does not display in the Animation Pane, click the audio icon on the slide, and then under Audio Tools, click the Playback button. In the Audio Options group, make sure that the Start is set for On Click.

3 Click the **Trigger button arrow**, and then point to **On Click of.** Compare your screen with Figure 5.31.

Notice the options to select for the trigger—Subtitle, Picture, Title, or the file name.

Figure 5.31

4 Click **Title 1**. Compare your screen with Figure 5.32.

At the right, in the Animation Pane, *Trigger: Title 1: Cross Oceans Music* is displayed at the top of the list. Notice that it is identified as the trigger.

Figure 5.32

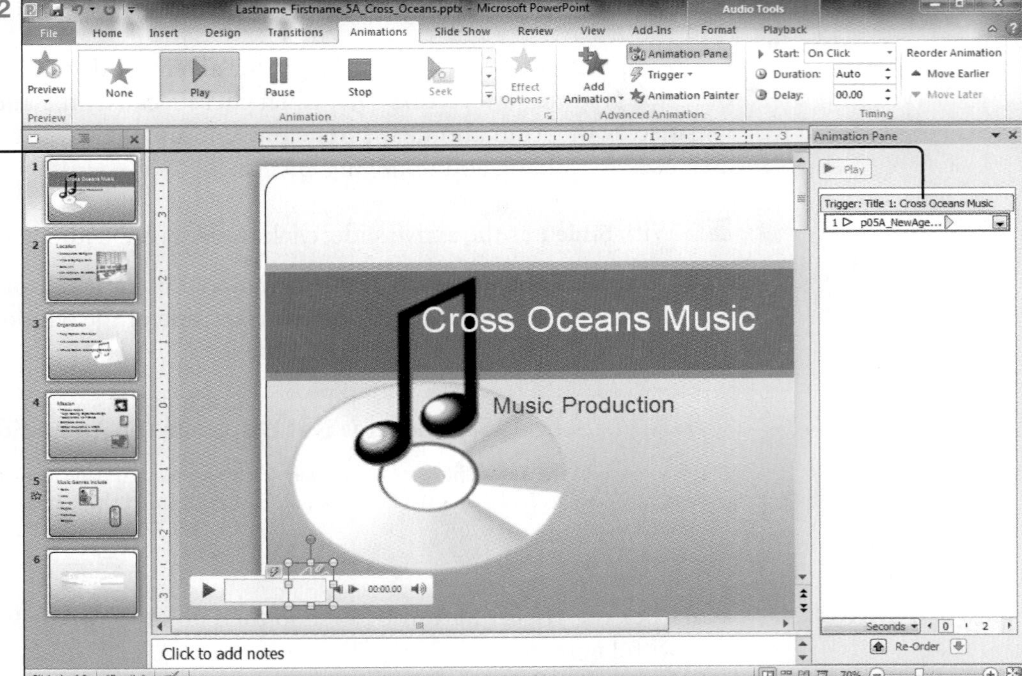

Trigger identified in the Animation Pane

5 Under **Audio Tools**, click the **Playback tab**. In the **Audio Options group**, click the check box for **Hide During Show**. **Close** [×] the **Animation Pane**.

6 Click the **Slide Show tab**. In the **Start Slide Show group**, click **From Current Slide**. Click the title *Cross Oceans Music* to start the audio. Press Esc.

7 **Save** your changes.

Activity 5.09 | Adding a Linked Video to a Presentation

In this activity, you will link a video to your presentation. Recall that you have previously learned how to embed a video. A presentation with a linked video is smaller in file size than a presentation with an embedded video. To prevent possible problems with broken links, it is a good idea to copy the video into the same folder as your presentation and then link to it from there. Both the video file and the presentation file must be available when presenting your slide show.

1 In the location where your data files are stored, locate **p05_Music_Video.avi**, and then copy it into your Chapter 5 folder.

> **Note | Copying a File**
>
> To copy a file on your storage device, display the Documents library, locate the file you want, right-click the file name, and then click Copy. Next, open the folder where you are saving your completed files, right-click, and then and click Paste.

2 Click **Slide 6**. Click the **Insert tab**. In the **Media group**, click the **Video button arrow**, and then click **Video from File**. Navigate to your data files, and then click **p05_Music_Video.avi**. In the preview area on the right, click **Play** to view the video. Click **Pause** to stop the video. In the lower right corner of the **Insert Video** dialog box, click the **Insert button arrow**. Compare your screen with Figure 5.33.

The options on the Insert list are Insert and Link to File.

Figure 5.33

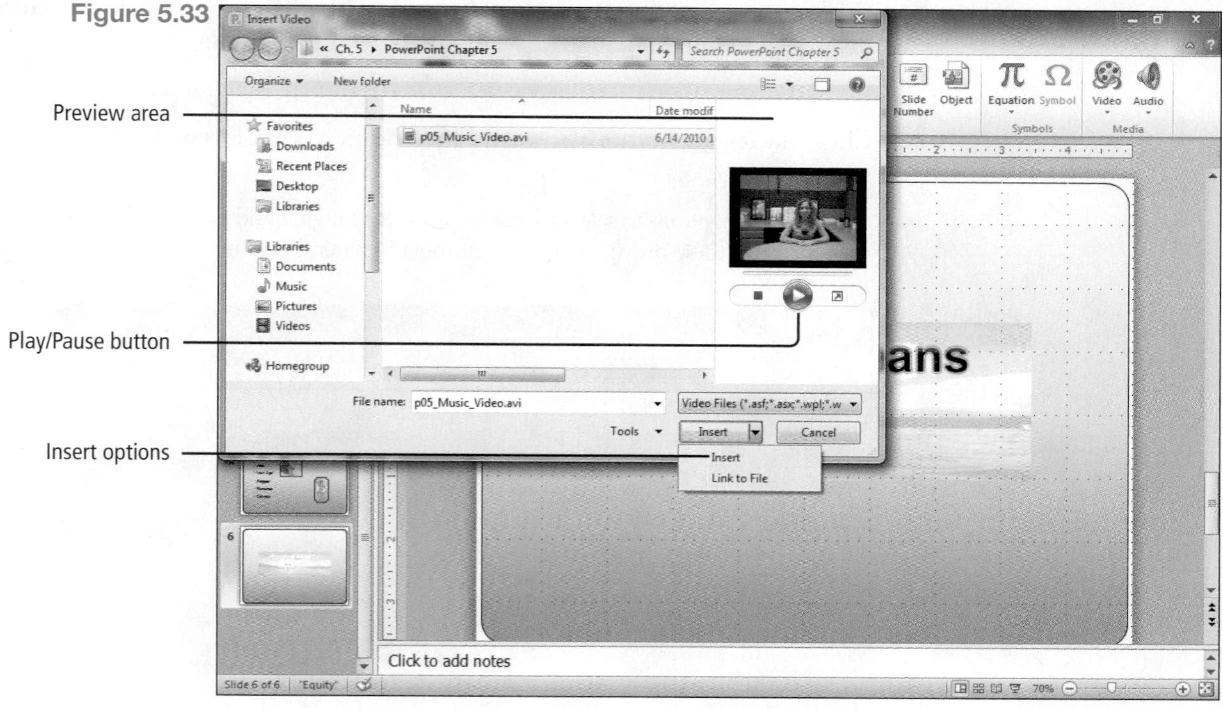

3 Click **Link to File**. In the **Size group**, change the **Video Height** to **1.5"**. Drag the entire video so the top aligns at **3.5 inches on the upper half of the vertical ruler** and the left side aligns at **4.5 inches on the left side of the horizontal ruler**. Compare your screen with Figure 5.34.

Moving the video allows you to see the content of the slide better. You can even resize the video if you wish.

Figure 5.34

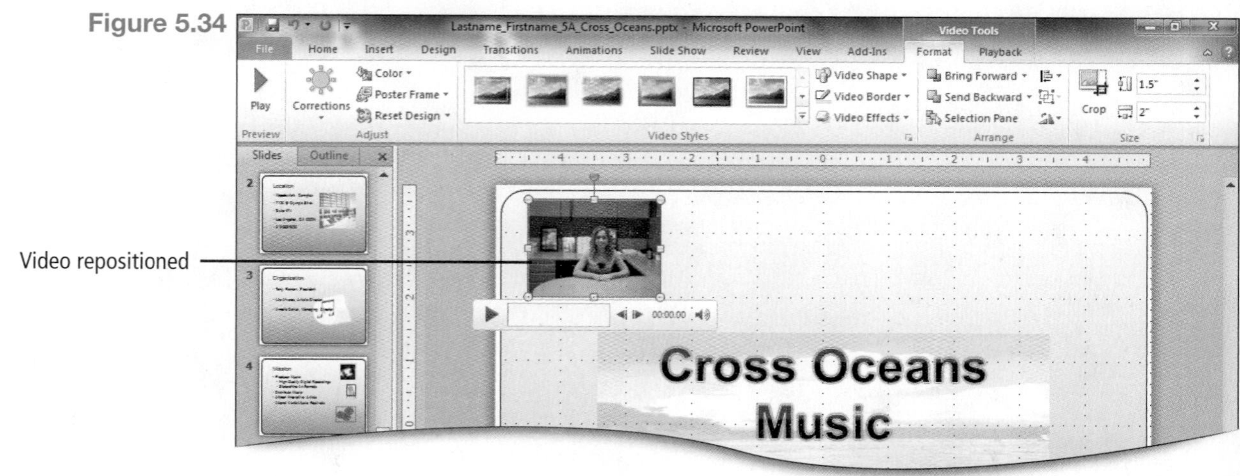

4 **Save** your changes.

Activity 5.10 | Changing the Trigger for a Linked Video in a Presentation

In this activity, you will use the Animation Pane to change the trigger that will play the video file from the video image to the WordArt shape. You will also set the video so it plays in full screen.

1 With **Slide 6** as the active slide, click to select the video, if necessary.

2 Click the **Animations tab**. In the **Advanced Animations group**, click **Animation Pane** to display the **Animation Pane** on the right side of the window.

In the Animation Pane, the video filename is displayed in the list.

3 Click the **Trigger button arrow**, and then point to **On Click of**. Compare your screen with Figure 5.35.

Notice the options to select for the trigger—Rectangle 1 and **p05_Music_Video.avi**. Rectangle represents the WordArt shape. The number in parentheses after Rectangle may vary.

Figure 5.35

4 Click **Rectangle 1**. Compare your screen with Figure 5.36.

Rectangle refers to the WordArt.

Figure 5.36

5 In the **Advanced Animation group**, click the **Animation Pane** button to close the **Animation Pane**. Under **Video Tools**, click the **Playback tab**. In the **Video Options group**, click the check box for **Hide While Not Playing**. Click check box for **Play Full Screen**. Compare your screen with Figure 5.37.

Figure 5.37

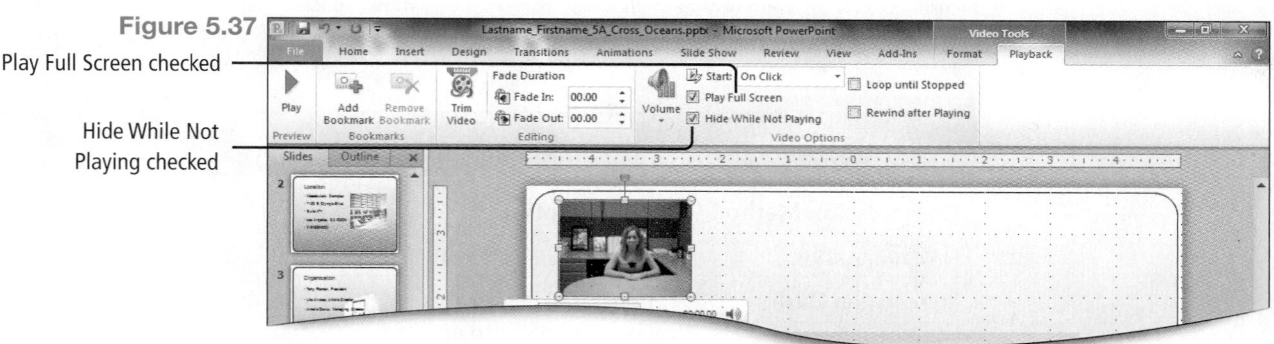

6 Click the **Slide Show tab**. In the **Start Slide Show group**, click **From Current Slide**. Click the *Cross Oceans Music* WordArt to start the audio. After the video plays, press Esc.

The video plays in full screen. Allow the video to play completely. If you stop the video, the video will display on the slide. For that reason, you might want to resize the video to a smaller size.

7 Press Esc. In the **Start Slide Show group**, click the **From Beginning** button to view the entire presentation. Click the trigger on **Slide 1** to hear the audio. Click the trigger on **Slide 6** to view the video. Press Esc.

8 In the **Documents library**, display the contents of your Chapter 5 folder. Observe that the size of the presentation file is much smaller than the size of the video file.

Because the presentation file contains a link to the video file, the actual video file is not a part of the presentation file size. For example, the video for this presentation is about 16,000 KB and the presentation file is about 2,000 KB. If you send this presentation electronically or transfer it to another location such as a USB drive, be sure to place both files in the same folder before sending or moving them.

Alert! | **Did You Change the Name of the Video File After Linking It to a Presentation?**

If you change the name of a video file after you link it to a presentation, the video will not play. You will have to link the file again.

9 On the **Insert tab**, in the **Text group**, click the **Header & Footer** button to display the **Header and Footer** dialog box. Click the **Notes and Handouts tab**. Under **Include on page**, select the **Date and time** check box, and then select **Fixed**. If necessary, clear the **Header** check box, and then select the **Page number** and **Footer** check boxes. In the **Footer** box, using your own name, type **Lastname_Firstname_5A_Cross_Oceans** and then click **Apply to All**.

10 Display **Backstage** view, click **Properties**, and then click **Show Document Panel**. Replace the text in the **Author** box with your own name; in the **Subject** box, type your course name and section number; and then in the **Keywords** box, type **mission, genres Close** the **Document Information Panel**.

11 **Save** your changes. Print **Handouts 4 Slides Horizontal**, or submit your presentation electronically as directed by your instructor.

12 **Close** the presentation, and then **Exit** PowerPoint.

More Knowledge | **Compressing Your Presentation Files**

If you are concerned about the size of your files or need to transmit them electronically, you may wish to consider using one of the compression methods. To display your options, in Backstage view, click Info, and then click Compress Media. Refer to Figure 5.38 for an explanation of compression qualities and the possible file sizes.

Compression File Size Comparison

Compression Method	Description	File Size Example
No Compression	The original size of the presentation.	18,010 KB
Presentation Quality	Reduced file size that maintains overall audio and video quality.	17,497 KB
Internet Quality	Quality comparable to media that is streamed over the Internet.	9,431 KB
Low Quality	Reduced file size sufficient for file sharing, such as sending as an e-mail attachment. Quality is not appropriate for a formal presentation.	2,766 KB

Figure 5.38

End **You have completed Project 5A**

Project 5B Business Photo Album

Project Activities

In Activities 5.11 through 5.13, you will create a PowerPoint photo album to display business photos of jazz musicians promoted and recorded by Cross Oceans Music. You will insert photos, add an attention-getting theme, and select a layout. You will also add frames to the photos and provide captions. You will experiment with tools that allow you to enter and format text in a text box and crop a photo to emphasize a key area of the photo. Your completed presentation will look similar to Figure 5.39.

Project Files

For Project 5B, you will need the following files:

New blank PowerPoint presentation
p05B_Jazz1.jpg
p05B_Jazz2.jpg
p05B_Jazz3.jpg
p05B_Jazz4.jpg
p05B_Jazz5.jpg
p05B_Jazz6.jpg
p05B_Jazz7.jpg

You will save your presentation as:

Lastname_Firstname_5B_Jazz_Album.pptx

Project Results

Figure 5.39
Project 5B Jazz Album

Objective 6 | Create a Photo Album

In the following activity, you will create a PowerPoint photo album. In PowerPoint, a ***photo album*** is a stylized presentation format to display pictures; you can display 1, 2, or 4 photos on a slide. The format may include a title or caption for the photo(s). A placeholder is inserted with each photo when the photo is added to the album. PowerPoint provides an easy and powerful tool to aid you in creating an exciting photo album.

Activity 5.11 | Creating a Photo Album

In this activity, you will create a photo album by inserting and customizing photos and selecting a theme. Each picture will be placed on its own slide.

1 **Start** PowerPoint. Click the **Insert tab**. In the **Images group**, click the **Photo Album button arrow**, and then click **New Photo Album**. Compare your screen with Figure 5.40.

The Photo Album dialog box provides an easy and convenient way to insert and remove pictures; rearrange and rotate pictures; apply brightness and contrast; insert captions; and select a layout, theme, and frame shape.

Figure 5.40

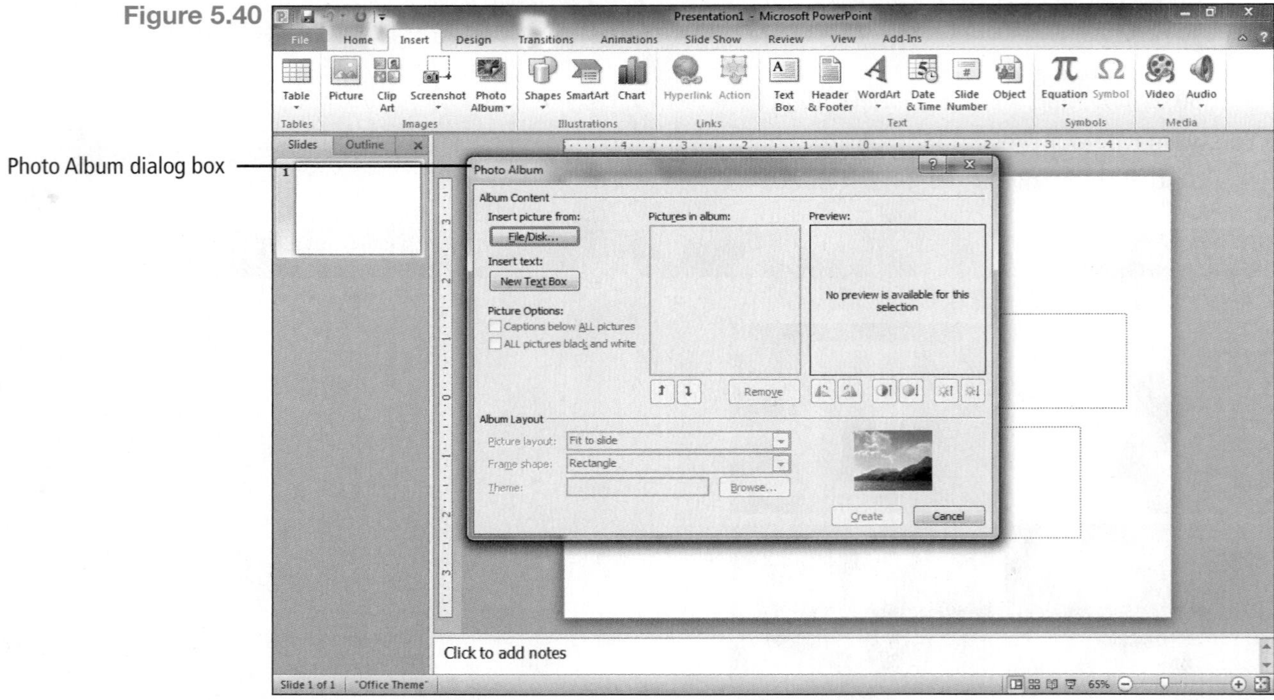

Another Way

When inserting pictures in the Photo Album dialog box, you can double-click the picture file name to insert it.

2 Under **Insert picture from**, click the **File/Disk** button to display the **Insert New Pictures** dialog box. Navigate to the location where your student files are stored, click **p05B_Jazz1.jpg**, and then click the **Insert** button. Compare your screen with Figure 5.41.

The file name displays as the first picture in the album, under Pictures in album, with a preview of the photograph.

Figure 5.41

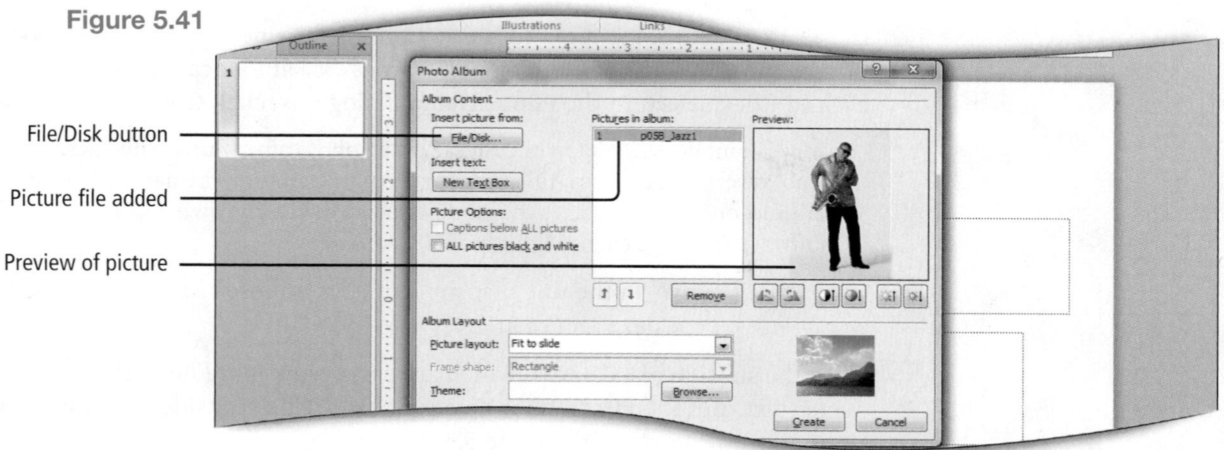

3 Using the technique you practiced, insert p05B_Jazz2.jpg, p05B_Jazz3.jpg, p05B_Jazz4.jpg, p05B_Jazz5.jpg, p05B_Jazz6.jpg, and p05B_Jazz7.jpg. Compare your screen with Figure 5.42:

Figure 5.42

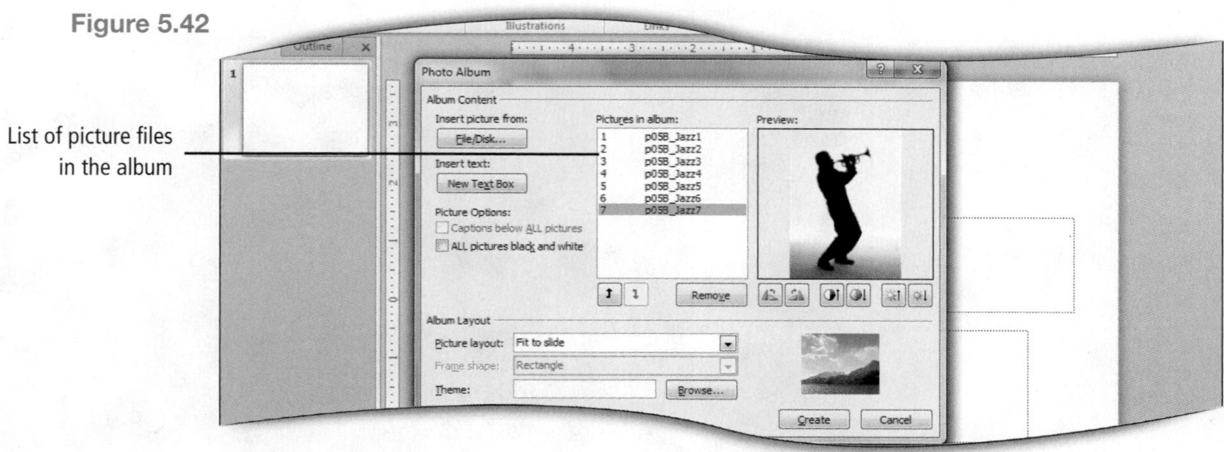

Note | **Inserting a Picture in the Photo Album Dialog Box**

If the pictures you want to insert into your photo album are listed in a sequence on your storage location, you can click on the first filename in the list, hold down the Shift key and click on the last picture in the list, and then click Insert. If the pictures are not in a sequence, you can hold down the Ctrl key while clicking the pictures individually, and then click Insert.

4 With **p05B_Jazz7.jpg** selected, under **Pictures in album**, click **Remove**.

The photo album now contains six pictures.

5 In the **Album Layout** section, click the **Picture layout arrow** to display the options.

You can choose to insert 1, 2, or 4 pictures on a slide, with or without a title, or you can choose Fit to slide.

6 Click **Fit to Slide** if necessary.

The Captions below ALL pictures check box is dimmed and therefore unavailable. Also, the Frame shape box is unavailable. In a photo album, the border around a picture is known as a ***frame***, and a limited number of styles are available. When you select ***Fit to slide***, the picture occupies all available space on the slide with no room for a frame or a caption.

> **Another Way**
> You can also double-click a document theme to select it.

7 In the **Album Layout** section, to the right of the **Theme** box, click the **Browse** button to display the **Choose Theme** dialog box themes. Scroll to locate **Perspective**, and then click it. Click **Select**. In the **Photo Album** dialog box, click **Create**.

PowerPoint does not apply the theme to the photo album until you click Create. Notice that PowerPoint creates a title slide for the photo album. The name inserted in the subtitle, on the title slide, is the name associated with the owner or license holder of the software. It can be changed on the slide.

8 With **Slide 1** active, in the title placeholder, click an insertion point to the left of the word *Photo*. Type **Jazz** and then press Spacebar.

9 Click the subtitle placeholder, which appears below *Jazz Photo Album*, delete the owner text, and then type **Cross Oceans Music**. Click outside the subtitle, and then compare your screen with Figure 5.43.

Cross Oceans Music now replaces the default owner or license holder of your software.

Figure 5.43

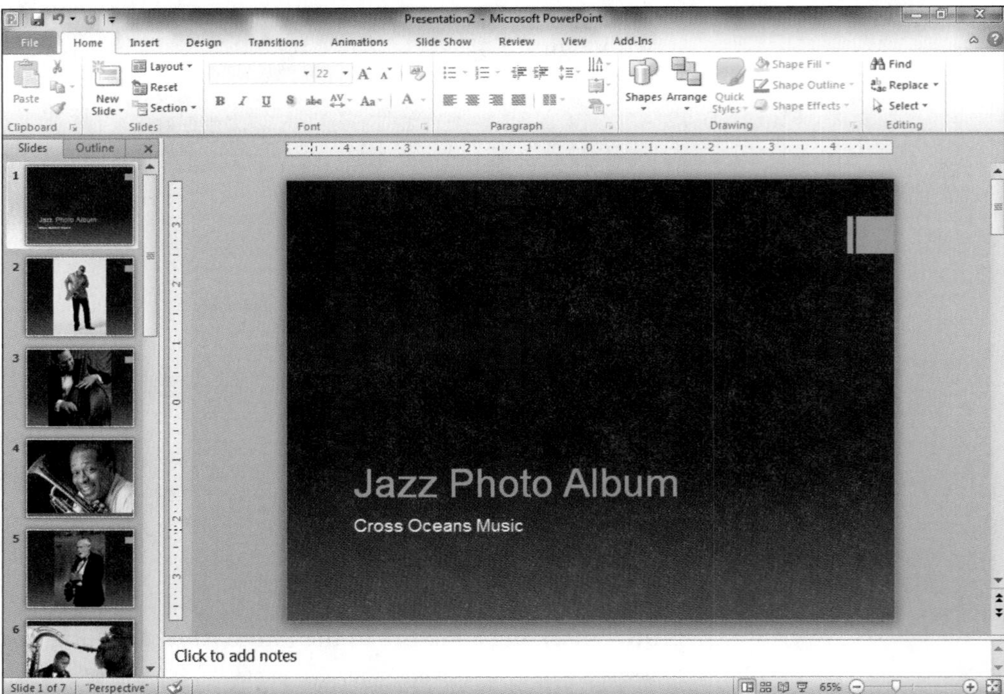

10 Display **Backstage** view, click **Save As**, and then navigate to the location where you are storing your projects for this chapter. Using your own name, save the file as **Lastname_Firstname_5B_Jazz_Album**

Because PowerPoint creates the photo album in a new presentation, you should wait until you click the Create button before saving the photo album. The original blank presentation that you started with is empty.

Objective 7 | Edit a Photo Album and Add a Caption

After you create a PowerPoint photo album, it is possible to format the background of the title slide by adding and customizing a caption for each photo. A ***caption*** is text that helps to identify or explain a picture or graphic.

Activity 5.12 | Editing a Photo Album and Adding a Caption

In this activity, you will edit a photo album, change the picture layout, and add captions.

1 With **Slide 1** as the active slide, right-click in the Slide pane to display the shortcut menu, and then click **Format Background**. In the **Format Background** dialog box, under the **Fill** options, select the **Picture or texture fill** option button.

2 Under **Insert from**, click **File**. Navigate to the location where your student files are stored, click **p05B_Jazz7.jpg**, and then click **Insert**. In the **Format Background** dialog box, click **Close**. Compare your screen with Figure 5.44.

This applies the background picture to the title slide only. Notice that the top of the picture is off the slide and the subtitle *Cross Oceans Music* is too light to read.

Figure 5.44

3 In the upper right corner of the slide, right-click, and then click **Format Background**. In the **Format Background** dialog box, under **Stretch options**, under **Offsets**, in the **Top** box, type **-20%**, and then click **Close**. Compare your screen with Figure 5.45.

This lowers the background silhouette to make the top visible on the slide. Because only the top was changed, the picture is a little distorted.

> **Alert! | Did Format Background Appear on the Context-Sensitive Menu?**
>
> If you did not see Format Background as a choice when you right-clicked the slide, you probably clicked on the Title or Subtitle placeholder. Right-click in another place on the slide, and you should see the appropriate options.

Figure 5.45

4 On **Slide 1**, select the text in the subtitle placeholder. Right-click the selected text to display the Mini toolbar, and then click the **Font Color button arrow** [A ▾]. In the first row, click the fourth color—**Orange, Text 2**. On the **Home tab**, in the **Font group**, click the **Text Shadow** button [S].

5 Click the **Slide Show tab**. In the **Start Slide Show group**, click the **From Beginning** button. Click through all the slides. Press [Esc] to return to Normal view.

The pictures fit to the slide and do not allow room for a caption.

6 Click the **Insert tab**. In the **Images group**, click the **Photo Album button arrow**, and then click **Edit Photo Album** to display the **Edit Photo Album** dialog box. Click the **Picture layout arrow** to display the options, and then click **1 picture**.

7 In the **Album Content** section, under **Picture Options**, select the **Captions below ALL pictures** check box, and then compare your screen with Figure 5.46.

Figure 5.46

8 Click **Update**, and then make **Slide 2** the active slide. Compare your screen with Figure 5.47.

Notice that, by default, the file name displays as the caption.

Figure 5.47

9 With **Slide 2** as the active slide, click to select the picture caption placeholder. Reposition the caption by dragging the entire placeholder down until the bottom edge of the placeholder aligns with the bottom edge of the slide.

10 Double-click to select the caption, and then press Del. Type **Tenor Saxophone** Compare your screen with Figure 5.48.

Figure 5.48

11 Using the technique you practiced, add the following captions to **Slides 3**, **4**, **5**, **6**, and **7**, and then reposition the captions to align with the bottom edge of the slide:

Slide 3	Bass
Slide 4	Trumpet
Slide 5	Alto Saxophone
Slide 6	Tenor Saxophone
Slide 7	Alto Saxophone

12 View the slide show **From beginning**. Click **Slide 1** when finished.

13 **Save** your changes.

Objective 8 | Crop a Picture

In the following activity, you will edit the PowerPoint photo album you created by cropping the picture. When you ***crop*** a picture, you remove unwanted or unnecessary areas of a picture. Images are often cropped to create more emphasis on the primary subject of the image. Recall that the Compress Picture dialog box provides the option to delete the cropped area of a picture. Deleting the cropped area reduces file size and also prevents people from being able to view the parts of the picture that you have removed. The ***crop handles*** are used like sizing handles to crop a picture, and the ***Crop tool*** is the mouse pointer used when removing areas of a picture.

Activity 5.13 | Cropping a Picture

1 Make **Slide 7** the active slide. Click the picture once to select the placeholder, and then click again to select the picture.

Because the placeholder is inserted at the time the picture is inserted, you must click the picture two times in order to gain access to the crop feature.

2 Under **Picture Tools**, click the **Format tab**. In the **Size group**, click the **Crop** button. Compare your screen with Figure 5.49.

> **Alert! | Is the Crop Button Inactive?**
>
> If you cannot display the Crop tool and crop lines, click the picture two times.

Figure 5.49

3 Position the Crop pointer just inside the middle cropping handle on the right edge of the picture.

The mouse pointer assumes the shape of the crop line, in this case a straight vertical line with a short horizontal line attached.

4 Drag the pointer to the left until the right edge of the picture aligns with approximately the **0-inch mark** on the **horizontal ruler**, and then release the mouse button. Compare your screen with Figure 5.50.

The dark area to the right represents the area that will be removed.

Figure 5.50

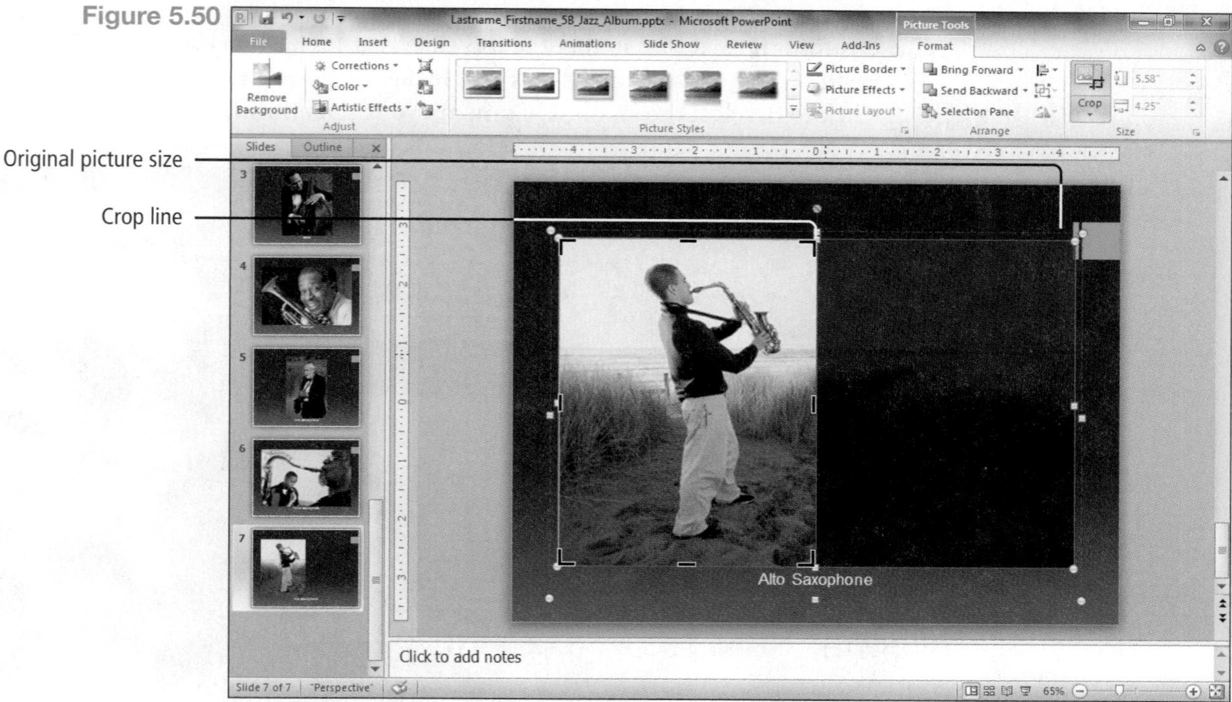

Another Way

You can also turn off the cropping button by pressing Esc or by clicking the Crop button.

5 Click outside the picture to turn off cropping.

6 Click the **Insert tab**. In the **Text group**, click **Text Box**, and then click one time to the right of the picture. Compare your screen with Figure 5.51.

Figure 5.51

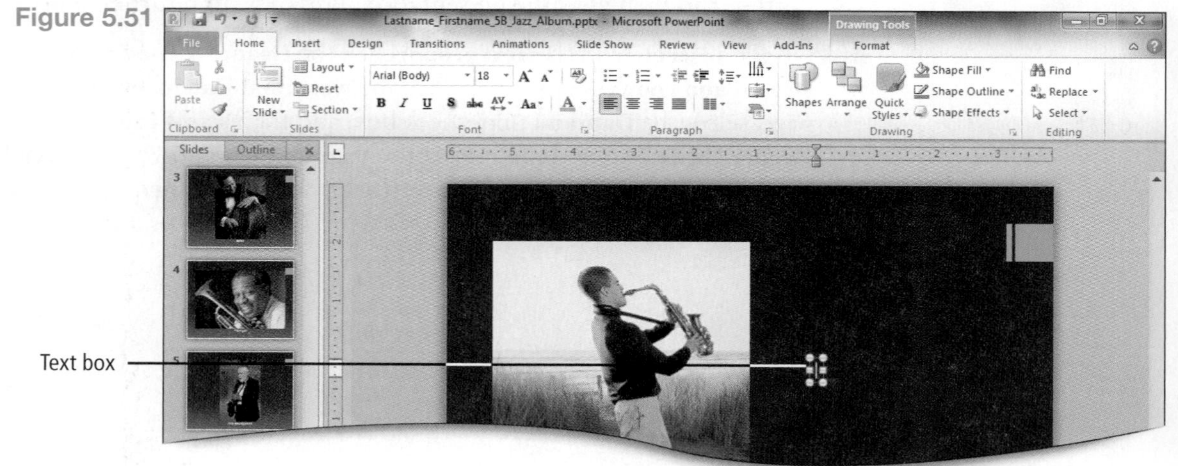

PowerPoint | Chapter 5

7 In the text box, type **Meet the newest addition to our jazz musicians.**

8 Position the insertion point to the left of *to*, and then press Enter to break the text to a second line. Select both lines of text in the text box, and then increase the font size to **24. Center** the text.

> **Note | Selecting Text in Placeholders**
>
> Recall that you can click the border of a placeholder to select text. When the border is displayed as a solid border, you know the text is selected.

9 Position the text box so that the top edge is at **1.5 inches on the upper half of the vertical ruler** and the left edge is at **.5 inches on the right side of the horizontal ruler.** Click to deselect the text box. Compare your screen with Figure 5.52

Figure 5.52

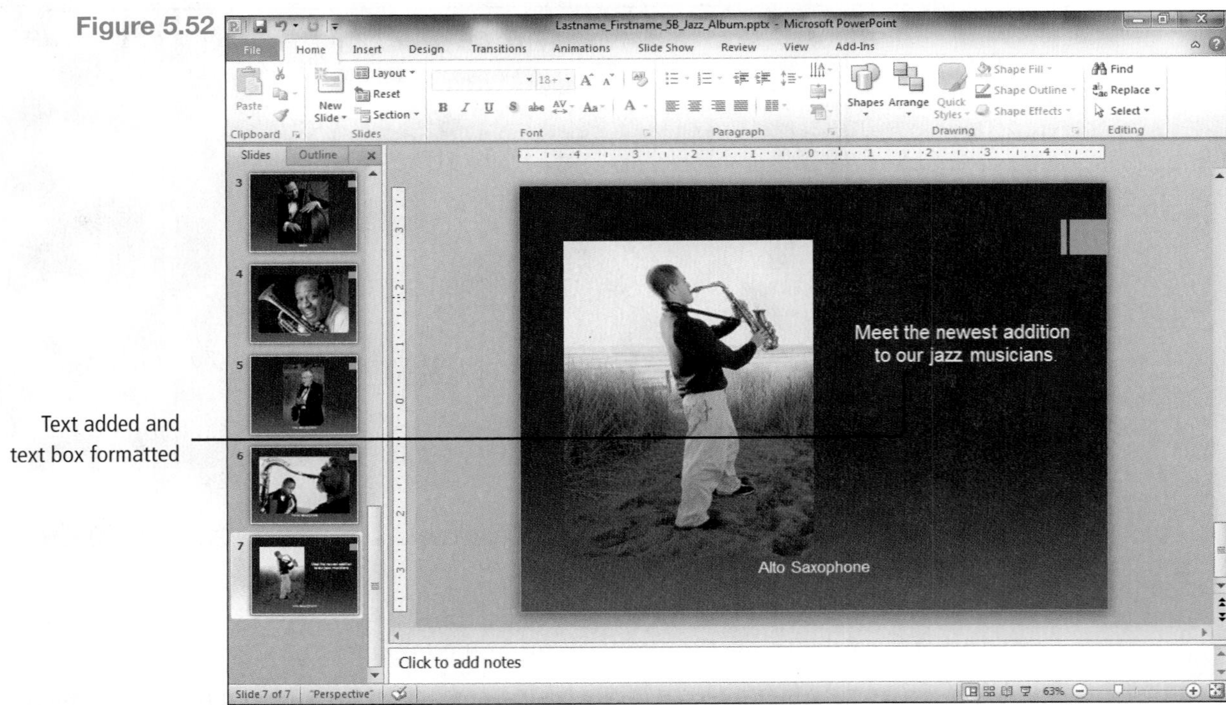

> **Another Way**
>
> To start the slide show from the beginning, make Slide 1 the active slide, and then press the F5 key or the Slide Show icon on the status bar.

10 Click the **Slide Show tab**. In the **Start Slide Show group**, click the **From Beginning** button, and then view the presentation. Press Esc to return to Normal view.

11 On the **Insert tab**, in the **Text group**, click the **Header & Footer** button to display the **Header and Footer** dialog box. Click the **Notes and Handouts tab**. Under **Include on page**, select the **Date and time** check box, and then select **Fixed**. If necessary, clear the **Header** check box, and then select the **Page number** and **Footer** check boxes. In the **Footer** box, using your own name, type **Lastname_Firstname_5B_Jazz_Album** and then click **Apply to All**.

12 Display **Backstage** view, click **Properties**, and then click **Show Document Panel**. Replace the text in the **Author** box with your own name; in the **Subject** box, type your course name and section number; and in the **Keywords** box, type **jazz, photo, album** **Close** the **Document Information Panel**.

13 **Save** your changes. Print **Handouts 4 Slides Horizontal**, or submit your presentation electronically as directed by your instructor.

14 **Close** the presentation, and then **Exit** PowerPoint.

End **You have completed Project 5B**

Content-Based Assessments

Summary

In this chapter, you practiced completing a PowerPoint presentation by inserting and modifying pictures and images, and by changing the sharpness and softness and also the brightness and contrast. Next, you added borders to images. You recolored pictures and added audio and video to a slide show. You changed the method by which audio and video play in a slide show and created triggers for starting them. You created and edited a photo album and you practiced cropping a picture and added captions to photos.

Key Terms

Matching

Match each term in the second column with its correct definition in the first column by writing the letter of the term on the blank line in front of the correct definition.

____ 1. The term used to describe the amount of light or white in a picture.

____ 2. The mouse pointer used when removing areas of a picture.

____ 3. The process of applying a stylized effect or hue to a picture.

____ 4. The pane used for adding and removing effects.

____ 5. The thickness of a line, measured in points.

____ 6. The term used to describe corners of a border that are angled to form a square.

____ 7. The term used to describe playing an audio file repeatedly until it is stopped manually.

____ 8. The term used to describe audio or video files that are saved as part of the PowerPoint presentation.

____ 9. The button that displays next to the slide thumbnail in the Slide/Outline pane that, when clicked, will play an audio file or an animation.

____ 10. A portion of text, a graphic, or a picture on a slide that, when clicked, will play an audio or video file.

____ 11. A frame or outline added to a picture or clip art.

____ 12. The text that displays beneath a picture in a photo album and, by default, is the file name.

A Animation
B Border
C Brightness
D Caption
E Crop handles
F Crop tool
G Embedded
H Line weight
I Loop
J Mitered
K Play Animations
L Recoloring
M Soften
N Track
O Trigger

_____ 13. The marks on a selected picture used to remove unwanted parts of a picture.

_____ 14. A feature that decreases the clarity of an image, making it look fuzzy.

_____ 15. A song from a CD.

Multiple Choice

Circle the correct answer.

1. The term for an .avi video file that is saved separately from a PowerPoint presentation is:
   A. embedded B. surrounded C. linked

2. In a photo album, which is the term used to describe a picture that occupies all available space on a slide, leaving no room for a caption?
   A. Unbordered B. Fit to slide C. Full screen

3. The term that describes a border around a picture in a photo album is:
   A. edging B. handle C. frame

4. The lines used to crop a picture are known as:
   A. crop handles B. sizing handles C. mitered corners

5. How lines display, such as a solid line, dots, or dashes, is referred to as:
   A. line weight B. line style C. line gradient

6. A single point in an image is called a(n):
   A. element B. pixel C. grid

7. The file size of a presentation with a linked video file, compared with a presentation with an embedded video file, is:
   A. larger B. the same C. smaller

8. A picture that has been formatted to look fuzzy is:
   A. cropped B. softened C. sharpened

9. The amount of difference between the light and dark extremes of color in an image is called the:
   A. contrast B. disparity C. brightness

10. A portion of text that, when clicked, causes an audio or video to play is called the:
    A. activator B. trigger C. frame

Apply 5A skills from these Objectives:

1. Use Picture Corrections
2. Add a Border to a Picture
3. Change the Shape of a Picture
4. Add a Picture to a WordArt Object
5. Enhance a Presentation with Audio and Video

Skills Review | Project 5C Celtic Instruments

In the following Skills Review, you will modify pictures in a presentation about the instruments used in the Celtic music genre for the Cross Oceans Music company. You will change the brightness, contrast, and shapes of pictures and add borders to some pictures for emphasis. You will also add audio files that demonstrate the various instruments used in this type of music and a video file. Your completed presentation will look similar to Figure 5.53.

Project Files

For Project 5C, you will need the following files:

p05C_Celtic_Instruments.pptx
p05C_Flute.wav
p05C_Harp.wav
p05_Music_Video.avi
p05C_Sheet_Music.jpg

You will save your presentation as:

Lastname_Firstname_5C_Celtic_Instruments.pptx

Project Results

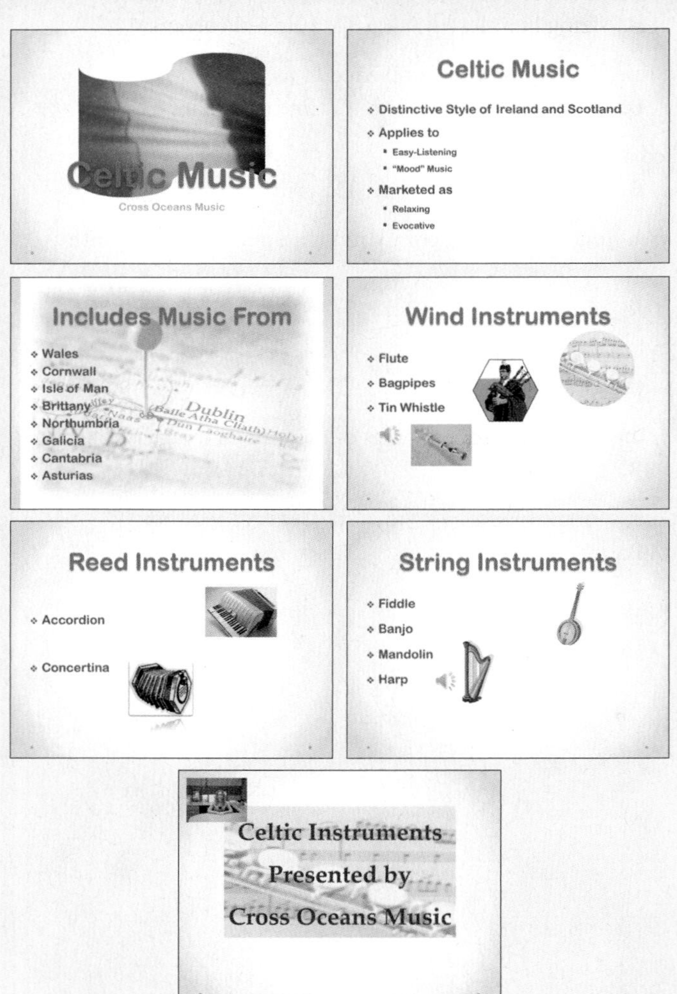

Figure 5.53

(Project 5C Celtic Instruments continues on the next page)

Content-Based Assessments

Skills Review | Project 5C Celtic Instruments (continued)

1 **Start** PowerPoint. Locate and open the file **p05C_Celtic_Instruments**. Using your own first and last name, save the file as **Lastname_Firstname_5C_Celtic_Instruments** in your PowerPoint Chapter 5 folder.

2 Click **Slide 1**, if necessary, and then click to select the image.

a. Under **Picture Tools**, click the **Format tab**. In the **Size group**, click the **Crop button arrow**, and then point to **Crop to Shape**. Under **Flowchart**, locate and click **Flowchart: Punched Tape**, which is in the second row, fourth from the left.

b. In the **Adjust group**, click the **Corrections** button, and then click **Picture Corrections Options** to display the **Format Picture** dialog box. Under **Sharpen and Soften**, drag the slider to the left to **-100%**. Under **Brightness and Contrast**, click the **Presets** button, and then in the first row, third column, click **Brightness: 0% (Normal) Contrast: -40%**. Click **Close**.

c. Drag the entire image so the top edge is at **3 inches on the upper half of the horizontal ruler**. In the **Arrange group**, click the **Align** button, and then click **Align Center**.

d. In the **Arrange group**, click the **Send Backward button arrow**, and then click **Send to Back**.

3 Make **Slide 3** the active slide, and then select the picture.

a. Under **Picture Tools**, click the **Format tab**, and then click **Selection Pane**. In the **Selection and Visibility pane**, click **Picture 3**. Close the **Selection and Visibility pane**. In the **Adjust group**, click the **Corrections** button. Under **Brightness and Contrast**, locate and click **Brightness: 0% (Normal) Contrast: +20%**, which is in the fourth row, third column.

b. In the **Arrange group**, click the **Send Backward button arrow**, and then click **Send to Back**.

4 Make **Slide 4** the active slide.

a. Click the **picture of the musician playing bagpipes**. On the **Format tab**, in the **Size group**, click the **Crop button arrow**, and then point to **Crop to Shape**. Under **Basic Shapes**, locate and click **Hexagon**.

b. In the **Picture Styles group**, click **Picture Border button arrow**, point to **Weight**, and then click **1 pt**.

c. Click the **picture of the sheet music with the flute**. On the **Format tab**, in the **Size group**, click the **Crop button arrow**, and then point to **Crop to Shape**. Under **Basic Shapes**, locate and click **Oval**.

5 Make **Slide 5** the active slide.

a. Click the **picture of the accordion**. On the **Format tab**, in the **Picture Styles group**, click the **More arrow**. Locate and click **Reflected Bevel, Black**, which is in the last row, first column.

b. In the **Picture Styles group**, click the **Picture Border** button, and then click **No Outline**.

6 Make **Slide 6** the active slide.

a. Click the **picture of the banjo**.

b. In the **Adjust group**, click the **Corrections** button. Under **Brightness and Contrast**, locate and click **Brightness: +20% Contrast: -20%**.

7 Make **Slide 4** the active slide.

a. Click the **Insert tab**. In the **Media group**, click the **Audio button arrow**, and then click **Audio from File**.

b. Navigate to the location where your student files are stored. Locate and insert **p05C_Flute.wav**.

c. Under **Audio Tools**, click the **Playback tab**. Click the **Start button arrow**, and then click **Automatically**. Click the **Hide During Show** check box.

d. Move the speaker icon to the left side of the picture of the tin whistle so it is under the word *Tin* in the last bullet.

8 Make **Slide 6** the active slide.

a. Click the **Insert tab**. In the **Media group**, click the **Audio button arrow**, and then click **Audio from File**.

b. Navigate to the location where your student files are stored. Locate and insert **p05C_Harp.wav**.

c. Under **Audio Tools**, click the **Playback tab**. Click the **Start button arrow**, and then click **Automatically**. Click the **Hide During Show** check box.

d. Move the audio icon close to the left side of the picture of the harp.

9 On the **Home tab**, in the **Slides group**, click the **New Slide button arrow**, and then click **Blank** to insert a new blank **Slide 7**.

a. On the **Insert tab**, in the **Text group**, click the **WordArt** button. In the third row, third column, locate and click **Gradient Fill – Gray, Outline – Gray**.

b. Type **Celtic Instruments** Press Enter, and then type **Presented by** Press Enter, and then type **Cross Oceans Music**

(Project 5C Celtic Instruments continues on the next page)

Skills Review | Project 5C Celtic Instruments (continued)

c. Select the lines of text. On the **Home tab**, in the **Paragraph group**, click the **Line Spacing button arrow**, and then click **1.5**. In the **Font group**, click the **Font Color button arrow**. Locate and click **Dark Green, Accent 5, Darker 50%**.

d. Drag the **WordArt** so the top edge is at **2.5 inches on the upper half of the vertical ruler**. Under **Drawing Tools**, click the **Format tab**. In the **Arrange group**, click the **Align button arrow**, and then click **Align Center**.

e. On the **Format tab**, in the **Shape Styles group**, click **Shape Fill**, and then click **Picture**. Navigate to the location where your student files are stored. Locate and click **p05C_Sheet_Music.jpg**, and then click **Insert**.

f. Under **Picture Tools**, click the **Format tab**. In the **Adjust group**, click **Color**. Under **Recolor**, locate and click **Dark Green, Accent Color 5 Light**. Right-click the **WordArt shape**, and then click **Format Picture**. Under **Sharpen and Soften**, drag the slider to **-100%**. Click **Close**.

10 In the location where your data files are stored, locate **p05_Music_Video.avi**, and then copy it into your **Chapter 5 folder**.

11 Click **Slide 7**, and then click the **Insert tab**. In the **Media group**, click the **Video button arrow**, and then click **Video from File**.

a. Navigate to the location where your student files are stored, click **p05_Music_Video.avi**, and then click the **Insert button arrow**. Click **Link to File**.

b. Under **Video Tools**, click the **Playback tab**. Click the check boxes for **Play Full Screen** and **Hide While Not Playing**.

c. Click the **Animations tab**. In the **Advanced Animation group**, click the **Trigger** button, point to **On Click of**, and then click **Rectangle**.

d. Click the **Format tab**. In the **Size group**, change the **Video Height** to **1.5"**. Move the entire video to the upper left corner of the slide, at **3.5 inches on the upper half of the vertical ruler** and **4.5 inches on the left side of the horizontal ruler**.

12 Click the **Slide Show tab**. In the **Start Slide Show group**, click **From Beginning**. Listen for the two audio files, and then click the **WordArt** on **Slide 7** to view the video.

13 On the **Insert tab**, in the **Text group**, click the **Header & Footer** button to display the **Header and Footer** dialog box. Click the **Notes and Handouts tab**. Under **Include on page**, select the **Date and time** check box, and then select **Fixed**. If necessary, clear the **Header** check box, and then select the **Page number** and **Footer** check boxes. In the **Footer** box, using your own name, type **Lastname_Firstname_5C_Celtic_Instruments** and then click **Apply to All**.

14 Display **Backstage** view, Click **Properties**, and then click **Show Document Panel**. Replace the text in the **Author** box with your own name; in the **Subject** box, type your course name and section number; and in the **Keywords** box, type **Celtic, instruments, Ireland, Scotland Close** the **Document Information Panel**.

15 **Save** the presentation. Print **Handouts 4 Slides Horizontal**, or submit your presentation electronically as directed by your instructor. **Exit** PowerPoint.

End You have completed Project 5C

Apply 5B skills from these Objectives:

- 6 Create a Photo Album
- 7 Edit a Photo Album and Add a Caption
- 8 Crop a Picture

Skills Review | Project 5D Celtic Album

In the following Skills Review, you will create a photo album for the Cross Oceans Music company. You will insert photos of musicians who record Celtic music and are represented by Cross Oceans. You will also include photos of some of the unusual instruments used to create this type of music. You will add captions and crop unwanted areas of photos. Your completed presentation will look similar to Figure 5.54.

Project Files

For Project 5D, you will need the following files:

New blank PowerPoint presentation
p05D_Mandolin.jpg
p05D_Flautist.jpg
p05D_Banjo.jpg
p05D_Violinist.jpg
p05D_Bagpipes.jpg

You will save your presentation as:

Lastname_Firstname_5D_Celtic_Album.pptx

Project Results

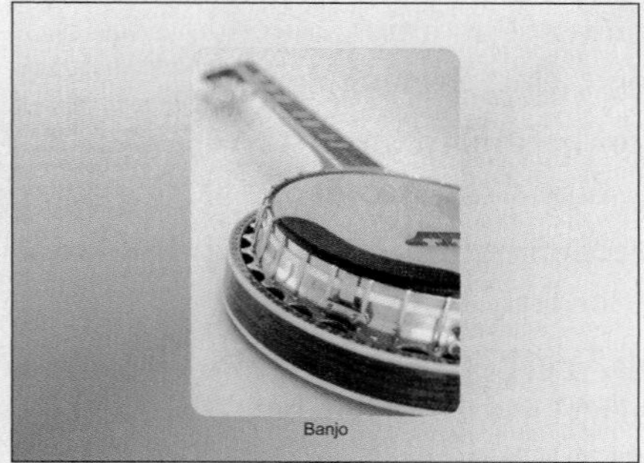

Figure 5.54

(Project 5D Celtic Album continues on the next page)

Skills Review | Project 5D Celtic Album (continued)

1 **Start** PowerPoint. Click the **Insert tab**. In the **Images group**, click the **Photo Album button arrow**, and then click **New Photo Album**.

2 Under **Insert picture from**, click **File/Disk** to display the **Insert New Pictures** dialog box. Navigate to the location where your student files are stored, click **p05D_Mandolin.jpg**, and then, if necessary, click the **Insert** button.

3 Using the technique you practiced, insert the following pictures into the photo album in this order: **p05D_Flautist.jpg**, **p05D_Banjo.jpg**, **p05D_Violinist.jpg**, and **p05D_Bagpipes.jpg**.

4 Under **Album Layout**, click the **Picture layout arrow** to display the selections. Click **1 picture**.

5 Click the **Frame shape arrow** to display the frame shape selections, and then click **Rounded Rectangle**.

6 To the right of the **Theme** box, click the **Browse** button to display the **Choose Theme** dialog box. Click **Clarity**, and then click **Select**. In the **Photo Album** dialog box, click **Create**.

7 Display **Backstage** view, click **Save As**, and then navigate to the location where you are storing your projects for this chapter and save the file as **Lastname_Firstname_5D_Celtic_Album**

8 Click **Slide 1**. Right-click to display the shortcut menu.

a. Click **Format Background**, and then click the **Hide background graphics** check box.
b. Select the **Gradient Fill** option, and then click the **Type arrow** and select **Rectangular**.
c. Click the **Color** button. In the first row, ninth column, click **Blue-Gray, Accent 5**.
d. Click the **Direction** button. Locate and click **From Bottom Left Corner**.
e. Drag the **Stop 2 position** slider to **75%**. Click **Apply to All**, and then **Close** the dialog box.

9 Position the insertion point to the left of *Photo Album*.

a. Type **Celtic Music** and then press **Enter**. The text will be in all capital letters.
b. Select both lines of the title—*CELTIC MUSIC PHOTO ALBUM*. Click the **Format tab**. In the **WordArt Styles group**, click the **Text Effects button arrow**, point to **Glow**, and then click **Gray-50%, 5 pt glow, Accent color 1**.
c. Click the **Text Outline button arrow**, and then in the second row, click **White, Background 1, Darker 5%**.
d. Increase the size of the title to **66 pts**, add **Bold**, and **Shadow**.

10 Delete the subtitle, and then type **Cross Oceans Music**

11 Click the **Insert tab**. In the **Images group**, click the **Photo Album button arrow**, and then click **Edit Photo Album**. In the **Edit Photo Album** dialog box, under **Picture Options**, select the **Captions below ALL pictures** check box, and then click **Update**.

12 Make **Slide 2** the active slide, and then click to select the caption. Select *p05D_*, and then press **Delete**. The caption should now read *Mandolin*.

13 Using the technique you practiced, edit the captions for **Slides 3**, **4**, **5**, and **6** as follows:

Flautist

Banjo

Violinist

Bagpipes

14 On **Slide 6**, click the **picture of the bagpipes**. Under **Picture Tools**, click the **Format tab**. In the **Size group**, click the **Crop** button.

a. Drag the right middle cropping handle left to **2.5 inches on the right side of the horizontal ruler**.
b. Repeat the procedure to crop the left side to **2.5 inches on the left side of the horizontal ruler**.
c. Click the **Crop** button to turn off cropping.

15 Click the **Slide Show tab**. In the **Start Slide Show group**, click **From Beginning**.

16 On the **Insert tab**, in the **Text group**, click the **Header & Footer** button to display the **Header and Footer** dialog box. Click the **Notes and Handouts tab**. Under **Include on page**, select the **Date and time** check box, and then select **Fixed**. If necessary, clear the **Header** check box, and then select the **Page number** and **Footer** check boxes. In the **Footer** box, using your own name, type **Lastname_Firstname_5D_Celtic_Album** and then click **Apply to All**.

17 Display **Backstage** view, click **Properties**, and then click **Show Document Panel**. Replace the text in the **Author** box with your own name; in the **Subject** box, type your course name and section number; and in the **Keywords** box, type **Celtic, music, album Close** the **Document Information Panel**.

18 **Save** the presentation. Print **Handouts 4 Slides Horizontal**, or submit your presentation electronically as directed by your instructor. Then **Close** your presentation and **Exit** PowerPoint.

End **You have completed Project 5D**

Content-Based Assessments

Apply **5A** skills from these Objectives:

1. Use Picture Corrections
2. Add a Border to a Picture
3. Change the Shape of a Picture
4. Add a Picture to a WordArt Object
5. Enhance a Presentation with Audio and Video

Mastering PowerPoint | Project 5E Reggae Music

In the following Mastering PowerPoint project, you will modify pictures in a presentation used in educational seminars hosted by Cross Oceans Music. The presentation highlights Reggae music and its roots in jazz and rhythm and blues. You will also add an audio file that represents this genre of music and format it to play across the slides in the slide show. You will also add a video file. Your completed presentation will look similar to Figure 5.55.

Project Files

For Project 5E, you will need the following files:

p05E_Reggae_Music.pptx
p05E_Reggae.wav
p05E_Music.jpg
p05_Music_Video.avi

You will save your presentation as:

Lastname_Firstname_5E_Reggae_Music.pptx

Project Results

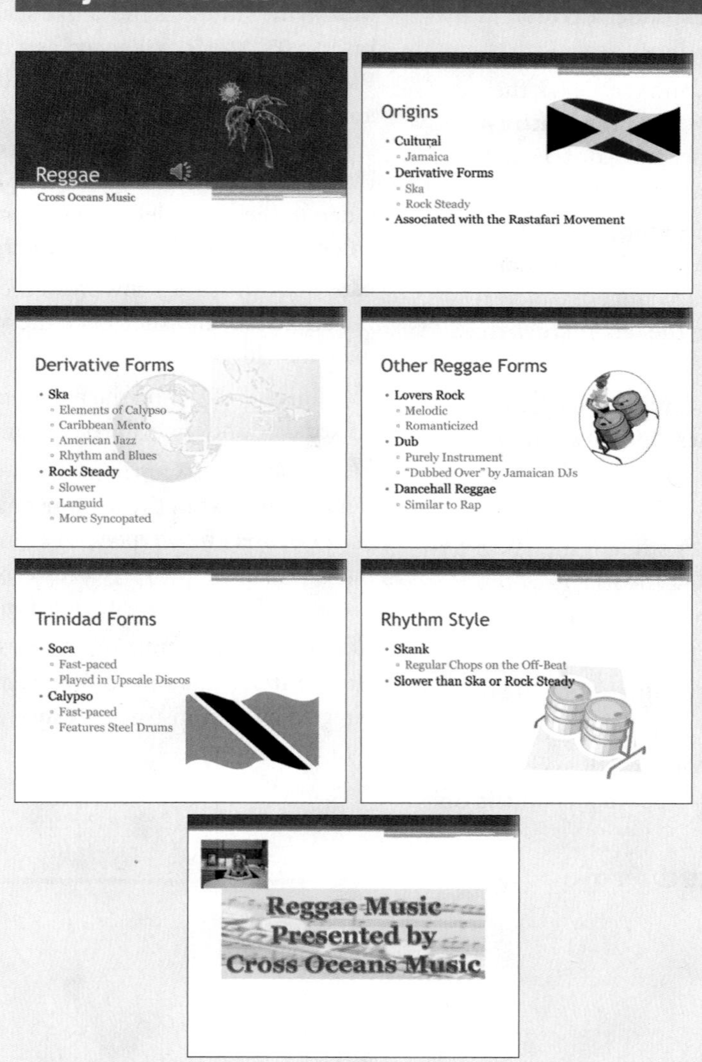

Figure 5.55

(Project 5E Reggae Music continues on the next page)

Mastering PowerPoint | Project 5E Reggae Music (continued)

1 **Start** PowerPoint. Locate and open the file **p05E_Reggae_Music**. Save the file in your chapter folder, using the file name **Lastname_Firstname_5E_Reggae_Music**

2 On the **title slide**, click to select the picture, click the **Format tab**, and then set the **Sharpen and Soften** to **0%**. Set the **Brightness** to **-15%**.

3 Make **Slide 2** the active slide, and then click to select the **picture of the Jamaican flag**. On the **Format tab**, click the **Crop button arrow**, and then crop the picture to the **Wave** shape, which is under **Stars and Banners**, in the second row, the seventh shape.

4 Make **Slide 3** the active slide. Click the **map and globe picture**, and the send the picture to the back. In the **Adjust group**, click **Color**, and then under **Recolor**, in the first row, fourth column, click **Washout**.

5 Make **Slide 4** the active slide, and then click the picture. Set the **Brightness** to **+20%** and the **Contrast** to **+20%**. Change the picture border to **Teal, Accent 2, Darker 50%**. Crop the picture to an **Oval** shape.

6 Make **Slide 5** the active slide, and then click to select the **picture of the flag of Trinidad**. Use **Crop to Shape**, and then under **Stars and Banners**, change the picture shape to **Double Wave**, which is in the second row, the last shape.

7 Make **Slide 6** the active slide, and then click to select the picture. Set the **Brightness** to **+40%**, and then **Send to Back**.

8 Make the **title slide** the active slide. Display the **Insert Audio** dialog box. From your student files, insert the audio file **p05E_Reggae.wav**. On the **Playback tab**, set the audio to **Hide During Show** and to start **Automatically**.

9 Click **Slide 6**, and then insert a **Blank** slide as **Slide 7**.

10 Make **Slide 7** the active slide, if necessary. On the **Insert tab**, click the **WordArt** button, and then click **Fill – Teal, Accent 2, Warm Matte Bevel**. Type **Reggae Music** on one line, type **Presented by** on the next line, and then type **Cross Oceans Music** on the third line. Change the **Font Color**
to **Teal, Accent 2, Darker 25%**. Drag the **WordArt** so the top edge is at **1.5 inches on the upper half of the vertical ruler**. On the **Format tab**, **Align Center** the WordArt shape.

11 With **Slide 7** as the active slide, use **Shape Fill** to insert from your data files the picture **p05E_Music.jpg**. Under **Picture Tools**, click the **Format tab**. Recolor the picture to **Teal, Accent color 2 Light**. Set the **Sharpen and Soften** at **-100%**.

12 In the location where your data files are stored, locate **p05_Music_Video.avi**, and then copy it into your Chapter 5 folder.

13 With **Slide 7** as the active slide. From your data files, insert **p05_Music_Video.avi** as a linked video. On the **Playback tab**, click the check boxes for **Play Full Screen** and **Hide While Not Playing**. On the **Animations tab**, set a trigger for the video to play **On click of** the WordArt rectangle. Change the **Video Height** to **1.5"**. Move the video to the upper left, at **3.0″ above 0 on the vertical ruler** and **4.5″ to the left of 0 on the horizontal ruler**.

14 Start the slide show from the beginning. Listen for the audio file, and then click the **WordArt** on **Slide 7** to view the video.

15 Insert a footer on the notes and handouts that includes a fixed date and time, the page number, and the file name.

16 Modify the **Properties** in the **Show Document Panel**. Replace the text in the **Author** box with your own name; in the **Subject** box, type your course name and section number; and in the **Keywords** box, type **Reggae, music** **Close** the **Document Information Panel**.

17 **Save** the presentation. Print **Handouts 4 Slides Horizontal**, or submit your presentation electronically as directed by your instructor. **Close** your presentation and **Exit** PowerPoint.

End **You have completed Project 5E**

Apply **5B** skills from these Objectives:

- **6** Create a Photo Album
- **7** Edit a Photo Album and Add a Caption
- **8** Crop a Picture

Mastering PowerPoint | Project 5F CD Cover

In the following Mastering PowerPoint project, you will create a photo album of pictures of island settings for a CD entitled *Reggae Revisited*. One of these cover designs will be chosen by Cross Oceans Music to be the cover of the soon-to-be-released CD of reggae and Jamaican music. Your completed presentation will look similar to Figure 5.56.

Project Files

For Project 5F, you will need the following files:

New blank PowerPoint presentation
p05F_Island1.jpg
p05F_Island2.jpg
p05F_Island3.jpg
p05F_Island4.jpg
p05F_Island5.jpg

You will save your presentation as:

Lastname_Firstname_5F_CD_Cover.pptx

Project Results

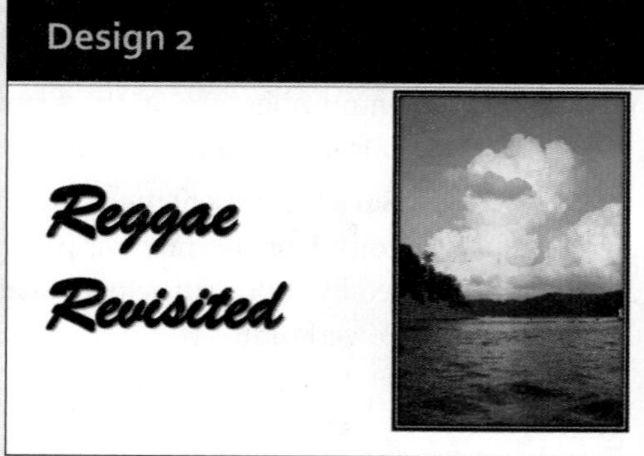

Figure 5.56

(Project 5F CD Cover continues on the next page)

Mastering PowerPoint | Project 5F CD Cover (continued)

1 **Start** PowerPoint. Click the **Insert tab**. In the **Images group**, click the **Photo Album button arrow**, and then click **New Photo Album**.

2 From the student data files, insert the following pictures into the photo album: **p05F_Island1.jpg**, **p05F_Island2.jpg, p05F_Island3.jpg, p05F_Island4.jpg**, and **p05F_Island5.jpg**. In the **Picture layout** list, click **1 picture**. Select the **Module** theme. Click the **Create** button.

3 Edit the **Photo Album**, and remove the last two pictures—**p05F_Island4** and **p05F_Island5** from the album. Change the **Picture layout** to **1 picture with title** and the **Frame shape** to **Compound Frame, Black**.

4 Save the file in your chapter folder, using the file name **Lastname_Firstname_5F_CD_Cover**

5 Make the **title slide** the active slide. Change the subtitle text, the first placeholder, to **Cross Oceans Music** Apply **Bold**, and then change the font size to **28**.

6 Delete the title text, *Photo Album*, and then type **Design Entries for CD Cover** Press **Enter**, and then type **Reggae & Jamaican Music** Select both lines of the title. On the **Format tab**, in the **WordArt Styles group**, click the **More** button. Under **Applies to All Text in the Shape**, in the first row, click the third style—**Fill – Aqua, Accent 2, Warm Matte Bevel**.

7 Make **Slide 2** active. Change the title to **Design 1** Drag the picture so the left side aligns at **4.5 inches on the left side of the horizontal ruler**.

8 Insert a text box in the blank area to the right of the picture. In the text box, type **Reggae** press **Enter**, and then type **Revisited** Change the font to **Bauhaus 93** and the font size to **72**. Position the text box so that the left edge aligns with **0 on the horizontal ruler** and the top edge aligns with **1 inch on the upper half of the vertical ruler**.

9 Make **Slide 3** active. Change the title to **Design 2** Drag the picture so the right side aligns at **4.5 inches on the right side of the horizontal ruler.**

10 Insert a text box in the blank area to the left of the picture. In the text box, type **Reggae** press **Enter**, and then type **Revisited** Change the font to **Brush Script MT** and the font size to **88**. Apply **Bold** and **Text Shadow**. Position the text box so that the left edge aligns with at **4 inches on the left side of the horizontal ruler** and the top edge aligns at **1 inch on the upper half of the vertical ruler**.

11 Make **Slide 4** active, and then change the title to **Design 3** Drag the picture so the right side aligns at **4 inches on the right side of the horizontal ruler**.

12 Insert a text box in the middle of the slide, to the left of the picture. In the text box, type **Reggae** press **Enter**, and then type **Revisited** Change the font to **Algerian** and the font size to **60**. Apply **Bold, Italic**, and **Text Shadow**. With the text box selected, on the **Format tab**, in the **WordArt Styles group**, click the **More** button, and then under **Applies to Selected Text**, in the third row, click the fifth style—**Fill-Aqua 2, Double Outline - Accent 2**. Position the text box so that the top edge aligns at **1 inch on the bottom half of the vertical ruler** and the left edge aligns at **4.5 inches on the left side of the horizontal ruler**.

13 Make **Slide 2** the active slide. Select the picture. On the **Format tab**, click the **Crop** button, and then drag the left middle cropping handle to at **4 inches on the left side of the horizontal ruler**. Click outside to deselect the picture.

14 Review your presentation from the beginning.

15 Insert a footer on the notes and handouts that includes a fixed date and time, the page number, and the file name.

16 Modify the **Properties** on the **Show Document Panel**. Replace the text in the **Author** box with your own name; in the **Subject** box, type your course name and section number; and in the **Keywords** box, type **design, CD, entries Close** the **Document Information Panel**.

17 **Save** the presentation. Print **Handouts 4 Slides Horizontal**, or submit your presentation electronically as directed by your instructor. **Close** your presentation and **Exit** PowerPoint.

End You have completed Project 5F

Content-Based Assessments

Apply 5A and 5B skills from these Objectives:

1. Use Picture Corrections
2. Add a Border to a Picture
3. Change the Shape of a Picture
4. Add a Picture to a WordArt Object
5. Enhance a Presentation with Audio and Video
6. Create a Photo Album
7. Edit a Photo Album and Add a Caption
8. Crop a Picture

Mastering PowerPoint | Project 5G Jazz Origins and Percussion Album

In the following Mastering PowerPoint project, you will edit a short presentation about the origins and elements of jazz by changing the brightness, contrast, and shape of pictures and adding a border. You will also format the presentation to play a short jazz video across slides during the slide show. Finally, you will create a photo album showing some of the percussion instruments used in Cross Oceans Music jazz recordings. The album will contain an audio clip of music. Your completed presentations will look similar to Figure 5.57

Project Files

For Project 5G, you will need the following files:

Presentation:
p05G_Jazz_Origins.pptx
p05_Music_Video.avi

Photo Album:
New blank PowerPoint presentation
p05G_Drums1.jpg
p05G_Drums2.jpg
p05G_Drums3.jpg
p05G_Drums4.jpg
p05G_Jazz.wav

You will save your presentations as:

Lastname_Firstname_5G_Jazz_Origins.pptx
Lastname_Firstname_5G_Percussion_.pptx

Project Results

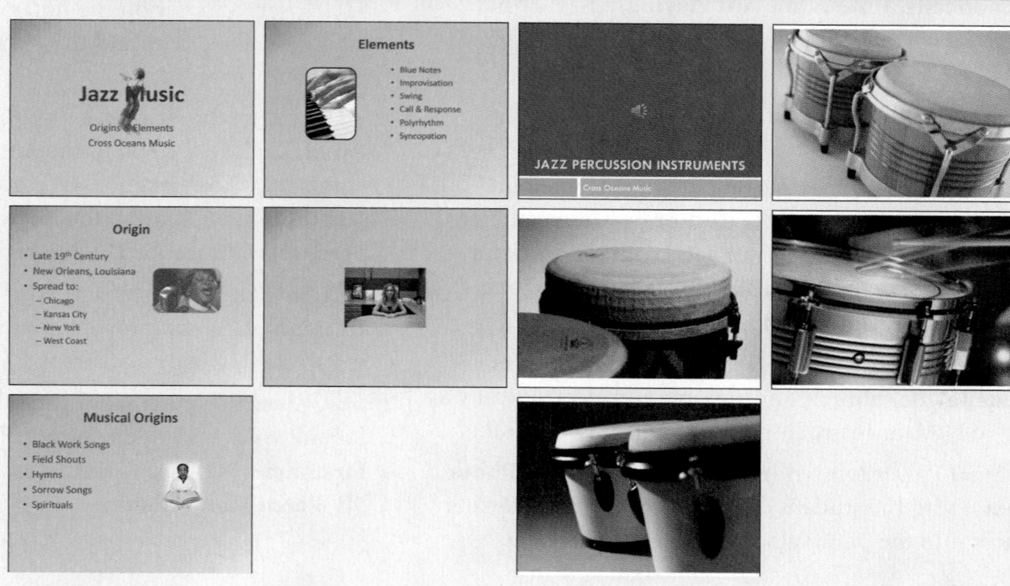

Figure 5.57

(Project 5G Jazz Origins and Percussion Album continues on the next page)

Content-Based Assessments

Mastering PowerPoint | Project 5G Jazz Origins and Percussion Album (continued)

1. **Start** PowerPoint. Locate and open the file **p05G_ Jazz_Origins**, and then save the file as **Lastname_ Firstname_5G_Jazz_Origins**

2. On **Slide 2**, change the picture **Color** to **Blue, Accent color 1 Light**, found under **Recolor** in the third row. **Crop** the picture to a **Rounded Rectangle** shape, found under **Rectangles**. Apply a **Picture Border—Orange, Accent 6, Darker 25%**, found in the last column.

3. On **Slide 3**, change the picture **Color** to **Temperature: 4700 K**, found under **Color Tone**. Change the **Picture Effects** to **Soft Edges, 25 Point**.

4. Display **Slide 4**. On the **picture of the hands on the piano keyboard**, apply **+20% Brightness**. Change the picture shape to **Flowchart: Alternate Process**, found under **Flowchart**, in the first row. Add a picture border that is **Dark Blue, Background 2, Darker 50%**, found in the last row, third column of the gallery. Set the border weight (also known as width) to **2¼ pt**.

5. Insert a new blank slide after **Slide 4**. In **Slide 5**, insert as a linked video **p05Music_Video.avi**. Set it to play **Automatically**, **Hide While Not Playing**, and **Play Full Screen**. View your presentation from the beginning.

6. Insert a footer on the notes and handouts that includes a fixed date and time, the page number, and the file name.

7. Modify the **Properties** on the **Show Document Panel**. Replace the text in the **Author** box with your own name; in the **Subject** box, type your course name and section number; and in the **Keywords** box, type **jazz, origin** **Close** the **Document Information Panel**.

8. **Save** the presentation. Print **Handouts 6 Slides Horizontal**, or submit your presentation electronically as directed by your instructor. **Close** your presentation.

9. **Start** PowerPoint, if necessary. Insert a **New Photo Album**. From the student data files, insert the following pictures into the photo album: **p05G_Drums1.jpg**, **p05G_Drums2.jpg**, **p05G_Drums3.jpg**, and **p05G_ Drums4.jpg**.

10. Set the **Picture layout** to **Fit to slide**. Use the **Median** theme. Click to select the box **ALL pictures black and white**, and then create the photo album. In the location where you are storing your projects, save the file as **Lastname_Firstname_5G_Percussion_Album**

11. Make **Slide 1** the active slide. Replace the title—*Photo Album*—with **Jazz Percussion Instruments** It will be in all capital letters. Drag the middle sizing handle on each side of the title placeholder so the placeholder occupies the entire width of the slide and the entire title fits on one line. **Center** the text horizontally. Select the **title**, and then apply **Bold** and **Text Shadow**.

12. Click to select the **subtitle**. Delete the subtitle, and then type **Cross Oceans Music**

13. On **Slide 1**, insert the audio file **p05G_Jazz.wav**. On the **Playback tab**, click the **Start** option **Play across slides**. Click the check box for **Hide During Show**. View the slide show **From Beginning** and test the sound.

14. Insert a footer on the notes and handouts that includes a fixed date and time, the page number, and the file name.

15. Modify the **Properties** on the **Show Document Panel**. Replace the text in the **Author** box with your own name; in the **Subject** box, type your course name and section number; and in the **Keywords** box, type **jazz, percussion** **Close** the **Document Information Panel**.

16. **Save** the presentation. Print **Handouts 6 Slides Horizontal**, or submit your presentation electronically as directed by your instructor.

17. **Close** the presentation, and then **Exit** PowerPoint. Submit your work as directed for both **Lastname_ Firstname_5G_Jazz_Origins** and **Lastname_Firstname_ 5B_Percussion_Album**.

End **You have completed Project 5G**

Apply a combination of the **5A** and **5B** skills.

GO! Fix It | Project **5H** Caribbean Music and Strings Album

Project Files

For Project 5H, you will need the following files:

Presentation:
p05H_Caribbean_Music.pptx
p05H_Caribbean.wav

Photo Album:
p05H_Strings_Album.pptx
p05H_Harp.jpg
p05_Music_Video.avi

You will save your presentations as:

Lastname_Firstname_5H_Caribbean_Music.pptx
Lastname_Firstname_5H_Strings_Album.pptx

In this project, you will edit slides in a presentation that describes the soca genre of Caribbean music. Modify the color and shape of the images and add audio. Next, edit a photo album depicting instruments used in the production of Cross Oceans Music recordings.

Open **p05H_Caribbean_Music**, and then save the file in your chapter folder as **Lastname_Firstname_5H_Caribbean_Music** Correct these errors:

- On Slide 3, the picture of the two drums should have the color changed to Tan, Accent color 2 Light, one of the Recolor choices. The picture should be Sent to Back.
- On Slide 4, the flag should be cropped to a Wave shape. The Picture Effects should be set for Reflection, Tight Reflection, touching. The picture border should be Black, Text 1, Lighter 5%.
- On Slide 1, the audio file p05H_Caribbean.wav should be inserted and set to start Automatically. The audio icon should be set to Hide During Show. The speaker icon should be at the lower right corner.
- Insert a Header & Footer on the Notes and Handouts that includes the Date and time Fixed, the Page number, and a Footer with the text **Lastname_Firstname_5H_Caribbean_Music** Document Properties should include your name, course name and section, and the keywords **Caribbean, instruments**

Open the file **p05H_Strings_Album**, and then save the file in your chapter folder as **Lastname_Firstname_5H_Strings_Album** Correct these errors:

- Edit the Photo Album. The theme should be Apothecary, and the picture p05H_Harp.jpg should be added as the last slide in the album.
- On Slide 1, the title should be **String Instruments**. Titles for the remaining slides should be: **Bass, Classical Guitar, Mandolin, Violin, and Harp**.
- On Slide 1, p05_Music_Video.avi should be inserted as a linked video, resized to a height of 1.5 inches, and positioned in the upper left corner with a Trigger set to the slide title. The video should play Full Screen and Hide While Not Playing.
- A Header & Footer should be inserted on the Notes and Handouts that includes the Date and time Fixed, the Page number, and a Footer with the text **Lastname_Firstname_5H_Strings_Album** Document Properties should include your name, course name and section, and the keywords **strings, instruments**

Submit your presentations electronically or print Handouts 6 slides per page as directed by your instructor. Close the presentations.

End **You have completed Project 5H**

Content-Based Assessments

Apply a combination of the **5A** and **5B** skills.

GO! Make It | Project 5I Salsa Music and Latin Album

Project Files

For Project 5I, you will need the following files:

Presentation:
p05I_Salsa_Music.pptx
p05I_Marimba.jpg
p05I_Dancer1.jpg
p05I_Salsa.wav
p05_Music_Video.avi

Photo Album:
New blank PowerPoint presentation
p05I_Exotic1.jpg
p05I_Exotic2.jpg
p05I_Music.jpg

You will save your presentations as:

Lastname_Firstname_5I_Salsa_Music.pptx
Lastname_Firstname_5I_Latin_Album.pptx

Start PowerPoint and open p05I_Salsa_Music. Save the file in your PowerPoint Chapter 5 folder as **Lastname_Firstname_5I_Salsa_Music**

By using the skills you practiced in this chapter, create the first two slides of the presentation shown in Figure 5.58. On the first slide, insert the picture p05I_Marimba.jpg. Recolor the picture to Brown, Accent color 4 Light, and then add a picture effect of Soft Edges at 50 Point. Position the picture so the text can be read. Insert p05I_Salsa.wav with a trigger on the title—*Salsa Music*. Move the audio icon to the bottom left corner. On the second slide, insert p05I_Dancer1.jpg, and then apply a hexagon shape to the picture and add a border—Gray-50%, Accent 1, Darker 25%. Insert p05_Music_Video.avi as a linked video with a trigger on the dancer picture. Resize video height to 1.5" and position it at the bottom left corner of the screen. Set the playback so the video will play full screen.

Insert a Header & Footer on the Notes and Handouts that includes the Date and time Fixed, the Page number, and a Footer with the text **Lastname_Firstname_5I_Salsa_Music** In the Document Properties, include your name, course name and section, and the keywords **Salsa, Latin** Save, and then print Handouts 4 slides per page or submit the presentation electronically as directed by your instructor.

Create a new Photo Album and create the first three slides as shown in Figure 5.58. Insert p05I_Exotic1.jpg and p05I_Exotic2.jpg, then apply the Opulent theme. Save the file in your PowerPoint Chapter 5 folder as **Lastname_Firstname_5I_Latin_Album** Insert p05I_Music.jpg on Slide 1, crop and position it as shown. The picture will be distorted. Crop the picture on Slide 2.

Insert a Header & Footer on the Notes and Handouts that includes the Date and time Fixed, the Page number, and a Footer with the text **Lastname_Firstname_5I_Latin_Album**. In the Document Properties, add your name and course information and the keywords **exotic, music** Save, and then print Handouts 4 slides per page or submit the photo album electronically as directed by your instructor.

(Project 5I Salsa Music and Latin Album continues on the next page)

GO! Make It | Project 5I Salsa Music and Latin Album (continued)

Project Results

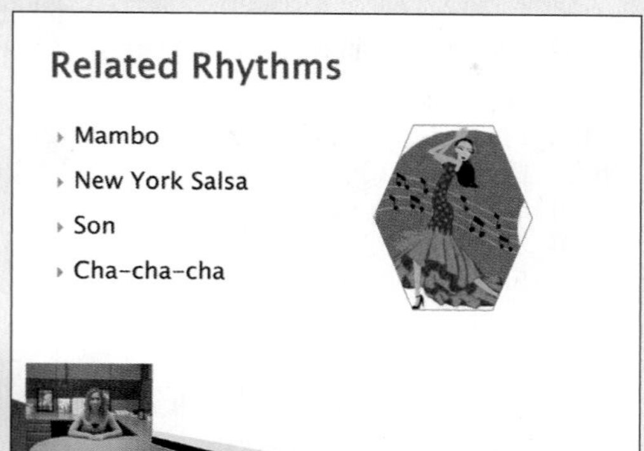

Figure 5.58

End **You have completed Project 5I**

Content-Based Assessments

Apply a combination of the **5A** and **5B** skills.

GO! Solve It | Project 5J Flamenco Music and World Album

Project Files

For Project 5J, you will need the following files:

Presentation:
p05J_Flamenco_Music.pptx
p05J_Flamenco2.jpg
p05J_Guitar1.jpg
p05J_Guitar2.jpg
p05J_Flamenco.wav
p05_Music_Video.avi

Photo Album:
New blank PowerPoint presentation
p05J_World_Music1.jpg
p05J_World_Music2.jpg
p05J_World_Music3.jpg
p05J_World_Music4.jpg
p05J_World_Music5.jpg
p05J_World_Music6.jpg

You will save your presentations as:

Lastname_Firstname_5J_Flamenco_Music.pptx
Lastname_Firstname_5J_World_Album.pptx

In this project, you will modify a presentation on the elements of Flamenco music and then create a photo album on World music. Demonstrate the skills you have covered in this chapter.

Open p05J_Flamenco_Music, and then save it as **Lastname_Firstname_5J_Flamenco_Music** Use the provided picture files or insert pictures of your own choosing. Add the provided audio and video files. Format the pictures and apply audio and video playback options.

Create a photo album to highlight other forms of World Music produced and distributed by Cross Oceans Music. Use the provided picture files or ones of your own choosing. Select a theme, and then place the photos on the slides in a manner that will highlight the performers. Add a title and subtitle on the title slide. Save the presentation as **Lastname_Firstname_5J_World_Album**

For both presentations, insert a header and footer on the Notes and Handouts that includes the fixed date and time, the page number, and a footer with the file name. Add your name, course name and section number, and the key words you feel are appropriate to the Properties. Print Handouts 6 slides per page or submit electronically as directed by your instructor.

		Performance Element		
		Exemplary: You consistently applied the relevant skills.	**Proficient:** You sometimes, but not always, applied, the relevant skills.	**Developing:** You rarely or never applied the relevant skills.
Performance Element	**Added and formatted pictures in the presentation.**	Used numerous picture formatting techniques that were appropriate for the presentation.	Demonstrated some of the picture formatting. What was completed was correct.	Little or no picture formatting was demonstrated.
	Inserted audio and video files and applied playback settings.	Inserted audio and video files in appropriate places and applied playback options. Both played correctly. May have used a trigger.	Inserted the audio, but either the playback options were not set or the audio did not play back correctly. May have used a trigger.	Inserted the audio, but either the playback options were not set or the audio did not play back correctly. May have used a trigger.
	Created a photo album, selected a theme, and inserted pictures.	The photo album had a theme, and the pictures were inserted.	The pictures were inserted, but there was no theme. Presentation lacked consistency.	The photo album was not created.

End **You have completed Project 5J**

Apply a combination of the 5A and 5B skills.

GO! Solve It | Project 5K New Age Music and Asian Album

Project Files

For Project 5K, you will need the following files:

Presentation:
p05K_NewAge_Music.pptx
p05K_Piano.wav
p05_Music_Video.avi

Photo Album:
New blank PowerPoint presentation
p05K_Asian_Music1.jpg
p05K_Asian_Music2.jpg
p05K_Asian_Music3.jpg
p05K_Asian_Music4.jpg
p05K_Asian_Music5.jpg
p05K_Asian_Music6.jpg

You will save your presentations as:

Lastname_Firstname_5K_NewAge_Music.pptx
Lastname_Firstname_5K_Asian_Album.pptx

In this presentation project, you will modify a short presentation that describes the elements of New Age music and create a photo album on Asian music. Demonstrate your knowledge of the skills you have covered in this chapter.

Open p05K_NewAge_Music, and then save it as **Lastname_Firstname_5K_NewAge_Music** Improve the presentation by including a title and subtitle, applying a theme, and modifying the photos in the slides. Add the provided audio and video files and set the playback options.

Using the graphic files provided, create a photo album to highlight Asian musical instruments, and add captions or titles, if necessary. Save the album as **Lastname_Firstname_5K_Asian_Music**

For both presentations, insert a header and footer on the Notes and Handouts that includes the fixed date and time, the page number, and a footer with the file name. Add your name, course name and section number, and appropriate key words to the Properties. Print Handouts 6 slides per page or submit electronically as directed by your instructor.

Performance Element		Performance Element		
		Exemplary: You consistently applied the relevant skills.	**Proficient:** You sometimes, but not always, applied, the relevant skills.	**Developing:** You rarely or never applied the relevant skills.
Performance Element	Modified photos in NewAge_Music.	Used a variety of picture corrections, shapes, and borders that enhanced the presentation.	Used some picture corrections, shapes, and borders to enhance the presentation.	Used few or no picture corrections, shapes, and borders to enhance the presentation.
Performance Element	Added audio and video files and applied playback options.	Inserted audio and video files in appropriate places and applied playback options. Both played correctly. May have used a trigger.	Inserted the audio, but either the playback options were not set or the audio did not play back correctly. May have used a trigger.	Inserted the audio, but either the playback options were not set or the audio did not play back correctly. May have used a trigger.
Performance Element	Created a photo album, inserted pictures, an added appropriate captions or titles.	The photo album had a theme, and the pictures were inserted. Used captions and titles as necessary and completed title slide.	The pictures were inserted, but there was no theme. Presentation and captions lacked consistency.	The photo album was not created.

End You have completed Project 5K

Outcomes-Based Assessments

Rubric

The following outcomes-based assessments are *open-ended assessments*. That is, there is no specific correct result; your result will depend on your approach to the information provided. Make *Professional Quality* your goal. Use the following scoring rubric to guide you in *how* to approach the problem and then to evaluate *how well* your approach solves the problem.

The *criteria*—Software Mastery, Content, Format and Layout, and Process—represent the knowledge and skills you have gained that you can apply to solving the problem. The *levels of performance*—Professional Quality, Approaching Professional Quality, or Needs Quality Improvements—help you and your instructor evaluate your result.

	Your completed project is of Professional Quality if you:	**Your completed project is Approaching Professional Quality if you:**	**Your completed project Needs Quality Improvements if you:**
1-Software Mastery	Choose and apply the most appropriate skills, tools, and features and identify efficient methods to solve the problem.	Choose and apply some appropriate skills, tools, and features, but not in the most efficient manner.	Choose inappropriate skills, tools, or features, or are inefficient in solving the problem.
2-Content	Construct a solution that is clear and well organized, contains content that is accurate, appropriate to the audience and purpose, and is complete. Provide a solution that contains no errors in spelling, grammar, or style.	Construct a solution in which some components are unclear, poorly organized, inconsistent, or incomplete. Misjudge the needs of the audience. Have some errors in spelling, grammar, or style, but the errors do not detract from comprehension.	Construct a solution that is unclear, incomplete, or poorly organized; contains some inaccurate or inappropriate content; and contains many errors in spelling, grammar, or style. Do not solve the problem.
3-Format and Layout	Format and arrange all elements to communicate information and ideas, clarify function, illustrate relationships, and indicate relative importance.	Apply appropriate format and layout features to some elements, but not others. Overuse features, causing minor distraction.	Apply format and layout that does not communicate information or ideas clearly. Do not use format and layout features to clarify function, illustrate relationships, or indicate relative importance. Use available features excessively, causing distraction.
4-Process	Use an organized approach that integrates planning, development, self-assessment, revision, and reflection.	Demonstrate an organized approach in some areas, but not others; or, use an insufficient process of organization throughout.	Do not use an organized approach to solve the problem.

Outcomes-Based Assessments

Apply a combination of the **5A** and **5B** skills.

GO! Think | Project **5L** Ragtime and African Music

Project Files

For Project 5L, you will need the following files:

Presentation:
p05L_Ragtime_Music.pptx
p05_Music_Video.avi
p05L_Entertainer.wav

Photo Album:
New blank PowerPoint presentation

You will save your presentations as:

Lastname_Firstname_5L_Ragtime_Music.pptx
Lastname_Firstname_5L_African_Album.pptx

In this project, you will edit a presentation about the history and makeup of Ragtime music. Open p05L_Ragtime_Music and save it as **Lastname_Firstname_5L_Ragtime_Music** Modify the images on the slides. Add audio and video to the presentation. Set the audio file to start automatically and play across slides. Create a photo album using the provided pictures. Insert p05L_Africa.jpg on the title slide. Save it as **Lastname_Firstname_5L_African_Album** Insert appropriate headers and footers, and then update the Properties on both files. Submit your files as directed.

You have completed Project 5L

Apply a combination of the **5A** and **5B** skills.

GO! Think | Project **5M** Indian Music and Indian Instruments

Project Files

For Project 5M, you will need the following files:

Presentation:
p05M_Indian_Music.pptx
p05M_Indian_Music.wav
p05_Music_Video.avi

Photo Album:
New blank PowerPoint presentation
p05M_Bagilu.jpg
p05M_Ghantis.jpg
p05M_Indian_Dancer.jpg
p05M_Khangling.jpg
p05M_Nagphani.jpg

You will save your presentations as:

Lastname_Firstname_5M_Indian_Music.pptx
Lastname_Firstname_5M_Indian_Album.pptx

In this project, you will modify a short presentation about the basic tenets of Indian music and prepare a photo album. Open p05M_Indian_Music, modify the photos and graphics and add the provided audio and video files. Save as **Lastname_Firstname_5M_Indian_Music**. Create a photo album using the provided pictures. Save the album as **Lastname_Firstname_5M_Indian_Album** Insert appropriate headers and footers, and then update the Properties on both files. Submit your files as directed.

You have completed Project 5M

Outcomes-Based Assessments

Apply a combination of the **5A** and **5B** skills.

You and GO! | Project 5N Swing Origins

Project Files

For Project 5N, you will need the following files:

Presentation:
p05N_Swing_Origins.pptx
p05N_Cakewalk.wav
p05N_Lindy_Hop.wav
p05N_Swing.wav
p05_Music_Video.avi

Photo Album:
New blank PowerPoint presentation
p05N_Violinist.jpg
p05N_Conductor.jpg
p05N_Strings.jpg
p05N_Horns.jpg
p05N_Orchestra.jpg
p05N_Orchestra2.jpg
p05N_Conducting.jpg

You will save your presentations as:

Lastname_Firstname_5N_Swing_Origins.pptx
Lastname_Firstname_5N_Orchestra_Album.pptx

In this project, you will modify a presentation about the origins and history of Swing music. Open p05N_Swing_Origins.You will improve the presentation by modifying and formatting the photos and graphics. Change the size and position of the images, where necessary, and adjust the transparency of the background graphic on Slide 5. Change the brightness and contrast, and recolor the images to emphasize the slide content. Where appropriate, add audio to the presentation by inserting the .wav files provided, and adjust how they will play in the presentation. If it is a lengthy audio clip, set it to Play Across Slides. On an appropriate slide, insert a linked video of your choice, or use p05_Music_Video.avi. Include a trigger for the video and set it to Play Full Screen. Save the presentation as **Lastname_Firstname_5N_Swing_Origins**

Insert a Header & Footer on the Notes and Handouts that includes the Date and time Fixed, the Page number, and a Footer with the text **Lastname_Firstname_5N_Swing_Origins** In the Document Properties, add your name and course information and the keywords **Swing, music** Save, and then print Handouts 4 slides per page or submit electronically as directed by your instructor.

In a new blank PowerPoint presentation, using the graphic files provided, create a photo album showing candid photos of one of the orchestras that appeared at a Music Festival sponsored by Cross Oceans Music. Save p05N_Conducting.jpg to use in the title slide.

Select a theme, and then place the photos on the slides with captions. Add frames to the photos and crop unwanted areas of pictures. Insert the image p05N_Conducting.jpg on the title slide. Add an informative title and subtitle. Save the album as **Lastname_Firstname_5N_Orchestra_Album**

Insert a Header & Footer on the Notes and Handouts that includes the Date and time Fixed, the Page number, and a Footer with the text **Lastname_Firstname_5N_Orchestra_Album** In the Document Properties, add your name and course information and the keywords **orchestra, instruments** Save, and then print Handouts 4 slides per page or submit electronically as directed by your instructor.

End You have completed Project 5N

Delivering a Presentation

OUTCOMES

At the end of this chapter you will be able to:

OBJECTIVES

Mastering these objectives will enable you to:

PROJECT 6A

Apply slide transitions and custom animation effects.

1. Apply and Modify Slide Transitions (p. 355)
2. Apply Custom Animation Effects (p. 360)
3. Modify Animation Effects (p. 371)

PROJECT 6B

Insert hyperlinks, create custom slide shows, and view presentations.

4. Insert Hyperlinks (p. 379)
5. Create Custom Slide Shows (p. 390)
6. Present and View a Slide Presentation (p. 395)

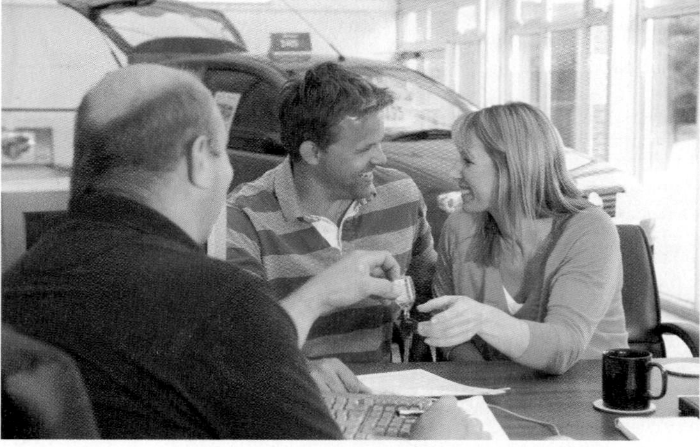

Monkey Business Images/Shutterstock

In This Chapter

Microsoft Office PowerPoint provides a wide range of tools that can turn a lackluster presentation into one that captivates the attention of the audience. Recall that SmartArt graphics can be used to add visual effects to text. SmartArt can also be animated. You can apply slide transitions, which are animation effects that occur as slides move from one to another when a slide show is played. Transitions and other animation effects can be applied to all slides or to selected slides. Animation can be applied to individual slides, a slide master, or a custom slide layout.

In addition, you can insert hyperlinks into a presentation to quickly link to a Web page, another slide, or a document. By inserting ready-made action buttons or creating your own action buttons, you can also link to a specific document or action. You may also want to create a custom show composed of selected slides. PowerPoint includes an annotation tool that enables you to write or draw on slides during a presentation.

Penn Liberty Motors has one of eastern Pennsylvania's largest inventories of popular new car brands, sport utility vehicles, hybrid cars, and motorcycles. Their sales, service, and finance staff are all highly trained and knowledgeable about their products, and the company takes pride in its consistently high customer satisfaction ratings. Penn Liberty also offers extensive customization options for all types of vehicles through its accessories division. Custom wheels, bike and ski racks, car covers, and chrome accessories are just a few of the ways Penn Liberty customers make personal statements with their cars.

Project 6A Informational Presentation

Project Activities

In Activities 6.01 through 6.08, you will add slide transitions and animation effects to a presentation that outlines the organizational structure and location of Penn Liberty Motors. Your completed presentation will look similar to Figure 6.1.

Project Files

For Project 6A, you will need the following files:

p06A_Penn_Liberty.pptx
p06A_Tada.wav

You will save your presentation as:

Lastname_Firstname_6A_Penn_Liberty.pptx

Project Results

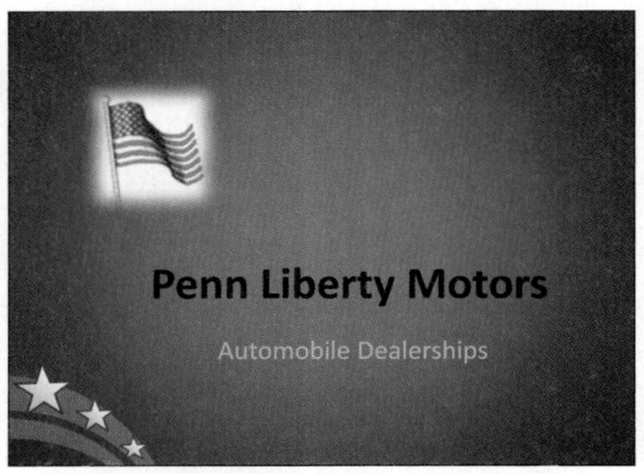

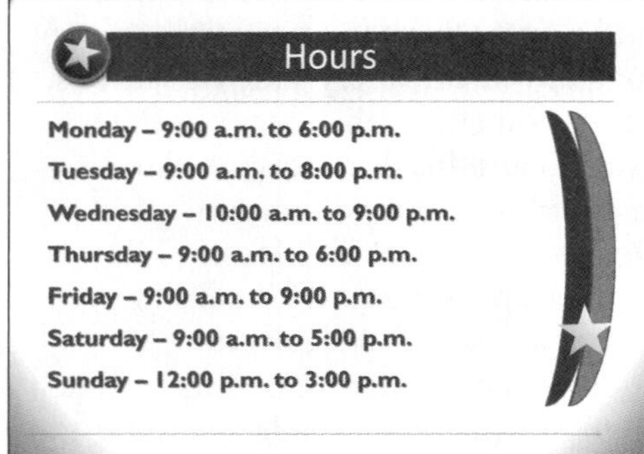

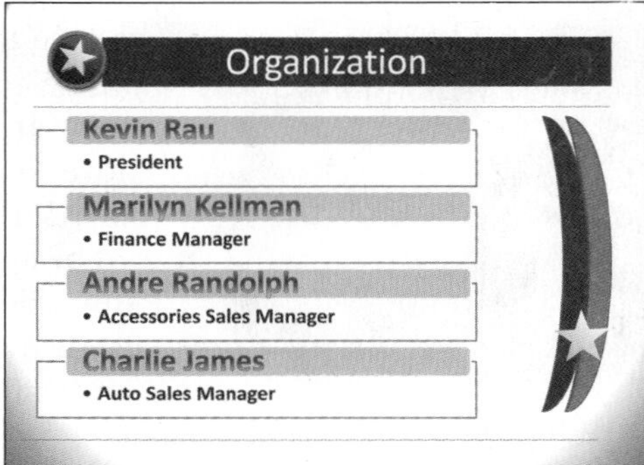

Figure 6.1
Project 6A Penn Liberty

Objective 1 | Apply and Modify Slide Transitions

Transitions are motion effects that occur when a presentation moves from slide to slide in Slide Show view and affect how the content is revealed. When referring to transitions, ***animation*** is any type of motion or movement that occurs as the presentation moves from slide to slide. Different transitions can be applied to selected slides or the same transition can be applied to all slides. Animation is also used in a second context in this chapter, meaning a special visual effect or sound effect that is added to text or an object.

You can modify the transitions by changing the ***transition speed***, which is the timing of the transition between all slides or between the previous slide and the current slide. It is also possible to apply a ***transition sound*** that will play as slides change from one to the next. Transition sounds are prerecorded sounds that can be applied and will play as the transition occurs.

Setting up a slide show also includes determining how you will advance the slide show from one slide to the next. You can set up the presentation to display each slide in response to the viewer clicking the mouse button or pressing the Enter key. You can also design the slide show so that the slides advance automatically after a set amount of time.

> **Note | Applying Transitions**
>
> In this project, you will learn how to apply and modify several kinds of transitions so that you are aware of how they work. When creating a presentation for an audience, however, you do not want to use too many transitions because they can be distracting and may destroy the professional appearance of your slide show. Remember, apply transitions in moderation.

Activity 6.01 | Applying and Modifying Slide Transitions

Slide transitions can be applied to all slides or to specific slides, and different transitions can be applied in one slide show. In this activity, you will modify slide transitions. In this case, modifications include changing the transition speed and sounds to be played during transitions.

1 **Start** PowerPoint. Locate and open the file **p06A_Penn_Liberty**. In the location where you are saving your work, create a new folder named **PowerPoint Chapter 6** and then save the file as **Lastname_Firstname_6A_Penn_Liberty**

2 Make the **title slide** the active slide. Click the **Transitions tab**. In the **Transition to This Slide group**, click the **More** button [▾] to display the **Transitions** gallery, and then compare your screen with Figure 6.2.

The Transitions gallery includes the following types of slide transitions: Subtle, Exciting, and Dynamic Content.

Figure 6.2

3 Under **Subtle**, point to the fifth selection—**Wipe**. As you point, notice that **Live Preview** displays how the transition will display.

If you were unable to see the transition, move the [pointer] pointer away, point to a different selection, and then point again to *Wipe*.

> **Another Way**
>
> To preview a slide transition, in the Slide pane, click the Play Animations icon that displays to the left of the slide thumbnail.

4 Click **Wipe**, and then in the **Timing group**, click the **Apply to All** button. On the **Transitions tab**, in the **Preview group**, click the **Preview** button. Compare your screen with Figure 6.3.

The Wipe transition played on Slide 1. In the Slides/Outline pane, a Play Animations icon displays next to every slide.

Figure 6.3

5 Click the **Slide Show tab**. In the **Start Slide Show group**, click the **From Beginning** button. Press Enter five times to view the entire slide show, and then press Enter or Esc to return to **Normal** view.

Because you selected Apply to All, the transition occurred between each slide.

6 Make **Slide 2** the active slide. Click the **Transitions tab**. In the **Transition to This Slide group**, click the **More** button.

7 In the **Transitions** gallery, under **Exciting**, take a moment to experiment with the different effects by pointing to—but not clicking—various thumbnails. When you are finished experimenting, in the first row, click the fourth column—**Clock**.

By not clicking the Apply to All button, the Clock transition will apply to Slide 2 only.

8 Using the technique you practiced, view the slide show **From Beginning**. When you are finished viewing the slide show, press Enter or Esc to return to **Normal** view.

The Clock transition occurs between Slide 1 and Slide 2. The transition between all the other slides remains set to Wipe.

More Knowledge | Animated GIFs and JPGs

Many images are ***GIF*** (Graphics Interchange Format) or ***JPG*** (Joint Photographic Experts Group, also JPEG) files. GIFs are usually drawings, and JPGs are typically photos. GIF files are smaller in size and display faster than JPGs. Because of this, GIFs are frequently used on Web pages. The image of the waving flag on the title slide is known as an ***animated GIF***. An animated GIF is a file format made up of a series of frames within a single file. Animated GIFs create the illusion of movement by displaying the frames one after the other in quick succession. They can loop endlessly or present one or more sequences of animation and then stop. The animation plays only when the the slide show runs.

9 If necessary, make Slide 2 the active slide. Click the **Transitions tab**. In the **Timing group**, click in the **Duration** box, type **3** press Enter, and then compare your screen with Figure 6.4.

The number of seconds it takes to reveal the slide content is now three seconds, which is longer than the default value of one second.

Figure 6.4

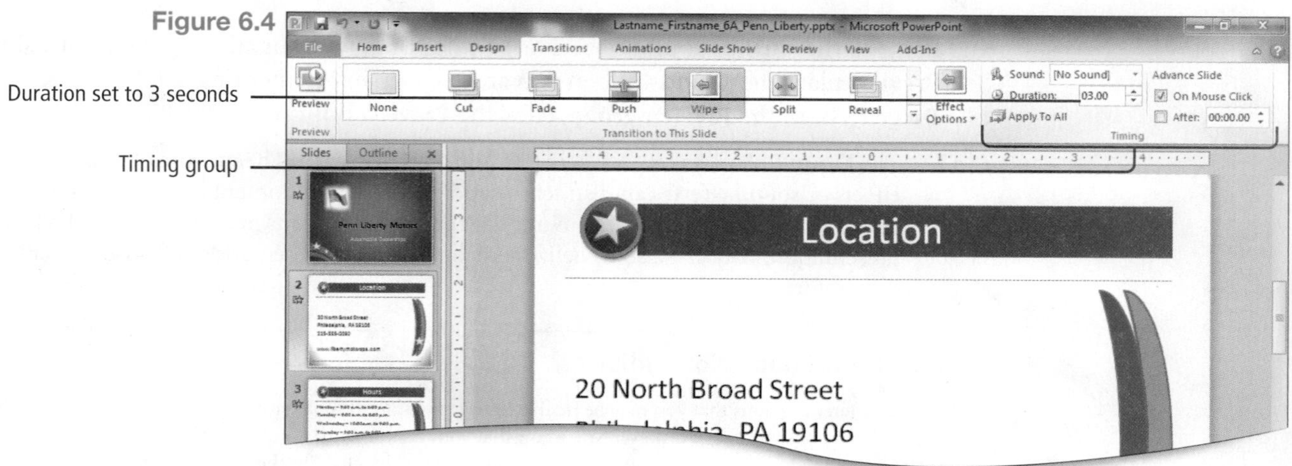

10 In the **Preview group**, click the **Preview** button.

The transition is displayed one time with the new speed setting. Slide 1 is displayed first and then three seconds later, slide 2 appears.

11 Make **Slide 5** the active slide. In the **Timing group**, click the **Duration spin box up arrow** to display **05.00**. On the **Slide Show tab**, in the **Start Slide Show group**, click **From Beginning**. Click or press Enter to view the slides. Click or press Esc when finished.

Notice that when you clicked slide 4 to advance to slide 5, the time delay was five seconds. Choose a speed that best displays the content.

12 If necessary, make **Slide 5** the active slide. On the **Transitions tab**, in the **Timing group**, click the **Sound button arrow**, and then compare your screen with Figure 6.5.

From the displayed list, you can choose from various prerecorded sound effects, choose your own sound effect by clicking Other Sound, or choose [No Sound] to remove a sound effect that was applied.

Figure 6.5

13 Point to the various sound selections. Notice that, without clicking the mouse, Live Preview plays the sounds. When you are finished experimenting, click to select **Drum Roll**. In the **Preview group**, click the **Preview** button.

The Drum Roll plays on Slide 4 before Slide 5 is displayed. The overuse of any animation effects or sound effects can distract the audience from the content of the presentation. Keep your audience and your intent in mind. Whereas animations may enhance a light-hearted presentation, they can also trivialize a serious business presentation or cause viewer discomfort.

Alert! | Is the Sound Not Audible?

There are different reasons that you may be unable to hear the sound. For example, your computer may not have sound capability or speakers. If, however, you know that your computer has sound capability, first check that your speakers are turned on. If they are on, open the Control Panel by clicking the Start button, and then clicking Control Panel. In the Control Panel window, click Hardware and Sound. Under Sound, click Adjust system volume. In the Volume Mixer – Speakers dialog box, click the Unmute Speakers button if necessary. If the device is not muted, use the slider to set the volume. The procedure used to adjust sound varies with different operating systems.

14 Make the **title slide** the active slide. On the **Transitions tab**, in the **Timing group**, click the **Sound arrow**, and then from the displayed list, click **Other Sound**.

15 In the displayed **Add Audio** dialog box, navigate to the location where your student files are stored, click **p06A_Tada.wav**, and then click **OK**. View the slide show **From Beginning**. Press Enter or click to advance each slide. Click or press Esc when finished.

The Wipe transition played on all slides except Slide 2. The Clock transition played on Slide 2. Sound occurred on Slides 1 and 5. The timing on Slide 2 was three seconds, and the timing on Slide five was five seconds. Transitions affect how the slide is revealed on the screen.

16 **Save** your changes.

Activity 6.02 | Advancing Slides Automatically

In this activity, you will customize a slide show by changing the Advance Slide method to advance slides automatically after a specified number of seconds.

1 Make **Slide 2** the active slide. Click the **Transitions tab**. In the **Timing group**, under **Advance Slide**, clear the **On Mouse Click** check box.

By clearing the On Mouse Click check box, viewers will no longer need to press Enter or click to advance the slide show. The slide show will advance automatically.

> **Another Way**
> To enter the time in the After box, click once in the box to select the current time, type 15, and then press Enter.

2 In the **Timing group**, under **Advance Slide**, click the **After spin box up arrow** to display **00:10.00**. Compare your screen with Figure 6.6.

The time is entered in number of seconds. This automatic switching of slides is only effective if no one is providing an oral presentation along with the slides.

Figure 6.6

3 On the **Slide Show tab**, in **Start Slide Show group**, click **From Beginning**. Press Enter one time to advance the slide show to Slide 2. Wait 10 seconds for the third slide to display. When **Slide 3** displays, press Esc.

> **Note | Previewing Slides**
> Previewing a slide will not advance to the next slide. Play the Slide Show From Beginning or From Current Slide in order to verify the time it takes to display the next slide.

4 Make **Slide 2** the active slide. On the **Transitions tab**, in the **Timing group**, change number in the **After** box to **5**. Compare your screen with Figure 6.7.

If no person is speaking, set the number of seconds to allow people sufficient time to read the content. However, you may need to consider adding time to allow a speaker to make key points.

Figure 6.7

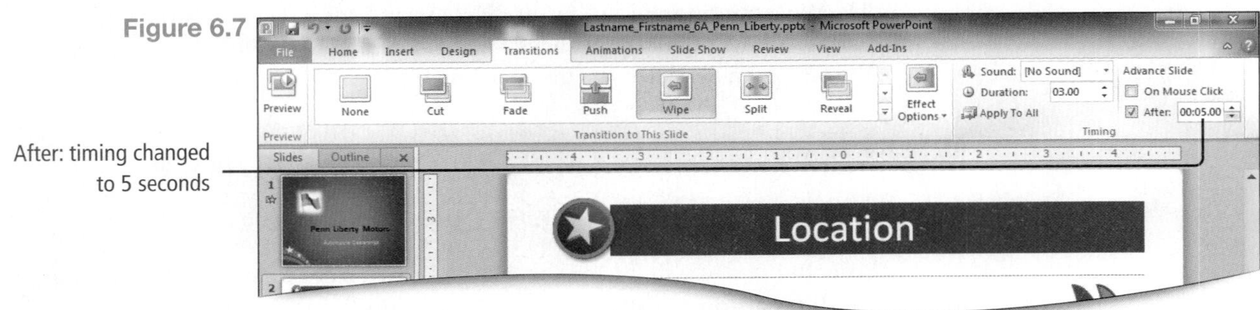

5 **Save** your changes.

Objective 2 | Apply Custom Animation Effects

Like other effects that you can customize in PowerPoint, you can customize animation effects. In this context, animation refers to a special visual effect or sound effect added to text or an object. You can add animation to bulleted items, text, or other objects such as charts, graphics, or SmartArt graphics.

Animation can be applied as an ***entrance effect***, which occurs as the text or object is introduced into the slide during a slide show, or as an ***exit effect***, which occurs as the text or object leaves the slide or disappears during a slide show. For example, bulleted items can fly into, or move into, a slide and then fade away.

Animation can take the form of a ***motion path effect***, which determines how and in what direction text or objects will move on a slide. Examples of an ***emphasis effect*** include making an object shrink or grow in size, change color, or spin on its center.

The ***Animation Pane*** is the area that contains a list of the animation effects added to your presentation. From this pane, you can add or modify effects.

Activity 6.03 | Adding Entrance Effects

In this activity, you will add entrance effects to text and objects by making them move in a specific manner as the text or graphic enters the slide.

1 Make **Slide 3** the active slide, and then click to select the body text placeholder. Click the **Animations tab**. In the **Advanced Animation group**, click the **Add Animation** button, and then compare your screen with Figure 6.8. Scroll the list to see all of the animation effects. Refer to Figure 6.9 for more information.

There are four groups of animations—Entrance, Emphasis, Exit, and Motion Paths. You have to scroll the list to see the Motion Paths animations.

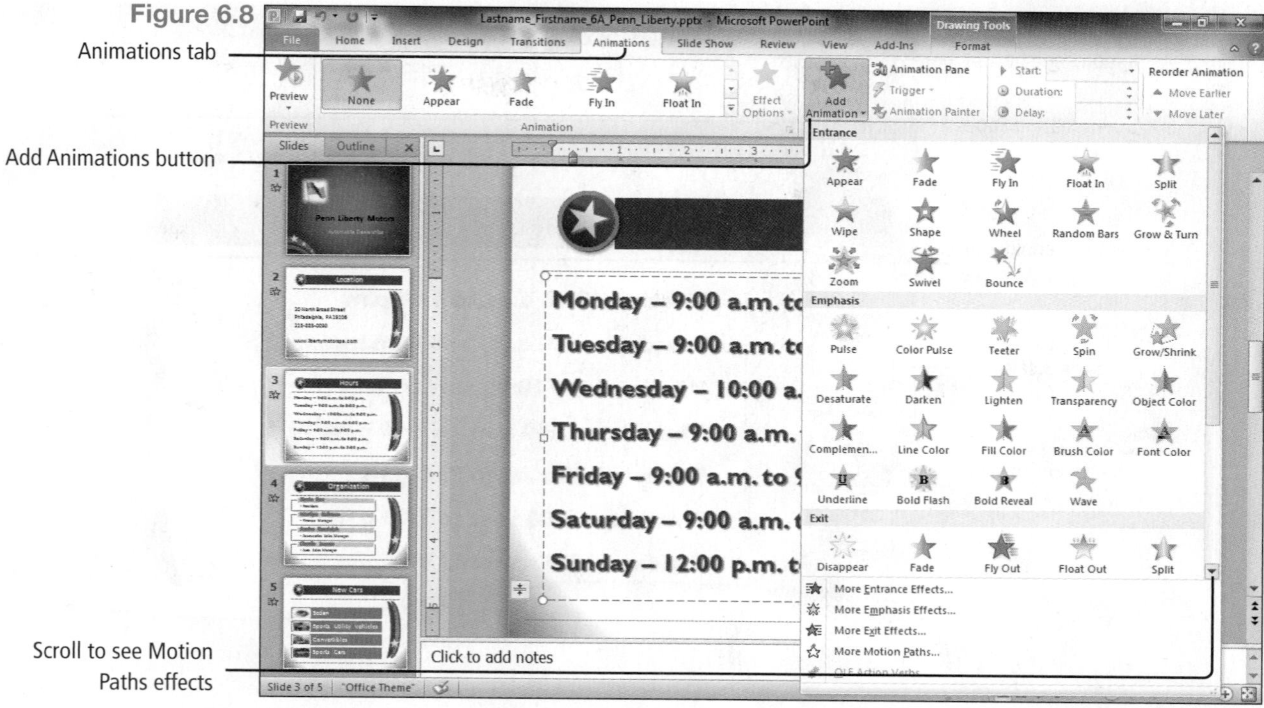

Animation Effects	
Animation Effects	**Examples**
Entrance	Fade gradually into focus, fly onto the slide from an edge, or bounce into view.
Emphasis	Shrink or grow in size, change color, or spin on its center.
Exit	Fly off the slide, disappear from view, or spiral off the slide.
Motion Paths	Move up or down, left or right, or in a star or circular pattern.

Figure 6.9

2 From the displayed list, under **Entrance**, point to **Fade**—but do not click—and watch the Live Preview. Experiment with some of the other Entrance effects, and then click **Fade**.

Clicking Fade sets the text on the slide to display the various bulleted items one after the other, in order from top to bottom. Choose an animation that enhances the content of the slide.

3 In the **Advanced Animation group**, click the **Animation Pane** button, and then compare your screen with Figure 6.10.

The Animation Pane displays with the results of the animation you applied on Slide 3. In this case, the Animation Pane displays with the effect applied to the content placeholder selected. Each item on the slide content placeholder displays with a number next to it to indicate the order in which the items will display.

Figure 6.10

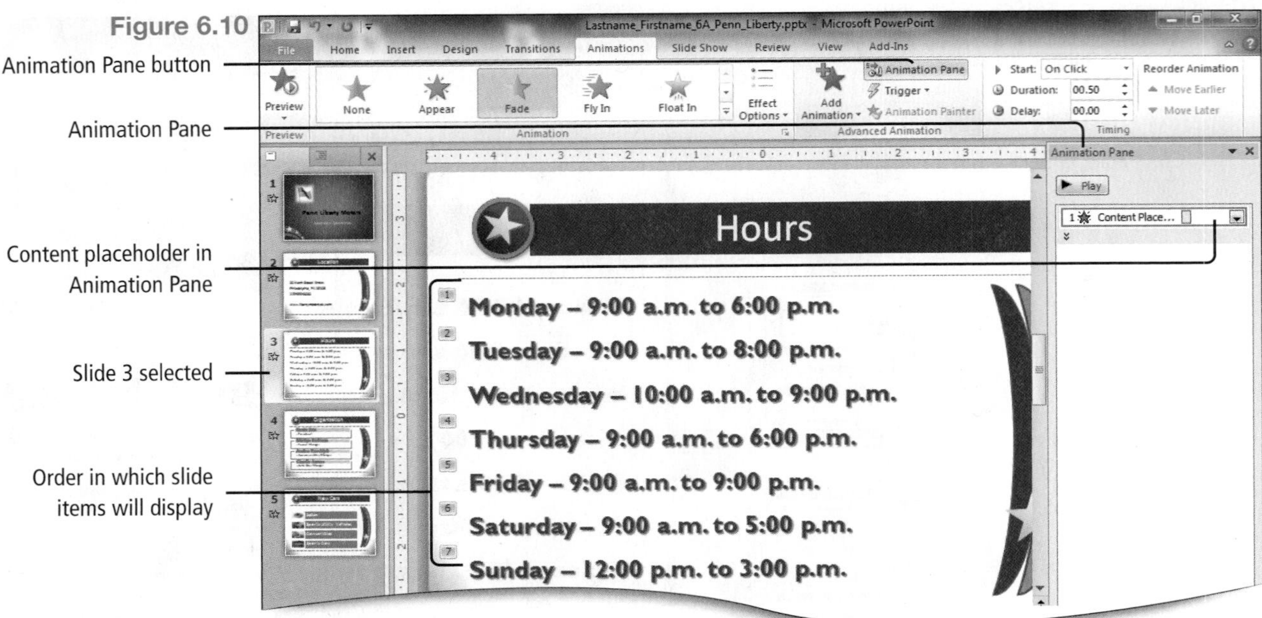

Alert! | Do You Have Extra Items Displayed in the Animation Pane?

If you clicked on an effect instead of pointing at it, you will have an extra item in the Animation Pane. Click the unwanted item in the Animation Pane, and then click the arrow and select Remove. If the item arrow does not display, click the correct placeholder on the slide or the item in the Animation Pane to make the item active.

Another Way

To remove an effect in the Animation Pane, right-click the effect to display the options, and then select Remove. You can also just click on the effect and press the Delete key.

4 In the **Animation Pane**, below *Content Placeholder*, point to the expand chevron to display the ScreenTip *Click to expand contents*. Compare your screen with Figure 6.11.

The ***chevron*** is a V-shaped pattern that indicates more information or options are available.

Figure 6.11

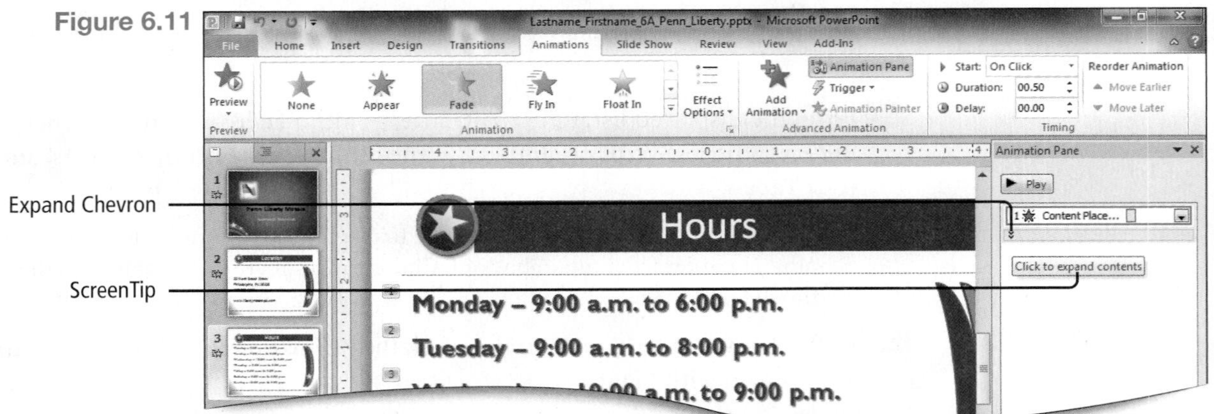

5 Click the chevron one time to expand the contents, and then compare your screen with Figure 6.12.

The numbers to the left of the items on the slide correspond with the numbers of the items in the Animation Pane.

Figure 6.12

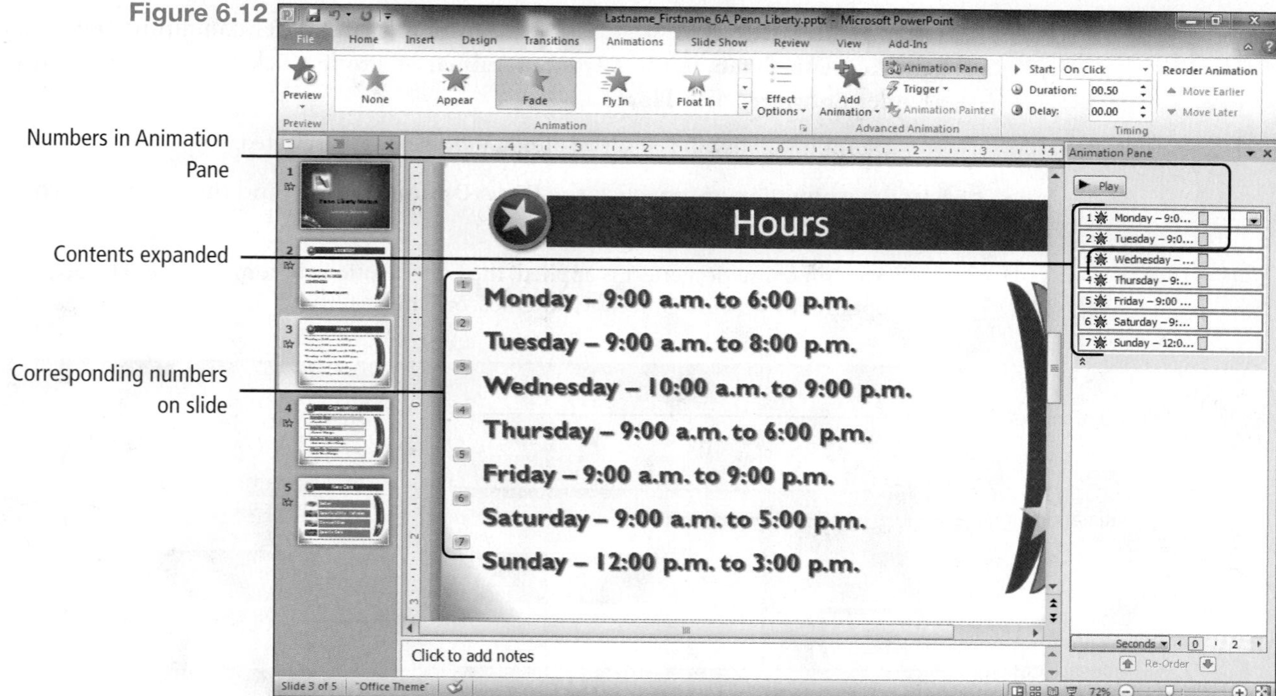

6 Right-click the entrance effect for the content placeholder, and then if necessary, click Show Advanced Timeline. In the **Animation Pane**, click the **Play** button to test the animation.

At the bottom right side of the Animation Pane, a ***timeline*** displays the number of seconds the animation takes to complete.

> **Alert! | Did the Timeline Display?**
>
> If you cannot see the timeline at the bottom of the Animation Pane, right-click the entrance effect for the content placeholder, and then click Show Advanced Timeline. If the timeline is visible, the option is displayed as Hide Advanced Timeline.

7 Click the hide chevron to hide the contents. Under the **Play** button, point to *Content Place ...*, read the ScreenTip, *On Click Fade: Content Placeholder ...*, and then compare your screen with Figure 6.13.

The ScreenTip identifies the start setting, which is On Click, and the Effect, which is Fade.

Figure 6.13

8. Make **Slide 5** the active slide. Click the content placeholder containing the cars. On the **Animations tab**, in the **Advanced Animation group**, click **Add Animation** button. Under **Entrance**, click **Float In**.

   The animations tab is inactive until a slide element is selected.

9. In the **Animation group**, click the **Effect Options** button, and then compare your screen with Figure 6.14.

   After an animation effect is applied, the Effect Options becomes active. The Sequence options are As One Object, All at Once, or One by One.

Figure 6.14

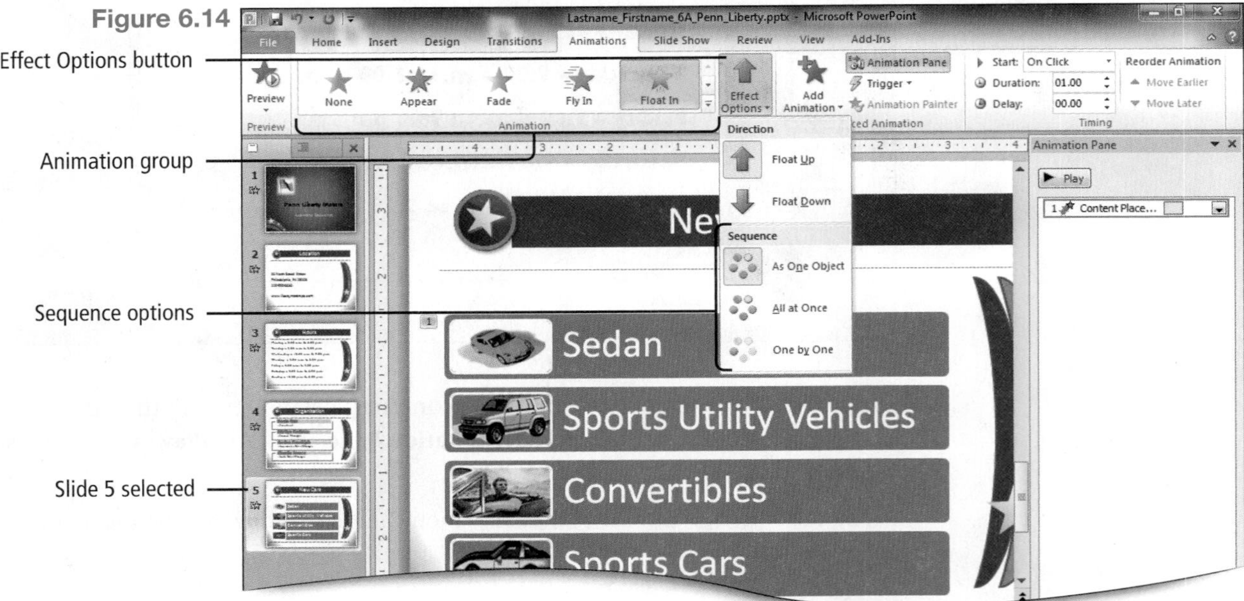

10. Under **Sequence**, click **One by One**. In the **Preview group**, click the **Preview** button.

    Clicking One by One sets the shapes in the SmartArt graphic on Slide 5 as individual objects that display one at a time.

11. Make the **title slide** the active slide, and then click to select the title placeholder—*Penn Liberty Motors*. In the **Advanced Animation group**, click the **Add Animation** button, and then click **More Entrance Effects**. In the **Add Entrance Effect** dialog box, under **Moderate**, scroll the list, click **Rise Up**, and then compare your screen with Figure 6.15.

    The Add Entrance Effect dialog box provides additional effects.

Figure 6.15

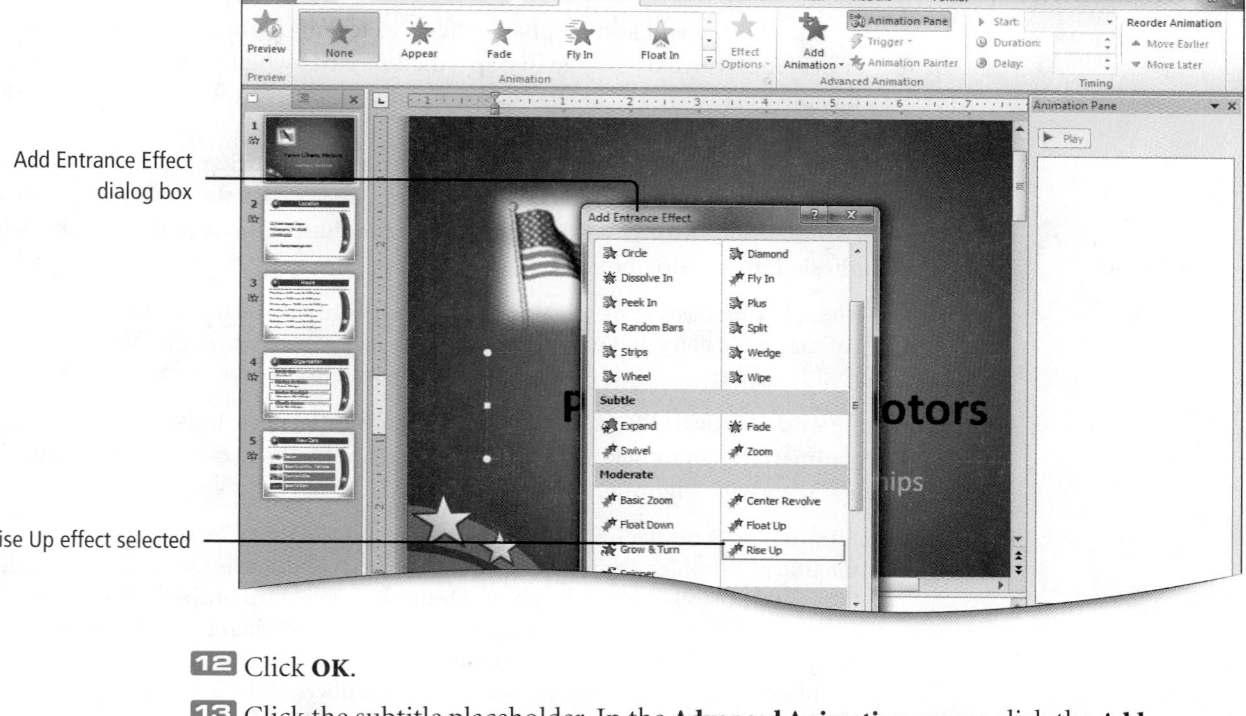

12 Click **OK**.

13 Click the subtitle placeholder. In the **Advanced Animation group**, click the **Add Animation** button, and then click **More Entrance Effects**. In the **Add Entrance Effect** dialog box, under **Moderate**, scroll the list, if necessary, and then click **Rise Up**. Click **OK**. Compare your screen with Figure 6.16. In the **Animation Pane**, click the **Play** button to test the animation.

The entrance effect for Slide 1 displays in the Animation Pane. The number 1 corresponds with the title placeholder. The number 2 corresponds with the subtitle placeholder. The numbers that appear on the slide in Normal view do not appear when you play the presentation.

Figure 6.16

14 **Save** your changes.

Activity 6.04 | Adding Emphasis Effects

In this activity, you will add emphasis effects to text and graphics. These effects make the text or graphics move or change in a specified manner when you click the mouse or press Enter while the text or graphic is displayed on the slide. You will also reorder the effects.

1 With the **title slide** as the active slide, click to select the title placeholder—*Penn Liberty Motors*. On the **Animations tab**, in the **Advanced Animation group**, click the **Add Animation** button, and then click **More Emphasis Effects** to display the **Add Emphasis Effect** dialog box.

The Add Emphasis Effect dialog box includes more emphasis effects than the Add Animations gallery and organizes them into groups—Basic, Subtle, Moderate, and Exciting effects. Use this dialog box if you do not find the effect you want in the gallery.

2 In the **Add Emphasis Effect** dialog box. Under **Subtle**, click **Pulse**, and then click **OK**. In the **Animation Pane**, click the **Play** button to see the Pulse effect on the title. Compare your screen with Figure 6.17.

A third item is displayed in the Animation Pane. The first one is for the entrance effect for the title placeholder, Penn Liberty Motors. The second one is for the entrance effect for the subtitle placeholder, Automobile Dealership. The third one is for the emphasis effect for the title. The Pulse effect for the title is set to occur when the presenter clicks the mouse button. To make an item in the Animation Pane active, click the item or click on the placeholder on the slide. Notice that the numbers to the left of the title and subtitle on the slide correspond with the numbers for the effects in the Animation Pane.

Figure 6.17

3 On the **Slide Show tab**, in the **Start Slide Show group**, click **From Current Slide**. Click to see the title entrance effect, click to see the subtitle entrance effect, and then click to see the title emphasis effect. Press Esc.

The sound effect played, the title moved up, the subtitle moved up, and then the title displayed the Pulse emphasis.

4 In the **Animation Pane**, click the third effect, the emphasis effect for the title—*3 Title1: Penn Li....* At the bottom of the **Animation Pane**, to the left of *Re-Order*, click the **move up arrow**. Compare your screen with Figure 6.18

Figure 6.18

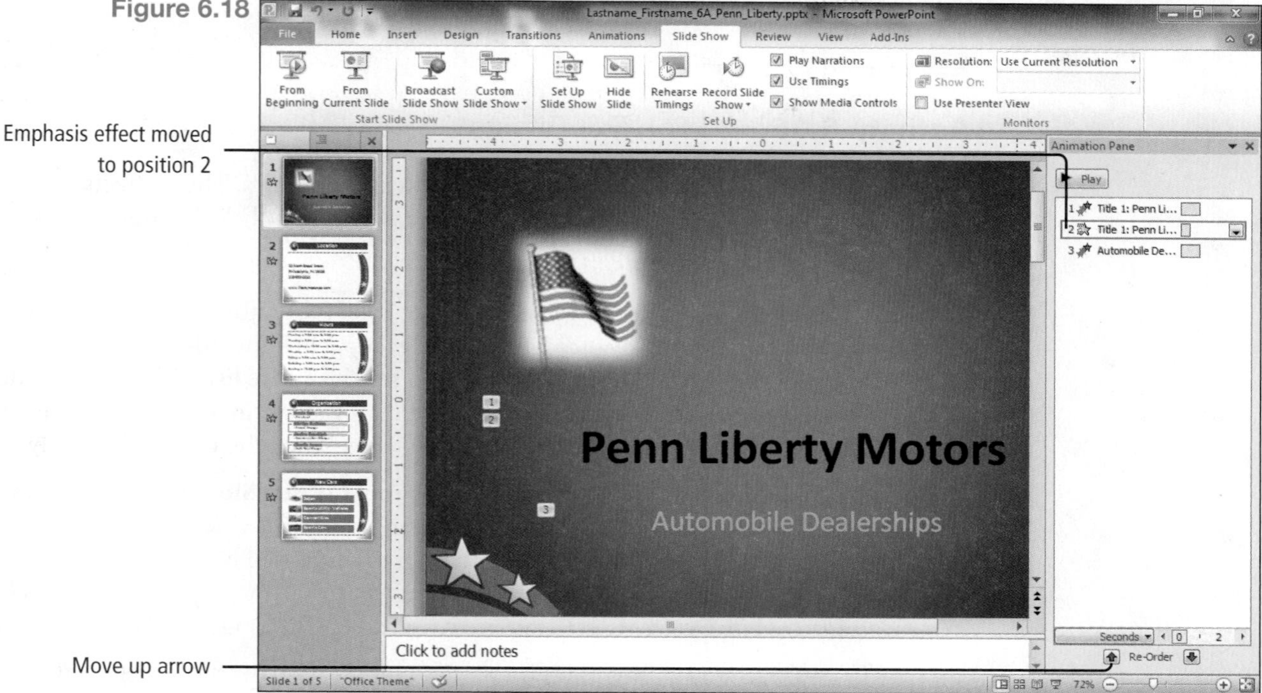

5 In the **Animation Pane**, click the **Play** button.

The order that the effects play is changed. The title moved up and displayed with the Pulse emphasis, and then the subtitle displayed. The sound effect does not play in the preview.

6 Make **Slide 4** the active slide, and then click to select the title placeholder—*Organization*. Using the technique you practiced, display the **Add Emphasis Effect** dialog box. Under **Subtle**, click **Bold Flash**, and then click **OK**. In the **Animation Pane**, point to the animation to display the ScreenTip—*On Click Bold Flash: Title 1: Organization*. Compare your screen with Figure 6.19.

Figure 6.19

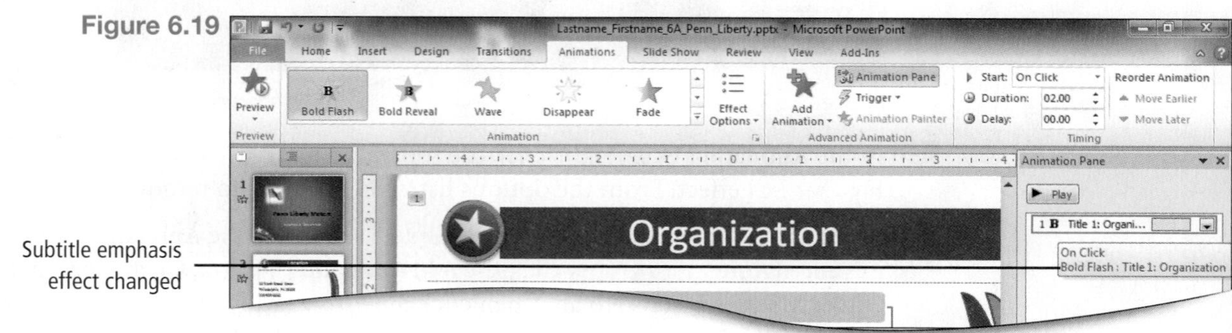

7 On the **Slide Show tab**, in the **Start Slide Show group**, click **From Current Slide**. Click to test the title emphasis effect. Click again to display Slide 5. When it appears, press Esc.

The title is displayed immediately. After the mouse click, the title blinks once and then returns to normal.

> **Alert! | Did the Title Blink More Than Once?**
>
> If the title blinked again on the second mouse click instead of advancing to Slide 5, you have applied the blink emphasis effect more than once. In the Animation Pane, right-click the extra effect, and then select Remove. Test the animation again.

8 **Save** your changes.

Activity 6.05 | Adding Exit Effects

In this activity, you will add exit effects to text and graphics. These effects make the text or graphics move or change in a specified manner when you click the mouse or press Enter while the text or graphic is displayed on the slide.

1 With the **title slide** as the active slide, click to select the subtitle placeholder. On the **Animations tab**, in the **Advanced Animation group**, click the **Add Animation** button. From the displayed list, under **Exit**, scroll to see the entire list. Point to—but do not click—**Disappear**, and then watch the Live Preview. Continue pointing at several of the effects. When you are finished, in the first row, click the third effect—**Fly Out**.

2 On the **Slide Show tab**, view the slide show **From Current Slide**. Click to display the title Rise Up entrance effect. Continue clicking to see the title Pulse emphasis effect, the subtitle Rise Up entrance effect, and then the subtitle Fly Out exit effect. Press Esc. In the **Animation Pane**, point to the fourth effect to see the ScreenTip *On Click Fly Out: Automobile Dealerships*. Compare your screen with Figure 6.20.

The order in which the effects play is determined by the sequence shown in the Animation Pane.

Figure 6.20

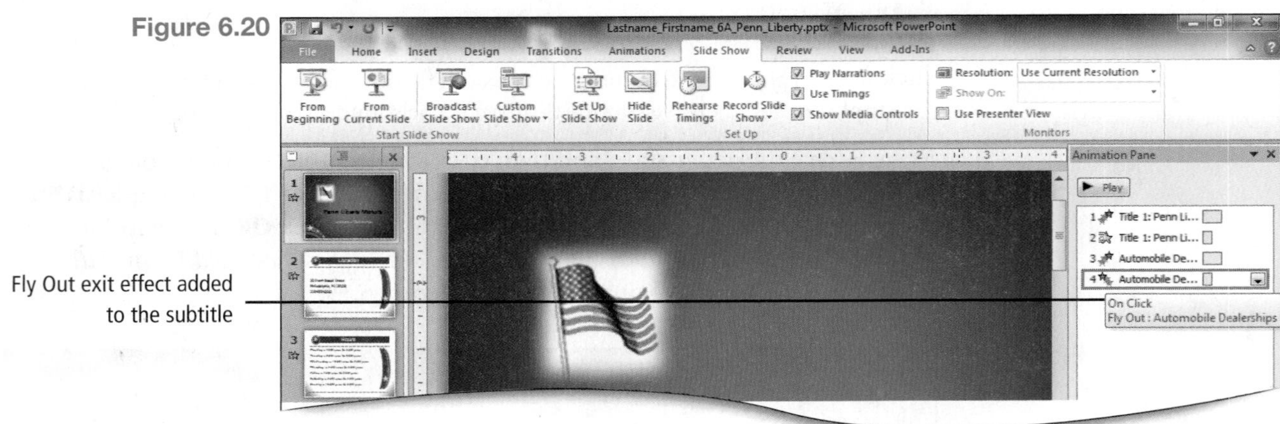

3 In the **Animation Pane**, right-click the fourth animations effect, which is the subtitle Fly Out exit effect. From the options list, select **Remove** to remove the effect.

4 Select the subtitle placeholder on the Slide 1 again. On the **Animations tab**, in the **Advanced Animation group**, click the **Add Animation** button. Click **More Exit Effects**. Under **Moderate**, scroll to and then click **Sink Down**. Click **OK**. In the **Preview group**, click the **Preview** button to see the Sink Down exit effect. In the **Animation Pane**, point to the fourth effect to see the ScreenTip—*On Click Sink Down: Automobile Dealerships*. Compare your screen with Figure 6.21.

In the Animation Pane, the entrance effect for the title is marked with a green star, the emphasis effect for the title is marked with a gold star, the entrance effect for the subtitle is marked with a green star, and the exit effect for the subtitle is marked with a red star. The stars are displayed with different actions to help define the pattern selected. The ScreenTip clarifies what specific effect was applied.

Figure 6.21

5 View the slide show **From Current Slide**. Click four times to activate the title entrance, the title emphasis, the subtitle entrance, and the subtitle exit effects. When Slide 2 displays, press Esc.

Slide 1 is displayed with the sound effect. With each click, the title enters in an upward direction, the title blinks, the subtitle enters, and finally the subtitle exits.

6 With **Slide 5** as the active slide, click the content placeholder to select the **SmartArt** graphic. On the **Animations tab**, in the **Advanced Animation group**, click the **Add Animation** button, and then click **More Exit Effects**. Under **Basic**, click **Wipe**, and then click **OK**. Compare your screen with Figure 6.22.

The first effect in the Animation Pane identifies the entrance effect for the SmartArt. Because there are four items in the SmartArt, the items are numbered 1 through 4 on the slide. The second effect in the Animation Pane identifies the exit effect for the SmartArt. The corresponding numbers on the slide are 5 through 8.

Figure 6.22

PowerPoint | Chapter 6

7. In the **Animation pane**, click the **Play** button to see the entrance and exit effects.

   Each item in the SmartArt graphic entered separately with the Float In entrance, and then the items exited separately with the Wipe exit.

8. View the slide show **From Current Slide**. After the sound effect, click four times to see the cars enter, and then click four more times to see them exit. Click two more times to return to Normal view.

   Because you are viewing the slide as it would be displayed in a slide show, you needed to click or press Enter in order to see the results.

9. **Save** your changes.

> **Note | Selecting Effects**
>
> Entrance, emphasis, exit, and motion effects may be selected from the Add Animation gallery or from the Add Effect dialog boxes. The Add Effect dialog box specific to each type of effect contains additional effects, which are categorized as Basic, Subtle, Moderate, and Exciting.

Activity 6.06 | Adding Motion Paths

Motion paths can also be applied to graphics. Built-in motion paths enable you to make text or a graphic move in a particular pattern, or you can design your own pattern of movement.

1. Make **Slide 2** the active slide. Click to select the title placeholder—*Location*. On the **Animations tab**, in the **Advanced Animation group**, click the **Add Animation** button, and then click **More Motion Paths**. In the **Add Motion Path** dialog box, scroll down, and then under **Lines & Curves**, click **Right**. Compare your screen with Figure 6.23.

Figure 6.23

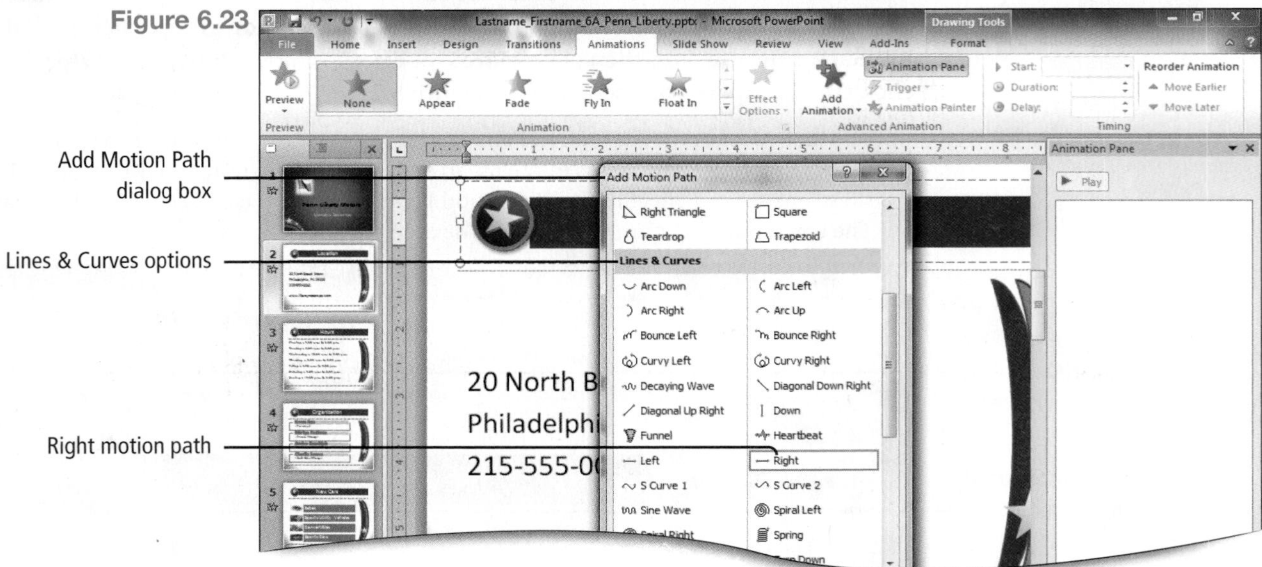

2. Click **OK**. View the slide show **From Current Slide**. Wait for the title to move to the right. When Slide 3 displays, press Esc.

   The transition on Slide 2 displayed first, and then the title moved to the right. Use motion paths very sparingly. They can be very distracting, and the audience may watch the path of the text or graphic instead of listening to the presenter.

3. Make **Slide 2** the active slide. In the **Animation Pane**, click the motion path effect. Compare your screen with Figure 6.24.

   The ScreenTip displays *On Click Right: Title 1: Location*. On the slide, the title placeholder displays a motion path graphic showing the direction of the movement.

Figure 6.24

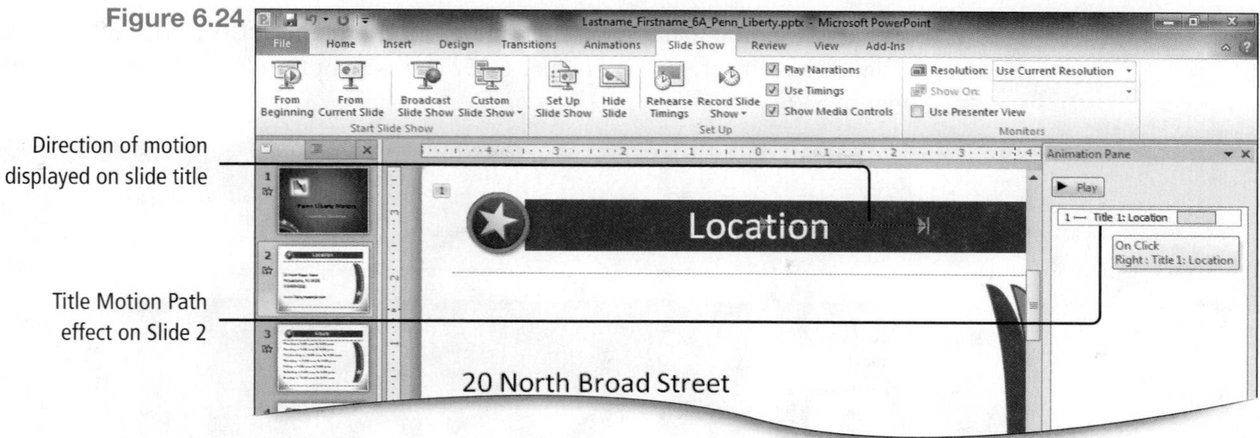

4 **Save** your changes.

Objective 3 | Modify Animation Effects

Entrance, emphasis, and exit effects as well as motion paths can be modified or customized by changing how they start, the speed at which they occur, and their direction. Effect settings such as timing delays and the number of times an effect is repeated can also be added. Effects can be set to start after a previous effect or simultaneously.

On Click allows you to start the animation effect when you click the slide or a trigger on the slide. On Click also allows you to display animation such as a motion path because the animation is triggered by the mouse click or, in some instances, by pressing Enter. Changing an animation start method to ***After Previous*** allows the animation effect to start immediately after the previous effect in the list finishes playing. Changing the start method to ***With Previous*** starts the animation effect at the same time as the previous effect in the list.

Activity 6.07 | Modifying Animation Effects

In this activity, you will modify the start method of some of the animation effects you added. You will also modify their speed and timing.

1 Click the **Slide Show tab**. In the **Start Slide Show group**, click **From Beginning**. Return to **Normal** view when finished.

On the title slide, you had to click for the title to enter, click for the title to blink, click for the subtitle to enter, and then click for the subtitle to exit. After clicking Slide 1, Slide 2 displayed after three seconds. Slide 3 advanced automatically after 5 seconds. On Slide 3, the hours of each day of the week displayed one by one as you clicked the mouse or pressed Enter. On Slide 4, the title effect occurred when you clicked the mouse. On Slide 5, each type of vehicle displayed with separate mouse clicks, and each one exited with separate mouse clicks.

Another Way

If animation has been applied to a placeholder or to an object such as a picture or graphic, you can select the object or placeholder by clicking the small number that displays on the slide. This number corresponds with the list of objects in the Animation Pane.

2 In **Normal** view, make the **title slide** the active slide, and then click to select the subtitle placeholder.

The title slide subtitle is displayed with two numbers. Number 3 represents the entrance effect, and number 4 represents the exit effect. Numbers 1 and 2 are for the title placeholder.

3 In the **Animation Pane**, right-click the subtitle exit effect, the fourth effect in the list. Compare your screen with Figure 6.25. The start options are defined in the table in Figure 6.26.

Figure 6.25

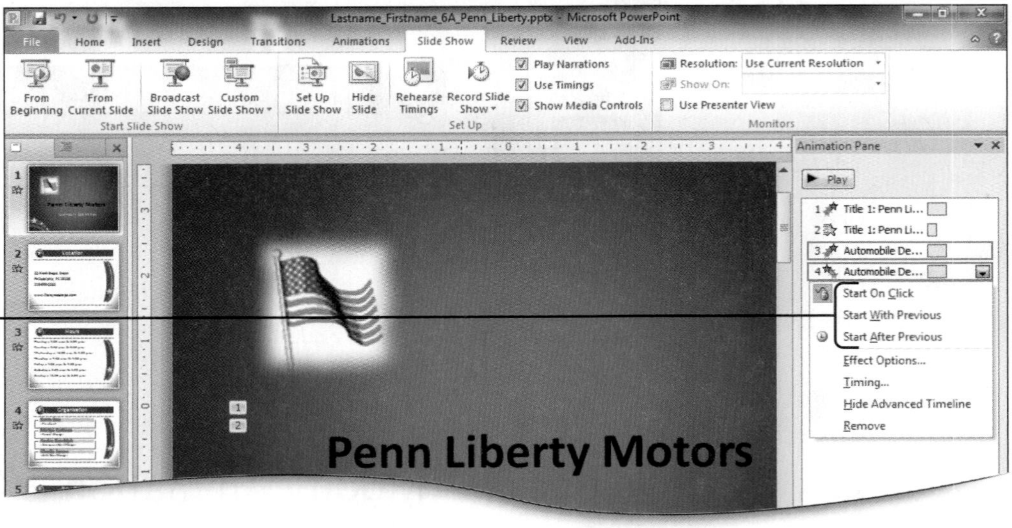

Subtitle exit effect start options

Start Options

Screen Element	Description
Start On Click	Animation begins when the slide is clicked. Displays with a mouse icon in the option list.
Start With Previous	Animation begins at the same time as the previous effect. One click executes all animation effects applied to the object. Displays with no icon in the option list.
Start After Previous	Animation begins after the previous effect in the list finishes. No additional click is needed. One click executes all animation effects applied to the object. Displays with a clock icon in the option list.

Figure 6.26

Another Way

To select a start method, on the Animations tab, in the Timing group, click the Start arrow, and then select the method.

4 Click **Start After Previous**. View the slide show **From Current Slide**. Click three times to display the title entrance, the title emphasis, and then the subtitle entrance and effects. Press Esc.

By changing On Click to After Previous, it was not necessary to click the mouse to initiate the subtitle entrance and exit effects. On the Animations tab, in the Timing group, the Start box now displays After Previous. Both the emphasis effect and exit effect applied to the subtitle displayed automatically. Notice that numbers 3 and 4 disappeared from the exit effect in the Animation Pane.

5 Make **Slide 3** the active slide. In the **Animation Pane**, right-click the entrance effect for the content placeholder, and then click **Effect Options**. In the **Fade** dialog box, click the **Timing tab**, and then click the **Start arrow**. Click **After Previous**.

6 Click the **Duration arrow**, and then select **1 seconds (Fast)**. Compare your screen with Figure 6.27.

The Fade dialog box is a context-sensitive dialog box for the entrance effect applied to the title. The name of the dialog box reflects which effect you are modifying. In this dialog box, you can modify more than one setting.

Figure 6.27

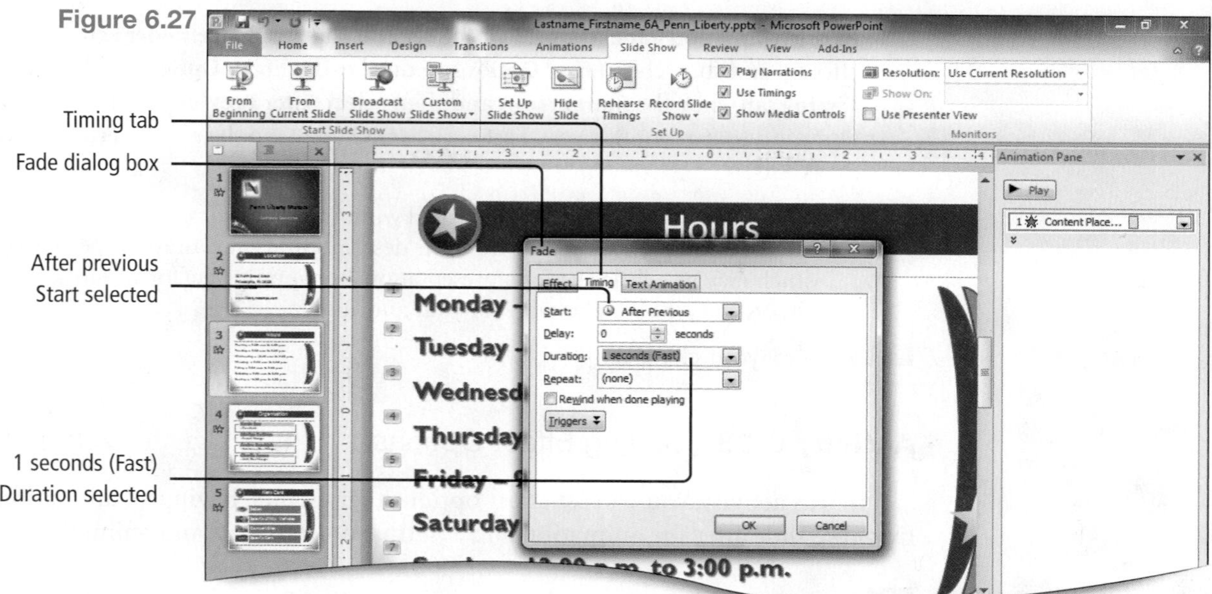

7 Click **OK**. On the **Slide Show tab**, in the **Start Slide Show group**, view the slide show **From Current Slide**. After the last day displays, press Esc.

Each day displayed automatically without any mouse clicks.

8 Make **Slide 2** the active slide, and then click to select the body text placeholder. On the **Animations tab**, click the **Add Animation** button, and then click **More Entrance Effects**. Under **Basic**, click **Fly In**, and then click **OK**. View the slide show **From Current Slide**. When **Slide 3** displays, press Esc to return to **Normal** view.

The title is displayed and then moved to the right. The items in the content placeholder fly in from the bottom one after the other. No mouse clicks were required.

9 Make **Slide 5** the active slide. In the **Animation Pane**, click the **Play** button, and then view the slide show **From Current Slide**. Press Esc.

The Play button displays all animations associated with the slide, in Normal view, regardless of how the animation is set to start. However, the From Beginning or From Current Slide button plays all animations applied to the slide in Slide Show view, and it displays them the way they will display in a slide show. If you are testing the effects with the Slide Show button and the animation is set to start On Click, you must click the mouse or press Enter to begin the animation.

10 In the **Animation Pane**, right-click the entrance effect for the SmartArt—the first effect. Click **Effect Options** to display the **Float Up** dialog box. On the **Timing tab**, click the **Start arrow**, and then select **After Previous**. Change the **Duration** to **.5 seconds (Very Fast)**. Click **OK**. View the slide show **From Current Slide**. Press Esc to return to **Normal** view.

The SmartArt items entered without mouse clicks. To view the exit effect, you had to click the mouse for each one. The Duration speed for the entrance effect was .5 seconds, which may be a little fast for a presentation, but appropriate for you to see the effect. Always choose a time suitable for your audience.

11 In the **Animation Pane**, right-click the second **Content Placeholder arrow**—the exit effect—and then click **Effect Options** to display the **Effect Options** dialog box. On the **Timing tab**, click the **Start arrow**, and then select **After Previous**. If necessary, change the Duration to .5 seconds (Very Fast). Click **OK**. View the slide show **From Current Slide**. Press Esc.

The SmartArt items entered and exited without mouse clicks. Notice that the pictures entered and exited separately from the descriptions. The Duration speed was .5 seconds, which may be a little fast for a presentation, but appropriate for you to see the effect. Always choose a time suitable for your audience.

12 **Save** your changes.

Activity 6.08 | Setting Effect Options

In this activity, you will set effect options that include having an animation disappear from the slide after the animation effect, setting a time delay, and animating text.

1 With **Slide 2** as the active slide, in the **Animation Pane**, right-click the second effect, the entrance effect for the content placeholder, and then click **Effect Options** to display the **Fly In** dialog box.

The Fly In dialog box has three tabs—Effect, Timing, and Text Animation. On the Effect tab, you can change the Settings and the Enhancements. You can change the direction of the Fly In, add sound, and change the way text is animated.

2 On the **Effect tab**, under **Settings**, click the **Direction arrow**, and then click **From Left**.

3 Under **Enhancements**, click the **After animation arrow**. Compare your screen with Figure 6.28.

You can apply a color change to the animated text or object. You can also automatically hide the animated object after the animation takes place or hide the animated object on the next mouse click. Don't Dim is selected by default.

Figure 6.28

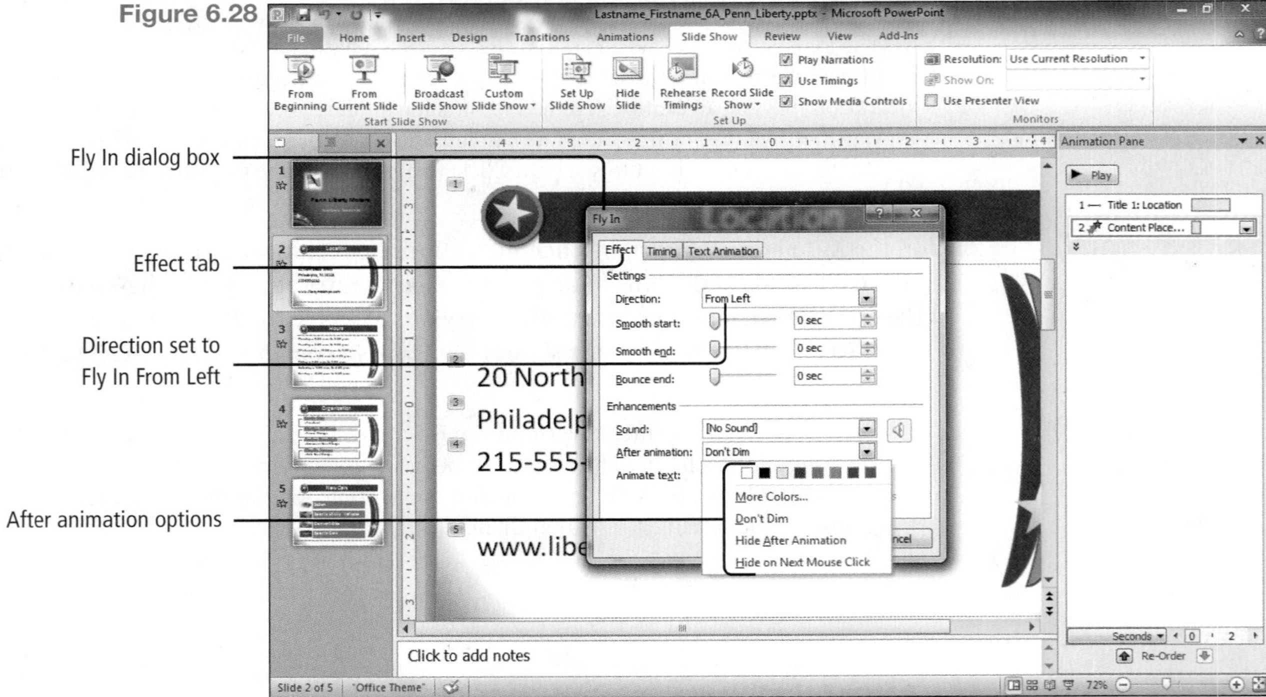

4 In the row of colors, click the second color—**Black**. Click **OK**. On the **Slide Show tab**, in the **Start Slide Show group**, view the slide show **From Current Slide.** When Slide 3 displays, press Esc.

The animation changes display automatically one at a time.

5 With **Slide 2** selected, in the **Animation Pane**, right-click the effect for the content placeholder, and then click **Effect Options**. In the **Fly In** dialog box, click the **Timing tab**. Click the **Duration arrow**, and then click **2 seconds (Medium)**. Compare your screen with Figure 6.29.

By using the Timing tab, you can change how the animation will start. You can also set a delay, in seconds, from when the slide displays until the text displays. You can select the speed and how many times you would like the animation to repeat. Selecting the *Rewind when done playing* check box will cause the animated text or object to disappear from the slide after the animation is completed, as opposed to remaining on the slide. From this tab you can also set a ***trigger***, which is a portion of text, a graphic, or a picture that, when clicked, produces a result. Recall that in the previous chapter you practiced inserting sounds into slides and selecting a placeholder or object that would start the sound when clicked. Triggers are created for animation purposes using the same technique.

Figure 6.29

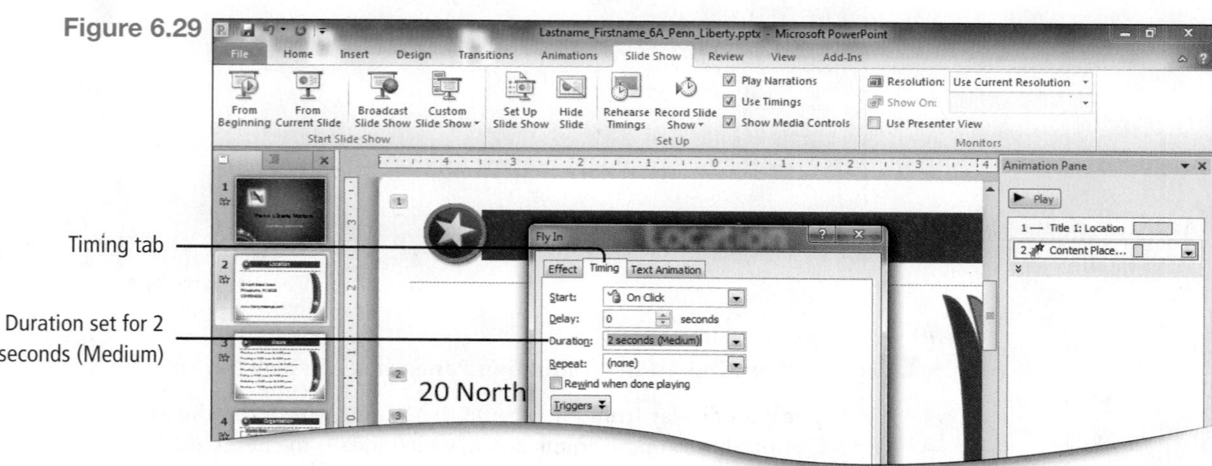

> **Note | Repeating an Animated List of Items**
>
> In the Fly In dialog box, on the Timing tab, if you elect to repeat a list of items that have animation applied to them, typing a number in the Repeat box will cause each line of text or each bulleted item to repeat before the next item displays. Repeating a list of two or three bulleted items might be used in a presentation as a special effect to emphasize the points but may produce unexpected and unwanted results, so be very cautious about using this option.

6 In the **Fly In** dialog box, click the **Text Animation tab**. Click the **Group text arrow**.

You can treat a list as one object and animate all paragraphs of text simultaneously. If your bulleted list has several levels of bulleted items, you can select how you want to animate the items. Use the Text Animation tab to set a delay in seconds, animate an attached shape, or reverse the order of the items.

7 If necessary, click By 1st Level Paragraphs, and then click **OK**.

Another Way

To set the direction and sequence of bullet points, use the Effect Options button in the Animation group.

8 With **Slide 2** active, click the content placeholder. On the **Animations tab**, in the **Animation group**, click the **Effect Options** button, and then compare your screen with Figure 6.30.

Figure 6.30

Another Way

To set the direction and sequence of effects, on the Animations tab, in the Animation group, click the Effect Options button, and then make your selection.

9 Click **From Top**. In the **Animation Pane**, click the **Play** button.

The lines display from the top. On the Animations tab, in the Animation group, the Effect Options button now points down, which means the items are coming from the top.

Another Way

To reorder effects in the Animation Pane, you can click on the effect, and then drag it to the new position.

10 With **Slide 2** active, click the title placeholder—*Location*. At the bottom of the **Animation Pane**, to the right of *Re-Order*, click the **down-pointing arrow**. Click the **Play** button. Compare your screen with Figure 6.31.

The order of the effects is changed. The address and Web site displayed first. The motion effect on the title is displayed last because the order of the effects was changed in the Animation Pane. You can easily reorder the list of animation sequences by selecting a placeholder and then clicking the Re-Order arrows at the bottom of the Animation Pane.

Figure 6.31

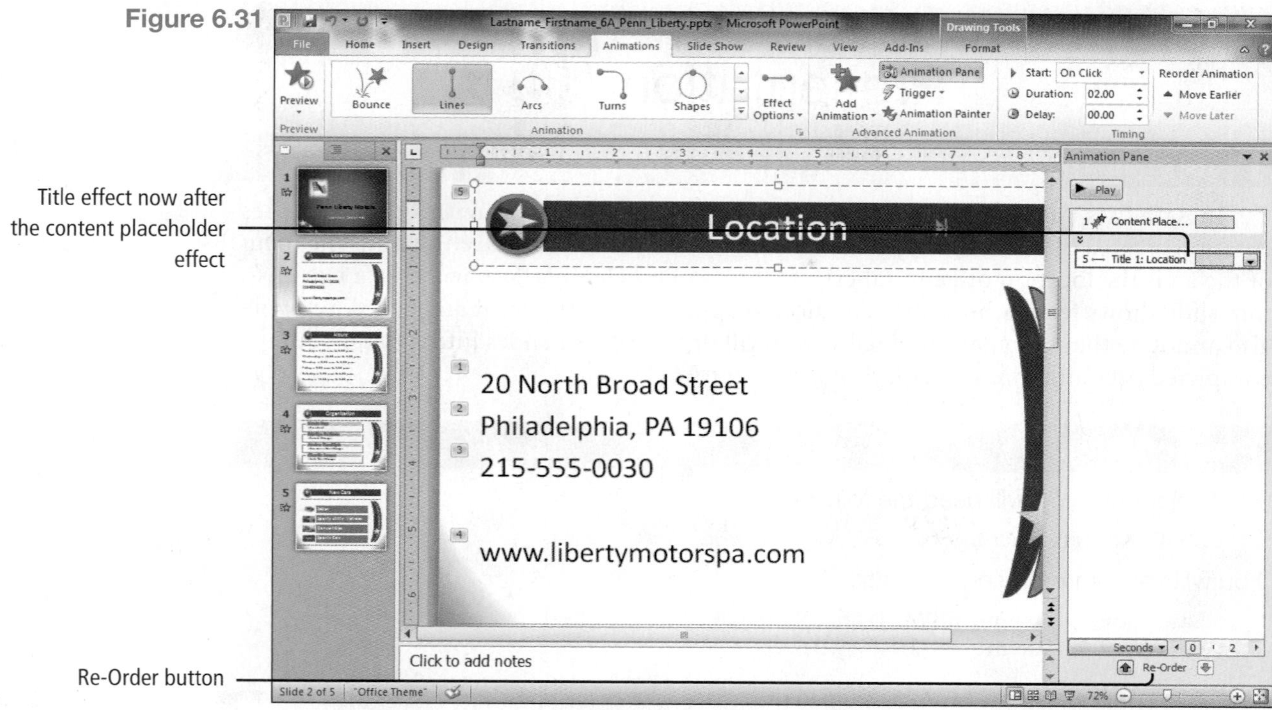

11 Under the **Content Placeholder**, click the chevron [icon], and then click the **Play** button and watch the timeline. Click [icon] to hide the contents.

12 View the slide show **From Beginning.** Click when necessary to advance the slides.

13 On the **Animations tab**, in the **Advanced Animation group**, click the **Animation Pane** to close the pane.

14 On the **Insert tab**, in the **Text group**, click the **Header & Footer** button to display the **Header and Footer** dialog box. Click the **Notes and Handouts tab.** Under **Include on page**, select the **Date and time** check box, and then select **Fixed.** If necessary, clear the Header check box, and then select the **Page number** and **Footer** check boxes. In the **Footer** box, using your own name, type **Lastname_Firstname_6A_Penn_Liberty** and then click **Apply to All.**

15 Display **Backstage** view, click **Properties**, and then click **Show Document Panel.** Replace the text in the **Author** box with your own name; in the **Subject** box, type your course name and section number; and in the **Keywords** box, type **hours, cars Close** the **Document Information Panel.**

16 **Save** [icon] your changes. **Close** the presentation, and then **Exit** PowerPoint. Submit your work as directed.

End **You have completed Project 6A**

Project 6B Advertisement Presentation

Project Activities

In Activities 6.09 through 6.19, you will insert various types of hyperlinks into a presentation created by Penn Liberty Motors as an advertisement for the company. The focus of the ad is the location of Penn Liberty Motors in Philadelphia. You will create two custom slide shows from a single presentation to appeal to two different audiences. You will also annotate the presentation. Finally, you will organize your slides into sections. Your completed presentation will look similar to Figure 6.32.

Project Files

For Project 6B, you will need the following file:

p06B_Advertisement.pptx

You will save your presentation as:

Lastname_Firstname_6B_Advertisement.pptx
Lastname_Firstname_6B_History.docx

Project Results

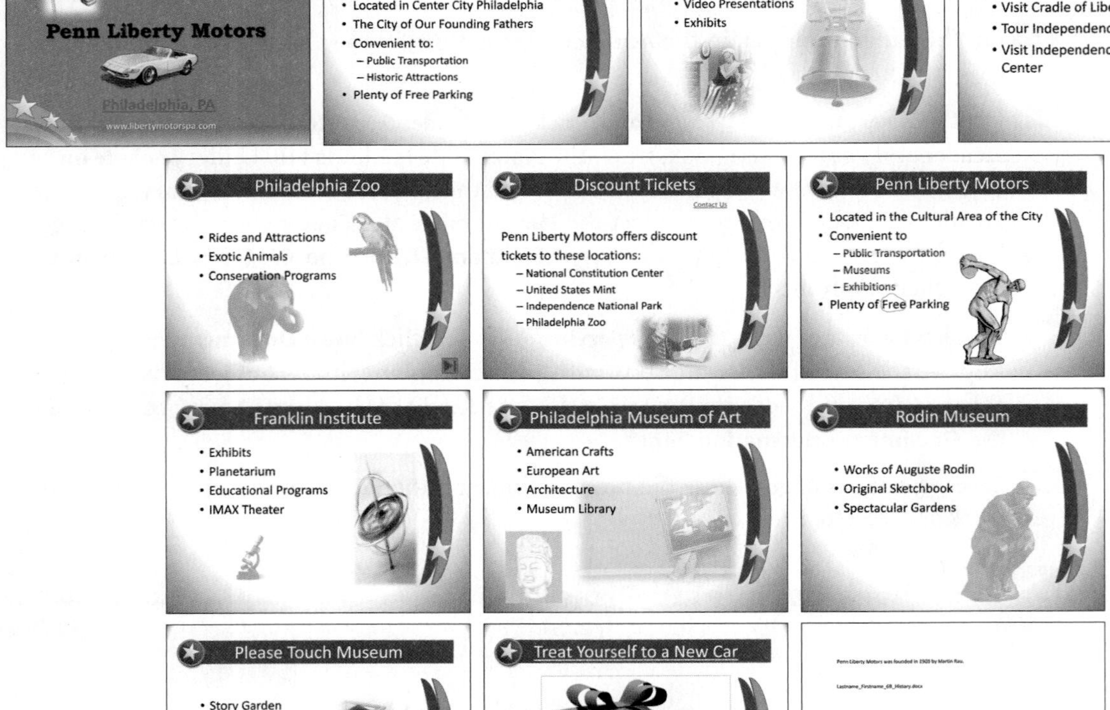

Figure 6.32
Project 6B Advertisement

Objective 4 | Insert Hyperlinks

In the following activities, you will insert hyperlinks into a PowerPoint presentation. Recall that ***hyperlinks*** are text or objects such as clip art, graphics, WordArt, or pictures that, when clicked, will move you to a Web page, an e-mail address, another document or file, or another area of the same document. In a PowerPoint presentation, hyperlinks can also be used to link to a slide in the presentation, to a slide in a different presentation, or to a custom slide show.

Activity 6.09 | Inserting a Hyperlink to Web Page

In this activity, you will insert a hyperlink into a slide that will connect to the Penn Liberty Motors Web page.

1 **Start** PowerPoint. Locate and open the file **p06B_Advertisement**. Navigate to the **PowerPoint Chapter 6** folder you created, and then save the file as **Lastname_Firstname_6B_Advertisement**

2 Make the **title slide** the active slide. Click to select the text box containing the Web page address *www.libertymotorspa.com*. Then click and drag to select the text.

3 Click the **Insert tab**. In the **Links group**, click the **Hyperlink** button to display the **Insert Hyperlink** dialog box. If necessary, under Link to, click Existing File or Web Page. Compare your screen with Figure 6.33.

The Insert Hyperlink dialog box provides an easy and convenient way to insert hyperlinks. You can link to an Existing File or Web Page (the default setting), a Place in This Document, Create New Document, or an E-Mail Address. You can also browse the Web, browse for a file, or change the text that displays in the ScreenTip.

Figure 6.33

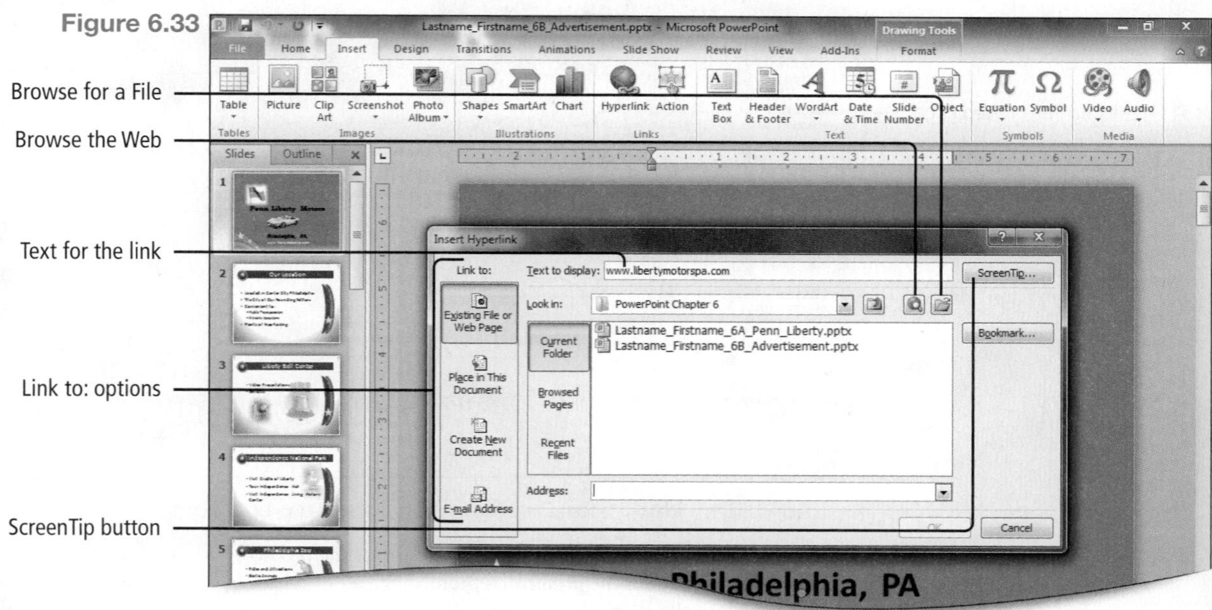

4 Click the **ScreenTip** button. In the **Set Hyperlink ScreenTip** dialog box, type **Penn Liberty Motors** Compare your screen with Figure 6.34.

Figure 6.34

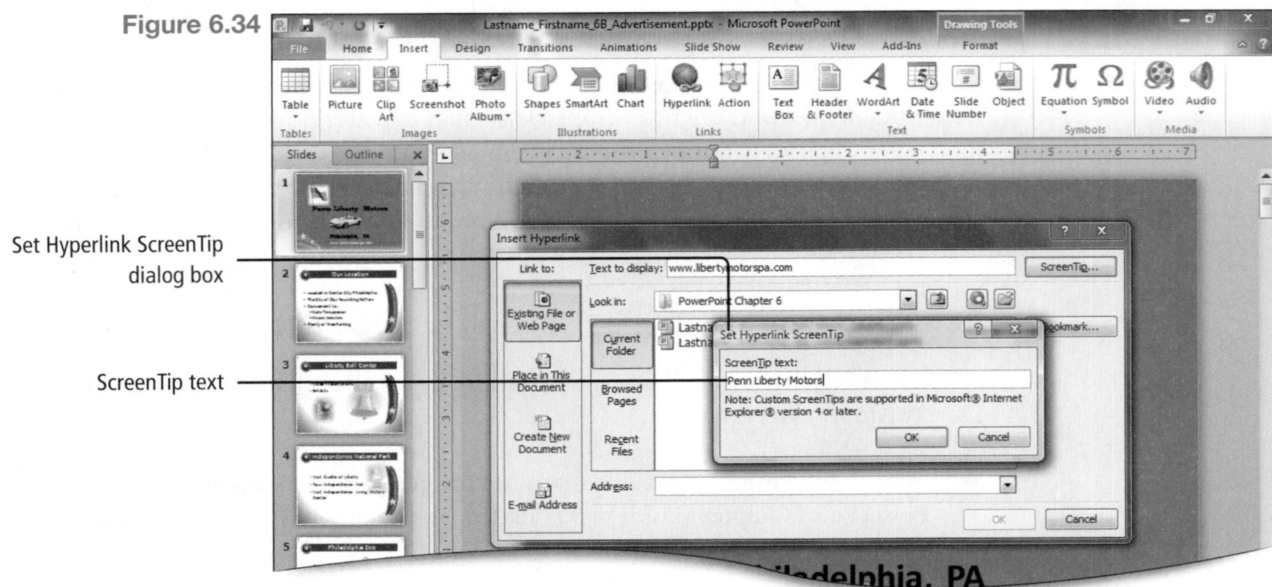

5 Click **OK**. In the **Address** box, delete the existing text, if any, and then type http://www.libertymotorspa.com Compare your screen with Figure 6.35.

The text you typed is a ***URL***, or ***Uniform Resource Locator***. A URL defines the address of documents and resources on the Web.

Figure 6.35

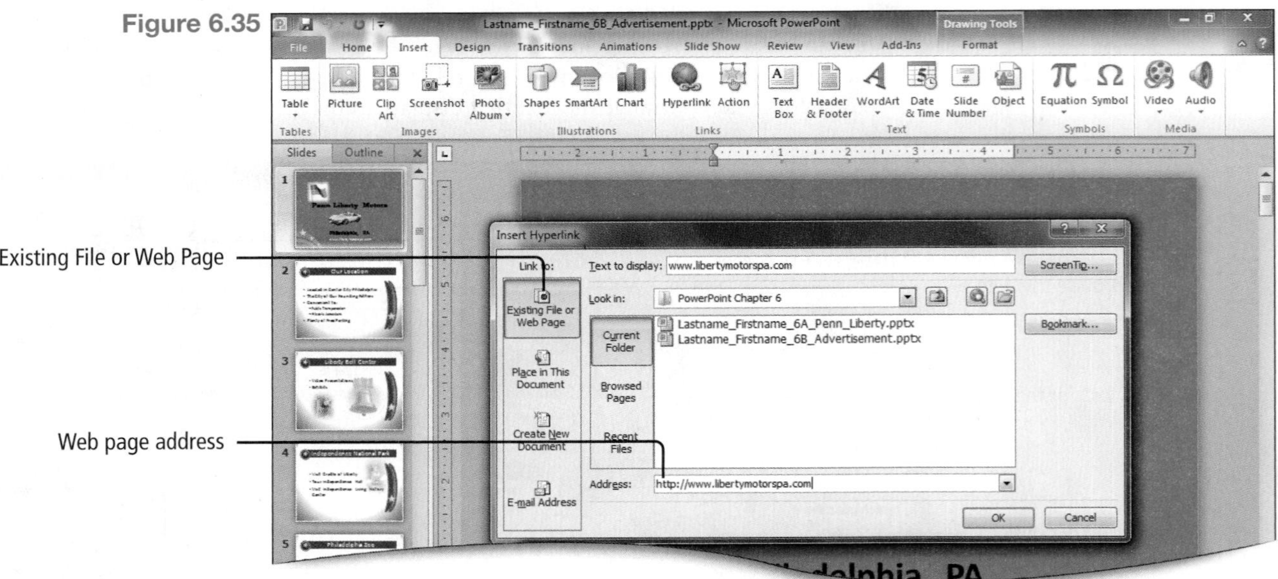

More Knowledge | Understanding Uniform Resource Locators

A Uniform Resource Locator, or URL, generally consists of the protocol and the IP address or domain name. The first part of the address is the ***protocol***. A protocol is a set of rules. ***HyperText Transfer Protocol (HTTP)*** is the protocol used on the World Wide Web to define how messages are formatted and transmitted. It also instructs the ***Web browser*** software how to display Web pages. Web browsers, such as Internet Explorer, format Web pages so that they display properly. The protocol is followed by a colon (:) and two forward slashes (//). The *www* stands for *World Wide Web*. The World Wide Web is a collection of Web sites. This is followed by the *domain name*. The domain name is a user friendly name that represents an *IP address*. An IP address, or Internet Protocol address, is a unique set of numbers, composed of a network ID and a machine ID, that identifies the Web server where the Web page resides. The *suffix* part of the domain name, the portion after the dot (.), is the *high level domain name (HLDN)* or top level domain name, such as *.com*, *.org*, or *.gov*. This is the upper level domain to which the lower level domain belongs.

6 Click **OK**.

The Web page address now displays with an underline and takes on the appearance of a hyperlink.

7 Start the slide show **From Current Slide**. On the **title slide**, without clicking, point to the address www.libertymotorspa.com, and then compare your screen with Figure 6.36.

The Link Select pointer displays. A ScreenTip displays with the text you typed.

Figure 6.36

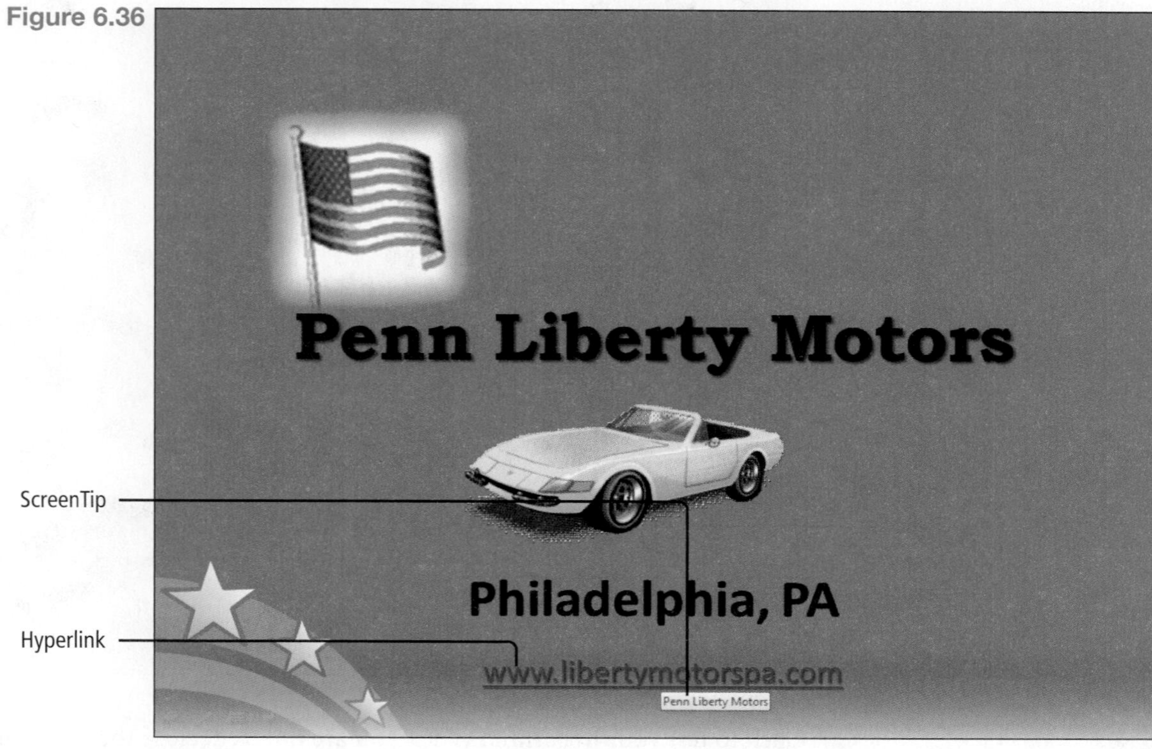

8 With the Link Select pointer, click the hyperlink.

The Web page is displayed if you are connected to the Internet.

> **Alert! | Did the www.libertymotorspa.com Web Site Not Appear?**
>
> As of this writing, the www.libertymotorspa.com Web site was active. You might receive an error message stating that the Internet server could not be located.

9 Close the Web page, return to PowerPoint, and then press Esc.

10 Right-click anywhere on the URL **www.libertymotorspa.com**, and then from the displayed shortcut menu, click **Remove Hyperlink**.

11 With the **title slide** still the active slide, drag to select the subtitle *Philadelphia, PA*. Click the **Insert tab**. In the **Links group**, click **Hyperlink**.

12 To the right of the **Look in** box, click the **Browse the Web** button.

If you are connected to the Internet, your selected home page will display. From there, you can browse for a particular page.

13 In the **Internet Explorer** address bar, type **www.google.com** and then press Enter.

14 In the **Google** search box, type **Philadelphia** and then press Enter. Click to display a Web page of your choosing.

15 On the status bar at the bottom of your screen, click the **PowerPoint** button. Click **OK**.

The Web site address is automatically displayed in the Insert Hyperlink dialog box Address box.

16 Start the slide show **From Current Slide**. Point to *Philadelphia, PA*, and then compare your screen with Figure 6.37.

It is not necessary to format the Web page hyperlink text in URL format as long as it is linked correctly to the Web page address. Any text or object can serve as a hyperlink.

Figure 6.37

Hyperlink

ScreenTip with Web page address

Penn Liberty Motors

Philadelphia, PA

http://www.phila.gov/

www.libertymotorspa.com

17 Click to test your hyperlink. When you are finished, close the Web page and return to PowerPoint. Press Esc to return to your presentation screen.

18 **Save** your changes. Close any other Web page that may have opened during this activity.

Activity 6.10 | Inserting a Hyperlink to a Slide in Another Presentation

In this activity, you will insert a hyperlink into a presentation that will link to the Location slide in a previously created presentation.

1 In **Normal** view, make **Slide 12** the active slide. Drag to select the title—*Treat Yourself to a New Car*. Click the **Insert tab**. In the **Links group**, click the **Hyperlink** button to display the **Insert Hyperlink** dialog box.

2 If necessary, under **Link to**, click to select **Existing File or Web Page**, and then using the technique you practiced, navigate to the **PowerPoint Chapter 6** folder and click **Lastname_Firstname_6A_Penn_Liberty**. Compare your screen with Figure 6.38.

Figure 6.38

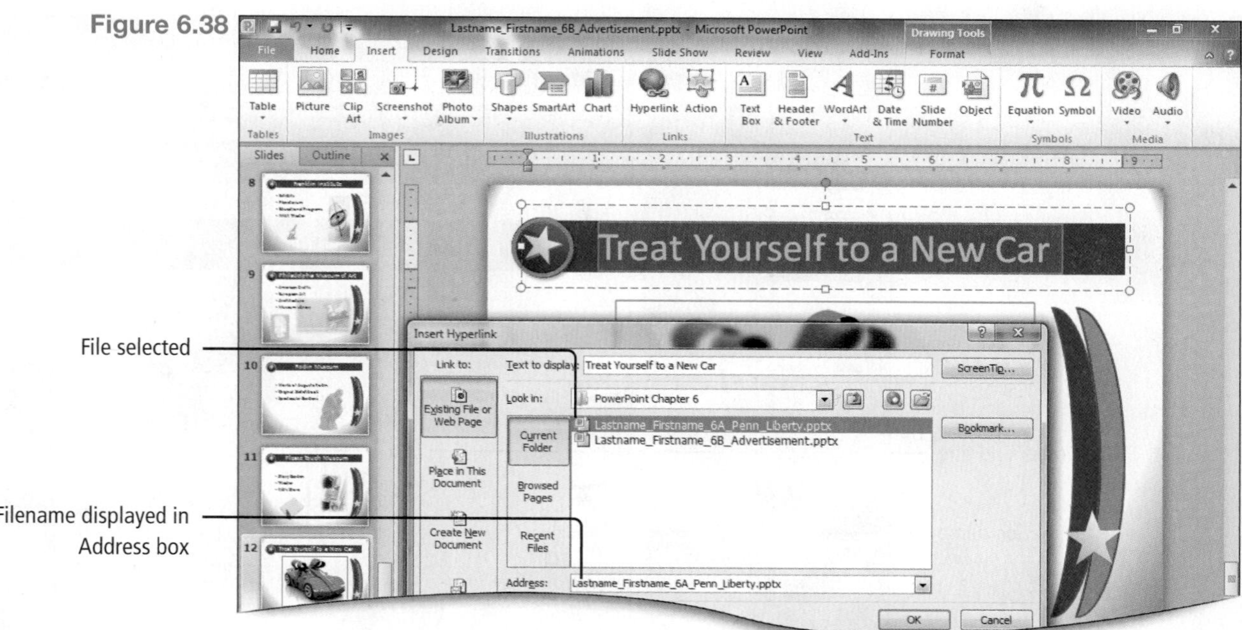

3 In the **Insert hyperlink** dialog box, click the **Bookmark** button to display the **Select Place in Document** dialog box. Compare your screen with Figure 6.39.

Notice that the slides from Lastname_Firstname_6A_Penn_Liberty are listed.

Figure 6.39

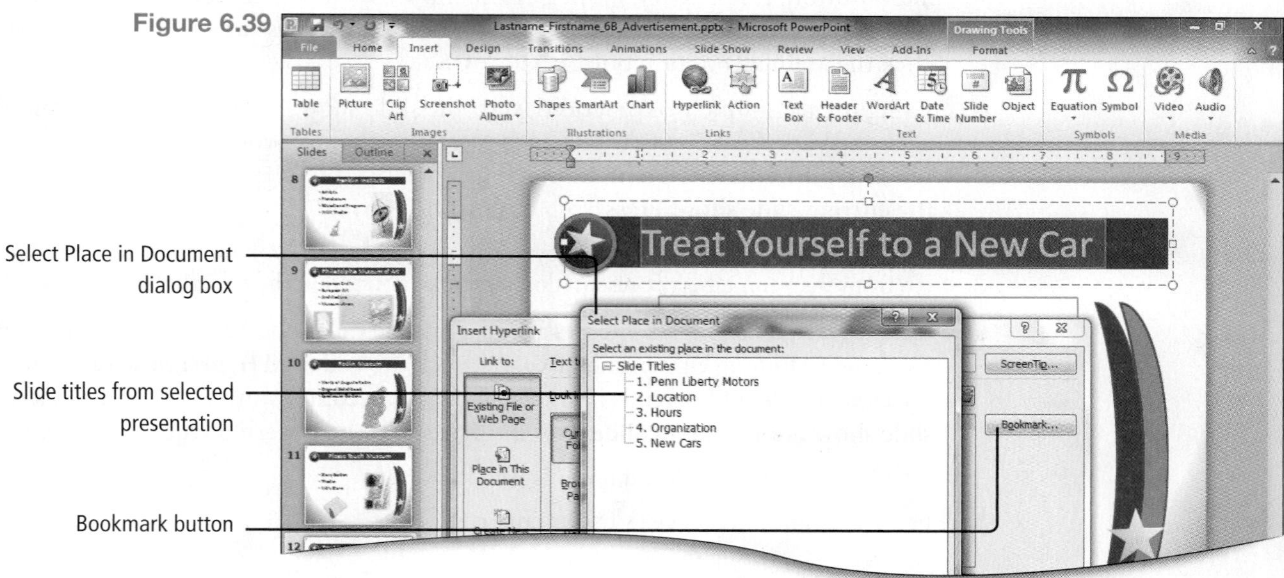

4 In the **Select Place in Document** dialog box, click the fifth slide—*New Cars*—and then click **OK**. Compare your screen with Figure 6.40.

The Address box contains the name of the presentation and the number and title of the slide.

Figure 6.40

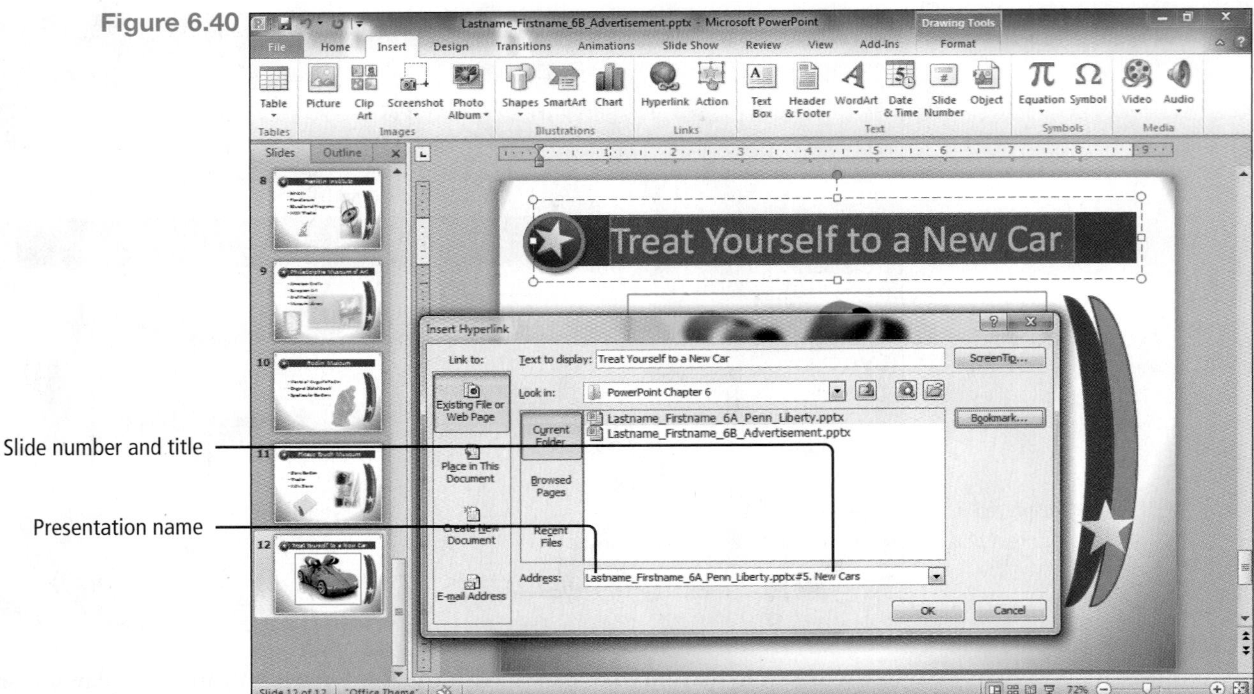

5 Click **OK**. Click the **Slide Show tab**, and then in the **Set Up group**, click the **Set Up Slide Show** button. If necessary, in the Set Up Show dialog box, under Show type, select the **Presented by a speaker (full screen)** option button. If necessary, under Advance slides, click the **Manually** option button. Click **OK**.

6 Using the technique you practiced, start the slide show **From Current Slide**, and then click the hyperlink on Slide 12. The hyperlink will move you to Slide 5 of the other presentation. When the animations finish playing, press Esc to return to Slide 12 of the current slide show. Press Esc to return to **Normal** view.

Because you selected Presented by a speaker (full screen), you were able to view Slide 5 from the Penn Liberty presentation. You may notice that the hyperlink is difficult to see.

7 On the **Design tab**, in the **Themes group**, click the **Colors** button, and then click **Create New Theme Colors**. Under **Theme colors**, click the **Followed Hyperlink arrow**, and then select **White, Text 1**, which is in the first row, the second column. Click **Save**. View the slide show **From Current Slide** so you can see that the hyperlinked text is easier to read.

The visited hyperlink text now displays in white.

8 Press Esc, and then **Save** your changes.

Activity 6.11 | Inserting a Hyperlink to an E-mail Address

In this activity, you will insert a hyperlink that will open an e-mail client and insert the recipient's e-mail address and subject.

1 In **Normal** view, make **Slide 6** the active slide. Drag to select the text *Contact Us*. Click the **Insert tab**. In the **Links group**, click the **Hyperlink** button.

2 In the **Insert Hyperlink** dialog box, under **Link to**, click to select **E-Mail Address**.

3 In the **E-mail address** box, type **kevin@libertymotors.com**

4 In the **Subject** box, type **Discount Tickets** and then compare your screen with Figure 6.41.

The word *mailto:* displays before the e-mail address. This is an *HTML* attribute instructing the Web browser software that this is an e-mail address. HTML stands for ***HyperText Markup Language*** and is the language used to code Web pages. The recently used e-mail addresses with the associated subject also display for easy selection. You may not have any in your list.

Figure 6.41

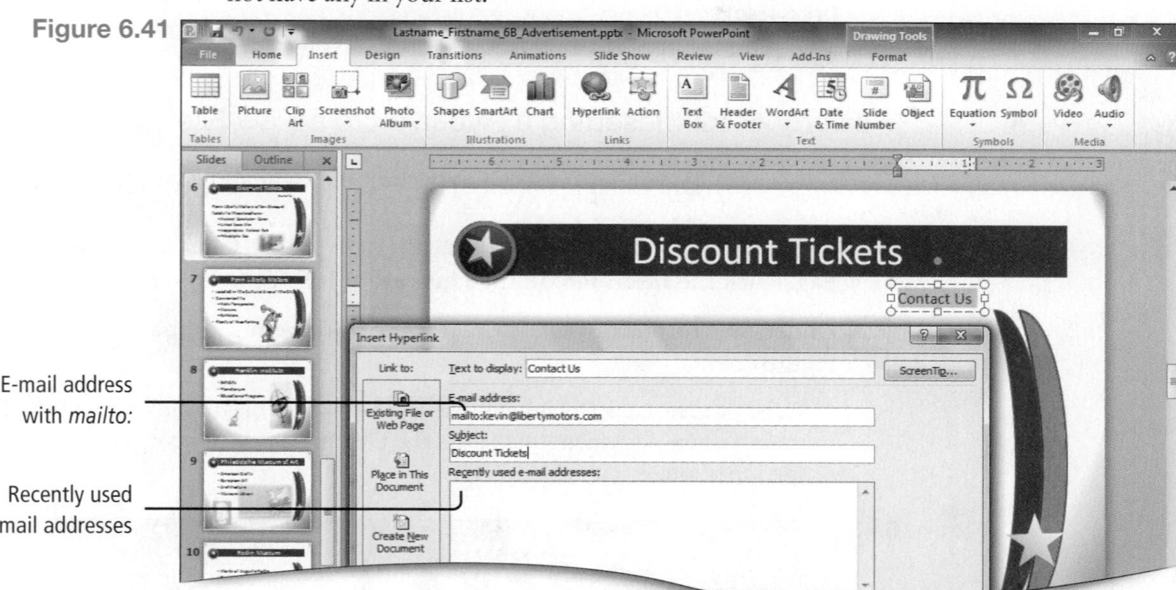

5 Click **OK**.

> **Alert! | Do You Have An E-mail Client to Use?**
>
> If you do not have an e-mail client that is configured to a mail service, skip the following steps in this activity. Instead, save your changes and proceed to the next activity.

6 Start the slide show **From Current Slide**, and when the slide show displays, click the hyperlink. Compare your screen with Figure 6.42.

An e-mail program opens with the e-mail address you typed in the To box. In this case, ***Microsoft Outlook*** opens. Microsoft Outlook is the program, or ***e-mail client***, that facilitates the sending and receiving of electronic messages. This enables you to type an e-mail message and click Send from within the PowerPoint presentation. An e-mail client is a software program that enables you to compose and send e-mail.

Figure 6.42

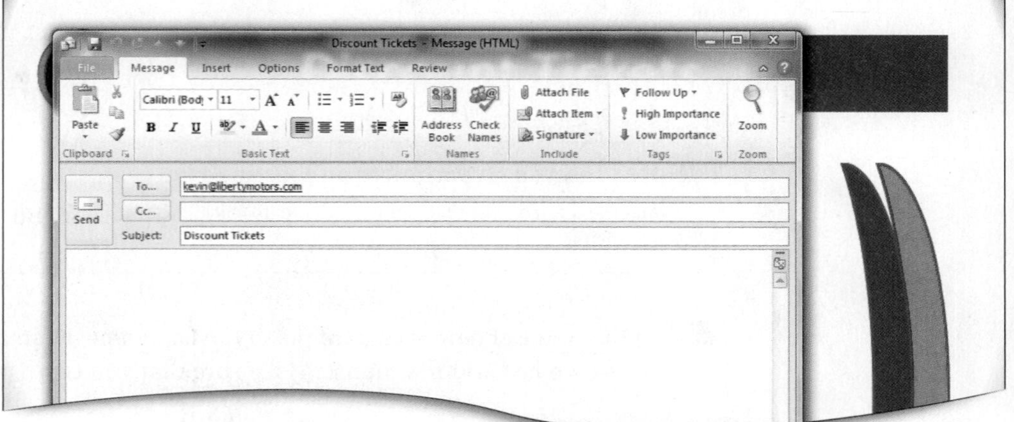

Alert! | **Does Your Screen Differ?**

If the e-mail client on the computer you are using is not Microsoft Outlook, the Discount Tickets window that displays will differ from the one shown in Figure 6.42. If you do not have an e-mail client, you will not be able to do this. If you get a startup screen when you click on the e-mail link, that means your client has not been configured.

7 **Close** the e-mail program without saving changes to the e-mail message, and then press Esc.

8 **Save** your changes.

Activity 6.12 | Inserting a Hyperlink to a New File

In this activity, you will insert a hyperlink that will allow you to create a new file.

1 In **Normal** view, make the **title slide** the active slide. Click to select the image of the flag. Click the **Insert tab**. In the **Links group**, click the **Hyperlink** button.

2 Under **Link to**, click to select **Create New Document**. Compare your screen with Figure 6.43.

When Create New Document is selected, the Insert Hyperlink dialog box allows you to create a new document on the fly. The file can be a document, a spreadsheet, or a presentation.

Figure 6.43

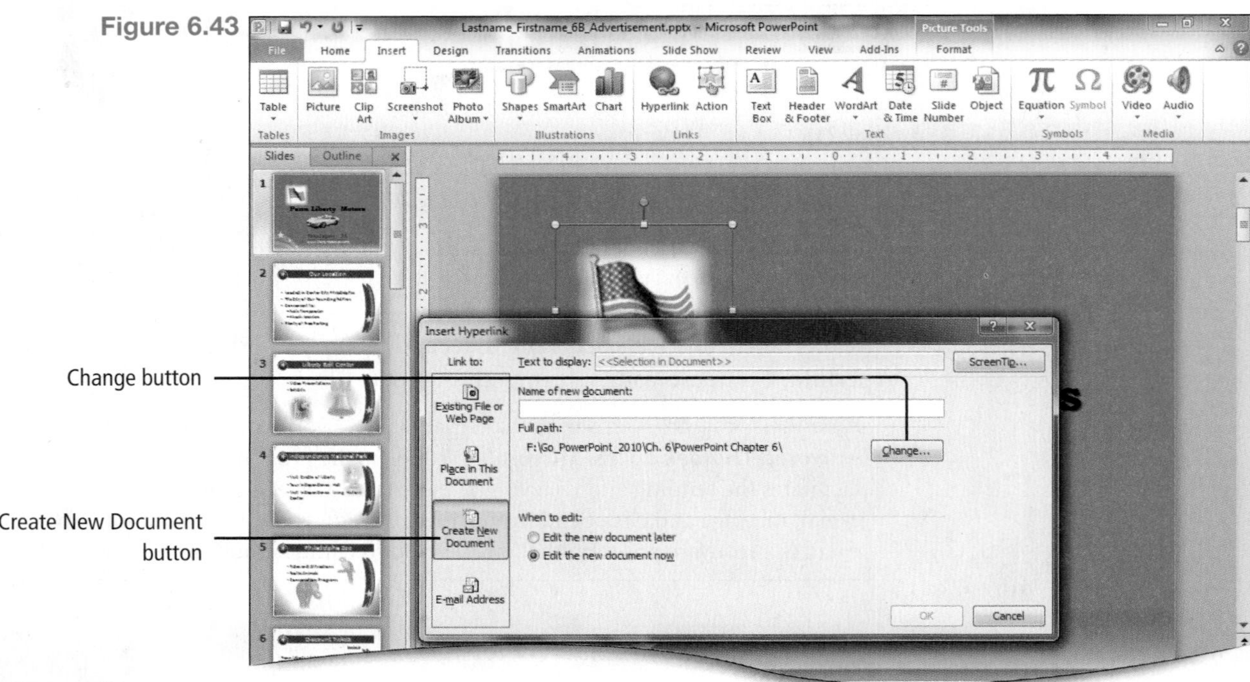

Note | **Insert a Hyperlink to an Existing File**

If you have created a file that you want to link to, click Existing File or Web Page (the default setting) and navigate to the file.

3 In the **Name of new document** box, type **Lastname_Firstname_6B_History.docx** using your own last and first name. Make sure that you type the file extension—.docx.

4 Click the **Change** button, and then navigate to your Chapter 6 folder if necessary. Click **OK**.

In this case, you are creating a Microsoft Word document. The ***file extension*** or file type identifies the format of the file or the application that was used to create it. If the ***full path*** listed is incorrect, click the Change button, and then navigate to the PowerPoint Chapter 6 folder you created. The full path includes the location of the drive, the folder, and any subfolders in which the file is contained.

> **Note** | **File Name and File Extension**
>
> Typing the file extension with the file name in the Name of new document box is the only way that Windows recognizes which application to start. If you do not type a file extension, Windows will assume you are creating a presentation and will start PowerPoint because you are currently using PowerPoint.

5 Under **When to edit**, make sure the **Edit the new document now** option button is selected, and then compare your screen with Figure 6.44.

Figure 6.44

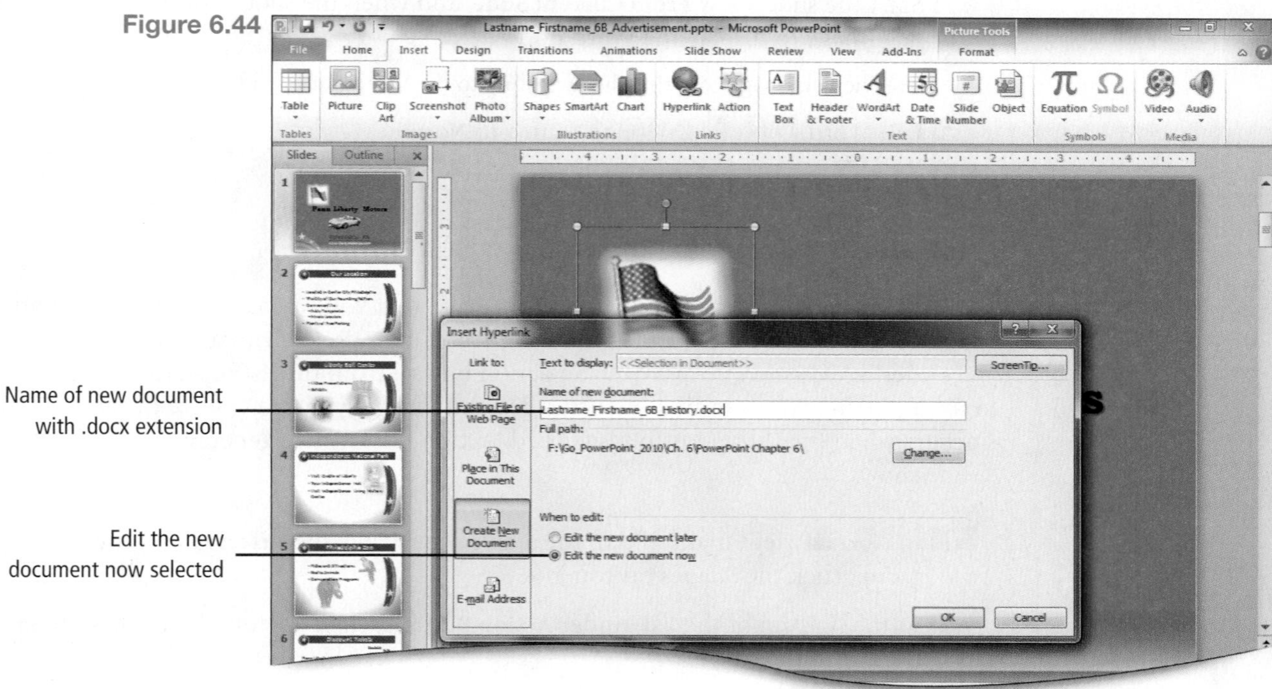

6 Click **OK** to open a new Microsoft Word file named Lastname_Firstname_6B_History.docx.

> **Alert!** | **Did You Have Trouble Displaying the Word Document?**
>
> If you made an error in the process of creating the hyperlink to create a new document and tried to do it again, you may find that the Word document does not display. If that happens, look in your chapter folder. If a file named Lastname_Firstname_6B_History.docx displays, delete the file. Return to PowerPoint, and then enter the hyperlink again.

7 At the top of the new Word document, type **Penn Liberty Motors was founded in 1903 by Martin Rau.** Press Enter two times, and then type **Lastname_Firstname_6B_History .docx** Compare your screen with Figure 6.45.

Figure 6.45

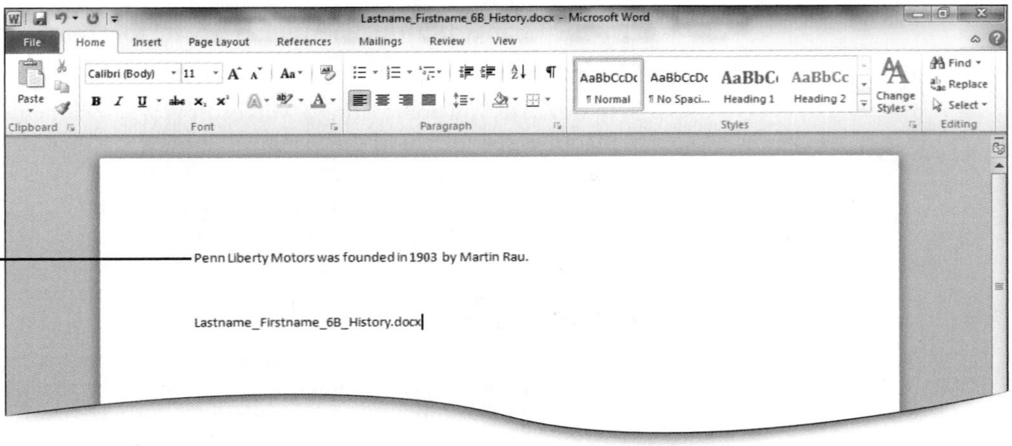

8 **Save** the document, and then **Exit** Microsoft Word.

9 Start the slide show **From Current Slide**, and when the slide show displays, click the flag image to display the Word document.

The flag image contains the hyperlink to the Word document.

10 **Exit** Word. Press Esc to return to **Normal** view.

11 **Save** your changes.

Activity 6.13 | Creating an Action Button

An ***action button*** is a built-in button shape that you can add to your presentation and then assign an action to occur upon the click of a mouse or with a mouse over. It is a type of hyperlink, created by inserting an action button from the list of shapes. Action buttons have built-in actions or links associated with them, or you can change the action that occurs when the action button is clicked. Action buttons are generally used in self-running slide shows.

1 In **Normal** view, make **Slide 5** the active slide. Click the **Insert tab**. In the **Illustration group**, click the **Shapes** button.

2 At the bottom of the list, under **Action Buttons**, click the fourth button—**Action Button: End**.

3 Position the + pointer at the lower right corner—at **4 inches on the right side of the horizontal ruler** and **3 inches on the lower half of the vertical ruler**. Click once to display the **Action Settings** dialog box.

The Action Settings dialog box displays. Because the action associated with the End button is to link to the last slide in the presentation, *Last Slide* displays in the Hyperlink to box. The action button on the slide is too large, but you will resize it later.

4 Click the **Hyperlink to arrow**, and then scroll to review the list of options, which includes other slides in the presentation, a custom show, a URL, a file, and another PowerPoint presentation. Click **Last Slide** to close the list, and then compare your screen with Figure 6.46.

There are two tabs in the Action Settings dialog box. You can set the action to occur on a Mouse Click or ***Mouse Over***. Mouse Over means that the action will occur when the presenter points to (hovers over) the action button. It is not necessary to click.

Figure 6.46

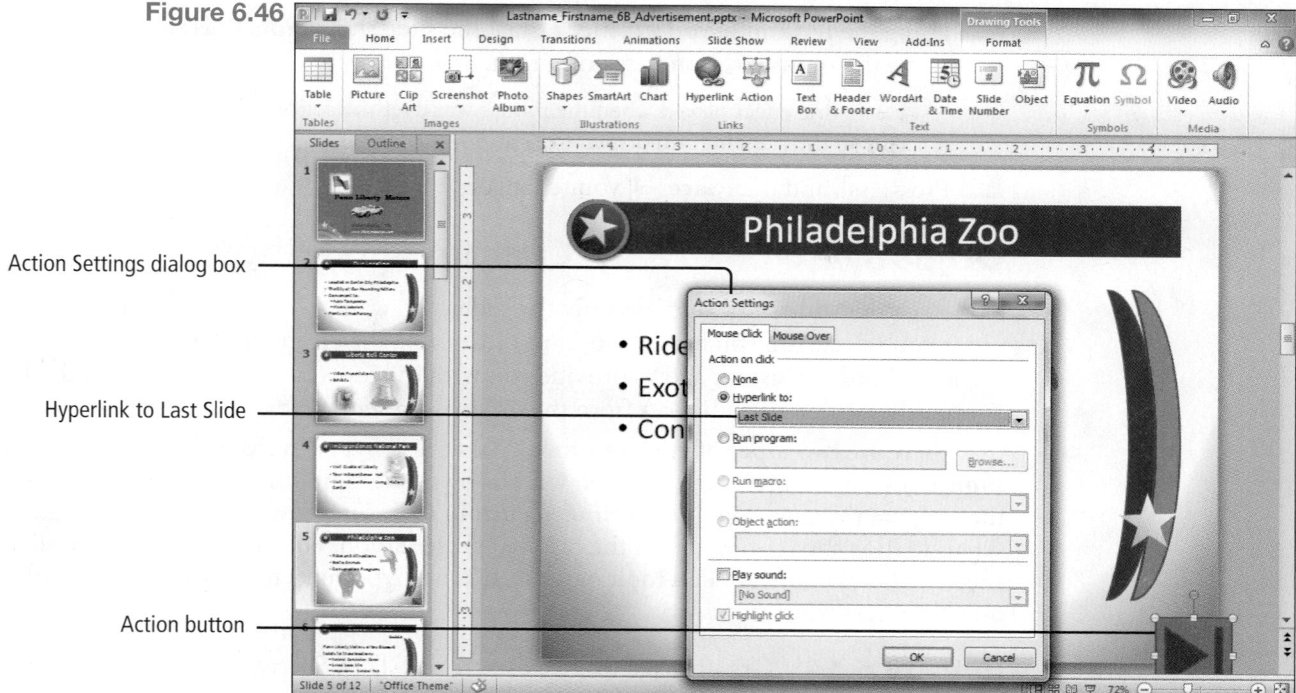

5 Click the **Mouse Over tab**. Click the **Hyperlink to** option, click the **Hyperlink to arrow**, and then select **Last Slide**. Click the **Play sound** check box, click the **Play sound check box arrow**, scroll down, and then click **Chime**. Click **OK**.

6 With the action button still selected, under **Drawing Tools**, click the **Format tab**. In the **Size group**, change the **Shape Height** to **.5"**. Change the **Shape Width** to **.5"**. Compare your screen with Figure 6.47.

The action button is displayed at the bottom right of the slide.

Figure 6.47

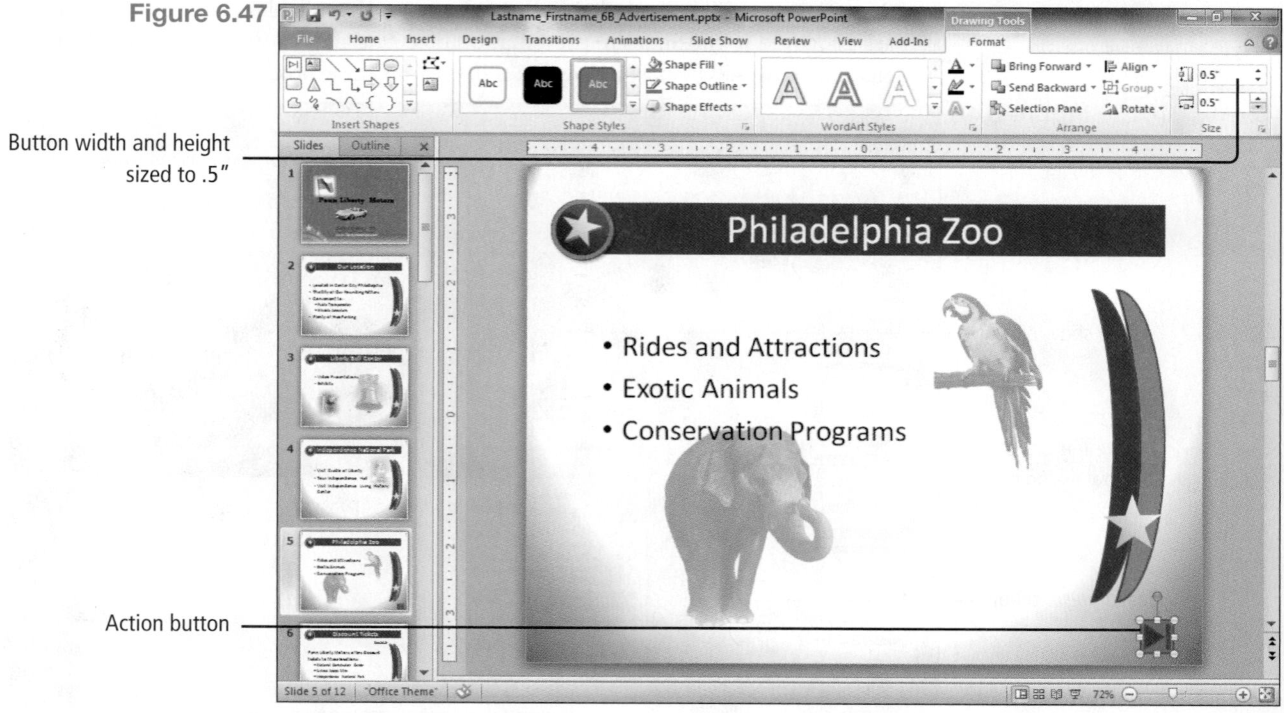

7 Using the technique you practiced, start the slide show **From Current Slide**, and then move the mouse over the action button.

The chime effect played when the mouse was over the action button, and then the last slide in the presentation displayed.

8 Press Esc, and then **Save** your changes.

Objective 5 | Create Custom Slide Shows

A ***custom slide show*** displays only the slides you want to display to an audience in the order you select. You still have the option of running the entire presentation in its sequential order. Custom shows provide you with the tools to create different slide shows to appeal to different audiences from the original presentation.

There are two types of custom shows—basic and hyperlinked. A ***basic custom slide show*** is a separate presentation saved with its own title containing some of the slides from the original presentation. A ***hyperlinked custom slide show*** is a quick way to navigate to a separate slide show from within the original presentation. For example, if your audience wants to know more about a topic, you could have hyperlinks to slides that you could quickly access when necessary.

Activity 6.14 | Creating a Basic Custom Slide Show

In this activity, you will create basic custom slide shows from an existing presentation. You will then save them as separate custom shows that can be run from the Slide Show tab.

1 Make the **title slide** the active slide. Click the **Slide Show tab**. In the **Start Slide Show group**, click the **Custom Slide Show** button, and then click **Custom Shows** to display the **Custom Shows** dialog box.

2 Click **New** to display the **Define Custom Show** dialog box, In the **Slide show name** box, type **Historic** and then compare your screen with Figure 6.48.

From the Define Custom Show dialog box, you can name a custom slide show and select the slides that will be included in the slide show. All the slides in the current presentation are displayed in the Slides in presentation box. The slides you want to include in the custom show will display in the Slides in custom show box.

Figure 6.48

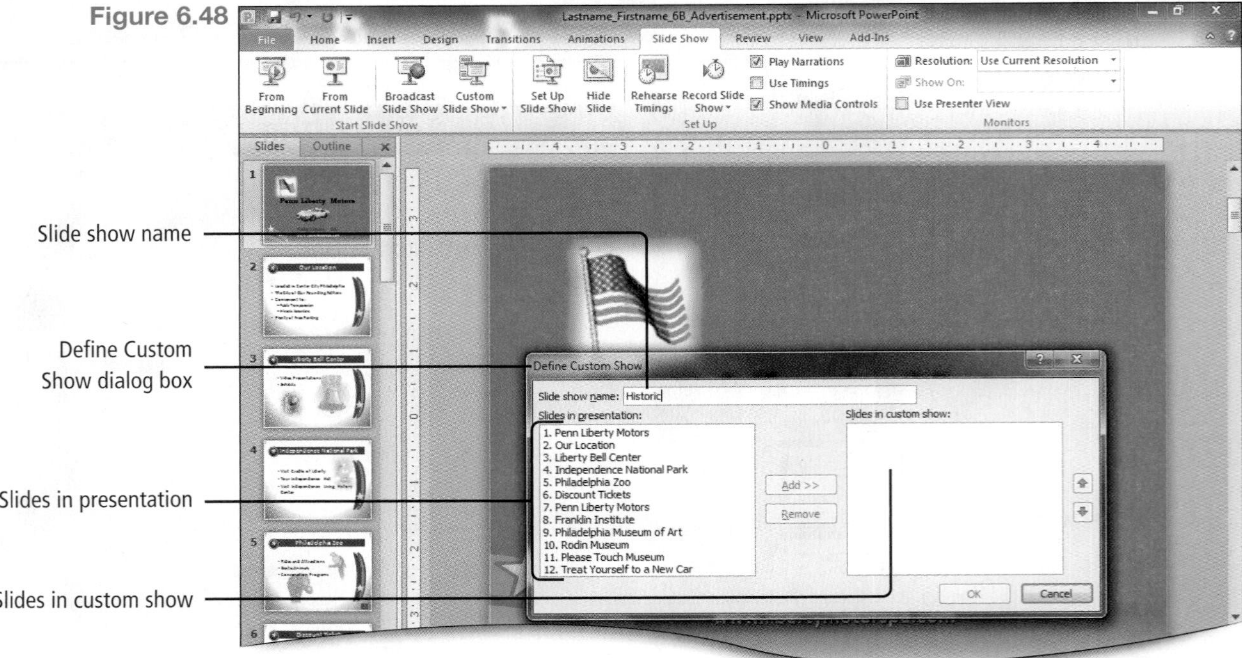

3 Under **Slides in presentation**, click **Slide 1**. Hold down ⇧ Shift, and then click **Slide 6** to select the six adjacent slides. Compare your screen with Figure 6.49

Figure 6.49

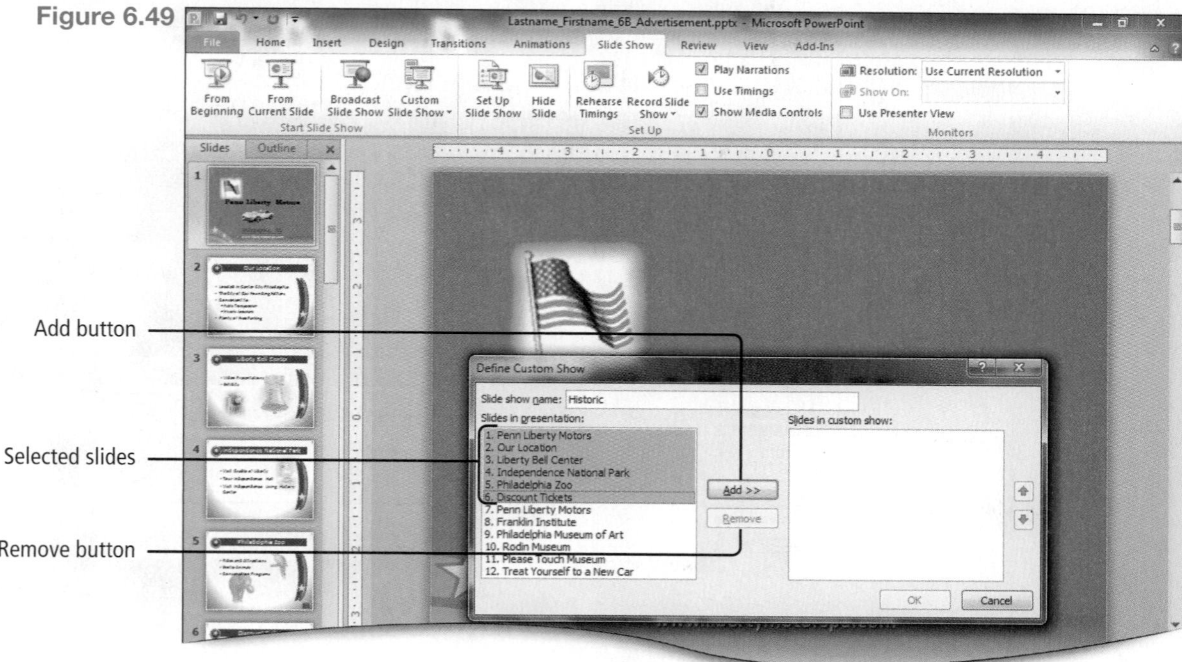

4 Click the **Add** button. Under **Slides in presentation**, double-click **Slide 12** to add it to the custom show. Compare your screen with Figure 6.50.

Slide 12 is renumbered as Slide 7 in the custom show.

Figure 6.50

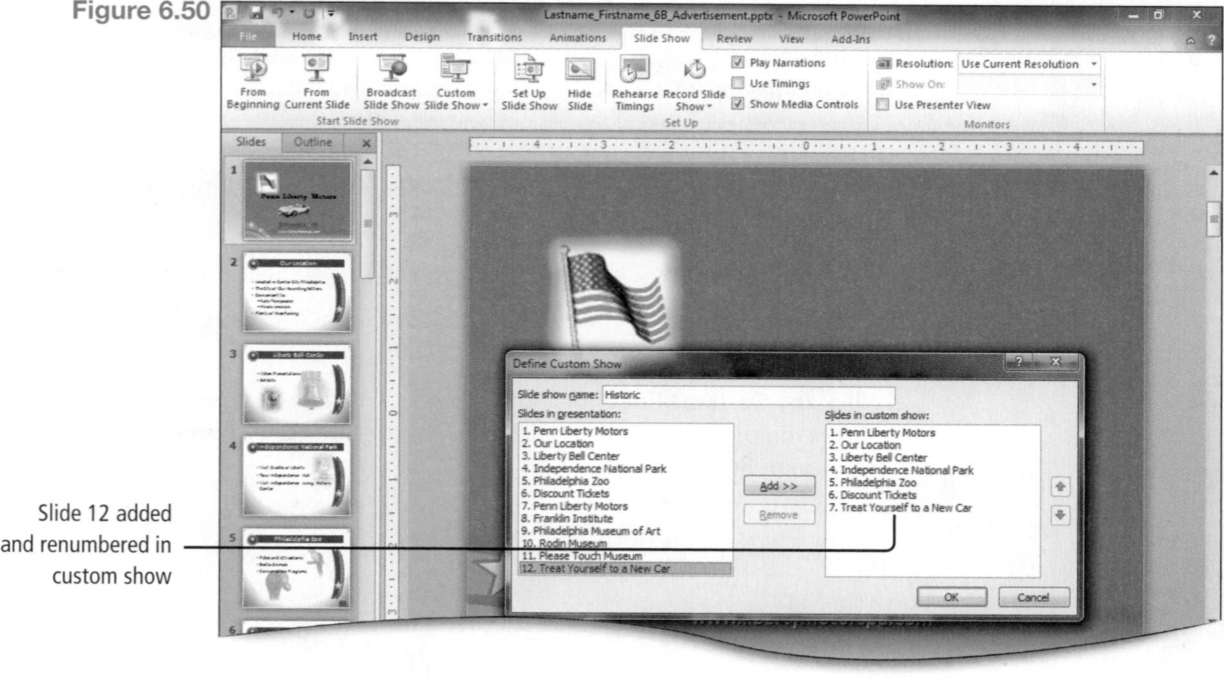

5 Click **OK**. Compare your screen with Figure 6.51.

Figure 6.51

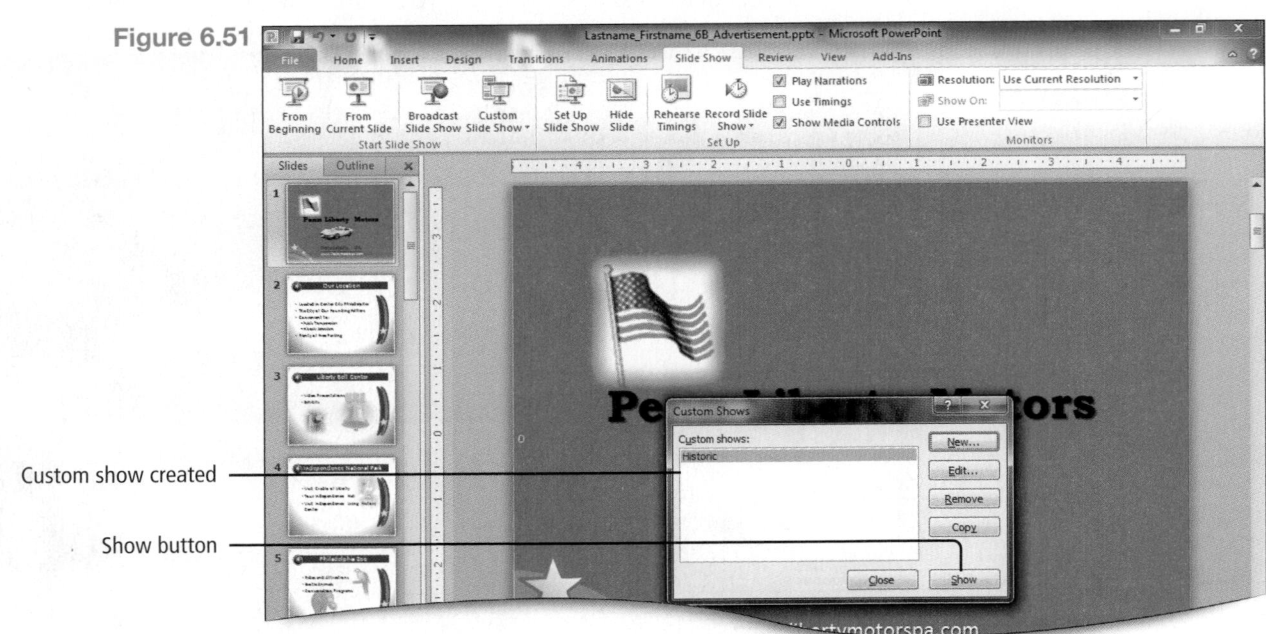

6 In the **Custom Shows** dialog box, click the **Show** button to preview your custom show. Click through the slides. When you are finished viewing the slide show, press Esc.

The custom slide show included only seven slides.

Alert! | **Did the Presentation Not Display?**

If the first slide of the presentation did not display automatically, press Esc. On the Slide Show tab, in the Set Up group, click the Set Up Slide Show button. In the Set Up Show dialog box, in the Show Type section, select the *Presented by a speaker (full screen)* option button, and then click OK.

7 On the **Slide Show tab**, in the **Start Slide Show group**, click the **Custom Slide Show** button.

The custom show—Historic—displays, and you can start the show from this list also.

8 Click **Historic**, and then view the slide show. When you are finished viewing the slide show, press Enter or Esc.

9 Click the **Custom Slide Show** button again. Click **Custom Shows** to display the **Custom Shows** dialog box, and then click **New**. In the **Slide show name** box, delete the text, and type **Cultural**

10 Under **Slides in presentation**, click to select **Slide 6**, hold down [⇧ Shift], and then click **Slide 12**. Click the **Add** button. Under **Slides in presentation**, double-click **Slide 1**.

Slide 1 is now Slide 8 in the custom show.

11 Under **Slides in custom show**, click **Slide 8**. Click the **Up arrow** seven times to move **Slide 8** so it is in the **Slide 1** position in the custom show, and then compare your screen with Figure 6.52.

Figure 6.52

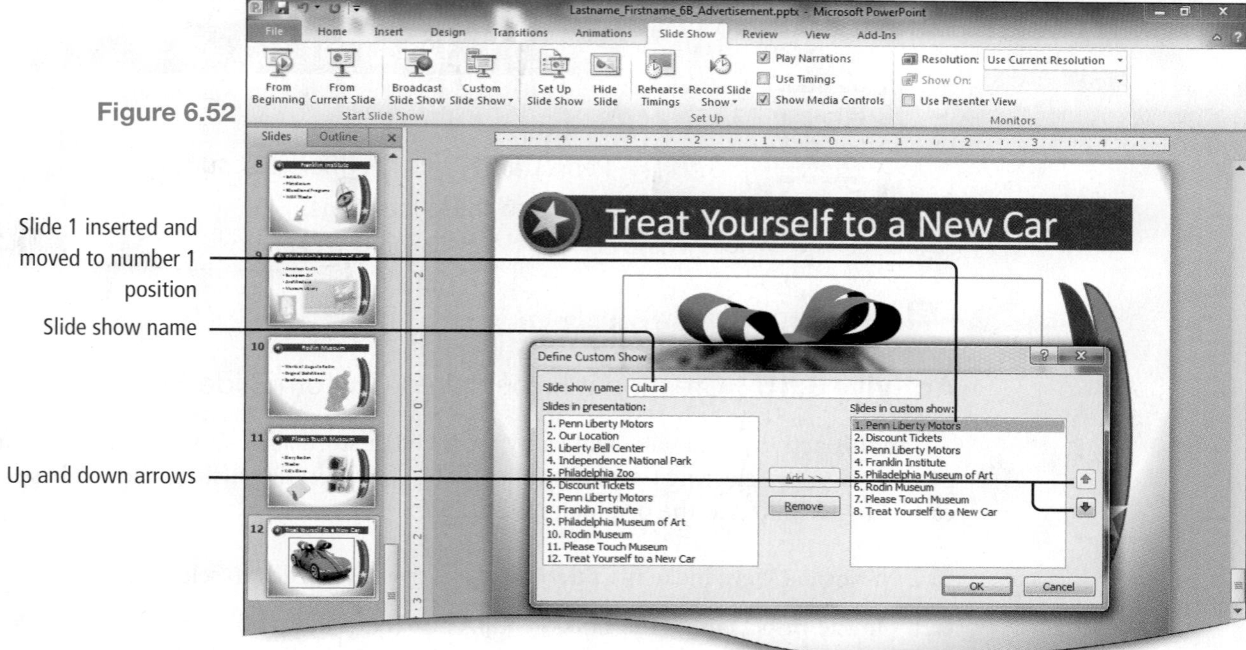

12 Click **OK**. In the **Custom Shows** dialog box, click **Show** to preview your custom show. When you are finished viewing the slide show, press [Enter] or [Esc].

Eight slides displayed.

13 In the **Start Slide Show group**, click the **Custom Slide Show** button. Click **Custom Shows** to display the **Custom Shows** dialog box. Click **Cultural**, and then click **Edit**. In the **Slides in custom show** list, click **2. Discount Tickets**, and then click the **Remove** button. Click **OK**. In the **Custom Shows** dialog box, click the **Show** button. Press [Enter] or [Esc] when you are done.

Seven slides displayed.

> **Alert! | Did You Click the Name of a Custom Show Instead of Custom Shows?**
>
> To edit a specific custom show, when you click the Custom Slide Show button, make sure you click Custom Shows to allow you to select the show and edit it. If you clicked a custom show by accident, press [Esc] and try again.

14 Click the **Custom Slide Show** button, and then click **Custom Shows** to display the **Custom Shows** dialog box. Click **New**. In the **Slide show name** box, delete the text, and then type **Location**

15 In the **Slides in presentation** box, click to select **Slide 2**, hold down [⇧ Shift], and then click **Slide 6**. Click the **Add** button. Click **OK**.

16 In the **Custom Shows** dialog box, click **Show** to preview your custom show. When you are finished viewing the slide show, press [Enter] or [Esc].

17 In the **Start Slide Show group**, click the **Custom Slide Show** button. Compare your screen with Figure 6.53.

Figure 6.53

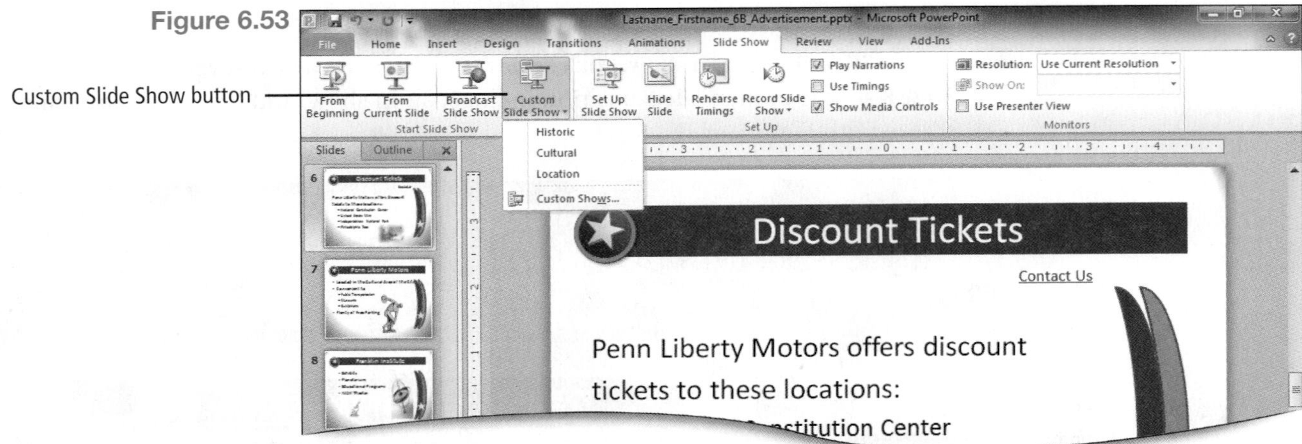

18 **Save** your changes.

Activity 6.15 | Creating a Hyperlinked Custom Slide Show

In this activity, you will create a hyperlinked custom slide show from an existing presentation by selecting the slides that will be shown in the custom show. These slides can be hyperlinked to the original presentation.

1 In **Normal** view, make the **title slide** the active slide. Click to select the picture of the car.

2 On the **Insert tab**, in the **Links group**, click **Hyperlink**. In the **Insert Hyperlink** dialog box, under **Link to**, click **Place in This Document**. In the **Insert Hyperlink** dialog box, scroll down to display the **Custom Shows**.

3 Under **Select a place in this document**, click **Location**, and then select the **Show and return** check box. Compare your screen with Figure 6.54.

Figure 6.54

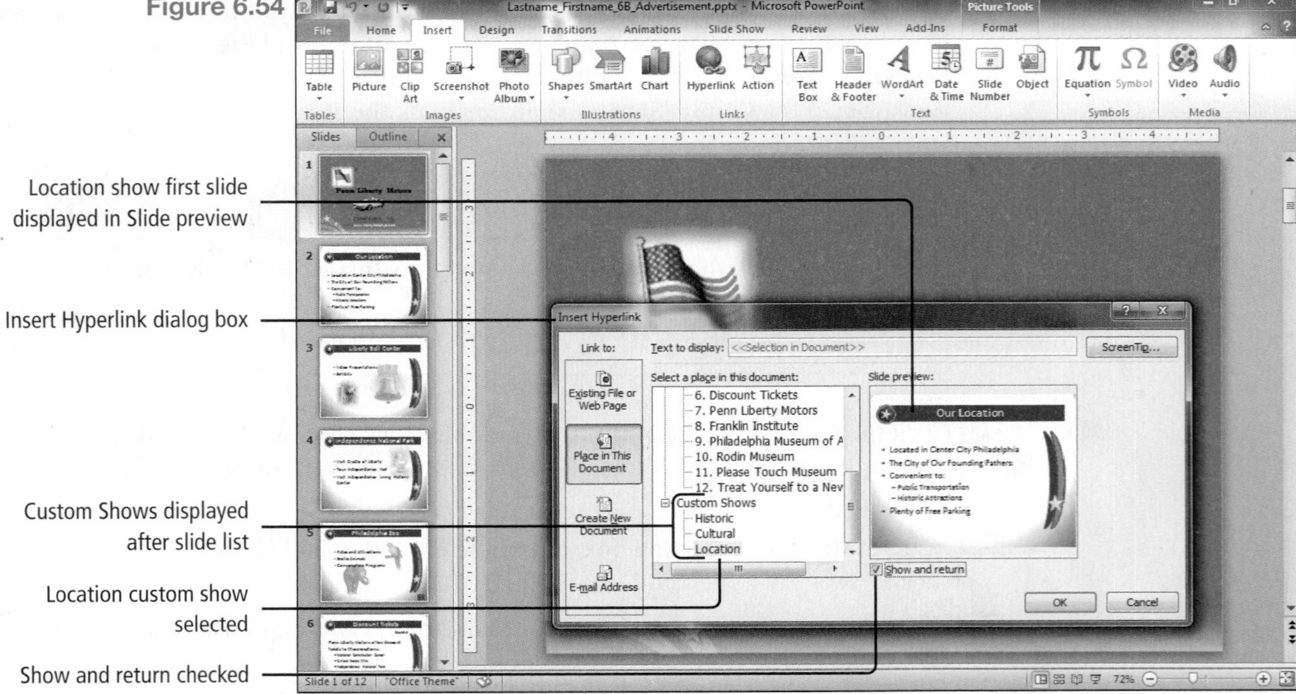

4 Click **OK**. Start the slide show **From Beginning**, and then click the picture of the car. When the title slide displays, press Esc.

The slides in the custom show—Location—will display, and after the last slide, the presentation will return to the title slide.

5 **Save** your changes.

Objective 6 | Present and View a Slide Presentation

In the following activities, you will use the navigation tools included with PowerPoint to view slide shows. You can start a slide show from the beginning or from any slide you choose. The ***navigation tools*** include buttons that display on the slides during a slide show that enable you to perform actions such as move to the next slide, the previous slide, the last viewed slide, or the end of the slide show. Additionally, you can add an ***annotation***, which is a note or a highlight that can be saved or discarded.

Activity 6.16 | Hiding a Slide

In this activity, you will hide the two slides so that they do not display during the slide show and unhide one slide.

1 Make **Slide 6** the active slide. If necessary, click the **Slide Show tab**. In the **Set Up group**, click the **Hide Slide** button. Scroll the thumbnail slides, and then compare your screen with Figure 6.55.

In the Slides/Outline pane, a hidden slide icon is displayed to the left of the slide thumbnail. The number inside the icon has a diagonal line through it.

Figure 6.55

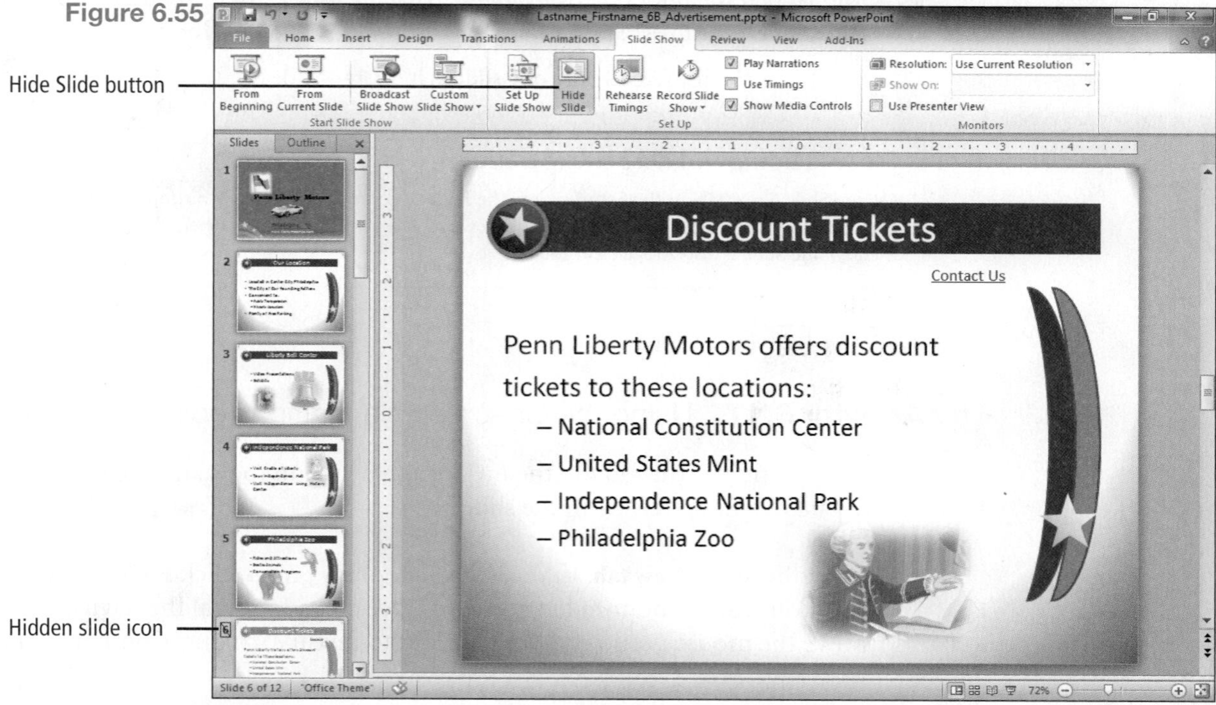

2 In the **Slides/Outline pane**, scroll to **Slide 12**. Right-click the thumbnail for **Slide 12** to display the shortcut menu, and then compare your screen with Figure 6.56.

You can hide a slide from the shortcut menu. Make sure you right-click the thumbnail.

Figure 6.56

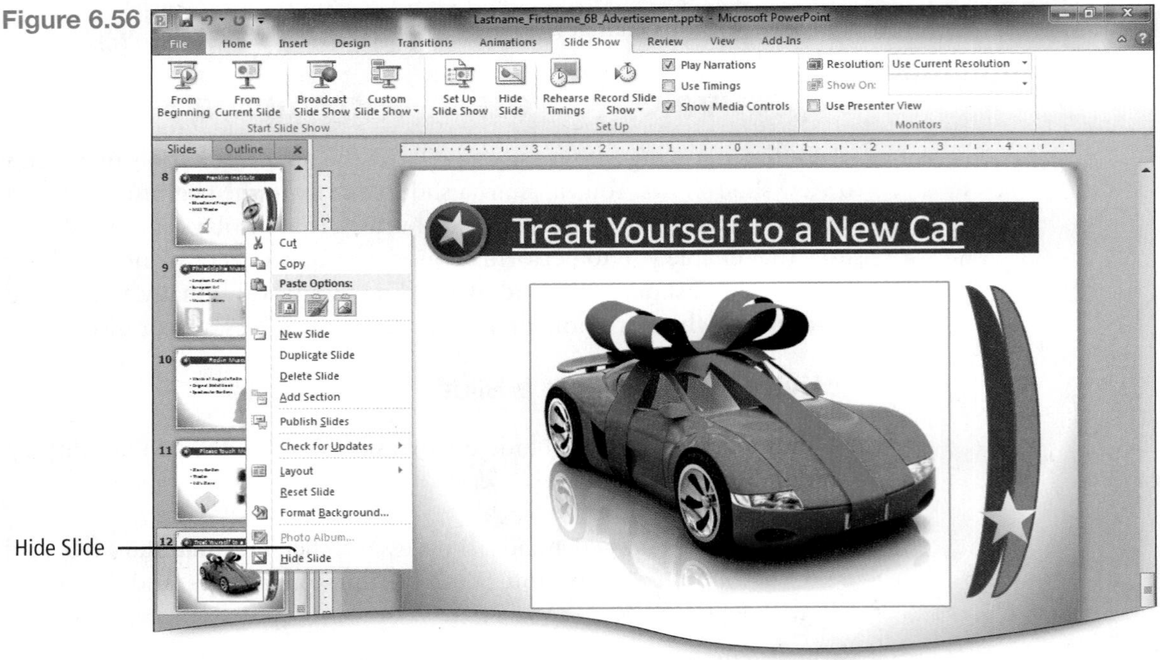

Hide Slide

3 Click **Hide Slide**.

4 Right-click the Slide 12 thumbnail to display the shortcut menu again, and then click **Hide Slide** to unhide **Slide 12**.

Slide 12 is displayed. Only one slide is hidden—Slide 6.

> **Note | Hiding and Displaying a Slide**
>
> On the Slide Show tab, in the Setup group, the Hide Slide button is a toggle button. Recall that a toggle button performs an action when clicked and then reverses the previous action when clicked again. In the shortcut menu, Hide Slide is also a toggle command.

5 **Save** your changes.

Activity 6.17 | Using the Onscreen Navigation Tools

In this activity, you will use the onscreen navigation tools and the slide shortcut menu to navigate to a desired slide in the slide show.

1 Click the **Slide Show tab**. In the **Start Slide Show group**, click **From Beginning**. Point the mouse at the bottom left corner of the screen to reveal the navigation buttons. Move the mouse pointer to the right to reveal each one. Compare your screen with Figure 6.57.

Notice that four semi-transparent buttons display for a few seconds and then disappear. If you move the mouse pointer, they display again for a few seconds. The buttons display as long as you are moving the mouse pointer or when you point to them.

Figure 6.57

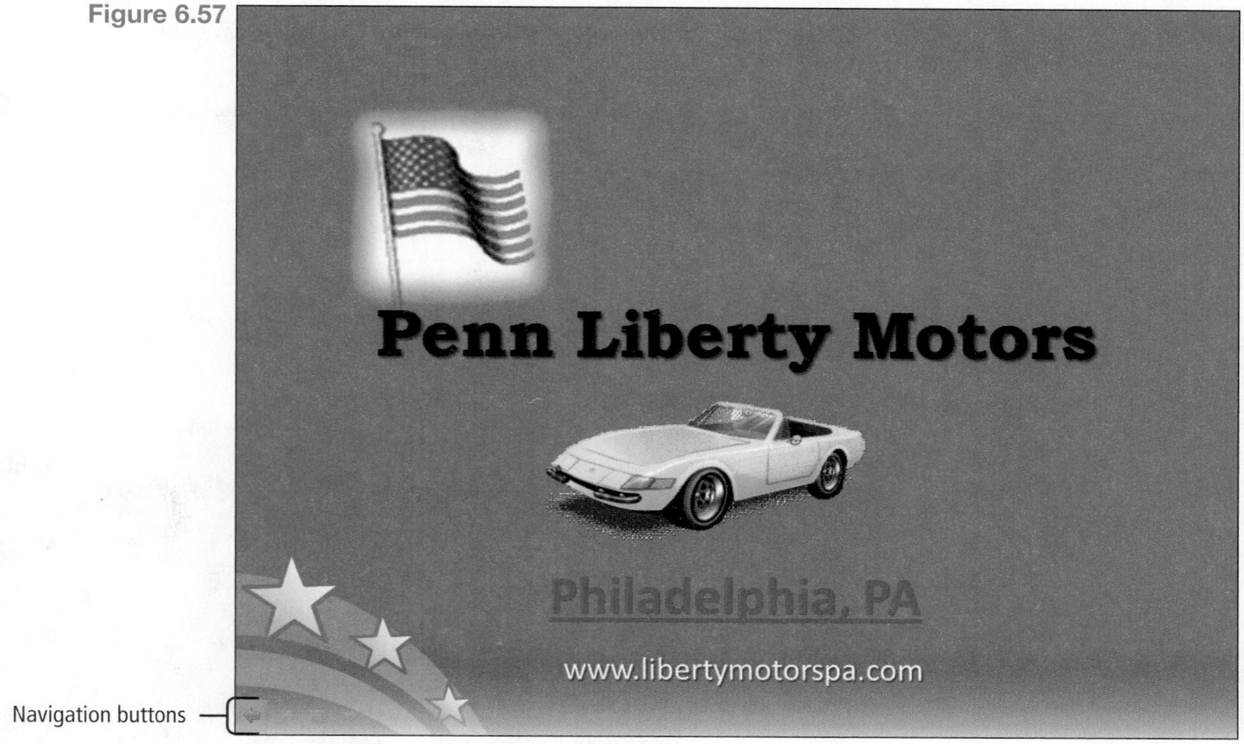

Navigation buttons
Penn Liberty Motors
Philadelphia, PA
www.libertymotorspa.com

2 Point to the second button—the **Annotation pointer** button. Compare your screen with Figure 6.58.

The Previous slide button displays as a blue arrow. The other buttons are Annotation pointer, Slide shortcut menu, and Next slide button. As you move the mouse over them, they can be seen.

Figure 6.58

Next Slide button
Slide shortcut menu
Annotation pointer
Previous Slide button
Penn Liberty Motors
Philadelphia, PA
www.libertymotorspa.com

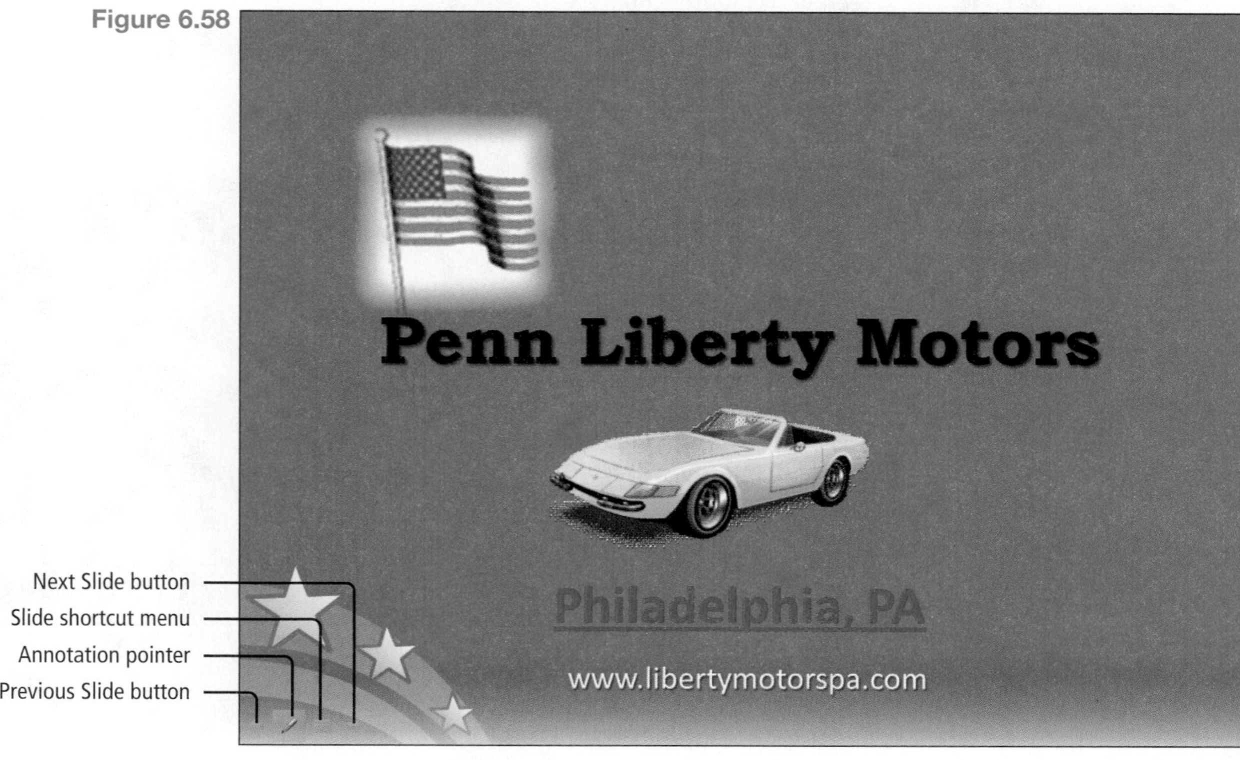

Another Way

To display the Slide shortcut menu, you can display the shortcut menu by right-clicking anywhere on a slide during a slide show. This shortcut menu also displays Pointer Options for the Annotation tool.

3 Click the third button—**Slide shortcut menu**. Compare your screen with Figure 6.59.

Pause is dimmed. In this presentation, the slides are advanced manually by a mouse click or by pressing Enter. Pause is available when the slides advance automatically.

Figure 6.59

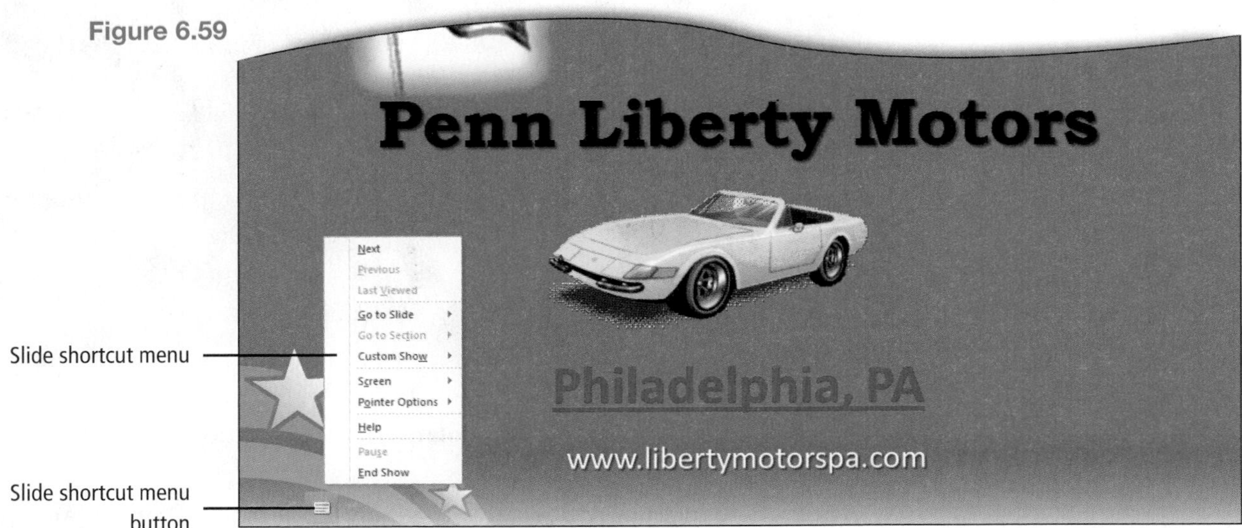

4 From the shortcut menu, click **Go to Slide**. Point to **Slide 7**, and then compare your screen with Figure 6.60.

The currently displayed slide has a check mark, and the number of the hidden slide (Slide 6) is in parentheses.

Figure 6.60

5 Click **Slide 7** to display Slide 7. Right-click anywhere on the slide, click **Custom Show**, and then click **Historic**. Click to view each of the slides in the custom show. When the slide show is finished, press Esc.

Slide 7 displayed. You also right-clicked Slide 7 to display the shortcut menu, and then you viewed the Historic custom show.

6 **Save** your changes.

Activity 6.18 | Using the Annotation Tool

In this activity, you will use the Annotation tool to highlight and annotate information on a slide.

1 Using the technique you practiced, start the slide show from the beginning. Right-click anywhere on the slide to display the **Slide shortcut menu**, click **Go to Slide**, and then click **Slide 7**.

2 At the lower left corner of the slide, click the second navigation button—**Annotation pointer**. Compare your screen with Figure 6.61. Take a moment to review the annotation options, as described in the table shown in Figure 6.62.

Figure 6.61

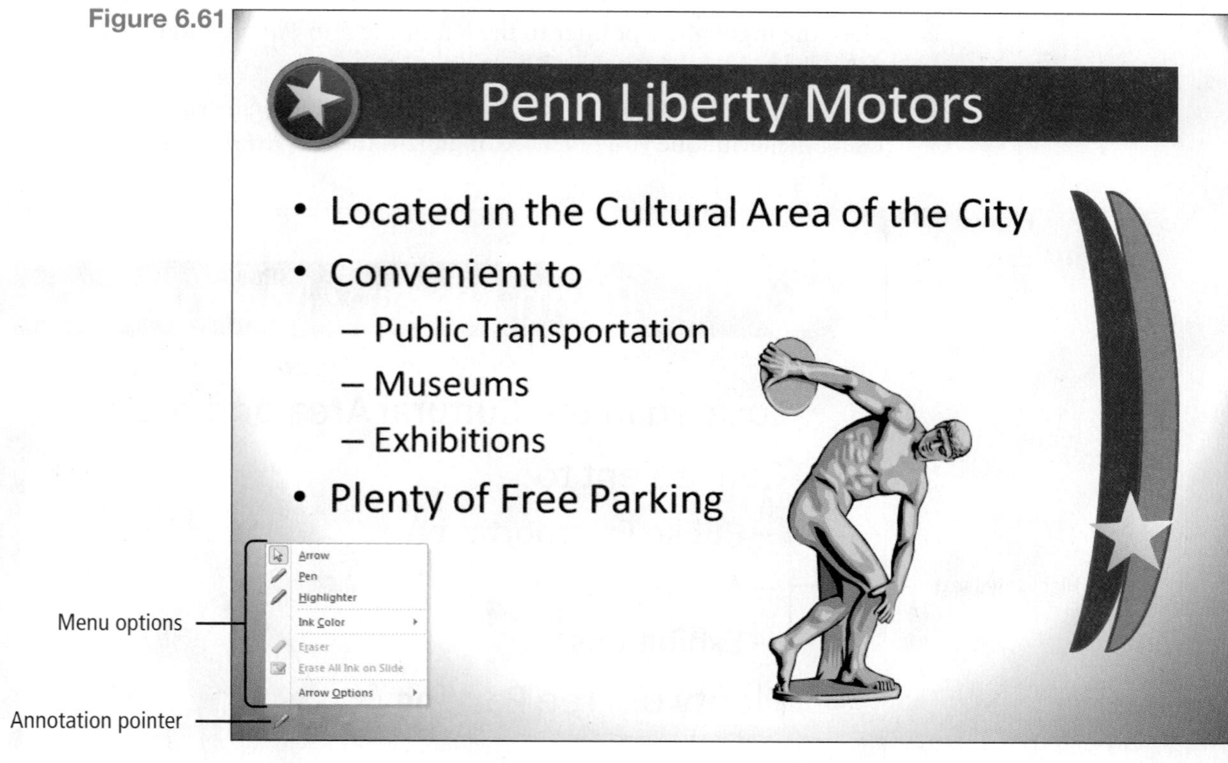

Annotation Pointer Menu

Screen Element	Description
Arrow	Denotes that the mouse pointer displays when the Arrow Options is set for Visible. When the Arrow Options is set for Hidden, the mouse pointer does not display.
Pen	Allows you to write or circle items on the slide.
Highlighter	Allows you to emphasize parts of the slide.
Ink Color	Displays a selection of colors for highlighting or writing with the pen.
Eraser	Removes areas of an annotation.
Erase All Ink on Slide	Removes all annotations on a slide.
Arrow Options	Enables you to hide the mouse pointer or to allow it to remain visible during a slide show. The default is Visible.

Figure 6.62

3 From the shortcut menu, click **Highlighter**.

The mouse pointer displays as a yellow rectangle.

4 Place the highlighter pointer to the left of the *P* in *Public*, and then click and drag to the right to highlight *Public Transportation.*

5 Point to the left of *Museums*, and then click and drag to the right to highlight *Museums.* Using the technique you practiced, highlight the text *Exhibitions.* Compare your screen with Figure 6.63.

Figure 6.63

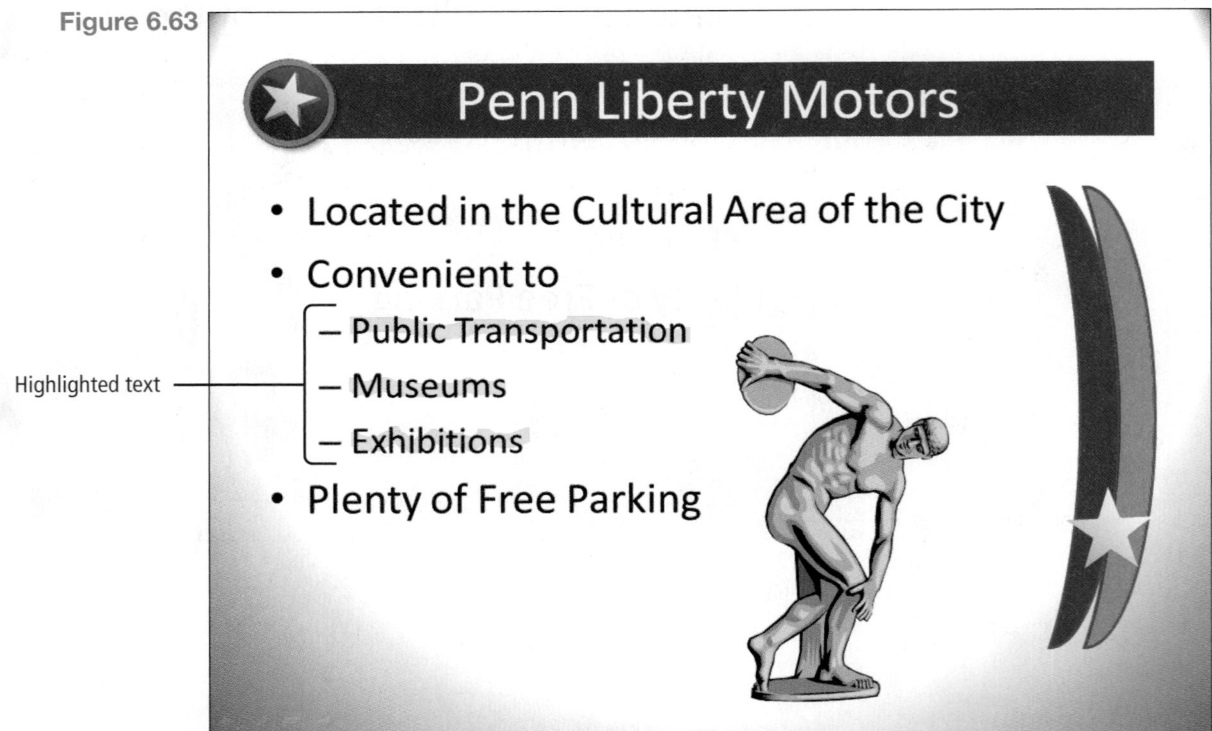

6 Click the **Annotation pointer** button. Click **Ink Color**, and then under **Standard Colors**, click the first color—**Dark Red**.

7 Click the **Annotation pointer** button, and then click **Pen**.

The annotation pointer displays as a small red circle or dot.

8 Point above the word *Parking*, and then click and drag to draw a circle around the word *Parking*. Compare your screen with Figure 6.64.

Figure 6.64

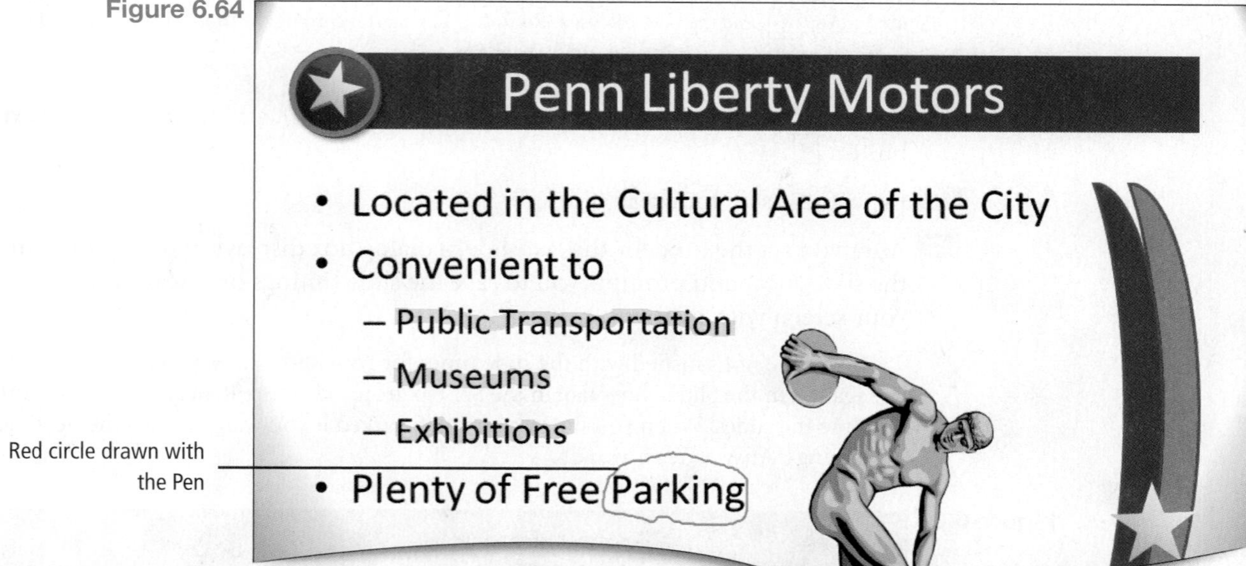

9 Click the **Annotation pointer** button, and then click **Eraser**. Click one time on the circle to remove the circle. It is not necessary to drag the eraser.

10 Click the **Annotation pointer** button, and then click **Pen**. Using the technique you practiced, draw a circle around the word *Free*.

11 Press Esc two times. In the displayed dialog box, which prompts you to keep your annotations, click the **Keep** button.

12 **Save** your changes.

Activity 6.19 | Creating a Self-Running Presentation

In this activity, you will set up a presentation to run without an individual present to run the slide show. Normally, self-running presentations run on a ***kiosk***. A kiosk is a booth that includes a computer and a monitor that may have a touch screen. Usually, kiosks are located in an area such as a mall, a trade show, or a convention—places that are frequented by many people.

1 With the **title slide** as the active slide, click the **Slide Show tab**. In the **Set Up group**, click **Rehearse Timings**. Compare your screen with Figure 6.65.

The Recording toolbar displays, and the Slide Time box begins timing the presentation.

Figure 6.65

PowerPoint | Chapter 6

Alert | Did Your Time Get Past 10 Seconds?

If you spent longer on the slide than 10 seconds, you can revise your timing. On the Rehearsal toolbar, click the Repeat button, and then click Resume Recording to restart recording the time for the current slide.

2. Wait until the **Slide Time** box displays **10 (seconds)**, and then click the **Next** button.

3. Repeat this step for every slide.

4. After you set the time for the last slide, a dialog box displays with the total time for the slide show and prompts you to save the slide timings or discard them. Compare your screen with Figure 6.66.

   If you are not satisfied with the slide times for your slide show, you can rehearse the times again. On the Slide Show tab, in the Set Up group, click the Rehearse Timings button, and time the slides. When you finish, you will be asked if you want to keep the new slide timings. Answer Yes if you do.

Figure 6.66

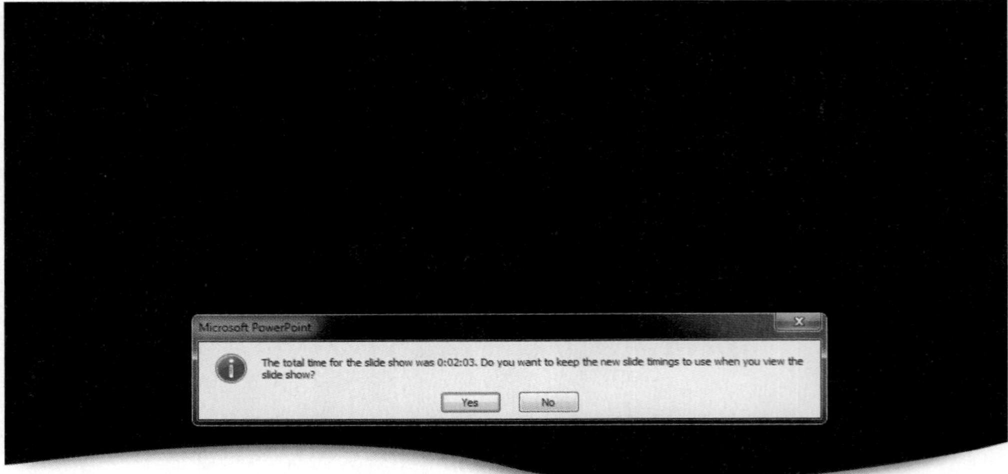

5. Click **Yes**. At the bottom right corner of the window, drag the Zoom slider to 70%. Compare your screen with Figure 6.67.

   Slide Sorter view displays with the time of each slide in the presentation. Your slide times may not be timed at exactly 10 seconds. There is a delay between the click and the actual time, but that is not critical.

Figure 6.67

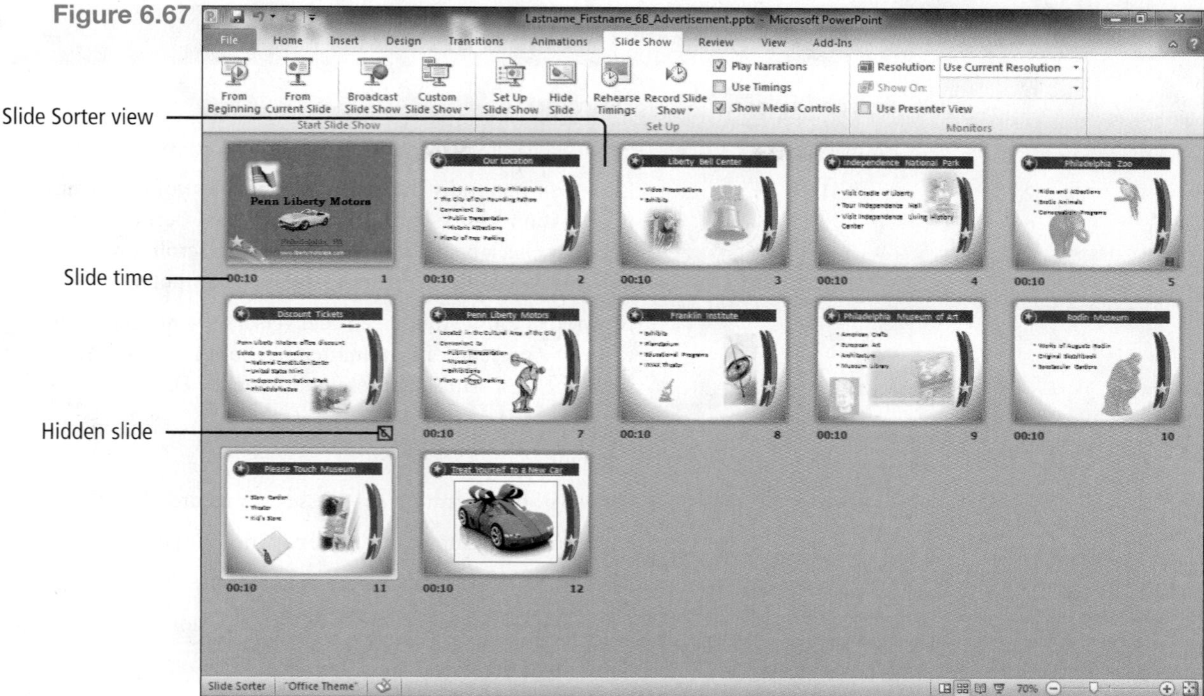

> **Alert! | Are Your Slide Times Longer Than the Time You Expected?**
>
> If you want your slide times to be an exact number of seconds, click the Next button early. For example, if you want each slide to be 10 seconds, click the Next button when you see 9 in the Slide Time box.

6 On the **Slide Show tab**, in the **Set Up group**, click the **Set Up Slide Show** button. Compare your screen with Figure 6.68.

The Set Up Show dialog box displays. The options in the Set Up Show dialog box are described in the table shown in Figure 6.69.

Figure 6.68

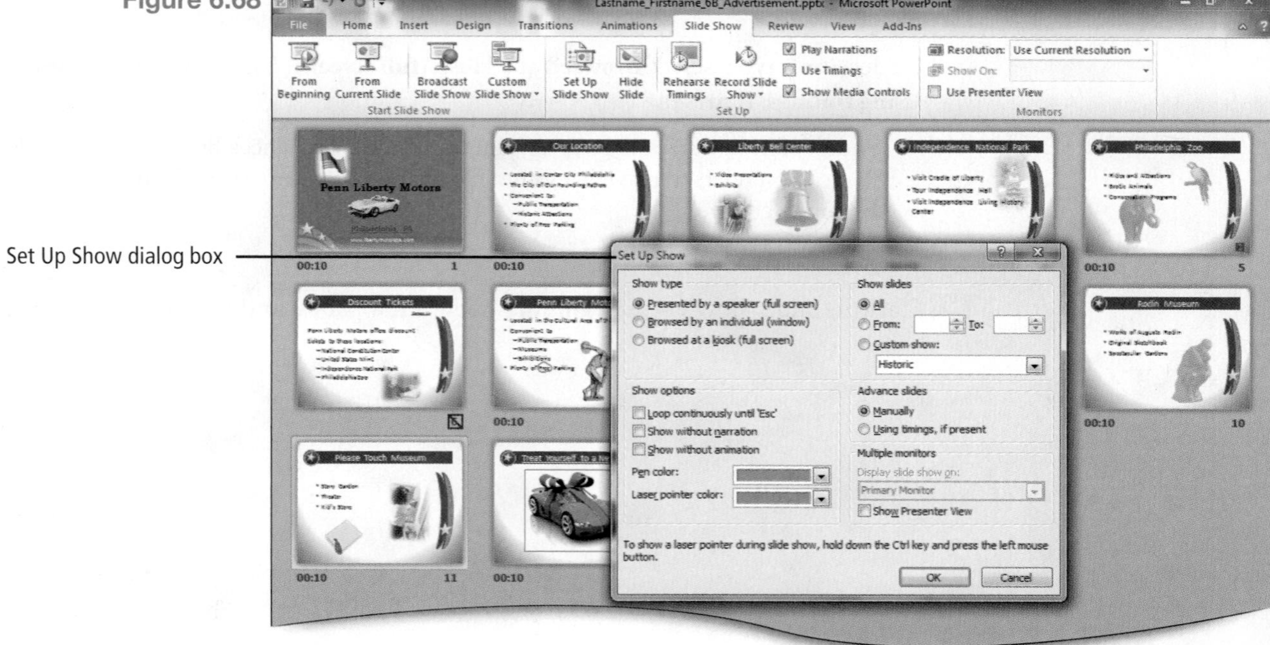

Set Up Show Options

Screen Element	Description
Show type	Presented by a speaker (full screen) is used to present to a live audience. Browsed by an individual (window) enables your audience to view the presentation from a hard drive, CD, or the Internet. Selecting the Show scrollbar check box allows the audience to scroll through a self-running presentation running on an unattended computer. Browsed at kiosk (full screen) delivers a self-running show that can run without a presenter in an unattended booth or kiosk. You can also send someone a self-running presentation on a CD.
Show options	Loop continuously until the Esc key is pressed is used when the show is unattended. Show without narration suppresses any recorded audio in the presentation. Show without animation suppresses the animation in the presentation. Pen color allows you to select a color for the slide show. Laser pointer color allows you to select a color for the slide show.
Show slides	Show all of the slides. Select a range of slides to view. Show a custom show.
Advance slides	Manually lets you advance the slides yourself. Using timings, if present, activates the timings you set for each slide.
Multiple monitors	If your computer supports using multiple monitors, a PowerPoint presentation can be delivered on two monitors. Show Presenter View allows you to run the PowerPoint presentation from one monitor while the audience views it on a second monitor. This enables you to run other programs that will not be visible to your audience.

Figure 6.69

7 Under **Show type**, select **Browsed at a kiosk (full screen)**. Under **Advance slides**, click **Using timings, if present**.

Under Show options, the Loop continuously until "Esc" check box is selected by default. This option refers to playing a sound file or animation continuously. It is also unavailable for you to change.

8 Click **OK**.

9 Start the slide show **From Beginning**. View a few slides, and then press Esc to end the show.

Note | To Change the Slide Show Timings

If you want new timings for your slides, you can rehearse the timings again. On the Slide Show tab, in the Set Up group, click the Rehearse Timings button, and then set new timings for each slide in the presentation. When all slides have been timed, you will be asked whether you want to keep the new timings or to cancel them and keep the old timings.

10 On the **Slide Show tab**, in the **Set Up group**, click **Set Up Slide Show** button. Under **Show type**, select **Presented by a speaker (full screen)**. Under **Advance slides**, click **Manually**. Click **OK**.

The timings are saved with the presentation. When you want to use them for a kiosk, click the Set Up Slide Show button, select Browsed at a kiosk (full screen) and Use timings, if present.

11 On the **View tab**, in the **Presentation Views group**, click the **Normal** button.

12 On the **Insert tab**, in the **Text group**, click the **Header & Footer** button to display the **Header and Footer** dialog box. Click the **Notes and Handouts tab**. Under **Include on page**, select the **Date and time** check box, and then select **Fixed**. If necessary, clear the Header check box, and then select the **Page number** and **Footer** check boxes. In the **Footer** box, using your own name, type **Lastname_Firstname_6B_Advertisement** and then click **Apply to All**.

13 Display **Backstage** view, click **Properties**, and then click **Show Document Panel**. Replace the text in the **Author** box with your own first name and last name; in the **Subject** box, type your course name and section number; and in the **Keywords** box, type **discount, tourist, attractions** **Close** the **Document Information Panel**.

14 **Save** your changes. **Close** your presentation, and then **Exit** PowerPoint. Submit your work as directed.

End You have completed Project 6B

PowerPoint | Chapter 6

Content-Based Assessments

Summary

In this chapter, you practiced various techniques related to viewing and presenting a slide show by adding and modifying slide transitions and various animation effects, including entrance, exit, and emphasis effects and motion paths. Within a slide show, you also inserted hyperlinks to link to a Web page, an e-mail address, other files, and other slides within a slide show. You practiced hiding slides and creating a basic custom slide show and a hyperlinked custom slide show. You created action buttons and used the onscreen navigation tools. You practiced annotating slides and created a self-running slide show.

Key Terms

Matching

Match each term in the second column with its correct definition in the first column by writing the letter of the term on the blank line in front of the correct definition.

_____ 1. Term used to describe any type of movement or motion.

_____ 2. File format used for graphic images.

_____ 3. A quick way to navigate to a separate slide show from within the original presentation.

_____ 4. File format used for photos.

_____ 5. The term applied to how and in what direction text or objects move on a slide.

_____ 6. An animation effect that, for example, makes an object shrink, grow in size, or change color.

_____ 7. A V-shaped symbol that indicates more information or options are available.

_____ 8. A graphical representation that counts the number of seconds the animation takes to complete.

_____ 9. The term that identifies the application used to create a file.

_____ 10. A portion of text, a graphic, or a placeholder on a slide that, when clicked, produces a result.

A Action button
B Animation
C Annotation
D Basic custom slide show
E Chevron
F Emphasis effect
G File extension
H GIF
I Hyperlinked custom slide show
J JPG (JPEG)
K Motion path effect
L Timeline
M Trigger
N URL
O With Previous

_____ 11. A separate presentation saved with its own title that contains some of the slides from the original presentation.

_____ 12. The term applied to describe a custom animation effect that starts at the same time as the preceding effect in the list.

_____ 13. The term that defines the address of documents and resources on the Web.

_____ 14. A built-in shape that you can add to your presentation and then assign an action to occur upon the click of a mouse.

_____ 15. A note or highlight on a slide that can be saved or discarded.

Multiple Choice

Circle the correct answer.

1. Animation effects that occur when a presentation moves from slide to slide are known as:
A. transitions **B.** entrances **C.** protocol

2. The animation effect that occurs when the text or object is introduced into a slide is called the:
A. beginning effect **B.** With Previous effect **C.** entrance effect

3. The animation effect that occurs when the text or object leaves the slide or disappears is called the:
A. exit effect **B.** emphasis effect **C.** chevron

4. The start method of an animation that allows the animation to occur after preceding animations on the slide is:
A. On Click **B.** After Previous **C.** With Previous

5. Text or objects that, when clicked, will transport you to a Web page, another document, or another area of the same document are:
A. animated GIFs **B.** hyperlinks **C.** kiosks

6. The term that refers to an action that will occur when the mouse pointer is placed on an action button is:
A. protocol **B.** resolution **C.** Mouse Over

7. A booth that includes a computer and a monitor that can include a touch screen is a:
A. custom slide show **B.** URL **C.** kiosk

8. Buttons that display on the slides during a slide show and that allow you to perform actions such as move to the next slide, the previous slide, the last viewed slide, or the end of the slide show are:
A. GIF buttons **B.** navigation tools **C.** motion path effects

9. Another name for the file type that defines the format of the file or the application that created it is:
A. file extension **B.** timeline **C.** trigger

10. The protocol used on the World Wide Web to define how messages are formatted and transmitted is:
A. URL **B.** HTTP **C.** HTML

Apply 6A skills from these Objectives:

1. Apply and Modify Slide Transitions
2. Apply Custom Animation Effects
3. Modify Animation Effects

Skills Review | Project 6C Vintage Car

In the following Skills Review, you will modify a PowerPoint presentation advertising the annual Vintage Car Event hosted by Penn Liberty Motors. You will apply slide transitions and custom animation effects to the slide show to generate interest in the event. Your completed presentation will look similar to Figure 6.70.

Project Files

For Project 6C, you will need the following file:

p06C_Vintage_Cars.pptx

You will save your presentation as:

Lastname_Firstname_6C_Vintage_Cars.pptx

Project Results

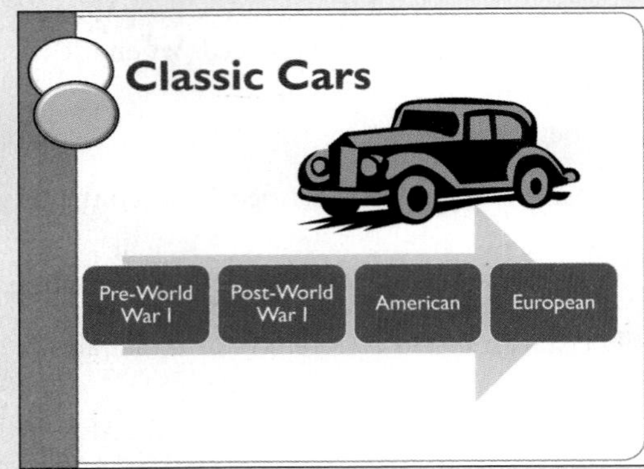

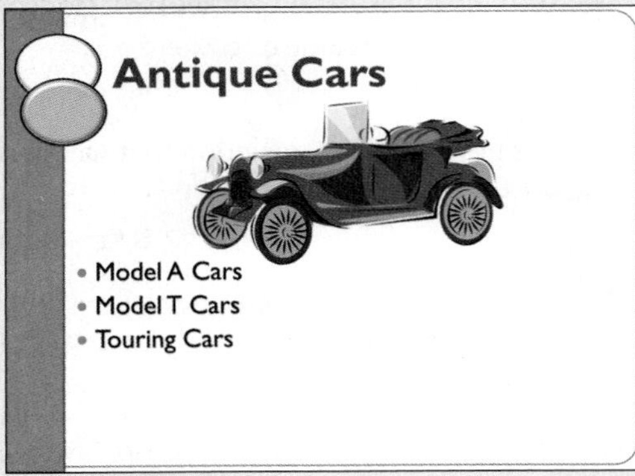

Figure 6.70

(Project 6C Vintage Car continues on the next page)

Skills Review | Project 6C Vintage Car (continued)

1 **Start** PowerPoint. Locate and open the file **p06C_Vintage_Cars**. Using your own first and last name, save the file as **Lastname_Firstname_6C_Vintage_Cars** in your **PowerPoint Chapter 6** folder.

2 Make the **title slide** the active slide.

a. Click the **Transitions tab**. In the **Transition to This Slide group**, click the **More** button. In the **Transitions** gallery, under **Subtle**, in the last row, click the first transition—**Shape**.

b. In the **Timing group**, click the **Apply to All**.

3 Make **Slide 2** the active slide.

a. In the **Transition to This Slide group**, click the **More** button. In the **Transitions** gallery, under **Subtle**, in the first row, click the fourth transition—**Push**.

b. Click the **Transitions tab**. In the **Timing group**, in the **Duration** box, click **spin box up arrow** to **02.00**, and then click the **Preview** button.

c. In the **Timing group**, click the **Sound arrow**, and then select **Click**. Click the **Preview** button.

d. In the **Timing group**, under **Advance Slide**, clear the **On Mouse Click** check box. Click once in the **After spin box**, type **3** and then press Enter.

4 Make **Slide 3** the active slide.

a. Apply the same transition, sound, and duration slide settings and advance slide mouse settings that you applied to **Slide 2**.

b. Click the **Slide Show tab**, and then view the slide show **From Beginning**. Wait for Slides 2 and 3 to advance after 3 seconds, and then press Esc.

c. On **Slide 3**, click the body text placeholder. On the **Animations tab**, in the **Advanced Animation group**, click the **Add Animation** button, and then under **Entrance**, click on **Fly In**.

d. In the **Advanced Animation group**, click the **Animation Pane** button. In the **Animation Pane**, below *Content Placeholder*, click the chevron to expand the contents. In the **Animation Pane**, click the **Play** button.

5 Make **Slide 4** the active slide.

a. Select the body text placeholder. On the **Animations tab**, in the **Advanced Animation group**, click the **Add Animation** button. Under **Entrance**, click **Wipe**.

b. In the **Animation group**, click the **Effect Options** button, and then select **All at Once**.

c. In the **Animation Pane**, click the **Play** button.

(Project 6C Vintage Car continues on the next page)

6 Make **Slide 1** the active slide.

a. Click to select the subtitle placeholder—*Penn Liberty Motors*. On the **Animations tab**, in the **Advanced Animation group**, click the **Add Animation** button. Under **Emphasis**, in the first row, click **Grow/Shrink**. In the **Animation Pane**, click the **Play** button.

b. Click the subtitle placeholder. In the **Advanced Animation group**, click the **Add Animation** button, and then click **More Exit Effects**. Under **Basic**, select **Disappear**. Click **OK**.

c. In the **Animation Pane**, right-click the second effect, which is the exit effect for the subtitle, and then click **Start After Previous**. In the **Preview group**, click the **Preview** button to view the effect.

7 Make **Slide 4** the active slide.

a. Click to select the text body placeholder. On the **Animations tab**, in the **Animation group**, click the **Effect Options** button, and then click **By Paragraph**.

b. In the **Animation Pane**, click the chevron to expand all effects. Right-click the first effect—**Model A Cars**, and then click **Effect Options** to display the **Wipe** dialog box. On the **Timing tab**, click the **Start arrow**, and then select **After Previous**. Change the **Duration** to **1 seconds (Fast)**. Click **OK**.

c. Click to select the title placeholder. Click the **Add Animation** button. Under **Motion Paths**, click **Shapes**.

8 Make **Slide 3** the active slide.

a. Click to select the **text body placeholder**. In the **Animation Pane**, right-click the first entrance effect—*Luxury Cars,* and then select **Effect Options** to display the **Fly In** dialog box. On the **Effect tab**, under the **Settings**, click the **Direction arrow**, and then click **From Bottom - Left**.

b. Under **Enhancements**, click the **After animation arrow**. In the row of colors, click the fifth color—**Teal**. Click the **Animate text arrow**, and then click **All at Once**.

c. On the **Timing tab**, click the **Duration arrow**, and then click **1 seconds (Fast)**.

d. On the **Text Animation tab**, click the **Group text arrow**, select **All Paragraphs at Once**, and then click **OK**.

e. Click to select the title placeholder. On the **Animations tab**, in the **Advanced Animation group**, click the **Add Animation** button. Under **Emphasis**, select **Pulse**. In the **Animation Pane**, click the **Play** button.

Content-Based Assessments

Skills Review | Project 6C Vintage Car (continued)

f. At the bottom of the **Animation Pane**, to the left of *Re-Order*, click the **up arrow** to move the title—*Title 1: Exotic Cars*—to the top of the list. Click **Play** in the **Animation Pane**.

g. Click on **Slide Show tab**, and then view the slide show **From Beginning**.

9 **Close** the **Animation Pane**.

10 On the **Insert tab**, in the **Text group**:

a. Click the **Header & Footer** button to display the **Header and Footer** dialog box.

b. Click the **Notes and Handouts tab**. Under **Include on page**, select the **Date and time** check box, and then select **Fixed**. If necessary, clear the Header check box, and then select the Page number and Footer check boxes. In the **Footer** box, using your own name, type **Lastname_Firstname_6C_Vintage_Cars** and then click **Apply to All**.

11 Display **Backstage** view, click **Properties**.

a. Click **Show Document Panel**. Replace the text in the **Author** box with your own first and last name; in the **Subject** box, type your course name and section number.

b. In the **Keywords** box, type **vintage cars, Penn Liberty**

c. **Close** the **Document Information Panel**.

12 Print **Handouts 4 Slides Horizontal**, or submit your presentation electronically as directed by your instructor.

13 **Save** the presentation. **Exit** PowerPoint.

End **You have completed Project 6C**

Apply **6B** skills from these Objectives:

4 Insert Hyperlinks
5 Create Custom Slide Shows
6 Present and View a Slide Presentation

Skills Review | Project **6D** Safety

In the following Skills Review, you will modify a PowerPoint presentation showcasing safety features of the cars sold by Penn Liberty Motors. You will insert hyperlinks to a Web page and the e-mail address of the company's safety director. You will also create custom slide shows of standard safety features available on all vehicles and custom safety features available on select vehicles. You will annotate the slide show and then create a self-running version of the presentation for use in a kiosk. Your completed presentation will look similar to Figure 6.71.

Project Files

For Project 6D, you will need the following files:

p06D_Safety.pptx
p06D_ESC.docx

You will save your presentation as:

Lastname_Firstname_6D_Safety.pptx
Lastname_Firstname_6D_ESC_Benefits.docx

Project Results

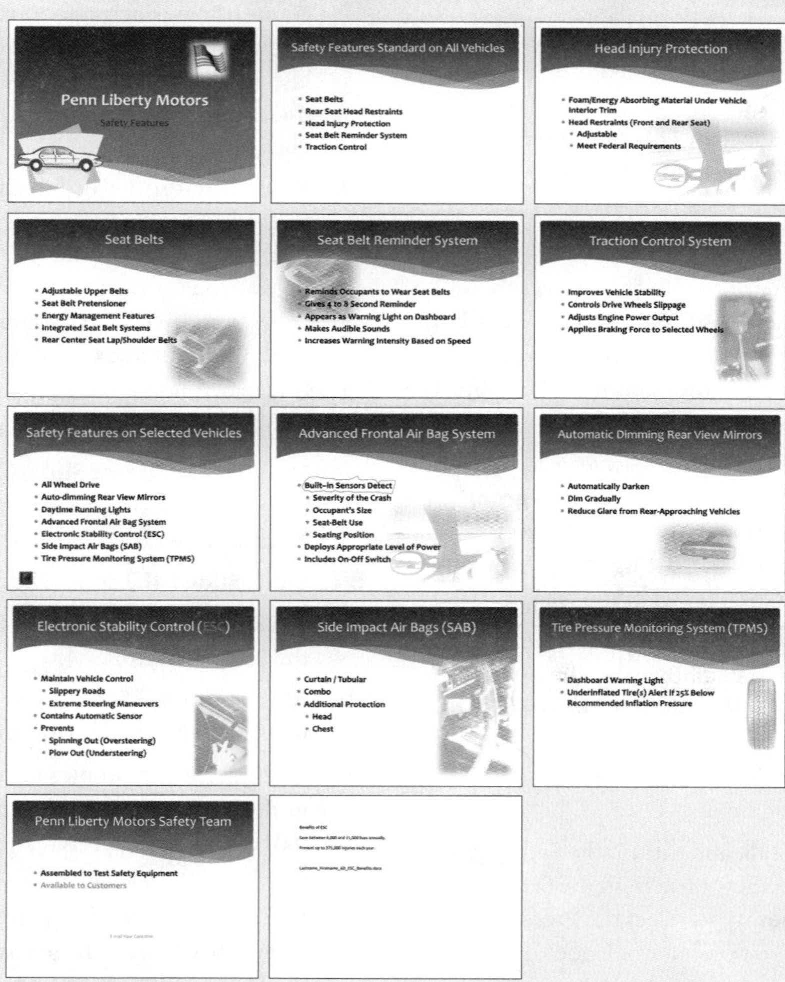

Figure 6.71

(Project 6D Safety continues on the next page)

Content-Based Assessments

Skills Review | Project 6D Safety (continued)

1 **Start** PowerPoint. Locate and open the file **p06D_Safety**. Save the file as **Lastname_Firstname 6D_Safety** in your **PowerPoint Chapter 6** folder.

2 Make the **title slide** the active slide.

a. Click to select the graphic of the car.

b. Click the **Insert tab**. In the **Links group**, click the **Hyperlink** button. In the **Insert Hyperlink** dialog box, under **Link to**, click **Existing File or Web Page**.

c. In the **Address** box, type **http://www.nhtsa.dot.gov** This is the Web site for the National Highway Traffic Safety Administration.

d. Click the **ScreenTip** button. In the **Set Hyperlink ScreenTip** dialog box, type **National Highway Traffic Safety Administration** Click **OK**. Click **OK** again.

3 Confirm that the **title slide** is the active slide.

a. In the subtitle, click and drag to select *Safety Features*.

b. On the **Insert tab**, in the **Links group**, click the **Hyperlink** button.

c. Under **Link to**, click **Place in This Document**. Scroll down, click **13. Penn Liberty Motors Safety Team**, and then click **OK**.

4 Make **Slide 13** the active slide.

a. Select *E-mail Your Concerns*. On the **Insert tab**, in the **Links group**, click the **Hyperlink** button. Under **Link to**, click **E-mail Address**. In the **E-mail address** box, type **safetyteam@libertymotors.com** In the **Subject** box, type **Safety First** Click **OK**.

b. Select the second bulleted item—*Available to Customers*. Click the **Insert tab**. In the **Links group**, click the **Hyperlink** button to display the **Insert Hyperlink** dialog box. Click **Existing File or Web Page**.

c. Navigate to the **PowerPoint Chapter 6** folder and select **Lastname_Firstname_6B_Advertisement**. In the **Insert hyperlink** dialog box, click the **Bookmark** button to display the **Select Place in Document** dialog box. Click the last slide—*Treat Yourself to a New Car*—and then click **OK**. Click **OK** to close the Edit **Hyperlink** dialog box.

d. Click the **Slide Show tab**, and then in the **Set Up group**, click the **Set Up Slide Show** button. In the **Set Up Show** dialog box, under **Show type**, select the **Presented by a speaker (full screen)** option button. Under *Advance slides*, click **Manually**, and then click **OK**.

e. View **From Current Slide**. Click the hyperlinks to test them.

5 Make **Slide 10** the active slide.

a. Click to select the photo of the dashboard. Click the **Insert tab**. In the **Links group**, click the **Hyperlink** button. In the **Insert Hyperlink** dialog box, under **Link to**, click **Existing File or Web Page**.

b. Click the **Browse for File** button, navigate to the location where your student files are stored, and then double-click **p06D_ESC.docx**. Click **OK**.

6 **Slide 10** should be the active slide.

a. In the title, select *ESC*. On the **Insert tab**, in the **Links group**, click the **Hyperlink** button. In the **Insert Hyperlink** dialog box, click the **ScreenTip** button. Type **Benefits** Click **OK**.

b. Under **Link to**, click **Create New Document**. In the **Name of new document** box, type **Lastname_Firstname_6D_ESC_Benefits.docx** using your own last and first name. Make sure the **Edit the new document now** option button is selected, and then click **OK**.

c. When Microsoft Word displays, type **Benefits of ESC** and then press Enter. Type **Save between 6,000 and 11,000 lives annually.** Press Enter. Type **Prevent up to 275,000 injuries each year.** Press Enter two times, and then type **Lastname_Firstname_6D_ESC_Benefits.docx**

d. **Save** your document in the **PowerPoint Chapter 6** folder, and then **Exit** Microsoft Word.

e. View **From Current Slide**. Click the hyperlinks to test them. **Close** Word, and then press Esc to return to **Normal** view.

7 Make **Slide 7** the active slide.

a. Click the **Insert tab**. In the **Illustrations group**, click the **Shapes** button.

b. At the bottom of the list, under **Action Buttons**, click the third button—**Action Button: Beginning**.

c. Position the + pointer at **4.5 inches on the left side of the horizontal ruler** and at **3 inches on the lower half of the vertical ruler,** and then click once to insert the shape and display the **Action Settings** dialog box.

d. In the **Action Settings** dialog box, click the **Mouse Over tab**. Click the **Hyperlink to** option button, click the **Hyperlink to** arrow, and select **First Slide**. Click

(Project 6D Safety continues on the next page)

Skills Review | Project 6D Safety (continued)

the **Play sound** check box, click the **Play sound check box** arrow, and then select **Chime**. Click **OK**.

e. On the **Format tab**, in the **Size group**, change the **Height** to **.5"** and the **Width** to **.5"**.

f. View the slide show **From Current Slide**, click the action button to test it. Press Esc.

8 If necessary, make the title slide the active slide.

a. Click the **Slide Show tab**. In the **Start Slide Show group**, click the **Custom Slide Show** button, and then click **Custom Shows**. In the **Custom Shows** dialog box, click the **New** button. In the **Slide show name** box, type **Standard Safety Features**

b. In the **Slides in presentation** box, click to select **Slide 1**, hold down Shift, and then click **Slide 5**. Click **Add**. Scroll to and then double-click **Slide 13** to add it to the slides in the custom show. Click **OK**.

c. Click the **Edit** button. Under **Slides in presentation**, double-click **Slide 6** to add it to the custom show. Under **Slides in custom show**, click **Slide 7**, and then click the **up arrow** so the new slide is before the *Penn Liberty Motors Safety Team* slide. Click **OK**.

d. In the **Custom Shows** dialog box, click the **New** button. In the **Slide show name** box, type **Optional Safety Features**

e. In the **Slides in presentation** box, click to select **Slide 7**, hold down Shift, and then click **Slide 13**. Click **Add**. Click **OK**, and then **Close** the **Custom Shows** dialog box.

f. In the **Start Slide Show group**, click the **Custom Slide Show** button. Click **Standard Safety Features**, and then view the slides. Repeat the procedure to view **Optional Safety Features**.

9 Make the **title slide** the active slide.

a. Click to select the picture of the flag. On the **Insert tab**, in the **Links group**, click **Hyperlink**. In the **Insert Hyperlink** dialog box, under **Link to**, click **Place in This Document**.

b. Under **Select a place in this document**, scroll down to display the **Custom Shows**. Select **Optional Safety Features**, and then click the **Show and return** check box. Click **OK**.

c. View the slide show **From Beginning**, and then click the flag. When the title slide displays, press Esc.

10 Make **Slide 7** the active slide. Click the **Slide Show tab**. In the **Set Up group**, click the **Hide Slide** button.

11 Make **Slide 8** the active slide.

a. In the **Start Slide Show group**, click **From Current Slide.**

b. At the bottom left corner of the screen, click the second navigation button—**Annotation pointer**.

c. From the shortcut menu, click **Pen**. Circle the first bulleted item—*Built-in Sensors Detect.*

d. Click the **Annotation pointer** button. Click **Ink Color**, and then under **Standard Colors**, click the sixth color—**Green**. Circle the last bullet—*Includes On-Off Switch.*

e. Click the **Annotation pointer** button, click **Eraser**, and then click to delete the green annotation on the last bulleted item.

f. Press Esc two times. In the displayed dialog box, which prompts you to keep your annotations, click the **Keep** button.

12 Make the **title slide** the active slide.

a. Click the **Slide Show tab**. In the **Set Up group**, click **Rehearse Timings**.

b. In the **Slide Time** display, wait for **4** seconds, and then click **Next Slide arrow**. Repeat for all slides. When prompted, click **Yes** to save the timings.

c. In the **Set Up group**, click the **Set Up Slide Show** button. In the **Set Up Show** dialog box, under **Show type**, select the **Browsed at a kiosk (full screen)** option button. Click **OK**.

d. View the slide show **From Beginning** and view all slides. When Slide 1 appears, press Esc.

e. On the **Slide Show tab**, in the **Set Up group**, click the **Set Up Slide Show** button. Under **Show type**, select **Presented by a speaker (full screen)**. Under **Advance slides**, select **Manually**. Click **OK**.

f. On the **View tab**, in the **Presentation Views**, click **Normal** to return to **Normal** view.

13 On the **Insert tab**, in the **Text group**:

a. Click the **Header & Footer** button to display the **Header and Footer** dialog box.

b. Click the **Notes and Handouts tab**. Under **Include on page**, select the **Date and time** check box, and then select **Fixed.** If necessary, clear the Header check box, and then select the Page number and Footer check boxes. In the **Footer** box, using your own name, type **Lastname_Firstname_6D_Safety** and then click **Apply to All**.

(Project 6D Safety continues on the next page)

Skills Review | Project 6D Safety (continued)

14 Display **Backstage** view, click **Properties**.

a. Click **Show Document Panel**. Replace the text in the **Author** box with your own first and last name; in the **Subject** box, type your course name and section number.

b. In the **Keywords** box, type **safety, seat belts, Penn Liberty**

c. **Close** the **Document Information Panel**.

15 Print **Handouts 9 Slides Horizontal**, or submit your presentation electronically as directed by your instructor.

16 **Save** the presentation. **Exit** PowerPoint.

End **You have completed Project 6D**

Apply **6A** skills from these Objectives:

1. Apply and Modify Slide Transitions
2. Apply Custom Animation Effects
3. Modify Animation Effects

Mastering PowerPoint | Project 6E Race Car

In the following Mastering PowerPoint project, you will modify a PowerPoint presentation advertising the Annual Race Car Rally hosted by Penn Liberty Motors. You will apply slide transitions and custom animation effects to the slide show to make the slide show more dynamic. The purpose is to appeal to race car enthusiasts. Your completed presentation will look similar to Figure 6.72.

Project Files

For Project 6E, you will need the following files:

p06E_Race_Car.pptx
p06E_Fast_Car.wav
p06E_Car_Horn.wav
p06E_Tires1.wav
p06E_Drag_Race.wav

You will save your presentation as:

Lastname_Firstname_6E_Race_Car.pptx

Project Results

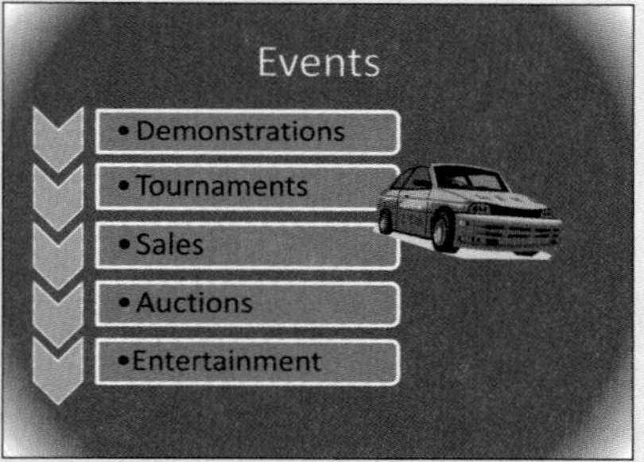

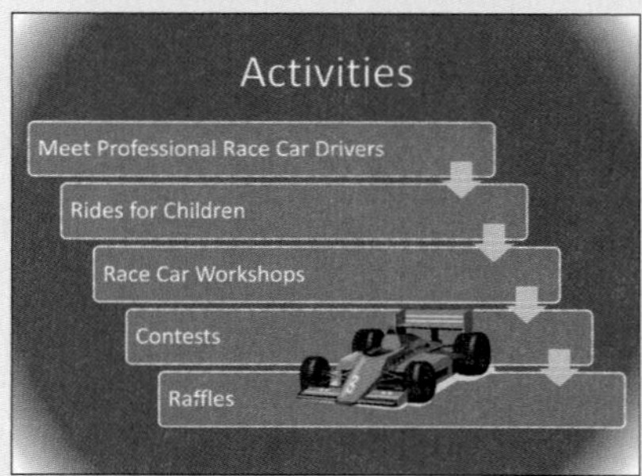

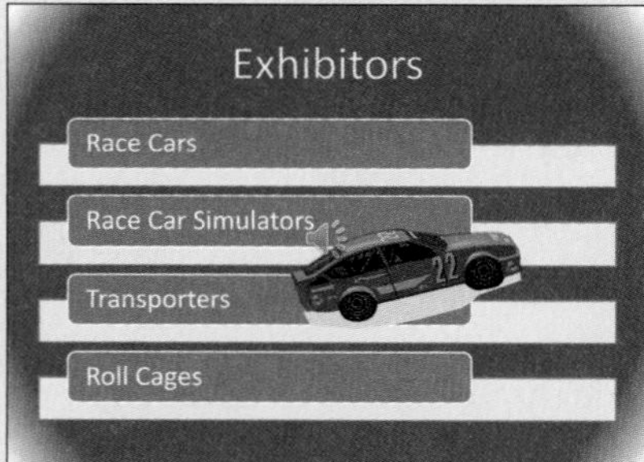

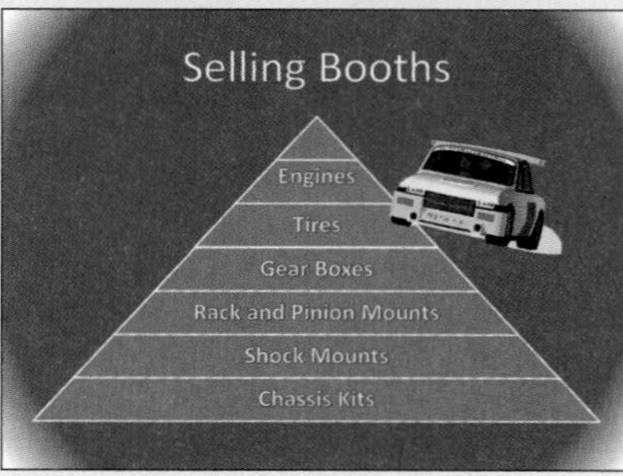

Figure 6.72

(Project 6E Race Car continues on the next page)

Mastering PowerPoint | Project 6E Race Car (continued)

1 **Start** PowerPoint. Locate and open the file **p06E_Race_Car**. Save the file in your chapter folder using the file name **Lastname_Firstname_6E_Race_Car**

2 Make the **title slide** the active slide. Display the **Transitions** gallery, and then under **Subtle**, in the first row, click the third transition—**Fade**. Set the **Duration** to **1.50**, and then click **Apply to All**.

3 Make **Slide 2** the active slide. Click the content placeholder to select the **SmartArt** graphic. In the **Add Animation** gallery, under **Entrance**, click **Fly In**. Click the **Effect Options** button. Under **Sequence**, choose **Level at Once**.

4 Open the **Animation Pane**, right-click the entrance effect for content placeholder, and then click **Effect Options**. Change the **Direction** to **From Left**. On the **Timing tab**, set the **Duration** to **1 seconds (Fast)**.

5 On **Slide 2**, click to select the car graphic, and then apply the **Fly In** entrance effect. Change **Direction** to **From Top-Left**, set the **Duration** to **2 seconds (Medium)**, and then set the **Start** to **After Previous**.

6 On **Slide 2**, click the **Transition tab**. In the **Timing group**, insert the sound file **p06E_Fast_Car.wav** from the student data files.

7 Make **Slide 3** the active slide. Select the **SmartArt** graphic, and then apply the **Fly In** entrance animation effect. Click the **Effect Options** button, and then select **One by one**. Click the **Effect Options** button again, and then select **From Top**. Change the **Duration** to **1 seconds (Fast)**. From the student data files, add the sound file **p06E_Car_Horn.wav**.

8 On **Slide 3**, click to select the car graphic, and then add the **Fly In** entrance effect. In the **Animation Pane**, right-click the entrance effect for the picture, select **Effect Options**, and then change the **Direction** to **From Top-Right**. Under **Enhancements**, add the sound **p06E_Car_Horn.wav**. Change the **Start** to **After Previous** and the **Duration** to **2 seconds (Medium)**.

9 View the slide show **From Current Slide** to test the transition and animation entrance effects on **Slide 3**.

10 Make **Slide 4** the active slide. Insert the sound **p06E_Tires1.wav**. Click to select the car graphic. Click the **Add Animation** button, and then click **More Exit Effects**. Under **Moderate**, click **Basic Zoom**.

11 View the slide show **From Current Slide** to test the transition and animation entrance effects on **Slide 4**.

12 Make **Slide 5** the active slide. Select the title placeholder. Click the **Add Animation** button. Select **More Motion Paths**, and then under **Lines & Curves**, select **Arc Up**.

13 On **Slide 5**, select the **SmartArt** graphic. Display the **Animations** gallery. Under **Exit**, click **Fade**. In the **Animation group**, click **Effect Options**, and then select **One by One**. Click to select the car graphic, and then apply the **Grow/Shrink** emphasis effect. Click the **Effect Options** button, and then select **Smaller**. Select the car graphic if necessary, and then insert the sound **p06E_Drag_Race.wav**.

14 View the slide show **From Current Slide** to test the transition and animation entrance effects on **Slide 5**.

15 Make the **title slide** the active slide. Click to select the title placeholder. Display the **Add Animation** gallery, and then click **More Entrance Effects**. Under **Basic**, select **Blinds**. In the **Animation Pane**, right-click the entrance effect for the title, and then click **Effect Options**. On the **Timing tab**, set the **Start** to **With Previous** and the **Duration** to **1 seconds (Fast)**. On the **Transitions tab**, in the **Timing group**, apply the **Whoosh** sound.

16 Start the slide show **From Beginning**, and then view the animation effects. When you are finished, return to **Normal** view.

17 Insert a footer on the notes and handouts that includes a fixed date and time, the page number, and the file name.

18 Modify the **Properties** in the **Show Document Panel**. Replace the text in the **Author** box with your own name; in the **Subject** box, type your course name and section number; and in the **Keywords** box, type **race, exhibition, events Close** the **Document Information Panel**.

19 Print **Handouts 6 Slides Horizontal**, or submit your presentation electronically as directed by your instructor

20 **Save** the presentation. **Exit** PowerPoint.

End You have completed Project 6E

Apply 6B skills from these Objectives:

- 4 Insert Hyperlinks
- 5 Create Custom Slide Shows
- 6 Present and View a Slide Presentation

Mastering PowerPoint | Project 6F Custom Detail

In the following Mastering PowerPoint project, you will modify a PowerPoint presentation listing many of the customization services available at Penn Liberty Motors to give a vehicle a unique appearance. You will insert hyperlinks and create custom slide shows of interior and exterior detailing. You will annotate the slide show and create a self-running version of the presentation for use in the automobile dealership. Your completed presentation will look similar to Figure 6.73.

Project Files

For Project 6F, you will need the following file:

p06F_Custom_Detail.pptx

You will save your presentation as:

Lastname_Firstname_6F_Custom_Detail.pptx
Lastname_Firstname_6F_Dashboard.docx

Project Results

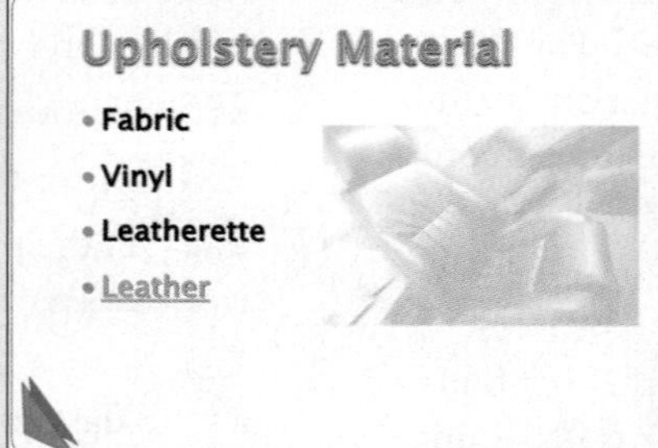

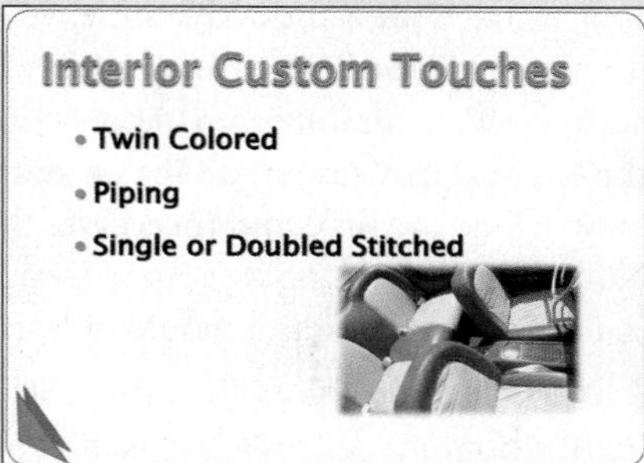

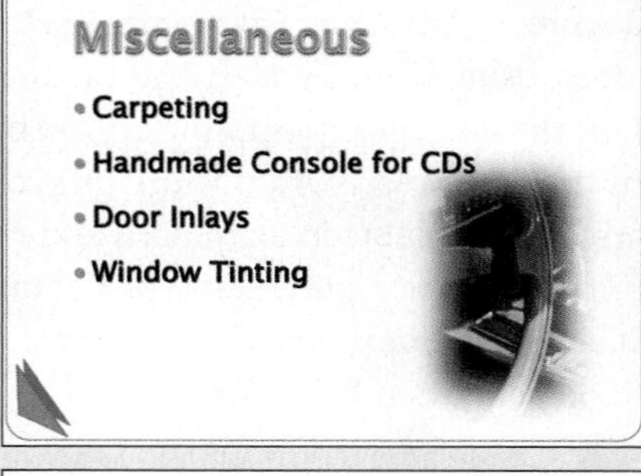

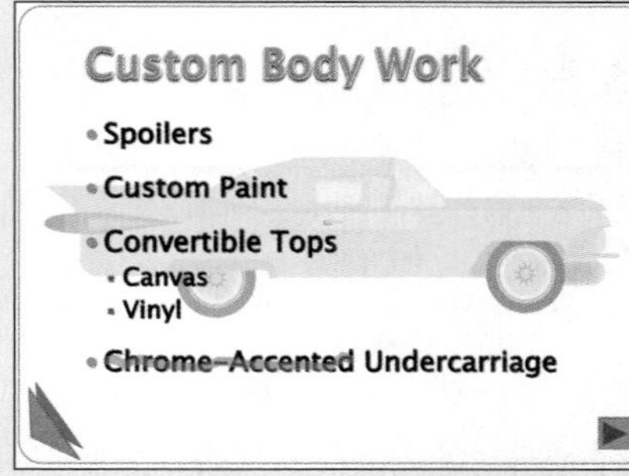

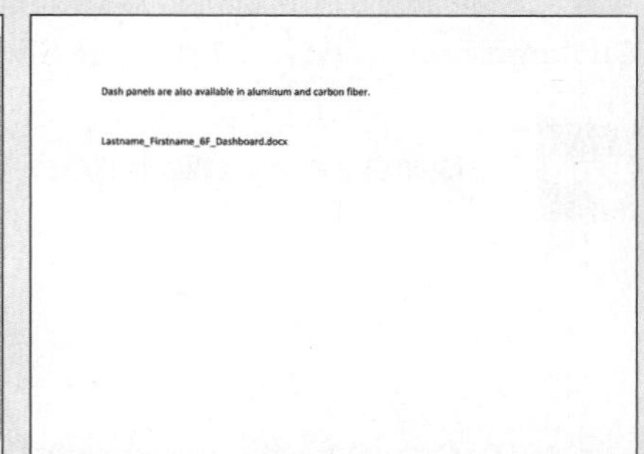

Figure 6.73

(Project 6F Custom Detail continues on the next page)

Mastering PowerPoint | Project 6F Custom Detail (continued)

1 **Start** PowerPoint. Locate and open the file **p06F_Custom_Detail**. Save the file in your chapter folder using the file name **Lastname_Firstname_6F_Custom_Detail**

2 Make the **title slide** the active slide. Click to select the graphic of the car. Display the **Insert Hyperlink** dialog box, and then type the **Address www.libertymotorspa.com** Include the ScreenTip **Liberty Motors Web site** View **From Current Slide** and test the link.

3 Make **Slide 7** the active slide. At the bottom right corner of the slide, insert an **Action Button: Forward or Next**, which is found in the last row of the **Shapes** gallery. Size the button about .5" wide and high. View **From Current Slide** and test the link.

4 Make **Slide 2** the active slide. Select *Leather*. Insert a hyperlink to **Place in This Document**, and then click **3. Interior Custom Touches**. Test the link.

5 Make **Slide 8** the active slide. Select *Contact Us*, and then add a **Hyperlink** to an **E-mail Address**. For the e-mail address, type **customteam@libertymotors.com** Include the **ScreenTip**, **Contact us for all your customization needs.** Test the link, and then close the e-mail program. Note: If you are using a campus computer, the actual e-mail may not work as it would at home.

6 Make **Slide 4** the active slide. Select the first bulleted item—*Handmade Dash Panels in Exotic Wood*. Set up a **Hyperlink** to **Create New Document**. In the **Name of new document** box, type **Lastname_Firstname_6F_Dashboard.docx** using your own last and first name. Make sure the **Edit the new document now** option button is selected. In the displayed Word document, type **Dash panels are also available in aluminum and carbon fiber.** Press Enter two times, and then type **Lastname_Firstname_6F_Dashboard.docx Save** the document in your chapter folder, and then **Exit** Word.

7 Create a new custom slide show named **Interior Customization** Add **Slide 1** through **Slide 6**. Create another custom slide show named **Body Customization** Add **Slide 1**, **Slide 7**, and **Slide 8**. Move the *Body Accessories* slide so it is number 2 in the list. Remove **Slide 1**.

8 Make the **title slide** the active slide. Double-click to select the subtitle *Customization*. Insert a hyperlink to **Place in This Document**. Scroll down to custom shows, and then click **Body Customization**. Select the **Show and return** check box, and then click **OK**. View **From Current Slide** and test the link to view the 2 slides, and then return to the title slide.

9 Hide **Slide 5**.

10 Use the onscreen navigation tools to go to **Slide 7**. Click the **Annotation pointer**, and then click **Highlighter**. Change the **Ink Color** to **Red**. In the last bulleted item, highlight *Chrome-Accented*. Highlight the first bulleted item—*Spoilers*. When prompted, keep your annotations.

11 Make the **title slide** the active slide. Set each slide to display for 4 seconds.

12 Remove the highlighting on *Spoilers*

13 Return to **Normal** view.

14 Set the presentation to be **Presented by a speaker (full screen)** and advanced manually.

15 Insert a footer on the notes and handouts that includes a fixed date and time, the page number, and the file name.

16 Modify the **Document Properties**. Replace the text in the **Author** box with your own name; in the **Subject** box, type your course name and section number; and in the **Keywords** box, type **dashboard, custom, accessories**

17 Print **Handouts 9 Slides Horizontal**, or submit your presentation electronically as directed by your instructor

18 **Save** the presentation. **Exit** PowerPoint.

End **You have completed Project 6F**

Apply 6A and 6B skills from these Objectives:

1. Apply and Modify Slide Transitions
2. Apply Custom Animation Effects
3. Modify Animation Effects
4. Insert Hyperlinks
5. Create Custom Slide Shows
6. Present and View a Slide Presentation

Mastering PowerPoint | Project 6G Repairs

In the following Mastering PowerPoint project, you will modify a PowerPoint presentation advertising Penn Liberty Motors' Repair Department, listing the types of repairs performed and the goodwill customer services available. You will apply slide transitions and custom animation effects, insert hyperlinks, and create custom slide shows. You will annotate the slide show and create a self-running version of the presentation. Your completed presentation will look similar to Figure 6.74.

Project Files

For Project 6G, you will need the following files:

p06G_Repairs.pptx
p06G_Emergency.docx

You will save your presentation as:

Lastname_Firstname_6G_Repairs.pptx

Project Results

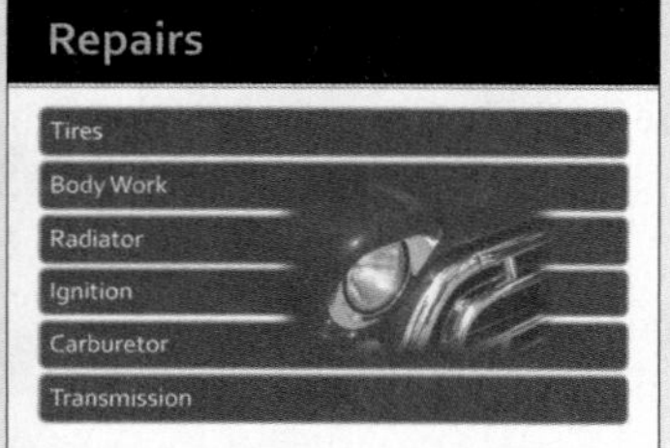

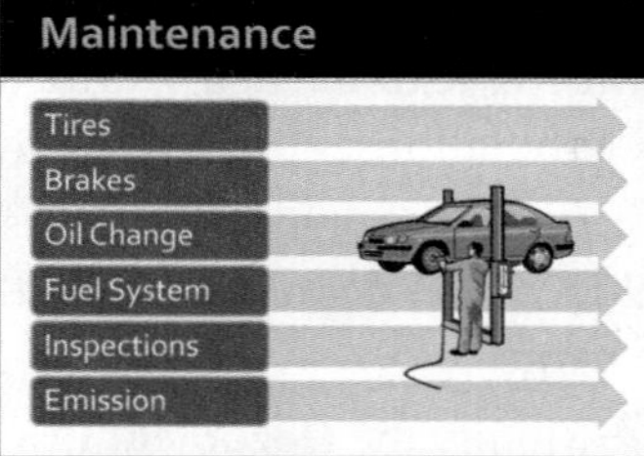

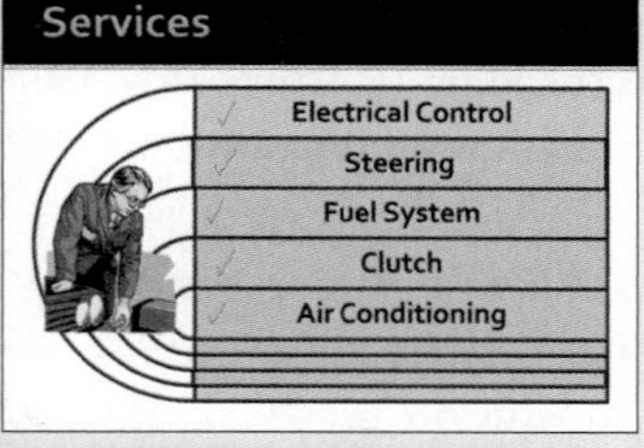

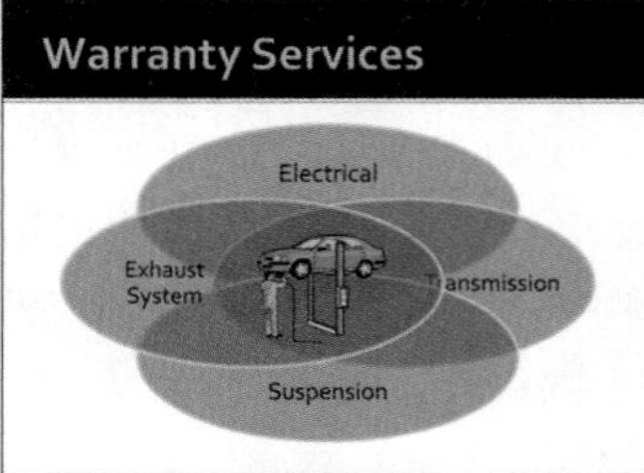

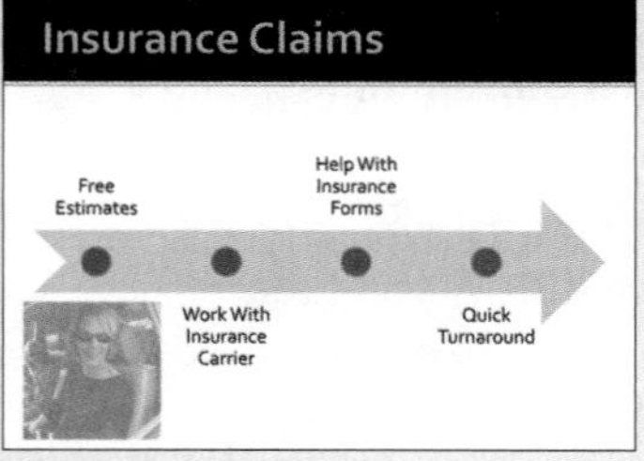

Figure 6.74

(Project 6G Repairs continues on the next page)

Mastering PowerPoint | Project 6G Repairs (continued)

1 **Start** PowerPoint. Locate and open the file **p06G_Repairs**, and then save the file as **Lastname_Firstname_6G_Repairs**

2 Make the **title slide** the active slide. Apply a **Wipe** transition to all slides.

3 Make **Slide 2** the active slide. Select the **SmartArt** graphic. Add the **Fly In** entrance effect, set the **Effect Options** to **One by One**, and then set the **Start** to **After Previous**. In the **Animation Pane**. select **Effect Options**. Set the **Direction** to **From Left**, and then change the **Duration** to **2 seconds (Medium)**.

4 Make **Slide 3** the active slide. Select the **SmartArt** graphic. Apply the **Fly In** entrance effect, set the **Effect Options** to **As One Object**, and then change the **Direction** to **From Left** and the **Duration** to **2 seconds**.

5 Make **Slide 4** the active slide. Select the **SmartArt** graphic, and then add the **Fade** entrance animation effect. Change the **Effect Options** to **One by One**. Change the **Start** to **After Previous**.

6 Make **Slide 5** the active slide. Using the same techniques, apply the same animation entrance effects to the **SmartArt** graphic as you applied to **Slide 4**.

7 Make **Slide 6** the active slide. Select the **SmartArt** graphic. Apply the **Wipe** entrance animation effect. Set the **Effect Options** to **One by One**, the **Start** to **After Previous**, the **Direction** to **From Left**, and the **Duration** to **1 seconds (Fast)**.

8 Make **Slide 7** the active slide. Using the same techniques, apply the same animation effects to the **SmartArt** graphic as you applied to **Slide 6**.

9 Make **Slide 7** the active slide. At the bottom right corner of the slide, insert an **Action Button: Home**, which is found in the last row of the **Shapes** gallery. Size the button about .5" wide and high. Test the link.

10 Make the **title slide** the active slide. Select the graphic of the repairman, and then set up a **Hyperlink** to **Link to** an **Existing File or Web Page**. Navigate to the location where your student files are stored, and then click **p06G_Emergency.docx**. For the **ScreenTip**, type **24-Hour Phone Number** Test the link.

11 Make **Slide 6** the active slide. Select the picture of the mother and child in the car, and then set up a **Hyperlink** to **Place in This Document**. Select *7. Customer Service*. Test the link.

12 Make **Slide 1** the active slide. Select *Contact Us*, and then set up a **Hyperlink** to an **E-mail Address**. For the **E-mail address**, type **repairs@libertymotors.com** Test the link.

13 Set up a new custom slide show named **Warranty and Maintenance** Add **Slides 1**, **3**, **4**, and **5** to the custom slide show. Set up a second custom slide show named **Insurance Claims** Add **Slide 6** and **Slide 7** to the custom slide show.

14 Make **Slide 2** the active slide. Select the picture of the car. Set up a **Hyperlink** to a **Place in This document**. Scroll down to the custom shows, and then click **Insurance Claims**. Click the **Show and return** check box. Test the link.

15 View the slide show **From Beginning**. Use the **Navigation tools** to go to **Slide 4**. Click the **Annotation pointer**, and then click **Pen**. In the gray area before each of the five text line items, draw a check mark. **Keep** the ink annotations.

16 Insert a footer on the notes and handouts that includes a fixed date and time, the page number, and the file name.

17 Modify the **Document Properties**. Replace the text in the **Author** box with your own name; in the **Subject** box, type your course name and section number; and in the **Keywords** box, type **insurance, maintenance, warranty**

18 Print **Handouts 9 Slides Horizontal**, or submit your presentation electronically as directed by your instructor

19 **Save** the presentation. **Exit** PowerPoint.

End You have completed Project 6G

Apply a combination of the **6A** and **6B** skills.

GO! Fix It | Project 6H Staff

Project Files

For Project 6H, you will need the following file:

p06H_Staff.pptx

You will save your presentation as:

Lastname_Firstname_6H_Staff.pptx
Lastname_Firstname_6H_Banks.docx

In this project, you will modify a PowerPoint presentation highlighting the employees of Penn Liberty Motors. Slide transitions and custom animation effects will add life to the slide show. You will also insert hyperlinks and create custom slide shows. You will annotate the slide show and create a self-running presentation.

Open **p06H_Staff**, and then save the file in your chapter folder as **Lastname_Firstname_6H_Staff** To complete the project, you will create a slideshow to do the following:

- Apply a Wipe transition and .5 Timing to all slides.
- On Slide 2, Slide 3, and Slide 6, apply the Wipe entrance animation to the SmartArt placeholder. Set the effect options to One by One, Start After Previous, Direction From Left, and Speed of Fast. Animate the salesman graphic on each slide with the Fade entrance effect starting after the previous effect.
- On Slide 4, animate the SmartArt placeholder with the Wipe entrance effect with the following options: One by One, Start After Previous, and Speed of Fast. Set the car graphic animation for an entrance effect of Fly In, From Left, Start After Previous, and Medium speed.
- On Slide 5, animate the SmartArt placeholder with a Fade entrance effect with the following options: One by One and Start After Previous. Add a Circle Motion path to the dollar sign graphic, and then apply Start After Previous. Use the dollar sign graphic to set up a hyperlink to Create New Document. Name the new document **Lastname_Firstname_6H_Banks.docx** In the Word document, type **We are committed to working with your bank, credit union, or other financial institution.** Press Enter two times, and then type **Lastname_Firstname_6H_Banks.docx** Save your document, and then exit Microsoft Word.
- Create a custom slide show named **Sales** that includes Slides 1, 2, and 3. Create a second custom slide show named **Service** that includes Slides 4, 5, and 6 to the show. On Slide 1, add a hyperlink to the flag graphic that takes you to the Service custom show. Set it to return to the title slide after showing.
- On Slide 4, highlight the bulleted item *Trained* and keep your annotation.
- Rehearse the slide show with timings of about 6 seconds for each slide. Set the slide show to advance the slide manually.
- Insert a Header & Footer on the Notes and Handouts that includes the date and time fixed, the page number, and a footer with the text **Lastname_Firstname_6H_Staff** Document Properties should include your name, course name and section, and the keywords **customer, quality, trainer**
- Save your presentation. Print Handouts 6 slides per page, or submit electronically as directed by your instructor.

End You have completed Project 6H

Content-Based Assessments

Apply a combination of the **6A** and **6B** skills.

GO! Make It | Project 6I Auto Show

Project Files

For Project 6I, you will need the following files:

p06I_Auto_Show.pptx
p06I_Registration.docx

You will save your presentation as:

Lastname_Firstname_6I_Auto_Show.pptx

By using the skills you practiced in this chapter, you will modify a presentation. Your presentation should look similar to Figure 6.75.

Start PowerPoint, open p06I_Auto_Show, and then save it in your chapter folder as **Lastname_Firstname_6I_Auto_Show** On the title slide, apply a transition to all slides and set a timing duration. On all slides, add an entrance effect for the content placeholder, and then apply effect options for direction, timing, and starting sequence.

On Slide 7, select the bell, and then add a hyperlink to the file p06I_Registration.docx, located in the student data files. Add an appropriate ScreenTip. On Slide 4, click the top auto, and then add an entrance animation with effect options for speed and starting sequence. On Slide 8, format the SmartArt placeholder for entrance and effect options. Link the last slide to the first slide using an action button.

On the title slide, format the text *Philadelphia International Auto Show* for exit animation and effect options. Hyperlink the text *Contact Us* to the e-mail address sponsor@libertymotors.com

Set up a new custom slide show. For the first show, use the name **Auto_Show** and add Slides 1, 2, 3, 4, and 5. For the second show, use the name **Convention_Center** and add Slides 6, 7, and 8. Hide Slide 4. On Slide 2, hyperlink the text *Pennsylvania Convention Center* to the custom show Convention_Center. Set up a slide show to be viewed on a kiosk with rehearsed timings for the presentation.

Insert a Header & Footer on the Notes and Handouts that includes the date and time fixed, the page number, and a footer with the text **Lastname_Firstname_6I_Auto_Show** In the Document Properties, add your name, course name and section, and the keywords **Pennsylvania, convention, trade** Save your file. Print Handouts 4 slides per page, or submit electronically as directed by your instructor.

(Project 6I Auto Show continues on the next page)

GO! Make It | Project 6I Auto Show (continued)

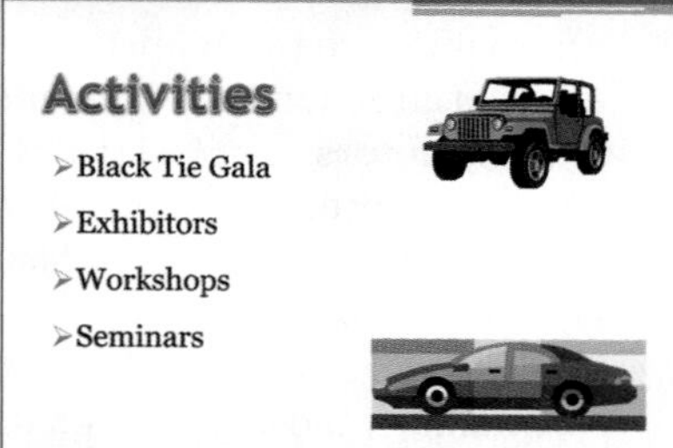

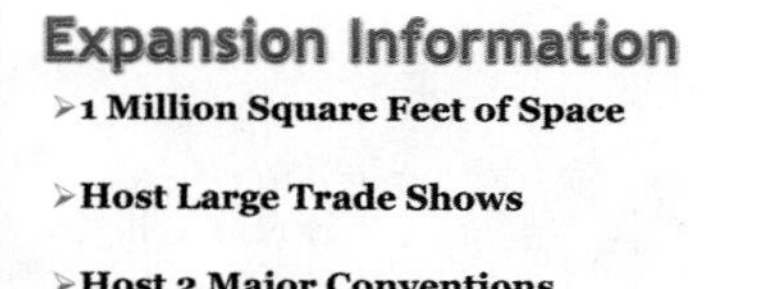

Amenities
Cutting Edge Technology
Wireless Access
Impressive Art Collection

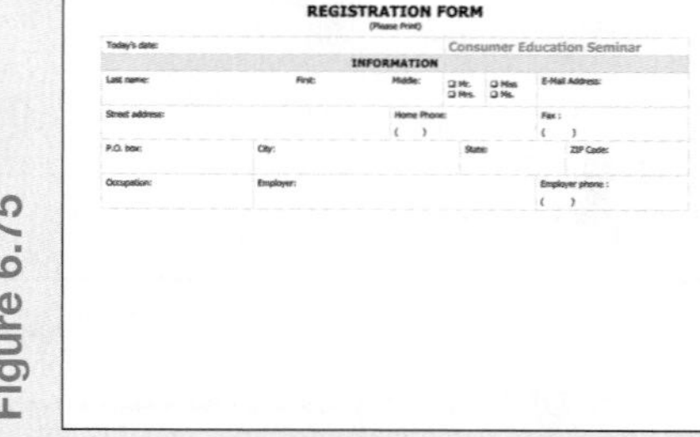
REGISTRATION FORM

Consumer Education Seminar

INFORMATION

Figure 6.75

End You have completed Project 6I

Content-Based Assessments

Apply a combination of the **6A** and **6B** skills.

GO! Solve It | Project 6J Leasing

Project Files

For Project 6J, you will need the following files:

p06J_Leasing.pptx
p06J_Terms_ Conditions.docx

You will save your presentation as:

Lastname_Firstname_6J_Leasing.pptx

Open the file p06J_Leasing, and then save it as **Lastname_Firstname_6J_Leasing** Apply transitions and add entrance, emphasis, exit, and motion path animation effects. Modify and set effect options to the animation effects.

Add an action button on one slide. Create a hyperlink to the following e-mail address: **leasing @libertymotors.com** Insert a hyperlink to the Word document p06J_Terms_Conditions.docx. Create one custom show, and then hyperlink it on one of the slides. Use the animation pen tool to annotate one of the slides and keep the ink annotations. Rehearse the timings, and then set up the show for a kiosk.

Insert a Header & Footer on the Notes and Handouts that includes the date and time fixed, the page number, and a footer with the text **Lastname_Firstname_6J_Leasing** In the Document Properties, add your name, course information, and the keywords **lease, value** Save your presentation. Print Handouts 4 slides per page, or submit electronically as directed by your instructor.

		Performance Level		
		Exemplary: You consistently applied the relevant skills.	**Proficient:** You sometimes, but not always, applied the relevant skills.	**Developing:** You rarely or never applied the relevant skills.
Performance Element	**Formatted slides with a variety of transitions and effects.**	Slide show included relevant transitions and effects.	Slide show included a variety of transitions and effects, but they were not appropriate for the presentation.	Slide show did not include transitions and effects.
	Added action button and hyperlinks as instructed.	Action button and requested hyperlinks were present and completely functioning.	Action button and some hyperlinks were present, but not all functioned correctly.	There is little evidence that action button and hyperlinks are present.
	Created a custom slide show and linked it on one slide.	Custom slide show was created and linked properly.	Custom slide show was created but not linked.	The custom slide show was not created.
	Set up slide show for a kiosk.	The kiosk worked correctly.	The slide show timings were rehearsed, but the show was not set up as a kiosk.	The slide show timings were not rehearsed.

End **You have completed Project 6J**

Apply a combination of the **6A** and **6B** skills.

GO! Solve It | Project 6K Special Orders

Project Files

For Project 6K, you will need the following file:

p06K_Special_Orders.pptx

You will save your presentation as:

Lastname_Firstname_6K_Special_Orders.pptx

In this project, you will customize a slide show showcasing special-order vehicles, such as limousines, motorcycles, and race cars, available at Penn Liberty Motors. You will apply innovative transitions and customized entrance and exit animation effects.

Open p06K_Special_Orders, and then save it as **Lastname_Firstname_6K_Special_Orders** Insert a hyperlink to the Penn Liberty Motors Web site: **www.libertymotorspa.com** Insert a hyperlink to the Special Order Department's e-mail address: **custom@libertymotors.com** Use hyperlinks to link the picture of a vehicle to its features. Create at least two basic custom shows to appeal to two different vehicle enthusiasts, and then insert a hyperlink to one of the custom shows. Create an action button.

Insert a Header & Footer on the Notes and Handouts that includes the date and time fixed, the page number, and a footer with the text **Lastname_Firstname_6K_Special_Orders** In the Document Properties, add your name, course information, and the keywords **classic, limousines** Save your presentation. Print Handouts 4 slides per page, or submit electronically as directed by your instructor.

Performance Element	Performance Level — Exemplary: You consistently applied the relevant skills.	Proficient: You sometimes, but not always, applied the relevant skills.	Developing: You rarely or never applied the relevant skills.
Formatted slide show with a variety of transitions and effects.	Slide show included relevant transitions and effects.	Slide show included a variety of transitions and effects, but they were not appropriate for the presentation.	Slide show contained no transitions and effects.
Inserted hyperlinks to Web site, to e-mail address, and to place in the slide show.	All hyperlinks worked correctly.	One of the hyperlinks did not work correctly.	Hyperlinks were not created, or they did not work correctly.
Created two custom slide shows and linked one of them.	Created two custom shows and one was linked correctly.	Created one custom show and may not have linked it.	No custom slide shows were created.
Created an action button.	The action button produced the intended result.	Action button was created but did not work properly.	No action button was inserted.

End **You have completed Project 6K**

Outcomes-Based Assessments

Rubric

The following outcomes-based assessments are *open-ended assessments*. That is, there is no specific correct result; your result will depend on your approach to the information provided. Make *Professional Quality* your goal. Use the following scoring rubric to guide you in *how* to approach the problem and then to evaluate *how well* your approach solves the problem.

The *criteria*—Software Mastery, Content, Format and Layout, and Process—represent the knowledge and skills you have gained that you can apply to solving the problem. The *levels of performance*—Professional Quality, Approaching Professional Quality, or Needs Quality Improvements—help you and your instructor evaluate your result.

	Your completed project is of Professional Quality if you:	Your completed project is Approaching Professional Quality if you:	Your completed project Needs Quality Improvements if you:
1-Software Mastery	Choose and apply the most appropriate skills, tools, and features and identify efficient methods to solve the problem.	Choose and apply some appropriate skills, tools, and features, but not in the most efficient manner.	Choose inappropriate skills, tools, or features, or are inefficient in solving the problem.
2-Content	Construct a solution that is clear and well organized, contains content that is accurate, appropriate to the audience and purpose, and is complete. Provide a solution that contains no errors in spelling, grammar, or style.	Construct a solution in which some components are unclear, poorly organized, inconsistent, or incomplete. Misjudge the needs of the audience. Have some errors in spelling, grammar, or style, but the errors do not detract from comprehension.	Construct a solution that is unclear, incomplete, or poorly organized; contains some inaccurate or inappropriate content; and contains many errors in spelling, grammar, or style. Do not solve the problem.
3-Format and Layout	Format and arrange all elements to communicate information and ideas, clarify function, illustrate relationships, and indicate relative importance.	Apply appropriate format and layout features to some elements, but not others. Overuse features, causing minor distraction.	Apply format and layout that does not communicate information or ideas clearly. Do not use format and layout features to clarify function, illustrate relationships, or indicate relative importance. Use available features excessively, causing distraction.
4-Process	Use an organized approach that integrates planning, development, self-assessment, revision, and reflection.	Demonstrate an organized approach in some areas, but not others; or, use an insufficient process of organization throughout.	Do not use an organized approach to solve the problem.

Outcomes-Based Assessments

Apply a combination of the **6A** and **6B** skills.

GO! Think | Project 6L Car Purchase

Project Files

For Project 6L, you will need the following files:

New blank PowerPoint presentation
p06L_Off_Lease.docx

You will save your presentation as:

Lastname_Firstname_6L_Car_Purchase.pptx

Penn Liberty Motors has launched a new sales initiative to sell used cars. In this project, you will create a presentation with a minimum of six slides comparing the benefits of buying a new car versus buying a used car. In addition, certified lease cars should be part of the presentation. Insert a hyperlink on one slide to link to the **p06L_Off_Lease.docx** file provided in the student files Include transitions and custom animation effects in the presentation. Create a self-running slide show.

Insert a Header & Footer on the Notes and Handouts that includes the date and time fixed, the page number, and a footer with the text **Lastname_Firstname_6L_Car Purchase** In the Document Properties, add your name and course information and the keywords **certification, lease** Save your presentation. Print Handouts 6 slides per page, or submit electronically as directed by your instructor.

You have completed Project 6L

Apply a combination of the **6A** and **6B** skills.

GO! Think | Project 6M Security

Project Files

For Project 6M, you will need the following files:

p06M_Security.pptx
p06M_Silent_Alarms.docx
p06M_Brakes.wav
p06M_Car_Alarm.wav
p06M_Siren.wav

You will save your presentation as:

Lastname_Firstname_6M_Security.pptx

In this project, you will transform the existing presentation regarding security and anti-theft devices for automobiles into a dynamic slide show. Open **p06M_Security**, and then apply transitions, customized animation effects, and sound effects—use **p06M_Car_Alarm.wav**, **p06M_Brakes.wav**, and **p06M_Siren.wav**. Add a hyperlink to the Microsoft Word document **p06M_Silent_Alarms.docx**. The sound files and the Microsoft Word document are provided. Keep in mind that the animation effects should enhance and not overwhelm the content of the slides. Create a custom show from the original presentation, and then create a self-running show for Penn Liberty Motors to present at the upcoming Annual Auto Show.

Insert a Header & Footer on the Notes and Handouts that includes the date and time fixed, the page number, and a footer with the text **Lastname_Firstname_6M_Security** In the Document Properties, add your name and course information and the keywords **alarms, keyless** Save your presentation. Print Handouts 6 slides per page, or submit electronically as directed by your instructor.

End **You have completed Project 6M**

Apply a combination of the 6A and 6B skills.

You and GO! | Project 6N Digital Sound

Project Files

For Project 6N, you will need the following file:

p06N_Digital_Sound.pptx

You will save your presentations as:

Lastname_Firstname_6N_Digital_Sound.pptx
Lastname_Firstname_6N_Pricing.docx

In this project, you will create a slide show for Penn Liberty Motors to showcase their new and innovative digital stereo systems to be offered on select automobiles.

Include transitions, sounds, and animation effects to spark interest in this new technology. Insert a hyperlink to the Web page www.digital.libertymotorspa.com Include a hyperlink to a new document you create named **Lastname_Firstname_6N_Pricing.docx** In the document, type: **Pricing is not yet available for our integrated digital stereo system. However, we are now taking orders. Please e-mail Penn Liberty Motors at orders@libertymotors.com.**

Create a custom slide show and annotate at least one slide.

Insert a Header & Footer on the Notes and Handouts that includes the date and time fixed, the page number, and a footer with the text **Lastname_Firstname_6N_Digital_Sound** In the Document Properties, add your name and course information and the keywords **pricing, digital** Save your presentation. Print Handouts 6 slides per page, or submit electronically as directed by your instructor.

You have completed Project 6N

Business Running Case

Razvan CHIRNOAGA/Shutterstock

In this project, you will apply the PowerPoint skills you practiced in Chapters 4 through 6. This project relates to **Front Range Action Sports**, which is one of the country's largest retailers of sports gear and outdoor recreation merchandise. The company has large retail stores in Colorado, Washington, Oregon, California, and New Mexico, in addition to a growing online business. Major merchandise categories include fishing, camping, rock climbing, winter sports, action sports, water sports, team sports, racquet sports, fitness, golf, apparel, and footwear. The company plans for expansion in other states in the west and into Vancouver, British Columbia.

You will develop a presentation that Irene Shviktar, Vice President of Marketing, will show at a corporate marketing retreat that summarizes the company's marketing and implementation plan to expand the footwear product lines. Your completed presentation will look similar to the one shown in Figure 2.1.

Project Files

For Project BRC2, you will need the following files:

- pBRC2_Goals.pptx
- pBRC2_Lake.jpg
- pBRC2_SkateSet.jpg
- pBRC2_Hiking.png
- pBRC2_Skating.jpg
- pBRC2_Sports.mid
- pBRC2_Target.wmf
- pBRC2_Athletic.jpg
- pBRC2_Sales.jpg

You will save your presentations as:

- Lastname_Firstname_BRC2_Goals_Template.potx
- Lastname_Firstname_BRC2_Goals.pptx
- Lastname_Firstname_BRC2_Goals.pdf
- Lastname_Firstname_BRC2_Album.pptx

Project Results

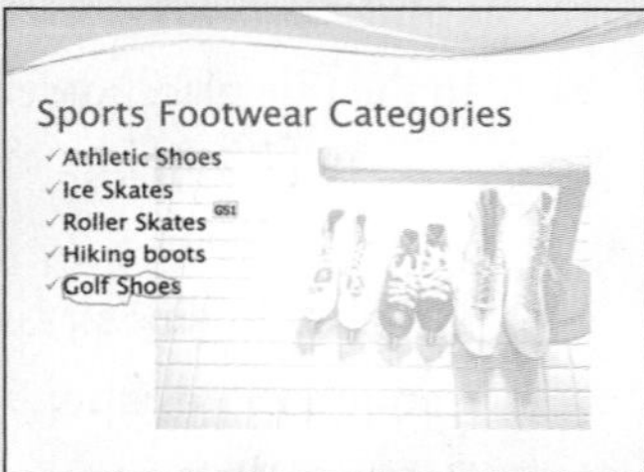

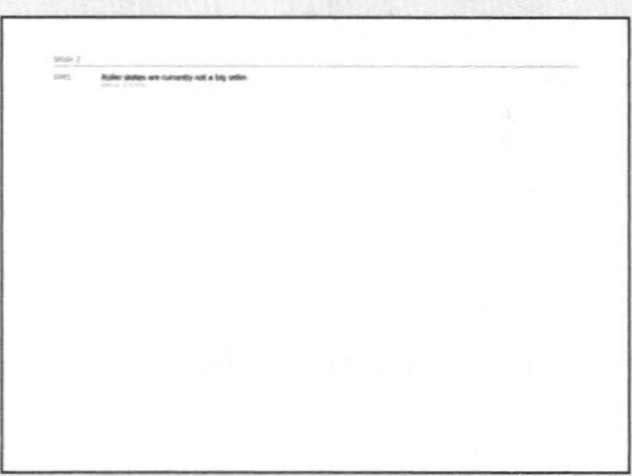

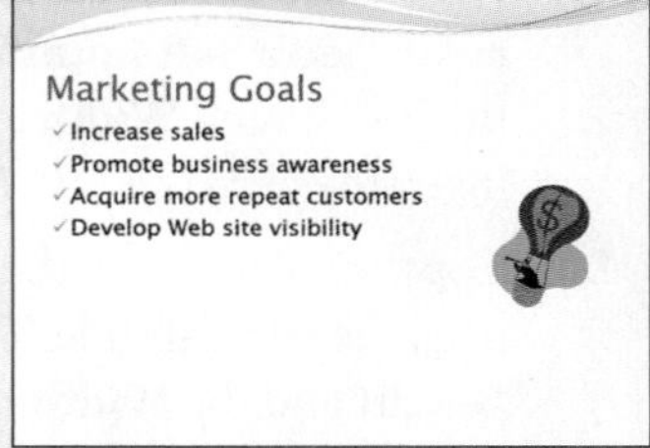

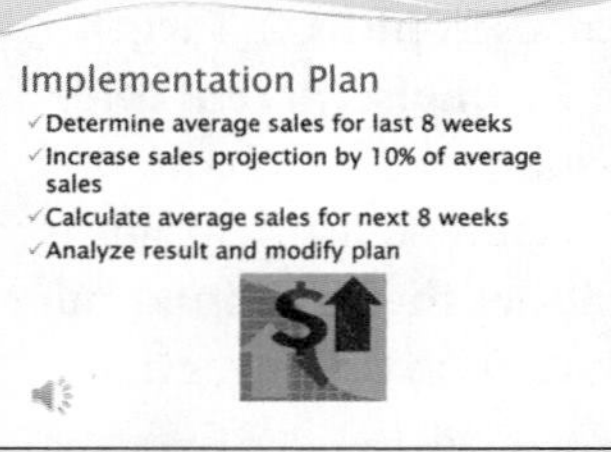

Figure 2.1

Business Running Case

Front Range Action Sports

1 **Start** PowerPoint. From the student files that accompany this textbook, locate and open **pBRC2_Goals.pptx**. Navigate to the folder you created for **Front Range Action Sports**, or create one if necessary, and then save the presentation as a **template** named **Lastname_Firstname_BRC2_Goals_Template.potx**

a. Display the **Slide Master** view. The Flow theme has already been applied. On the **Flow Slide Master**, change the **Master title style** font to **Lucida Sans** and the **Font size** to **40**. Change the content placeholder font to **Lucida Sans**. Change the bullets on the first line to **Arrow Bullets**.

b. On the **Title Slide Layout**, change the **Background Style** to **Style 11**. Format the **Background** with a **Gradient fill** set with a **Linear** type. Position the **middle gradient stop** at **45%** with the color **Blue, Accent 1, Darker 50%**, and then close the dialog box, without applying to all. Change the **Font size** of the Master title placeholder to **40**.

c. On the **Title Slide Layout**, from **Basic Shapes**, insert the **Cloud** shape—the eleventh shape in the third row—at **4.25 inches on the left half of the horizontal ruler** and **3 inches on the upper half of the vertical ruler**. Add a **Soft Round Bevel** shape effect. Change the **Height** and **Width** to **1.5"**. From your data files, insert the picture **pBRC2_Skating** as a **Shape Fill**.

d. Copy the shape, and then paste a second copy of it onto the current slide, **Title Slide Layout**. Change the **Height** and the **Width** of the copied shape to **1.2"**. Move the shape so the right side aligns at **4.25 inches on the right half of the horizontal ruler** and the bottom aligns at **3 inches on the lower half of the vertical ruler**.

e. **Close** the **Master View**. **Save** the template and **close** it, but do not exit PowerPoint.

2 Display **Backstage** view, click **New**, and then click **New from existing**. Click **Lastname_Firstname_BRC2_Goals_Template.potx**, and then create a new presentation. Save the presentation as **Lastname_Firstname_BRC2_Goals.pptx**

3 On **Slide 1**, in the title placeholder, type **Front Range Action Sports** In the subtitle placeholder, type **Footwear Promotion**

4 Insert a **New Slide** with the **Title and Content** layout as **Slide 2**.

a. In the title placeholder, type **Sports Footwear Categories** In the content placeholder, type the following bulleted items:

Athletic Shoes

Ice Skates

Roller Skates

Hiking Boots

Golf Shoes

b. Display the **Slide Master**. On the first thumbnail at the left, change the first-level bullets to **Checkmark Bullets**. Close the **Master View**.

c. On **Slide 2**, insert the picture **pBRC2_SkateSet.jpg**. Change the height to **4.5"**. Position the picture so the top is at **1.5 inches on the upper half of the vertical ruler** and the right side is at **4 inches on the right side of the horizontal ruler**. Apply **Send to Back**. Set the color to **Washout**, which is under **Recolor**, the first row, fourth color.

d. Insert the following comment after *Roller Skates*: **Roller skates are currently not a big seller.**

5 Insert a **New Slide** with the **Title and Content** layout as **Slide 3**.

a. In the title placeholder, type **Marketing Goals** In the content placeholder, type the following:

Increase sales

Promote business awareness

Acquire more repeat customers

Develop Web site visibility

b. In the content placeholder, insert **pBRC2_Target.wmf**. Change the color to **Turquoise, Accent color 3 Dark**, which is under **Recolor**, the second row, the fourth color. Position the picture so the right side is at **4 inches on the right side of the horizontal ruler** and the bottom is at **2.5 inches on the lower half of the vertical ruler**.

6 Insert a **New Slide** with the **Title and Content** layout as **Slide 4**.

a. In the title placeholder, type **Implementation Plan** In the content placeholder, type the following:

Determine average sales for last 8 weeks

Increase sales projection by 10% of average sales

Calculate average sales for next 8 weeks

Analyze result and modify plan

(Business Running Case: Front Range Action Sports continues on the next page)

Front Range Action Sports (continued)

b. Insert **pBRC2_Sales.jpg**. Set the **Brightness** to **-20%** and the **Contrast** to **40%**. Change the color to **Turquoise, Accent color 3 Dark**. Change the **Height** to **2"**, and then position the picture so that the bottom aligns at **3 inches on the lower half of the vertical ruler**. **Align Center**.

7 Insert a **New Slide** with the **Title Only** layout as **Slide 5**.

a. In the title placeholder, type **Review**

b. In the blank content area, insert a **WordArt** with a **Fill – Turquoise, Accent 3, Outline – Text 2**. In the text box, type **Winning** Press Enter, and then type **Strategies** Insert the picture **pBRC2_Lake.jpg** as a **Shape Fill**. Change the **Height** to **4"** and the **Width** to **6"**. Position the top edge at **1.5 inches on the upper half of the vertical ruler**, and then **Align Center**.

8 Make **Slide 4** the active slide. Insert the audio file **pBRC2_Sports.mid**. Set the **Volume** to **Medium**, and then check **Hide During Show**. Add a trigger to activate the audio **On Click of** the **Picture**. Position the speaker at the lower left corner of the slide.

9 Make **Slide 2** the active slide. View your slide show **From Current slide**. Use the **Highlighter** annotation tool to highlight *Athletic Shoes*. Use the **Pen** annotation tool to circle *Golf Shoes*. Make sure you **Keep** the annotations.

10 Insert a **Header & Footer** for the **Notes and Handouts**. Include the **Date and time fixed**, the **Page number**, and a **Footer** with the file name **Lastname_Firstname_BRC2_Goals** In the **Properties**, add your first and last name, course name and section number, and the **Keywords marketing, goals**

11 **Save** and **Close** the presentation, but do not exit PowerPoint.

12 Display a new blank presentation, and then insert a new **Photo Album**.

a. Insert the following pictures in this order: **pBRC2_Hiking**, **pBRC2_Skating**, and **pBRC2_Athletic**.

b. Set the picture layout to **1 picture**, the Frame shape to **Rounded Rectangle**, and then select the **Flow** theme. Include **Captions below ALL pictures**.

c. On **Slide 1**, replace the title text with **Athletic Footwear** and the subtitle text with **Front Range Action Sports**

d. For the pictures, use these captions:

Slide 2: **Hiking Boots**

Slide 3: **Skates**

Slide 3: **Athletic Shoes**

e. Save the album as **Lastname_Firstname_BRC2_Album**

f. Insert a **Header & Footer** for the **Notes and Handouts**. Include the **Date and time fixed**, the **Page number**, and a **Footer** with the file name **Lastname_Firstname_BRC2_Album** In the **Properties**, add your first and last name, course name and section number, and the **Keywords album, footwear**

g. Print **Handouts 4 Slides horizontal** showing all comments, or submit your presentation electronically as directed by your instructor. **Save** and **Close** the presentation.

13 Open Lastname_Firstname_BRC2_Goals.pptx.

a. Apply a **Fade** transition to all slides.

b. On **Slide 2**, set **Advance Slide** to **After 3** seconds, and then uncheck **On Mouse Click**.

c. On **Slide 3,** add a **Fade Entrance** animation effect to the Title to start **After Previous**.

d. On **Slide 4**, add a **Fade Entrance** animation effect to the Title to start **After Previous**.

e. On **Slide 1**, on *Footwear Promotion*, insert a hyperlink to the **Existing File** *Lastname_Firstname_Album_pptx*.

f. Create a **Custom Slide Show** named **Goals** and include **Slides 3 and 4**.

g. On **Slide 5**, on *Review*, insert a hyperlink to the **Goals** custom show. Click **Show and return** before clicking **OK**.

14 View the slide show from the beginning and check your links and the audio.

15 Create a PDF Document with the options to publish **Handouts** with **6 Slides per page** and **Include comments**.

16 **Save** your presentation. Print **Handouts, 6 Slides Horizontal**, or submit your presentation electronically as directed by your instructor.

17 Mark the presentation as **Final**, and then **Close**.

End **You have completed Business Running Case 2**

Glossary

.potx File extension for a PowerPoint template.

.pptx File extension for a PowerPoint presentation.

.wav (waveform audio data) A sound file that may be embedded in a presentation.

Action button A built-in button shape that you can add to your presentation and then assign an action to occur upon the click of a mouse or with a mouse over.

Address bar The bar at the top of a folder window with which you can navigate to a different folder or library, or go back to a previous one.

After Previous An animation command that begins the animation sequence for the selected PowerPoint slide element immediately after the completion of the previous animation or slide transition.

Alignment The placement of paragraph text relative to the left and right margins.

All Programs An area of the Start menu that displays all the available programs on your computer system.

Animated GIF A file format made up of a series of frames within a single file that creates the illusion of animation by displaying the frames one after the other in quick succession.

Animation 1. Any type of motion or movement that occurs as the presentation moves from slide to slide. 2. A special visual effect or sound effect added to text or an object.

Animation Painter A feature that copies animation settings from one object to another.

Animation Pane The area that contains a list of the animation effects added to your presentation. From this pane, you can add or modify effects.

Annotation A note or highlight on a slide that can be saved or discarded.

Application Another term for a program.

Artistic effects Formats applied to images that make pictures resemble sketches or paintings.

AutoPlay A Windows feature that displays when you insert a CD, a DVD, or other removable device, and which lets you choose which program to use to start different kinds of media, such as music CDs, or CDs and DVDs containing photos.

Back and Forward buttons Buttons at the top of a folder window that work in conjunction with the address bar to change folders by going backward or forward one folder at a time.

Background Removal A command that removes unwanted portions of a picture so that the picture does not appear as a self-contained rectangle.

Background style A slide background fill variation that combines theme colors in different intensities or patterns.

Backstage tabs The area along the left side of Backstage view with tabs to display various pages of commands.

Backstage view A centralized space for file management tasks; for example, opening, saving, printing, publishing, or sharing a file. A navigation pane displays along the left side with tabs that group file-related tasks together.

Basic custom slide show A separate presentation saved with its own title and that contains some of the slides from the original presentation.

Black slide A slide that displays at the end of an electronic slide show indicating that the presentation is over.

Body font A font that is applied to all slide text except titles.

Border A frame around a picture.

Brightness The relative lightness of an image.

Caption Text that helps to identify or explain a picture or a graphic.

Category label A chart element that identifies a category of data.

Cell The intersection of a column and a row.

Cell reference The identification of a specific cell by its intersecting column letter and row number.

Center alignment The alignment of text or objects that is centered horizontally between the left and right margin.

Chart A graphic representation of numeric data.

Chevron A V-shaped symbol that indicates more information or options are available.

Click The action of pressing the left button on your mouse pointing device one time.

Clip A single media file, for example art, sound, animation, or a movie.

Column chart A type of chart used to compare data.

Command An instruction to a computer program that causes an action to be carried out.

Comment A note that you can attach to a letter or word on a slide or to an entire slide. People use comments to provide feedback on a presentation.

Common dialog boxes The set of dialog boxes that includes Open, Save, and Save As, which are provided by the Windows programming interface, and which display and operate in all of the Office programs in the same manner.

Compatibility Checker A feature that locates potential compatibility issues between PowerPoint 2010 and earlier versions of PowerPoint.

Compatibility mode Saves a presentation as PowerPoint 97-2003 Presentation.

Compressed file A file that has been reduced in size and thus takes up less storage space and can be transferred to other computers quickly.

Context sensitive command A command associated with activities in which you are engaged.

Contextual tabs Tabs that are added to the Ribbon automatically when a specific object, such as a picture, is selected, and that contain commands relevant to the selected object.

Contrast The amount of difference between the light and dark extremes of color in an image.

Copy A command that duplicates a selection and places it on the Clipboard.

Crop A command that reduces the size of a picture by removing vertical or horizontal edges.

Crop handles Used like sizing handles to crop a picture.

Crop tool The mouse pointer used when removing areas of a picture.

Crosshair pointer A pointer that indicates that you can draw a shape.

Custom slide show Displays only the slides you want to display to an audience in the order you select.

Cut A command that removes a selection and places it on the Clipboard.

Data marker A column, bar, area, dot, pie slice, or other symbol in a chart that represents a single data point; related data points form a data series.

Data point A value that originates in a worksheet cell and that is represented in a chart by a data marker.

Data series Related data points represented by data markers; each data series has a unique color or pattern represented in the chart legend.

Default The term that refers to the current selection or setting that is automatically used by a computer program unless you specify otherwise.

Deselect The action of canceling the selection of an object or block of text by clicking outside of the selection.

Desktop In Windows, the opening screen that simulates your work area.

Details pane The area at the bottom of a folder window that displays the most common file properties.

Dialog box A small window that contains options for completing a task.

Dialog Box Launcher A small icon that displays to the right of some group names on the Ribbon, and which opens a related dialog box or task pane providing additional options and commands related to that group.

Document properties Details about a file that describe or identify it, including the title, author name, subject, and keywords that identify the document's topic or contents; also known as *metadata*.

Double-click The action of clicking the left mouse button two times in rapid succession.

Drag The action of holding down the left mouse button while moving your mouse.

Edit The actions of making changes to text or graphics in an Office file.

Editing The process of modifying a presentation by adding and deleting slides or by changing the contents of individual slides.

Ellipsis A set of three dots indicating incompleteness; when following a command name, indicates that a dialog box will display.

E-mail client A software program that enables you to compose and send e-mail.

Embed Save a file so that the audio or video file becomes part of the presentation file.

Emphasis effect An animation effect that, for example, makes an object shrink or grow in size, change color, or spin on its center.

Enhanced ScreenTip A ScreenTip that displays more descriptive text than a normal ScreenTip.

Entrance effect An animation effect that occurs when the text or object is introduced into the slide during a slide show.

Exit effect An animation effect that occurs when the text or object leaves the slide or disappears during a slide show.

Extract To decompress, or pull out, files from a compressed form.

File A collection of information stored on a computer under a single name, for example a Word document or a PowerPoint presentation.

File extension Also called the file type, it identifies the format of the file or the application used to create it.

File list In a folder window, the area on the right that displays the contents of the current folder or library.

Fill The inside color of an object.

Fill color The inside color of text or of an object.

Fit to slide The photo album option that allows the picture to occupy all available space on a slide with no room for a frame or caption.

Folder A container in which you store files.

Folder window In Windows, a window that displays the contents of the current folder, library, or device, and contains helpful parts so that you can navigate.

Font A set of characters with the same design and shape.

Font styles Formatting emphasis such as bold, italic, and underline.

Footer A reserved area for text or graphics that displays at the bottom of each page in a document.

Footer (PowerPoint) Text that displays at the bottom of every slide or that prints at the bottom of a sheet of slide handouts or notes pages.

Format Painter An Office feature that copies formatting from one selection of text to another.

Formatting The process of establishing the overall appearance of text, graphics, and pages in an Office file—for example, in a Word document.

Formatting (PowerPoint) The process of changing the appearance of the text, layout, and design of a slide.

Formatting marks Characters that display on the screen, but do not print, indicating where the Enter key, the Spacebar, and the Tab key were pressed; also called *nonprinting characters*.

Frame The border around a picture in a photo album.

Full path Includes the drive, the folder, and any subfolders in which a file is contained.

Gallery An Office feature that displays a list of potential results instead of just the command name.

GIF Stands for *Graphics Interchange Format*. It is a file format used for graphic images.

Gradient fill A gradual progression of several colors blending into each other or shades of the same color blending into each other.

Gradient stop Allows you to apply different color combinations to selected areas of the background.

Groups On the Office Ribbon, the sets of related commands that you might need for a specific type of task.

Handout Master Includes the specifications for the design of presentation handouts for an audience.

Header A reserved area for text or graphics that displays at the top of each page in a document.

Header (PowerPoint) Text that prints at the top of each sheet of slide handouts or notes pages.

Headings font The font that is applied to slide titles.

HTML (HyperText Markup Language) The language used to code Web pages.

HTTP (HyperText Transfer Protocol) The protocol used on the World Wide Web to define how messages are formatted and transmitted.

Hyperlinked custom slide show A quick way to navigate to a separate slide show from within the original presentation.

Hyperlinks A navigation element that, when clicked, will take you to another location, such as a Web page, an e-mail address, another document, or a place within the same document. In a PowerPoint presentation, hyperlinks can also be used to link to a slide in the presentation, to a slide in a different presentation, or to a custom slide show.

Icons Pictures that represent a program, a file, a folder, or some other object.

Info tab The tab in Backstage view that displays information about the current file.

Insertion point A blinking vertical line that indicates where text or graphics will be inserted.

JPEG (JPG) Stands for Joint Photographic Experts Group. It is a file format used for photos.

Keyboard shortcut A combination of two or more keyboard keys, used to perform a task that would otherwise require a mouse.

KeyTips The letter that displays on a command in the Ribbon and that indicates the key you can press to activate the command when keyboard control of the Ribbon is activated.

Kiosk A booth that includes a computer and a monitor that may have a touch screen.

Landscape orientation A page orientation in which the paper is wider than it is tall.

Layout The arrangement of elements, such as title and subtitle text, lists, pictures, tables, charts, shapes, and movies, on a PowerPoint slide.

Legend A chart element that identifies the patterns or colors that are assigned to the categories in the chart.

Library In Windows, a collection of items, such as files and folders, assembled from various locations that might be on your computer, an external hard drive, removable media, or someone else's computer.

Line chart A chart type that is useful to display trends over time; time displays along the bottom axis and the data point values are connected with a line.

Line style How the line displays, such as a solid line, dots, or dashes.

Line weight The thickness of a line measured in points.

Link Save a presentation so that the audio or video file is saved separately from the presentation.

List level An outline level in a presentation represented by a bullet symbol and identified in a slide by the indentation and the size of the text.

Live Preview A technology that shows the result of applying an editing or formatting change as you point to possible results—*before* you actually apply it.

Location Any disk drive, folder, or other place in which you can store files and folders.

Lock aspect ratio When this option is selected, you can change one dimension (height or width) of an object, such as a picture, and the other dimension will automatically be changed to maintain the proportion.

Loop The audio or video file plays repeatedly from start to finish until it is stopped manually.

Mark as Final Makes a presentation file read-only in order to prevent changes to the document. Adds a Marked as Final icon to the Status bar.

Metadata Details about a file that describe or identify it, including the title, author name, subject, and keywords that identify the document's topic or contents; also known as *document properties*.

Microsoft Access A database program, with which you can collect, track, and report data.

Microsoft Communicator An Office program that brings together multiple modes of communication, including instant messaging, video conferencing, telephony, application sharing, and file transfer.

Microsoft Excel A spreadsheet program, with which you calculate and analyze numbers and create charts.

Microsoft InfoPath An Office program that enables you to create forms and gather data.

Microsoft Office 2010 A Microsoft suite of products that includes programs, servers, and services for individuals, small organizations, and large enterprises to perform specific tasks.

Microsoft OneNote An Office program with which you can manage notes that you make at meetings or in classes.

Microsoft Outlook An Office program with which you can manage e-mail and organizational activities. An example of e-mail client.

Microsoft PowerPoint A presentation program, with which you can communicate information with high-impact graphics.

Microsoft Publisher An Office program with which you can create desktop publishing documents such as brochures.

Microsoft SharePoint Workspace An Office program that enables you to share information with others in a team environment.

Microsoft Word A word processing program, also referred to as an authoring program, with which you create and share documents by using its writing tools.

Mini toolbar A small toolbar containing frequently used formatting commands that displays as a result of selecting text or objects.

Mitered A border corner that has been angled to fit precisely in a square.

Motion path effect An animation effect that determines how and in what direction text or objects will move on a slide.

Mouse Over Refers to an action that will occur when the mouse pointer is placed on (over) an Action button. No mouse click is required.

Navigate The process of exploring within the organizing structure of Windows.

Navigation pane (Windows) In a folder window, the area on the left in which you can navigate to, open, and display favorites, libraries, folders, saved searches, and an expandable list of drives.

Navigation tools Buttons that display on the slides during a slide show that allow you to perform actions such as move to the next slide, the previous slide, the last viewed slide, or the end of the slide show.

Nonprinting characters Characters that display on the screen, but do not print, indicating where the Enter key, the Spacebar, and the Tab key were pressed; also called *formatting marks*.

Normal view (Excel) A screen view that maximizes the number of cells visible on your screen and keeps the column letters and row numbers close to the columns and rows.

Notes Master Includes the specifications for the design of speaker's notes.

Notes page A printout that contains the slide image on the top half of the page and notes that you have created on the Notes pane in the lower half of the page.

Notes pane The PowerPoint screen element that displays below the Slide pane with space to type notes regarding the active slide.

Office Clipboard A temporary storage area that holds text or graphics that you select and then cut or copy.

Office Theme Slide Master A specific slide master that contains the design, such as the background, that displays on all slide layouts in the presentation.

On Click An animation command that begins the animation sequence for the selected PowerPoint slide element when the mouse button is clicked or the spacebar is pressed.

Open dialog box A dialog box from which you can navigate to, and then open on your screen, an existing file that was created in that same program.

Option button A round button that allows you to make one choice among two or more options.

Options dialog box A dialog box within each Office application where you can select program settings and other options and preferences.

Paragraph symbol The symbol ¶ that represents a paragraph.

Paste The action of placing text or objects that have been copied or moved from one location to another location.

Paste Options Icons that provide a Live Preview of the various options for changing the format of a pasted item with a single click.

PDF (Portable Document Format) file A file format that creates an image that preserves the look of your file, but that cannot be easily changed; a popular format for sending documents electronically, because the document will display on most computers.

Photo album A stylized presentation format to display pictures.

Pixel The term, short for picture element, represents a single point in a graphic image.

Placeholder A box on a slide with dotted or dashed borders that holds title and body text or other content such as charts, tables, and pictures.

Play Animations button The small star-shaped icon displaying to the left of a slide thumbnail that, when clicked, plays the sound or animation.

Point The action of moving your mouse pointer over something on your screen.

Pointer Any symbol that displays on your screen in response to moving your mouse.

Points A measurement of the size of a font; there are 72 points in an inch, with 10-12 points being the most commonly used font size.

Portrait orientation A page orientation in which the paper is taller than it is wide.

Preview pane button In a folder window, the button on the toolbar with which you can display a preview of the contents of a file without opening it in a program.

Print Preview A view of a document as it will appear when you print it.

Program A set of instructions that a computer uses to perform a specific task, such as word processing, accounting, or data management; also called an *application*.

Program-level control buttons In an Office program, the buttons on the right edge of the title bar that minimize, restore, or close the program.

Protected view A security feature in Office 2010 that protects your computer from malicious files by opening them in a restricted environment until you enable them; you might encounter this feature if you open a file from an e-mail or download files from the Internet.

Protocol A set of rules.

Pt. The abbreviation for *point*; for example when referring to a font size.

Quick Access Toolbar In an Office program, the small row of buttons in the upper left corner of the screen from which you can perform frequently used commands.

Quick Commands The commands Save, Save As, Open, and Close that display at the top of the navigation pane in Backstage view.

Read-Only A property assigned to a file that prevents the file from being modified or deleted; it indicates that you cannot save any changes to the displayed document unless you first save it with a new name.

Reading view A view in PowerPoint that displays a presentation in a manner similar to a slide show but in which the taskbar, title bar, and status bar remain available in the presentation window.

Recolor The term used to change all the colors in an image to shades of one color, often used to make the colors match a background or apply a stylized effect or hue to a picture.

Reviewer A person who inserts comments into a presentation to provide feedback.

Ribbon The user interface in Office 2010 that groups the commands for performing related tasks on tabs across the upper portion of the program window.

Ribbon tabs The tabs on the Office Ribbon that display the names of the task-oriented groups of commands.

Right-click The action of clicking the right mouse button one time.

Rotation handle A green circle that provides a way to rotate a selected image.

Ruler guides Dotted vertical and horizontal lines that display in the rulers indicating the pointer's position.

Sans serif A font design with no lines or extensions on the ends of characters.

ScreenTip A small box that that displays useful information when you perform various mouse actions such as pointing to screen elements or dragging.

Scroll bar A vertical or horizontal bar in a window or a pane to assist in bringing an area into view, and which contains a scroll box and scroll arrows.

Scroll box The box in the vertical and horizontal scroll bars that can be dragged to reposition the contents of a window or pane on the screen.

Search box In a folder window, the box in which you can type a word or a phrase to look for an item in the current folder or library.

Select To highlight, by dragging with your mouse, areas of text or data or graphics, so that the selection can be edited, formatted, copied, or moved.

Serif font A font design that includes small line extensions on the ends of the letters to guide the eye in reading from left to right.

Shapes Lines, arrows, stars, banners, ovals, rectangles, and other basic shapes with which you can illustrate an idea, a process, or a workflow.

Sharpen Increase the clarity of an image.

Shortcut menu A menu that displays commands and options relevant to the selected text or object.

Sizing handles Small circles and squares that indicate that a picture is selected.

Slide A presentation page that can contain text, pictures, tables, charts, and other multimedia or graphic objects.

Slide handouts Printed images of slides on a sheet of paper.

Slide Master Part of a template that stores information about the formatting and text that displays on every slide in a presentation. There are various slide master layouts.

Slide pane A PowerPoint screen element that displays a large image of the active slide.

Slide Sorter view A presentation view that displays thumbnails of all of the slides in a presentation.

Slide transitions The motion effects that occur in Slide Show view when you move from one slide to the next during a presentation.

Slides/Outline pane A PowerPoint screen element that displays the presentation either in the form of thumbnails (Slides tab) or in outline format (Outline tab).

SmartArt graphic A visual representation of information that you can create by choosing from among many different layouts to communicate your message or ideas effectively.

SmartArt Styles Combinations of formatting effects that you can apply to SmartArt graphics.

Soften Decrease the clarity of an image or make it fuzzy.

Split button A button divided into two parts and in which clicking the main part of the button performs a command and clicking the arrow opens a menu with choices.

Start button The button on the Windows taskbar that displays the Start menu.

Start menu The Windows menu that provides a list of choices and is the main gateway to your computer's programs, folders, and settings.

Status bar The area along the lower edge of an Office program window that displays file information on the left and buttons to control how the window looks on the right.

Style (PowerPoint) A collection of formatting options that can be applied to a picture, text, or an object.

Subfolder A folder within a folder.

Table A format for information that organizes and presents text and data in columns and rows.

Table style Formatting applied to an entire table so that it is consistent with the presentation theme.

Tabs On the Office Ribbon, the name of each activity area in the Office Ribbon.

Tags Custom file properties that you create to help find and organize your own files.

Task pane A window within a Microsoft Office application in which you can enter options for completing a command.

Template A predefined layout for a group of slides saved as a .potx file.

Text alignment (PowerPoint) The horizontal placement of text within a placeholder.

Text box (PowerPoint) An object within which you can position text anywhere on a slide.

Theme A predesigned set of colors, fonts, lines, and fill effects that look good together and that can be applied to your entire document or to specific items.

Theme (PowerPoint) A set of unified design elements that provides a look for your presentation by applying colors, fonts, and effects.

Theme colors A set of coordinating colors that are applied to the backgrounds, objects, and text in a presentation.

Theme font A theme that determines the font applied to two types of slide text—headings and body.

Thumbnails (PowerPoint) Miniature images of presentation slides.

Timeline A graphical representation that displays the number of seconds the animation takes to complete.

Timing options Animation options that control when animated items display in the animation sequence.

Title bar The bar at the top edge of the program window that indicates the name of the current file and the program name.

Title slide The first slide in a presentation the purpose of which is to provide an introduction to the presentation topic.

Toggle button A button that can be turned on by clicking it once, and then turned off by clicking it again.

Toolbar In a folder window, a row of buttons with which you can perform common tasks, such as changing the view of your files and folders or burning files to a CD.

Track A song from a CD.

Transition sound A prerecorded sound that can be applied and will play as slides change from one to the next.

Transition speed The timing of the transition between all slides or between the previous slide and the current slide.

Transitions Motion effects that occur when a presentation moves from slide to slide in Slide Show view and affect how content is revealed.

Trigger A portion of text, a graphic, or a picture that, when clicked, causes the audio or video to play.

Trim The action of deleting parts of a video to make it shorter.

Triple-click The action of clicking the left mouse button three times in rapid succession.

Trusted Documents A security feature in Office 2010 that remembers which files you have already enabled; you might encounter this feature if you open a file from an e-mail or download files from the Internet.

URL (Uniform Resource Locator) Defines the address of documents and resources on the Web.

USB flash drive A small data storage device that plugs into a computer USB port.

Views button In a folder window, a toolbar button with which you can choose how to view the contents of the current location.

Web browser A software application used for retrieving, presenting, and searching information resources on the World Wide Web. It formats Web pages so that they display properly.

Window A rectangular area on a computer screen in which programs and content appear, and which can be moved, resized, minimized, or closed.

Windows Explorer The program that displays the files and folders on your computer, and which is at work anytime you are viewing the contents of files and folders in a window.

Windows taskbar The area along the lower edge of the Windows desktop that contains the Start button and an area to display buttons for open programs.

With Previous An animation command that begins the animation sequence on a PowerPoint slide at the same time as the previous animation or slide transition.

WordArt A gallery of text styles with which you can create decorative effects, such as shadowed or mirrored text.

XML Paper Specification (XPS) Microsoft's file format that preserves document formatting and enables file sharing. Files can be opened and viewed on any operating system or computer that is equipped with Microsoft Viewer. Files cannot be easily edited.

Zoom The action of increasing or decreasing the viewing area on the screen.

Index

C

D

E

F

T

U

V

W

X–Z

SINGLE PC LICENSE AGREEMENT AND LIMITED WARRANTY

READ THIS LICENSE CAREFULLY BEFORE OPENING THIS PACKAGE. BY OPENING THIS PACKAGE, YOU ARE AGREEING TO THE TERMS AND CONDITIONS OF THIS LICENSE. IF YOU DO NOT AGREE, DO NOT OPEN THE PACKAGE. PROMPTLY RETURN THE UNOPENED PACKAGE AND ALL ACCOMPANYING ITEMS TO THE PLACE YOU OBTAINED THEM. *THESE TERMS APPLY TO ALL LICENSED SOFTWARE ON THE DISK EXCEPT THAT THE TERMS FOR USE OF ANY SHAREWARE OR FREEWARE ON THE DISKETTES ARE AS SET FORTH IN THE ELECTRONIC LICENSE LOCATED ON THE DISK:*

1. GRANT OF LICENSE and OWNERSHIP: The enclosed computer programs ("Software") are licensed, not sold, to you by Prentice-Hall, Inc. ("We" or the "Company") and in consideration of your purchase or adoption of the accompanying Company textbooks and/or other materials, and your agreement to these terms. We reserve any rights not granted to you. You own only the disk(s) but we and/or our licensors own the Software itself. This license allows you to use and display your copy of the Software on a single computer (i.e., with a single CPU) at a single location for academic use only, so long as you comply with the terms of this Agreement. You may make one copy for back up, or transfer your copy to another CPU, provided that the Software is usable on only one computer.

2. RESTRICTIONS: You may not transfer or distribute the Software or documentation to anyone else. Except for backup, you may not copy the documentation or the Software. You may not network the Software or otherwise use it on more than one computer or computer terminal at the same time. You may not reverse engineer, disassemble, decompile, modify, adapt, translate, or create derivative works based on the Software or the Documentation. You may be held legally responsible for any copying or copyright infringement which is caused by your failure to abide by the terms of these restrictions.

3. TERMINATION: This license is effective until terminated. This license will terminate automatically without notice from the Company if you fail to comply with any provisions or limitations of this license. Upon termination, you shall destroy the Documentation and all copies of the Software. All provisions of this Agreement as to limitation and disclaimer of warranties, limitation of liability, remedies or damages, and our ownership rights shall survive termination.

4.DISCLAIMER OF WARRANTY: THE COMPANY AND ITS LICENSORS MAKE NO WARRANTIES ABOUT THE SOFTWARE, WHICH IS PROVIDED "AS-IS." IF THE DISK IS DEFECTIVE IN MATERIALS OR WORKMANSHIP, YOUR ONLY REMEDY IS TO RETURN IT TO THE COMPANY WITHIN 30 DAYS FOR REPLACEMENT UNLESS THE COMPANY DETERMINES IN GOOD FAITH THAT THE DISK HAS BEEN MISUSED OR IMPROPERLY INSTALLED, REPAIRED, ALTERED OR DAMAGED. THE COMPANY DISCLAIMS ALL WARRANTIES, EXPRESS OR IMPLIED, INCLUDING WITHOUT LIMITATION, THE IMPLIED WARRANTIES OF MERCHANTABILITY AND FITNESS FOR A PARTICULAR PURPOSE. THE COMPANY DOES NOT WARRANT, GUARANTEE OR MAKE ANY REPRESENTATION REGARDING THE ACCURACY, RELIABILITY, CURRENTNESS, USE, OR RESULTS OF USE, OF THE SOFTWARE.

5. LIMITATION OF REMEDIES AND DAMAGES: IN NO EVENT, SHALL THE COMPANY OR ITS EMPLOYEES, AGENTS, LICENSORS OR CONTRACTORS BE LIABLE FOR ANY INCIDENTAL, INDIRECT, SPECIAL OR CONSEQUENTIAL DAMAGES ARISING OUT OF OR IN CONNECTION WITH THIS LICENSE OR THE SOFTWARE, INCLUDING, WITHOUT LIMITATION, LOSS OF USE, LOSS OF DATA, LOSS OF INCOME OR PROFIT, OR OTHER LOSSES SUSTAINED AS A RESULT OF INJURY TO ANY PERSON, OR LOSS OF OR DAMAGE TO PROPERTY, OR CLAIMS OF THIRD PARTIES, EVEN IF THE COMPANY OR AN AUTHORIZED REPRESENTATIVE OF THE COMPANY HAS BEEN ADVISED OF THE POSSIBILITY OF SUCH DAMAGES. SOME JURISDICTIONS DO NOT ALLOW THE LIMITATION OF DAMAGES IN CERTAIN CIRCUMSTANCES, SO THE ABOVE LIMITATIONS MAY NOT ALWAYS APPLY.

6. GENERAL: THIS AGREEMENT SHALL BE CONSTRUED IN ACCORDANCE WITH THE LAWS OF THE UNITED STATES OF AMERICA AND THE STATE OF NEW YORK, APPLICABLE TO CONTRACTS MADE IN NEW YORK, AND SHALL BENEFIT THE COMPANY, ITS AFFILIATES AND ASSIGNEES. This Agreement is the complete and exclusive statement of the agreement between you and the Company and supersedes all proposals, prior agreements, oral or written, and any other communications between you and the company or any of its representatives relating to the subject matter. If you are a U.S. Government user, this Software is licensed with "restricted rights" as set forth in subparagraphs (a)-(d) of the Commercial Computer-Restricted Rights clause at FAR 52.227-19 or in subparagraphs (c)(1)(ii) of the Rights in Technical Data and Computer Software clause at DFARS 252.227-7013, and similar clauses, as applicable.

Should you have any questions concerning this agreement or if you wish to contact the Company for any reason, please contact in writing:

Multimedia Production,
Higher Education Division,
Prentice-Hall, Inc.,
1 Lake Street,
Upper Saddle River NJ 07458.